GETTING BA
INTO PLAC

Toward a Renewed Understanding
of the Place-World

SECOND EDITION

Edward S. Casey

Indiana University Press
Bloomington & Indianapolis

This book is a publication of

Indiana University Press
601 North Morton Street
Bloomington, IN 47404-3797 USA

http://iupress.indiana.edu

Telephone orders   800-842-6796
Fax orders   812-855-7931

First edition © 1993 by Edward S. Casey
© 2009 by Edward S. Casey
All rights reserved

♾ The paper used in this publication meets the minimum
requirements of the American National Standard for Information
Sciences—Permanence of Paper for Printed Library
Materials, ANSI Z39.48-1992.

Manufactured in the United States of America

Library of Congress Cataloging-in-Publication Data

Casey, Edward S., date
Getting back into place : toward a renewed understanding of
the place-world / Edward S. Casey. — 2nd ed.
    p.   cm. — (Studies in Continental thought)
Includes bibliographical references and index.
ISBN 978-0-253-22088-2 (pbk. : alk. paper) 1. Place (Philosophy) I. Title.
B105.P53C37   2009
2008052939

3   4   5   14   13   12

Dedicated to my colleagues and students at Stony Brook,
Where I have come back into place—
And in honor of the spirit of other memorable places
From which this book has taken inspiration,
Among them: Enterprise, Abilene, Topeka, Asheville,
New Haven, Chicago, Paris, Fairfield, Guilford, Quogue,
Sound Beach, Yarlung Valley

Contents

PREFACE

Being before Place

We do not live in "space."
—J. J. Gibson, *An Ecological Approach to Visual Perception*

Wherefore you ought to have regard to the greatness of places.
—Andrea Palladio, *The Four Books of Architecture*

Consult the *Genius* of the *Place* in all.
—Alexander Pope, "An Epistle to Lord Burlington"

Give me a place to stand, and I will move the world.
—Archimedes

I

AN OPENING QUESTION: Can you imagine what it would be like if there were no places in the world? None whatsoever! An utter, placeless void! I suspect that you will not succeed in this thought-experiment, which is not just difficult to perform (can you really eliminate any trace of place from your experience of *things*?) but also disturbing (can you really picture yourself in a *world* without places?). Our lives are so place-oriented and place-saturated that we cannot begin to comprehend, much less face up to, what sheer place-lessness would be like. For just this reason, we rarely pause to consider what being no place or having no place might mean. Even when we are displaced, we continue to count upon *some* reliable place, if not our present precarious perch then a place-to-come or a place-that-was. While we easily imagine or project an ideal (or merely a better) place-to-be and remember a number of good places we have been, we find that the very idea, even the bare image, of no-place-at-all occasions the deepest anxiety.

The prospect of no-place is dismaying not only when pulling up stakes or in wartime (part of the horror of nuclear war is its annihilation of places as well as persons) but at many other times: indeed, every time we are out of place, whether we are lost in a snowstorm, or our house has burned down, or we are simply without lodging for the night. In such situations we find ourselves entering into a special form of panic: place-panic. For we confront the imminent possibility of there being no place to be or to go. We feel not so much displaced as *without place*. The Greek word *atopos* (literally, "no place") means "bizarre" or "strange." No wonder we feel estranged when we are out of place. In fact, we would be devastated if consigned to an unending life in placeless "waste lands" vast in their vacuity.[1] No wonder, either, that fleeing in the face of our own panic, we resort to elaborate stratagems to avoid the void that looms before us.

The emotional symptoms of placelessness—homesickness, disorientation, depression, desolation—mimic the phenomenon itself. Each of these symptoms involves a sense of unbearable emptiness. Separation from place is perhaps most poignantly felt in the forced homelessness of the reluctant emigrant, the displaced person, the involuntary exile. Yet place-separation ensues not only when we are literally without a home. We can feel out of place even *in* the home, where *Unheimlichkeit*, the uncanny anxiety of not feeling "at home," may afflict us. Separation anxiety sets in early, by most accounts before twenty-four months of life. Thereafter, for the rest of our life we suffer from a series of separations, all of which involve aspects of place: separations from caring parents, from siblings and childhood friends, from a native region and its characteristic beliefs and dialect, from things we have done or witnessed. As Freud, Bachelard, and Proust all suggest, to refind place—a place we have always already been losing—we may need to return, if not in actual fact then in memory or imagination, to the very earliest places we have known. And even this return may not prevail against episodes of place-panic that hold us in their grip more than we may care to admit.

Philosophers have responded to such panic in a revealing way. With rare exceptions they have tried to sidestep the void by arguing that, despite certain appearances, the universe is chock-full of places. Such is the Parmenidean path: Being is everywhere full, Nonbeing is nowhere at all. Since ontological plenitude must be situated, no-place does not exist in or for a plenitudinous world. Being guarantees Place. As a result, the idea of the void is voided out. We need only think of the passionate struggle on the part of ancient philosophers, from Parmenides to Plotinus, to reject the *kenon*, the strict void, of the Atomists. Topology came to triumph over atopia.

On this issue, ancients and moderns are in considerable accord: wherever possible, abolish or at least deny the void! For the void, that which is utterly empty, threatens to undermine the reassurance promised by plenary presence. In the early modern era, the void loomed ever larger inasmuch as mathematics, physics, and astronomy posited an implacable infinity of empty (or almost empty) space. As Pascal put it in the middle of the seventeenth century, "The eternal silence of these infinite spaces terrifies me."[2] The infinity and silence of space reflect its emptiness. They also signify the absence of place. For space as a vast vacuum does not allow for places, even though one might think that there would be plenty of room for them! In such space there are no places for particular things; indeed, there are not even *empty places*. Thinkers of "the century of genius" fell into *horror vacui*, the unbridled terror occasioned by the mere contemplation of an entirely vacuous space. Such terror was felt by such otherwise dispassionate figures as Descartes and Pascal, Newton and Leibniz, each of whom attempted to deal with his phobia by papering over the abyss with philosophical and scientific speculation.

Several centuries later, we still suffer from the vista of a cosmic abyss and still paper over the unsettling prospect. By now this abyss has become incorporated into ourselves, in the vast inner space of the unconscious, not to mention the vacuum of the contemporary narcissistic self. Eliot's "Waste Land" (1922) captured this late modern *malaise* in haunting images of empty minds and lives cast adrift in a place-resistant city: "Unreal city / Under the brown fog of a winter dawn / A crowd flowed over London Bridge, so many, I had not thought death had undone so many."[3] Eliot suggested that we suffer not so much from anomie as from atopia. (In fact, anomie, a lack of social norms or values, often stems from atopia.) More recently an Anselm Kiefer painting entitled *Horror Vacui* shows nondescript human subjects huddled together under an enormous empty dome that is the very shell of a placeless world. Other works by Kiefer depict desolate and ravaged fields and buildings, evoking the dire state of mind wrought by placelessness in the twentieth century.

In philosophy the threat of atopia calls forth a veritable ontomania, an irrational desire to have and to know as much determinate presence as possible; in short, to put Being *before* Place. Whether the philosopher is Parmenides or Plato, Aristotle or Plotinus, Descartes or Spinoza, Hegel or Whitehead, the aim remains the same: to fill up, to populate, the empty field with as much determinate Being as possible. The motivation remains remarkably constant: panic before the empty field, the dark vision of no-place-at-all. Philosophers' endemic fear of having an empty mind, being "empty-headed," is another expression of the same panic-stricken state. The soul, asserts Aristotle, is "a place of forms"—where place itself is conceived by Aristotle as a strict container.[4] A mind or soul empty of forms, sensations, memories, and thoughts is as threatening as a universe empty of places. In view of such aversion to the void we may emend a celebrated dictum of Nietzsche's: it is not that "man would sooner have the void for his purpose than be void of purpose" but that human beings would rather be void of purpose than have the void as their purpose.[5]

II

A tree stands in its own place. Its life is sedentary. It is a life in one place, a life without anxiety. Not only is a tree in its place; it actively contributes to its place, filling it up with its own organic substance. It knows no menacing void, even though to move from its own place is to risk the death of the organism. "With its adjacent surroundings," writes Hans Jonas, "the plant forms one permanent context into which it is fully integrated, as the animal can never be in its environment."[6]

Animal life refuses the immobility of the plant. Animals, including human animals, are not only able to change their places, they *must* do so if they are to survive. No given place suffices indefinitely. Appetite, along with memory and desire, calls for a continual change of place and hence moving to locations where the enhancement of survival or simple "animal satisfaction" beckons. Only by foraging in *another* place can the insufficiencies of the present place—its lacks and privations—be overcome. Human beings are among the most mobile of animals. We are beings of the between, always on the move between places. When one place threatens to become vacuous (uninteresting, unsatisfying, desolate, or empty), we hasten on to another. Pascal also remarked that "all of human unhappiness stems from one thing: *not to know how to remain in repose in a room*."[7] Changing places is not only a matter of tedium or restlessness. Our desires and interests, our very metabolism and musculature, conspire to keep us moving. Even when practical needs are not at issue, we keep putting themselves into motion, getting out of one place and into another, and then still another.

Getting out of place is therefore a basic action of all animal, including all human, life. But with the freedom to change places—made ever more feasible by the development of the central nervous system, bipedalism, and upright posture—comes the danger of getting lost. A plant, having no place to go, is never lost. A mobile animal, however, continually confronts the unhappy prospect of disorientation, of not knowing its way between places. Still more dire is the experience of being *unplaced*, which constant movement brings with it. Not only may the former place be lost but a new place in which to settle may not be found. With increased mobility and range comes increased risk, above all the risk of having no proper or lasting place, no place to be or remain. A transitory place is better than none at all, but it only spurs on further searching for an enduring or at least reliable place. In the face of this risk, it is not surprising that human and nonhuman animals alike have come to rely on "territoriality" as a means of maintaining the stability and security of a home-place or home-region as defined by an appropriate "biotope" or "ecological niche."[8] The home territory embodies the plenitude that being placeless so painfully lacks.

To say "I have no place to go" is to admit to a desperate circumstance. Yet we witness daily the disturbing spectacle of people with no place to go: refugees from natural catastrophes or strife-torn countries, the homeless on the streets of modern cities, not to mention "stray" animals. In fearing that "the earth is becoming uninhabitable"—a virtually universal lament—we are fearing that the earth will no longer provide adequate places in which to live. The incessant motion of postmodern life in late-capitalist societies at once echoes and exacerbates this fear. Rushing from place to place, we rarely linger long enough in one particular place to savor its unique qualities and its local history. We pay a heavy price for capitalizing on our basic animal mobility. The price is the loss of places that can serve as lasting scenes of experience and reflection and memory.

III

Despite the costly character of an accelerated life, it remains the case that where we are—the place we occupy, however briefly—has everything to do with what and who we are (and finally, *that* we are). This is so at the present moment: where you are right now is not a matter of indifference but affects the kind of person you are, what you have been doing in the past, even what you will be doing in the future. Your locus deeply influences what you perceive and what you expect to be the case. Even if you are merely "passing through" an airport, this is so: just to be there as a *passenger* already says a great deal about you. Your immediate placement—or "implacement," as I prefer to call it[9]—counts for much more than is usually imagined. More, for instance, than serving as a mere backdrop for concrete actions or thoughts. Place itself is concrete and at one with action and thought.

Yet we rarely accord to place any such importance. Descriptions of place tend to reduce it to bare position in space, where "position" implies an arbitrary location. "If I weren't still here in Chicago, I'd be back on Long Island," I say to myself idly in O'Hare airport, as if changing places were just a matter of exchanging positions in a geographical board game having no significant stakes. Philosophy and physics, followed closely by psychology, also often operate on a model of manipulable positions in empty space— "sites," as I shall call them.

But what if place is not something so easily exchanged or merely manipulated? What if place is not a matter of arbitrary position? What if the stakes in the game of place are much higher than we think? Where then will we find ourselves?

Not in empty space. As J. J. Gibson reminds us (in one of the epigraphs to this preface), "We do not live in 'space.'" Instead, *we live in places*. So it behooves us to understand what such place-bound and place-specific living consists in. However lost we may become by gliding rapidly between places, however oblivious to place we may be in our thought and theory, and however much we may prefer to think of what happens in a place rather than of the place itself, we are tied to place undetachably and without reprieve.[10]

The pervasiveness of place and its plurality of forms are such that we can grasp the perplexing phenomenon of displacement, rampant throughout human history and especially evident at the present historical moment, only in relation to an abiding implacement. (The reverse is also true.) Although we acknowledge the suffering occasioned by personal or collective displacement, we tend not to trace it back to the loss of a vital connection with place itself. But the disoriented and the dispossessed are bereft precisely of such connection. They lack not just permanence of place but its very availability, its minimal resources. The result is a suffering not limited to the experience of exile: in a "dromocratic," speed-bound era, every mobile person is a victim of placelessness in one guise or another.[11]

The phenomenon of displacement derives in large measure from a failure to link up with places, beginning with local places and including more capacious places such as those occupied by entire cities and regions, cultures and societies, and ultimately the natural world. A related failure is conceptual: the nonrecognition place has received in the hands of most modern thinkers. Taking these failures into account, I shall in effect rejoin Hegel's view that geography is the single most efficacious basis of history, a view that Braudel has borne out recently in his massive history of the Mediterranean world.[12] Everywhere we turn we find place at issue in the alienation and violence from which human beings have suffered so devastatingly in modern times. More often than we realize, the alienation is *from* (a given) place and the violence has been done *to* (some) place, and not only to people in places. If it is distinctively postmodern to wish to return to place, this is so even if the most promising patterns for the return are often distinctively premodern in inspiration.

In the past three centuries in the West—the period of "modernity"— place has come to be not only neglected but actively suppressed. Owing to the triumph of the natural and social sciences in this same period, any serious talk of place has been regarded as regressive or trivial. A discourse has emerged whose exclusive cosmological foci are Time and Space. When the two were combined by twentieth-century physicists into the amalgam "space-time," the overlooking of place was only continued by other means. For an entire epoch, place has been regarded as an impoverished second cousin of Time and Space, those two colossal cosmic partners that tower over modernity.

But we would not endorse this put-down of place so readily if only we turned our concerted attention to the glaring discrepancy between the official doctrine of belittling place and the prominence of place in ordinary life. "Where are you from?" we ask a stranger whom we have just met, not reflecting on how acutely probing such a mundane question can be and how deeply revealing the answers to it often are. As the conversation proceeds, we rarely pause to consider how frequently people refer back to a certain place of origin as to an exemplar against which all subsequent places are implicitly to be measured: to their birthplace, their childhood home, or any other place that has had a significant influence on their lives. Indeed, many human beings are enthusiastic or nostalgic, at home in the world or out of sorts there, in relation to just such an ur-place. To lack a primal place is to be "homeless" indeed, not only in the literal sense of having no permanently sheltering structure but also as being without any effective means of orientation in a complex and confusing world. By late modern times, this world had become increasingly placeless, a matter of mere sites instead of lived places, of sudden displacements rather than of perduring implacements.

IV

Others have begun to address the elusive phenomenon of place in the past few decades. Heidegger, in writings dating from at least 1950, thematized "location" and "region" in contrast with space.[13] I am deeply indebted to him as well as to Bachelard, whose *Poetics of Space* (1957) rejoined Heidegger's emphasis on the importance of dwelling places. Neither philosopher, however, adequately assessed the role of the human body in the experience of significant places. A later wave, stemming from the 1970s and frankly topophiliac in character, was composed of ecologically minded geographers who attempted to reinstate place as a central category within their own discipline.[14] A recent undercurrent of architects, sociologists, anthropologists, ethicists and theologians, feminists, and social observers is still gathering force.[15] But as yet there has been no concerted, extended *philosophical* treatment of place in all its amplitude and complexity.

My primary aim in this book is to articulate an exact and engaged analysis of place more fully, and to trace out its philosophical consequences more completely, than has been done by other students of the subject. Instead of succumbing to topophilia, I will pursue what Bachelard has aptly termed "topo-analysis."[16] I shall accord to place a position of renewed respect by specifying its power to direct and stabilize us, to memorialize and identify us, to tell us who and what we are in terms of *where we are* (as well as where we are *not*).

To be in the world, to be situated at all, is to be in place. Place is the phenomenal particularization of "being-in-the-world," a phrase that in Heidegger's hands retains a certain formality and abstractness which only the concreteness of *being-in-place*, i.e., being in the *place-world* itself, can mitigate. Can we rediscover and redescribe that concreteness? Can we regain and restore a sense of the full significance of place?

V

In attempting to answer these questions, I shall take up the topic of place in five parts. In part one I consider place as it figures in such diverse situations as navigation and myths of creation, the nature of mind, and the character of rhetoric. I invoke early Greek discussions of place and space and contrast them with modernist efforts to reduce place to space and to assert the primacy of time. This leaves unaddressed the question of *how* we are in place. In part two I propose that we are in place primarily by means of our own bodies, and accordingly I scrutinize such basic parameters of implacement as dimension and directionality, both of which contribute importantly to orientation. Embodied implacement requires structures in which to reside—structures devised by human beings to reflect and support their desires and needs. In part three I thus explore how we *dwell* in places and, in particular, what it means for places to become *built*. Built places, however, are surrounded—eventually, if not immediately—by the wild places of the natural world. In part four, I ponder place in its unbuilt and uncultivated aspects, its ecological horizons and wilderness modes. A final part considers how the experience of making a journey between particular places illuminates our life in the place-world at large, especially in home-places.

Readers may take various paths through this book. Although its topics are pursued in an exfoliating order, the book need not be read serially. Those with special interests in architecture may wish to read the two introductory chapters and then skip to part three, which treats constructed places. Ecologically minded readers may prefer to concentrate on part four, "Wild Places." Part two, which treats the role of the body in place, is doubtless the most demanding and rigorous section of the book. It is also the most explicitly phenomenological in its approach, building on the inaugural work of Husserl and Merleau-Ponty. Although it is not necessary to read it in order to grasp the rest of the book, I conceive of it as the narrow defile of the text through which more comprehensive and more familiar vistas of the place-world may be glimpsed.

VI

Getting Back into Place is the third in a series of books in which I have attempted to take another look—a considered and persistent look—at everyday phenomena that have been passed over or systematically misconstrued in the theorizing of Western philosophers and other thinkers. These phenomena are imagination, memory, and place. They are complementary in character. Just as imagination takes us forward into the realm of the purely possible—

into what *might be*—so memory brings us back into the domain of the actual and the already elapsed: to what *has been*. Place ushers us into what *already is*: namely, the environing subsoil of our embodiment, the bedrock of our being-in-the-world. If imagination projects us out *beyond* ourselves while memory takes us back *behind* ourselves, place subtends and enfolds us, lying perpetually *under* and *around* us. In imagining and remembering, we go into the ethereal and the thick respectively. By being in place, we find ourselves in what is subsistent and enveloping.

If we are rarely securely in place and ever seemingly out of place, it behooves us to understand what place is all about. This entails a sustained reflection on what it means to be in place—in the first place. Unless we undertake this reflection, we shall not find for the combined work of memory and imagination the proper field of their own distinctive gravity. Still more seriously, until we open up this field our own lives will continue to be as disoriented and displaced, as destabilized and dismaying, as we know them to be at this imperiled postmodern moment.

Acknowledgments

I N THE CASE of the present book, it might seem to be more appropriate to acknowledge particular places than particular people. But many persons were indispensable to the making of this book—many more than I can here name. My earliest ruminations on place, occurring over a decade ago, arose in the challenging company of James Hillman and Peter Manchester. At later moments I came under the enlightening influence of Keith Basso and David Martinez concerning the importance of place among native peoples, and of Janet Gyatso with regard to place's role in South Asian life and culture. I am grateful to J. B. Jackson, premier theorist of landscape, for a memorable conversation at his home outside Santa Fe, and to Ulrich Neisser for correspondence on psychological aspects of place. Several pioneers of place, none known to me personally, have also been significant in my thinking: Yi-Fu Tuan and E. V. Walter, Wendell Berry and Gary Snyder.

My understanding of built places was deepened by ongoing conversations with Kent Bloomer, David Seamon, and Tom Brockelman. Elizabeth Behnke, independent scholar, bestowed her extraordinary command of Husserl, and of recent work in the phenomenology of the body, to bolster my fledgling descriptions of the role of the lived body in matters of implacement. For insights and references regarding the dimensional parameters of such implacement, I am grateful to Nancy Franklin, my colleague in the Psychology Department at Stony Brook, and to Henry Tylbor, independent researcher. Drew Leder was prescient and precise in his analysis of my first descriptions of bodies in places, and I benefitted greatly from several talks with Glen Mazis. As I found my way into the place-logic of wild places, I was fortunate to have such excellent guides as Irene Klaver and Anthony Weston, with both of whom I met during a semester of intense discussion of wilderness; I am especially indebted to the former for her penetrating reading of several other portions of the book. David Abram and David Strong, philosophical naturalists and recent graduates of the doctoral program at Stony Brook, were also guiding presences. Strong led me straight into the heart of the Crazy Mountains, a wild place indeed. Bruce Wilshire, himself a man of the mountains, encouraged me to discern exactly what makes a place wild.

When it came to turning a tortured torso into a polished text, I was given invaluable assistance by Kurt Wildermuth, who helped me to economize verbiage and still to do descriptive justice to complex phenomena.

Melvin Woody, once again, supplied telling suggestions for making my lines of argument more forceful. Bernard Dauenhauer's skepticism was salutary. Jeffrey Gaines, Sharon Hartline, and Steve Michelman all provided close and constructive readings of the book in its middle-aged versions, and the last-named composed the index. Eric Casey, burgeoning classicist, kept me honest regarding ancient tongues.

Introduction to the Second Edition

I

NO ONE DOUBTS that place is indispensable to daily living. After all, it is the concrete basis of location, inhabitation, and orientation on the part of human beings and other animals. But philosophers have acted as if they did not know this—as if place were a mere annex of space or something subordinate to time or history. Though sometimes touching on aspects of place, philosophers have not acknowledged its full scope and more complete significance. This book attempts to make such acknowledgment on the basis of a thorough phenomenological description and thus to justify the common persuasion that place is integral to the everyday life-world.

When this book first appeared fifteen years ago, place was far from central to the preoccupations of philosophers. Sartre had addressed it in *Being and Nothingness*—in several pages devoted to "My Place"—and Bachelard pursued "topoanalysis" in his later writings, while Heidegger had come to recognize its importance in several late essays.[1] Otherwise, if mentioned at all, it was consigned to margins and footnotes. I had come to it belatedly myself. Only in facing up to the fact that most episodic memories require a scene of enactment was I led to write a chapter on "Place Memory" in an earlier book on memory.[2] In the course of writing that chapter I realized that place not only had been neglected by philosophers but is a very complex subject that calls for its own treatment. The handwriting was on the wall: I felt that the time had come for a detailed treatment of place. Little did I know when I took this step that place would become my primary philosophical focus for nearly two decades. This focus derived from the passionate conviction that *place matters*, both in everyday existence and in philosophical analysis. The result was the first full-scale philosophical assessment of this elusive entity.

When the first edition of *Getting Back into Place* was published in 1993, "spatial studies" amounted to an isolated bookcase with this label at City Lights Bookstore in San Francisco. Since that time, it has become an entire arena of contemporary research and thought. Spatial studies are now a whole industry in the humanities and the social sciences. A spatial turn has been taken, with dramatic and far-reaching consequences. At the heart of this turn has been a recognition of the formative presence of place in people's lives and thoughts. Place is now a prominent theme in literary theory, cultural geography, psychoanalysis, and architectural theory.[3] At least two new journals devote themselves largely to issues of place: *Society and Space* and *Space and Culture*. An important book, *Experience and Place,* by Jeffrey Malpas, examines the human subject's experience of place.[4] *Senses of Place,* a collaborative volume, argues for the primacy of place in anthropological fieldwork.[5] A recent survey of contemporary models of "socio-spatial relations" gives a prominent position to place, along with territory, scale, and network as the primary ways of conceiving these relations.[6] A new field has emerged, "computational models of place," in which place is studied from the standpoint of such diverse areas as geomatics, geoinformatics, applied linguistics, geographical information systems, and robotics.[7]

To turn to place is to effect a paradigm shift away from temporocentrist understandings of human culture and personal development—understandings that assume time to be the operative medium of human experience, whether in Kant's claim that the formal intuition of time is the only truly universal presupposition of such experience, in the Hegelian and Diltheyian extensions of this thesis into the realm of human history, or in Kierkegaard's and Heidegger's pursuit of the primacy of time in human existence pervasively. By the later twentieth century, it had become a virtual dogma in philosophy that time precedes space—with place regarded as a mere sector of space. *Getting Back into Place* contested both claims by arguing that place is irreducible to space and that in relation to time it is, if anything, a first among equals. (My more recent thought proposes that time and place are coeval partners in the constitution of *events* taken as the primary ontological terms.)[8]

I attempted to effect this sea change by pursuing a phenomenological account of place—also the first of its kind to have appeared. Such an account provides an attentive description of place as it forms part of daily (and nightly) life—a description that is often missing in other accounts, philosophical or otherwise. *Getting Back into Place* offered such a description even if it did not follow phenomenological method in any strict or traditional sense. It was the first of my books to pursue a more informal but more expansive brand of analysis. In particular, I departed from the act/content distinction that is the basis of an intentional analysis in which consciousness is privileged. We are indeed conscious of place, but often with a markedly peripheral awareness that is not reducible to a mode of intentionality. It was as if place itself, in its pervasive and often subtle presence, led me to modify hitherto normative phenomenological technique.

Beyond its increasing recognition in philosophy and other academic disciplines, place-awareness has been rising in the past fifteen years. This emerging awareness derives from several sources—among them globalization, screen and video culture, and the effects of forced migration. Each of these three sources has thrust place into a position of paradoxical salience in world culture: paradoxical insofar as place is usually considered of limited local significance. Let us consider each briefly:

(a) Marshall McLuhan's idea of the "global village" foresaw what is now called "globalization": precisely as technology connects innumerable human beings across many cultures, it has the effect of emphasizing the special virtues of one's own place vis-à-vis a world culture that is more and more massively homogeneous at the level of commercial products (many of which are now made in China) and technological devices (e.g., cell phones). Valorization of local differences arises in the very face of global capitalism and global communication networks: partly as resistance to them but still more so from a renewed appreciation of the felt familiarity of the places one inhabits with one's lived body.[9]

(b) Place also comes into prominence from the sheer fact that much of global culture is now conveyed by screens, whether those of video and television, or those giving access to the unending resources of the worldwide web. The fact is that a considerable portion of daily experience for human beings everywhere is mediated by what they see on screens—which can be construed as miniature and tightly framed micro-places that rivet viewers in the particular positions from which they are looking at these circumscribed visual fields.

(c) At the same time, the massive upsurge in forced migrations among millions of human beings—it has been estimated that fully 40 percent of humans are now on the move, most of them settling into urban slums—has reinforced an acute sensitivity to the loss of the place of origin: precipitating not just nostalgia but a deeply felt place-mourning that I take up at several points in this book.[10]

In each of the three geopolitical contexts to which I have just alluded—globalization, screen-mediated informational and entertainment networks, and forced migration—place (or its loss) has been felt with ever-augmenting intensity.

II

The attraction of place as a response to these three contexts—a response that can be characterized as an espousal of the "local absolute" in Deleuze and Guattari's phrase[11]—brings with it a series of new challenges for thinkers of place. These challenges can be met if we are willing to ponder a set of four topics closely associated with place: its cultural and political aspects, the status of territory, the effects of global warming, and the role of regions. In the next few sections, I shall comment on each of these various topics, to which insufficient attention was paid in the first edition of this book.

The desire for a lively local community has been revived in many people's consciousness by the stark absence of any analogue to the ancient agora in Athens or to Hyde Park in London. By the tacit logic of longing-for-place-in-the-face-of-its-absence, the role of place as a necessary basis for community action and thought has emerged as intensely desirable in many parts of the contemporary world. As international corporations and national governments become increasingly indifferent to the interests and requirements of ordinary citizens, local governments have stepped into the breach. For example, a number of municipalities in the United States have declared themselves cities of refuge or hospitality for immigrants from Mexico and Central America. As many as sixty cities have "moved not to adopt national initiatives that would require local police to be involved in the enforcement of immigrations laws, and in particular not to ask about the immigration status of those who require police assistance, medical care, or social services (unless federally mandated for particular programs)."[12] In order to reach this point of concerted political action, public discussion must first occur locally in particular places such as town halls, high school auditoriums, parks, and other suitable venues. Public dialogue on controversial or pressing political and social issues requires a containing space such as these places provide. It is not sufficient to communicate by electronic means to reach genuine consensus on such complex issues as immigration or education. Useful as these means can be for disseminating information and for signing electronic petitions by many citizens in a very short stretch of time, they do not replace face-to-face talking and debating among those concerned with a given issue.[13] However compromised and rare public spaces have become, they remain indispensable: for instance, debates among candidates for the American presidency are viewed in person only by a small number of people, but they are broadcast into millions of homes via television: in this technologically mediated way, they make their way into a local place, the family living room, where they are contained and framed. Yet this is still not sufficient for genuine political discourse, for it excludes the voices of other citizens in the neighborhood or region. This is why genuinely open spaces that encourage and support public dialogue are required for the full expression of the "multi-voiced body" that is the active basis of political life.[14]

The specific implacement of communitarian discussion and political action reflects the deep pervasion of place itself by cultural factors. Among such factors, I include social and political forces, ethnic and gender differences, and family and institutional histories: each of which pervades place in its own characteristic way. If place in the public dialogical format just outlined is required for its power to hold and enhance verbal discourse and other expressive forms taken by the interplay of gestures and voices in human society, place is able to play this role effectively thanks to its absorptive virtues. I refer to its characteristically porous boundaries, that is, its special capacity for admitting the different and diverse into its midst. Rather than stressing its closely held material and historical identity—e.g., in the case of Union Square in New York, as a place for debates and discussions of the Labor movement after World War I, and more recently, as a place of mourning in the immediate wake of 9/11—now we consider a particular place from the standpoint of all that it incorporates and reflects: such as the history of a class, its endemic culture, its associated beliefs and thought. Seen in this perspective, place is quite mutable and is the very converse of what the Romans sought in the ideal of *stabilitas loci*. In other words, place becomes an *event*, a happening not only in space but in time and history as well. To the role of place as facilitative and locatory we need to add the role of place as eventmental: as a scene of personal and historical happening.

In order to make this move, we should think of culture, ethnicity, gender, class, etc., as furnishing *dimensions* of a place beyond its exact location in geographic space and chronometric time. These dimensions are not themselves events, but they form part of the event of place itself. They act as indwelling forces that contribute to a place its non-physical and non-geographic dimensions. As such, their status is generic rather than specific: that is, they operate as *types* or *kinds* rather than as particulars or individuals. Thus, Union Square as it exists today is suffused with the history of American working-class people taken not in their sheer individuality but as members of a certain socioeconomic class that has its own history. The character of this class, taken as a generic fact, infuses Union Square as an integral part of its history. So, too, does the atmosphere felt there in the immediate aftermath of 9/11: a mood at once sad, angry, confused, and commemorative.[15] One and the same place undergoes both of these very different avatars—which, instead of competing with one another, coexist, albeit at different levels. The inherent generality, drawing upon "the value of the vague" in William James's phrase, adumbrates many possibilities of such complex co-existence; were the dimensions more determinate, they would be much more likely to conflict by vying for the same space.

The two poles here at stake—place as locatory vs. place as an event with cultural/historical dimensions—are not exclusive of each other: one and the same place can support both poles just as it can exemplify widely variant cultural vicissitudes. This is precisely the case with Union Square. Its rather circumscribed triangular shape has served as a locus for countless happenings, some dramatic and significant, others merely circumstantial or convenient (e.g., the tent-shops that are set up on its steps in the Christmas season). Beyond being a place for these particular events, however, *Union Square is itself an event*. Things happen *in it*, but *it happens too*—it has its own historicity, its own eventmentality. It has its own architectural and cultural history, its own evolving role in the history of lower Manhattan, and its changing status in the midst of the neighborhoods that surround it in the area of 14th Street east of Fifth Avenue.[16]

Considering place in this bipolar, multidimensional way does not disagree with what I maintained in the first edition of this book, but it offers a very different emphasis from that which I sought fifteen years ago. At that time, my concern was not with place's cultural parameters as such, even though I did address them at several points in the book.[17] My most insistent urge then was to bring place out of the shadows into which it had fallen since at least the High Middle Ages, and to put it into the light of day by a close description of how it occurs in concrete modalities in the human life-world—where "concrete" signifies lived experience, especially its bodily modalities. Without denying the cultural aspects of place, I was nonetheless not focusing on them. Other writings of mine since that time have picked out particular cultural dimensions of place—especially those associated with its representation in maps, landscape paintings, and earth-works—but still did not single out this factor as such. The first essay appended to this new edition of *Getting Back into Place* attempts to make amends for this inattention by pursuing more intently several of the directions to which I am here only alluding.

III

Territory and place: these notions are deeply intertwined even if their relationship is not symmetrical. Every territory is a place of some kind, but not every place counts as territory. The latter requires, minimally but essentially, a more or less distinct border—that is, a defining limit that is geographically specific. This limit is set up by members of a given animal species in an effort to establish an area within which its members can assert dominance and control. Once created by various means (e.g., urinary trail, foliage foraging, laying down of scent, etc.), this border takes on a certain unrevisability, as to say: this far and no farther! In the case of the human species, other means are employed to proclaim a border: perhaps signs that say in no uncertain words: No Trespassing! or, at the level of representation, a map that indicates borders in imagistic and/or linear formats. Around every territory, human or nonhuman, there is a comparatively clearly indicated delineation, as if to underscore the implicit imperative to *draw the line* in both senses of this latter phrase: to demarcate and to declare strict limits (regarding entry, movement, exit, etc.). The line itself need not be literally linear or visual, as in the case of a map or a No Trespassing sign; it can be aromatic or even acoustic (as when wolves announce territorial claims by their nocturnal howls). But its sensible base must be such as to carry a straight-forward message to anyone who comes into the vicinity: watch out, you are on the edge of possible danger to yourself and your companions, and you'd better take note before you come to regret it! In this sense, the borders of a territory are always, in some significant sense, defensive structures: they fend off undue or unwanted intrusions into their space.

Territories are also political in character: they are established to protect and support a certain population, whether this is made up of members of a given animal group or of human beings who claim local sovereignty. Both animals and humans seek homogeneity of population, but human beings go to greater lengths to assure that this is so—e.g., by policing borders, requiring certain papers in order to pass through, and formulating laws to regulate the behavior and movements of residents. Hence the power of the "territorial imperative" that justifies violence in defense of the home territory—as well as in the extension of this territory into neighboring areas: an imperialist activity that is often designated as a matter of "territorial ambition."[18] The human establishment and enforcement of a territorial border allows the territory to be as assertively sovereign as it wishes to be within these same edges: in control and thus able to direct its own destiny. No wonder that political communities in the West, ever since the days of the Athenian League, have insisted on their own "constitution" and on the right to determine the rules by which their citizens will live.[19] Even when there is no formal statement of these rules, no written constitution, some equivalent of such a declaration of sovereignty is found in every humanly established territory, large or small, ancient or recent, democratic or dictatorial in its governance.[20]

A territory, then, is a part of space delimited by a carefully demarcated border that announces: This space begins (or ends) just here; inside it, the rightful inhabitants (i.e., the "citizens") have the right to decide what they can do and cannot do; outside it, a different world looms—one to which denizens of the territory are comparatively indifferent (unless they have imperialist designs upon it!). But the definiteness of territorial borders and the claim to self-determination within them should not obscure the fact that a given territory, like place itself, has features that are redolent of the character of the more encompassing region to which the territory belongs—the environing forest or plain for a territorial enclave located within it, or an entire continent for the individual countries that make it up. Just as there is no territorial border that exists in isolation from what lies around it, so there is no territory that is independent of the embracing geographical and biological life-worlds to which it belongs.

Territories, then, are distinguished from places and regions by the fact that they are never simply given or found but are made up. They require specific actions of fabrication and reinforcement, among which the single most crucial is the setting up of definite borders that give definition and identity to the living beings they enclose. Despite their artificial status, they often collude with the local or regional topography: the Kansas-Nebraska Territory incorporated the flat underlying earth of the high plains, considered as a coherent bioregion that differs dramatically from the mountainous area just to the west, in what was to become Colorado and Wyoming. This nineteenth-century territory brought together a tacit acknowledgment of the planiform earth with a claim to possession and geographic determination (as is evident in the early maps of the region). At the same time, a comparable claim came to alter the landscape itself as settlers sought to inhabit the arid soil within this territory. In this way, the territory shows itself to be no static entity but something closer to an action or event. As Deleuze and Guattari put it, "The territory is in fact an act that affects milieus and rhythms, that 'territorializes' them."[21]

IV

In the case of global warming, we are again thrust back onto the local by something happening at a global scale—in this case, the global as a matter of massive climate change and the local as valued for the sake of the life it sustains. Given that the entire earth is caught up in the dire effects of greenhouse gases, any and every place on earth is subject to fateful dangers. Not only will some actual localities be submerged under rising ocean levels, but many other places will be put at high risk: e.g., in the meltdown of the polar ice caps and in large areas of the American Southwest where desertification is now setting in. Whole species of animals are struggling to survive in increasingly rigorous conditions, while many plants (less adaptable because of their comparative immobility) are perishing outright. The availability and distribution of fresh water are becoming highly problematic as underground aquifers and major rivers are depleted. Millions of human beings have inadequate access to clean water supplies, with a consequent spread of diseases that are waterborne.

In the face of this gathering ecological disaster, place emerges as ever more important—prized not merely as secure and familiar turf to which inhabitants retreat before the plunge into the unknown but, more positively, for the quality of life still possible. Place is increasingly regarded as a natural reserve in which to care for existing life-forms—to be sure that they will be nurtured and protected despite the encroaching environmental threats. Local place becomes a sanctuary of sorts, a *hortus cultura,* or "cultivated garden," for ongoing life in which surviving species discover their deep interdependencies. Here we are at another extreme from where we began in my brief assessment of the revalorization of place in the face of global culture and technology. We are also somewhere else than in communities and territories. No longer in the realm of logos (the space of dialogue and discourse), we enter the domain of life, where place figures more as scene of sustenance than as forum for debate. This is not the realm of territory, since there are no strictly drawn borders in the biological world; and there is not any aim of achieving homogeneity of population within a given place (profusion of species being a sign of ecological health), much less anything like a constitution that would order and supervise the activities of the denizens of that place (the spontaneous interaction of species takes the place of any regulatory decrees).

Still more significant is the emergence of a new principle, that of *specific uptake*. In treating communitarian and cultural aspects of place, I stressed the principle of pervasion, whereby various dimensions suffuse themselves across and into places without consideration of the particularity of the places themselves: what mattered was the way in which factors of culture and class, gender and ethnicity, characterized these places *all the way through*. Now we are confronted by a very different circumstance, in which the specificity of a place has everything to do with how a global pandemic is absorbed and reflected there. Global warming shows up very differently in different places—in lakes and rivers, mountainous areas and deserts, farms and suburbs. A given human culture, such as that of the Inuit, also manifests itself differently in varied locales where these native peoples live in northern Canada, but there is an overall continuity and substantial identity from place to place that allows anthropologists to speak of "Inuit culture" throughout. Global warming has no such steady identity as it is exhibited in particular locales. It is taken up in each locale in quite distinctive ways—in a specific uptake so nuanced that the layperson often cannot tell that global warming is the common source of such differences (hence the need to consult ecologists and climatologists for an accurate assessment of what is happening).

Another crucial difference in the fate of place emerges when we consider that global warming affects not just discrete places but whole regions (usually referred to as "bioregions"). Such warming, stemming as it does from changes in the atmosphere surrounding the earth as a whole, is making a difference to all parts of the planet, but the most capacious units of its uptake—where it becomes most palpable—are entire bioregions: the rainforest and cloudforest belt of Central America, sub-Saharan Africa, etc. The basic reason for these broad patterns of effect is evident: a given bioregion is composed of organisms that are interconnected in distinctive ways in and through the area they share. Thus a climatological parameter such as temperature or comparative aridity will be assimilated by the colonies of these same organisms in intimately parallel ways; and these colonies in turn will impact the well-being of other organisms in the same bioregion. In an increasingly dry period, the root systems of Ponderosa pine trees will be forced to sink ever deeper into the earth as the overall water table lowers, and in this downward movement they will encounter and influence the root systems of bushes and grasses in the same ecosystem; and these latter will in turn alter the character of the topsoil in that same system—and thus the life of creatures who live on (or in) that soil, ranging from microorganisms to worms, from gophers to squirrels. When all such specific uptakes concatenate, we have a distinctively regional expression of global warming. The consistency of this expression reflects the ramified character of local effects as they spread from a discrete place into an entire region.

Territories also call for close cooperation among their inhabitants; but unlike bioregions, their insistence on homogeneity of population and commonality of goals forecloses the full operation of anything like specificity of uptake. This is above all true of those territories established by human beings, who characteristically insist on rigidly reinforced borders and strict monitoring of the activities of citizens of the territory. In contrast, animal territories act in closer concert with bioregions, setting themselves up on their exacting terms and respecting their characteristic makeup. Despite this close collaboration between animal community and bioregion, territories can complicate the collaboration itself—for instance, at the level of the borders that are laid down by members of the primary species living there and that often cut across the organic diversity of bioregional life. This life often suffers from borders—especially those constructed or imposed by human beings for their own independent interests, as occurs at the formidable security wall that has been built along many stretches of La Frontera, the U.S.-Mexico border.

V

The very concept of region that is forced upon our attention by the specter of global warming was not fully considered in the first edition of *Getting Back into Place*. Although I pointed to certain "powers and virtues" of regions such as their ability to "gather out," crucial questions were left unanswered.[22] Is a region a mere collection of places? A place of places? A super-place? I have since taken steps to address such questions, for example, in a study of John Constable as a painter of the region of East Anglia, England. There I wrote that a region is "a group of closely concatenated places that are (1) spatially contiguous with each other . . . ; (2) temporally coexistent and thus cohistorical—that is, possessing a shared history."[23] Let us agree that a region is, minimally, *a coherent collocation of places*—where the places are not necessarily the same in extent, composition, or overall character. They can be very diverse and yet belong to the same region, as we see in the case of the American Southwest, which combines Native American reservations and towns, cities populated mostly by Anglos, and farming communities: all this in the midst of mountains and deserts, variety of plants, and considerable wildlife. But a region is also something more than a collocation of places: the Southwest is an entity of its own, with its history and fate that allow us to refer to it as an identifiable part of the earth.

Every region is circumscribed by a characteristic edge, a boundary that is highly permeable. This is what distinguishes a region from a territory, whose perimeter is a more or less impervious (or at least clearly marked) border. Regions, especially bioregions, are subject to penetration by many species of animals and plants—and all too often by enterprising humans! Consider, for example, a bioregion such as a watershed, which is porous throughout its rambling extension across different landscapes, confluences of rivers and streams, and human and animal communities. Around the watershed we can imagine an approximate outer limit; but this limit will never be anything so distinctly delineated as a border.[24] Even if it is depicted on a map of the bioregion of which it forms part, its full character cannot be captured in any strictly linear terms. If we try to locate where the cartographic contour of the watershed is to be found on the rude earth, we shall never encounter anything but indeterminate edges of waterways, rough-hewn earth formations, vaguely limned rock structures, and other naturally given features of the regional landscape. Moreover, these various edges will change position and aspect over time. As Gary Snyder puts it, "The lines between natural regions are never simple or clear, but vary according to such criteria as biota, watersheds, landforms, elevation."[25]

Regional boundaries are not confined to those that circumscribe a given region from the outside—i.e., those that distinguish one region from another. They are also internal to the region, which is subdivided in myriad ways, depending on which natural system is at stake: a certain wildflower will have its own boundaries of growth, these boundaries will intersect in turn with those of various grasses in a crisscrossing pattern, and both sorts of boundary will be contained within the bioregion to which they belong jointly. Rock formations will form their own patterns on the land, as will particular species of trees that leave a trail in their wake. An ocean has its own regions, internally differentiated by currents and other flows. A region is a complex of internal and external boundaries, and this holds true for urban regions as well as wild ones: a borough in New York City, such as Queens or Brooklyn, though having a formal outline on official maps, is composed of a dense congeries of neighborhoods, each of which has its own indeterminate boundaries that are internal to the borough of which it is a part. Nor is the external boundary of an urban region any more clear: where does Spanish Harlem begin? What is the exact extent of this area of Harlem? Only the inhabitants can tell you, and their accounts will vary depending on their individual and collective experience there, reflecting idiosyncratic family histories, ties of personal friendship, the local positioning of the subway stations, and the block-to-block variations in patterns of socializing.

Internal and external boundaries stitch together the multifarious content of a region, but the same region is also unified by its *material essence:* that is, the quality or set of qualities that gives to the region its distinctive character and that helps to make it *this* region and not another.[26] The Maine coast is distinguished as a bioregion by the unique coastline it forms, its edge on the Atlantic Ocean, as this has been described in Rachel Carson's classic book on the subject.[27] This coastline is a telling instance of an external boundary that is shared out between sea and land. It is characterized by a certain kind of rock formation in which outsize boulders are perched casually on enormous flat stone shelves. These shelves run under the sea and are often fully submerged at high tide; but their upper parts abut dense forest, with pine trees and soil coming to the very edge of the rock. Considered as a collective mass, these distinctive stone outcroppings hold earth and sea together and constitute a unique material essence of the coastal region of northeastern New England. In a different but parallel way, the material essence of Spanish Harlem is built up from a combination of building styles (apartment buildings of three or four stories that were constructed early in the last century), streams of pedestrian traffic (where individual walkers are absorbed in their stride, and only rarely glance at others on the street), a certain grittiness in the air that stems from a high proportion of buses on the main streets, etc. This composite material essence (whose full description would require a much more extensive treatment) differs markedly from that accruing to the Upper West Side, even though the latter directly touches Spanish Harlem on its western edge. Although it would be difficult to say *just where* the transition from Spanish Harlem to the Upper West Side occurs—that is to say, where a distinct border is to be found, much less at what literal street address—one senses unequivocally the difference between the two regions upon walking from one to the other.

Thanks to its material essence, a region possesses a certain generality—a lasting (even if not permanent) sameness of aspect and constitution—that obtains for all the places contained within it: they are unmistakably the places *of that region*. Thus the neighborhoods of Spanish Harlem belong to it as constituent parts, integral to its overall character. The specificity of such parts—each neighborhood being a unique place—contrasts with the generality of the region in which these parts inhere. In fact, one calls for the other: a region with no placially specified parts would be empty indeed—as empty as the wide open ocean or a cloudless sky—while places that pertain to no region whatever would be as isolated as oases in a vast desert.

This suggests that *place and region are coeval and co-requisite*. They are exemplary of what Deleuze and Guattari call "reciprocal presupposition," that is, a relationship in which each, to be what it is, presumes the presence of the other.[28] This interdependent relationship, though glimpsed in the first edition of this book, was not spelled out in any detail. The primacy of place—my emphatic focus in the edition of 1993—needs to be complemented by a more complete consideration of region: the region to which any given place belongs. The danger of regarding place as something autonomous—a danger that lurks in the first edition—is mitigated by situating place within the compass of region, while emphasizing that region itself is not self-standing. Just as there can be no place without a region in which it is enclosed, so there is no region that is not replete with places. Place and region are in effect two poles of being located anywhere on earth: poles that reach out to embrace each other. This new bipolarity rejoins that recognized earlier in this introduction—the bipolarity of place itself as locatory and eventmental. We need only add that region is also both of these latter: it too serves to situate and is itself, in its fullest expression, an event; but what it locates in its midst are places themselves, and in this very act of implacing places it constitutes an event of regional scope.

VI

Just as in my first work on place I had to narrow down to place in its sheer particularity to make a strong case for its singular status over against the hegemony of an abstract and universal space, so I am now suggesting that place itself needs to be amplified if we are to attain to the level of region: region is at once a partner of place and an indispensable supplement to it. Indeed, the analysis of place ("topoanalysis" in Bachelard's term) calls for expansion on two major fronts: on the one hand, so as to include more expressly its cultural and com-munitarian instantiations and, on the other, to account for its relation with ter-ritory and especially region. Here I have been arguing for both of these forms of augmentation as if they were separate directionalities. But in fact they are quite intimately connected. This becomes evident if we think of both of them as situ-ated on an axis that stretches between nature and culture, thereby facilitating movement back and forth between these basic parameters.

Territory and region, as well as place itself, are at once natural and cultural: all three manifest both of these parameters and are fully activated and embodied through their co-presence. Earlier, I underlined the twofold status of territory as something that is equally a creation of nonhuman animal species (hence "natu-ral") and of human societies (to this extent "cultural"). The very word "terri-tory" and its equivalents in modern European languages (*territoire, Gebiet, ter-ritorio*, etc.) reflect this intrinsic ambiguity. (So too does a *terroir*, the region in whose soil is cultivated a certain wine varietal that flourishes in, and reflects, that very place.)[29] Much the same obtains for region, which combines encultured aspects (not just as urban culture but also in the impingement of human pres-ence on wilderness) with natural components remote from human intervention. And the natural/cultural dovetailing obtains as well for ordinary places, which are rarely entirely wild—and, just as rarely, entirely civilized.

But to allude to ambiguity and impingement, intervention and dovetailing, is still to maintain a dichotomy between the natural and the cultural that the very experience of places, territories, and regions belies. In this experience, we are only rarely presented with a choice between something stemming exclusively from the natural world (e.g., the deepest part of an ocean, a remote mountain peak) over against something deriving wholly from cultural antecedents (e.g., a scientific laboratory). For the most part, we encounter a much more subtle commixture—an intertanglement of the natural and the cultural in which each is fully intertwined with the other, even if in different measures and modali-ties: territories usually include a stronger component of the cultural (e.g., as enforced borders), while regions often favor the natural (e.g., in forests and watersheds); given places almost always combine the two factors (e.g., cities, parks, landscaped vistas). Despite these differential compositions, the collusion of the natural with the cultural virtually everywhere in the place-world is so deep that "everything is cultural in us (our Lebenswelt is 'subjective') (our perception is cultural-historical) and everything is natural in us (even the cultural rests on the polymorphism of the wild Being)."[30] To these words of Merleau-Ponty's, I would add only that the convergence of the natural with the cultural in a com-mon "plane of immanence" (Deleuze) is not only *in us* but is also, and espe-cially, *in places, territories, and regions.*

We witness the interfusion of the natural and the cultural in the notion of "the commons" as this term was construed in early modern British and Ameri-can history. The commons is a public space set aside at the edge of a human settlement that is used for collective gardening and livestock raising. It is at once communitarian and cultivated (as actively shared by all members of the settlement), and contiguous with wilderness (i.e., in the form of wholly un-cultivated areas). The equivalent of the traditional New England commons is found in such different circumstances as the acequia system of northern New Mexico (in which members of a local community collectively maintain a system of ditches that irrigate surrounding fields)[31] and in the communal gardens that have sprung up in certain empty building lots in New York City (tended by members of the immediate neighborhood). In all such versions of a commons, we can detect an intimate relationship between nature and culture: nature in the guise of land that is not built upon as well as the weather hovering overhead, culture as a set of shared practices that act to modify the land in ways beneficial to the local citizenry. What Snyder says of the original commons is equally true of acequias and New York City neighborhood gardens: "the commons is a level of organization of human society that includes the nonhuman."[32]

Still more pointedly, Snyder suggests that if we were able to return to what he calls "the old ways"—i.e., ways of living in the natural world before the advent of European civilization—we would find that nature and culture inter-penetrate as thoroughly as Merleau-Ponty had claimed.[33] In pre-civilized life, knowing nature from up close *is* culture; such intimate acquaintance is the cul-ture that counts. In Snyder's words: "In the old ways, the flora and fauna and landforms are *part of the culture*."[34] An intensive knowledge of one's local places and the bioregion in which they are situated amounts to a cultural knowledge that is notable not just for its practicality but also for its considerable specificity, its attention to detail. On the basis of this compresence of the natural and the cultural, native peoples settle into those places and bioregions in which they acquire such "natural knowledge" and become identified with them over time.[35] In the old ways, the parallel between cultural practices and customs on the one hand and place and region on the other runs deep—so deep that they are finally inextricable from each other.

From this inextricability we may infer two significant implications. First, my initial discussion above of the communitarian locus of particular places and the cultural as providing dimensions that pervade these places needs to be extended to the territorial and regional levels—where communitarian and cultural factors may also be formative even if less conspicuous. To make this move, we need not call for a return to aboriginal life, even if it is in this latter that the inseparability of nature and culture is most salient. We can search for analogues in modern and postmodern times: for instance, "the South" regarded as a region of the United States that combines characteristic climatic and landscape features (e.g., hot and humid in the summer; frequent pine forests) with culturally distinctive behaviors and attitudes (certain accents, dialects, biases and attitudes, etc.); or contem-porary China regarded as a vastly complex but identifiable region of consistent cultural practices that interact intimately with natural landscapes (earlier, in the form of contemplative retreats and landscape painting; much more often today, in an aggressive exploitation of nature by extensive industrialization, mining, and damming of rivers).

Second, the juggernaut of globalization, from which my reflections in this introduction took their initial rise, should not be merely set over against place-specific customs and practices. The increasing consciousness (and attendant appreciation) of place to which I have pointed does indeed represent a constructive response to the forces of globalization in communicational, technological, economic, climatological, and migratory contexts. These same forces induce an enhanced awareness not just of place but also of regions and territories: for instance, that of Eastern Europe as a set of interlinked countries and histories or of Appalachian forests as compromised by acid rain. But the more that region and territory as well as place are recognized as emerging cynosures of contemporary life, the more will the ancient model of the intertwining of the natural with the cultural become pertinent to our current global predicament. In this rising recognition, we must avoid reifying regions (their porous and shifting boundaries discourage this in any case) and isolating territories (given that they are continuous with regions) but see both as exemplary models of the merging of culture and nature at another scale, and with different stakes, than particular places provide.

VII

Since the publication of *Getting Back into Place* in 1993, I have continued to write on place and region as they figure into several contexts. The immediate successor was entitled *The Fate of Place: A Philosophical History* (1997); it traced the vicissitudes of place's consideration (and more particularly its devalorization) by philosophers since the pre-Socratics. This book pointed to a special resilience in the very idea of place, whose significance was never entirely lost sight of despite its repeated marginalization in the hands of thinkers such as Plato, Descartes, and Kant.[36] In *Representing Place in Landscape Painting and Maps* (2002), I showed how place and region, even if demoted in philosophical and scientific theory, remained central in landscape painting and in mapping, both of which set forth places and regions in imagistic form. This book, which belongs to art theory and cartography as much as to philosophy, explored the painterly and (to a lesser extent) the photographic depiction of place, contrasting these modes of visual representation with those found in cartographic and other map-like representations of place. A direct sequel to this last book, *Earth-Mapping: Artists Reshaping the Landscape* (2005), examined the role of place in contemporary painting and earthworks, both of which embody innovative forms of mapping that are transfigured into radically new forms of art.

My recent work on glance and edge continues to meditate on place, albeit somewhat more obliquely. In *The World at a Glance* (2007), I detail how the darting glance picks out crucial features of the place-world, especially in environmental and interpersonal settings, while also being a primary basis for orientation in space. The glance seeks out surfaces everywhere, many of which belong to the local place where the person glancing is situated. A companion to this book, *The World on Edge,* will consider how edges offer crucial inroads into things and surfaces, people and events—as well as places and regions. Almost everything we experience possesses edges that are direct or indirect constituents of places. Edges take many forms, but borders and boundaries—which have figured into this introduction—are particularly prominent. Borders and boundaries encompass places as well as the regions in which they inhere. As a consequence, the collusion between edge and place, territory, and region is very close.

The present book remains the inaugural text in this series of writings on place and region. It makes the basic statement that set the stage, and opened lines of research, for further inquiry into the place-world in its many peregrinations.

In addition to this introduction, I have added to this new edition two essays written after the publication of the first edition: "How to Get from Space to Place in a Fairly Short Stretch of Time" and "Smooth Spaces and Rough-Edged Places: The Hidden History of Place."

I wish especially to thank Dee Mortensen of Indiana University Press for her generous and imaginative support of this new edition of *Getting Back into Place.*

PART I

Finding Place

For times and spaces are, as it were, the places as well of themselves as of all other things. . . . It is from their essence or nature that they are places.

—Isaac Newton, Scholium to the Definitions,
Mathematical Principles of Natural Philosophy

Created things have their particular place in space, and their particular place in time. . . . They embrace each other. . . . the whole of each is in every part of the other.

—Thomas Reid, *Essays on the Intellectual Powers of Man*

1

Implacement

Place possesses a manifest reality [whereas] time on the other hand possesses
an obscure one, since it exists only as conceived by mind.

—Simplicius, *In Aristotelis Categorias Commentarium*

A cry off.
Where are we at all? and whenabouts in the name of space?
I don't understand. I fail to say.
I dearsee you too.

—James Joyce, *Finnegans Wake*

I

THINK OF WHAT it would be like to be lost at sea, not only not knowing
the way but also not knowing one's present place, where one is. "Where
are we at all? and whenabouts in the name of space?" Joyce's double-edged
question, posed near the end of *Finnegans Wake*, might have been asked in
this very extremity.[1] It was an extremity experienced in many early sea voyages in the West, especially those in which land was no longer visible as one
headed into the vast void of the Atlantic Ocean.

One of these voyages proved to be particularly fateful. In 1707 a fleet of
British ships under the direction of Admiral Cloudesley Shovel ran into
heavy fog returning to England from Gibraltar. For eleven days the fleet
drifted, increasingly uncertain as to where it was located. On the twelfth day
the navigators thought the fleet was safely west of Brittany. But that same
night the ships crashed into the Scilly Islands to the southwest of England.
Two thousand men, including Admiral Shovel, were killed, and four ships
were lost. These losses meant in effect that *place had been lost*, dissolved in a
soup of space. The way to avoid such situations in the future was, paradoxically, through the administration of time.

The British government responded to the disaster by passing a bill in
1714 "providing a publick reward for such person or persons as shall discover
the Longitude." The munificent reward of twenty thousand pounds—a sizable fortune at the time—was to be given to the person who could come up

3

with a device for the accurate determination of longitude, the position east or west of the prime meridian established at Greenwich, England. Although many contenders presented themselves to the specially appointed Board of Longitude, the reward was to languish undisbursed for fifty years. The reason for this delay was that the solution lay in the invention of a marine chronometer such as the world had never seen. To solve the problem of longitude the exact measurement of *time* at sea was necessary: time had to be brought to bear on space. For longitude is not merely a matter of spatial position. It is a matter of where one is *at a certain time*—"mean" or "local" time—relative to the time it then is at the prime meridian. To determine longitude is thus to trade on the truth of Simplicius's prescient remark that "the 'when' and the 'where' have a cognate mutual relationship."[2]

In the actual practice of navigation, space cannot be held apart from time. Despite the initial impression that one is simply moving over a spatial expanse at sea, time must be continually invoked. Indeed, in the case of longitude, space is *equivalent* to time. Knowing the difference between local and Greenwich times in minutes and seconds, one can establish the longitude of one's position at sea (also given in minutes and seconds), the difference in time being equivalent to the difference in longitude. To be three minutes earlier than the time at the prime meridian is to be fifty-one miles westward in space from Greenwich and hence at a particular meridian of longitude. For millennia the determination of just where one is situated at sea in relation to a given fixed point had eluded satisfactory resolution. If it could be said with confidence that "the navigator always knows his latitude"—for the distance between parallels of latitude is fixed and thus easily measured—the same cannot be said of longitude, whose nonparallel meridians diverge from one pole only to merge at the other.[3] "Now there be some that are very inquisitive to have a way to get the longitude," lamented a disconsolate navigator in 1594, "but that is too tedious for seamen, since it requireth the deep knowledge of astronomy, wherefore I would not have any man think that the longitude is to be found at sea by any instrument, so let no seamen trouble themselves with any such rule."[4] Not even Magellan mastered the mystery of longitude, and certainly not Christopher Columbus—who deliberately doctored his readings of longitude to reassure his own crew.[5] Richard Eden wrote at the close of the sixteenth century that "some doo understand that the knowledge of the Longitude myght be founde, a thynge greatly to be desyred, and hytherto not certaynly knowen, although Sebastian Cabot, on his death-bed told me that he had the knowledge thereof by divine revelation."[6]

It seemed indeed that divine revelation was required to illuminate the mystery. Even the likes of Galileo could not propose a feasible solution: his suggestion to the Dutch government in 1636 to make use of the regular ro-

tation of the satellites of Jupiter was impracticable, since it called for an unwieldy telescope almost twenty feet in length that would have to remain
trained on Jupiter even in the roughest of seas![7] A still earlier use of the
method of "lunar distances"—Amerigo Vespucci appears to have employed
this method in a 1497 voyage to the country auspiciously named after him—
proved to be unperfectable after centuries of continuous investigation by the
Royal Observatory at Greenwich.

In fact, it was not until the latter part of the eighteenth century that the
reliable determination of longitude came within the reach of the ordinary
navigator. Until then, most sailors could not aim directly at their destination
but had to engage in "parallel sailing," first gaining the destination's parallel
of latitude and then staying on this parallel until the destination was reached.
Such sailing along the proper parallel meant the loss of many nautical miles
and the frequent misestimate of the expected time of arrival, not to mention
the danger of shipwreck.

By the end of the seventeenth century it had become evident that to
determine longitude in space—the surface space of the earth-sphere—one
must call upon the dimension of time. Even Jupiter's satellites or "Cosmian
stars" were considered important by Galileo only because of the temporal
regularity of their appearance and disappearance, not because of their spatial
positions.[8] The immediate issue, however, was not *their* celestial regularity
(or that of any other heavenly bodies) but the trustworthiness of a time-
keeper that could measure the time while at a given position at sea in comparison with the time at the prime meridian. A first step toward creating a
consistently accurate marine chronometer was made by Christian Huygens,
the Dutch scientist and mathematician. Pursuing a hint given by Galileo, he
constructed in 1661 a pendulum clock that was remarkably precise. But his
earnest efforts to adapt this clock to turbulent motions at sea were un-
availing.

The solution was reached by John Harrison, an uneducated carpenter's
son who could not resist tinkering with clocks. Born in 1693, he had, by the
age of twenty-seven, constructed a gridiron pendulum that (unlike Huygens's
clock) could withstand extreme temperature changes. By 1735 he built his celebrated "No. 1 chronometer," which proved to be amazingly accurate on a
first sea trial to Lisbon. But this machine was too bulky for easy placement
on ships. The Board of Longitude was impressed enough to give Harrison
five hundred pounds sterling to build a more usable clock. Thanks to this
underwriting, Harrison built three more timepieces. The last of them, "No.
4," was constructed in 1759 and tested in 1761 on a voyage to Jamaica by his
son. On this two-month passage, the new clock, which resembled a large
watch worn suspended at the waist, was only five seconds slow, well within
the criterion of two minutes posited by the Board of Longitude as requisite

for obtaining the coveted prize. Harrison boasted: "I think I may make bold to say, that there is neither any other Mechanical or Mathematical thing in the World that is more beautiful or curious in texture than this my watch or Time-keeper for the Longitude."[9]

The Board of Longitude, however, was dominated by astronomers who still hoped to find a solution through observations of the moon or the planets. It balked at the innovation of the unheralded Harrison. A new trial was arranged, and Harrison was asked to hand over his working drawings and all four of his personally constructed marine clocks in order to receive the first ten thousand pounds of the reward. Even though No. 4 was carried to the Royal Observatory in triumph, Harrison was asked to build two successor clocks to be tested in Hudson's Bay before he could receive the second half of the prize. He dutifully built No. 5, which was exhibited at King George III's private observatory at Kew. Exclaiming "By God, Harrison, I'll see you righted," the much-impressed king intervened in person to assure that Harrison—now eighty years old—be given the remainder of the coveted reward.

I recount this tale of perseverance and deferred success in order to underscore one basic point. It required time to resolve the problem of determining exact location in space. Not only did it take time—many centuries of it—but it was *by means of* time, captured and regulated in the frame of a marine chronometer, that this problem was finally resolved. The winning logic was this: when lost in space, turn to time. In other words, *where* one was became equivalent to *when* one was. The determination of the latter allowed the specification of the former. The measure of space was taken by time.

The success of "Longitude Harrison" is revealing not only because the enigma of longitude was at long last resolved. Harrison's ingenious contrivance concretized, literally put into one's hands, the characteristically modern domination of space by time. If it is true that "cunningly concealed from prying eyes beneath the plate [of No. 4] was a mechanism such as the world had never seen,"[10] it is also true that concealed within the triumph of No. 4 was a form of domination such as the Western world had never known: the subordination of space to time, or "temporocentrism," as we may call it. In the modern world, to be "whenabouts in the name of space" is to know one's whereabouts in the form of time. Harrison's clever clock instituted temporocentrism in its purely mechanical guise.

II

"Time will tell": so we say, and so we believe, in the modern era. This era, extending from Galileo and Descartes to Husserl and Heidegger, belongs to time, the time when Time came into its own. Finally. And yet, despite the fact that history, human and geological alike, occurs in time (and has been doing so for quite a while), time itself has not long been singled out for separate scrutiny. Thus it comes as something of a surprise to learn that "it was only late in the Middle Ages that the role of time as the fundamental variable parameter in physical processes was clearly understood."[11] Once it was understood, it was not long before time assumed a predominant position in physics and philosophy. By the middle of the eighteenth century, time had become prior to space in metaphysics as well as in physics. If, in Leibniz's elegant formula, "space is the order of co-existing things," time proved to be more basic: as "the order of *successive* things," it alone encompasses the working of causal interaction. As Kant argued in his *Critique of Pure Reason*, objective succession in time is the schematic expression of causality in the physical world order. By the moment when Kant could assert this, time had won primacy over space. We have been living off this legacy ever since, not only in philosophy and physics but in our daily lives as well.

These lives are grasped and ordered in terms of time. Scheduled and overscheduled, we look to the clock or the calendar for guidance and solace, even judgment! But such time-telling offers precious little guidance, no solace whatsoever, and a predominantly negative judgment ("it's too late now"). Harrison's marine chronometer, perfected just twenty years before the publication of Kant's *Critique* in 1781, was prototypically modern. For all its engineering brilliance, however, it did not actually give *guidance* to sailors at sea (this only comes from the combination of destination with motivation), much less solace or shrewd judgment.[12] Faced with time, indeed in its very clock-face, the modern subject is unguided and disconsolate. It doesn't take the poet to let us know that "time eats away our lives" and that it is our most insidious "enemy."[13] Modern subjects are thus in the desperate position of Admiral Shovel's foredoomed sailors: lost on the sea of time as well as space, and still lost even after the invention of the marine chronometer. We are lost because of our conviction that time, not only the world's time but *our time*, the only time we have, is always running out or down. All time, it seems, is "closing time." No sooner have we settled in somewhere than we hear "Hurry up, please! It's time!"[14]

In the modern era, in this epoch of time as the primary world-order, there is not "world enough and time."[15] *Had we* but world enough and time . . . but we don't, and we don't precisely because we have come to conceive the world itself as a predominantly temporal ordering of events. When events are ordered on a time-line—just as Descartes, Leibniz, and Kant all proposed (and as Galilean and Newtonian physics seemed to affirm)—then we should not expect anything other than the running down or out of these events, their literal ex-haustion.[16] Our lives also run out and down if we conceive them on this kenotic model of self-emptying time. And if we construe world-order as time-order, then the world, including our own world, is at all times in imminent demise.

Aristotle's assurance that "time will not fail" falls on deaf ears in modern times.[17] We only have time enough to see time itself lapsing from the line of its own appearance. On this line, appearance is tantamount to disappearance. No sooner does an event occur *in* time than it goes *out of* time. Into what? Presumably into the sea of absolute flux, where (as both Heraclitus and Husserl would assert) it is lost and perhaps irretrievable. At least it is not retrievable as a discrete event, to be simply relocated on the time-line of the modern world-order.

What are we to do in dealing with such a disappearing act? What does *doing* itself mean in a world so ordered? Have we not stymied ourselves in time, thanks to the modernist conception of time? Has not the problem become quite literally *diachronic*, so "chronic" indeed that we cannot act or think effectively in (terms of) time any more? We don't even have time for time itself. Taking two steps forward in chronological time, we are set back three in lived time. The result is not just discrepancy but dead time, *temps mort*. No assurance, much less any remedy, is forthcoming in this perplexing circumstance and we have *done this to ourselves*. We have effected our own double-binding of time: of it to ourselves and of ourselves to it. To be absorbed in a linear time of our own making is to be consumed by the artifact itself.[18]

The crux of the problem is that time is conceived in such a way that everything else is made subjacent to it, beginning with place and ending with space. The subordination of place to space culminates in the seventeenth century; the subordination of space to time continues during the next two-and-a-half centuries. In 1925 Rudolf Carnap could still claim to show "the dependency of the properties of space on those of time."[19] Carnap's claim is echoed in Hans Reichenbach's statement that "time is . . . logically prior to space."[20] We see the long arm of modernism reaching into these twentieth-century propositions. This arm is none other than the arm of linearized time—the time of "progress" and of infinite succession—compared with which space and place cannot be anything but derivative and secondary.

But is the primacy of linear time truly *primary*? Can we, in the dawning of a new era called proleptically "postmodern," accept without questioning the paradigm laid down for us by the early modern philosophers and physicists? Is the putative priority of the time-line an unquestionable "absolute presupposition"?[21] Is it not time to question it? Not because time is running out but because the very notion of time entailed by the linear model is (in Nietzsche's prophetic word) "untimely": made for another time. And because we must, in postmodern times, begin to appreciate once more the intrinsic ingredience of place in our time-bound and spaced-out lives.

III

"Time on the Mind": this phrase also epitomizes the occasion of the modern. It was hardly accidental that Descartes located successive time in the mind, putting "duration," or eventful process, outside in physical things. If time is monolinear, its natural site is mental. The rapid emerging and evanescing of thoughts, their sudden appearance and disappearance in the thinking mind (*res cogitans*), is a prototype for the arising and demising of events in extended things (*res extensa*).[22] But it is difficult to conceive of "time out of mind." For, outside the mind, many entities display a durational permanence that does not fit the idea of sheer succession. Hence Kant's First Analogy: "the permanence of the real in time." Such permanence—or "enduringness," as we might also translate Kant's *Beharrlichkeit*—is not found within the mind. In the midst of mind, cogitations come and go with ceaseless celerity in what Whitehead called the "immediate rush of transition."[23] No wonder that confronted with this confusing and sometimes dazzling spectacle, we are tempted by the idea of a continuous line of time, to which our onrushing thoughts can cling as to a life-line at sea. In being thus tempted, we do not notice that we have ourselves constructed the line and thereby insidiously imported a specifically spatial model into our experience of succession in time, at once abstracting from this experience and homogenizing it. Nor do we notice that we project this same constructed line back onto the world.[24] Whenever we think of time as a stringlike succession, we spatialize it, giving to it—supposedly an exclusively mental concern—predicates such as "continuous" and "linear," which we borrow surreptitiously from the "external" world of space (a world into which we just as surreptitiously reimport these same predicates in order to reinforce its exteriority).

We also borrow certain properties from the world of place. If the time-line is spatial in its continuity and homogeneity, it is at the same time "placial" in its constitution by means of *positions*, that is, a series of points arranged on the line and grasped, all together, *as* the line. As Bergson writes in *Time and Free Will*, "We could not introduce order among terms without first distinguishing them and then comparing the *places which they occupy*; hence we must perceive them as multiple, simultaneous, and distinct; in a word, we set them side by side, and if we introduce an order in what is successive, the reason is that succession is converted into simultaneity and is projected into space."[25] Bergson's celebrated critique of the "spatialization" of time is just as much a critique of its "placialization," its representation as a set of densely juxtaposed positions on a time-line. Yet it is as important to separate place from space (construed as a homogeneous and isotropic medium) as it is to distinguish such space from true time (grasped as heterogeneous anisotropic multiplicity). In failing to make the first separation and by his insistence on the second, Bergson unwittingly falls prey to the modernist myth that place can be discounted and set aide for the sake of space or time. By the same token, he explicitly endorses the predominance of time over space that we have seen to be an integral part of this same myth.

The *gigantomachia* between Time and Space—a contest of giants orchestrated by Newton and Leibniz, Descartes and Kant, Galileo and Gassendi—is a struggle that overlooks Place. Place undoes the presumed primordiality of Time over Space as well as the equiprimordiality that both Newton and Reid ascribed to them (see the epigraphs to this part). It is remarkable that in these same ascriptions the priority of Place over Space and Time is at least tacitly affirmed. But we are getting ahead of our story.

For the moment, let us agree with Simplicius (in his epigraph to this chapter) that time possesses "an obscure [reality], since it exists only as conceived by mind."[26] Or rather, it has an obscure reality precisely to the extent that it is conceived as taking place in the mind; and the obscurity consists in the subreption (the illicit transposition) of space, and more particularly of place, into what is putatively nonspatial and nonplacial. Yet because of this subreption the reprojection of time into the world can take place in equal obscurity. Since we do not notice that space and place have been imported into the heart of time to begin with (it took Bergson's discernment to bring this importation to our collective notice), we remain unaware of the reexternalizing of spatialized and implaced time into the world as its own presumptive order.

IV

Aristotle remarks that we can tell time even in the dark.[27] He might well have said: especially in the dark, where time and the mind collude most intimately. Time's obscure origins, its hybrid birth and hydra-headed existence, lead us to obsess about it even when we cannot see its imprint left lucidly in the world-order. The darkness of time-telling reflects its ambivalent position between Cartesian interiority and an equally Cartesian exteriority, each the shadow of the other. The darkness is also Saturnian: grim Saturn is the time-keeping god of regular measure and exact division. "Saturn will shape order slowly through time," James Hillman remarks.[28] Neptune's realm was Saturnized by Harrison's marine chronometer, which facilitated regular and predictable voyages across the sea's outer surface. But in the depths, where profit and loss are forgotten, another time is to be found: "a succession of qualitative changes, which melt into and permeate one another, without precise outlines, without any tendency to externalize themselves in relation to one another, without any affiliation with number . . . pure heterogeneity."[29] This nonlinear dissolving time, which Bergson labeled "*durée ré-elle*" (in contrast with Cartesian duration), refuses to be located either in the mind or in the world; indeed, its very existence deconstructs that Cartesian bifurcation by introducing a conceptual sea-change whose momentous consequences are still not fully appreciated. When Bergson finished his *Essai sur les données immédiates de la conscience* just over a century ago, in 1888, he was taking the first crucial step beyond the modern view of time and toward a distinctively postmodern conception. Looking back on this step several decades later, he commented that "before the spectacle of this universal mobility, some among us will be seized by vertigo."[30]

The pandemic obsession with time from which so many moderns have suffered—and from which so many postmoderns still suffer—is exacerbated by the vertiginous sense that time and the world-order, together constituting the terra firma of modernist solidity, are subject to dissolution. Not surprisingly, we objectify time and pay handsome rewards (such as that offered by the Board of Longitude) to those who can tie time down in improved chronometry. Although the modern period has succeeded brilliantly in this very regard, it has also fallen into the schizoid state of having made objective, as clock-time and world-time, what is in fact most diaphanous and ephemeral, most "obscure," in human experience. We end by obsessing about what is no object at all. We feel obligated to tell time in an objective manner; but in fact we have only obliged ourselves to do so by our own sub rosa subreptions, becoming thereby our own pawns in the losing game of time.

V

Is there any way out of this double-bind, which we have managed to impose on ourselves so stealthily and yet so destructively? We can't do without time, and yet we can't live *with* the time we have devised for ourselves. Is there an exit or passage leading out of this impasse, this *aporia*? Place, that most innocuous and taken-for-granted item in our experience, offers a way out, if we are willing to reconsider our prejudices and to question our all-too-absolute presuppositions regarding time and space. We need to get back into place so as to get out of (the binding and rebinding of) space and time. But this is not so simple a step as it may seem. Not even Bergson, as we have seen, was sensitive to the special properties of place in contrast with space.[31] Insensitive as well were other philosophers who should have known better, including even such otherwise resolute anti-Cartesians as Merleau-Ponty, James, Dewey, and Whitehead. Heidegger alone of postmodern thinkers has thematized place, albeit fragmentarily and inconsistently.[32] It is as if the modern obsession with time—an obsession that continues into the postmodern period—comes coupled with a resistance to place. What are we to make of this resistance?

Following Bergson's lead, we can note that many of the descriptive terms and phrases that we apply unthinkingly to time are spatial in character: a "stretch" or "interval" of time; indeed, a "space of time."[33] Notice also that when we talk about being "before" and "after" in time, we are invoking a spatial distinction, as is evident when one object is said to be placed "before" or "after" another. Yet we can trace the distinction between before and after still further back—all the way back to place. "The before and after," avers Aristotle, are "in place (*en topoi*) primarily."[34] The ultimate source of the distinction between before and after resides in the way that a given place disposes itself: as having both a "forward" area that is accessible to and continuous with our own embodied stance and a "back" region in which the same place eludes our grasp and view. The room in which I am now writing these words is such a bipartite place. Its forepart is oriented toward the dormer windows out of which I look as I write; its rearward portion lies around and behind me. The epicenters established by these fore and aft regions lend to this room a characteristic dynamism that is lacking in a merely homogeneous space. The dynamism generated by the before and after in place is such that it comes to shape our very idea of time as always having the double aspect of the before and the after. "Here is a place of disaffection / Time before and time after / In a dim light."[35] But all too often we assume that the before and after belong to time *to begin with*, an instance of subreption in its strictly logical sense, whereby we draw a fallacious inference from an initial misrepresentation.[36]

Or take Saint Augustine's offhand observation that "we speak of a 'long time' and a 'short time,' though only when we mean the past or the future."[37] But where do we first understand the sense of "long" and "short" themselves if not from our experiences of being in more or less accommodating or demanding, more or less extended or compressed, *places*? It is nonsensical to speak of *space* as long or short, at least of space in its modern Newtonian conception as "always similar and immovable."[38] Newton's notion of homogeneous and infinite space resists determination as merely long or short. Yet any given place as we experience it invites just this kind of description. "This is a very long valley!" I exclaim upon first viewing the Yarlung in Tibet. "That is quite a short street," I say upon entering a cul-de-sac. In each case, I also mean that it would take a long or short time to traverse the place I have just encountered; but the temporal estimates follow upon the perception of the extensiveness of the places, and not the reverse. (The actual motion of traversing these places would bring place and time together.) The most appropriate—though not necessarily the exclusive—source of the long and the short in time is to be sought in predicates of place.

Saint Augustine's own celebrated formula for time is *distentio animi*, "an extendedness of the soul."[39] Augustine muses that "it seems to me that time is merely an extension, though of what it is an extension I do not know."[40] My conviction is that time is an extension of the extensiveness of place itself as superimposed, or subincised, on time—so forgetfully so that we do not realize how many of time's supposedly ingredient properties are borrowed from place to start with.[41]

Hence we can applaud Simplicius's statement that "the 'where' and the 'when' are, so to say, siblings."[42] But we must go on to ask: where is the root of the "where" (*pou*) that forms one of Aristotle's ten leading metaphysical categories? Certainly not in abstract and empty space, an Atomistic notion (anticipatory of Newtonian space) roundly rejected by Aristotle; and certainly not in time, which Aristotle makes dependent on motion. *Where else but in place*, on which motion is in turn dependent? Simplicius himself observes that "place and time are akin to each other, both being measures essential for generation."[43] But they are akin not as identical twins, much less as parent and child. Instead, place is a *primus inter pares*, a first among equals; and the same holds for the relationship between place and space.

VI

How can place, mere place, be *"prior to all things"*?[44] We must seek other than merely historical or philological grounds for this strong claim of Aristotle's, a claim from which it follows that (as Aristotle also avers) "the power of place will be a remarkable one."[45] In this section I shall examine one such ground, logical (or perhaps more properly cosmological), as it reveals itself in a group of very diverse phenomena.

It is a striking fact, on which we do not often enough reflect, that while we can certainly *conceive* of entirely empty spaces and times—radical vacua in which no bodies (in space) or events (in time) exist—such spatio-temporal voids are themselves placelike insofar as they *could be*, in principle, occupied by bodies and events.[46] Moreover, once bodies are found or even merely posited, they *require* places in which to exist. There are no "actual occasions" (in Whitehead's composite term for objects as well as events) without places for these occasions. Although there may be displaced occasions, there are no *non*placed occasions, i.e., occasions without any form of implacement whatsoever. To exist at all as a (material or mental) object or as (an experienced or observed) event is to have a place—*to be implaced*, however minimally or imperfectly or temporarily. For this to be so, the object or event need not be well formed, regular, or predictable. Even Chaos has a shape and a place into which that shape fits, as Hesiod early on realized and as "chaos theorists" of the present moment are rediscovering.

Aristotle was acutely sensitive to this fundamental point; it is the main basis for his claim that place is prior to all things:

> One might suppose that place is something over and above bodies, and that every body perceptible by sense is in place. Hesiod, too, might seem to be speaking correctly in making Chaos first . . . because he thinks as most people do that *everything is somewhere and in place*.[47]

"Everything is somewhere and in place": despite its definite tone, this statement is by no means original with Aristotle. It stems from the Pythagorean Archytas of Tarentum (428–347 B.C.), who wrote a lost treatise on place. Only fragments survive; one of them is cited by Simplicius:

> Since everything that is in motion is moved in some place, it is obvious that one has to grant priority to place, in which that which causes motion or is acted upon will be. Perhaps thus it is the first of all things, since all existing things are either in place or not without place.[48]

Aristotle, then, merely paraphrases Archytas when he comments in the *Physics* that "that, without which no other thing is, but which itself is without the others, must be first (for place does not perish when the things in it cease to be)."[49] Place is "prior to all things" according to Aristotle for the very reason which Archytas gives: place's indispensability for all things that exist. *To be is to be in place*: this is Archytas's message, dutifully preserved and transmitted by Aristotle (and by Simplicius commenting on Aristotle).

In modern and postmodern times we are so inured to the putative primacy of time that we rarely question the temporocentrist dogma that time is the first of all things. Nor do we often notice how frequently we subscribe to this dogma by passing on and repeating Saint Augustine's remarkably modern question: "What, then, is time? I know well enough what it is, provided that no one asks me; but if I am asked what it is and try to explain, I am baffled."[50] Twentieth-century thinkers such as Husserl and Waismann still repeat this aporetic Augustinian question at the very beginning of their inquiries into time. It has become an obligatory and ritualized starting point for almost every modern philosophical investigation of time.[51] In contrast, we certainly do not ask any comparable question concerning place. Nor is there any tradition of place-consciousness on which we can draw, as Aristotle and Simplicius drew from Archytas, repeating his primal gesture of designating place as "the first of all things."[52]

An Archytian thinker holds, then, that *there is no being without place*. But is this so? Archytas himself provides the most persuasive answer:

> It is peculiar to place that while other things are in it, place is in nothing. For if it were in some place, this place again will be in another place, and this will go on without end. For this very reason it is necessary for other

things to be in place, but for place to be in nothing. And so for the things
that exist there always holds the relation of the limits to the things limited,
for the place of the whole cosmos is the limit of all existing things.[53]

The point is that place, by virtue of its unencompassability by anything other
than itself, is at once the limit and the condition of all that exists.

It is the *limit* inasmuch as there is nothing beyond the place of an actual
occasion—except another place for another occasion. This leads to a regress
that is benign, not vicious. Archytas is thought to have been the first to pose
the conundrum that obsessed later Greek thinkers: what happens when a
javelin thrower throws his javelin into the space surrounding the *last*, outermost cosmic place of the known cosmos? Archytas answered that there is no
surrounding space that is not itself of the nature of place. If the javelin can
be thrown at all, it must be thrown *into another place*; otherwise it cannot
occupy any place other than the place it already occupies as not yet thrown.
Although the Archytian perspective induces a shell game of places-within-
places, it posits a cosmological limit in the form of "the place of the whole
cosmos." This is coextensive with the "universe" (as we now prefer to call
the totality of all that is). Beyond this outer limit there is "nothing," not the
nothing of an Atomistic void (i.e., empty space) but the peculiar nothing of
no-place-at-all. That is why Archytas says with disarming simplicity that
"place is *in* nothing." In other words, there can be *no other* nonplacial entity,
medium, or container (not even an infinite and vacuous one) into which
place, whether the tiniest locale or the cosmos at large, could be deposited.
Instead there is simply the boundary of any given place and, at the limit, the
boundary of the physical universe, its own limit. The limit of place is thus
the limit of every actual occasion as well as the limit of the universe (*to pan*)
that contains all actual occasions. Place provides the absolute edge of everything, including itself.[54]

At the same time, place serves as the *condition* of all existing things. This
means that, far from being merely locatory or situational, place belongs to
the very concept of existence. To be is to be bounded by place, limited by
it. "Boundary" (*horos*) or "limit" (*peras*) is not the nugatory notion of mere
cutting off; nor is it the geometric concept of perimeter (itself the linear
reduction of placial limit to an abstract residue comparable to the time-line).
Boundary or limit, construed cosmologically, is a quite positive presence.
When Archytas says that "for the things that exist there always holds the
relation of the limits (*perata*) to the things limited," he is saying nothing
other than that the limit of an existing thing is intrinsic to its being, a condition for its very existing.

Through such an eminently cosmo-logical line of reasoning, we reach the
conclusion, not expressly stated by Archytas but implied by all he says, that

the boundary or limit of a thing determines its place. A thing is not merely *in* a place—that is the important but not the exhaustive sense of place-as-container that Aristotle was to adopt in his *Physics*—but *a thing constitutes its (own) place*. But it does so only to the extent that place is its boundary, its limit-of-being, its way of not being nothing, its edge on the void that does not exist. Only the unlimited is nothing and calls for cosmic vacancy.

One direct implication is that as regards place at least, there is no difference in principle between the universe in toto ("the whole cosmos" in Archytas's words) and the most minute thing in that universe (down to the most exiguous subatomic particle). For both alike, and for all that lies in between, place-being is part of an entity's own-being.

VII

If to be is to be in place, it also follows that even the most unlikely candidates can be regarded as placial: numbers, the mind, rhetoric, God, creation, time itself. To call these things "places" or even "placelike" is to risk excommunication from the realm of rational human being, especially in modern times. Yet consider an idea held by Archytas's Pythagorean colleagues: "every number is in its proper place."[55] Not only is each number in its place; it is also *at* its place, for it *is* its very position in the number-series. As Bergson, by no means a Pythagorean, attests,

> Space is, accordingly, the material with which the mind builds up number, the medium in which the mind places it. . . . if we did not already localize number in space, science would certainly not succeed in making us transfer it thither. From the beginning, therefore, we must have thought of number as of a juxtaposition in space.[56]

The reference to "space" should not mislead us; numerical space, the space of numbers, is (as Bergson expressly indicates) a highly *localized* space, a space "in which the mind places" numbers. True, as composed of serially arranged positions it is an abstractly placialized, a pointillistic, space. But numerical space is genuinely placeful, inasmuch as the place of a number is its limit, a limit that determines its contour and exact quantity.

The mind that does the placing of numbers is itself a place: "The mind is its own place, and in itself can make a Heaven of Hell, a Hell of Heaven."[57] Milton has been preceded by Aristotle, who regarded the mind (as we have seen) as "a place of forms," including the forms of numbers.[58] To regard the mind as a place of forms is to engage in more than metaphor. It is to recognize a basic capacity of mind to grasp and retain what comes into its ken. The mind holds cognized items not just in memory (itself a store-place) but in other arenas that serve as place-holders for mindfulness of many sorts—indeed, for the reflective noting of any experience whatsoever. Here, too, place functions as a limit, i.e., as a limit to what we can know or remember or at least notice. And it remains intrinsic and not just adventitious to what we know, remember, or notice.[59]

Part of minding is arguing and, in particular, using the argument-forms of rhetoric. The rhetorician is someone who knows how to employ the places of an argument effectively: how to be well positioned in the crossfire of dialectic. Thus Simplicius observes that "the dialectical proofs are called 'common-places,' for instance, arguments by opposites or by similars, or by genera or by species."[60] Common-places (*topoi*) are general argument-forms that are applicable to many given cases.[61] As such, they at once delimit and facilitate the actual arguments set forth by the dialectician. They are cognitive places from which one argues and in terms of which one makes "moves" in discussions with others. At the present moment in historical time, dialectical and rhetorical *topoi* would be studied under the heading of "informal logic." But we need not study them formally or informally in order to make use of them, which we do spontaneously in the course of daily talk. Even idle chatter or gossip involves moving between the common-places by which we economize, locate, and limit our discourse—to the point of engaging in mere commonplaces! It all remains a matter of where we are, and where we are going, in our talk.

But God? Here is no object of fallen speech but a supreme object of thought and will. In contemplating God, it might seem that we pass beyond place into meta-place, into an ethereal realm ("heaven," "svarga," "pure land") in which the earthbound configurations of place, and above all its limits, no longer obtain. Yet we need only think of the fact that the Hebrew word *Makom*, the name of God, means precisely Place. " 'Place' as a synonym for God," writes Shmuel Sambursky, "became a generally accepted expression in the Hebrew language from the first centuries of the Christian era onwards."[62] If the Archytian position is correct, this is not an anomalous but an altogether expectable development. A rabbinical commentary on Genesis exclaims, "Why is God called place? Because He is the place of the world, while the world is not His place."[63] Philo of Alexandria follows suit in words that could have been written by Archytas: "God Himself is called place, for He encompasses all things, but is not encompassed by anything."[64] Philo's creative conjunction of Judaism and late Neoplatonic thought is carried forward by the Cambridge Platonist Henry More, a correspondent of Descartes and an important influence on Newton:

> There are not less than twenty titles by which the Divine Numen is wont to be designated, and which perfectly fit this infinite internal place (*locus*) the existence of which in nature we have demonstrated; omitting moreover

that the very Divine Numen is called, by the Cabalists, MAKOM, that is, Place (*locus*).[65]

God as Place—well, why not? Surely this conception generates fewer problems than the more usual idea of God as a divine Person. It allows us to depersonalize God and to turn God into a cosmic occasion, or rather the place of every occasion.[66] But as such, God remains a limit of all that exists: Its (not Her or His) celestial status and divine being (not to mention the role of that status and being in worship) change nothing when it comes to the fundamental fact that, *as a place*, God is a source-limit, both limit and source, of the universe. From God's Place the universe proceeds—and comes continually to end.[67]

It follows as an immediate corollary that if God is a place, the act of creation undertaken by any such deity will also be place-bound. When we think of the creation of the world, we tend to think in terms of *entia creata*, of created things like animals and trees and human beings, rather than of the scene of creation. But if we ask ourselves not *what* was created or even *how* it was created but *where* creation occurred, we realize that it could not have happened just anywhere, much less nowhere. If things and ultimately the world-whole were indeed created, then they will have to be brought into being (from) *somewhere*. The exact character of this somewhere differs from cosmogony to cosmogony. In the first chapter of Genesis, the "Deep" already exists when God decides to become cosmically creative:

> In the beginning God created the heavens and the earth. The earth was without form and void, and darkness was upon the face of the Deep; and the Spirit of God was moving over the face of the waters.[68]

Not only does the Deep (*tehom*) precede the act of creation; it also has a "face" and is determinate enough in shape to be moved *over* by God. In other words, it has enough consistency and form to be a *place*, a place for and of creation. If it is true that in the beginning was the Word, it is also true that in the beginning was the Place.

In other accounts, the aboriginal state is still less definite in its specification and might seem to be no place at all. Consider Hesiod's notion of Chaos as at the origin:

> Verily first of all did Chaos come into being, and then broad-bosomed Gaia [earth], a firm seat of all things for ever, and misty Tartaros in a recess of broad-wayed earth, and Eros, who is fairest among immortal gods. . . . Out of Chaos, Erebos and black Night came into being; and from Night, again, came Aither and Day. . . . [69]

Chaos may not be a well-ordered place, but it is nonetheless a place both differentiated and differentiating. *Chaos* signifies chasm or gap, and thus a certain primal shape.[70] Indeed, it signifies space itself if Aristotle, commenting on the above passage from the *Theogony*, is right: "Things need to have space first [of all]."[71] The word for "space" in this last sentence is *chōra*, the very word with which Plato characterizes the initial state of the universe in his account of creation in the *Timaeus*. Choric space has its own determinacy. Not only is it characterized by "necessity" (*anankē*); it is also filled with sensible qualities grouped loosely into four "regions" (*chorāi*) that correspond to the ancient elements of fire, air, earth, and water. Plato's cosmogonic model, enormously influential in subsequent Western accounts of creation, not only posits space as there from the beginning in the form of regions but also traces out their progressive concretization into particular "places" (*topoi*). In Plato's synoptic vision, *cosmogenesis occurs as topogenesis*. Aristotle, in an unusual homage to his teacher, remarks that "while everyone says that place is something, he alone tried to say what it is."[72]

Chaos is by no means an exclusive invention of Western cosmogony. In an early Taoist text, chaos is again the source of a primary separation:

> In the beginning there was chaos. Out of it came pure light and built the sky. The heavy dimness, however, moved and formed the earth from itself. Sky and earth brought forth the ten thousand creations . . . and all of them take the sky and earth as their mode.[73]

Likewise, in a southern Chinese creation myth of the third to sixth century A.D., the creator god P'an Ku, after bursting out of the cosmic egg, "went to work at once, mightily, to put the world in order. He chiselled the land and sky apart."[74] Peoples as distant from each other as the Japanese and the Celts identify the primal state of creation as a scene of scission.[75] If earth and sky must be separated as the very first act of creation, then they must emanate from some place where they were first of all together.

The medieval dictum that *ex nihilo nihil fit* ("from nothing nothing can be made") here finds another application. There is no creation without place. Cosmogenesis is not from no-place to place but from less determinate to more determinate places. Creation in the first place both presupposes a preexisting first place and consists in the further constitution of other primary (and eventually secondary) places. Once more, place remains both source and limit. In creation as in the deity that creates, there is *no getting around* place, no getting *before* it, much less *behind* it.

And what of time? It too is a source and a limit: a source of events and processes and a limit to these same events and processes. Indeed, time is a place—its own kind of place. We have seen how this is so in the modeling of time as linear: the controlling image of the line, composed of positions that are indefinitely densely juxtaposed, is a covert borrowing from place.[76] But we can take a further step by asserting that almost all philosophical theorizing about time, from Plato to McTaggart, is place-determined. When Plato talks of time as "a moving image of eternity,"[77] he describes this image as a circle that imitates the regular path of the planets, that is to say, the circular *place* of the planets, their own way of moving-in-place. Augustine imports place even more explicitly into his description of time:

> If the future and the past do exist, I want to know *where they are.* . . . While we are measuring [time], *where is it coming from*, what is it passing through, and *where is it going*? It can only be coming *from* the future, passing *through* the present, and going *into* the past. In other words, it is coming *out of* what does not yet exist, passing through what has no duration, and moving into what no longer exists.[78]

The prepositions italicized in this passage demonstrate the extent to which Augustine's account of time is deeply imbued by the search for location: for *the place of time*. Taken literally, these prepositions signify the pre-positions of time in place. They inform Augustine's description of time from within in terms of its inner limits, its own infrastructures.[79]

We find the same placialization at work in the many characterizations of time as "passage."[80] For time's passing is a moving from one place to another, whether the places in question belong to the psyche or to the physical world, to rhetoric or to God, to the notes of a melody or to the words of a recited psalm (in Augustine's example).[81] This is perhaps most evident in McTaggart's celebrated discussion of time as a combination of an "A series" (i.e., past, present, and future) with a "B series" (i.e., of earlier and later, the before and the after). Far from such series being merely or sheerly temporal in character, their very description depends on place predicates. Thus in introducing his distinction McTaggart says that

> positions in time, as time appears to us *prima facie*, are distinguished in two ways. Each position is earlier and later than some of the other positions. . . . In the second place, each position is either Past, Present, or Future.[82]

How else are we to understand this move on McTaggart's part except as a matter of *placing time* by a determination of its distinctively implacing "positions"? Such positions are no less place-specific than the positions that make up the time-line posited by Descartes, Locke, and Kant. McTaggart admits that "it is very usual to contemplate time by the help of a metaphor of spatial movement."[83] But the matter is more than that of receiving assistance from a metaphor. It is a matter of the constitution of time from within by aspects of place on which McTaggart, no less than Augustine and Husserl, manifestly draws: e.g., in his statement that "no fact about anything can change, unless it is a fact about its place in the A series."[84]

As in the other cases we have examined (and building on earlier observations as well), place proves to be a deeply constitutive, indeed an irreplaceable, factor in the phenomenon of time and its understanding. There is *no (grasping of) time without place*; and this is so precisely by virtue of place's actively delimiting and creatively conditioning capacities. Place situates time by giving it a local habitation. Time arises *from* places and passes (away) *between* them. It also vanishes *into* places at its edges and *as* its edges. For the "positions" of time are its effective limits, without which it would not appear as time at all—indeed, without which time itself would not be able to present itself to us, would not be timelike or temporal in the first place.

The indispensability of place is evident, then, in the disparate instances of rhetoric and number, God and creation, time and mind. In each case we witness a version of what Aristotle calls tellingly the inherent and unborrowed "power" (*dynamis*) of place.[85] This power is considerable. It is much more considerable than we are willing to grant as modernists—and now as postmodernists—whose obsession with time and space has blinded us to the forgotten but formidable presence of place in our lives.

2

Displacement

It is not down in any map; true places never are.

—Herman Melville, *Moby Dick*

In a certain sense, everything is everywhere at all times.

—Alfred North Whitehead, *Science and the Modern World*

I

B UT ENOUGH of logic, including the cosmo-logic into which we have been
so indelicately drawn. Let us turn to the actual experience of place. This
is so pervasive and yet so elusive that most of us simply do not notice it.
But it is to our own peril that we do not. For we risk falling prey to time's
patho-logic, according to which gaining is tantamount to losing.

Consider only the immediate circumstance in which you, my reader, find
yourself at this very moment. However forlorn or lost you may feel, you are
not adrift in what Locke calls "the undistinguishable inane of infinite
space."[1] Nor are you lost in any comparably undistinguishable void of infinite
time that (in Newton's words) "flows equably without relation to anything
external."[2] Wherever you are, you are distinctly (if not simply) located in
space and time. Let us assume that you are now in your living room as you
read these words. The room itself serves to distinguish you, at least as much
as does the time of day or year. You are *there* in your room *now*, comfortably
ensconced in space and time. Your existence is reflected and supported by
the room as a distinguishing mark, a "specific difference" in an otherwise
undistinguished world of homogeneous space and equably flowing time.
Room is cognate with the German *Raum*, which means "space." But as a
space in which you are located, a living room is a particular *place*, a place
for living.

The same is true of other, more encompassing spaces, which you are
simultaneously occupying at this very same moment: the apartment or house
in which your living room is lodged, your neighborhood, your city, your
state. Although their fit is looser, you are also distinguished by these places.
You are *in* them not as a puppet stuffed in a box—as would be true on a

strict container view of place—but as living in them, indeed, *through* them.[3] They too are living rooms. They serve to implace you, to anchor and orient you, finally becoming an integral part of your identity. "Where do you come from?" we ask each other on first meeting. Our answers—"upper West Side," "Topeka," "the Midwest," "Stony Brook"—place and identify us. They do so as surely as does an account of our life history, which we come to only later in the conversation and which itself includes still further place-names.[4]

In making such commonplace observations, I am saying something more than that our existence is indicated deictically ("here," "now") or even prepositionally ("in," "through"). Locatory adverbs and prepositions do express and specify our implacement; but despite their particularity of use and reference, they are intrinsically universal in scope, as Hegel argues in *The Phenomenology of Spirit*.[5] Implacement itself, *being concretely placed*, is intrinsically particular. It is occasion-bound; or more exactly, it binds actual occasions into unique collocations of space and time. To be *here in* this room—to be "herein"—is not only not to be in the room down the hall or in a room in the next building. It is to be *somewhere in particular*: a peculiar somewhere in space that situates the "somewhen" in time. Whereabouts pin down whenabouts. The idiolocal (*idios kosmos*) is the truth of the common world (*koinos kosmos*). Just to be here, I in my room and you in your room, is to exemplify the simple but profound truth of Aristotle's assertion that "things that exist are somewhere."[6] To be somewhere is to be in place and therefore to be subject to its power, to be part of its action, acting on its scene.

The power a place such as a mere room possesses determines not only *where* I am in the limited sense of cartographic location but *how* I am together with others (i.e., how I commingle and communicate with them) and even *who* we shall become together. The "how" and the "who" are intimately tied to the "where," which gives to them a specific content and a coloration not available from any other source. Place bestows upon them "a local habitation and a name" by establishing a concrete situatedness in the common world. This implacement is as social as it is personal. The idiolocal is not merely idiosyncratic or individual; it is also collective in character.

Place-names embody this complex collective concreteness despite their considerable brevity. A locution such as *Roanoke* or *the Great Plains* acts both to designate a particular city or region and to institutionalize this name in a geographic and historical setting (e.g., the history of Virginia or an account of Plains Indians).[7] The importance of place-names is such that an entire branch of mapmaking is devoted to "toponymy"; in England one could until recently make a living as a toponymist. Toponyms are as crucial in fiction as they are in fact: Proust gives to a long and central section of *Remembrance of Things Past* the suggestive title "Place-Names: The Place." An extension of place-naming occurs in the bestowal of proper names on built places.

"Linsley-Chittendon," "Kresge Hall," "Brentano Hall," "Harriman Hall": these buildings in which I have studied or taught all bear the imprint of particular patrons or illustrious predecessors. Not only do these building names historicize and personalize the edifices to which they are attached; their invocation indicates that the educational places constituted by such buildings are as unique as the people they commemorate.

But the power of places is no more exhausted by the place-names attached to them than it is by their deictic and prepositional designators. In order to see this, we need to expand the scope of our analysis to include a term that does not fit easily into any neat spatial series: *landscape*. Beyond the house and the neighborhood lies the landscape. We tend to construe landscape as natural—paradigmatically, as wilderness—but in fact a city constitutes a landscape, a "cityscape," as surely as does the surrounding countryside. There is landscape wherever there is a felt difference unrecuperable by the usual designators of place. As Jean-François Lyotard remarks,

> There would appear to be a landscape whenever the mind is transported from one sensible matter to another, but retains the sensorial organization appropriate to the first, or at least a memory of it. The earth seen from the moon for a terrestrial. The countryside for the townsman; the city for the farmer.[8]

Does this mean, as Lyotard concludes, that a landscape is "the opposite of a place"?[9] This is to go too far. Let us say instead that a landscape is what encompasses those more determinate places, such as rooms and buildings, designated by the usual idiolocative terms. It is a curious fact that we do not normally *name* a landscape, even though the land on which it is located may have its own proper legal name. This is not because of any inherent diffuseness, much less numinousness, in the landscape itself. A landscape has its own determinacy. If it did not, how could it be painted or photographed, discussed or remembered, or even merely gazed at? When I look at a group of mountains whose name I do not know, I witness a spectacle that, however indeterminate or overwhelming it may be on first perception, is nevertheless just *this* mountainscape. It is also evident to me that I am standing in a particular place (also, perhaps, unnamed) and standing before a particular spectacle: this spectacle and no other. Still, as a spectacle it does not bear a name of its own.

Another curious fact is that I do not name my own standing body, even though as a person I have a name that applies by extension to that body. My friend Nancy Franklin would not call her *body* "Nancy Franklin." By the same token, if someone told me that the mountains I am looking at are the Grand Tetons I would not call the landscape *view* "Grand Tetons."[10]

Pondering both curiosities, I am led to ask: are these two nonnamed—

but intensely present—phenomena, landscape and body, somehow covertly connected when it comes to matters of place?

II

A landscape seems to exceed the usual parameters of place by continuing without apparent end; nothing contains it, while it contains everything, including discrete places, in its environing embrace. The body, on the other hand, seems to fall short of place, to be "on this side," the near edge, of a given place. Nevertheless, body and landscape collude in the generation of what can be called "placescapes," especially those that human beings experience whenever they venture out beyond the narrow confines of their familiar domiciles and neighborhoods.

Vilhjálmur Stefánsson, who explored Eskimo territory in northern Alaska, reports this revealing episode:

> In December, 1910, when we were traveling along Horton River in a district unknown to my companion, Natkusiak—who, by the way, is the best of all Eskimo hunters that I have known—was away from camp two days in the pursuit and killing of some caribou. When he came to camp, he reported to me that he would have to go upstream about ten miles, which meant south in that case, until he would be opposite the place where the meat was [stored]. . . . He went off early in the morning, going south; in the afternoon, while sitting on a hill three miles east of our camp spying out the country with my glasses for caribou, I saw a sled coming from the south. At first this astonished me very much, for I had no sleds to expect in that country except our own. And sure enough, it was our own sled and Natkusiak coming almost directly toward me. . . . It turned out that he had shot the caribou about four miles northeast of our camp and that he had gone something like twenty-five miles out of his way to follow the trail by which he had come home. So much for the idea of the Eskimo having a compass in his head.[11]

Stefánsson is most struck by the inefficiency of Natkusiak's trajectory, by his failure to realize how close the store of caribou meat was to the camp in terms of a straight line drawn between the two sites.[12] In Stefánsson's thinking, the straight line of time (i.e., the "least time") is interchangable with the equally straight line of space. Or more exactly, the two lines merge into one arrow-line in keeping with the Euclidean proposition that "a straight line is the shortest distance between two points." What is shortest in space is also shortest in time, and vice versa. A recipe, in short, for efficiency and especially for the meeting of deadlines.[13] In order to apply this lethal prescription to the situation as described, one would have to abstract from the circumstance and form a flattened-out mental image of the scene. One could then read off the shortest route not from the circumstance itself but *from this image*, whose viewpoint is that of someone (but *who* exactly?) suspended over the scene.

But what if one is actually *in* the circumstance described and not inclined—not having been trained this way—to depict the spatiality of the scene in such an abstractive, suspended, and formal-geometric manner? What if one does not think of landscape in terms of linear representations and "properties of angles"?[14] One would first of all look for landmarks. But in the snowbound tundra here in question, stretching endlessly in every direction, there were no conspicuous landmarks.[15] In this circumstance, one would naturally turn to one's *own marks*, i.e., the trail one had made on a previous occasion in getting to a certain place. Natkusiak did just this. The fact that his journey was "the long way around" pales in significance when compared with the assurance his own trail gave to him.

Whether guided by landmarks or by one's own pathmarks, I rely on my body as the primary agent in the landscape. Landmarks call for perception (typically, but not exclusively, visual), while the trailsigns of my own trajectory are the concrete precipitates of my bodily movements on the land. In the latter case, my body marks its way through an otherwise unmarked landscape. To retrace the steps of one's own making is to remark one's own marks, and thus to find one's way.

But what if my body finds itself in a situation in which it cannot leave a lasting trail? What if I am on the open sea, where every wake is soon obliterated? Will I not then be utterly lost, having neither landmarks nor pathmarks?

While Europeans had to wait until 1761 for an effective technique of navigation, the Puluwat of the Caroline Islands in Micronesia have been successfully navigating the Pacific Ocean for many centuries. Puluwatan navigators transform into a reliable scene of sure directedness what would be for Europeans an acutely disorienting prospect, i.e., an endless expanse of water that is a virtual void (perhaps even the oceanic equivalent of empty Newtonian space). Puluwatans navigate hundreds and sometimes thousands of miles in open ocean without the use of compasses or other navigational instruments and only rarely fail to reach their destination. How is this possible?

Ever since the native guide "Tupaia" astonished Captain Cook with his ability to point definitively toward Tahiti at any moment of a voyage—even after a circuitous journey of more than two thousand leagues—Westerners have been fascinated with the Polynesians' and Micronesians' powers of navigation.[16] Only recently have these been more adequately understood. It turns out that the Puluwatans (who have been the most closely studied of the Pacific Island navigators) make use of a complicated system of signals from the seascape and skyscape surrounding them at all times. From the sea, they observe ocean currents and flotsam and above all the exact size and character of ocean swells, including the jet spray as waves strike the hull of their canoes. They also pay close attention to signs of underwater reefs, e.g., changes in the coloration of the water. These unlikely and often seemingly trivial factors constitute veritable "seamarks."[17] From the sky, navigators pick out a certain star seen as standing over a "reference island," itself located beyond the horizon. By noting the changing star bearings of the reference island— which, though unseen, is conceived as "moving" backward on an imaginary line parallel to the horizon—the navigator tallies the "etaks," or segments, of the journey thus far traversed. When the destination is reached, the position of the reference island has moved to its final star bearing (i.e., the bearing from the goal island to the reference island).[18]

In the Puluwat system, then, landmarks in the conventional sense of perceptually prominent objects have been replaced by barely perceptible seamarks and, most importantly, by dimly visible stars and an altogether out-of-view island.[19] The latter is not perceived but "envisioned in [the navigator's] mind's eye."[20] The navigator thus takes advantage of the horizon's capacity to contain what is not yet visible in the actual seascape; what might seem to be an obstacle for navigation, i.e., minimal or zero visibility, here becomes a distinctive virtue. (The reference island is navigationally valuable precisely because it is conceived as changing places over the horizon.) Conversely, what appears to be a virtue in the case of a standard landmark, its unmoving rigidity, is now a disadvantage, since a stationary physical object, once overtaken and out of sight, is rendered useless for the remainder of a given journey.

The Micronesian method of orientation is anything but "dead reckoning" in the derogatory sense of merely estimating one's position (and direction and speed) by experience or probable judgment.[21] And the Puluwatans' reckoning is anything but dead when it comes to the role of the body in navigating. Their acute visual powers enable them to read and follow the myriad nocturnal constellations with close discernment. But they are by no means entirely dependent on vision, since difficult weather conditions can render unaided sight useless. Not only do they actively imagine the unseen reference island over the horizon; they sometimes deliberately shut out sight (even when it is unobstructed) in order to draw more fully upon the other bodily senses. This is particularly true of estimating the direction and identity of ocean swells: to become fully sensitive to these deep currents, Puluwatans "steer by the feel of the waves under the canoe, not visually."[22] One navigator reported that he would sometimes "retire to the hut on his canoe's outrigger platform, where he would lie down and without distraction more readily direct the helmsman onto the proper course by analyzing the roll and pitch of the vessel as it corkscrewed over the waves."[23] Here the navigator is relying on auditory and kinesthetic data—including sensations in his testicles—as they form rhythmic patterns within his lived body.[24] At other times, the sense of smell or even of taste is exploited: "The oceans are by no means featureless, and when all else fails, the Polynesian navigator dips his hand in the water, places it to his lips, and can judge from its temperature and/or salinity, if not precisely, at least the general area into which a particular current or wind has drifted him under overcast skies."[25] It is evident, then, that the Puluwat navigational method makes systematic use of at least three basic variables: moving and sensing human bodies, far horizons as the common edge of sea- and skyscapes, and oceanic and celestial regions as the encompassing areas within which particular places are to be located.[26]

The examples of the Eskimo hunter and the Puluwat navigator both point to the intimate interaction of body and landscape in the achievement of orientation. In particular they show that to become oriented it is not enough to rely on the perception of actually given features of the landscape, for a landscape or seascape may be ambiguous or even drastically lacking in orientational cues, i.e., landmarks or seamarks. But it is also not sufficient to count on the body alone. Left to its own devices, one's body may drift in the direction of the least resistance, which is not necessarily the direction of one's chosen destination![27] If I am to get oriented in a landscape or seascape (especially one that is unknown or subject to sudden or unpredictable variation), I must bring my body into conformity with the configurations of the land or the sea: e.g., by retracing my precise path in snow or attending to the exact shape of the sea-swells. The conjoining of the surface of my body with the surface of the earth or sea—their common integumentation—generates the interspace in which I become oriented. Then I am able to find my way about in a placescape that to a significant degree is marked and measured, as well as perceived and remembered, by my own actions.

The foregoing foray into the subject of orientation and navigation portends a still more basic point. If it is true that "the oceans are by no means featureless"—if deserts are not trackless after all, and if arctic tundra is far from nondescript—then we have come back around to place from something that strangely resembles the modern idea of space as empty and endless. The purpose of navigating and getting oriented is to transform an apparently vacuous expanse, a Barren Grounds of unmarked space, into a set of what can only properly be called *places* (even if these places still lack proper names). "What begins as undifferentiated space," says the geographer Yi-Fu Tuan, "ends as a single object-situation or place. . . . When space feels thoroughly familiar to us, it has become place."[28] What is true for the Puluwat and the Eskimo, the Bedouin and the Temne, is also true for ourselves.[29] Confronted with the actual emptiness of modernist space, each of us attempts to move

from the discomfort of disorientation in such space to the comparative assurance of knowing our way about. We do so by transmuting an initially
aimless and endless scene into a place of concerted action, thereby constituting a dense placescape that, in close collaboration with our active bodies,
guides us into orientation. Unplacement becomes implacement as we regain
and refashion a sense of place.

Moving bodies on land or at sea provide us with oriented and orienting
placescapes. From being lost in space and time (or, more likely, lost *to them*
in the era of modernity), we find our way in place.[30]

III

Body and landscape present themselves as coeval epicenters around which
particular places pivot and radiate. They are, at the very least, the bounds of
places. In my embodied being I am *just at* a place as its inner boundary; a
surrounding landscape, on the other hand, is *just beyond* that place as its outer
boundary. Between the two boundaries—and very much as a function of
their differential interplay—implacement occurs. Place is what takes place between body and landscape. Thanks to the double horizon that body and
landscape provide, a place is a locale bounded on both sides, near and far.[31]
Unlike the double-bind of time, however, the double bound of place is open-
ended. Far from being constrictive in the manner of a deadline, the lifeline
extending from body to landscape (and back again) is as porous as a sieve.
Thanks to the mutual enlivening of body and landscape, a place constantly
overflows its own boundaries. Uncontainable on its near edge, it flows back
into the body that subtends it; uncontainable on its far side, it flows outward
into the circumambient world. Place's inflow and outflow are such that to
be fully *in* a place is never to be confined to a punctate position; it is to be
already on the way out.[32] The Puluwat navigator, bodily implaced in his canoe, is already steering into the next etak of his journey. He is both in the
near-place of his canoe and beyond it, toward the far-places over the distant
horizon and toward the stars.

Another current in place's overflowingness is its distinctively *cultural* dimension. If body and landscape are the concurrent epicenters of place, this
does not mean that they must be natural givens. This interpretation was as
tempting to the Greeks as it remains in the modern era. It proceeds from
what Husserl calls the "natural attitude," the concerted tendency to construe
any given object as real, as "simply there" (*einfach da*) in the manner of a
material thing. His celebrated counsel to suspend the stranglehold of this
attitude allowed the phenomenologist to be newly sensitive to neglected aspects and dimensions of the phenomenal world. Some of these aspects and

dimensions are nonmaterial, and among them are to be found cultural as well as eidetic structures.

We too must suspend any dogmatic naturalism in approaching place through body and landscape. In particular we must resist the temptation to make place absolute or transphenomenal—a "thing in itself"—by regarding it as a cluster of physicalistic predicates, including those bestowed by the human body and the environing landscape. To begin with, we need only observe that both body and landscape are always already imbued with cultural determinants. Not even the human body—perhaps especially not this body—is a natural given. Consider the discrepancy between being a fur-clad Eskimo and a virtually unclad Puluwatan. The discrepancy is not just a matter of amount or type of clothing. It resides in the total manner in which a human body, however it is clad, makes its way through a given landscape. The Eskimo lives out his or her body in ways that reflect a culture intent on surviving in arctic extremities. These ways include forms of domestic architecture, social rituals, styles of hunting, and (as we have seen) techniques of trailmarking in the tundra.[33] The Puluwatan incorporates—and ex-corporates—his or her culture differently. One difference manifests itself in just how the Puluwat's seafaring body relates to the seascape. Yet the seascape itself is no more a natural given than is the body of the seafarer. Material as it is in its constitution and perception, the seascape acts as a cultural screen onto which certain astronautical beliefs (e.g., concerning orienting stars in relation to reference islands) are projected. As such a screen, the seascape becomes a lived map of navigable places.

The places that precipitate out from the body–landscape interplay are cultural entities from the start. Their cultural dimensions help to distinguish them from the bare positions at stake in the determination of longitude in modern Western mapping. To know your longitude at sea is not—not yet—to know your place there. However important such knowledge is for navigational purposes, it yields only a world-point expressed in abstract numbers: seventy-two degrees longitude, seventeen degrees latitude. Precisely as a *point*, this position is interpretable as spatial or temporal—indeed, indifferently both. (The indifference supports the spatio-temporal linearism of early modern thinking.) As a theoretical posit, such a position is itself a cultural object. But precisely as a posit, it is not an experiential object; no one, not even John Harrison, nor anyone else dependent on a longitude-measuring device, ever *experienced* longitude at sea.

Places, like bodies and landscapes, are something we experience—where *experience* stays true to its etymological origin of "trying out," "making a trial out of."[34] As John Dewey emphasized, to have an experience is to make a trial, an experiment, out of living. It is to do something that requires the proof of the senses, and often of much else besides. A posited object, e.g., a particular line of longitude, is not experimentally entertained; instead, it is imposed as a pure position in world space-time. It is *employed* but not experienced as such. Concerning it, no significant change, much less improvement, is possible.[35]

To recognize the experimentalism of places is to undermine the belief that they are pregiven natural absolutes.[36] This recognition does not contradict Aristotle's assertion that places are prior to all things. Their priority, however, is not metaphysical or even epistemological. It is phenomenological as well as ontological: places are primary in the order of description as in the order of being.

Places are also primary in the order of culture. Just as there can be no disembodied experience of landscape, so there can be no unimplaced cultures. If "things that exist are somewhere," among these existing things are human cultures; they too are in place.

Thus we are driven to acknowledge the truth of two related but distinct propositions: just as every place is encultured, so every culture is implaced.

Taken as encultured, places (along with the bodies and landscapes that bound, and sometimes bind, them) are matters of experience. We make trial of them in culturally specific ways. This principle obtains not just for the familiar places to which we are accustomed but also for the faraway places visited on ambitious voyages: the English had mainly economic motives in their transatlantic traffic, the Eskimos visited by Stefánsson were mostly concerned with survival, and the Puluwats still seek tobacco and certain domestic items on their oceanic outings. If a position is a fixed posit of an established culture, a place, despite its frequently settled appearance, is an essay in experimental living within a changing culture.

IV

Implacement is an ongoing cultural process with an experimental edge. It acculturates whatever ingredients it borrows from the natural world, whether these ingredients are bodies or landscapes or ordinary "things."[37] Such acculturation is itself a social, even a communal, act. For the most part, we get into places together. We partake of places in common—and reshape them in common. The culture that characterizes and shapes a given place is a shared culture, not merely superimposed upon that place but part of its very facticity.

Place as we experience it is not altogether natural. If it were, it could not play the animating, decisive role it plays in our collective lives. Place, already cultural as experienced, insinuates itself into a collectivity, altering as well as constituting that collectivity. Place becomes social because it is already cultural.[38] It is also, and for the same reason, historical. It is by the mediation of culture that places gain historical depth. We might even say that culture is the third dimension of places, affording them a deep historicity, a *longue durée*, which they would lack if they were entirely natural in constitution.

Buildings are among the most perspicuous instances of the thorough acculturation of places. *A building condenses a culture in one place.* Even if it is more confining than a landscape, a building is more densely saturated with culture than is a landscape (unless the landscape is a cityscape). As itself a place, a building is a *focus locorum*—indeed, a *locus locorum*, a place for places. It exists between the bodies of those who inhabit or use it and the landscape arranged around it. If it gives dwelling to these bodies, it gives cultural mission to that landscape. Within the ambience of a building, a landscape becomes articulate and begins to speak in emblematic ways.

Take, for example, an early Greek temple. Such a building was oriented by the lay of the land, often by the establishment of an axis formed by the temple and a nearby double-peaked mountain (symbolizing the horns of a primal earth goddess). Thus the temple, the most sacred of cultural artifacts, was situated in relation to the landscape, itself regarded as sacred. As Vincent Scully writes of the temple complex,

> The formal elements of any Greek sanctuary are, first, the specifically sacred landscape in which it is set and, second, the buildings that are placed within it. The landscape and the temples together form the architectural whole. . . . Each [such] sanctuary necessarily differs from all others because it is in a different place.[39]

This is more than a merely local issue. By this I do not mean just that such orientation of buildings by landscape occurs elsewhere—in Knossos, in Lisbon, in San Francisco. I also mean that the very intertwining of culture and nature as it arises in oriented constructions specifies a fundamental aspect of place itself. In this interaction it is the *meaning* of landscape that is at stake: "Its meaning . . . is developed as the buildings [of a given culture] are placed within it."[40] As landscape comes to orient buildings, the very significance of the landscape changes, in keeping with the cultural values embodied in these buildings and in reflection of the larger culture from which these values stem. In a culture such as that of Greece in the Dorian period, the landscape becomes "the complement for *all* Greek life and [not just] the special component of the art of Greek temples."[41] Landscape becomes a forceful presence, harboring the powers of the gods worshiped in these same temples.

This remains the case even if such buildings are given additional orientation from the sky as well as from the land, as occurs in post-Doric temples such as the Parthenon, which is primarily situated in relation to the sun's rising on the morning of the anniversary of its own founding. As in directional guidance from nighttime constellations, cultivated by navigators in many cultures, celestial "orientation" (here living up to its name by being eastern in outlook) links up with sublunar situation.[42] But now an entire culture allows itself to be oriented by earth and sky taken together, to live collectively from their conjoint "Dimensionality."[43] This is by no means unique to ancient Greece but also is found at Stonehenge and Avebury, as well as in the ancient Chinese, classical Maya, and Pueblo cultures. In all of these latter instances, the orientation provided by the four cardinal directions (each with multiple cultural connotations) is an indispensable feature, further specifying the interaction between culture and place.[44] For the Saulteaux Indians of Manitoba the main directions *are themselves places*, so that natural place here draws cultural place into a common orbit.[45]

If limits have to do with distinctions between nature and culture, orientation takes us to the point of their merging. We see this perhaps most dramatically in the earthworks of the Nazca Plain in Peru. On this plain, the land itself has been reshaped on an extensive scale (sometimes more than a mile in width or length) to form gigantic geometric and organic figures. Paradoxically, these figures are best seen from the sky, to which they seem to be magnanimous and open-armed votive offerings. (In this case, the aerial-suspended view *is* appropriate.) Their mysterious provenance and unknown meaning serve to remind us that the building of culturally determinate places out of indeterminate elements in the land is by no means a precise or predictable matter. Such constructing involves a virtually alchemical transformation whose laws we shall not soon, if ever, discover. No chronometer will resolve this mystery, nor will a modern scientific understanding of space reveal its concealed meaning.[46]

The cultural dimension of place—along with affiliated historical, social, and political aspects and avatars—adds something quite new to the earlier analysis, something we had not yet encountered in our reflections on the logic and experience of place.[47] This dimension contributes to the felt density of a particular place, the sense that it has something lasting in it.

To be lasting, however, is to be in time. We say that *things* last in time, yet so do *places*. Places last not just by the perdurance of material constituents but also by the binding force of cultural constraints. Thanks to these constraints and their applications and inscriptions, time reenters the scene of place. It reenters not in the form of a line but as something distinctively multidimensional, that is, ramified in diverse directions.[48] For what is paramount in a culturally specified place is not the end-point of destination, much less the shortest route to it. What matters most is the experience of *being* in that place and, more particularly, *becoming part of the place*. The time of cultural implacement (and the time experienced *in* that implacement) is that which informs a place in concert with other human beings, through one's bodily agency, within the embrace of a landscape.

V

We have moved from a predicament of unplacement—of not knowing one's whereabouts at sea—to several situations of secure implacement. These latter included such complicated circumstances as the discovery of longitude and the etak method of navigation, one archetypally modern in inspiration, the other resolutely premodern. But we have also considered the comparatively uncomplicated circumstance of retracing a trail left by footprints in the snow. And we have pondered the metaphysical claims for the priority of place that were articulated by Archytas and then restated by Aristotle; these claims also bear on situations of implacement, albeit in a highly theoretical vein. In contrast, the experience of place engendered through the conjoint contributions of body and landscape heightened the sense of how implacement is attained in more concrete registers. A consideration of the cultural dimension of place—a dimension as problematic as it is uneliminable—allowed us to appreciate the importance of social and historical aspects of implacement.

But let us not rest assured. Displacement threatens implacement at every turn. Harrison's No. 4 cost 450 pounds sterling, making it impracticable for ordinary voyages, which continued to go astray until a less expensive model became available. Even those who, like the Puluwat, do not rely on advanced technology are certainly capable of getting lost at sea, despite their considerable finesse. Eskimos lose their way on snowbound terrain they know quite well, but which suddenly takes on a very different visage during a severe storm.[49] Indeed, our own bodies, normally quite reliable indicators of implacement, can lead us astray; if myopic or intoxicated, we may suddenly find ourselves in places we never intended to be. Landscape itself, usually a most accommodating presence, can alienate us. (Lyotard goes so far as to assert that "estrangement (*dépaysement*) would appear to be a precondition for landscape.")[50] Entire cultures can become profoundly averse to the places they inhabit, feeling atopic and displaced within their own implacement. If Freud and Heidegger are correct, this dis-implacement, or "dysplacement" as it could also be called, is endemic to the human condition in its ineluctable "uncanniness"; *Unheimlichkeit*, not-being-at-home, is intrinsic to habitation itself.[51]

If from being unplaced we have discovered several ways of being and becoming implaced, from implacement in turn the way is all too short to displacement (although it is rarely a straight line). One concrete contemporary case of displacement will serve as a sober reminder of the immense value of human implacement, precisely in view of the equally immense fragility of human being-in-place.

I refer to the plight of the Dinéh Indians in northeastern Arizona. The

Dinéh, better known as the Navajo, have been subjected to literal displacement by the United States government as a result of the Navajo-Hopi Land Settlement Act of 1974. This settlement action has proved to be profoundly unsettling, for it has meant the forced relocation of thousands of Navajos who found themselves on the wrong side of the barbed-wire fence erected to separate them from the Hopi, with whom they had been able to coexist in a mostly peaceful way for over a century. The results of the relocation (a notion for which the Navajo say there is no word in their language) have been disastrous. A quarter of those relocated have died, including an unusually high number from suicide. Alcoholism, depression, and acute disorientation are rampant. Not only that, but significant parts of the land cleared for purposes of relocation are slated for coal and uranium mining and for the dumping of nuclear waste products, all of which if effected will render the area uninhabitable into the indefinite future.

What we witness in the case of the Navajo has been observed before in situations of coercive displacement. A report of 1979 states that "the results of over 25 studies around the world indicate, with no exceptions, that the execution of compulsory relocation among rural populations with strong ties to their land and homes is a traumatic experience for the majority of the relocatees."[52] What is striking in the Navajo tragedy—and poignantly pertinent to our topic—is the explicit acknowledgment by relocated people themselves that the loss of the land was the *primary* loss in the circumstance. The Navajo consider it to be an unalterable premise that "there is no land like this land. Our land is our life."[53] It follows as a devastating deduction that to take away the land is to take away life, that the major cause of illness is not something "physical" or "psychological" in the usual bifurcated Cartesian senses of these words but, instead, the loss of landed place itself. In fact, the Navajo believe that illness proceeds from a distorted relationship with the land: "To take from the Earth without reciprocating, without having first become a part of the life of the place, is to disrupt a sacred balance and ultimately to grow ill."[54] To take a people's land away altogether, so that reciprocating with it is not even possible, is to disrupt the sacred balance even more drastically.

Displacement has two dimensions for those Dinéh who have been directly affected. First, it represents the loss of particular places in which their lives were formerly at home. As one relocated man put it, "We need a hogan [the circular earth-covered structure that is the characteristic domicile] to have singing ceremonies in. I was already told by a medicine man [that] he can't perform in a square house. We also need a farm with a big enough place to store our corn and melons. We can't do it here [in the relocated region]."[55] Another laments: "There is nothing to live for. There is no land; there is no hogan. . . . I'm not used to this world. . . . I would have liked (at least) a small area of land like the one I had with a hogan on it."[56] Second, beyond the relinquishment of particular places, there is the still greater loss of an entire land, a region. The Navajo call this larger landed entity "the Great Self." It includes plots of land, particular landscapes, landmarks, the tribe, families, the ecosystem, and ancestors. Each of these factors constitutes a discrete place or set of places in the encompassing region of the Great Self, whose very identity "depends upon the continuation of a devotional connectedness to earth, ground, community, and ancestral place."[57]

The land construed by the Dinéh as the Great Self has two distinct but interrelated aspects, one of which is situated outside and around the individual self while the other is internal to this self. On one hand, the land as a whole is characterized by certain actual features of the environing landscape. Circumscribing the native land, for example, are four sacred mountains that demarcate the four cardinal directions. Each family traditionally owned a medicine bundle whose contents, taken from these four mountains, included earth as well as sacred stones, which were used in prayer ceremonies. On the other hand, the system of sacred places was deeply internalized by the Navajo and became essential to their self-identities. As Paul Shepard writes in *Nature and Madness*,

> Individual and tribal identity are built up in connection with widely separated places and the paths connecting them. Different places are successfully assimilated or internalized. They become distinct, though unconscious elements of the self, enhanced by mythology and ceremony, generating a network of deep emotional attachments that cements the personality. Throughout life those places have a role in the evocation of the self and group consciousness.[58]

The internalized system of places may also be said to underlie history as well as time. For the Navajo people, "closeness to the land and to their place on the land is their way of being grounded in tradition, in the traditional ground of their tribal ancestors. Their sense of history and even their sense of time itself are dependent on this closeness to their land."[59] The Navajo thus help us to realize that the priority of place over time obtains whether a given place is out there in the landscape or inherent in the psyche.

The Navajo experience of displacement rejoins certain other themes we have encountered in this chapter. In addition to a belief in the "spirit of place" in the form of the Great Self, the Navajo affirm the continuity of culture and landscape. Since they conceive their land as an ancestral dwelling place and since all significant learning proceeds ultimately from ancestors, culture is almost literally *in the land*. It follows that to learn something is not to learn something entirely new, much less entirely mental; it is to learn how to connect, or more exactly to reconnect, with one's place.[60] At the same time, to reconnect with that place is to engage in a form of collective memory of one's ancestors: to commemorate them. To be dis-placed is therefore to incur both culture loss and memory loss resulting from the loss of the land itself, each being a symptom of the disorientation wrought by relocation.[61]

Pauline Whitesinger, a contemporary Navajo, says that "to move away means to disappear and never be seen again."[62] To lose one's land is tantamount to losing one's existence. Heeding Whitesinger, we thus rediscover, by *via negativa*, a truth about place we first learned from Archytas of Tarentum. In the language of Archytas, not to be in place is not only to be nowhere; it is not to exist. The displaced Pythagorean (Tarentum was a Greek colony in Italy) anticipates the dolorous experience of the displaced Navajo.

VI

If Archytas and Whitesinger, situated as they are at opposite ends of the earth and at disparate cultural and historical times, seem remote from your own situation, I would remind you that each of us is caught in the toils of displacement. As moderns and postmoderns in the Eurocentric West, we too are displaced persons, "D.P.s," and inescapably so. Our symptoms may seem milder than those of the Navajo, but they are no less disruptive and destructive.

Among these symptoms, nostalgia is one of the most revealing. At the moment, our own culture suffers from acute nostalgia. Proust, living on the edge between the modern and the postmodern periods, described the drama of an entire life delivered over to nostalgia.[63] But we do not need to turn to literature for evidence of the pervasive presence of nostalgia; we witness its cinematic expression in certain of Woody Allen's films and its commercial exploitation in Disney World.

Nostalgia, contrary to what we usually imagine, is not merely a matter of regret for lost times; it is also a pining for *lost places*, for places we have once been in yet can no longer reenter (any more than the Navajos can reenter their lost land).[64] Sven Birkerts observes:

> No matter what plea or adjustment I make, I cannot catch hold of the peculiar magic of those [childhood] places. . . . No effort of will can restore to me that perception, that view of the horizon not yet tainted by futurity—it runs through me sometimes, but I cannot summon it. And yet everything I would say about place depends on it, and everything I search for in myself involves some deep fantasy of its restoration. My best, truest—I cannot define my terms—self is vitally connected to a few square miles of land.[65]

These lines put their finger on the problem. To lose "a few square miles of land" is to lose one's "best, truest self," one's most intimate identity, as surely as the Navajo feel they have lost their deeply grounded collective identity in being removed from their native land. For the sense of self, personal or collective, grows out of and reflects the places from which we come and where we have been. As Lawrence Durrell writes, "We are the children of our landscape. It dictates behavior and even thought in the measure to which we are responsive to it."[66]

No wonder we are nostalgic (literally, "pained at the [non]return home"), not just over cherished childhood places but over many now inaccessible or despoiled places, often in consequence of ecological damage or negligence. Such massive nostalgia is a speaking symptom of the profound placelessness of our times, in which we have exchanged place for a mess of spatial and temporal pottage. As Durrell suggests, the placeless is the thoughtless; and if we fail to honor and remember places, this is a direct reflection of our unthinking and increasingly ill condition. Another telling sign is the fact that "for the modern self, *all places are essentially the same*: in the uniform, homogeneous space of a Euclidean-Newtonian grid, all places are essentially interchangeable. Our places, even our places for homes, are defined by objective measures."[67]

The uniformity of space and the equability of time have replaced, or more exactly displaced, the priority of place. If nostalgia is a characteristically modern malaise, this may be due to its covert recognition that a time once existed when place was "the first of all things," when time and space in their modern (dis)guises were not yet fatally at work. For in the pathos of nostalgia, "space and time [are] not yet separable concepts, [they are] scarcely concepts at all."[68] But in the modern era we have accepted and incorporated space and time in their objectivity and (in)difference. In "the age of the world picture," we have become what we have allowed ourselves to behold.[69] We calculate, and move at rapid speeds, in time and space. But we do not live in these abstract parameters; instead, we are displaced in them and by them. Nevertheless, time and space remain the outgrowth, the alienated expression, of the very places that form their common matrix.

It is a disconcerting fact that, besides nostalgia, still other symptoms of place pathology in present Western culture are strikingly similar to those of the Navajo: disorientation, memory loss, homelessness, depression, and various modes of estrangement from self and others. In particular, the sufferings of many contemporary Americans that follow from the lack of satisfactory implacement uncannily resemble (albeit in lesser degree) those of displaced Native Americans, whom European Americans displaced in the first place. These natives have lost their land; those of us who are nonnatives have lost our place.

Natives and nonnatives alike are embroiled in a shared predicament of placelessness and its aftermath, and the only way out of this predicament is to regain living contact with place itself, to remember that place is a remarkable thing. This will take more than nostalgic glimpses backward into personal or collective history or forward-looking gazes into utopias or the exotica of outer space. Nostalgia (as well as the exoticism with which it is so often allied) is part of the problem, and it does not contain the solution. The solution may lie in a belated postmodern reconnection with a genuinely premodern sense of place, a sense such as the Navajo once had and may lose altogether unless something is done to restore them to their land.

A special report issued in 1980 stated that while the Navajo "often visited the Indian Health Service Hospitals for counseling, the only real solution [for their ills] would be the resumption of their original way of life."[70] In this way of life, place was paramount. Can we, in the postmodern period, recapture and relive some significant vestige of an original way of life, one that is as attuned to place as the modern era has been to time?

PART II

The Body in Place

There is nothing to allow us to assert that the distinctions applied to space are anterior to those that concern [the] body.

—Robert Hertz, "The Pre-eminence of the Right Hand"

Far from my body's being for me no more than a fragment of space, there would be no space at all for me if I had no body.

—Maurice Merleau-Ponty, *Phenomenology of Perception*

3

Directions

When there was no heaven,
no earth, no height, no depth, no name,
  when Apsu was alone,
the sweet water, the first begetter; and Tiamat
  the bitter water, and that
return to the womb, her Mummu,
  When there were no gods—

When sweet and bitter
mingled together, no reed was plaited, no rushes
  muddied the water,
the gods were nameless, natureless, futureless, then
  from Apsu and Tiamat
in the waters gods were created, in the waters
  silt precipitated.[1]

THESE ARE THE opening lines of the *Enuma Elish*, a creation liturgy that probably dates to 1900 B.C., before the reign of Hammurabi. In this text we witness an initial merging of body and place in the figure of Tiamat, as well as a subsequent emerging of place from her body. In contrast with the account given in Genesis, in the *Enuma Elish* no earth whatsoever is present at first, not even an earth "without form and void." Instead we find *two bodies of water in a shared elemental matrix.* For Apsu (ocean; literally, "abyss") and Tiamat (primeval waters) are the names of primeval regions in which sweet and bitter waters reside respectively. From these waters "silt precipitated"; that is, earth came to be.

"The coil of Tiamat," lament the Sumerian gods, "is too deep for us to fathom."[2] For this very reason, Marduk must set out to destroy her. As the architect of the new world order, Marduk can only comprehend and tolerate measurable entities. His preordained confrontation with Tiamat is not merely a matter of settling old accounts or of defending himself and other gods against her procreative powers (she gives birth to eleven monsters). The confrontation arises when "he surveyed her scanning the Deep."[3] Marduk *surveys* while Tiamat *scans*. Not only does Tiamat scan the Deep; she *is* the Deep. (*Tehom*, Hebrew for the Deep, stems from *Tiamat*.) Too deep for measurement or survey, she must be overcome in a cosmogony that celebrates the triumph of the architectonic over the chaotic and in which mastery of the unruly matrix is the overriding concern.

Before construction must come destruction. Marduk masters the Tiamatian matrix by crushing her in combat. In a vividly portrayed battle scene, he unleashes on Tiamat (now transformed from water into the figure of an Old Hag) a vast net and a tumultuous tempest. Entangled in the net and tumescent with ingested wind, Tiamat is brought low and killed by Marduk's virile arrow.

But order arises not just from disorder. Triumph in battle is not sufficient for the building of a cosmos. As master builder, Marduk must build *from* something. The materials from which he builds are found nowhere else than in Tiamat's slain body:

> The lord rested; he gazed at the huge body, pondering how to use it, what to create from the dead carcass. He split it apart like a cockle-shell; with the upper half he constructed the arc of sky, he pulled down the bar and set a watch on the waters, so they should never escape.[4]

From Tiamat's body, then, Marduk creates sky as a region distinct from water. Marduk next endows the new world with basic directions, which are also body-based: "through her ribs he opened gates in the east and west, and gave them strong bolts on the right and left; and high in the belly of Tiamat he set the zenith."[5] Not only the cardinal directions but also the body-relative directionalities of right and left and up and down are established. The creation of an ordered world full of places becomes ever more specific:

> Then Marduk considered Tiamat. He skimmed spume from the bitter sea, heaped up the clouds, spindrift of wet and wind and cooling rain, the spittle of Tiamat.

> With his own hands from the steaming mist he spread the clouds. He pressed hard down the head of water, heaping mountains over it, opening springs to flow: Euphrates and Tigris rose from her eyes, but he closed the nostrils and held back their springhead.

> He piled huge mountains on her paps and through them drove water-holes to channel the deep sources; and high overhead he arched her tail, locked-in to the wheel of heaven; the pit was under his feet, between was the crotch, the sky's fulcrum. Now the earth had foundations and the sky its mantle.[6]

In these decisive steps Marduk creates the earth's atmosphere and the terrain (including the subsoil) of the earth: its basic topography. He does so by reshaping—literally reimplacing—particular features of Tiamat's prone body: her eyes, nostrils, breasts, tail, crotch. The carcass of Tiamat becomes a source of earth-places within an encompassing sky-region.

The creation of the world narrated in the *Enuma Elish* is at once *from* something and *of* something. What is most notable in the Babylonian text is that the something from which creation arises is a *body*—Tiamat's gigantic recumbent body—and the something created is a set of distinct *places.* Marduk's cosmogonic action brings about ever more particular places from the primal undifferentiated region that is Tiamat's own body. Not unlike Plato's "mythical" recounting in the *Timaeus* (whose Demiurge is remarkably reminiscent of Marduk), the *Enuma Elish* depicts a progression from inchoate regions to well-formed places. But what Plato designates as "Space," "Necessity," or "the Receptacle"—none of which connotes the idea of an organic body—the anonymous author of the *Enuma Elish* specifies as the fallen body of an elemental goddess.[7]

If the Babylonian legend is telling us anything, it is that body and place belong together from the very beginning. Their fate is linked—not only at the start but at subsequent stages as well.

Despite this common fate, in ancient and modern Western philosophy there is rarely any serious discussion of the role of body in the determination of place.[8] Among ancient thinkers in the Western tradition, Aristotle alone at least *recognized* the importance of the human body in regard to place when he said that the dimensions of place, such as above and below, right and left, "come to be in relation to our position, *according as we turn ourselves about.*"[9] Aristotle emphasized that these dimensions "are not just relative to us . . . in nature each is distinct and separate."[10] Only certain mathematical objects (e.g., points) possess positions entirely relative to our own bodily position, yet these points do not themselves constitute places or even parts of places.

Early critics of Aristotle invoked the human body in the form of that hypothetical javelin thrower (to whom I alluded in chapter 1) situated at the outer limit of the spherical heavens: where would this ambitious athlete toss his javelin if space came to an end at the edge of the outermost sphere?[11] After the concerted exploration of this simple but provocative thought-experiment we find no significant theorizing in the West concerning the role of the active and supple body in space.[12] The virtual disappearance of this body in favor of the rigid material body goes hand in hand with an abating of interest in place as distinct from space. At first glance, the convergence of diminished attention to the lived body and to experienced place might seem to be merely coincidental. But in fact the respective destinies of body and place are closely connected in philosophical thinking; as *body* came to designate the hard physical body of *res extensa,* so *place* came to mean a mere segment of infinite space.

The Hellenistic and medieval preoccupation with the infinite and the void brought with it a marked obliviousness to the contribution of the active body to concrete implacement.[13] To the extent that the agency of this body in the constitution of place was forgotten or repressed (or perhaps never fully suspected) during the millennia that separated mythical from modern ruminations on space, the fate of place as a philosophical concept was subject to the vicissitudes of changing fashion. From a period of preoccupation in the wake of Aristotle—Simplicius, elaborating on Aristotle, devoted an entire treatise to the notion of place[14]—philosophical concern with place vacillated, finally waning as the High Middle Ages gave way to the nominalism and skepticism that preceded the Renaissance revival of Platonism. The increasing fascination during the Renaissance with the idea of an infinite universe, so deftly delineated in Alexandre Koyré's *From the Closed World to the Infinite Universe,* spelled an increasingly bodiless and placeless tale. This is hardly a surprising development. The more one considers space as unlimited—whether as an actual infinite in the manner of Crescas, Bruno, Gassendi, and Newton or as an indefinite infinite in the conception of Descartes—the less one will be concerned with the position of the human body in the vastness of space. Only if explicit attention is given to the lived body in relation to its whereabouts does the importance of place in distinction to space become fully evident.[15]

In the preceding chapter I pointed to the active role of the human body in Puluwatan navigation—where both vision and kinesthesia are at stake—as as well as in Eskimo orientation (in which the trail left by one's own footprints is a crucial clue). The somatic symptomatology of dispossessed Navajos indicated the ingrediency of the lived body in displacement as well as in implacement. If it is true that body is on the "near side" of place and that place is in turn the "far side" of body (with landscape in turn on the far side of particular places), then the differential destinies of body and place are indeed deeply conjoined.

In this chapter I shall explore the intimate interinvolvement of body and place. Apart from foreshadowings in myths, where better to look for a renewed appreciation of place than in our own bodily enactments? *Where else* can we look for it, given that all human experience emerges from the facticity of being a body-in-the-world? Just as we may say with Kant, "There can be no doubt that all our knowledge begins with experience," so we can say that knowledge of place begins with the bodily experience of being-in-place.[16] This is all the more true if we are to come to know place from within, in its own distinctive being.

II

> There is, therefore, another subject beneath me, for whom a world exists
> before I am here, and who marks out my place in it. This captive or natural
> subject is my body.
> —Maurice Merleau-Ponty, *Phenomenology of Perception*

I begin with a concrete instance of being bodily in place.

I am in my living room, a rectangular room with two entrances and a number of windows. (How many? I'd have to count them concertedly to know.) The piano, whose surface has been newly finished, is covered with sheets to protect its gleaming wood from wayward paws. The pillows on the couch are in deliberate disarray to discourage Pippin, the dog, from sleeping on it. A bookcase contains volumes (most of them stemming from my Kansas forebears), rocks, and various memorabilia. A diptych painting, purchased this year from my friend Eve, hangs on the wall over the couch. Pale lavender geraniums are perched on a small oval table on my left. The fireplace, dormant for the summer, is on my right. I am seated in a low-cut white fabric chair near one of the south windows.

Already in this bare sketch a cardinal direction has been invoked, along with a divergence between right and left. A room, a living room, is coming to descriptive life. Despite this room's rectilinearity, certain idiosyncratic details (e.g., piano, painting, books) animate its otherwise static being. Some of these details, even as they populate my immediate space, take me far back into time, and thus into other places. Several objects reflect or solicit bodily action in the present. The cover on the piano and the helter-skelter pillows on the couch allude to the possible incursion of animal bodies in domestic space. Also within this space as I experience it is a "seat" for my writing, itself a quite bodily endeavor. Two entrances suggest possible motions in and out of the living room. Movement, even action, is afoot.

I stand up and walk to the bookshelf, where I search in vain for the copy of *Emerson's Essays* I thought was there. Disappointed, I return to my chair, resigning myself to writing without the assistance of Emerson's Oversoul. Suddenly Pippin enters and lunges onto the couch in spite of its forbidding cushions. I implore him to get off this precarious perch, and my daughter Erin, hearing the commotion, rushes in. The phone rings. I go to answer it while Erin lectures Pippin on his bad canine manners. I am now out of the living room and into the kitchen: in another place, with its own peculiar characteristics. Were I to stay there, this new place might call for yet other movements of my body, such as bending over, reaching up, etc.

In this sequel to the initial scene, I set my body into motion. I get up twice, first to retrieve a book and then to answer the telephone. In so doing, I move from the immediate locus of the chair in which I am writing to the region of the bookshelf and then to the kitchen, each of which, upon my approach, becomes a new scene for bodily action. At the same time, I engage in an interchange of proximity and distance as I move from one place to another: I am now here, now there, and as I draw close to certain things I am farther from others. The sudden entry of Pippin and then of my daughter brings other active bodies into an originally solitary scene. With them, my own body forms a momentary pact, literally, a "com-pact." Each of us positions him or her self in relation to the moving body of the other. Despite the settled character of the room as architecture, this has become a highly kinetic circumstance. It is mobile in time as well as in space, constantly changing aspect and content.

My body continually *takes me into place*. It is at once agent and vehicle, articulator and witness of being-in-place. Although we rarely attend to its exact role, once we do we cannot help but notice its importance. Without the good graces and excellent services of our bodies, not only would we be lost in place—acutely disoriented and confused—we would have no coherent sense of place itself. Nor could there be any such thing as *lived* places, i.e., places in which we live and move and have our being. Our living-moving bodies serve to structure and to configurate entire scenarios of place.

It is at once convenient and economical to consider the constituting and shaping of places by bodies in terms of a series of dyadic structures. The binary character of these structures reflects upright posture, the bilaterality of our body—its disymmetricality of organ and function—and, more generally, the function of the lived body as a basis of orientation. In keeping with its own ambidexterous proclivities, this body tends toward bifurcation (not to be confused with geometric bisection), arranging its choices, directions, and movements, as right–left, near–far, up–down, above–below, etc.[17] Even as it acts to project a field of possible actions, my body closes down the prospect of unlimited choice. Hence it poses to itself constantly (even if often only implicitly) determinate choices between, say, going forward and retreating. Being in the center of things, my body can always move here *or* there, up *or* down, this way *or* that. This dimorphous structuring does not, of course, preclude still other possibilities, but it does bestow on a given field of possibilities a coherent set of routes. A spontaneous corporeal mapping or somatography arises in which, as on an actual map, meaningful alternative directions are available at each important juncture.[18]

Even in an architecturally delimited space, I can move in any number of directions. At every moment (assuming that I am not constrained by a disabled body or by an extremely severe architecture), the options, far from being imposed in advance in the shape of rigidly determined choices, offer themselves to me as permitting ever new possibilities of action. I can say of such options what Derrida says of deconstructed binary oppositions: they are "*simultaneously* either or."[19] In such a circumstance, the all-too-definite dyad of an exclusive choice gives way to the "indefinite dyad" proposed in the *Philebus*. But where Plato spoke of the like and the unlike, the odd and the even, I shall examine the here and the there, the near and the far, the before and the after, and other corporeally specified but still indefinite dyads. Every time I move myself about in my living room—or in other rooms, other places—I find myself in the midst of a scene constructed by such dyadic pairs, an open situation that nevertheless brings with it the minimal structure of a choice between x *and* y or among x *or* y and m *or* n and a *or* b.[20] Anesthetized conceptions of space consider just three dimensions—height, breadth, and depth—and think of these in turn as strictly orthogonal to each other; e.g., as three perpendicular axes that conjoin in an abstract zero-point. Such a point—not to be confused with what Husserl calls the "null-point of orientation"—gives rise to lines and planes that extend into infinity. Such a model not only leaves no room for place or region; it forecloses serious consideration of the lived aspects of the binary pairs being discussed here.

When dimension is assumed to be formal and geometric in this manner, two difficulties arise. First, we presume that there are only *three* dimensions of space. But do we know this for sure? Buddhists take space to have ten dimensions: the four cardinal points of the compass, the four midpoints between the cardinal points, and up and down. Relativity theory posits a four-dimensional space (the fourth dimension being time), and modern topology proposes the idea of n-dimensional spatial manifolds. Even short of Buddhist cosmology or advanced mathematics and physics, are we restricted to length, height, and depth in our experiences of lived place? Are there not oblique directions that do not map onto any of these classical and all too tidy dimensions? Do we not experience certain untidy dimensions every time we walk over uneven terrain? Indeed, do we ever experience height or length or depth *pure and simple*?

Second, and more important, is the divorce between dimensionality and directionality that belongs to the Cartesian model and its conceptual progeny. Instead of regarding dimensionality as abstract and objective and directionality as concrete and merely subjective, dimensionality needs to be seen as a reflection of the lived directionality by which embodied implacement occurs. The tables need to be turned on the view—still very much alive—according to which three-dimensional space exists first and foremost in comparison with directionality as a merely derivative phenomenon.[21] On the contrary, the classical conception of tridimensionality is itself *derivative from directionality*, in which it resides, as Heidegger says, in a "still veiled" state.[22] Directionality in turn is anchored in bodily postures and movements whose description calls for intrinsically ambiguous terms such as "over there" and "way down yonder."

To say that "spatializing" space precedes "spatialized" space, as does Merleau-Ponty, or that "spatiality" precedes "space," as does Heidegger, or that bodily kinesthesias precede the idealizations of space in the manner of Husserl, is to claim that the directionality inherent in the lived body in place precedes the dimensionality of inert matter in space.[23] To maintain such precedence is not to revert to a rampant subjectivism. The lived body that is the (re)source of directionality and dimensionality alike is neither subjective nor objective. It is the "common, but to us unknown, root" of all that comes to be classified in rigidly stratified ways in modern Western thought.[24]

III

Hiersein ist herrlich.
—Rainer Maria Rilke, *Duino Elegies*

Here I stand. I cannot do otherwise.
—Martin Luther, speech at the Diet of Worms, 1521

As I sit in my living room, and as I move around in and then out of it, I find myself at every moment *here*. No matter where I am in relation to the precise layout of the room, I remain just here and not *there*. Seated, I am here in this white upholstered chair; standing at the bookshelf, I am here looking for the book of Emerson's essays; and walking into the kitchen, I am still here. I am here even when I occupy precisely what had formerly been a "there," e.g., the kitchen viewed from my chair in the living room. I am here even when I am there, at that destination which had been my goal as I searched for a book or as I came to answer the telephone. Indeed, I am never *not* here.

If the "now" is often a point of obsessive concern, we do not wonder often enough about the "here," that ubiquitous locative we continually engage in our experience. Between the here and the there, the paired members of this primal placial dyad, we have always already made a choice in favor of the here. Or more exactly, we have not so much chosen the here as we have *exemplified* it: I *am* here. And I exemplify it by *embodying* it: I am here in/as my body. *You* are here, too, in and with your body. However distant from me you may be as you read these lines, you are just as fully, as corporeally, here in your world as I am here in mine. (To indicate this biplex situation I shall sometimes employ a special graphism: you are *[t]here*.)

Thus it is by my body—my lived body—that I am here. My lived body is the vehicle of the here, its carrier or "bearer" (*Träger*), as Husserl called it.[25] My own body (my *Eigenleib*) is at once the necessary and the sufficient condition of being (located) here. When it comes to the here, my body has plenipotentiary power: a fully invested power to situate my embodied subjectivity here, *just here*. For this reason, Husserl designates the here to which the body brings me as the "absolute here."[26] An absolute here is one that cannot be diminished or compromised; to be here at all by means of the body is to be *altogether* here. It is patently nonsensical to say that "I am partly here"; or, if we do say this sometimes, we mean that, being distracted, we are torn between two or more competing heres. Each particular here nevertheless remains absolute in its demands and its opportunities; we are distracted by another here only when we feel that it, like the here we now occupy, is imperious in its requirements.

To be here is therefore an all-or-nothing affair. By this I mean not only that being-here is a matter of life or death (which is also true, since a dead person loses, along with life, the here that is the prerogative of his or her living body). I also mean that the fate of the here is tied entirely and exclusively to that of the body. If there are experiences in which my body does not figure, then these experiences will lack a here, or will possess only a quasi or pseudo here. Hence herelessness inheres in certain intellectual and mystical experiences in which we rejoin a conceptual or religious "there," an "on the other side" (*jenseits* in German) that has no proper here. But we do not have to go so far afield as this to find circumstances in which the here is apparently absent: e.g., experiences of "attuned space" (such as euphoria, fugue states, and "charged" situations into which we are precipitated without having gained any secure sense of our own bodily hereness) in which we find ourselves floating in an atmosphere not anchored, much less centered, in our own body.[27] In such experiences we are literally disoriented, since we can regard it as axiomatic that to be without a here is to lack orientation. Beyond instances of acute disorientation occasioned by immersion in attuned space, there are disorientations due to difficulties more fully internal to the organism itself, whether these be caused by Korsakoff's syndrome, temporal lobe epilepsy, Parkinson's disease, or severe emotional distress. In such extremities as these, one is all the more impressed at the lived body's capacity to regain orientation or at least to integrate lostness within an ongoing situatedness. But to the extent that the lived body is still capable of guidance, a sense of here will remain in play. "H. M.," a patient with catastrophic temporal lobe damage, was able to navigate successfully around his room and through the halls of the hospital to which he was confined. To this exact extent he knew at least that he was *(t)here* in these halls.[28]

It follows that even when we become acutely disoriented, *so long as we have at least a residual sense of where we are bodily*, we are never entirely un-oriented in space, never wholly lost in its "undistinguishable inane," never without some vestigial hereness. Only if space itself were as intrinsically di-rectionless, as indifferent and neutral, as it came to be regarded in the mod-ern era, would we be threatened with anything like a complete lack of orientation, that is to say, sheer herelessness. In other words, we are never not oriented to some degree and more or less successfully in the places we inhabit. Long before we learn astronomy or geography (much less modern physics), we already have reliable orientational knowledge of these places; thanks to our "knowing body," we know how to find them and live in them, how to be here in their presence.[29]

Hence we may say without hesitation: if I feel a lived body as such (and as mine), it provides a distinct sense of (my) being here. And conversely: if I feel that I am here, I must also feel my lived body as the basis, the very vehicle, of this here.[30]

An immediate corollary is that if my here were to be detached from my current place—my here-place—*I would have to go with it*. I cannot become not here and remain (myself). Part of the absoluteness of the here is that I cannot detach it from my body-self and thus from the place to which this body-self now gives access.

But being here—what does this mean? Even if we grant that all being-here occurs through centration in the lived body, i.e., through what Husserl calls my "central body,"[31] there is not just one way to be here. We may in fact distinguish five modes of here-being.

1. *Here in part.* First of all, even *within* my lived body, I can distinguish a corporeally localized here from the here that is coextensive with my body as a whole. At this level, my here is often identified with my head, and even more particularly with a region between or behind the eyes.[32] But it can very well migrate into other parts of the body, e.g., my torso or hips when I am dancing.[33] Wherever the exact center of the here may be, when localized in this discrete way it is capable of being opposed to another part of my body taken as there: say, my feet.[34] Although we may not be accustomed to think-ing of a particular body part as the habitual locus of a here in relation to other body parts as theres, the fact that such a here–there relationship ob-tains indicates that the body, taken as a single intact entity, *is itself a place*—if it is the case that anything that exhibits a here–there structure counts as a place in some minimal sense.

2. *Here of my body proper.* The body itself as a unitary entity constitutes a second kind of here. Indeed, the body *tout court* is often assumed to be the sole effective here-place.[35] When I felt securely *here* in my living-room chair, I was feeling here not just *in my body* but, more exactly, *as my body*. Indeed, the implicit corporeal equation "here = body = place" may lead me to take this

particular implacement of the here for granted or, contrastingly, to assume that it may be the only such implacement. Luther's "Here I stand" draws on this same equation to powerful rhetorical effect; we stand only with our full body, not with part of it. This is what we imply when we say revealingly, "As I stand here, I tell you . . . "[36]

3. *Here of my by-body.* We often stand in order to move, and when we move we experience yet another kind of hereness, one that moves *with* and *by* my body. *With* is Whitehead's term for the way we experience things through the agency of our body, by its intermediary presence, as it were. The epitome of such withness is doubtless found in situations in which my body plays an instrumental role, as when I use my body in order to locate a book or to answer the phone. Then I am moving here in this particular way so as to realize a given goal over there at the bookcase or in the kitchen. But the here of the by-body (i.e., my body as that *by which* I realize a certain action) is not confined to what I accomplish in instrumental activity. Every time I move my body out of a strictly stationary posture, I experience such a here. It consists in an active area at once clinging and expansive: clinging to my body proper as it moves (it takes its clue entirely from this kinetic body) and yet expanding outward from the lived-moving body, giving to it a leeway of spontaneous action. At the limit, this leeway becomes an entire *range* of free actions when we consider all of the various paths which my body can pursue even in such a narrowly circumscribed place as my living room.[37]

4. *Regional here.* When the range of the here includes not just the place through which I am now moving (and which therefore reflects my immediate bodily movement) but all of the places to which I can effectively move, I experience a properly regional here. Examples include the entire house in which I reside (sometimes with its yard attached), a block on which I live, an entire neighborhood, even a county or state or nation. I take myself to be *here* in this house or block or neighborhood, in this state or nation, whenever I am convinced that (a) I can in principle move (in person or by proxy) to any part of this region, however far-flung this part might be; (b) some other more or less comparably extensive region stands opposed to my current here-region: *another* neighborhood, *another* state, over there and in relation to which I am now truly here, on *this* side (*diesseits*) of whatever boundary or difference demarcates the two regions in question. A region, therefore, is a concatenation of places that, taken together, constitutes a common and continuous here for the person who lives in or traverses them.[38]

5. *Interpersonal here.* The majority of Husserl's speculations concerning the here—there structure evolved out of his desire to acount for the constitution of other human beings in our midst. In a characteristic passage he writes that "[the other's] body in the mode *There*, which presents itself in *my* monadic sphere and is apperceived as another's live body (the animate organism of the alter ego)—that body indicates 'the same' body in the mode *Here*, as

the body experienced by the other ego in *his* monadic sphere."[39] Here Husserl points to the structure of the (t)here in the interpersonal realm: what is there for me as the other's lived body is, for that other himself or herself, a here of self-presence. What is at stake is not just *my* own body but also the other's body as it relates to, and differs from, mine (and vice versa). My own here remains mine, yet I am aware of another here precisely as *another's here*: a here that is conveyed to me only indirectly by the other's body as *there* in my perception. In this circumstance, more than a dialectic of self and other is at play; the other's (t)here is actively resistant to my here, which thereby meets an intrinsic limit of its own range.[40]

Let us grant, then, that the here is multilocular and that it has at least the five forms just outlined.[41] Let us also grant that these five forms are subject to considerable variation of aspect and appearance, according to vicissitudes of climate, history, temperament, gender, etc. Still, we find ourselves wondering, *where* is *here*? Notice that I can know that I am here without knowing just where I am. Whitehead observes that "a traveller, who has lost his way, should not ask, Where am I? What he really wants to know is, Where are the other places?"[42] This means that to become oriented again I have to know the respective *theres* of my changing here. To know where I am is to know that I am determinately (t)here—bodily here in relation to an already known there or set of theres.

More basically still, the very concept of here includes reference to a corresponding there; or more exactly, "each Here has many Theres."[43] Some of these theres are actual, that is, situated in currently perceived parts and places of my surrounding world. Other theres are only virtual; I *might* perceive them were I to move to the appropriate locations. Any given singular here may be coupled with an indefinite plurality of actual and virtual theres (including theres that correspond to the five sorts of here just discussed). Even though this circumstance is not an evenly balanced one, its very asymmetry suggests the complementarity of the One and the Many. What the here lacks as a strict singularity, the there possesses in its plurivalency.[44] Such a here–there complementarity occurs continually in the course of everyday life.

The telephone call I have just received brings with it the request that I attend a demonstration concerning the suppression of human rights in Tibet. The demonstration is to be held simultaneously in two locations: New York and Boston. *Here* in Connecticut I am situated between these two cities. I am therefore suddenly confronted with the lures of two distinctly different but equally possible theres. At the level of political action, there is only *one* there: that inhering in the action of demonstration, wherever it may take place. But at the level of concrete geography, being just here, I am faced with a double there: Boston-as-there and New York-as-there.

In this instance, two possible theres link up with the stable here established by my body.

Further, I may be committed to an overarching There (e.g., the destination of a long journey) but find myself diverted by a series of episodic theres along the way. Odysseus is determined to return to his native land, yet he manages to take a quite convoluted route to get there. Each convolution possesses its own unique group of theres to which Odysseus's bodily being-here is oriented as he makes his way home. So too in the Odyssey of our own lives. Encounters with Calypso or Cyclops, with Nausicaa or the Lotus Eaters, are woven into a greater fabric: the There of our determined seeking after lasting and significant aims.

More important than the plurality of theres or their differential hierarchy is the inherent structure of the here–there relation, which possesses two distinctive features. First, this relation *splits* the very field it serves to structure. Whether the field in question be purely visual (as in Husserl's notion of *Sehraum*) or synesthetic (as in Merleau-Ponty's model of a multilayered perceptual field) or social (as in Schutz's analysis of interpersonal space), the here–there dichotomy at once exhausts the field and divides it. By "exhausts" I mean that the sectors of here *and* there, taken together, are coextensive with the experiential field as a whole, leaving no remainder. Everything in the field, even the minutest detail, is designatable *either* as "here" *or* as "there." As I sit in my study, for example, my body (including its various leading parts), the clothes I am wearing, the book I am reading, and the chair in which I am seated are all *here* for me. They constitute what we might call my "proto-place." Everything else in the room, as well as other rooms in the house, the house itself, and its surroundings, are *there* for me inasmuch as I am seated here. They are somewhere "over there" in a series of "zonal places" that arrange themselves around my proto-place. This is the case even though I may not be able to discover any exact line of demarcation between the various items that make up my proto-place here and those items that constitute its covalent zonal places there. Nothing is located *on* any such line that enables me to say it is *neither* here nor there or *both* here and there. The distinction between here and there therefore has the remarkable property of being at once definitive and indefinite.

A second feature of the here–there relation is the *tensional arc* it exhibits. We feel the tension between here and there much more acutely in certain situations than in others, often most acutely in interpersonal settings. For instance, we become aware of our failure to understand another person "from her point of view," which is to say, from the standpoint of her own somatocentric here. Husserl speaks of an "abyss" between myself and another opening at such moments, while Levinas refers to the "infinity" separating me from the other.[45] In these circumstances, the here and the there are in such tension that they seem to break apart, even to repel each other. We are then confronted with a "counter-place," a place that exists by opposing us. What might have been projected as a merely imaginary line of demarcation becomes a wall of difference (often felt emotionally as indifference).[46]

During moments of minimal tension, the here seems to be continuous with the there. This happens, for instance, when I walk over to a bookcase, knowing just which book I am seeking: no sooner have I thought of a particular book here, in my chair, than I find myself over there, at the appropriate bookshelf. Only if I fail to find the book am I suddenly polarized by the barren there of an unyielding object. Short of such disappointment, many of our spontaneous actions manage to put here and there into nondisruptive combinations that can be termed "com-places." In a com-place here and there are in open interplay, a free exchange, as it were. The there is suddenly here "before I know it." This last phrase reflects the special power of the com-place to bring here and there into an intimate embrace in which otherwise divisive differences of body and place are suspended.

The here–there relation is not only manifold in its appearance and type. It is remarkably variable in scale, since it applies to places of almost every size, ranging from the micro-place of my own body to the macro-locus of the earth. This scalar diversification allows the here–there pair to combine readily with other dimensional dyads in constantly varying combinations. Thus we speak spontaneously of "up there," "down here," "back there," "over there," "near here," etc. This combinatory power suggests that the here–there dyad may be the most comprehensive of the binary pairs that structure the body–place plexus. All other such pairs are, if not derivative from, at least beholden to this primal pair, which is in this regard truly *primus inter pares*.[47]

IV

> The relation between nearness and remoteness is not that of spatial places which are next-to or with each other.
>
> —Erwin Straus, *The Primary World of Senses*

> Making the farness vanish [is] making the remoteness of something disappear, bringing it close.
>
> —Martin Heidegger, *Being and Time*

> The nearness and remoteness of things open up to the subject.
>
> —Elisabeth Ströker, *Investigations in Philosophy of Space*

Despite the manifest importance of the here–there polarity, the lived body finds its way in/to place in manifold ways. Its orientation in place is more than a matter of aligning my own here with a set of surrounding (or opposing, or congenial) theres. A second pair of terms, near and far, is also crucially ingredient in the relationship between body and place, as we can see from a continuation of the earlier vignette.

> The telephone call I received earlier has led to a decision: I shall go to the demonstration in Boston. It is late, however, and I risk missing the action if I do not hustle. I get into my car and begin to drive more rapidly down the turnpike than the speed limit permits. As I begin my journey, I am acutely aware of how far away Boston seems. It seems far even when I am well over the Massachusetts border. Only when I reach Boston itself and realize that I shall be in time to participate in the demonstration does the city begin to seem genuinely near.

This otherwise banal situation brings with it a telling insight into the character of the near and the far. What I experience as near or far is not only resistant to geographic actuality but may be quite independent of it. As I rush to Boston in haste, my sense of the far is so intrusive that my knowledge that the normal driving time is only about two-and-a-half hours offers no consolation. My destination seems so far that I despair of arriving in time for the demonstration. The felt farness has vanquished the actual geographical proximity. Or more exactly, felt farness has set proximity aside, suspended it as an item of knowledge. A convergence of the two occurs only at a more relaxed moment, when the farness has vanished.[48]

What are we to make of the fact that we do not speak (in English) of going "therer," but we do say that we go "farther"; nor can we come "herer" (or even "more here"), while we do speak of getting "nearer" to something? This seemingly trivial linguistic difference points to something important: near and far are both subject to progressive intensification (or deintensification). The here and the there retain an all-or-nothing character, but this does not hold for the near and the far. We can engage more or less fully in nearness or farness. Moreover, the near and the far are themselves subject to commixture.[49] I can go *far from the near* or draw *near to the far*. The latter is in effect what I was doing as I came closer to Boston, and as I might do still more emphatically were I to reach the low-lying hills surrounding a distant mountain. The hybridizing of near and far is made possible by the fact that both near and far are matters of degree. The fact that each term is an expression of gradual differences facilitates their combination with each other. In the end, their relationship is characterized by continuous transition and by the fact that they form a complemental series, i.e., the more of one, the less of the other.

In their very continuity and differentiation by degree, the near and the far are remarkably porous, taking on changing aspects of the situations in which they are immanent. Thus my anxious mood of fearing that I was going to be late qualified my perception of Boston as farther than the cartographic fact indicated. On other occasions, far and near assume quite different casts; e.g., a catastrophic involution of the near when I am feeling under attack by real or imagined persecutors or a cozy contraction of space when I sense that someone I care for is "close to me," although he or she is located distantly in terms of objective world-space. Not only emotional factors but cognitive and memorial elements also structure the experience of the near–far in decisive ways. To return to my childhood home, even when it is comparatively close in geographic terms, may seem to be a far trip indeed; the distant root of my memories is parlayed into the current perception of my home as spatially remote. In its absorptiveness, the near–far pairing often mirrors my total milieu: "Far and near vary with health and illness, with walking and standing, with hurrying and resting."[50] More than any other locatory dyad, the near–far is attuned to—and thus reflects—the particular way I am inserted into my life-world at a given moment.

Two corollaries follow from this attunement. First, just because the near and the far are so fully reflective of my entire situation, they are especially *averse to exact determination* of a metric sort, including determination by geographical distance. One cannot *add* nearnesses in order to attain a "sum" of farness. Nor can one find out their precise perimeter or outer limit. How far is far? How near is near? How far is near from far? Even though I can *perceive* the far as continuous with the near, I can no more *reach* the far than I can reach the end of a rainbow. To be reachable is to be within a calibratable distance from where I am now located. Yet where I *am* now located, my own "near," is not specifiable by metric means. Indeed, any effort to measure the near or the far—to gauge them, singly or together, on a scale of uniformly distributed marks or numbers—not only misses the phenomena themselves but undermines their very identity.[51]

The second corollary is that the near–far is thoroughly *spatio-temporal* in its experience and presentation. Where the here–there is primarily spatial, the near–far can be temporal or spatial, and is often both at once.[52] When I felt myself to be so frustratingly far from Boston, I experienced myself as distant from it both in space and in time. What Husserl refers to as the inherent "spatio-temporality" of the life-world becomes most apparent in the case of the near and the far, which continually combine spatial with temporal features.[53] This combinatory capacity is doubtless itself part of the general ability of the near–far to mirror the self-world relationship as a whole. In this relationship, the spatial and the temporal are inextricably intertwined; when I want you to be near me, I want you to be close to me not just *where I am* but *at the time I am* at this same where. I want it both ways, and this is just what the near delivers to me when it is fully experienced. (The far, in appropriate contrast, is remote in both spatial and temporal respects: "Long ago and far away" is practically a pleonastic phrase.)

Both of the foregoing corollaries are body-based. As at once kinetic and kinesthetic (moving and feeling-itself-moving), my lived body is what offers the ultimate—and the first—resistance to determination in strictly spatial terms. This body's movements *through* space, its elliptical saunterings and sidewise turnings (its literal con-siderations), defy calibrated measurement. Even its straight courses are never altogether rectilinear; even when I am moving unequivocally toward a given goal, I continue to turn and twist my serpentine body along the way. The amorphousness of my lived body (Merleau-Ponty would say its "ambiguity") ensures that my connection with the near and the far will be indeterminate, both in space and in time.

Neither the near nor the far—much less their various concatenations—would appear without my corporeal intentionality, my directedness to the world through my bodily bearing. As Straus observes, "Only insofar as I am directed toward the world, striving for and desiring that which I do not have, and in so desiring the other am myself changed, only then can there exist for me the near and the far."[54] The intentional body, then, is a *desiring body*; when we experience ourselves as far from or near to things, a factor of attraction or repulsion is almost always involved. If we are rarely entirely indifferent to what we feel to be distinctly near or far away, this is due to our embodiment as creatures of desire, interest, wish, and concern.

Here we must delve deeper into the immanent structures of the near and the far as these form their own realms or "spheres."[55]

What is near to us is *within our reach*, or what dancers call "reach space." Such space is not "space" at all in the modernist sense, since it is neither homogeneous nor isotropic. It comes to us as highly and often oddly configurated. "Reach" itself is complex, extending into the areas of those things within *actual* reach at the present moment as well as those within *potential* reach. To be within actual reach is to occupy a location so nearby that I do not have to move, or move much, to attain it. Here are found things that are ready-to-hand, now present, in earshot, unambiguously visible, etc. Spatial as well as temporal, the modalities of actually reachable nearness are multiple. The criterion for such nearness is less that of distance (i.e., literal proximity) than advertability.[56]

The potential reach of the near sphere includes an even more extensive group of possibilities. Now it is not merely a matter of immediately attainable items but of all the things we *could* reach. The volume of Emerson for which I sought in vain is a member of this category. It lay (in Schutz's phrase) within "restorable reach," even if I failed to find it in fact. Restorability of reach signifies that I can reenter a certain near sphere and grasp the item I once perceived or used. Thanks to the accumulation of many such restorable reaches, my everyday life becomes at once facilitated and complexly sedimented.

My near sphere also includes numerous things attainable even if not yet (or ever) actually attained. If I hear a cat fight outside the house, I can rush to the place of the fight or I can choose to ignore it. The fight-place is an attainable arena in my near sphere. It is no less an integral part of my current near sphere for my not actually entering it. How is such attainability ascertained? Largely on the basis of typifications of situations; I know the *type* of circumstance in question—here, animals fighting each other—and thanks to this knowledge, itself sedimented from a variety of like occasions, I include the fight-place in my near sphere.[57]

Perhaps most striking of all is the readiness with which we move between and among the various actually and potentially reachable parts of any given near sphere. To be near at all is to be reachable by definite, enactable doings. In a normal circumstance, the reachability is easy; but even when obstructed in our actions, we are assured that, were the obstacles to vanish, we might well attain our aims. (The perception of an intractable obstacle, e.g., paralysis on my part or a permanently locked door, has the effect of transferring the item I wish to reach into the far sphere even when it lies close by in terms of objective distance.)[58]

My near sphere, then, is a nexus of differentially available reachables, connected and traversed by multiple pathways. These paths of access are themselves potential as well as actual. The obvious routes from my chair to the two entrances to my living room are supplemented by a myriad of possible paths I *could* take if I were to try to reach this or that object (person, event, etc.). A pattern of nodal points (constituted by particular reachables) and connecting paths (ways to attain the reachables) is an implicit infrastructure of every given place. As I move about and modify my position, the pattern itself shifts, thereby reflecting my altered bodily locus. Exhibited here is a quite specific version of the body's intentional arc, not now the tensional arc of the here–there relation but an *arc of reachability* stretching between my body on one hand and pathways-cum-reachables on the other.[59]

The far is not the distant. Even if distance sometimes contributes substantially to effects of farness, sheer amount of distance does not guarantee farness. Things remote in space and time can enter our near sphere, most notably through technological intermediaries such as telescopes and telephones, cameras and television sets.[60] When something presents itself to us as genuinely *far*—i.e., as part of the far sphere—we experience "range." Where our main action in the near sphere is that of reaching, in the far sphere we find ourselves ranging. The ranging itself need not be literal wandering; it can occur in a purely perceptual (or memorial or imaginary) mode whereby we tranpose ourselves into the far and pick out features in it. The far sphere is the domain where ranging is expected and encouraged.

My movement in the far sphere is often described as "broad-ranging." When I range broadly, I move across and over a given expanse of the earth, sometimes *around* it as well; in circumambulating a distant mountain such as Mount Kailash on a pilgrimage in western Tibet, I am ranging broadly around it. In this latter case my ranging is purposive, and the far sphere is filled with a determinate religious significance. In other instances, e.g., when I stroll idly around Paris as a *flâneur*, I am exploring the byways of a far sphere that beckons without offering any definite purpose. I meander in its wide embrace. Sometimes, of course, purposive and nonpurposive ranging combine, as in serendipitous discoveries. The far sphere allows for the planned and the unplanned alike to occur as I range broadly in its midst.[61]

The single most prominent feature of the far sphere is the *horizon*. As uncontainable in any simple delineation, the horizon is a boundary, not a limit. The "horizon line" is a fiction foisted upon perceptual experience by the graphic requirements of depicting recession in depth. In fact, we experience the horizon of the far sphere not as a line but as itself a sphere (or more exactly, as the inner surface of a sphere).[62] The horizon of the far sphere includes the enormous concave dome of the sky as well as the land or sea that spreads out before us as it draws into remoteness. Were it a mere line, the horizon would be something we could in principle attain, but it is at once too massive and too elusive to be reachable.

The unreachability of the horizon in no way constricts its range. On the contrary, the horizon provides maximum range for any given situation. It is even a range of ranges, encompassing as it does all regional rangings. Its own range is, in Gurwitsch's phrase, "susceptible to indefinite continuation," and it even includes things not visible, much less tangible, from our own standpoint: "things un-perceived, unknown, things to appear in perceptual experience under the conditions of appropriate movement when we proceed in one or another direction."[63] Things lying on the other side of the horizon possess only one certain property: they are in principle *perceivable* if only the requisite bodily motions place us in their presence.

Horizons as boundaries of the far sphere exhibit further peculiar properties. First, the horizon itself, though an intrinsic feature of the far sphere, may present to me a near and a far aspect. The Himalayas (and it is not accidental that we speak of such mountains as forming a "range") viewed from the high plateau of Tibet show to me a near-side paired with a non-visible but adumbrated far-side. This near-side—i.e., the peaks and slopes present in my current perception—is very distant, in fact many hundreds of miles, from me. I know this fact, and I also know that *this* nearness forms no part of my own near sphere. In this way I encounter a nearness of the far that belongs to the far itself. Second, the horizon itself, even as thus complicated, recedes as I approach it. "The really striking fact about the horizon," says van Peursen, "is that it recedes."[64] Whatever my efforts to stride toward it—to reach it—the horizon is always evading me.

The horizon of the far sphere is not itself an object but a boundary *for* objects. It is not so much *in* the world—indeed, it "adds nothing" to the world's inventory and is in this respect an "unreality"—as *with* the world as an outermost part.[65] This in turn reflects the fact that the lived body in moving toward the far requires for its very movement (again: virtual as well as actual) the notion of an ever-expanding range of action. To move into the far is ipso facto to move into what cannot be attained as a determinate object or limit or line, even if what we move into must be bounded and unified in some way. As Derrida observes, "A horizon is always virtually present in every experience; for it is at once the unity and the incompletion for that experience—the anticipated unity in every incompletion."[66]

How then does my body figure into the experience of the horizon? Without the mobility my body provides, I would have no meaningful sense of perspective, and without perspective I could have no experience of the horizon. If we were entirely stationary beings, we would lack continually varying viewpoints. To lack these changing standpoints would be in turn to lack something essential to horizonality. Whereas a given object can be approached from one vantage point only, a horizon calls for multiple ingressions on the part of my lived body. I approach it there in its farness from the closeness my body realizes in each successive here.[67]

The paramount fact about the horizon for our purposes is that it is the ultimate *perimeter of places*. It encompasses *all* places, those in the far sphere most decisively (around these it forms a firm boundary), but those in the near sphere as well (since the near sphere is itself contained within the far sphere). Such inclusion is no static matter, as if it were a question of pre-established cosmic geography. The horizon at once holds and distributes the places within its embrace, but only because of its sustained animation by my lived and moving body.

Moving in the near and into the far is always done *in regard to the horizon*. This is not merely a matter of fact but points to a condition of possibility: there would be no places to which to move unless any given place were what it is in relation to an encompassing horizon. Nor would there be any reach or range in and among places without such a horizon. Moving—reaching and ranging—in the natural light of the horizon, we encounter the places the horizon itself makes possible. To the two kinds of intentional arc previously identified, tensional and reachable, we must therefore add a third: the *horizonal* arc. Within this arc is contained all that we have discussed under the heading of the near and far spheres.

Body–horizon–place: in the mutual enlivening of this dynamic triad the near and the far realize their most effective interaction. Rather than the resistance or Secondness inherent in the relation between the here and the there—which polarize even as they conjoin—we witness here a more subtle complicity as we move from the near into the far within the circumambient horizon. No wonder near and far are so absorptive in character; their constant entanglement within the arc of the horizon predisposes this pair of terms to be maximally reflective of each other and of the places they contain and connect.

The same entanglement ensures that the dialectic of near and far leaves little room for a void in our experience of the circumambient life-world. Since every place within a given horizon presents itself as near or far—or as a changing combination of these two adverbial terms—no place will be utterly devoid of spatial specifications. Every place experienced as close or remote (and as having closeness and remoteness within it) is a place that is already internally differentiated. To the extent that the near and far are present there can be no empty places; and for the same reason there can be no non-places, no Space without Place. But we are immersed in plenitudinous places only because we are beings for whom the near and the far, along with the here and the there, are inherent features of an embodied experience.

V

The here and the there, the near and the far, are the most pervasive parameters of place. Given that *parametrein* means "to measure out," we can say that every place we encounter (and know and remember) is measured out, given its full extent, by these four locative predicates. Such measuring out is not to be confused with measuring *in*, as in the expression "measuring in miles." Rather than being mere means of measurement like yardsticks placed against raw lumber, here–there and near–far are themselves ingredient in what they measure, being *measurants* in Merleau-Ponty's term.[68] This means that they span what they measure out. As a consequence, nothing falls outside the far and the there (nothing is farther than far, more there than there); nor does anything fall short of the here and the near (nothing is closer than the near, more here than here). Everything in place, including place itself, is brought to com-parison in the nonmetric measuring effected by these paired terms ("to compare one thing by another" is another meaning of *parametrein*).

Everywhere we turn, we turn in place as measured out by here versus there, near together with far. To be in place, to *be* place(d), is to be located here or there, near or far. No place is not here or there, not near or far.

Conversely, to be neither here nor there, neither near nor far, is not to be (in) place. ("It's neither here nor there," we say, meaning that it doesn't matter *in this place/time*: the topic doesn't call for a continuing *topos*.)

What turns in parametric place is my lived body, which acts as "the *origo* of the deictic field."[69] *From* and *with* my body I turn *to* and *in* place and move between places as well. This bodily origin of implacement does not mean that my body acts as a mere thing, a determinate presence in place. On the contrary, only as animated and changing can a lived body be the effective *origo* of implacement. Even a seemingly stationary plant moves in the very place in which it is grounded; it grows in place and often literally turns in place. Plants may even have an elemental sensibility concerning the here and the there, as exhibited in their capacity to shape themselves in accordance with the configuration of their immediate circumstance or to turn toward the distant sun. To move *between* places, as virtually all animals do, is to become acutely aware of the differences between here and there and especially between near and far. Animals are above all sensitive to the latter inasmuch as their nutrition depends on overcoming the farness of food.

In the case of human animals, the here–there and near–far are culturally (and linguistically) conditioned as well. This is most readily apparent in the case of the far sphere, where what counts as constitutive varies greatly from culture to culture. For the Greeks, the Heavens (*to ouranos*), composed of circular spheres encased in each other, constituted the far realm as viewed from the "middle" realm of Earth. The Navajo designate the far as the Sky and imagine it not as circular but as an enormous flat disk lying on top of the Earth and conjoined to the latter at its edges. Contemporary Western astrophysics is continually revising its conception of what lies far out in the physical universe by positing black holes, quarks, exploding galactic "walls," etc., all *far* out *there*. Indeed, since at least the time of Copernicus the far sphere has been subject to such frequent reconception that the near sphere might seem by comparison to be constant in its parametrical properties. Yet this is not so; the furniture of the local environment is as carpentered as the posits at the outermost fringes of the known universe.[70] Open places for stopping and talking in a Greek *agora* disappear in the gridlocked streets and crowded sidewalks of a modern metropolis. Not just the contents but the very structure of the near sphere may therefore differ drastically between cultures and even between different epochs of the same culture, for instance in radically changing ideas of one's "home-world" in contrast with the "alien-world."[71]

The same effects of enculturation are evident in how the body-in-place is conceived. Even if this body acts in general like a corporeal analogue of Kant's transcendental mind, it is no cultural constant to be taken for granted. Its means and modes of placing—its exact ways of assuring implacement and of falling into displacement—vary considerably. As the conception of the body alters, the notion of place changes with it. When Locke links labor with value through the common term of *property*, he is thinking of the body as a specifically working body that gains the right to own and shape the land on which it labors. Locke can think of a place as appropriated from the non-place of unworked wilderness—in short, as deserved property—only because he views the human body as primarily destined for concerted manual labor that accumulates and possesses material goods.[72] By contrast, in ancient Sybaris, the human body, conceived as a body of pleasure rather than of labor, constituted places as hedonic scenes of ritualized indulgence.

Despite the cultural specificity of both bodies and places, we can recognize general traits that characterize the here–there, near–far parameters: non-simple location and primal depth.

I take the term *simple location* from Whitehead, for whom such location means that "whatever is in space is *simpliciter* in some definite portion of space."[73] A simply located object is *just here* or *just there*, existing in splendid isolation from other objects. Its relations with these objects are entirely extrinsic and are not in any way essential to its being, much less its well-being. By the same token, a simply located place is isolated from other places: "As soon as you have settled, however you do settle, what you mean by *a definite place* in space-time, you can adequately state the relation of a particular material body [including the human body] to space-time by saying that it is just there, *in that place*; and so far as simple location is concerned, there is nothing more to be said on the subject."[74] When place has been subjected to simple location, it becomes what I shall call "site." Site is place reduced to being "just there."

But as embodied beings are we ever *just there*? The poet doubts it: "I can only say, *there* we have been: but I cannot say where."[75] An indeterminate "there" is not to be confused with a determinate "where"; and the same is true of "here," which is not reducible to a pinpointed simple location. Place, insofar as it is spanned by the tensional arc of the here–there, cannot be construed as site if we are to be true to what is proper to place itself. In a simply located site, embodied heres and theres have become indifferent "whereats" that are the shrunken residues of lived whereabouts.[76]

Simple location, which for Whitehead is the "fundamental assumption" of the entire modern era in physics and philosophy, falls into the Fallacy of Misplaced Concreteness, the error of "mistaking the abstract for the concrete."[77] In the concreteness of actual bodily experience, Whitehead writes, there is no such thing as simple location: "Among the primary elements of nature as apprehended in our immediate experience, there is no element whatever which possesses this character of simple location."[78] Least of all place as characterized by the oppositional dyad of here–there! For neither here nor there is a simple location. Reflecting the amorphousness of the lived body (itself not simply situated), each is at once too complex and too diffuse to be considered a mere position of the sort at stake in the determination of longitude (or, for that matter, in the intersection of lines in the maplike grids of Descartes's analytical geometry). Although the here is certainly contrasted with the there—especially in the case of counter-places—it lacks a determinate locus. Even the "absolute here" of my body is not a simple location but a moving locus that relates in a continually changing way to its various theres. Despite my body's fate to be always insistently *here* and yet never simply positioned in space, it is also its fate to be implicated in the theres that surround it, thereby exemplifying Whitehead's notion that "every location involves an aspect of itself in every other location."[79]

In Whitehead's view, far from being a simply located bit of matter, an organic body is a "total event" that reaches out to many locations continuous with this body's immediate here. I feel these locations *with* my body and sometimes even *in* my body when I internalize them. In contrast with Descartes's or Newton's conception of nature as "merely, and completely, *there*, externally designed and obedient,"[80] I experience nature and the world as there-with/in-my-body. My body brings together their thereness with my own hereness. My being-here, with its various modulations, is no more a pinpointed position than their being-there is the site of an indifferent thing or quality:

> if green be the sense-object [I perceive], green is not simply at A where it is being perceived [i.e., "here"], nor is it simply at B where it is perceived as located [i.e., "there"], but it is present at A with the mode of location in B.[81]

Modal location stems from the implacing power of my body, its distinctive ability to determine "location elsewhere" in terms of its own inherent prehensive power.[82] It ensues that the relation between the here of the perceiving body and the there of perceived objects is not merely indicative but adumbrative and inclusive. The here and the there, both nonsimply located, connect as the ever-changing epicenters of any given place, whether that place is an antagonistic counter-place or a congenial com-place. Within the *common place* of the here–there—even when the scene is conflictual—"the obvious solidarity of the world" becomes apparent.[83]

When we engage in the near and the far, we find ourselves dealing in *depth*. To move near to something is to move into its depth; to move far from it is to leave its depth and to join another. Either way, depth makes the near and far possible as distinguishable but inseparable parameters; it is also what serves to connect them as aspects of one differentiated field. For the depth of the near and that of the far belong ultimately to one continuous primal depth. Just as the horizon encompasses the discrete things and places it embraces in its comprehensive sweep, so primal depth encompasses the horizon in turn. The horizon is depth taken to the limit of presence—which is to say, all the way to absence.

But what is depth? Berkeley conceived of it as length or "breadth seen from the side."[84] The depth of a perceived object is the distance I pace off or that which, seen by another subject observing my line of sight, is interpreted by this second subject as the length of that line. God, as the ultimate subject of subjects and as someone who possesses all points of view, sees every depth as breadth: "For God, who is everywhere, breadth is immediately equivalent to depth."[85] Thus depth dissolves into breadth or length regarded as determinate distance. Hegel took the next logical step by considering breadth, depth, and height to be "indifferent" dimensions interchangeable without remainder: "It is a matter of indifference whether we call a certain direction height or depth; it is the same with length or breadth, which is also often called depth, for nothing is determined in this way."[86] Berkeley's God and Hegel's Absolute Spirit share one pertinent trait in that each is bodiless. To take their incorporeal point of view is *eo ipso* to convert depth into distance without noticing that depth, experienced in bodily terms, is unreducible to distance. Berkeley and Hegel are "as forgetful as anyone else of the originality of depth."[87] Indeed, they are *more* forgetful than the ordinary person, who, sensitive to the deliverances of his or her lived body, knows depth to be something quite distinctive.

Merleau-Ponty insists on the distinction between "objectified depth" and "primordial depth." Objectified depth is depth as a determinate dimension (thus comparable, albeit in a different spatial register, to simple location). Such depth is "a relation between things or even between planes . . . [which is] detached from experience and transformed into breadth."[88] Primordial depth is "original" precisely in its unreducibility to any of the three classical dimensions. As "the most 'existential' of all dimensions," it is to be understood as "a pre-objective standard of distances and sizes."[89] Merleau-Ponty means that *before*, or better *under*, objectified or measured depth there is another depth that includes all determinate depths and acts as their common measurant. Discrete depths measure out, and into, this primal parameter. Primordial depth is more like a *medium* than an axis or line (i.e., the predominant metaphors for the traditional three dimensions). This depth exhibits "the thickness of a medium devoid of any thing."[90] As an indeterminate matrix, primordial depth resists reduction not only to the spatial determinacy of a Cartesian triaxial analytical system but also to the temporal determinacy of clock time.

Such depth (which I prefer to call "primal") is therefore not a matter of space or time. It is a matter—perhaps even *the matter*—of place. The uniqueness of place, its idiotopism, is best seen in its depth-dealing power. While determinations of time and space cling to the homogeneous surface, place goes into the depth. From primal depth place takes its rise, and to it place returns.

The intimate interplay of depth and place is based on the active intervention of the lived body. This intervention does not occur, as Berkeley imagined, by pacing off distances or by spectating from the sidelines. Rather, it stems from the way in which my body realizes the near and the far in my ongoing life. As Merleau-Ponty writes,

> When we say that an object is huge or tiny, nearby or far away, it is often without any comparison, even implicit, with any other object, or even with the size and objective position [i.e., the simple location] of our own body, but merely in relation to a certain "scope" of our gestures, a certain "hold" of the phenomenal body on its surroundings.[91]

"Scope" and "hold" are parametrical actions of the lived body. Scope is closely related to what I have called "horizonal arc"—the horizon is the outer boundary of the body's gesticular ambit—while hold reflects the way the near and far are grasped together within the compass of any given horizon. Scope has to do with range, hold with reach.

This brings us to the crux of the matter. Near and far are held together *in depth by the body*, but how precisely does this happen? Recall that I claimed in my description of near–far that the members of this dyad are continuous with each other, shade off into one another, even form something like a complemental series. This deep-lying connection bespeaks a common basis. The basis is provided by a particular feature of primal depth—reponsible for its "originality"—namely, envelopment or overlap. Primal depth, according to Merleau-Ponty, is "the dimension in which things or elements of things envelop each other, whereas breadth and height are the dimensions in which they are juxtaposed."[92] While juxtaposition acts to set objects merely *next to* each other—i.e., as simply located at contiguous points in planiform space— envelopment arranges objects *around* each other in a scene of mutual implication and simultaneous presence. What primal depth as a thick medium makes possible is thus the overlapping of near and far, which continually *intertwine in depth*.

Consider any given case of being near and far in a particular place. As I come close to something in that place, my body's motions effect an action of "nearing nearness" tantamount to delving further into the depth of place.[93] An initially far object gets nearer, resituating itself in the primal depth, not at simple locations in that depth but at indeterminate intervals, which change as I make the farness vanish by my bodily movements. Each such interval is a shifting mixture of near and far; the closer I get, the more the near predominates over the far in that interval. If primal depth "is merely a stage in arriving at a perceptual faith in one single thing," such depth nevertheless sets the scene for the altering ratios of near and far.[94] Within that scene the near and far relate to each other not only in place but *as* place. For place manifests itself in the indeterminate envelopment of nearness by farness and of farness by nearness, in accordance with the bodily actions that bring one into the vicinity of the other.

In a remarkable passage in "Eye and Mind," Merleau-Ponty brings together depth, envelopment, and place around an enigma.

> The enigma [of depth] consists in the fact that I see things, each one in its place, precisely because they eclipse one another, and that they are rivals before my sight precisely because each one is in its own place. Their exteriority is known in their envelopment and their mutual dependence in their autonomy.[95]

This means that the near and the far at once envelop *and* exclude one another and that precisely in this conjoint (and only seemingly contradictory) action, they call upon place as their common ground. "One carves in a being," says a working note of Merleau-Ponty's, "that *remains in its place*."[96] The combination of inclusion and occlusion that primal depth brings with it requires an abiding *place for* the near and the far in their game of mutual occultation, which can happen only *in* a place, *by* a body, and *with* a depthful indeterminacy that sustains the game itself.

This result may be generalized beyond any one scene of envelopment and exclusion. At the limit, as Merleau-Ponty adds, primal depth as the medium of this scene entails the notion of "a global 'locality'—everything in the same place at the same time, a locality from which height, width, and depth are abstracted . . . a voluminosity we express in a word when we say that a thing is *there*."[97] "Everything in the same place at the same time": here we rejoin Whitehead's insistence that the critique of simple location suggests that "in a certain sense, everything is everywhere at all times."[98] The "certain sense" is precisely that provided by primal depth, which acts as the connective tissue of the world of places to which my body brings me.

"I can only say, *there* we have been: but I cannot say where." The Anglo-American poet, like the French phenomenologist, literally underlines the "there" in order to indicate its nonpunctate status as not merely another particular "where." Eliot adds: "And I cannot say, how long, for that is to place it in time."[99] The there, understood in its full range, takes us everywhen as well as everywhere, into cosmic whenabouts as well as global whereabouts. Neither map nor clock can tell us the true positions of nonsimple locations in the space-time of primal depth.

We may infer that nonsimple location and primal depth possess an elective affinity for each other. Perhaps they are merely alternative descriptions of the same phenomenon of the body-in-place, the former prevailing when the here–there configuration is prominent, the latter when the near–far is at issue. To be in primal depth is not to be at a simple location. To be diffusely located is to be in primal depth.

We may also infer that if the determination of longitude is appropriate and valuable on the surface of the sea, it is inappropriate and useless in the depths—in *tehom*, the Deep from which the known world is said to have come in the first place.

In the first place there is depth. Primal depth, at once constituted and discovered by body, yields places. Places, gathered into a detotalized totality, yield world. Neither space nor time—nor universe—issues from these origins, except by way of abstraction and attenuation. Only a misplaced, or more exactly an unplaced, concreteness leads to such universalist terms, as consistent as they are superficial. But an implaced concreteness, bodily bound, engenders a world in depth.

As the legend of Tiamat first intimated, the world of places or place-world derives from the massive facticity of the lived body. Just as there is no place without the spread of nonsimple location—and no place without its own depth—so there is no depth or place without this body's irreplaceable contribution. Nor is there any world except for, by, and with the same corporeal contribution. *Cosmos* and *chōra*, "world" and "place," combine in bodily actions that lack simple location even as they find their way in depth, here and there, near and far, and somehow (somewhere, somewhen) both together.

4

Dimensions

When he wanted to show that I was many, he would say that I have a right and a left side, and a front and a back, and an upper and a lower half, for I cannot deny that I partake of multitude.

—Plato, *Parmenides*

The Here pointed to, to which I hold fast, is similarly a *this* Here which, in fact, is *not* this Here, but a Before and Behind, an Above and Below, a Right and Left.

—G. W. F. Hegel, *Phenomenology of Spirit*

I

THE MORE I try to pin down the here—to grasp it as a *"this* Here"—the more I find it dissolving between my philosophical fingers. The same thing happens when I address my own body as a sheer this: "O! that this too too solid flesh would melt, thaw and resolve itself into a dew."[1] Hamlet does not have to undertake the "self-slaughter" he contemplates for this melting to occur. His body, self-addressed, is already dissolving. The here occupied by this same body dissolves just as rapidly. Even the expression *my body* sheds its presumptive concreteness and is an "abstract universal," in Hegel's language. My body and its here alike—even my body taken as an "absolute here"—are designated by "shifters" that, despite their univocal meaning, are empty in their semantic cores. *I, my, this, here*: there is rarely any ambiguity as to who or what is meant when one employs these demonstrative and locative (deictic) terms on a given occasion, yet their exact range of application shifts in accordance with context and use.[2] *You* can say "my body" or "this" as unambiguously and with as much linguistic right as can *I*, even though when you do so you will indicate something that is not the same (e.g., a different body) as what I indicate when I use the same expressions. Put otherwise, the *origo* is shifting and thus nonoriginal; "I" or "you" is not a concrete person but a role a person assumes.[3] In regard to the *origo*, it doesn't matter *who*—who precisely—is using expressions such as *I, my body,* or *this,* nor do they tell us anything informative about their users. They point only to the bare facts that (some) speaker is speaking, that this speaker has a body, and that the same speaker is picking out an object in his or her immediate vicinity. But we already know these facts if we are part of the communicative situation itself. To this extent, the expressions are redundant and empty place-markers: they mark, or rather re-mark, the scene of the utterance. Yet since this scene is a merely formal one, it is in effect only the *site* of speaking or picking out.

The same is true for the demonstrative adverbs described in the preceding chapter: *here, there, near, far*. In each case, what is quite specific in one respect is, in another respect, abstract and empty. We have seen that "just there," *that* there, dissipates into a plurality of theres. Even the "near" is a matter of degree (which is to say, never strictly singular in its reference) and is directly dependent on the local context: what counts as near in one situation is not felt as near at all in another, although the objective distance may be exactly the same in both cases. "Far" vanishes finally into the encompassing horizon. Merleau-Ponty puts the matter thus: "The vertical and the horizontal, the near and the far are *abstract designations* for one single form of being in a situation, and they presuppose the same setting face to face of subject and world."[4]

In the face of such dissolution and disappearance, such absence and abstraction, what is left that is truly (and not merely apparently) concrete? Hegel suggests that the concrete remainder—the *"restance"* in Derrida's word—is "a Before and Behind, an Above and Below, a Right and Left." These pairs of terms are concrete in two senses. First, even if the here disintegrates upon analysis, I retain six much more particular placial terms. The abstractness of here gives way to the concreteness of right and left, front and back, up and down: a gain in the shadow of a loss! The here's very absoluteness is de-absolutized, ab-solved, by virtue of this unanticipated acquisition (an acquisition I already possess). The same situation obtains for the other initial absolutes. The near, the there, and the far dissolve into a rightward and a leftward portion, dispose themselves into up and down, and fall in front of or behind me.

Such concretion does not stem from a condensation or instantiation of the two primary placial parameters—which, taken on their own terms, remain abstractly universal—but by dint of the organic body as pivot. For it is around and in terms of my live and moving body that right and left, above and below, before and behind come into concrete play and interplay. In each instance, my body is at once differentiating (as continually bifurcating) and organizing (as connecting the variously portioned parts of place in accordance with the disposition of my bodily members). The precipitate of this differentiation-cum-organization is the very place, indeed the many places, my body assumes and inhabits.

One of the most remarkable properties of the six concrete dimensions is that, despite their specificity of locative reference, their *own* location is far from simple. In fact, each dimension hovers uneasily *between* the embodied subject and the surrounding world that benefits from their structuring. Where is up? Where is right? Where is behind? (The "where," inappropriate to designate the "here" and "there," now finds legitimate employment.) At the very least, "above" or "up" exceeds my body even as it includes it. The top of the tree is up over my head, seemingly apart from me, yet I grasp this up-phenomenon only because my head is itself felt to be up above the rest of my body. What is right of me just now—say, an entire part of my study as I sit at my desk—is both part of the room's perceived character *and* part of my own body (my "right side"). The area behind me is "back there" in some dark recess of the nonseen, and yet it stems from my own back (my "back side"). In each case—and in the remaining dimensions as well—I find a curious indeterminacy or vacillation between location in an "outer" region and location in my *corps propre*. This bi-location (or "bi-presence" in Lévy-Bruhl's word)[5] deconstructs any effort to provide a straightforward singular locus for the six dimensions—*either* in my body (i.e., as organic substrate) *or* in the environing world. The locus is somehow *in both at once.*[6]

In the literal ambi-valence of their locus, the three dimensional dyads offer a convincing case for the nonsimple location of the places they serve to structure. As existing indeterminately (somewhere) between body and world and yet as their most intimate link, they exist in place. For a place, viewed in this light, is nothing but the multidimensional composition of a lived body and its circumambient region.

A region, let it be noted, exceeds a given discrete place, whether this be a proto-place, a zonal place, a counter-place, or a com-place.[7] But in what does the excess consist? If we consider the term *region* to designate a collection or gathering of places, *place* retains that particularity essential to its description from the *Timaeus* onward. For places are the particular parts or portions of regions. But this is not to say that regions are abstract totalizations of places. Regions possess their own concreteness, as we realize when we consider the specificity of a regional landscape with which we are thoroughly familiar. (A landscape can be considered the phenomenal or sensuous manifestation of a region.) On the other hand, if regions do act to collect or gather places, this is not because they serve as mere containers, as "the first unchangeable limit of that which contains."[8] Regions are no more containerlike *things* than places are bare *positions*. Regions are forms of gathering, and in this capacity they have powers and virtues of their own, which are not foreign to the dynamisms of lived bodies that make possible the configuration of places.

In fact, lived bodies serve both to animate and to connect places and regions. Just as I have been led to speak of "implacing" when considering the interaction between body and place, so we might speak of "regioning" when considering the ways in which bodies relate to regions as active gatherings of places. For the lived body's peculiar combination of being at once a "general medium for having a world"[9] and something quite idiosyncratic and personal (as always *my* body) enables it to ensure the concreteness of the regions in which we are immersed in implacements.

A place can also be said to "gather." It gathers *in* the dimensions and directions indicated by the body's insertion into it. Such in-gathering is distinctively different from the out-gathering accomplished by a region. The latter collects not directions or dimensions but places toward which the body is already directed and with which it is also connected dimensionally. A region thus gathers places *out*. It puts them alongside one another; it is the shared outsideness of places to one another, and thus the reflection of their mutual differences.

When such gathering-out is interpreted as an empty scene for the simple location of material objects, it is set on the slippery slope toward pure space. Pure space is the reduction of region to a mere platform for places, themselves construed as sheer positions. In such space there is no room for places as lived by bodies. Regions reduced to pure spaces are nothing but containers for disembodied sites. Already in the *Timaeus*, regions signify collections of similar sensible qualities, and in this capacity they furnish the ancient prototype for the modern notion of space as homogeneous and isometric throughout.[10] But it took the notion of a strict void—first proposed by the Greek Atomists and refined by medieval and early modern thinkers—to evacuate space altogether of regionalization as well as any significant sense of implacement. Space and void (especially as combined in the idea of "empty space") represent the abstraction of region into a formal container of material objects. Missing is the presence of the lived body that is the dynamic bond to place. This presence is also the basis of a revived notion of region as the active scene of multiple implacement.

II

Plato, doubtless inspired by Pythagoras, seems to have been the first writer in the West to recognize the concrete specificity of the six dimensions and to have linked this specificity to the organic body. In the epigraph from the *Parmenides* at the head of this chapter, he characterizes these dimensions as the basis of the body's manyness. In the *Timaeus* he blames the "six motions" for the way in which the infant, not yet attuned to the rationality of the World-Soul, "advance[s] at hazard without order or method . . . straying every way in all the six directions."[11] The disorderly motions at issue are those of the infant's body, not yet endowed with a rational soul. But adult bodily motion also takes place in at least six major dimensions—and in many intermediate ones as well. The body is indeed "many" in its motions, and this manyness brings with it the configured concreteness of the dimensions in which it can move.

But what about the relationship between the six dimensions and *place?* Concerning this relationship Plato says very little. Aristotle, building on Plato's opening moves, speaks of above and below, ahead and behind, right and left as the "parts and kinds of place."[12] That he could consider them not only as "parts" of place but also as *"kinds"* of place reflects his overall view that places regarded as cosmological *topoi* have inherent power. As a consequence, the right or the below or the behind constitutes its *own* place with distinctive properties in each case. "In nature," writes Aristotle, "each [dimension] is distinct and separate."[13] But Aristotle also considers how the six parts or kinds of place exist in relation to the "position" of someone in a particular place:

> These [six dimensions] are not just relative to us. [But when we consider them] relatively to us, they—above, below, right, left [etc.]—are not always the same, but come to be in relation to our position (*thesis*), according as we turn ourselves about, which is why, often, right and left are the same, and above and below, and ahead and behind.[14]

This passage (part of which I cited in chapter 3) subverts our expectation that Aristotle, out of his commitment to the cosmological objectivity of natural places, would refuse to acknowledge any relativity of such places, much less a relativity that bears upon the human body.[15] Yet Aristotle does not tell us how this latter relativity (designated cryptically by the phrase "in relation to our position") is to be characterized. In particular, Aristotle does not provide a description of the specifically bodily basis of "our position" insofar as this basis bears on the determination of the parts of place considered as the six dimensions.

Much the same neglect recurs when Descartes, positing the three dimensions of height, breadth, and depth as ultimate in the realm of *res extensa*, fails to examine what it is about the human body that predisposes the mind to apprehend space in just these particular dimensions. The predisposing factor is found in the way the human body orients itself in terms of above and below (resulting in "height"), right and left (i.e., "breadth"), and front and back (i.e., "depth").[16]

To embed the six dimensions in the realm of extension is in effect to locate—to *simply locate*—them in space. The Cartesian spatialization of the dimensions is a characteristically modern reduction of the importance of the "parts and kinds of place," a reduction that is carried still further when height, breadth, and depth are compressed into the X, Y, and Z axes of Descartes's analytical geometry. Thus is inaugurated a modernist tradition that reaches an apogee in Kant's early effort to derive the three-dimensionality of space from Newton's inverse square law of gravitation![17]

Our own task is to provide an account of the bodily contribution to the parts and kinds of place without falling into the Fallacy of Misplaced Concreteness; without, that is, subsuming body and place under site and space. What is called for in particular is a description of the embodied implacement of the six dimensions. This will constitute an at least minimal account of how our body finds its way in place in the most concrete manner.

For the sake of convenience and because they fall together in these groups in descriptive fact, I shall treat the ancient sextet of directions by dividing them into the three pairs of above–below, before–behind, and right–left. This grouping seems to be acknowledged in every known human language: "In all languages there appear to be pairs of lexical items that name asymmetrical axes of spatial orientation: the up/down, the front/back, and the left/right. The referential functions for these lexical polarities may be compared across languages, for they are ultimately anchored in the human body itself."[18]

III

The upright direction has always been the most salient, constant, and unique direction in our world.

—Roger Shepard and Shelley Hurwitz, "Upward Direction, Mental Rotation, and Discrimination of Left and Right Turns in Maps"

Top and bottom . . . are not given to the subject with the perceived contents, [but] are at each moment constituted with a spatial level in relation to which things arrange themselves.

—Maurice Merleau-Ponty, *Phenomenology of Perception*

In book 4 of his *Physics* Aristotle remarks that

each body, if not impeded, moves to its own place, some above and some below. . . . "Above" is not anything you like, but where fire, and what is light, move [to]. Likewise, "below" is not anything you like, but where heavy and earth-like things move [to].[19]

In his discussion of natural places Aristotle privileges those regions that can be classified as "above" or "below" on an imaginary vertical axis extending between the earth and the heavens. Is this merely a quirky belief of early Greek cosmology? Or does it not answer to something quite real—and still quite contemporary—in our experience of being bodily in place? To stand on earth and look up into the sky: is this not one of the most telling experiences we can have as embodied beings? Another basic experience is that of standing. Standing and standing *up* are as nearly synonymous as are sitting and sitting *down*. Just to raise one's body from the earth—or merely to be radially symmetrical as is a starfish, which knows *only* the above–below dimension— is already to experience the difference between up and down. Even a stationary plant may grow toward the sun: its spontaneous heliotropism pays homage to "vertical Being" as persuasively as do anchorites and sun-worshipers.[20]

Aristotle's apparently arbitrary claim is thus not arbitrary at all. It is grounded in two fundamental facts: gravitation and the up-standing body. But the upright body and gravitation—concerning whose effects Aristotle and Newton find themselves in anachronistic accord—are internally related. We stand up *against* the force of gravity: "The body is continuously adjusting itself to the downward pull of gravity to maintain an upright posture."[21] Thanks to the collusion between the body and gravity (the connecting term is the mass that links body and earth as material entities), vertical movements are especially prominent; and this is so even though we move mainly on horizontal planes on Earth.[22]

We find signs of this same predominance in linguistic expressions of dimensionality. In a chapter devoted to orientational metaphors in *Metaphors We Live By*, Lakoff and Johnson attend exclusively to instances of up–down.[23] Cross-cultural linguistic studies indicate that the up–down distinction is both the most fully differentiated and the most inclusive of the dimensional dyads:

> Bodily asymmetries do not differentiate the three axes [i.e., of height, breadth, and depth] to the same degree: the up/down has the most differentiation, then the front/back, and, finally, the left/right. This order is also reflected in the degree to which each axis is viewed as intrinsically belonging to other entities in the physical world. In effect, we view more entities as possessing up/down orientation than front/back or left/right.[24]

This claim makes it clear that the up–down distinction, however much rooted in the body's upright posture, also characterizes entities in the surrounding world. Above and below, refusing to be located exclusively in the world or in the bodily self, are inherently bivalent phenomena whose loci are indeterminate.[25]

We witness this indeterminacy not only in language—e.g., in such phrases as "coming right up to me" or "walking down the street," wherein the exact locations of the "up" and the "down" in relation to "me" or "the street" are indeterminate—but in concrete perceptual situations as well. In these situations, the bivalence is redoubled: the up and (to a lesser degree) the down are projected onto the axis of the before and behind. Thus I tend to experience whatever lies *before* me as up, even if the plane on which it stands is perfectly flat and on the same level as my own current position. This plane is perceived as tilted slightly upward; hence, if I move into it, I would be implicitly moving "uphill," although in fact I am remaining on the same incline. Conversely, if I perceive this same object moving toward me, I take it to be moving *down* to where I am. In such cases, the up–down is directly embedded into the field normally perceived as simply lying ahead of or around me.[26]

We find a closely related phenomenon in the ordinary use of road maps. Disregarding any alignment between the cardinal direction designated "north" on such a map and actual magnetic north, a map reader may unselfconsciously rotate the map until the route-to-be-followed is perceived as moving upward from the indicated position where one knows oneself to be. In this case, up is projected not only onto the direction "ahead" but also onto the "there," while down is assimilated to "here": "I am *down here* and I need to get *up there*." The here and there are particularized for pragmatic purposes, and the ahead is rendered even more specific than it is in ordinary circumstances. "You are here" maps are virtually worthless unless the pathway to be pursued is depicted as "up" on the map in relation to a here represented below it. More than one time in four, readers of an inverted map will follow a route that is at least ninety degrees wrong in its directionality.[27]

Up and down span the most primitive and the most encompassing dimension, and (doubtless for this very reason) the one that resists measurement most fiercely. They mete out verticality even if they do not measure it in meters.[28] Indeed, as Merleau-Ponty says, "We cannot catch it in the ordinary run of living, because it is then hidden under its own acquisitions."[29] We tend to concentrate our efforts on the seemingly more measurable flatlands that are specified as in front or in back of us, to the right or to the left.

In consequence of this buried state, the above and the below find expression in highly mediated, symbolic forms. In such forms, they become the basis for those value hierarchies in which "high" and "low" are axiologically definitive. Think only of the contrasts—at once moral and metaphysical—between celestial–infernal, high road–low road, high-minded–meanspirited, etc. As Straus observes,

> The direction upward, against gravity, inscribes into space world-regions to which we attach values, such as those expressed by high and low, rise and decline, climbing and falling, superior and inferior, elevated and downcast, looking up to and despising. On Olympus, high, remote, inaccessible, and exalted, dwell the Homeric gods. On Mount Sinai, Moses receives the Ten Commandments. Below, in the depths, is Hades and the world of shadows.[30]

Such powerful symbolic valorization is ultimately rooted not in theology but in the concrete body. Yet this rooting is so deeply sedimented that we become aware of it only when our habitual sense of what is properly up or down comes into question. One such situation is found in the celebrated Stratton experiment, in which a subject is fitted with glasses that turn the visual world upside down. At first, everything seems to be suddenly inverted. By the second day, the landscape "rights" itself, and the subject feels his or her body to be upside down. From the third to the seventh day, the same body gradually seems to reassume an upright position, with the result that visual inputs tally with kinesthetic and tactile data and a measure of equilibrium is restored. In less extreme circumstances, equilibrium is regained more rapidly; in an experiment of Wertheimer's, a room taken at first to be tilted at an angle of forty-five degrees (it is perceived in a mirror set at this angle) resumes an orthogonal verticality after only a few minutes.[31]

In both experiments, the lived body is at play. What else but this body would have such a stake in rectifying a topsy-turvy situation of the two sorts just described? (A *mind* might be fascinated with the out-of-kilter circumstances and thus have no desire to rectify them.) Doubtless the physiological body—especially its semicircular canals and its proprioceptive system, both of which are designed to help us establish vertical posture in relation to the pull of gravity and to changing positions and velocities of the body—is important here.[32] But what I have been calling the "lived body" has the major interest in the matter, and in two quite basic ways.

1. Whenever possible, my lived body seeks to establish and to enjoy a sense of comparative stability in its environment, that is, a baseline of equilibrium in the form of a persisting *"spatial level"* (in Merleau-Ponty's term). This level is disturbed when two or more conflicting sets of impressions— e.g., visual and tactile—reach the lived body regarded as "the natural subject of perception."[33] Although it would be presumptuous to claim that the lived body possesses this sense of level innately, the effort to maintain it is continually at work, and all the more so in experimental and pathological predicaments, when it becomes imperative to reestablish a steady orientation in the world.[34]

To reestablish level is to equilibrate the relation between above and below. As Merleau-Ponty comments,

> Let us say that perception before the [Wertheimer] experiment recognizes a certain spatial level, in relation to which the spectacle provided in the experiment first of all appears oblique, and that during the experiment this spectacle induces another level in relation to which the whole of the visual field can once more seem straight.[35]

By "straight" Merleau-Ponty means upright, or *vertical*. Of the two axes involved in the establishment of spatial level, i.e., vertical and horizontal, the vertical axis is most important in matters of orientation. For the disequilibration of above–below is more disorienting than confusion concerning right–left and front–behind locations (all of which organize things in accordance with a horizontal axis). Even the horizon, at once the epitome and limit of the horizontal plane, serves primarily to separate "above" from "below."

2. Although Merleau-Ponty is the first philosopher to recognize the importance of spatial level, nowhere does he indicate precisely what the bodily basis might be. This basis is found in the *upright posture* of human beings. Without such a posture, which represents the basic gesture of our body as it stands or walks on earth, it is difficult to explain just why verticality has such immense significance in orienting us in the world. If the vertical is indeed a "constancy phenomenon" in human experience, it is due to the constancy of the upright stance, whose absence betokens illness or powerlessness.[36] (No wonder the gnostics, many of whom reviled the human body, accorded to this posture such a special place in their theology. They considered it a divine gift, exceeding anything the "archons" of the universe could create.)[37]

Our own upright bipolarity of upper and lower body is reflected in an environmental bipolarity of places above and below. Thus our erect stance is not indifferently related to how "space has been split up into places."[38] As distended along a vertical axis, we connect more fully and more sensitively with the vertical relation between earth and sky or between soil and those things that grow upward from it. My uprightness is manifested in the uprightness of the world's body, and the latter's upward-tendingness is embodied in my own standing-upness. This reciprocal relationship is the source of medieval and Renaissance views on the *concordia mundi*, whereby the head and the sky as well as the genitals and the sublunar region correspond with each other.[39]

The above and the below present themselves, then, both in my everyday posture and in the complex of places to which that posture, stationary or moving, gives me access. When I spontaneously designate the wall as "above" the rug in my living room or certain cliffs as "below" me as I drive along Highway 1 in Big Sur, I distinguish between segments of my lived world in ways that parallel the manner in which I distinguish, just as spontaneously, between my head and my neck or between my shoulder and my hand at my side. The point is not that the world is like a super-standing person or that my person is a mere microcosm of its environing world—such is the position of the *Corpus Hermeticum*—but that the above and the below belonging to my upright body anticipate, and articulate with, the above and the below accruing to the world. The articulation itself amounts to the establishment of a spatial level by which I manage to orient myself as something standing or walking upright in the world. In the end, it does not matter which above-below pair comes first in regard to onto- or cosmogenesis; what matters is the continual interleaving of body and place effected by the interaction of both pairs of terms. "Place" would not be place as we know it without the critical distinction between up and down; nor would our bodies be "lived" as they are without a comparable distinction in a specifically somatic format. Our bodies would certainly not be *in place* at all without the dialectic into which both distinctions enter.

Above and below impose an intrinsic asymmetry that belies any claim to isotropism within the vertical axis they co-constitute. Given the two-way directionality of this dimension, the motion of "up" is stressed more than that of "down," as we see in expressions such as "upright posture," "standing up," "coming up to him," etc. "Down" tends to denote deficient or degraded situations, e.g., "feeling down," "getting down on him," "down times." It is as if the downward draw of physical gravity gives rise to a compensatory emphasis on the upward motions of the human body, which seeks not only to be equal to gravity but, *per impossibile*, to be independent of it. The result is a privileging of places located *up above* in what Binswanger calls the "ethereal world" (e.g., the celestial spheres of Plato, the outermost heaven of Aristotle, the Christian Heaven, the Buddhist Pure Land) while places situated *down below* in the "tomb world" (underearth *chthōn*, the eleven circles of Dante's Inferno) are regarded with disgust or disdain.[40] In between is the "middle realm" of earth, where good and bad places alike abound and where above and below are more often relative in status (this tree stands above that house, the hill stands under the brow of the mountain, one person is taller than another, my right arm passes under my left, etc.).

Such differential axiological aspects, which attach primarily to the asymmetrical extremities of up and down, reproduce and reinforce the asymmetry of the *origo* of the situation—i.e., my own lived body—as we see in the sheer fact that my head and chest bear no resemblance whatsoever to my feet and legs. The "topology of the body is ethically axiologized," which is not to say that the body is a simple source of structures and values.[41] If the lived body is an origin, it is one split against itself and seeking its own foundations elsewhere. For this body often takes its crucial clues from the world outside as well as from the heart within. But the dialectic whereby the unequal status of up versus down is found both in the world and in the self is a comparatively advanced phase of a process whose ontogeny in the individual and phylogeny in the species stems from a profound, albeit obscure, sense that as upright creatures we discover the first model for the pervasive asymmetry of above and below in our own anisotropic bodies.

How could it be otherwise? To expect to find symmetry everywhere would be to start not with our imperfect bodily state but with the perfected sphere of Euclidean or Cartesian geometry, where isotropism guarantees symmetry.[42] It would be to start with pure space. Yet we are always already starting with impure bodies and equally impure places. We begin with the concretely discordant rather than with the abstractly harmonious; we begin with basic discrepancies such as those between hairy heads and bare feet, awkward arms and akimbo legs, flat chests and bulbous abdomens, strong shoulders and weak hips, and egregious sexual differences.

No wonder that the places most important to us are anisotropic and inhomogeneous! When Aristotle maintained that above and below are "not anything you like," he meant that they are concrete and idiolocal in character. This is just what we would say of the human body, which is as heterogeneous and polydirectional—as asymmetrical—as the places it subtends and sustains.

IV

> The terms of spatial organization, the words for "before" and "behind,"
> "above" and "below" are usually taken from man's intuitions of his own
> body: man's body and its parts are the system of references to which all
> other spatial distinctions are indirectly transferred.
>
> —Ernst Cassirer, *The Philosophy of Symbolic Forms*, vol. 2

"Up ahead" we say unhesitatingly, as though the two terms had an elective affinity for each other. It remains the case, however, that ahead, in concert with behind, has its own structuration and vicissitudes and that ahead and behind are of critical significance in human implacement and orientation. Only as differentiated into frontside and backside can organisms like ourselves also discern right from left in any systematic way. Still more basically, ahead and behind tease apart the world of our lived experience into two overlapping fields, with our own body acting as middle ground. Whereas we move *in*, *into*, and *out of* near and far areas as these are distributed around us in various configurations and volumes, we are always *between* front and back. To move in front of where we now are is to find ourselves between a new frontal sector and the former frontal area (now become a zone behind us). If we merely turn our body to the right, we are confronted by another front region continuous with the front we knew when we were merely looking "straight ahead." To turn around 180 degrees is to exchange front with back sectors, while remaining in between them throughout. There is no getting around, much less out of, the double-bind of ahead and behind: we are incurably forward-tending creatures haunted by our rearward wake.

Unlike the here (which is borne *by* my body and found *at* the nonsimple locus of my body) and in contrast with the there (which stands *away from* me in apparent independence), the ahead and behind encircle me, clinging to my body on pain of being nothing at all (to paraphrase *Timaeus*, 52c). What is ahead is never entirely severed from what lies behind; the two regions are connected by intermediate, peripheral regions—side spaces, as it were—and, most basically, by the fact that they encompass my body.

This sense of confined encirclement distinguishes itself from the way the up–down dyad constitutes an independent dimension of which my upright body is merely a part. At the limit, the up and the down form a cosmic axis originating far below me (perhaps in an imaginary center of the earth or at the antipodes) and continuing far above me into the atmosphere and even into outer space. In comparison, what lies ahead of me or behind me is delimited. Typically it is a finite sector of my visual (or auditory or tactile) field, a locale in my near sphere and often *just before* or *just behind* me; at the most, it may extend to the horizon. But I still perceive what lies on the horizon as something ahead of me that is viewed from *here where my body is*. Every horizon calls for the perspective of the absolute here of my bodily implacement. And *beyond* the horizon? Sometimes we speak of what lies ahead of us as "over the horizon," but such a place is never as indefinitely distant as are, say, the stars. In any case, whatever lies over the horizon still involves a tacit reference to my bodily here.[43] (Often what is grasped as beyond the horizon is an *event*, e.g., a concert this evening at Norfolk, Connecticut. The further ahead or behind something is, the more it will take on an eventmental status. Whereas in my near sphere a placial analysis can be exhaustive, or at least adequate—I simply describe what I see before me in a timeless present—the perceptual unavailability of items beyond the horizon leads me to search for a more complete set of descriptive terms even if each term is comparatively empty, e.g., "a concert/this evening/at Norfolk.")

The delimitations of the arena of the ahead and the behind point all the more insistently to the immanent link between body and place. It is with my body that I directly encounter places around me or in the middle distance, finding myself saturated with their presence, as it were, while I *project* a spatio-temporal status for those items out of the range of my bodily grasp at this moment. Space and time alike, and hence the events they configurate, are thus more appropriately invoked for a distant realm that has *not yet* shown itself to be a set of discrete places ahead or behind my lived body in their actual midst.

Perhaps the most distinctive trait of the ahead–behind dyad is a special form of asymmetry. The asymmetry is found at the level of action. We look and touch, move and manufacture, primarily *in front of* ourselves. Only rarely do we act in comparable ways *behind* us.[44] As Franklin and Tversky state, "The front/back axis separates the world that can be viewed and manipulated from the world that cannot be easily seen or manipulated."[45] This orientational asymmetry no doubt reflects the frontal–dorsal asymmetry of the human body, i.e., the fact that our face, chest, hands, and feet all point forward, while our backside is comparatively undifferentiated. The fact that our eyes look forward gives a decisive visual advantage to this direction, an advantage that also exists at the level of manipulative action. We must not, however, rely on such anatomical differences; anatomy is no more destiny here than in the case of gender identity. Nor can we rely on linguistic expressions of these same differences, revealing as these expressions may be.[46] Let us concentrate instead on just how ahead and behind form part of our ongoing experience of the world in and with our bodies.

"Ahead" (or "anterior," "front") is clearly the dominant member of the dyad here under scrutiny. "Ahead" signifies the most concertedly intentional—and thus the most broadly effective—aspect of our bodily insertion into place. Indeed, the single most potent expression of corporeal or operative intentionality is found in facing forward. To be bodily "directed toward"—in the phrase Brentano applied to mind alone—is to be actively engaged in, or at least open to, what lies before us. We are ahead of ourselves not just in time (as Heidegger emphasizes in his notion of anticipatory, ecstatic temporality) but also in space. Or rather, *in place*. For I face a world of particular places, not a totality of neutral spaces. In this always already configured world, I take up a succession of "advance positions," each of which entails a concrete corporeal connection to one or several places toward which I am tending. In this way, I keep on going or getting ahead, both of myself and (in competitive circumstances) of others. Given the implicit progressivism (not to be confused with any actual progress) of human existence, it is difficult to dispute Clark's statement that "*ahead of* metaphorically indicates positive direction on any scale to which it can be applied."[47]

The primacy of vision contributes powerfully to the dominance of the forward direction. Sight is, after all, the most definitive sense when it comes to dealing with places in front of us.[48] Seeing directs us to what is be-fore us, and it is by seeing that we (quite literally) con-front phenomena, meshing our active and percipient bodies with the presented front sides of encountered objects. As Straus observes,

> Language expresses this relation in signifying the whole, the face, through its dominating part—the eyes, as in the English and French word "visage," in the German *Gesicht*, and in the Greek *prosōpon*. While the origin of the Latin word *facies* [i.e., front, surface]—and therefore, also, of the English noun "face"—is uncertain, the verb "to face" reassumes, in a remarkable twist, the original phenomenological meaning: to *look* at things straight ahead and to withstand their thrust.[49]

We look at things straight ahead, but we also look around and beyond the focal points of vision. When we actually *move* ahead, however, we occupy loci that involve successively new forward vistas. In each of these vistas, we look beyond the near sphere into the margins of a given forward field and into its horizon. Thus we must distinguish between the *just ahead*—which lies between my body and the inner surface of the near sphere—and *way ahead*, which belongs to the far sphere. But if it is true that "the horizons retreat in an ever growing radius"—a circumstance on which Puluwatan navigators capitalize—this is only because what lies immediately ahead is continuous with what is seen to be far ahead.[50]

It is with my entire body, not just my forward-looking sight, that I am able to transcend any given place just ahead of me and link up with other places further ahead. Not only do I move ahead (and not backward in crab-wise fashion) by taking my whole body with me in a forward direction, but I move in such a fashion that in going ahead *my front side or surface confronts with the front portion or surface of that which lies ahead of me.*[51] I say "confronts" because the two surfaces need not literally touch each other (as when I actually move into the anterior part of my study from the hallway). The con-frontation can happen by means of sound or aroma or sight, even when I am not moving my body but merely attending to what lies ahead of me. In either case, the intermeshing is of two distinctly different but closely affiliated "aheads": the forward part *of my (attending-moving) body* and the forward part *of the place(s) before me.* As in the case of the above and the below, a cycle of continuing connection is set up in which each forward part has approximately equal status. But in this cycle the ahead accruing to the front side of my body is a "first among equals." Without this corporeal front I could not connect so effectively or so vividly—perhaps I could not connect at all—with the fronts of places ahead of me. I, being before them, make possible their being before me.[52]

"Behind" (or "back," "posterior," or "rear") is an intrinsically recessive member of the dyad under discussion. Precisely because it is for the most part out of sight (and often difficult to touch), "the back-field disappears," bringing with it a factor of hiddenness.[53] The hiddenness itself is of two sorts. On one hand, it refers to that which is *behind my body* as not-present-in-perception: a hidden object or person, something "out of view" because it fails to fit into the forefield of my vision. On the other hand, the hiddenness includes the backward depth *of my own body*, i.e., part or all of my backside. Both of these modes of hiddenness are body-based, since the first exists *in relation to* my body and the second *forms part of* my body. What is behind, what I cannot see, is behind *me*, behind those anterior parts of my body with which my forward-looking self tends to be identified (my head, my chest, my midriff). What is behind is on "my other side," the side from which I feel most vulnerable; hence my fear of being "stabbed in the back," of being gossiped about "behind my back." When I become paranoid, I feel that others are speaking about me—or plotting against me—*from behind.* We imagine darkness and evil, "the primitive terror," as occurring in this "dark backward and abysm," where we are not so much disoriented as essentially *non*oriented.[54] (So as not to orient his followers too explicitly by showing his face, and as a reminder that we are not to make any graven images of Him in his frontal majesty, YHWH exhibits only his hind quarters.)

Nevertheless, we often find ourselves in place through our backsides, and in ways that are not wholly lacking in orientation. When I return to my chair in the living room after receiving a telephone call in the kitchen, I "back into" this piece of furniture without having to review how my backing is to occur, much less how the backside of my body is accurately directing itself onto the seat of the chair. In general, we have a remarkably discerning sense of where items in back of us are situated. In habitual haunts, we know more or less precisely how they are disposed in those parts of the near- and far-spheres that lie behind us. This sense has its own acuity and directedness. Even if it lacks visual presence, the behind-in-place has its own multisensory modalities, which keep us in touch with the milieu in back of us at any given moment.

In contrast with the ahead—especially in regard to the active articulation between the forefront of my body and the foreparts of place—the behind brings with it a very different circumstance, in which my virtually unknown (and in any case unperceived) backside colludes with places behind it. It is as if the comparative lack of differentiation of my posterior parts answers to the comparative unavailability of objects and places behind me. Instead of meeting these objects and places on their own terms, my backside seems to connive with them in a conspiracy of common oblivion.[55]

"Right back in place," "backing into place," not to mention the very title of this book: such phrases point to the peculiar place-sensitivity that the dimension of the behind brings with it. They also indicate a specifically temporal aspect of place—its sedimented history, a density of duration facilitating my return to place from behind. Where I *have been* is somewhere that I might *come back to*, as to a familiar zone. Indeed, the very phrase "where/I have been" parses into a spatio-temporal doublet. The having-beenness of (my experience of a) place is the temporal analogue—indeed, it is the necessary condition—of its being behind my forward-moving body. Not only the ominous and the threatening but the elapsed facticity of experience is found behind me. I observe this every time I drive steadily in one direction; I have just traversed the road behind me, a route on whose surface the history of my driving has been traced, however lightly.[56]

Despite their considerable differences, the ahead and the behind intermesh in certain basic ways in the human experience of place. In *hearing*, I am attuned to all that goes on "around" me. This is so even if I have a proclivity to attend more fully to sounds emanating from in front of me than to those coming from behind me. The ears are located precisely at the midway point between the front and rear sides of my body, and in this medial position they are appositely stationed to receive the auditory givens that stream in from both directions. But my ears are also "cocked" forward, thus at least initially favoring what lies ahead. At a concert I am at first aware of the musical sounds as emanating from the stage in front of me and of myself as facing them; but as the concert proceeds, I tend to lose myself in a confluence of sounds found as much behind me and at my side as before me. By that later point, the sounds are *everywhere* in relation to my body, no longer situated simply in front or in back of this body. In the active *motion* of my body I observe yet another instance of continuous transition, this time not between near and far but between ahead and behind. As I walk to the city center, what is plainly before me at one moment passes by (and sometimes under) my moving body in the next, thereby gaining the status of something nonvisible yet indubitably behind me on my journey. I confront another walker coming toward me "face to face," but as I pass her she too recedes behind me, becoming faceless and even bodiless. Here the ahead and the behind—along with their corresponding temporal counterparts, the before and the after—pass into each other "before my very eyes," at least insofar as my eyes allow what was initially focal to become increasingly marginal. In *pivoting* my body around, I witness a still different mode of interaction between the ahead and the behind. Not only do items at the edge of the visual or tactile field change their right- and left-hand status in relation to my frontside (this much Aristotle observed),[57] but the ahead and behind *in place* are exchanged and reversed, items formerly in front of me now being in back of me and vice versa. Pivoting in place is an instance—rolling over is another—of a single bodily motion that has the immediate effect of interchanging the members of a dimensional dyad in one fell swoop. Moreover, the ahead and behind effectively *segment*—even as they effectively *share*—the here of my own immediate place. Front and back conjoin in the very here they sever by being two disjunctive sides of my own lived body. Their interaction is a function of their disjunction—and vice versa. (A similar pattern of collaboration-cum-opposition occurs in the instance of the near and the far. Not only is the near split up into the near-in-front and the near-in-back, but a subtle coordination between near and far occurs when my body moves forward. On one hand, a place far-in-front becomes nearer for *both* my front and back sides as I walk toward it; on the other hand, a place far-in-back becomes ever farther from the same two sides as I move away from it. This is so even if I am related to the former far-place primarily via my front side and to the latter far-place mainly via my back side.)

My analysis of ahead–behind would be termed egocentric in the language of certain contemporary linguists, who point to ways in which front and back—as well as up and down—sometimes belong to objects as "intrinsic" to them. The car in which I drive down the road has a proper front side and a proper back side, as does the house in which I live. When I say things like "that oak tree is in front of the house" or "the child is walking in back of the car," I orient myself by the front–back properties *belonging to the house or the car*. But the egocentric–intrinsic distinction—which corresponds roughly to deictic–nondeictic expressions in language—fails to recognize that a genuinely *somatocentric* analysis puts this very distinction into question. It does so not by positing my body as a simple source but as an *origo* that is always already split between taking its own stance as definitive for orientation and taking its cues from the environing world. *Both* options are continually available to the body-as-*origo*, which sometimes situates itself in regard to front–back (and up–down) from a sense of itself as a center of orientation but at other times acts from an awareness of signs inherent in the situations in which it finds itself. Either way, it is *on the basis of the body's perception*—whether self-perception or other-perception—that the determination of direction and dimension is made.[58] For I am continually getting my bearings from my body's sense of what is before and behind, whether this sense itself bears on my own body or on the circumambient world.

The course of the body in place is an itinerary composed of anteriorities and posteriorities, and of anteriorities *of* posteriorities (as well as the converse). As a bodily being, I am before and behind myself in place. Whether stationary or in motion, my body experiences parts and kinds of place in front of and behind me. But this is only because my body is itself an entity having before and after parts.

V

Dimensionality consists in a reaching out that opens up.
—Martin Heidegger, "Time and Being"

Even our judgments about the cosmic regions are subordinated to the concept
we have of regions in general, insofar as they are determined in relation to
the sides of the body.
—Immanuel Kant, "On the First Ground of the Distinction
of Regions in Space"

Right and left might seem to constitute a dimensional dyad of quite delimited significance when it comes to matters of body and place. Charles J. Fillmore has claimed plausibly that there could be no distinction between right and left in our experience without the prior differentiation of front from back and up from down.[59] Moreover, as Ernst Mach was perhaps the first to observe, the perceptual discrimination of right from left is markedly more difficult than that of up from down.[60] Confusion between right and left is common; many people cannot distinguish between their own right and left hands on the basis of mirror images of these hands.[61] Soldiers in tsarist Russia tied hay to their left legs and straw to their right legs in order to follow right versus left commands without hesitation. We say of someone who is confused, "he can't tell right from left" (and of someone who is *very* confused we say, "he can't tell up from down"). Nevertheless, the association of right- and left-handedness with the basic bilaterality of the human body hints that we are dealing with a nontrivial form in which body ties us into place. We move into place and stay in place with both sides of our body and in such a way that each remains distinct from the other. When we altogether lose our ability to differentiate right from left, as occurs in the "hemi-inattention" induced by certain strokes, we find ourselves deeply displaced.[62]

In part, of course, the significance of such a loss resides in the fact that as human beings we divide our body and our circumambient world into right and left parts and regions. As Rodney Needham remarks, the right versus left distinction is "an exhaustive discrimination; there is no intermediary or residual category, and the binary quality is therefore not prefabricated."[63] Yet we have seen that the other dyads bring with them much the same exhaustiveness. Is there, then, something specifically physical or physiological about the left–right dyad that would serve to distinguish it from other dyads? Tempting as this line of thought may be—especially in light of the hemispheric differentiation of the brain—it proves to be moot in the end. As Robert Hertz asked in 1909, "Of these two phenomena [i.e., the domination of the right hand and the specialization of the left brain] which is the cause and which the effect?"[64] Since we cannot say for certain which is which— given that it may have been socially reinforced conditioning that led to hemispheric specialization and not the other way around—it would be precipitous to fall back on a neurological explanation of the left–right distinction.

This leaves us in a quite paradoxical situation. On one hand, the noticeable differences between left- and right-handedness are grounded, as Hertz observed, on "an almost insignificant bodily asymmetry."[65] This slight asymmetry is due to the fact that our hands (feet, knees, ears, elbows) are counterparts yet are incongruent in shape, "enantiomorphs" in the technical term. Disposing themselves on either side of the body's vertical axis, left and right hands are alike in every important respect except that they cannot occupy precisely *the same place*. (This basic fact may not become evident to us until we attempt to put a left-handed glove onto our right hand.) Nor will we find any more obvious differences when we consider the comparative dexterity of the two hands. The existence of ambidexterity, in addition to the preferential training of the right hand in almost all known societies (with the clear implication that the other hand *could* also be so trained), argues for the protean status of handedness at the level of habitual body skills. Despite the empirical preponderance of right-handedness (hence the bias evident in the word *dexterity*), doing things with our left hand always remains a possibility, as right-handed people realize each time they write something out, however clumsily, with their "other hand."

At the same time, right and left exhibit a "trenchant and profound heterogeneity" found in human societies of the most diverse descriptions.[66] As Hertz puts it in the opening lines of his seminal essay,

> What resemblance more perfect than that between our two hands! And yet what a striking inequality there is! To the right hand go honors, flattering

designations, prerogatives: it acts, orders, and *takes*. The left hand, on the contrary, is despised and reduced to the role of a humble auxiliary: by itself it can do nothing; it helps, it supports, it *holds*. The right hand is the symbol and model of all aristocracies, the left hand of all plebeians. What are the titles of nobility of the right hand? And whence comes the servitude of the left?[67]

In Western civilization, we can trace back the honorific status of the right hand and the corresponding denigration of the left hand to Homeric times, when omens coming from the right were regarded as auspicious and those from the left as unlucky, when the "lucky direction" was from the left *toward* the right, and when the right hand alone was used to pour libations and to offer pledges.[68] The early Greek words for left were either euphemisms or meant something ill-omened or awkward (as survives today in "sinister" and "gauche"). Aristotle, summing up an already existing tradition of thought, privileged the right over the left, holding that animals' locomotion naturally proceeds from the right; right is classed with above and front as an *archē*, a first principle of change, growth, and sensation:

> As a whole, unless some more important object interferes, that which is better and more honorable tends to be above rather than below, in front rather than behind, on the right rather than on the left.[69]

With the exception of the ancient Chinese and the Zuni Indians, this valorization of the right over the left is pervasive in virtually all known cultures. The Nyoro people of Africa, for example, espouse a scheme of symbolic classification that includes the following items:[70]

Right	Left
normal, esteemed	hated
boy	girl
king	queen
man	woman
chief	subject
good omen	bad omen
health	sickness
joy	sorrow
fertility	barrenness
wealth	poverty
life	death
good	evil
purity	impurity
moon (beneficent)	sun (maleficent)
order	disorder

Our concern is not with the credibility or consistency of the dual coding of right versus left within a given culture, or even with the degree of its generality among all cultures.[71] Nor need we attempt to answer Hertz's question as to why the right hand is so highly valued and the left so vilified on so many occasions. (Any adequate answer must stem from a combination of ethnological and semiological analysis, brought into conjunction with neurological findings.) But we can at least try to determine how the right versus left hand dichotomy, expressed and reinforced so powerfully by its symbolic extensions, reflects a special aspect of being bodily in place. About this aspect we receive a clue when we look at another table of paired terms, this one deriving from the Amboyna people of Indonesia:[72]

Right	Left
male	female
land or mountain-side	coast or sea-side
above	below
heaven or sky	earth
worldly	spiritual
upwards	downwards
interior	exterior
in front	behind
east	west
old	new

Beyond its predictable associations of right with male and old and of left with female and new, this list is noteworthy for its inclusion of three place-specific groups of features: (1) other dimensional dyads (upwards–downwards, above–below, in front–behind); (2) cardinal directions (east–west); (3) elements of the environing world (land–coast, sky–earth). Each of these groups is body-based.

   1. To begin with, given the transposability of dimensions and directions on the part of the lived body—whose manifold kinesthesias and synesthesias facilitate just such displacements—we should not be surprised at the linking of members of the basic dyads of dimension. Furthermore, the association of right with above, upwards, and in front represents an association with an *already established* asymmetry of the lived body. One suspects that there is an inner affinity between the privileged members of the dimensional dyads: right–above–front versus left–below–back. Not every human culture will stress this affinity, but, *mutatis mutandis*, there is a bias in its favor.
   2. Less obvious is the tie between the bilaterality of the body and the cardinal directions. Many cultures, however, make this connection. The *Iliad* (book 12, lines 238ff.) identifies left with the "misty west" and right with the

sunlit east. The Nuer tribe associates east with life and the right side and
west with death and the left side.[73] Sometimes the role of the body is expressly singled out. The Osage Indians of the Missouri River posit a gigantic
symbolic man who faces east and to whose left (i.e., north) the Tsízhus tribal
division is located and to whose right (i.e., south) is found the Hónga division.[74] Not entirely unlike this conception of a directional mega-body is the
ancient Chinese notion that on important occasions the emperor always faces
south, which means that his left side, aligned with the auspicious east of the
rising sun, is considered superior to his right side.[75] In most cultures, however, east is associated with the right. For these cultures (e.g., the Meru and
the Temne as well as the Amboyna), "facing east is the primary orientation."[76] To face east is to turn the body—normally directed to the north—to
the right. In this way, the pre-eminence of the right hand (or side) merges
with the pre-eminence of the easterly direction, with the turning body as
the central pivot.

3. What, then, of the third group, i.e., elements of the environing world
or *landscape features* as we may call them? When the Amboyna posit a bond
between right and mountain-side, sky, and interior, and between left and
sea-side, earth, and exterior, this means that certain actions and movements
of the body involving the right hand or right side are expressly tied with
going upward or inward. Conversely, the left hand or side is invoked when
going down into the sea, or out into a particular space. The issue is not
whether this is in fact the case for everyone; not everyone may "lead with
the right" when climbing a mountain, or even be aware of leading with any
side of the body in such a situation. What matters is that the body, in its
asymmetrical sidedness, is actively engaged in movements of ascent or ingression, descent or egress, and that these movements are themselves engaged
in—and by—certain specific kinds of places.

But what exactly does such concerted engagement entail? What is it about
right- versus left-handedness (or -sidedness) that makes it especially valuable
for corporeal connection with particular places? The answer is found in the
fact that right and left offer more extensive possibilities of *articulation* with
these places than do front and back, above and below. By this I mean that
the right and left hands and more generally all parts of our body that lend
themselves to right–left differentiation (including feet, arms, chest, buttocks,
and even our head), allow us to engage our bodies in ways that more effectively realize the aims of specific projects than do actions drawing exclusively
on the other two dyads.[77] The very word *articulation* is derived from the
same root as is *arm*: *ar-*, "to join." Arms allow us to join ourselves to our
immediate environs in a more articulated way than can be done with, say,
the sheer trunk of our body. The trunk is important for the sense of up and
down, yet it is much less effective as a means of linking with the idiolocal

infrastructures to which active implacement must be sensitive. Thanks to having differential sidedness, we become more fully acquainted with these infrastructures and are thereby better able to complete projects in which body and place are both at stake. Our body articulates with what surrounds it by the multiple means of fingers and hands, toes and feet, arms and legs, all of which in their double articulation of left versus right contribute significantly to finding our way in place.

What is most remarkable about these various articulatory items is less their anatomical resemblance when grouped into pairs (e.g., of hands, legs) than the fact that this same resemblance lends itself to specialized actions calling for the close coordination of both members of a given pair. Right and left hands are at once the most adept and the most revealing of these organic pairings. Their coordination in the practical sphere is such that while one hand holds an object (including one's own body as object) the other is rendered free for a specific action taken with regard to (or by means of) that object. My left hand holds the nail, my right hand hammers it into the board; one hand steadies the log, the other chops it; with my left hand I hold the steering wheel, with my right I shift gears; one finger of one hand holds down the key marked *shift*, allowing the "same" finger of the other hand to press a letter key that is instantly capitalized on the computer screen.

Bilateral symmetry may have been immensely adaptive from an evolutionary point of view insofar as it facilitated forward motion (i.e., by the rhythmic movement of pairs of arms and legs or even, as with snakes, by the sinuous interaction of two sides of one body) and because it allows an animal to defend itself from both sides at once.[78] But when higher primates became upright, their hands were no longer of direct value in locomotion. They were set free for other useful and adaptive actions that, paradoxically, called for *asymmetrical* handedness. It seems likely that the basic pattern of holding-cum-acting, in which one hand is dominant and the other compliant, became the basic pattern for right- versus left-handedness and that (via a continuous feedback loop) the corresponding hemispheres of the brain also became progressively specialized.[79]

Whatever the ultimate reasons for the evolution of a slightly lopsided handedness, the question remains: what is the inner relationship between the dimension designated as right–left and *implacement*, a relationship as manifest in Amboyna categories as in our own daily lives? The crucial clue, I suggest, is found in the fact that we are constantly coordinating our two hands (as well as our two arms, legs, and feet) not just in relation to each other but both together *in relation to place*. In particular, I use my hands (and other two-sided appendages) as means for inserting myself actively and yet sensitively into the places I inhabit or toward which I move. The very asymmetry of the use of my bodily members, rather than being a drawback, aids me in this insertion. For the pattern of holding-and-acting made possible by this asymmetry extends beyond the mere manipulation of objects in hammering, driving, etc., into the action of implacement itself. When I am getting or being placed, I perform a two-fold movement of (a) putting my body into place and *maintaining* it there; (b) undertaking specific actions *in that place*, e.g., exploring, settling in, socializing. In this way, the micro-drama of holding and acting—most noticeable in activities of construction or manipulation, both of which take place close to the actor's body—is played out in more expansive scenarios of implacement.[80]

When I act in such scenarios, my hands (arms, legs, and feet) trace out a unique *articulatory arc*. This arc is most obvious in actual gestures of pointing, beckoning, "motioning," but it is implicit even in my bare intention to designate, occupy, avoid certain places. Such gesturing and intending, along with still other basic actions, serve to lift places out of surrounding regions; or more exactly, they pick out places already immanent in such regions and give to them a more nuanced articulation. The comparative detachment of my various limbs from my body's central mass renders them uniquely suited for this articulation of places through actions of reaching and grasping and climbing and walking, in fact all that I am able to do as an armed and legged and upright being. My outer parts (including my orbiting head) are located *between* the obdurate central mass of my body and the places that subtend and surround me, and in this intermediate position they bring body and place into ongoing and intimate connection.

Suddenly we realize that the articulatory arc also provides an aegis for the diverse sets of contrasting values associated with right and left in various cultural settings. The actional, perceptual, and environmental articulation effected by brachiated bodies-in-place underlies such ever-proliferating lists of differential terms. Many items on these lists are explicit expressions of a circuit extending between bilateral bodies and surrounding places: "sea-side," "earth," "mountain-side," "west," "moon," etc. Moreover, the many possible ways in which these bodies can insert themselves into places allow such lists to be as numerous as they are seemingly inconsistent.

Immanuel Kant was the first thinker in the West to suspect the deep attachment between two-sided bodies and environing places. In a prescient essay of 1768, "On the First Ground of the Distinction of Regions in Space," Kant argued that we could not become oriented in "world-regions" (*Weltgegenden*) unless we made effective use of our constitutional bilateralism. Even reading a simple map on which places are straightforwardly represented calls for an alignment of east and west with the left and right sides of our bodies. In Kant's example, an astronomic chart is of no value until I hold it in both hands and align its eastern end with my right hand and its western portion with my left hand.[81] Kant maintains that much the same circumstance is found in the ordinary life-world:

> [Not only] our geographical knowledge, [but] *even our commonest knowledge of the position of places*, would be of no aid to us if we could not, *by reference to the sides of our bodies*, assign to regions the things so ordered and the whole system of mutually relative positions.[82]

If we substitute "especially" for "even" in translating the German word *ja*, we can say that it is *especially* our ongoing knowledge of the position of places around and under us that depends on the activity of our two-handed body. Only on a purely relativist model of space such as that proposed by Leibniz would one think that "the position of places" could be determined independently of reference to human bilaterality (i.e., by inclusion in a "whole system of mutually relative positions"). Yet when we find ourselves in any given region, do we not relate to that region *through* or *with* our own body? And if our body is de facto two-sided, will this not make a decisive difference in how we relate to particular places within that region, for instance concerning how we approach, enter, and act in them?

Kant puts to Leibniz another difficult question: if the first thing God created was a single human hand, would it not have to be *either* a right *or* a left hand? This first hand could not be indifferently right or left, given Leibniz's own axiom that there must be a sufficient reason for everything that exists. Moreover, right and left hands, although symmetrical to sight, are in fact "incongruous counterparts" in the sense discussed earlier. Because of this incongruity, there remains an "inner difference," which may not be outwardly perceptible but which we *feel* nevertheless from within. Indeed, "the different feeling (*Gefühl*) of right and left sides is of such necessity to the judgment of the [location] of regions" that we could not accomplish a locational judgment without this slender but significant feeling.[83]

A century and a half after the publication of Kant's essay, Hertz, in "The Pre-eminence of the Right Hand," attempted to locate the origin of the fateful polarity between right and left not in an anatomical anomaly but in the dualism between the sacred and the profane: "The obligatory differentiation between the sides of the body is a particular case and a consequence of [this] dualism, which is inherent in primitive thought."[84] But Hertz admits uncertainty when he asks immediately afterward, "How is it that the sacred side should invariably be the right and the profane the left?"[85] How indeed, if not as rooted somehow in the lived body? In the end, Hertz himself is "forced to seek in the structure of the organism the dividing line which directs the beneficent flow of supernatural favors towards the right side."[86] What Hertz fails to underline is that this organic structure—as experienced by the embodied person and not just as a natural fact—is itself a positive resource and not merely something we are "forced" to posit. For if the incongruently right–left body engages in a multiple incursion into place, then it is not just one entity among others, one which (like all others) cannot "escape the law of polarity [between sacred and profane] which governs everything."[87]

Hertz in effect rewrites Kant's dictum that "even our judgments about the cosmic regions are subordinated to the concept we have of regions in general, *insofar as they are determined in relation to the [two] sides of the body.*"[88] Hertz also seems to paraphrase Kant when he writes that "a no less significant concordance links the sides of the body to regions in space . . . right and left transcend the limits of our body to embrace the universe."[89] The terms *concordance* and *embrace* both designate relationships between body and region in which purely functional criteria such as malleability and manipulability are no longer apposite. To be in concordance with something and to embrace it is to relate to it as something possessing more than a merely instrumental significance. This is above all the case when we are speaking about the relationship between our bodies and the regions they inhabit. To be in concordant embraces with regions through our bodies is to know regions as familiar parts of our experience.

Right and left themselves constitute regions: "If the left hand is despised and humiliated in the world of the gods and of the living, it *has its domain* where it commands and from which the right hand is excluded; but this is a dark and ill-famed region."[90] Yet neither Hertz nor Kant specifies just how such a thing as right versus left takes up *its own region*. The reason for this may lie in their almost exclusive emphasis on right- versus left-*handedness*. The saliency of two-handedness and its equally evident utility (as signaled in the term *ready-to-hand*) act to obscure what is in fact the more pertinent phenomenon so far as being-in-place is concerned: namely, the oriented articulation of places and regions through the bilateral but asymmetrical action of the two-sided *body*. Such bilaterality entails being bidirectional in an orientation roughly perpendicular to the axis of the ahead–behind and the above–below.[91] Furthermore, this same two-sidedness has its *own* dual structure. A given side of my body, whether right or left, is predelineative of place and region by virtue of possessing not just one element such as the hand but a series of connected articulatory factors, including arms, fingers, legs, toes, etc. My right hand *belongs to* my right arm, which in turn belongs to a movable shoulder, and this in turn to a mobile neck, etc. All of these closely coordinated body parts, acting together as an articulatory arc, reach out to circumambient places and regions in continual outbursts of corporeal intentionality.

But this "reaching out that opens up"[92] would not attain its aim unless these interdigitated body parts and finally my body as a whole constituted places of their own, proto-places *by* and *with* which we articulate the zonal places, counter-places, and com-places that lie around and beyond us. One kind of place, circumambient in nature, calls for the other, corporeal in its core. Evidence for such a claim is to be found in many quarters. When Marduk kills Tiamat and creates world-regions from her carcass, he does so with the full swing of his spear-wielding *arm*. From her aboriginal body-place and by means of his own active body-place, he creates the regions of a world to come. In Nuer society the right arm alone bears a spear, and Evans-Pritchard observes that such a spear is not merely an instrument but something itself fully "animate" and continuous with the arm by which it is grasped.[93]

In the end, the issue is not that of right *versus* left, hand *versus* arm, arm *versus* leg. There is no contest, much less any fixed hierarchy, within the lived body. Not pre-eminence but difference is what is critical. Instead of undermining our being-in-place, the asymmetries and incongruencies represented by such dichotomies contribute to the unity and vitality of our being and moving in places. Differences between right and left hands, arms and legs, feet and shoulders, act to extend the articulatory arc in directions and dimensions otherwise not possible to attain. Acting in concert as differential vectors of the living-moving body, they achieve implacement in the world in ways at once elastic and lasting.

VI

I began this chapter by remarking on the comparative concreteness and specificity of the dyadic pairs up–down, above–below, and right–left. I have attempted to bear out this claim by detailed accounts of each pair in succession, that is to say, by appeal to direct experiential evidence. But collateral evidence, in the form of cultural expressions and explanatory hypotheses, has arisen along the way. Prominent among the explanatory hypotheses were gravity and the upright posture in the case of up–down, structural differences between the front and back sides of the human body in regard to ahead–behind, and certain adaptive and evolutionary aspects of right–left handedness. Although it is not the proper concern of a descriptive account to settle the intrinsic merits of these hypotheses—as explanatory, they have to do with the genesis or epigenesis of the very phenomena I have described mainly in experiential terms—it is striking that such explanatory models should suggest themselves just here. No comparable hypotheses came up for discussion in my treatment of here–there and near–far. The reason for this difference, I suspect, is that the latter are much more sweeping in their scope and therefore do not demand the specific explanatory constructs called for by the three dimensional dyads in their very discreteness of appearance and operation. Since we are ineluctably here versus there and always engaging in comparative nearness and farness, to explain these parameters would be to explain why we are bodily and mobile creatures on earth to begin with. But that we turn and move in the particular directions of up–down, right–left, and front–back entails a sense of open choice that calls out for explanation, if not justification.

It will be noticed, meanwhile, that the three dimensional dyads under scrutiny here all imply a specific *somatic axis*. Thus, ahead–behind, strictly speaking, is linked by an axis that extends in front and behind, as well as through, my lived body. The same single axiality is true of left–right, which, however, runs in one side of my body and out the other. Beyond a comparable but now vertical axis, above–below also entails a three-dimensional "reference object." To be *above* something is to be above some *thing*, something solid that stands under something else; and the same analysis applies for being *below* something. Furthermore, above–below refers at least tacitly to a ground level—ultimately provided by the surface of the earth—that subtends both the solid reference object *and* that which is above or below it on the one implicit vertical axis. The idea of ground level is built into the simplest descriptions; when I say "the pen is on top of the desk," I *imply*, but need not say, that both objects are above the ground level of the floor on which the desk rests.[94] The often unacknowledged but persisting presence of ground level may elucidate the otherwise curious finding that objects situated near one's feet are easier to pick out than objects near one's head.[95]

Such disparity between the three dyads is a crucial antidote both to the Cartesian presumption that these pairs, as mere functions of the three classical dimensions, are indifferently disposed in space, and to Kant's similar attempt to derive the three dyads from the fact that "in physical space, on account of its three dimensions, we can conceive three planes which intersect one another at right angles."[96] Neither Descartes's presumption nor Kant's derivation adequately conveys the anomalies and asymmetries to which Kant himself pointed so cogently.

It is also to be noticed that each successive pair of terms described in this chapter finds its most characteristic locus *in increasing proximity to the human body*. The above and below belong to a cosmic column experienced as unending in either direction. No capping of this colossal dimension is ever convincing; even the "outermost sphere" implies a region beyond (as is signified in Archytas's conundrum of the javelin thrower), while the circles of Hell proliferate below. Although we experience the up–down dimension through the agency of our upright body, the vertical dimension so far exceeds this body's immediate locus as to seem (in the words of Lao Tzu) "empty without being exhausted."[97] The situation alters perceptibly in the case of ahead and behind. Now a middle realm presents itself in the form of place-islands forming a virtual archipelago around the body. At the limit, I can project my body ahead of itself just over the horizon, but I am not swept up in anything that exceeds "restorable reach." Instead, I am concerned mainly with places in an encircling middle distance, e.g., in what is "somewhere ahead" or "somewhere behind." In further contrast, what is right and left of me tends to be located close to or right at my body's periphery, literally at my fingertips (or toe tips). Right and left places are found in, indeed *as*, my present locus; they are its very portioning out. Thus, as I am seated at my computer typing these words, the keyboard and the table on which it sits seem to fall immediately into right and left sectors of my visual-tactile field. The immanent differentiation and specialization of my two hands extend out into these contiguous sectors. The "flesh of the world" is at one with my own flesh through the skin of fingers connecting my body with these closely connecting zones within my workplace.[98]

We observe, then, an ever-narrowing gyre as we track the preferred (or predisposed) nonsimple locations of the three dimensional dyads vis-à-vis our lived body. The movement is from an initially cosmocentric to an increasingly somatocentric series of implacements. But at every stage, including even that of up–down in the colossal column of cosmic space, the ingrediency of the concrete body remains indispensable. Without this body's various distinctive contributions, above all its articulatory arc, there would be no significant directedness toward, in, and between places nor any openness to the regions of which these places form part.

If we compare the pairs of terms discussed in this and the preceding chapter, we notice that all five pairs share one particular property: my body cannot locate itself simultaneously at more than one of the two positions assumed by the members of any given pair. I cannot be both here and there, just as I cannot turn both left and right. But beyond this mutually exclusionary character of each dyad, two differences readily emerge on closer inspection:

1. The members of the three pairs taken up in this chapter exhibit a pattern of alternation and internal opposition that is in each case the product of an at least implicit *choice*. In a given situation, we must choose between right *or* left, ahead *or* behind, front *or* back. Concerning the two members of a given pair, we find ourselves constantly at a crossroads of choice. No such forced choice obtains in the case of near–far or here–there. Indeed, there is no meaningful choice at all to be made. We are always *here* rather than *there* and *near* rather than *far*, however much we may wish to be there or far away. For, once we are *at* the there, we are ineluctably here and near again. Not only this, but in these two instances we are drawn either into a

dialectic (of the here/there) or a continuum (of the near/far) in which the two contrasting terms coexist as poles of a common field of action. In contrast, the binary terms of the pairs above–below, front–back, and left–right do not form distinctive polarities of a field shared in common. At the most, these six terms specify the implicit axes that traverse the fields whose respective epicenters are here and there, near and far.

2. Moreover, we find ourselves always at *one end* of these two fields. For my body is at the epicenter—indeed, *is itself* one of the two epicenters—of the circumstance. Such is my absolute here and my near sphere. From this here–near extremity there stretches out a series of ever more remote places or regions as these latter constitute the other end of the same scene. In the case of the three dyads, however, I find myself poised—precariously or stably, depending on the exact circumstance—approximately midway *between* the members of a given pair of dimensional terms: between right and left, before and behind, up and down. Instead of being *at* the here or *in* the near, and instead of being oriented only *toward* the there or the far, I am drawn out—and sometimes strung out—between alternatives that delineate axes rather than open up fields or spheres.

VII

It is not my intention to claim that the five pairs of terms on which I have focused in this part of the book provide anything like an exhaustive description of body-in-place. What they do furnish is a minimal description of how we find our way in and to place, on the basis of which other, more extensive descriptions can be undertaken. But we should recognize two hazards in restricting analysis to these binaries.

1. The geometric connotations of the pairings may subtly, or not so subtly, influence subsequent descriptions. To the extent that this occurs, we risk falling into what could be called the Fallacy of Misplaced Abstractness. This would happen, for example, if we were to assume that the three dimensional dyads stake out the *only* significant dimensions along which the human body meaningfully directs itself to and in places. Not only is it clear that "objects may be located at oblique angles in directions *between* the three canonical axes,"[99] but the absurdity of any such restrictive assumption becomes evident when we consider an orienting device such as the magnetic compass. Despite the considerable utility of the compass, its four cardinal directions in no way limit or predetermine the number of trajectories we may undertake when we employ it. Between north, east, south, and west are an indefinite number of intermediate directions, any one of which we can pursue if we are sufficiently mobile. As Thoreau intimates, starting from any given point (e.g., one's own

home), one can move out in so many different directions, each separated from the other by only a few degrees of the compass, that it would take more than one lifetime to explore all the routes indicated by these directions.[100]

2. An analysis of the sort I have undertaken in these pages might be taken to imply that places are somehow *constituted by bodies*. Yet important as bodies are to the composition and comprehension of places, to maintain that they bring places into existence would be to commit a converse Fallacy of Misplaced Concreteness. A simple thought experiment reveals the Fallacy: if my body's contribution to the sense of being above/below, ahead/behind, and right/left were suddenly suspended, would I not still exist in a scene having *some* dimensional structure? If this suspension itself seems unimaginable, take instead an inanimate physical object, say, a yellow legal pad lying before you on your desk: does *it* not exist in a locale with certain definite dimensions, mostly if not entirely independent of anything your own body might add to the circumstance? Is it not still located *above* the top of the desk, to the *right* of a certain book, and *behind* the cup of tea you are drinking? Isn't it *near* the telephone over *there* on the small desk? (On the other hand, you will not be able to imagine the legal pad as *here* unless you pick it up and place it on or next to your body. The here remains absolute and body-based—absolute *as* body-based—in every such circumstance. *Right* and *behind*, on the other hand, remain relative to my bodily position, even though they are not dependent on it.)

It is thus difficult to deny that certain dimensional structures inhere in things and places themselves and may reflect little if any influence from the incursion of human bodies into their midst. The most obvious case in point is that of wild places from which human beings are altogether absent. But even in vernacular landscapes in which human bodies are manifestly present, it would still be implausibly somatocentric to claim that the presence of these bodies is responsible for their very constitution. Getting oriented in these landscapes depends much more on attending to clues immanent *in them* than on any innate sense of directionality belonging to the human body. Recall the way in which the Eskimo rely on—in addition to their own surviving footprints—such environmental indicators as wind, ice texture, and low-hanging clouds whose lower surface reflects what lies below them. Or think of how desert nomads read the faintest rills in constantly shifting sands in order to orient themselves in what seems barren wasteland to the nonnative.

Even in less exotic circumstances, I find myself continually relying on environmental markers, some of which are constructed by other human beings. As I drive northward from the Connecticut coast in a raging storm at night, the bright light on top of a certain tall building in the far distance lets me know that I am approaching Hartford. This light presents itself to me as something existing independently of my personal needs and interests; as a landmark, it *stands on its own*, offering itself to me as a locative sign of where I am or, more exactly, can come to be.[101]

If we are alert to the danger of geometrizing the human body and if we grant that this body's contribution to orientation varies considerably from situation to situation, we can nevertheless affirm that the five body-based binary pairs remain important in orientation and implacement of every kind. Even when the crucial clues come from the distant environment, it is my body that must apprehend and act on them. I could not comprehend what "low-hanging clouds" mean as a natural phenomenon unless I already know how "low" signifies a downward direction with which I am familiar as part of my body's own relationship to the underlying earth. Nor could I grasp the night-light at Hartford as "far up ahead" unless I had a sure sense of what "up," "ahead," and moving there into the far sphere mean in bodily terms. In such situations, my body's role is to *follow through*: to take up the indications given by the landmark in accordance with an emergent direction-ality that is the conjoint product of my body and the place or region it co-inhabits with the landmark. Direction, like dimension, arises from the body's ingression into places, however indirect or subtle this body's contri-bution may be. In the end, the very structure of these same places colludes with the corporeal intentionality most decisively instantiated in the five dyads under examination.

The human body brings with it what has recently been called a "spatial framework," organized in terms of the three dimensional dyads. We need not consider this framework hard-wired within us to recognize it as invaluable in finding our way in place. All we need to claim is that such a framework renders "certain directions more accessible than others, depending on the natural axes of the body and the position of the body with respect to the perceptual world."[102] Because the axes are inherent and not superimposed by a geometric model, such a framework is always already in operation when bodies become oriented in places. The same framework also includes the dy-namic fields whose epicenters of force are here and there, near and far. And because this framework is not merely that of the human body in isolation but is operative "with respect to the perceptual world," it is a matter of bodies as they enter, and are taken up, into places. Indeed, it is a matter of *bodies as they already belong to places*.

It is equally the case, however, that *places belong to bodies*. We witness this latter inherency in the phenomenon of body memory. A major component of such remembering has to do with how bodies remember certain places to have been and how to orient and reorient themselves in regard to these same (and like) places. Similarly, cognitive maps, regarded as internalized representations of places, play a powerful role in orientation, often acting in conjunction with body memories. In both instances, places ingress into bodies in enduring and significant ways.[103]

Whether the primary emphasis is placed on how bodies enter into places or on how places become interior presences within bodies (as well as within minds in the case of cognitive maps), the active spatial framework composed by here—there and near—far and by above—below, ahead—behind, and left—right is of crucial consequence throughout. For these binaries are the *via media* of body and place; they give the structures of a common interspace. As such, they make possible the embodiment of place as well as the implacement of body.

Such five-way dyadic interplay may be said to furnish the intimate inseams of body and place alike, stitching the two together in one coherent fabric. By a continuous cross-stitching, the three dimensional dyads thread these two entities together into the single garment of BODY × PLACE. Within this same double-sided garment, here—there and near—far act as overseams that extend its length and take its full measure. Cross-seams and overseams conjoin in the dense double stitchery of body-in-place and place-in-body.

We might say, in sum, that body and place are *congruent counterparts*. Each needs the other. Each suits the other. Put otherwise, *place is where the body is*. It is certainly *nowhere else*. How could it be if it is by the body that we are introduced to a place, move into (and away from) it, and abide in it? It is not surprising, then, that we cannot find place, or even region, within the Atomistic void or the purified space of the modern atomism of Newton. Since there is no way for the lived body to inhabit such serenely empty spaces (except by imaginative projection, which is no genuine inhabitation), there can be no places within such spaces. Newton's notion that places are simply "parts" of spaces misleads us deeply.[104] Parts *of space* cannot be places if it is the case, as I have been maintaining, that there are *no places without bodies*. Lived bodies put us in places, orient (and disorient) us there, and allow for egress into other places as well.

Even if we vacate a place and it stays unoccupied, it does not become an instant void or revert to being a mere part of space. So long as we (or other living organisms) have once been there, it has become a place—and it *remains* a place, insofar as it bears the sedimented traces of our presence. These traces, which act to shape and identify a place and not just to haunt it, need not be externally, much less eternally, engraved; they can be inward memory traces possessed by all who have shared that place. Whatever their exact character, such traces establish what might otherwise be a mere locus or site *as a place*, a status which, once gained, is perhaps never entirely lost.

Instead of denigrating Aristotle for his limited appraisal of the role of body in place, it would be more profitable to invoke his idea of place's inherent power and say that a considerable portion of this power is taken *on loan*, as it were, from the body that lives and moves in it. For a lived body energizes a place by its own idiosyncratic dynamism, intensifying that place's own idiolocal character. If we were to begin to think in this direction, our understanding of place itself—place as lived and imagined and remembered—would gain by deepening.

Just as there is no place without body—without the physical or psychical traces of body—so *there is no body without place*. This is so whether we are thinking of body in relation to its own proto-place, its immediately surrounding zonal places, its oppositional counter-places, its congenial complaces, or in relation to landscaped regions as configured by such things as landmarks and lakes, towers and trees. For the lived body is not only locatory in the particular ways that have been described in this part; it is always already *implaced* (which is not to say that it is always securely *in place*).

Although displaced bodies are frequently found, an unimplaced body is as difficult to conceive as is a bodiless place. The two oxymorons conjoin in their common failure to reflect the interarticulated nexus of the place-world. If there is no void where lived body is (or has been), there where the lived body is (or has been) *there* is (already) place, place aplenty, place in its plenipotentiary power.

It ensues that to know that we are embodied-in-place is not to have to suffer from the *horror vacui* that afflicted Pascal and other place-deprived souls in the early modern era. Anxiety about being or having no place at all might well be justified in the placeless desert of the Cartesian or Newtonian universe, a universe still very much our own. But we need not be overcome by such anxiety in a life-world packed with places. In this world we have the assurance that our own embodiment brings implacement—as well as continual reimplacement—in its immediate wake. Within such a world, *some place* is always forthcoming, however minimal (as when a distant landscape is cautiously but cannily inserted into the margins of an Italian Renaissance portrait) or provisional (as in a child's first halting steps to places only a few paces away). If Aristotle is right to declare that "time will not fail," let us say in turn that *place will not lack*.[105]

Places will not fail to be found in the lives of embodied entities who make their way from place to place and who cannot do otherwise. Much as we might like to think that we could do otherwise (and much as we may be drawn to theories of placelessness in an age of spatial and temporal nihilism), we are *bound by body to be in place*.

If places will not be lacking, this is above all thanks to the lived body. It is this body which, more than any other entity, ensures that space has been, in every instance and from the very start, "split up into places." This body, my body, is not only the continuing source of my own oriented implacement in the life-world; it is the abiding resource of all the places I know, in whatever regions they may come to be gathered. My lived body is the locatory agent of lived places, the subtender of sites, the *genius loci* of all that has come to be called "space" in the West.

PART III

Built Places

Architecture is a robed and ornamented body.

—George Hersey, *Pythagorean Palaces*

5

Two Ways to Dwell

A dwelling should be not a retreat from space, but life *in* space.

—L. Moholy-Nagy, *The New Vision*

The relationship between man and space is none other than dwelling, strictly thought and spoken.

—Martin Heidegger, "Building Dwelling Thinking"

To dwell means to belong to a given place.

—Christian Norberg-Schulz, *The Concept of Dwelling*

I

BEING LOST AT sea, the situation with which this book began, means lacking place in an endless space-world. Yet we can even have exact bearings in such a world and still not be fully placed. Our knowledge of local seamarks may be intact and modern navigation may pinpoint our position in world-space, but in terms of implacement something remains missing.

To be on the high sea is to be constantly exposed in the midst of something constantly changing. Enclosed only by the horizon that lures even as it obscures, we feel we could go anywhere, yet we may be nowhere in particular. Any stability we experience is precarious. Even though we know where we are in relation to other places, we lack a sure sense of where *our own place* is. What we lack, therefore, is twofold: *stabilitas loci* ("stability of place") and inhabitancy in place.

To find such stability and inhabitancy, it is not enough to disembark. On land we may gain stability underfoot, but we will still be exposed overhead. Unless we discover a hospitable cave or a very dense rainforest, we must take special action. When we cannot find a habitable place, we must set about *making* or *building* such a place to ensure stable inhabitation. The place made, a "built place," occurs in a distinctly limited sphere of space. We gain thereby not just a measure of security but a basis for dwelling *somewhere in particular*. The freedom of movement possible in an open sphere—a freedom whose price is the danger of being lost or exposed—gives way to the circumscription of movement in the closed domain of the near.

Granting that we need a reliable dwelling place of some sort, on what basis are we to create one? Until now I have emphasized the contributions of the lived body to implacement, which has been approached *from the body out*, as it were. Accordingly I have been stressing the "spatial framework," or what could also be called the "a priori of our own bodily spatiality."[1] My treatment has stationed the body literally in the *advance position*, where any connection with place is first and foremost corporeal in character. Although I have made reference to orientational markers belonging to the landscape, the hero of the day has been the lived body as the principal locatory agent of implacement. While Kant situated the a priori of human experience squarely in the mind, I have attempted to relocate it resolutely in the body, especially when place is on the agenda—and place is always on the agenda at the first level of human experience. Although place is held to be a mere epiphenomenon by those who regard space and/or time as first in the order of being, *in the order of knowing* place comes first. It is "the first of all things" because we know it from the very beginning. But we know it thus only because our bodies have always already, i.e., a priori, given us access to it.

Such somatic transcendentalism may be a salutary step beyond modern mentalism—it is certainly so in matters of memory—but it soon encounters limits of its own in a study of place. For in the place-world there are other bases beyond those inhering in the lived body. If we are to avoid a nascent "idealism of the body"—i.e., the tendency to posit the body as some kind of epistemological or metaphysical absolute—we must seek out other a priori structures. It is not sufficient to replace the priority of mind with the priority of body; reversal of terms or values is essential but (as Derrida insists) only the first stage of a deconstruction. Beyond reversal there is dissemination.[2]

I have already taken a first disseminative step by introducing the notion of "arc" at several critical junctures in the two preceding chapters. By means of arc, one moves not just *from* the body *to* a place—such is the main vector of corporeal intentionality—but more actively *away* from the body and fully *into* a place. The body opens out onto a world. Thus the "arc of reachability" sweeps out a circle of attainable things located in places belonging to the near sphere, while the "horizontal arc" draws us out of ourselves into increasingly remote places situated in the far sphere. The "tensional arc" sets forth the sheer difference between here and there, whose dialectic teases apart the densely woven fabric of place itself. An "articulatory arc" is sketched out by our many two-sided gestures. Finally, what we could call an "arc of embodiment" gathers the other corporeal arcs together in one massive display of somatic implacement.

Taken in its summative force, the arc of embodiment demonstrates that the true ecstasy of human experience may not be temporal, as Kierkegaard and Heidegger both believed it was. Nor is it spatial, as Descartes and Merleau-Ponty thought. It is *placial*, for it is in place that we are beside ourselves, literally ec-static. In becoming implaced, we emerge into a larger world of burgeoning experience, not only by ourselves but with others. Kant's Copernican turn inward needs to be supplemented—if not altogether transcended—by a Ptolemaic turn outward. (Ironically, Kant himself pointed in this direction by his invocation of "cosmic regions" in the context of orientation.)

Although the arc of embodiment considerably extends the range of our relation to place—without it, we would be confined to the immediate locus of an immobilized body—it leaves us in a most vulnerable position. My body's various dyadically disposed bearings take me *out there*, all the way through the near sphere and into the horizon and beyond, as well as indefinitely far up and down and in other directions. Yet even in such considerable outreach I remain *without inhabitable places in which to remain*. I find my way and, thanks to an embodied arc, I open my route, but I still have *nowhere to stay*.

An important part of getting back into place is having a place to get back into. Since we don't have any such place by the mere fact of existing on earth, we must build places in which to reside. In creating built places, we transform not only the local landscape but ourselves as subjects: body subjects become fabricating agents. These same agents are social subjects and no longer individual pathfinders. If the lonely navigator draws upon corporeal a priori structures, *homo faber* is engaged in a characteristically collective enterprise that entails social a priori structures.[3] This collectivity is already evident, for instance, in the *Enuma Elish*. After Marduk has carved world regions out of Tiamat's defeated body, he goes on to build an entire city, Babylon, speaking to the assembled gods with these words:

> In the former time you inhabited the void above the abyss, but I have made Earth as the mirror of Heaven, I have consolidated the soil for the foundations, and there I will build my city, my beloved home. A holy precinct shall be established with sacred halls for the presence of the king. When you come up from the deep to join the Synod you will find lodging and sleep by night. . . . It shall be Babylon, the home of the gods. The masters of all the crafts shall build it according to my plan.[4]

Cities are places people inhabit together. They provide for masses what homes furnish for a limited set of closely affiliated persons. In both cases, built places stave off the chaos, "the void above the abyss," found in a dis-aggregated natural order.

Such building ultimately means constructing places in which we are able to *dwell*, and dwelling places offer not just bare shelter but the possibility of sojourns of upbringing, of education, of contemplation, of conviviality, lin-gerings of many kinds and durations. Built places in which human beings dwell may be said to constitute intermediate entities in the tale of topogene-sis. That is, they exist midway between oriented bodies and the wilderness (in which building is absent and orientation is put into question). Built places also lie in between the designing architect—whose prototype is Marduk or Plato's Demiurge, each full of schemes to convert raw space into crafted places—and the undesigning land, which has no plans of its own (so far as we know) but proffers many wild places. Buildings in places, buildings *as* places, serve as the mediatrix between the artless earth and the skillful body. Every building is in this respect a compromise formation: a middle ground between nature and culture, given that its material constituents are taken (directly or ultimately) from the natural world, while its exact shape and actual use stem from the world of human purposes.

A building is also a compromise formation at another level. Thanks to such features as stability and enclosure, it arrests accelerated movement and allows the lived body to rest. If the same body reenters the open world, it often seeks to return to the habitation from which it set out.

A final compromise is between buildings and dwellings themselves. A dwelling must be constructed well enough to be continuously habitable; a building must be sufficiently accommodating to be a dwelling place. But do we know what building really means? Do we know how dwelling actually happens?

II

Consider two personal experiences, one drawn from memory and the other from the present moment:

I am striding through one of my childhood haunts: the indoor shopping arcade that stretches between Crosby's Department Store and the Hotel Jayhawk. The gentle L-shaped corridor welcomes the slow gait of the win-dow shopper as well as the hurried pace of the hotel guest or the business-man heading to the weekly meeting of the Optimist's Club. My own traversal of this enclosed and sheltering space is part of a voyage to the movies, for the Jayhawk Theater is also located in this sacred arcade. The Jayhawk always has the best movies—better in any case than the Orpheum, just around the corner, and usually better than its main rival, the Grand

Theater, just down the street. Having bought a ticket to the movie outside the arcade, in the box office on Jackson Street, and barely glancing at the currently fashionable clothes on display in the great glass cases to my right, I gratefully disappear into the darkened theater farther down the arcade. The theater itself is a haven of cool comfort set deep within the Kansas earth, whose surface is unbearably hot in the summer. The images I perceive inside take me into yet another world. Even if it contains frightening scenes, this world is welcome in comparison with the harsh world of heat, personal ambition, and family tension I know to exist outside the theater but wish to forget for the time being.

In the present, I am getting back into place by clearing out my study after years of systematic neglect. I am struck by the way that a room I had virtually abandoned as uninhabitable—such was the chaos of unanswered letters and unread papers, of books bought and never opened, of paintings begun but not finished—this room is beginning to assume an unaccustomed aura of habitability. Before long, I hope, it will become a place in which I can stay for those hours of the day in which I am working on this book and other philosophical pursuits. The study will be a haven not just from the summer sun but from the world of pressing professional commitments. In place of that world, I seek a world not of soothing cinematic images but of ideas whose outlines and inlines I can delineate in words. Supporting that longed-for world are a number of concrete objects: a computer desk; a Macintosh seated defiantly astride the desk and sharing space with a Kachina doll, a small black pot from the Pueblo Santo Domingo, and a crudely sculpted frog; an ancient card table bearing the load of my research on place and space over the past eight years; a photograph of my children taken in England fifteen years ago; selected samples of a rock collection; books everywhere, many still on the floor awaiting proper placement; a set of small plastic shelves for financial matters; a bulletin board filled with quotations, memorable photographs, poems, and other miscellany; paintings of mine and of Jim Hunt, my favorite Topeka artist, on the walls. Although it is the smallest room in the house, the study is regaining a surprising expansiveness, which it had lost in its era of neglect, and it feels just large enough to contain and foster a new world of thoughts.

At first glance, these two autobiographical accounts may not appear to bear on dwelling at all. Neither depicts what many would take to be the archetypal case of dwelling in a built place: being at home in an established dwelling room, e.g., the dining room, bedroom, or living room. Still, my study is a place in which to linger for purposes of reflection and writing, as well as to escape the bustling activity of the house and various institutional demands farther away. I certainly look forward to residing there for protracted periods.

But how can the first scene be considered a case of dwelling? In this instance, I moved in memory from place to place: from the box office, along the curving arcade, and into the awaiting theater. The theater itself, however welcome as a place of respite, hardly seems to be a dwelling place. It shares with the study an aspect of evasion, but I do not remain in the theater for more than three hours at a time. At best it seems a stopping-place, a place of momentary sojourn. The same is true of the Crosby Brothers Department Store, in which I long ago shopped during the day, and is literally true of the Hotel Jayhawk. Is not a room in a hotel the very essence of transiency, of *not* dwelling somewhere, of merely passing through on one's way to somewhere else?[5]

Nevertheless, I once dwelled in the Jayhawk arcade just as much and as fully as I am now dwelling in my study. The arcade may not have offered the conventional, reliable residing I found in my own home, about thirty minutes away by bus. Yet it was a genuine dwelling place in my hometown world.

Dwelling as nonresiding? What does that mean? We can find an important clue by tracing the word *dwell* back to two apparently antithetical roots: Old Norse *dvelja*, linger, delay, tarry, and Old English *dwalde*, go astray, err, wander.[6] The second root, though rarely invoked, fits my memory of the arcade rather well. There the passerby is encouraged to wander off the street and into a world of film images and images of fashion. One may *dwalde* in that kind of world, drift with it, follow its lead (and not just one's own lead, as occurs in the concerted activity of the study). Dwelling is accomplished not by residing but by wandering.

The dwelling places that figure into my memory of the arcade as well as into my current perception of my study do, however, share one basic trait. They are both *built* places, buildings or parts of buildings. Buildings are constructed objects: "fabricks" as they were once called, "edifices" in the literal sense of "built out." Built places range from the permanent to the transitory, from the Pyramids to pitched tents. Strictly construed, a built place is any place transformed from an unbuilt, pregiven state by the manipulation of natural or artificial materials. The manipulation—i.e., the act of construction proper—aims at an arrangement of the circumstance in accord with particular predelineated purposes. Many of these purposes concern dwelling-as-residing, but other purposes may be served as well: commemoration (cenotaphs and tombs), defense (military fortifications), bringing up children (houses and schools), art (e.g., earthworks), athletic contests (stadia, courts, fields), and so on. Just as building and dwelling are distinct activities that nonetheless often combine in fact, so built places and dwelling places overlap without being conterminous. Even if dwelling usually calls for at least a minimal building (as in the case of a simple campsite), I can dwell momentarily in a place altogether unbuilt, just as I can build a place without dwelling in it in any significant sense.

Most built places, including those at stake in my two personal scenarios, are constructed to last for some significant period, not forever in the manner of the Pyramids, nor just overnight as in the campsite. The choice of materials reflects this concern for middle-range perdurance: in my examples, brick and glass, concrete and wood. So too the style of building often aims at a middling recognizability, a bland but serviceable mixture of motifs—a midwestern medley in the case of the Hotel Jayhawk, modified "Garrison Colonial" in the northeastern town in which I now reside.

Despite these similarities in materials and motifs, there remain telling differences. The spatiality of the Jayhawk arcade was at once sinuous and expansive. Its constantly curving corridor described an arc that, by occluding a full view of what lay ahead, generated a feeling of at least mild anticipation. Along this corridor were doors that opened onto ever-larger spaces, those of the department store, the theater, the hotel upstairs (via a connecting stairway), as if the architects of this modest arcade had subscribed to Lipps's dictum that "everything spatial expands."[7] On the other hand, in my study I experience a space closed in upon itself and quite discontinuous with surrounding spaces. In the arcade I was free to take up any of several courses and to exit at several points, whereas in my study I am literally cornered and have only one possible exit.

Even from this brief conspectus we can see that a dwelling place is not one kind of thing; nor does dwelling occur in only one way. Dwelling places range across a considerable gamut of styles and types, of uses and destinies, only several of which have been touched on thus far. Some dwellings encourage permanent residence, some reflect purely transient uses; a mobile home is as much a dwelling place as is an English country house. And just as we cannot restrict dwelling places to those experienced in the present (as we see from my memory of the Topeka arcade), so we cannot confine them to what is factually or historically real (as we witness in the case of dwellings forming part of utopian schemes). Parks, which are not "buildings" in any usual sense, sometimes not offering the barest shelter or any domestic amenities, can be dwelling places. Indeed, the places where people spontaneously congregate such as street corners and stoops of apartment buildings, are genuine dwelling places, and yet they may possess even less of a designed structure than do parks. We may even dwell in automobiles, as commuters do daily.

Given the remarkable spread of the subject, I shall restrict my attention for the most part to full-fledged dwelling places. When I say "full-fledged" I have in mind two necessary if not sufficient conditions that built places must meet if they are to qualify as places for human dwelling. First, such places must be constructed so as to allow for repeated return. This does not require permanency of structure or even sameness of implacement. The Bedouins continually change places, but they pitch their tents night after night in approximately the same configuration. Despite the marked transiency of their life-style, they continually reoccupy the same *dwellings* and can be said to reside in their tents. (They also return to the same areas of encampment year after year on a seasonal basis.) Second, a dwelling place must possess a certain felt familiarity, which normally arises from reoccupation itself. That to which one returns is increasingly inhabited by the spirit of the *familiaris*, the indwelling god of inhabitation.[8]

Beyond reaccessibility and felt familiarity, I shall not single out any further general traits of dwelling places. Even such a plausible candidate as "spatial interiority" is a contingent feature, given the case of the anchorite, for whom residence atop an exposed column is a legitimate (and sometimes long-lasting) mode of dwelling. Both the anchorite's perch and the open park teach us that not even something as basic as "shelter" is intrinsic to dwelling.[9]

III

Of one thing we can be certain: both the continuing accessibility and the familiarity of a dwelling place presuppose the presence and activity of the inhabitant's lived body. This body has everything to do with the transformation of a mere *site* into a dwelling *place*. Indeed, *bodies build places*. Such building is not just a matter of literal fabrication but occurs through inhabiting and even by traveling between already built places. Constructing, inhabiting, and traveling, as well as those actions in which residing and wandering combine, are bodily activities. Tourism, *Wanderlust*, pilgrimage, and walking through arcades all involve journeys in which bodies leave home residences only to return to them.[10] In each of these ways, the living-moving body converts the flatland of sheer sites into the variegated landscape of habitable or traversible places. But how can bodily movement, seemingly spontaneous and unrehearsed, be so crucial in the artificially constructed and deliberately designed environments that built places so often provide?

We begin to answer this question when we realize that our own body is not merely one thing among others, simply and indifferently disposed in spatio-temporal situations (in the manner of many natural and technological things). As a "lived" entity, a *Leib*, the body is not only situated but situating; no mere instance of *natura naturata*, it is instead an exemplar of *natura naturans*, "nature" in its active and dynamic aspect and thus something that "holds sway."[11] To *hold* sway is precisely not to be under the sway of circumstances, passively positioned and pinned down by the course of external events but rather to have a hand in the determination of these circumstances themselves, including their situatedness in space and in time.

This is not to say that the lived body is always directly or explicitly at stake in the determination of a particular built place. A remote and unattended lighthouse, for instance, may be determined—mechanically—in its admonitory function without anyone's actual presence in the building. And the alternation of seasons will significantly affect an already constructed place, whether that place is located in wilderness or in civilized space and regardless of whether it is presently occupied or not. In such cases as these, lived bodies are not directly determinative of built places; at most, they are marginal in status.

The picture changes dramatically when we consider the role of the body in dwelling places of a distinctly residential character.[12] From a peripheral position, the lived body here moves to an indisputable centrality, for it is by and with our bodies that we inhabit dwellings. In residing we rely on the body's capacity for forming "habit memories"; that is to say, memories formed by slow sedimentation and realized by the reenactment of bodily motions.[13] But in inhabitation, the body is an engine of exploration and creation as well as an agent of habit. Thanks precisely to the familiarity established by habitual body memories, we get our bearings in a place of residence, the interior analogue of orientation in open landscape. We are empowered to discover novel features of built structures or to create such features ourselves by rearranging the materials already present in a given residence.

The mere fact that we *stand up* in buildings represents another bodily dimension of dwelling-as-residing. Although we also sit and recline, we stand upon entering and leaving and sometimes during our entire stay (stay and stand are etymological cousins). In a built place we continually *take a stand*, adopting an upright posture appropriate to the configuration of particular rooms. Such standing is the effective basis of our staying. Just as the body's mobility is indissociable from dwelling-as-wandering, so the same body's uprightness is integral to dwelling-as-residing.

The *upward* action is more significant than we might suspect. Andrea Palladio devoted an entire chapter of his celebrated treatise *The Four Books of Architecture* to "The Heights of the Rooms."[14] What does this special concern with height bespeak? Why height and not length or width? When human beings stand in rooms, they are especially sensitive to their height, which echoes their own uprightness as beings. Palladio was convinced that the height of a room both mimics and symbolizes the upright stance of the human body. Moreover, to be upright signifies self-assertion and ambitious reaching up and out—values highly prized in the Italian Renaissance—just as it also connotes moral forthrightness ("an upright character") and artistic achievement ("he has risen in the art world"). The architectural expression of this valorization of verticality internalizes within built places the privilege Aristotle accorded to the vertical dimension of the physical world.

Bodies and built places alike contend with gravity, since both must make a stand in the world. If it is true that "in getting up, man gains his standing in the world," it is no less true that buildings take up stands in the world as well.[15] They gain an *estate* there and hence become the primary basis for "real estate."[16] They also gain *constancy* of form and shape. One of the aims of architects, even those of deconstructionist bent, is to make objects having structures consistently stable over time and in space. No less than Palladio's Neoclassical buildings, the skewed and nonrectilinear structures of buildings designed by contemporary architects such as Frank Gehry and Peter Eisenman are designed to last and not to collapse (their precarious appearances notwithstanding). Neoclassical and deconstructionist architects join forces in designing *places whose standing and staying powers foster our own staying and standing in their midst.*

In view of the intimate relationship between the human body and the dwellings in which it is placed (and where it places itself), it is only to be expected that dwellings will themselves be likened to bodies. Michelangelo wrote that "there is no question but that architectural members reflect the members of Man."[17] Implicit here are two closely related but distinguishable claims. The first is that buildings may actually *resemble* the bodies of human beings; the second is that they should be constructed according to *proportions* borrowed from the relationships of bodily parts. The second claim is explicitly made by Vitruvius in his *Ten Books on Architecture*: "Since nature has designed the human body so that its members are duly proportioned to the frame as a whole, it appears that the ancients had good reason for their rule, that in perfect buildings the different members must be in exact symmetrical relations to the whole general scheme."[18] Inspired by this same rule of proportionality, Alberti wrote in his *De re aedificatoria* that

> beauty will result from the beautiful form and from the correspondence of the whole to the parts, of the parts amongst themselves, and of these again to the whole; so that the structures [i.e., of a building] *may appear [as] an entire and complete body*, wherein each member agrees with the others and all members are necessary for the accomplishment of the building.[19]

The claim as to actual resemblance may be extended still further. Houses and bodies can resemble each other not only by parallel proportions of parts but by intrinsic features as well. Such resemblance is not limited to the fact that sculpted or painted human figures are sometimes explicitly attached to a building, as in the row of statues at the top of Sansovino's Library in Venice and the friezes on the Parthenon. Nor is it only a matter of the biomorphism by which the shape of the human body becomes integral to the overall contour of a building, as notably occurs in the Latin cross design of

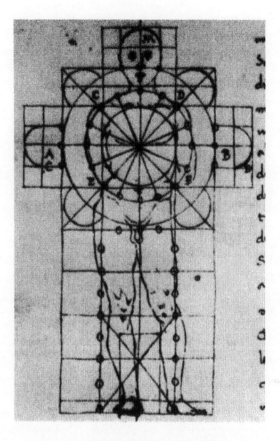

Fig. 1. Francesco di Giorgio, drawing for a
church, A.D. 1525.

many medieval churches, in which the body of Christ is explicitly inscribed
(figure 1).[20]

Still more dramatically, an entire building may resemble a human body
part by part. Construed as a mega-body, the building can be said to have a
face (revealingly called a "facade") with windows for eyes and a front door
for a mouth. The Bodhanath stupa in Kathmandu, Nepal, for example, has
enormous eyes painted on the base of its spire, which thereby resembles a
head set upon the body of the lower temple. But the resemblance may also
be metonymic or metaphoric in status. Thus in many ordinary homes the
hearth stands in for the heart and the neglected backside of the house is
reminiscent of the nether parts of the human body.[21] Palladio was quite sensitive to such implicit but aesthetically powerful analogies:

As our Blessed Creator has ordered these our [bodily] members in such a manner, that the most beautiful are in places most exposed to view, and the less comely more hidden; so in building also, we ought to put the principal and considerable parts, in places the most seen, and the less beautiful, in places as much hidden from the eye as possible.[22]

Built places, then, are extensions of our bodies. They are not just places, as the Aristotelian model of place as a strict container implies, *in which* these bodies move and position themselves. Places built for residing are rather an enlargement of our already existing embodiment into *an entire life-world of dwelling*. Moreover, thanks to increasingly intimate relationships with their material structures, the longer we reside in places, the more bodylike they seem to be. As we feel more "at home" in dwelling places, they become places created in our own bodily image.

If it is true (as Heidegger remarks) that "the world is the house where mortals dwell," a house is in turn a body, or bodylike.[23] Not only does a house mirror a body by its very structure; it is often functionally similar to a body, taking in dwellers, holding them in its interior, and offering egress to them as well. "Ah!" exclaims Emma Woodhouse. "There is nothing like staying at home for real comfort."[24] But more than comfort is at issue in the elective affinity between houses and bodies: *our very identity is at stake*. For we tend to identify ourselves by—and with—the places in which we reside. Since a significant part of our personal identity depends on our exact bodily configuration, it is only to be expected that dwelling places, themselves physical in structure, will resemble our own material bodies in certain quite basic respects. The resemblance, moreover, is two-way. A dwelling where we reside comes to exist in our image, but *we*, the residents, also take on certain of *its* properties. *How we are*, our bodily being, reflects how we reside in built places. Such traits as "reclusive" or "expansive," "sinuous" or "straight," can characterize our somatic selves as well as the houses we inhabit.

IV

We must consider all claims to attribute existence to what cannot be represented in space as completely meaningless.
—Gabriel Marcel, *Metaphysical Journal*, entry of January 20, 1914

Finding ourselves in built places is no straightforward matter. In fact, it is often decidedly circuitous, both in time (requiring not only much time but many different times) and in space (where we must often move *between* places to find the "right" place and where byways may be more significant than the straight path). Between the extremes of exploration and inhabitation lies an entire middle realm, for the most part neglected in previous investigations of built place, that calls for our concerted attention.

In exploration the primary issue, so far as place is concerned, is orientation. Unless we are oriented to some degree in the places through which we pass, we do not even know what we are in the process of discovering: witness Columbus's confusion as to just what he had come upon in the New World. But finding our way *in place* by means of orientation—whether technologically assisted or not—is not tantamount to being *implaced*. When we are moving among places in an exploratory manner, we are acutely aware of not having a place to be; however efficient and successful our voyaging may be and however many places we discover, we remain essentially homeless. For we are then between shores and between destinations, *somewhere else* than home, not "settled in." If we can be said to dwell en route, this is dwelling-as-wandering.

In stark contrast stands the settled state of dwelling-as-residing, i.e., being *somewhere in particular*. The paradigmatic case is the home, but we can also reside in schools, military camps, and other such stable places. In these circumstances, orientation is a given; we are already situated with regard to prominent or subtle landmarks, and our bodies are attuned to the dimensions and parameters of the particular place. The primary issue now becomes a matter of *inhabitation*, for we are not merely *at* our destination but fully *in* it, so much so that we often take the place for granted and cannot say in what it consists. "There is nothing like staying at home" precisely because *at home* we do not usually have to confront such questions as "Where am I?" "Where is my next meal coming from?" or "Do I have any friends in the world?"

Between finding our way and having a residence—between orientation and inhabitation—there is a whole domain of encroaching implacement. In this domain we are neither disoriented nor settled. We wander, but we wander in the vicinity of built places we know or are coming to know. Not discovery but better acquaintance is our aim. Or perhaps we prefer to loiter in the interspace, luxuriating in the fact that we are neither strictly in nor altogether outside, as when Americans linger on porches wrapped around their homes. Places are built not only for such obvious purposes as shelter or prestige or comfort; they also foster experiences that appear purposeless at first glance.

We enter here an architectural realm that might be called "transitional" pace Winnicott, since it shares with his notion of transitional space such characteristics as freedom of movement (within certain definite limits) and plasticity of aim. Just as the child in transitional space exists between harsh external reality and self-serving internal fantasy, so the person on the porch—or in other comparable intermediate places—exists between private and public or between the rigors of the journey and the comforts of inhabitation. Instead of being merely transitory, i.e., a superficial way station, a truly transitional space is often a place for creative action, providing enough protection to encourage experimentation (if not outright exploration) without being overly confining. In Freud's metaphor, such a situation is like a "reservation" set aside so that certain actions not possible elsewhere can be undertaken here.[25]

Thus we discern the special character of *indirection* in built places, their *non*straightforward aspects and roundabout features. Far from being merely anomalous, such aspects and features are much more commonly characteristic of built places than we might first imagine. It is true that on religious or state occasions we tend to focus on the formal entrances to buildings and approach them straight-on, e.g., in the T'ai-ho Tien, the Audience Hall in the Forbidden City of northern Peking.[26] But even on such formal occasions, the role of lateral approaches may be considerable, as in the palace at Persepolis, whose official stairway divides and sends visitors to the sides of the structure. Even in the most ordinary suburban houses the side and back entrances are in constant use, while front doors are often reserved for the arrival of guests, strangers, or relatives.[27]

Beside the architectural work, i.e., the massive central structure or "building" proper, there is the by-work of indirect approach and indirect knowledge. Such indirection is often supported by a series of micro-structures through which we come to experience (and afterward to remember) a given building in indirect terms. We designate these subtle but effective structures by such prepositions as *around, alongside, with, between, inside,* and *outside*. In fact, only *in* has been formally recognized and discussed by philosophers such as Aristotle and Heidegger, neither of whom pursues the ramifications of the term in architecture.[28] All such prepositions, however, articulate various concrete modes of ingression into buildings via the intimate interface between our living-moving bodies and built places. These modes are prepositional in status not just because they are named by particular prepositions, but more crucially because they are *pre-positional* in character. They specify forms of relating to built places *before* fixed positions, i.e., settled stances, are taken up.

Let us consider a series of paired pre-positionings in an effort to grasp more fully how the lived body dwells in architectural settings.

Outside and inside. Wolfgang Zucker has claimed that setting up boundaries between outside and inside is "the primaeval architectural act."[29] To build a structure at all and then to dwell in it is to presuppose (and to build in terms of) the difference between being out and being in. Indeed, it is to live from this very difference, which we can no more elude than we can elude being here versus there. But while we are *always* here—whether we are out or in—we are not always in a building and may even be forcibly barred from certain buildings, as when we try to enter a heavily fortified or specially sanctified place.[30] Nevertheless, in many cases the distinction between inside and outside is a comparatively complex matter, allowing us to experience an in *in* the out (e.g., a front porch) or an out *within* the within (e.g., an inner courtyard contained within a house).

The thoughtful architect or builder is aware of these diverse modalities of the in-out relation. The modalities exceed the bare functional requirements of doorways, dormers, and skylights, at stake when we are concerned only with letting in (or excluding) people or light. They bear on practically all aspects of building, since every built place, however humble, possesses some rudimentary distinction between inner and outer. Robert Venturi writes that "architecture occurs at the meeting of interior and exterior forces of use and space."[31]

The articulation of inside with outside or outside with inside is not limited to a simple exchange of items in and out of built structures, of information, decoration, air, private or public life, etc. Only on an Aristotelian model of place as a contained vessel would the relationship of inside and outside be a simple matter. The fact is that the interchange between the inside and the outside in built places is often complicated and variegated. Asymmetry is frequently involved; rarely is an edifice, even one built in accordance with a quite classical or modernist design, constructed with perfect symmetry of structure within and without. Reversal of position is frequently employed, as when a garden, normally outside, is incorporated into a glassed-in porch. (Conversely, a living room, usually considered unambiguously interior, may be made continuous with the outside by giving directly onto a balcony or patio.) Thus we can agree with Bachelard that in built places

> outside and inside are both intimate—they are always ready to be reversed,
> to exchange their hostility. If there exists a border-line between such an
> inside and outside, this surface is painful on both sides.[32]

The border-line itself, complicated by conjunctures and openings, is much more than a line. A glance at a blueprint design for an ordinary house demonstrates the many points at which inside and outside meet, not only at doorways and windows but also at corners and even at solid walls. Through such open or opaque points of transition, possibilities of coming and going in and out are projected or ruled out. In the constitution of these possibilities, the lived body is centrally at stake. What else but such a body can so reliably negotiate such a two-way action? As if to underline this fact, architects often design areas of transition that in some way reflect the size and upright posture of the human body, as well as its need for movement and light. In Anasazi architecture, for instance at the Pueblo Bonito in Chaco

Canyon, New Mexico, doorways provide openings that represent the body (i.e., by being just its size) *and* the load it bears on its back (by the use of a heavy and prominent capstone). In monumental architecture, on the other hand, the very disparity of scale between openings and bodies reminds us of the body's comparatively diminutive proportions.

In entering built places, most acutely at official entrances, though also on steps and stoops, patios and porches, we experience ourselves as between inside and outside. Movements through such thresholds contribute to a sense of the porousness of built places. Thus what is cause for difference and exclusion may be the very basis of fluid transition and inclusion. Rudolf Arnheim formulates this paradox:

> Perceptually and practically, the worlds of outside and inside are mutually exclusive. One cannot be in both at the same time. And yet they border directly on each other. . . . The great challenge to the architect, then, derives from the paradoxical contradiction between (1) the mutual exclusiveness of autonomous, self-contained interior spaces and an equally complete outer world, and (2) the necessary coherence of the two as parts of the indivisible human environment.[33]

Nevertheless, this contradiction is no greater than that between the enclosed inner surfaces and the exposed outer surfaces of one's own body—surfaces which, despite their manifest differences, must be ultimately continuous with each other. In fact, only insofar as we successfully resolve the tension between inner and outer at the level of our lived bodies are we able to deal with it effectively in the experience of architecture. Dealing with this tension within our organic selves, we need not find the differences between built insideness and outsideness to be alien or alienating. The result is another instance of architectural biomorphism; the dialectic of bodily incorporation and excorporation anticipates (and often facilitates) that of going in and out of a built place.

This biomorphism, however, coexists with an important difference: I cannot get entirely into my own body or be fully surrounded by it, since I *am* it. Taken by itself and without the contingency of clothing, my lived body has no external container that belongs to it properly; if contained at all, it is contained within my flesh alone. Nor can I get wholly outside my own body; as Husserl remarks, I cannot throw my body (or any part of it) *away from itself*.[34] In contrast, I can be wholly *in* a building so as to be surrounded by it, just as I can also be altogether *out* of it. To be in or out of a building is to exist in relation to something that exceeds the ingressing or egressing body itself. The merest lean-to exceeds the lived body that inhabits it, furnishing for this body a constructed carapace, a built outside for the body inside; and when the same body steps outside, it literally ex-ceeds the building it has left.

Alongside and around. Short of going into a building—even before we get to the predicament of being on the threshold—we may "hang around" or "stay alongside" that same building. In such hanging and staying, we relate to the building before it has become for us a settled site, fixed in place. *Situs*, Latin for "site," is closely related to *thesis*, Greek for "position." To be along-side or around a built place in a pre-positional way is to be pre-thetically related to it. *Getting into position to take up a position* means being near the edifice, in its environs, and in a prereflective, unpremeditated manner.[35]

Such pre-positioning is accomplished by particular bodily motions. In moving *around* a building, I circumnavigate it in such a way as to "stake out," explicitly or implicitly, its outer dimensions and certain positions I may eventually take up. "Casing the joint" is a case in point. Here I move around a built place warily and get to know it from the outside before entering it and knowing it from within. Every new station within such a circumambu-lation offers new approaches to and vistas of the building I am checking out. Apart from a thorough scrutiny, I may go around a building merely in order to gain a preliminary feeling for it, that is, to get a sense of its structure, its outline. In tracing out the aroundness of a building I confront its outer limit, its perimeter, what "goes around" (as *peri-erchesthai* means literally in Greek).

In a second (and often closely related) maneuver, I move myself closer to a built place, "sidle up" to it, and put myself *alongside* it. Then I am in a pre-position of proximity that stops just short of actually entering the place and engaging in the dialectic of inner and outer. Even if I intend to enter the building, I may pause and linger in its immediate environs, perhaps on the porch. To be alongside implies that I am close to the building's outer wall and that I have enough mobility to move in either direction along the wall. If I choose to follow the wall in this way, I find I am in fact going around the building. In this circumstance going around and being alongside coincide. As a concrete instance of this double pre-thetic movement, let us consider a plan of Andrea Palladio's Palazzo Chiericati in Vicenza, Italy; con-structed in 1550 (figure 2).[36]

Even in this view from above, Palladio's building expresses—indeed, it actively solicits—the dual pre-positions of around and alongside. To begin with, its variegated outer shape invites exploration *around* its entire perimeter. In particular, the arcade on the facade (i.e., the long rectangle at the bottom of the diagram) calls for movement back and forth *alongside* the front of the building within the portico, or formal porch. This movement is outside the interior of the dwelling and yet inside the outer shape of the building as a whole. It is midway between the enclosure of the interior and the full expo-

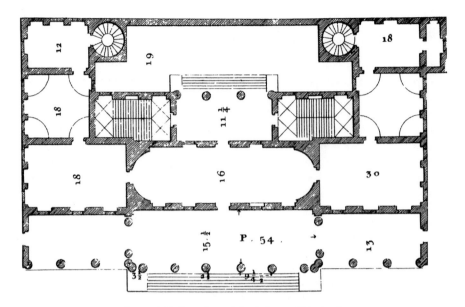

Fig. 2. Palladio, plan of the Palazzo Chiericati.

sure of the Piazza Isola in front of the building. In the piazza and beyond, one wanders unprotected and seemingly at random, whereas *inside* the palazzo, in the central *sala* (a reception hall) or in one of the attached rooms in the wings, one feels a sense of encompassing protection. Unpredictable peregrinations in the surrounding city are replaced by an assured habitation in the palazzo. Mediating between dwelling-as-residing and dwelling-as-wandering, the portico serves as the intermezzo between the palazzo and the piazza, alongside both, as both are in turn around it.

Between and with. Palladio's porch, then, is *between* interior and exterior, house and square, private and public. Regarded structurally, it is between open and closed; a roof is overhead (not represented in this diagram), yet openings abound on all its sides. To be in its semi-enclosure is to be able to pause between duties or errands, tarrying alongside the building to which the porch gives access. Then one can look *within*—through the entrance and flanking windows—and also look *without* onto the open square. An interspace, or rather an *interplace*, between inner and outer as well as between front and back, right and left, and up and down, this interstitial structure does not importune the visitor to go either in or out. (The porch is raised from the square in front yet is only the beginning of a full ascent into the second story of the house. Only inside the palace must one decide to turn one way or another, going farther in or up or turning to the right or left wings.)

Fig. 3. Palladio, facade of the Palazzo Chiericati.

The Chiericati portico is thus a two-way affair. One must cross it every time one enters or leaves the house from the official front entrance, but one can also stroll along it in leisure. Indeed,

> The design of Palazzo Chiericati was inspired by two traditions: that of the medieval row-house with covered street arcades . . . and that of a stoa-like public building alongside a square, like the Basilica [in the Roman Forum], [Sansovino's] Library in Venice (1537), or Michelangelo's Capitoline Hill (1538). [This] caused a conflict between the external and public function, which required circulation along the front, and the internal private or official function, which required finding an entrance and going inside.[37]

But the "conflict" between public and private is mediated—if not actually resolved—by the placement of the portico between the inside of the palace and the outside of the square. Occupying a middle ground, the porch can be at once public arcade and private entrance.

This intermediacy stakes out a domain that suits the lived body in its ambiguous being. As itself a *metaxu*, or intermediary, the body situates us in intermediate places by taking up successive but continuous pre-positions between established spaces. Able to move in at least two directions at any given moment, the body locates us in middles at which the explicit and the inexplicit, the propositional and the pre-positional, meet. Palladio graphically represents just such betweenness in his engraving of the facade of the Palazzo Chiericati (figure 3).[38]

Colonnaded in every part except the upper middle region (where there are bas-relief pilasters only), this facade is an amalgam of betweens. Looking at its elegant design, we find ourselves moving, by an imaginary bodily motion, between upper and lower stories, right and left ends (i.e., the wings), the numerous columns and pilasters that punctuate the facade, and the facade itself and whatever lies behind it. At the same time, the darkly shaded doors and windows lure us into the building in a seductive manner. Penetrating the facade toward the inner space of the edifice, we find ourselves drawn in a direction running perpendicular to the lateral direction implicit in strolling along the porch.

We are betwixt and between two directions in another sense as well. Just as we are not utterly excluded from the Chiericati when we view it from the outside, so we are not wholly included in it by this action of penetration. Palladio's engraving leaves us just where our own body always deposits us: in an intermediate zone between the extremities of light and dark, inside and outside, not knowing at all and overt propositional knowing. In engaging us in this ambi-valent betweenness, our bodily praxis at once foreshadows and makes possible the intermediacy of built places.

If the lived body is (in Bergson's phrase) a "place of passage," then it is itself a creature of the between.[39] As such, the body mediates between my awareness of a place and that place itself, moving me between one place and another and taking me into the intimate interstices of any given place. These interstices include such things as hallways, corridors, doorways, and windows, not to mention windowsills, wainscotting, and other ornamental features of a room. The Palazzo Chiericati possesses a plethora of such in-between elements. If it is true that "architecture should be conceived of as a configuration of intermediary places clearly defined," the Palazzo is a paradigm case.[40] To be anywhere in this building is to be involved in some significant betweenness. If I station myself on the arcaded porch, I am between walls and columns; if I am in the back courtyard, I am between the two rear wings of the building. Once inside the building, I am not merely between walls but between entire groupings of rooms, finding myself on visual-kinetic axes that connect whole suites of rooms, running between them like Ariadne's thread. Wherever I turn, inside or outside, I find myself caught up in a veritable labyrinth of modes of betweenness, a "multifarious between."[41]

At the same time, however, I find myself *with* the palazzo as I approach or enter it, linger alongside or circumambulate it. As I come to know it, this building becomes a com-presence in my experience, and I become compresent to it. Such double withness underlies my sense of being-at-home-with a built place. As signified by the German *bei* and the French *chez*, I then feel familiar with being in its ambiance. I feel that I belong there not because I have been there for an allotted stretch of time but because I am so much with the place—and it is so much with me—that we seem to belong to each other.

To be with a given built place is not just a matter of being in its literal presence, as though one object (i.e., a building) were simply to be juxtaposed with another (i.e., my body). In place of such a contingent (and typically once-only) juxtaposition, the with is an abiding and subtle *being*-with. Part of becoming intimately acquainted with a particular place is sensing it as with me at all times, not only physically in the manner of something present-at-hand or instrumentally like a ready-to-hand entity but as something I remember stays with me over time and in different places. In memory as in architecture, the things I *am with* help to constitute an ongoing "aura," an enveloping atmosphere, which surrounds me.[42]

The things of memory *remain with me*, within me. They occupy interior psychical (and doubtless also neurological) places and are the determinative loci of my life. I remain *with them* as well by returning to them in diverse acts of remembering. Much the same two-sided dialectic of the "with" obtains in the experience of built places, thanks in large measure to what Husserl calls "retaining-in-grasp" (*noch im Griff behalten*, that is, "bearing in mind" or, more appositely here, "bearing in body"). As I move in and around the Chiericati, I remember having been there at other times. I bear my former experiences of this building, and my retention of them is no less effective for often being quite tacit. Not only do I stay with the Chiericati by lingering on its rectilinear portico or in its ovoid *sala*, but these places remain with me as I move from one part of the building to another and as I move out of the building itself. They remain with me when I leave the piazza in front of the Chiericati and even when I depart from the town, Vicenza, in which the palazzo is located.

The measured proportionality with which Palladio designed the dimensions of the rooms aids the process of memorial being-with by establishing a sequence of memorable ratios through which I pass as I move through the building. However dim my awareness of these ratios themselves may be, I sense that an ordered progression is occurring, thus helping the building to stay with me as I move through it and out of it. As James Ackerman remarks, "In a sequence of rooms [in the Chiericati] there is not only an ascending or descending order of size, but a relationship of number: one dimension of the preceding rooms is *retained* while the other changes."[43] The dimension "retained" is not retained in mind alone but is also held by the moving body. Such bodily-memorial retention does not, however, require Renaissance *proportionalità*; it can occur whenever we find ourselves comfortably ensconced in the concrete with-world of a building.

Just as the "in" cannot be restricted to the inside surface of a room, so the "with" cannot be confined to the objective measurements of the walls of that room. To be within these walls is not to be limited by them, for in perceiving or sensing walls, one is already beyond them. This is so whether or not there are windows in the room or hallways leading from it. The word *room* itself is derived from Old English *rûm*, open land or space (as is also connoted in the German cognate *Raum*). This openness inheres in the with by which the body situates itself in the room's space. Even within a room, one is without as well. Such spatial ecstasis—such standing-out—cannot be incarcerated in a room conceived as an empty volume defined by its present-at-hand walls, ceiling, and floor. The felt voluminousness of a room may relate to ratios established by exact measurements—this much we learn from Palladio—but it is not to be reduced to these measurements. What William James calls "the feeling of crude extensity" exceeds the strict confinement of measured shapes.[44]

Thanks to the active ingrediency of the with, *the space of building becomes the place of dwelling*, which is non-volumetric, non-present-at-hand, and not even ready-to-hand. Getting acquainted with a building *as a place* is to enter a with-world that is at once porous and plenary. The more I am attuned with a building, the more it becomes a place I "live" in, a lived place. From being just one built place among others, it becomes a place for dwelling—dwelling in the sense of residing. The preliminary and provisional movements of going around and alongside give way to being between parts of the building itself and then to the sense that I am with it and not just by it or at it. This process of enhanced familiarity, abetted by continual return, may reach a point where I feel that I am *one with* the building. It is at this moment that I can be said truly to *in-habit* it.

Bodies, we may infer, are the agents of inhabitation. They are indispensable to living in, even merely relating to, buildings. Without the anticipatory and memorial powers of our own bodies, we would be lost in architectural space. We might find our way to a built place by simply wandering there (and thus by dwelling in its errant mode), but we would not be able to inhabit it (and thus to dwell in it by residing there). Nor will the accurate positioning effected by precise navigational methods—crucial as these may be to orientation at sea or on land—suffice to bring us to the point of inhabitation. Along the long and often circuitous path from orientation to inhabitation, we must assume and experience a series of connected corporeal stances and movements: pre-positions on the path to residence.

V

In "The Origin of the Work of Art," Heidegger writes of the fateful "strife" (*Streit*) between earth and world. In this struggle, a particular building, e.g., a Greek temple, offers a "common outline" (*Umriss*) between the conflicting forces, something "fixed in place" for the enactment of the strife itself.[45] Overlooked in Heidegger's forceful description, however, is the role of the human body in making the conflict between earth and world possible in the first place. The lived body is the concrete medium of this conflict, which is fought on *its* terms. My body brings me into place—whether it is a "place of conflict" (*Streitraum*) or a "place of openness" (*Spielraum*)—and maintains me there.[46] As itself a proto-place, the body constitutes my corporeal here. But precisely in its action of proto-placement, my body takes me up against counter-places, including conflictual places, at every moment. In this countering (and being encountered), the body constitutes the crossroads between architecture and landscape, the built and the given, the artificial and the natural. Were it not for the body as a proto-place, existing in opposition to counter-places, the earth/world confrontation itself could not occur; there would be no "common ground" for this confrontation and no basis for the mediation effected by the work of art, e.g., the temple at Paestum taken as exemplary in Heidegger's essay of 1935.[47]

The human body also establishes zonal places, areas of leeway in which free movements relatively unencumbered by the burdens of strife can be undertaken. *Leeway* is the English equivalent of *Spielraum*, place of openness (literally, "play-space") and is at work in Heidegger's notion that the task of the artist or architect is "to liberate the Open (*Offenen*) and to establish it in its structure."[48] But where Heidegger locates such liberation in the action of *Streit* itself, I would situate it in the near sphere. Leeway is the full arc swept out in the near sphere by the bodily modulations of zonal places.[49]

These modulations include the relations of inside–outside, alongside–around, and with–between, each of which is at once pre-positional and post-conflictual. As pre-positional, each such relation adumbrates a specific way of being in the leeway of built places. As post-conflictual, each explores and articulates this leeway, within which free movement is found and fostered (and sometimes also obstructed). Even if it is not always true that "everything spatial expands"—to claim this is to overlook possibilities of compression and miniaturization—an expansive structure is enhanced exponentially by the provision of leeway for the occupants of a given dwelling place. Such leeway is not to be measured in feet, inches, or *braccia* (literally, "arms," the unit of measurement used by Palladio and other architects of the Italian Renaissance). It is a matter, rather, of architectural elbow room, a sense of "crude extensity" not to be confused with Cartesian *extensio*. When Palladio said the architect "ought to have regard to the greatness of places," he meant the architect should attempt to inculcate a feeling of leeway wherever and however possible.[50]

Thanks to the provision of leeway within zonal places, not only do I connect more openly with the many counter-places and com-places of my environing world; I also broaden my sense of the span or spread of a built place, its "architectural arc." Guided by its configurated form, I move as freely as I can in this place; indeed, I actively contribute to the architectural arc. In this way I experience an opened-up implacement which then brings about expanded possibilities of residing. This happens, for example, when I come to know a building "inside and out," as often occurs poignantly during childhood. In the child's exploration of intimate corners and nooks, the merest bungalow seems to be a palace of possibilities; hence the shock at returning to one's childhood home and finding it so diminutive and unprepossessing. Nevertheless, the expanded space of the original scene, its "intimate immensity," still attaches to the place, if not as literally perceived by the adult, then as remembered in revery.[51]

We tend to accord credit for the expansiveness of dwelling places to buildings, to the architects who designed them, or, *faute de mieux*, to Being—as if buildings or their architects or Being could themselves bring about leeway, unassisted by those who live in them! Even if it is (just barely) imaginable that space exists without the contribution of lived bodies, it is *not* imaginable that a dwelling place could exist independently of corporeal contributions. We deal with dwelling places only by the grace of our bodies, which are the ongoing vehicles of architectural implacement. A bodiless architecture is as unthinkable as a mindless philosophy.[52]

VI

The various pre-positionings of architectural experience rejoin and reinforce the fundamental twofoldness of dwelling. On one hand, to move "around" a built place instead of entering it, to be "outside" it, to be constantly "between" (especially when taken to a nomadic extreme), is to dwell in a migratory, unsettled sense in which displacement is much more evident than implacement, homelessness than habitation. Nevertheless, far from being merely privative or secondary or just a means to an end of implacement, this sense has its own placial properties and represents a basic form of dwelling in the world.[53] On the other hand, my pre-positional body also leads me to dwell in another manner, in which delaying, tarrying, and finally inhabiting are more prominent and where the most exemplary bodily actions are those of moving "in," "alongside," and "with." Now I move toward, near to, and then into a built place. Thanks especially to my habitual body, I abide there, in-dwelling and staying-on, being-with. The external wandering abates as I settle into a place designed for residing.

The second, settled sense of dwelling is not merely the end-phase of a journey, in the manner of Odysseus returning to Ithaca. Just as wandering can happen within residing (as when I meander through the interior rooms of the Chiericati), dilatory dwelling may occur at many points along the way. At Calypso's cave, for instance, or in the land of the Phaicians, Odysseus discovers that sojourning en route can become the way itself. For dwelling-as-residing is not necessarily sedentary; not the literal absence of motion but finding a comparatively stable place in the world is what matters in such dwelling. Such finding is possible even when in motion. The earth offers continual if sometimes uncomfortable accommodations as one moves across its surface. If human beings may peregrinate in place, so they may also dwell stably even as they move from place to place. The two aboriginal senses of dwelling are not, then, simply diametrical opposites; they form a complemental series in which coexistence counts for more than exclusion and in which dialectical interplay allows for many unanticipated combinations. Let us call the exemplary extremes of this series—i.e., the two primary modes of dwelling—"hestial" and "hermetic."

Hestia was the Greek goddess of the hearth, at the center of the home and family life, of household economy in the broadest sense (*economy* derives from *oikos*, abode, house, household). Altars to Hestia were built in every private home in Greece as well as in front of the prytaneion (town-hall) of capital cities.[54] Honored by a sacred fire, she was invoked at the beginning and the end of feasts and sacrifices:

> Hestia,
> you who take care of the holy house of Apollo
> who shoots so far,
> the house at sacred Pytho,
> a liquid oil flows forever from your hair.
> Come on into this house of mine,
> Come on in here with shrewd Zeus,
> Be gracious towards my song.[55]

To invoke Hestia was to invoke a presence dwelling within the home. Credited with having been the first deity to construct a house, she was a somewhat lonely and retiring being (so retiring that the Athenians did not hesitate to replace her image with that of Dionysus when portraying the twelve major deities on the Parthenon). In Greek houses the hearth was located at the center of the house, and it was here that Hestia traditionally presided.[56] She was also a central presence at temples (e.g., at Delphi and, much later, at the temple of the Vestal Virgins in the Roman Forum). Both the hearth and the temples were circular in structure, a shape that exemplifies self-enclosure and promotes attention to the center.

Any built place that aims at encouraging hestial dwelling will therefore tend to be at once centered and self-enclosed. The implicit directionality will be from the center toward the periphery and will thus obey the architectural counsel to "extend inner order outward." Greek domestic architecture echoes this counsel:

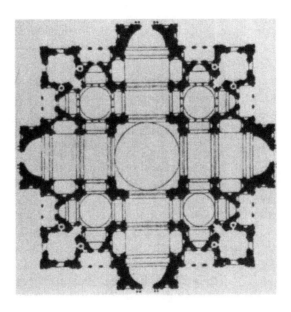

Fig. 4. Bramante, plan of Saint Peter's Basilica.

[Hestia's] circular altar, placed in the center of an utterly introverted house . . . is the symbol of the visceral relationship between home and earth (Rhea) and between family lineage and the continuity of time (Kronos). Actually, the Greek house is crossed by a vertical axis that, through the hearth, binds together the depths of earth with the summit of the heavens.[57]

More generally, hestial architecture exemplifies two tendencies: a penchant for centralized structure and a sensitivity to the vertical dimension (as the hearth extends into an *axis mundi* connecting earth and sky). Both tendencies gained particular prominence in the Italian Renaissance. Consider, for example, Bramante's design for Saint Peter's in Rome (figures 4 and 5).[58]

The plan in figure 4 shows a rigorous centralization. Rectangles and circles conjoin in a concentric pattern, which converges on the central circle directly beneath the dome. Of regular figures, the circle is the most perfect form of enclosure, hence its aptness in a temple that attempts to capture the Holy Spirit here below. The vertical view (figure 5) shows the dome not only rising skyward but resembling the vault of the sky itself. Here the human spirit rises up even as the divine essence is lured down. We see much the

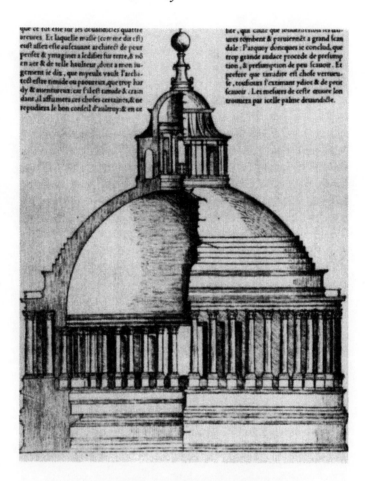

Fig. 5. Bramante, dome of Saint Peter's Basilica.

same combination of centralization-cum-elevation in Palladio's design for the Villa Rotonda, a residence just outside Vicenza (figures 6 and 7).[59]

The plan reveals that no matter how one maneuvers within this elegant dwelling (built in 1566–70), one is moving around the central reception hall. More forthrightly than the official *sala* in the Chiericati, this overtly circular room both facilitates and symbolizes the return to the center. The dome overhead, however, complicates the picture. Viewed from within, this dome inculcates the literally "domestic" virtues of remaining and residing inside. Seen from outside, the same dome moves the gaze upward into the sky and outward onto the surrounding hills. As in the case of Saint Peter's, though more gently, a double action of enclosure and transcendence is induced. The

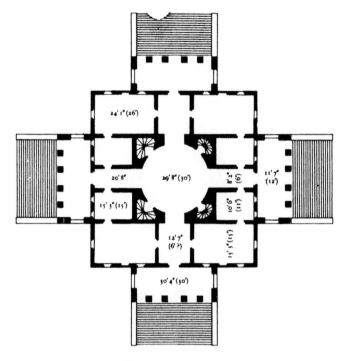

Fig. 6. Palladio, plan of Villa Rotonda.

dome demonstrates that hestial dwelling is not merely a matter of staying inside and tending the central fire. The upward motion of the fire itself leads up and out of the enclosure within. Indeed, the Navajo hogan, another circular and domed building, has an opening at the top of its roof for the release of flame and smoke (figure 8).[60]

In contrast with practices in the Italian Renaissance, here the domestic and the religious expressions of the two countervailing hestial tendencies combine in one and the same structure. The hogan is home, but the Navajo also consider it sacred and associate its escaping smoke with "holy wind."[61]

Despite the legendary patience and receptivity of Hestia, we detect, therefore, an important complication when it comes to building in a hestial manner. Insofar as the implicit verticality of the hearth (as exhibited in the upward motion of its smoke into the heavens) is extended into a built structure such as a dome, a movement *out of* domestic enclosure and into another domain is strikingly suggested. What Frank Lloyd Wright liked to call "interior spaciousness" is at once complemented and contested by the dome, which extends from the comforts and protection of the domicile into the uncomfortably vertiginous realm of the heavens.[62] Domestic life cannot be

Fig. 7. Elevation of Villa Rotonda.

contained, much less fully contented, in this upward and outward motion. The indwelling locatives of being in/within/down/here/near give way to locatives of being out/without/up/there/far.

Swiftly moving Hermes is at once "the God of motion, communication, guidance, and barter."[63] He acts as a guide to human souls on their journey into the underworld and yet is prone to mislead these souls by his cunning and guile. Either way, he moves in the public sphere and is the tutelary deity of the assemblies situated in the open space of the *agora*, which is discontinuous with the private sphere of the household. Associated with the heaps of stones that mark crossroads and territorial boundaries in ancient Greece—his name connotes "heap" or "cairn" of stones—Hermes is also the god of roads and of wayfarers. As a god of intersections, he is responsible for the disposition of entire regions of public space:

> Hermes permeates the whole world because of his possibility of making connections, and [because of] his commerce with, and constellation of, the other Gods from his borderline. He is the connection-maker and he is the Messenger of the Gods.[64]

This description of a deity at once deceptive and generous, moving through open space and marking its borders, always *out there*, resonates with a mode of dwelling experienced in its very outwardness. If the hestial mainly gathers in (and only lets out by escape or indirection), the hermetic moves out res-

Fig. 8. Navajo hogan.

olutely. The hermetic represents the far-out view, a view from a moving position, in which the slow motions of the caretaker/homemaker give way to
the impatient rapidity of the thief, the trespasser, and the traveler. Under the
sign of Hermes, the con-centric becomes ec-centric.

In dwelling places modeled on hermetic principles, the circular and the
vertical yield to the straight and the horizontal. In architecture, the straight
line appears in rectilinear rooms and especially in hallways, walkways, and
roads. From a straight hallway, one's vision shoots like an arrow out of the
building. (Hermes is usually depicted with winged feet and carrying an
arrow-straight rod.) If one then walks outside, into a civic space structured
by "squares" and "blocks," one is soon enmeshed in a dense grid of inter-
locking lines. Domestic curvilinearity becomes urban rectilinearity. At the
city limit, one can survey the laid-out linearism in the imperial manner of a
Demiurge. In the hermetic mode—not to be confused with "cloistered,"
much less with "occult"—the aim is to "observe [an object] from the outside, to organize it as an object other than oneself."[65]

An immediate consequence of being thrust outside and onto the borderlines is to lack a center. Not to have a center calls for a mode of building
that is both public and orthogonal:

THE AGORA

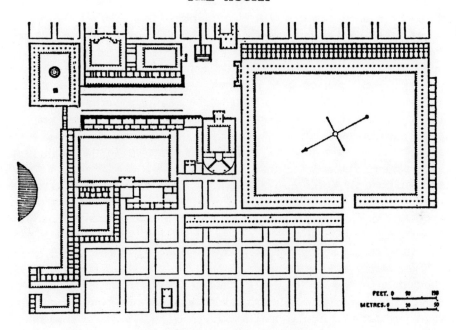

Fig. 9. City plan, Miletus, Asia Minor.

[Hermes] represents the centerless dynamic space, oriented toward many directions which, in the absence of a center, can only congregate into parallel lines, perhaps set into grid-like patterns (linear cities, urban *quadrillages*).[66]

No wonder that city planners, ancient and modern, are so often drawn to rectilinear designs as ideal urban (and suburban) configurations. In these designs, everything is a border and nothing a center (if there is a center, it is just another empty square). As a case in point, consider the city plan for Miletus in Asia Minor (figure 9).[67]

In urban space staked out in this style—just as it was a millennium earlier in the alluvial fields of Egypt, where geometry as "earth measurement" may have been born—what else can one do but flee hermetically from one indifferent corner to another? Instead of being encouraged to take up residence behind walls in a comfortable, centralized domestic space, one is cast adrift in a maze of rectangles. Many centuries later, in rationally planned cities, citizens who live in houses or apartment buildings constructed in a fixedly orthogonal "International Style" feel rootlessly positioned and impermanently housed.[68]

Nevertheless, the *agora* of Miletus also shows something running athwart the purely hermetic. The rectilinearity of this agora—located at the upper right corner of figure 9—is strikingly self-enclosed, having only one narrow entrance at its base. As R. E. Wycherley remarks, "In late Hellenistic and Roman times there was a greater tendency to plan the main agora-square [so as] to make it an enclosed building *turning in upon itself*."[69] It is as if Hermes, instead of darting outward to the edge of town, had come back into the city, if not to its exact center at least to a place whose shape is sharply self-enclosed. Has Hermes here joined forces with Hestia, taking up residence at her very doorstep? Just as we detected the hestial escaping up and out (e.g., through the dome of Palladio's Villa Rotonda), so we now find the hermetic working from within. Could it be that each architectural mode, and thus each answering kind of dwelling, *calls for* and *complements* the other? Might it be that just as earth and world share a "common outline" despite their conflictual differences, the hestial and the hermetic can constructively coexist in the very face of their manifest distinctness?[70]

The hestial and the hermetic also entail two kinds of bodily behavior subtending human dwelling. The centered, long-suffering, and measured movements of Hestia at the hearth epitomize the habitual body motions and memories that are part and parcel of domestic life. That is, the residents of a given household must be sufficiently habituated to their domicile to make their way around it without having to premeditate every movement. The intimacy and memorability of domestic space depend on a thorough acquaintance with a residence from within its walls.

> Linked to the earth (space) and to lineage (time), to the continuity of the human race and to its nourishment, Hestia presents the steady, deep being *with* and *in* things through which the meaning of the multiplicity of phenomena can be pierced.[71]

By contrast, the mercurial movements of Hermes, god of thieves, are suited to the nonhabitual, de-centered actions of traversing open spaces rapidly, and in particular of going *around* a public square or *between* houses and *outside* established limits. The introversion of Hestia's bodily motions, continually pivoting on herself, yields to the extraversion of mobile actions that proceed swiftly and in decidedly linear fashion. Once more, however, combination is perfectly possible. One can walk swiftly from room to room in the Palazzo Chiericati, and philosophers paused as they moved peripatetically around rectilinear stoas. Even the track inside a stadium—which is as self-enclosed as the Milesian *agora*—has straight stretches on its two long sides for fleet-footed runners to traverse.

Just as the hestial and the hermetic adumbrate two ontological categories (earth and world) and call upon two ways of being bodily in the world (stationary and mobile), so they also evoke two ways in which to build: "topological and participational," on one hand, and "geometry-bent and conceptual," on the other.[72] We become acquainted with the first form of building by empathetic connection, e.g., by sensory channels that tie the body as in-the-center of a situation to other bodies and objects in the same situation. Thanks to these centered empathetic-sensory interrelations, the body and other items in the scene—whether these be other human beings, pieces of furniture, paintings on the walls, the walls themselves, or whole buildings— co-participate in creating a place. This common place is a genuine *koinos topos* with all of the integrity and enclosedness that "topological" implies in modern topological mathematics, in which notions of vicinity and neighborhood are crucial.

Participational-topological buildings resist construal on a model of strict containment, i.e., "cellular sequestration" in Frank Lloyd Wright's phrase.[73] They are more encompassing than proto-places (tied as these latter are to the here of my own body) or counter-places (linked to a determinate there). Thanks to its collusion with the lived body, a truly participational building creates its own near sphere constructed in terms of zonal places and com-places. Such a building brings with it its own locale or vicinity, in which every topologically pertinent ingredient participates. The result is a truly porous built place, which opens onto the environing world through numerous apertures. Examples abound in architecture, and include such seemingly simple *topoi* as rooms, porches, and courtyards (filled with "pores" of windows, doors, and screens all experienced from within in their full sensuous being) as well as more complex structures (such as those found in the dense interior of the twelfth-century Romanesque church of the Madeleine in Vézélay).

Buildings "geometry-bent and conceptual," on the other hand, are constituted on a very different basis. Here the guiding principle is the disposition of space in accordance with previous ideation rather than in terms of immediate sensuousness. The prevalent form of such ideation in Western architecture since early Greek times has been formal (i.e., plane and solid) geometry. Such geometry allows the architect to organize space by means of coordinate systems composed of points and lines. I have been calling such a conception of space a "site," and I have located its apogee in the Cartesian notion of a pure extensional space at once three-dimensional, infinite in extent, and identical with the totality of the material bodies that occupy it. Examples in architecture include such diverse instances as eighteenth-century Neoclassical buildings in France and England (often, as in the case of Inigo Jones, designed in deliberate imitation of Palladio) and twentieth-century modernist constructions in the International Style. But the guiding geometry may be Euclidean rather than Cartesian, as we see in the layout of Miletus (one of the earliest instances of fully geometrized city planning in the West).[74] In the implicit imperialism of this geometrism, we witness a potent tendency to suppress a participational sense of built place, much as in the young child's cognitive development an initially topological grasp of space gives way to projective and finally to Euclidean modes of spatial organization. The child anticipates the history of architecture, since the Euclidean never triumphs entirely over the topological but enters into a complicated dialectical exchange with it that lasts into adulthood.[75]

Speaking experientially rather than developmentally or formally, the difference is between being part of a lively public festival on a plaza—where participation is spontaneous, yet respects the felt shape of the square—and surveying this same plaza in order to determine its metrically exact size. The formal dimensions of the square (i.e., its breadth and length) are precisely *not* the dimensions most pertinent to the lived bodies who throng it (i.e., right–left, before–behind, near–far, alongside, between, with). Geometric-formal dimensions are traced out by imaginary lines projected by the surveyor of the scene. These lines, whose continuity permits no porosity, are superimposed on the place, which in its own participational-topological reality exhibits no such pure products of the surveyor's ideology and practice.

Plaza and *place* both stem from Latin *platea*, broad street. In laying out streets—or other features of the built environment—continuous lines are essential, but the length designated by these lines does not capture the breadth of the experience undergone in the streets themselves, much less in the plazas to which they lead. The same is true of the depth of experience possible in such places.

VII

Plato's Demiurge, that arch-geometer and hermetic spirit of the ancient Greek world, must first make connection with the chaotic realm of *chōra*. The necessity of this connection—*chōra* is said to be Necessity itself—is most revealing. For choric space is at once hestial (it is said to be the "seat" of the emerging cosmos) and topological-participational (since it is elemental and pregeometric).[76] This connection suggests that if they are to describe the places in which human beings dwell, the two dichotomies under discussion in the preceding section must allow for the confluence of their separate terms. Just as the topological-participational must realize creative combinations with the geometric-conceptual, so the hestial and the hermetic tendencies in architecture must effect equally constructive conjunctions for human beings to undergo the most rewarding experiences of dwelling.

In fact, the Greeks considered Hestia and Hermes to be partners in a number of respects. Both deities symbolized beginnings. Each facilitated the making of connections.[77] Hermes protected a family's fertility, while Hestia

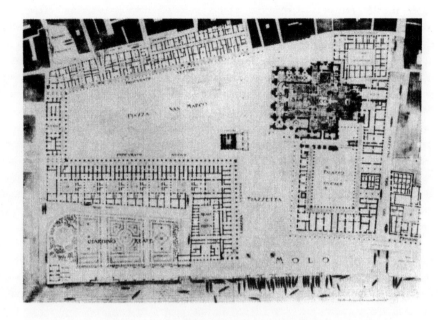

Fig. 10. Plan of the Piazza San Marco, Venice (Duomo at upper right).

guarded its actual household. Moreover, they cooperated with each other expressly:

> Hermes . . . stands outside the house to conduct the traveler away from the shelter of Hestia's fire. The traveler returns guided by Hermes to the more central and ever-abiding origins of self, family, and nation.[78]

In my own language, Hermes not only superintends dwelling-as-wandering but contributes to dwelling-as-residing by returning travelers safely to their hestial origins. Indeed, we may go further and assert that under the benevolent and mutual protection of Hermes and Hestia, the two basic modes of dwelling act to enhance each other's presence. A notable case in point is found in the building complex of San Marco in Venice (figure 10).[79]

Here, in a single "region" of urban space, we witness both a decidedly participational-topological form of construction and an equally concerted formal-geometric mode; the first is as hestial as the second is hermetic.[80] I refer respectively to the Duomo (Cathedral) of San Marco and to the piazza set in front of it. As the word suggests, the Duomo is concave and concentric in structure. Its multiple domes cover inner spaces that are powerfully ingathering. The interpenetration of these inner spaces—places within the

Place of the Duomo—engender a receptivity reinforced by the extremely thick walls and arches of the cathedral and by a particolored mosaic inlay throughout the interior surface. The Greek cross design of the building highlights the central arena at the heart of the edifice directly underneath the primary dome. The church as a whole lures the visitor to come ever closer to its center by proffering an immensely inviting interiority. To be within the building is to feel oneself solicited by hestial virtues of steadiness and slowness. Participation in religious rituals held inside bears out further, at a communal level, the hearthlike character of the darkened nave and transepts and chancel, their burnished gold glittering like late embers of a fire tended by Hestia.

But once outside the Duomo and onto the piazza, one is suddenly thrust into an imposing public space bordered by two rows of receding buildings on the north and south sides, terminating at the far end in another row closing off the piazza. The effect is that of confronting an enormous (and slightly skewed) trapezoid, egress from which is possible only by the smaller piazzetta on the south or by the corridor of shops to the north of the Duomo. Everything about this trapezoidal space is linear and geometric, ranging from arabesque patterns on the pavement of the piazza itself to the rigidly upright columns and rectangular windows of the bordering buildings. These latter present a repetitive motif of arches and bays that regularizes the perceptual space still further. Given the prevalent rectilinearity and the sheer externality of the setting, Hermes might feel at home in this late Renaissance *agora*. Even the overtowering Campanile (located on the southeastern corner of the piazza) contributes a distinctly hermetic note of arrow-straight verticality.

The insistent geometricity of the Piazza San Marco, its densely crisscrossing lines, make it a complex crossroads. If it is true that "any crossing marks a place," this is a very special place indeed.[81] Instead of deliberate, meditative, hestial movements, such as are encouraged within the Duomo, this open secular space inspires hermetic alacrity of body motion. The temptation to engage in religious ritual (or, short of that, in ordinary reflection) is replaced by the inclination to survey the scene, to *take in* instead of being *gathered in*.

Yet the intensely contrastive character of the scene is not in the least divisive. The two primary architectural components—Duomo and piazza—together compose a single, deeply satisfying situation. As one moves from the cathedral onto the square or vice versa, the transition is decisive but not abrupt or discontinuous. The in-gathered interiority of one kind of dwelling place answers to the geometrized exteriority of the other. No wonder almost everyone in Venice, resident or visitor, keeps coming back to this crucial place, sometimes several times a day, whether passing through with the celerity of Hermes or lingering thoughtfully in the manner of Hestia, not only in the cathedral but also in the cafés and restaurants on the edges of the piazza.[82] In this architecturally dual setting, the characteristic activities of the two gods conjoin as amiably and spontaneously as do the two kinds of human dwelling place to which they offer aegis from beyond.

Two sorts of scene; two superintending deities; two kinds of bodily engagement; two means of staying in space; two forms of place; two ways of dwelling-in-place. But dichotomy and difference do not have the last word when it comes to dwelling in place. Just as in Plato's metaphysical world the indefinite dyad brings together the like and the unlike, the odd and the even, so the dyads of near and far, inside and outside, right and left, with and between, before and behind, here and there, alongside and around, above and below all come together in the concrete realm of built implacement.[83] They come together as Hestes and Hermes come together: as presiding presences of dwelling. Like these two deities, they are finally two-in-one, the binarism of opposition yielding to the internally differentiated unity of dwelling twice over in the same place.

6

Building Sites and Cultivating Places

All architecture is what you do when you look upon it.

—Walt Whitman, "A Song for Occupations"

Where a place is to be formed, he who disposes the ground and arranges the plantations ought to fix the situation at least.

—William Mason, speaking of Capability Brown

We need these two homes, a green one and a brown one, a grown one and a built one, two worlds in tension.

—Robert Harbison, *Eccentric Spaces*

I

WE ARE STILL at sea regarding the elusive and vexing matter of place. Like the tide, the murky waters of this matter keep returning with insistent and difficult questions. What is place in contrast with space? What does orientation in place really mean? How is place built? What does it mean to dwell in a place? How are dwelling places related to the environing natural world?

In attempting to find our way in this virtual Sargasso Sea of confusion, we have enlisted the aid of a series of paired terms. Whether these terms are etymological or prepositional, perceptual or mythical, their initially oppositional standing in a given pair has turned out to be complementary on further scrutiny. But the skeptical reader may be asking: are not any such binary pairs artificially imposed? Are they not instances of what Husserl would call a "garb of ideas" (*Ideenkleid*) forced upon a recalcitrant subject matter (thus distorting it)? Or, alternatively, are they not tailor-made to fit this matter (thus merely reflecting it)? Other doubts may arise from the quasi-mathematical language of "dyad" or from an apparently too great reliance upon verbal resources. Perhaps the binarism of pairs, while valuable in linguistics (i.e., in describing paired bundles of distinctive phonemic features) or in molecular biology (e.g., RNA/DNA), is suspiciously neat when applied to the muddy matters in which implacement seems to plunge us. If the invocation of the mythical figures of Hermes and Hestia helped to clarify the difficult matter of dwelling, we should also remember that "mythical metaphors are not etiologies, causal explanations or name tags. . . . They give an account of the archetypal story in the case history, *the myth in the mess.*"[1]

The difficulty is not just that the distinctions in question are artificial, splitting in two what was originally one; *any* purely binary distinction may be artificial either in origin or in ultimate application. The problem is often that such distinctions allow too much to flow through their exclusively two-way mesh. In particular, a given pair may let pass many things intermediate between the two controlling terms, as well as many things that fall outside their scope. What is gained in conceptual clarity is lost in experiential nuance. But, then, this critique can be leveled at every attempt to distinguish one thing from another in purely conceptual terms.

In the final analysis, the only justification for the various dichotomies I have employed lies in whether they clarify the material at hand and allow us to view this material in a new, or a more searching, light. There is nothing the matter with binary concepts if they illuminate an intractable subject matter, just as there is nothing wrong with tailoring concepts to fit the subject if the fit itself is revealing.

Nonetheless, it is time to account for one factor in the experience of place that fiercely resists dichotomization of any kind. I refer to the natural world, or "nature." In its history ("natural history" precedes, and will doubtless outlast, human history), its forcefulness (felt in hurricanes, volcanic eruptions, and other "natural catastrophes"), and its independence (*its* will often seems to have nothing whatsoever to do with *our* will), nature does not submit gracefully to human categorizing. This is not to say that the natural world is disorderly; as we learn from the existence of "laws of nature," such as those that govern the evolution of organic matter, order is everywhere present in the natural world. In fact, this world possesses *its own order*, one frequently and perhaps finally beyond human ken.

We began with the predicament of being lost at sea. In assessing this predicament—that of not knowing where one is in the face of natural forces—we focused on how to achieve orientation and stability in a perilous environment. Orientation led us to a consideration of the body's concrete role in place, and stability drew us into a discussion of built places. But bodies and buildings, indispensable as they are to implacement, soon become self-centered and closed off if their potential outreach (by which I mean such things as the arc of embodiment and the architectural arc) is ignored. Once our bodies are comfortably ensconced in buildings, we simply tend to close out the larger world of nature. Yet the natural world surrounds every body and every building, finally if not immediately. Even if this wider world seems independent of human beings' cherished aims and interests, it *remains around us* as a mute presence tacitly waiting to be acknowledged.

Toward that acknowledgment, in this chapter I shall focus on how the natural world enters the experience of built places *from the edges*. Although literally marginal, these edge regions are not of merely peripheral significance. This becomes clear when we realize that the basic act of building consists in establishing two distinguishable zones: a central or main structure, which is the "building" proper, and an outlying area beyond the building yet belonging to the place.[2] In stressing the security of enclosure, it is tempting to concentrate on the edifice per se and to disregard its own lawn, yard, or sidewalk. I fell prey to this temptation as I traced the body's "progress" from the periphery of a building into its interior, e.g., from lingering alongside the Palazzo Chiericati to inhabitation within its central *sala*. My subsequent consideration of hestial dwelling only reinforced the inward movement by ignoring what lay just beyond a residence in the horizontal plane.

I made progress of another kind, however, by recognizing an ec-centric flight from the sedentary center of dwelling. An imaginary hermetic visitor to the Chiericati might rush out through the same inviting porch by which he had entered the building, darting into the Piazza Isola and then into the city streets of Vicenza. But this mercurial figure would soon become enmeshed in the rectilinearity of the urban grid. Even when he finally reached the city limits, he would stop short of the open countryside. Although Hermes presides at the crossroads, he is powerless in the face of a trackless nature.

It is thus time for us to move outside the city limits and into the margins of built place, into the peripheral areas where the natural and the cultivated conjoin and where we finally confront nature. In order to do so, we need not move far in terms of distance. If one turns left on exiting from the Duomo San Marco and walks through the piazetta and past the Doge's Palace—instead of walking straight into the main piazza—one very soon reaches an extension of the Adriatic Sea. In a matter of minutes, one's body moves out of the deep enclosure of the Duomo and into an embracing aqueous world that is not more than a few hundred yards away, bypassed in my analysis of Venice at the end of the preceding chapter.

Similarly, in my discussion of Palladio's Villa Rotonda I made only a passing reference to the circumambient hills of Vicenza. Yet these hills, visible from every window in the Rotonda, surround the building in a near sphere of mutual support. As Goethe wrote upon visiting the Rotonda in 1786: "Just as the house can be seen in all its splendour from every point of the surrounding countryside, so the views of the countryside from the house are equally delightful."[3]

If there is a felt harmony between the Villa Rotonda and its encircling hills—a harmony underlined by the resemblance between their rounded shapes and the Rotonda's graceful dome—no such equilibrium exists between Venice and its watery environs: the Queen of the Adriatic is at risk in her own element. The Adriatic not merely surrounds Venice (i.e., in its lagoonlike extensions), but through an intricate network of canals the sea insinuates itself into every corner of the city. Though Venetian commercial and military power was established from the sea, the sea's presence is also a distinct danger, for from it disease, death, and defeat have come to the Venetians at diverse moments in their long history. Even today the encroaching waters, slowly gaining on the sinking and rotting foundations of ancient buildings, threaten the survival of the city as a whole. Goethe, freshly arrived from Vicenza, had his first direct experience of the sea at the Lido just outside the city:

> We went ashore and walked across the spit of land. I heard a loud noise: it was the sea, which presently came into view. The surf was breaking on the beach in high waves, although the water was receding. . . . What a magnificent sight the sea is! I shall try to go out in a boat with the fishermen; the gondolas dare not risk putting out to open sea. . . . The Venetians must make every effort to protect the Lido, so that the angry element cannot destroy or alter that which man has already conquered and to which he has given shape and direction for his own purposes.[4]

Awestruck by the sea, Goethe is convinced that its force must be resisted by the counter-force of built places. But what does it mean to stand up to nature—to resist it—or, perhaps, to enter into equilibrium with it?

II

Building calls for heeding the parameters of the natural setting: a building, like a mythology, "reflects its region."[5] Not to heed the natural features of a region is to build unreflectively; it is to occupy a site rather than to construct a place adequate to its setting.

Building so as to reflect a region is not merely submitting to the obdurate materiality of that region but *contending* with it, entering into a constructive contest with the givens of a natural place. The ensuing contestation takes two different courses, which we can label "contentious" and "contented." In a contentious confrontation a building stands up to the natural world and challenges it. The Campanile in the Piazza San Marco, for example, not only looms over the square below but looks defiantly out to the sea beyond; Goethe first glimpsed the Adriatic from the top of this tower. In a contented connection, a building realizes an equipoise with its natural setting. We find such equipoise accomplished elegantly in Palladio's Villa Rotonda and in Wright's "prairie houses."

Another way of grasping the relationship between built places and unbuilt environments involves making a distinction between *boundaries* and *monuments*, claimed by one architectural historian to be the primeval forms of all human building.[6] Buildings attentive to their boundaries—whether these be marked by hedgerows, pathways, or border stones—take account of "the lay of the land." This is so even if the purpose of a particular boundary is to deny access to the building itself; the fence or wall announcing a property line hugs the very land it encloses. Other less forbidding boundaries let in the natural world around them, for instance, by allowing native flora to grow freely across them. The boundary may be so subtle, in fact, that one has the impression of unbroken continuity between a built place and its natural environs.[7] In monuments, on the other hand, a very different circumstance obtains. The issue is no longer one of continuity or delimitation but of building in such a way as to resist, ignore, or even flout the natural world. In the central mall in Washington, D.C., the predominant horizontality of the boundary—here present in a radial grid of receding city streets—is overpowered by a headstrong verticality epitomized in the Washington Monument, a sheer spire thrusting audaciously into space. A series of monuments and monumental office buildings sets itself off from a severely truncated natural setting as if to say that more important things are going on here than the mere growth of grass and trees.

Nature was certainly the force to be contended with in the earliest human dwellings. These rudimentary structures show themselves to be ingenious compromises between boundary and monument, contentment and contentiousness. Such compromise formations are evident in the recently discovered dwellings at Terra Amata in southern France, near Nice, only a few hundred miles west of Venice and Vicenza. Over 400,000 years old, these huts were situated at the beach in a cove that sheltered them from the prevailing northwest winds. "Shelters" themselves, they were built for periodical inhabitation in the late spring of each year. As a result, they were often constructed on top of the remnants of former buildings. Each hut—there were some twenty clustered together at a time—was made from branches or saplings set into the sand and converging at the top in a longitudinal axis supported by several posts. Inside, a hearth occupied the middle of a living area surrounded by sleeping spaces and, slightly farther out, by working spaces (figure 11).[8]

In this oldest known human dwelling, "a spot of earth" was converted into "a special place."[9] As in the case of pit houses, we find an already differentiated structure, fitting snugly into existing niches: "an architecture of shelter contained in the pleats of the earth."[10] In this instance at least, the

Fig. 11. Prehistoric hut at Terra Amata.

Aristotelian model of place as a container is quite apt: the huts serve as closely fitting containers for their inhabitants.

Although they do not set out any formal boundaries of their own, in being situated on a beach they are located on the boundary between land and sea. And in being constructed on the ruins of the previous year's dwellings, they are in effect commemorations of these latter: monuments *to them* even if not literally monumental in height or volume. The huts are thus at once boundary-bound and quasi-monumental. By the same token, these burrowlike buildings exist between the contentious and the contented. They stand up to nature, yet there is nothing defiant in their earth-hugging stance; and while they must have fostered contentment within, their sheer transiency belies any sense of being merely complacent.

In much more recent Old Stone Age dwellings such as those found not far from Terra Amata at Altamira and Lascaux, the earth-pleats are actual caves. Now the differentiation of space is more complex, thanks to the inclusion of whole rooms—we might call them "galleries"—filled with invocative and propitiatory images of animals and humans. Since no obviously utilitarian function for the galleries has been discovered, dwelling here seems to exceed mere housing or shelter. Enhanced by the painting of iconic images, rooms become more like numinous temples. But if there is iconic and even narrative representation, there is no building proper in the circumstance.

Nature here permits inhabitation without calling for construction (just as, conversely, there can be constructed places that are uninhabitable, such as false ruins and "follies").

Architecture and nature meet in a most effective manner at Betatakin, an Anasazi cliff-dwelling located in northeastern Arizona. Built between A.D. 1260 and 1280 and abandoned by 1300—the period during which the construction of Gothic cathedrals was in full tilt—this settlement of some 135 rooms is nestled within an enormous arch under an overhanging cliff. The overhang is some five hundred feet high and protects the settlement from rain and snow, shielding it from the direct glare of the sun in the summer while allowing sparser rays to penetrate in the winter. The construction itself is compact and ingenious: granaries, kivas (ceremonial chambers), and homes all cling tenaciously to the uneven floor and the lower back side of the arch.[11] Similar to the art work in the Old Stone Age caves in Europe, petroglyphs here depict animals, human beings, and certain insignia (e.g., the Fire Clan). A spring at the base of the settlement provides fresh water, and once cultivatable land spreads out along the narrow canyon floor.

At Betatakin the built structures fit into the natural givens gracefully, as though contented to be there; even their coloration (from a mixture of local limestone and adobe) is continuous with the surrounding rock canopy. But these same structures assert themselves in contending with the enormous arch under which they are built: they are mini-monuments of human presence, leaving indelible architectural autographs on the natural landscape.

Here we rejoin an earlier theme: every built place takes up a stand. Now we can add that the stand is taken toward a natural setting. This may occur as contentiously and monumentally as occurs in the dome of Saint Peter's, the Campanile at Venice, and the Washington Monument, or it may happen as a more modest and conciliatory integration of human purposes with natural resources, a "standing-with," as at Terra Amata, Lascaux, and the Villa Rotonda.

When human beings inhabit (or travel between) built places that are contentiously or contentedly related to natural settings, their bodies adumbrate whole segments of the surrounding world. These adumbrative actions are designated by such additive locutions as "way over there," "deep down under," "clear up above," etc. The concatenation of adverbs and/or prepositions echoes an extended exchange between body and environment. This exchange is not randomly realized but links up with the double axiality of the horizontal and the vertical in human experience.[12] Thus "way down below" and "high up there" indicate regions along the vertical axis stretching from under the earth to the upper sky, while "just over here" and "way over there" are situated on the horizontal axis reaching from one horizon to another. In contrast with the orientational dyads—which cluster between the lived body and the built places it occupies—these triads take us *out* of body and building and *into* the natural world. In this capacity, they can be considered ecologically pertinent variables.

Much as the body of the itinerant or the inhabitant is the seat of the dyads of orientation, the world of nature is the matrix of the various eco-variables. The direction implicit in realizing "inner order outward"—a direction most evident when building as such is on the agenda—is here complemented by the counter-direction of *outer order moving in*: out from nature and into the body, the common vehicle of journeying and inhabiting. These two basic directions constitute a virtual palindrome of lived place, a forward and backward movement whereby the built and the unbuilt, architecture and nature, enter into circular relationship with one another.[13]

It follows almost as a practical syllogism that buildings take their cue not only from the proclivities of the lived body but also from the propensities of the encompassing environment. (So much so that building in such places as Betatakin or Venice, where nature seizes the lead, means employing nature against itself, whether in the form of canals against the sea or adobe-and-stone against stone.)[14] Vitruvius observed that "designs for houses ought . . . to conform to the country and to diversities of climate."[15] In this spirit he recommended that the disposition of rooms in a house ought to have regard for the prevailing winds, the four quarters of the sky, and the direction and kind of natural light.[16] Palladio, much indebted to Vitruvius on this point, includes in his own treatise on architecture a close consideration of the natural settings of country houses, singling out climate, ground, rivers, and swamps; he espouses the general maxim that "architecture (as all other arts are) being imitative of nature, accounts nothing tolerable which is estranged [from nature], [or] differs from that which is natural."[17] The ancient principle of imitation implies that the model comes from without, from something extrahuman (natural if not supernatural), belonging properly and first of all to the environing world.

III

We will endeavour to shew how the aire and genious of Gardens operat upon humane spirits towards virtue and sanctitie. . . . How Caves, Grotts, Mounts, and irregular ornaments of Gardens do contribute to contemplative and philosophicall Enthusiasms.

—John Evelyn, letter of 1657 to Sir Thomas Browne

There are many ways of taking a stand vis-à-vis the natural world. One may stand *up* and build accordingly, from ziggurats and pyramids to skyscrapers and malls (in the Washington manner). Or one may stand *out* and build prairie houses, roads, and malls (in the original British sense of tree-lined promenades). One may also stand *in*, in which case, constructing houses and offices, rooms and hallways will follow. But one can also combine the three stances, standing *out* and *in* by standing *up*. This last, comparatively complex action is the characteristic stand human beings assume when in the actual presence of the natural world. In that presence, I walk or stand (up), and I find myself (out) in nature, (in) its embrace. (The up–out–in of this situation suggests another triadic eco-variable.) But if I discover myself thus in a natural scene, it is far from clear what kind of building corresponds to the experience. How should I build—indeed, why should I build at all—when, *ex hypothesi*, I am simply standing or walking in the midst of the natural world?

Gardens are forms of building that answer to this circumstance. They are built, or perhaps we should say contrived, places and yet are largely if not entirely composed of natural things. Even if I am not yet in wilderness, in a garden I am in the presence of things that live and grow, often on their own schedule.

When I stand in a garden, I find myself in a scene intermediate between the completely constructed and the frankly wild. For I am then in between a monument (e.g., a house) and a boundary (that of the property in which the garden is located). I have edged out of domestic enclosure and am moving toward exposed fields of uncultivated land. In getting myself into this cultivated but not fully constructed scene, I have decommissioned myself with respect to familial and professional duties. I have become marginal, halfway between the sacred and the profane, yet have somehow gained a very special place to be.

The situation is reminiscent of being on a porch, another halfway station. Both gardens and porches are interplaces that allow us to move freely into and out of residences and to vacillate between a private and a public life. But a garden is something very different from a porch. What sort of intermediacy does a garden possess? What kind of a place does it provide? What sort of building does it call for? What kind of dwelling does it encourage? What does it mean to speak of "cultivating" a garden?

Although gardens rarely offer shelter or any other practical service, they are not merely ephemeral or superficial in status. They are the primary forms of landscape architecture and have been important presences from the time of ancient Mesopotamia and early China until the present moment. In certain cultures, e.g., Persia between the seventh and tenth centuries A.D., gardens were more significant than residences, from which they were detached and given walls of their own to emphasize their special standing. If "a garden is partly an extension of architecture—a fragment of a city—and partly natural paradise,"[18] Persian gardens were an attempt to establish paradise on earth.

Behind their walls was a miniature cosmos in which a central body of water flowed into the four quarters of the world. Indeed, the word *paradise* is derived from the ancient Persian *pairidaēza*, meaning walled-in park or garden. "Paradise lost" is a garden lost—a point not lost on John Milton.[19]

Even when strictly self-contained and accorded quasi-sacred status, however, gardens remain *liminal* phenomena.[20] They are liminal just insofar as they are at the threshold between a series of things: between a building (domestic or institutional) and circumambient nature; between dwelling-as-residing and dwelling-as-wandering; between sky and ground, horizon and path; and between standing stock-still and running. Even if we pause from time to time, for the most part we *perambulate* in gardens.[21] *Perambulate* as a transitive verb means to inspect the boundaries of a place; perambulation rituals exist from ancient Rome to colonial New England. But in the case of gardens *the place itself is a boundary*. To perambulate here is not restricted to going *around* a place but includes walking *through* it (thus rejoining the literal meaning of "per-ambulate"). Indeed, the boundary *of* a garden can be obscured and even removed at the limit, but the garden as such is already and always a liminal presence.

The most consequential liminal feature of gardens is the uneasy boundary they maintain between building and nature. Gardens are "literal worlds in which artifice strains against senseless growth."[22] They hold artificiality and naturalness apart—often putting their differences into sharp relief—while at the same time bringing them back together in revealing ways. The bringing together, the "art of the garden," is tantamount to *cultivation*. A cultivated garden (a virtual pleonasm) domesticates wilderness, either by importing wild items such as herbs or flowers into the garden plot or by letting the plot itself "grow wild." Since cultivation is a matter of degree—a given patch of ground can always be *more or less* cultivated—there is a proliferation of possible garden types in accordance with the extensiveness of cultivation. As J. B. Jackson remarks, "Like the dwelling the garden has no single, universally accepted form; like the dwelling it is much more than the product of a design or of environmental influences, and like the dwelling it serves many needs and is thought of in many ways."[23]

In the face of this proliferation, I shall limit consideration of gardens to three leading types only (and these only in certain English and French versions): early enclosed gardens, formal gardens, and "informal" landscape gardens.

Even before the Norman Conquest of 1066, there was in early medieval England and France a lively interest in the natural grouping of living things. Aelfric's school (circa A.D. 995), for instance, drew distinctions between *mudu*, a wood, *bearu*, a grove, and *holt*, a copse. But there is no evidence before the Conquest of an interest in the concerted cultivation of the natural world, the re-orchestration of "fields" or smaller plots of land into parks and gardens.[24] At Le Mans in 1145, Bishop Guillaume de Passavant planted a garden (*viridarium*) "with many sorts of trees for grafting foreign fruits, [all] equally lovely; for those leaning out of the hall windows to admire the beauty of the trees, and others in the garden looking at the fair show of the windows, could both delight in what they saw."[25] In this prototypical circumstance, trees, originally denizens of the forest, were *brought into* the enclosure of the garden so as to be cultivated within its walls (e.g., grafted with exotic fruits) and, in this very captivity, to be enjoyed as aesthetically pleasing. The reverse action, *going into* a forest and creating a garden there, was also pursued, in this case by Hugh de Noyers, bishop of Auxerre, in the years 1183–1206:

> The woods, beset with briars and undergrowth and thus of little value, he cleared and brought into cultivation. There he made gardens and planted trees of different sorts so that, apart from deriving pleasure from them, he also got great quantities of fruit. He surrounded a large part of the wood with a ring fence.[26]

The combination of practical and hedonic motives is striking; pleasure mixes with yield, giving to the primordial act of cultivation a twofold aspect, which continues to be reflected in later medieval practices of including orchards and herbaries (small plots of herbs) in gardens. Nature is "brought into cultivation" as a nourishing as well as a pleasing presence.[27]

Also significant was the multiplicity of garden types from the very beginning of this Anglo-Norman tradition. At Winchester Castle, for example, a herbary was created in 1178, a lawn garden (*pratellum*) was added in 1252, and in 1306 a queen's garden was constructed in which a channel of water flowed through an enclosure in grass.[28] Elsewhere, parks and warrens, chases and circumscribed "forests"—all of which contained game for hunting in various formats—began to populate the English landscape.[29] Holding together this considerable variety was a common respect for nature in its untamed format. Trees in particular were greatly valued for their aesthetic and therapeutic potential.[30] In this early veneration of trees, which, unlike bushes and shrubs, are difficult to reconfigure into artificial shapes, we detect an attitude that will inform the English approach to gardens for many centuries.

We thus arrive at a first way in which gardens are cultivated places. The way itself is twofold. On one hand, gardens enclose a variety of vegetation within a carefully circumscribed space whose border may be a wall, a hedgerow, or a dense cluster of trees. The effect is often that of a bower, an intimate garden scene more suited to meditative walking and sitting than to promenading or sauntering. (*Bower* is a linguistic cousin of *build* and *boundary*.) On the other hand, despite their self-absorbed character, such gardens

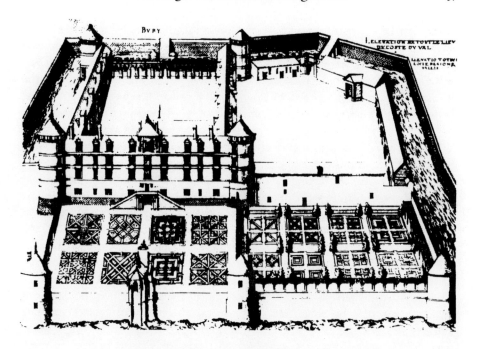

Fig. 12. Castle and garden, Bury (1511–24).

aim at bringing parts of the surrounding natural world into their care and "almost imperceptibly improving" them.[31] Such embowered enclosedness, whose origins doubtless derive from the fourfold Persian *pairidaēza* model as channeled through Spain, does not prevent these gardens from keeping important links with the natural environment outside their walls. The medieval English horticultural garden is, in effect, the continuation of nature not just by other means but often by the very same means supplied by nature itself.[32]

The attraction of enclosed gardens continued in England until at least the early seventeenth century. In Italy and France, where gardens had become increasingly monumental in the period of the Renaissance, enclosure remained an integral feature. In French châteaux of the late fifteenth and early sixteenth centuries, "the garden experience was still enclosed, limited, and inward-looking, with something of the protective, cloistered spirit that enveloped the medieval *hortus* with its high walls, covered arbors, and four-square divisions."[33] At Amboise, Blois, Bury, and Gaillon, walled-in gardens existed alongside the château, presenting the appearance of extended "kitchen gardens" (figure 12).[34]

By the middle of the sixteenth century, the rediscovery of the world of classical antiquity in Italy had spread to France, with the result that formerly austere gardens began to be adorned with statues, grottoes, and extravagant pageantry. "Nature succumbed to the whims of the exalted,"[35] as in the case of Fontainebleau, whose gardens teemed with reminders of the glory that was Greece. More telling than direct references to the ancient world was the invocation of classical criteria of architectural order: proportion, symmetry, balanced distribution, eurythmy, etc. Alberti, whose writings on architecture had a profound impact on French garden designers, had underlined these Vitruvian principles, and it was not long before entire castle complexes were being designed in accordance with them.

Paradoxically, the artificiality and formality of gardens constructed in this newly emerging French manner did not require the containment so characteristic of earlier English and French gardens. If embowerment and immurement were ways of keeping wilderness at bay, by the middle of the seventeenth century artifice had conspired with wilderness to eliminate enclosure altogether. It was above all André Le Nôtre who, at Vaux-le-Vicomte and Versailles (and at other less extravagant places), "broke down the very walls of Eden."[36] In Le Nôtre's ambitious schemes, walls became obstacles rather than protective structures. They stood in the way of extending estate gardens straight and deep into the surrounding countryside, and they interfered with the continuous vistas into the landscape that he wished to open up. At the same time, his grandiose designs pushed the untamed natural world so far afield that enclosure was no longer of any practical or symbolic value.

The garden as a place of intimacy, meditation, and family solidarity—as well as a place for the production of essential herbs, fruits, and vegetables— was set aside in favor of an open and unending visual spectacle, a coherent amalgam of infinite vistas seen from privileged viewing points. The inclination to enclose nature and to pamper it within walls gave way to a passion for reconfiguring the garden world by any means available, especially those that accorded with formal-geometric norms. These norms were ruthlessly applied, even if this meant the razing and linearizing of a given landform and its native flora.

Le Nôtre brought the formalization of gardens to a pitch of perfection and a magnitude of execution unequaled before or since in the Western world. His major constraints came from geometry rather than from nature. All avenues for promenading (*allées*), as well as the axes of concatenated garden features, traced out perfectly straight lines. Every determinate area in a garden, even the most minuscule, had the shape of a regular (if sometimes complex) geometric figure. This hypergeometrizing is evident in the overall plan of Versailles in two of its later versions (figures 13 and 14).[37]

At Versailles geometry not merely encroaches on the landscape but manifestly dominates it. The radial symmetry of the *étoile* (especially evident in

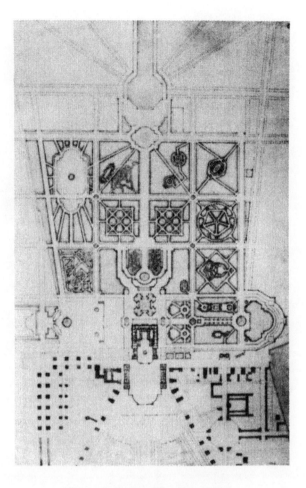

Fig. 13. *Petit parc*, Versailles (1680).

figure 14) carries an aggressive and expansive energy that seems almost literally to pin down the earth on which the radiating patterns are superimposed. The place of landscape has become the site of sheer spatial positions organized in accordance with geometric forms. These forms themselves are aligned, directly or indirectly, along the central axis that originates in the royal chambers of Louis XIV, continues through the Basin of Apollo and the longer arm of the great canal, passes over grottoes, and extends finally to the vanishing point on the horizon. This royal axis, itself the concrete symbol of the Sun King's absolute power, both collects and disperses all of the subsidiary axes and their attached plots, fountains, *bosquets*, and *quincunx*.

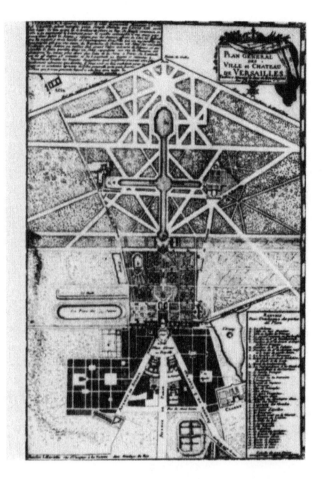

Fig. 14. Full plan of Versailles, end of Louis
XIV's reign (1693).

Nevertheless, what is manifest to us as we look at a schematized representation of Versailles seen from above—much as it was manifest to the king,
gazing westward from his elevated bedchamber along the primary *allée*—is
less perspicuous to the perambulator of the garden below. For, when walking, one is easily (and delightfully) diverted into numerous side paths.[38] Even
the vanishing point at the end of the central axis, when seen from the ground
as surrounded by ever-expanding spaces on both sides, acts to mitigate the
oppressive geometrism of the scene. "We are released to infinity," writes Vincent Scully, "or at least to indefinitely expanding space."[39]
    In fact, what makes Versailles a perpetually fascinating architectural scene

is less its rigid domination of nature than a complex dialectic between formalism and naturalism. Where other gardens of the time were unremittingly formal and geometric—notably that of the Château Richelieu, which boasted a *"jardin de l'intelligence"*[40]—Versailles offered moments of relief in its grottoes (its most important grotto, that devoted to Thetis, was situated off the central axis, on the north side of the palace), its varied waterworks, and its adroit use of trees in a *charmille* design (whereby the lower parts of trees were carefully trimmed, leaving the upper parts to grow naturally). Indeed, after building the great canal, Le Nôtre turned to ways of "relieving the predictable monotony of the main outlines."[41] The addition of the Grand Trianon and, above all, the Petit Trianon, with its seemingly unplanned woods and quasi-rustic cottages, further diluted the formalism of the central gardens.

A close consideration of the formal French gardens of the latter half of the seventeenth century reveals a consistent pattern of repressed but potent counter-formalism, even a covert collusion with wilderness. The simplicity of the basic layout of a garden often masks a complexity of construction rivaling nature itself in endless proliferation and seeming unpredictability. Saint-Simon reported that during a six-week period at Marly, Louis XIV's hermitage near Versailles, "fountains were altered a hundred times, and waterfalls redesigned in countless different ways."[42]

This self-deconstructing situation was mirrored in an ambivalent attitude toward geometry in high French formalism. On one hand, the study of geometry was *de rigueur* for aspiring architects. Jacques Boyceau's influential *Traité du jardinage selon les raisons de la nature et de l'art* (1638) recommended the study of geometry, draftsmanship, architecture, and aesthetics in addition to practical horticultural work. According to Boyceau, strict rules obtain for the design of garden structures; for example, the width of the side pathways or *palissades* branching off from a major *allée* must be exactly two-thirds of the width of the main avenue. Controlling the composition of the garden was an entire set of proportions significantly similar to the proportional ratios ruling Palladio's designs for the Palazzo Chiericati.[43] Designers even regulated walking by prescribing a correct cadence attuned to the spatial positions of fountains and statues![44] On the other hand, the French displayed a poignant sense of the magical power of geometry. The central axis at Versailles, for example, was not simply a line imposed on a flat plane—had it been merely this, it could not have been such a cynosure—but, in its dynamic force, a condensed expression of regal power. It can be said that the general plan of Versailles "is all vast, straight, linear, simple, formal, strong, and generous, a pattern that speaks of power."[45] Indeed, the French regarded the power of lines and numbers as Hermetic, here drawing on another property of Hermes: his penchant for secrecy and silence.[46]

Given such an ambivalent use of geometry in the conception and design of gardens, we are left wondering how the two currents could coexist in one and the same "site" (a word which itself betokens the dominance of geometry). The answer is: *not just by way of contrast or even complementarity but by outright compromise*, a compromise between the (projected) perfectionism of the plan and the (imputed) irregularity of nature. The place of the garden is the compromised (and decidedly illusory) in-between of these two extremes. To its creation many things contribute. For instance, when certain *parterres* at Versailles were employed as theaters, a wholly artificial backdrop, presenting an imaginary scene, would sometimes cut off the actual view down an *allée*; at other times, an elaborate artificial frame would surround an *un*impeded view but give the impression that the view as a whole had been painted. In the end, we can regard the entire enormous estate at Versailles as a theater, in which otherwise antithetical terms such as the contrived and the natural, the formal and the numinous, the geometric and the political, conjoined in endless combinations.[47]

Gardens thus deployed in the service of illusion are exemplary cases of transitional space as discussed in the preceding chapter. They exist between the abstractness of a formal plan and the concreteness of surrounding nature, between "the manmade and the natural at the level of the entire visible environment."[48] Lacking the fixity of the plan, they possess more regularity than nature in its wilder outreaches. This is not to say, however, that a formal garden is a mere go-between. It has its own peculiar properties of ephemerality, fluidity, dynamism of appearance, ease of access and exit, and aptitude for masking and occluding. Although illusory garden space is *on* the earth, it is not *of* the earth. Nor does it set forth a completely coherent world, being too transitional for worldhood as well. The Heideggerian option of earth versus world fails to capture the garden in its illusoriness and transitionality.

Heidegger's model of strife-torn space is at odds with a scene of playful illusion where magical transformations can occur. At Versailles the visual sensations of looking and the kinesthesias of walking, far from being discrepant, come together in a momentary but exhilarating union. Compresent in this union were plants and flowers, scenes acted and painted, the sounds of fountains and caged birds, along with music and declaimed poetry. The garden became a veritable *Gesamtkunstwerk*, a total work of art.

The paradox is that just such scenographic placefulness lends itself to extreme formalization. The French formal garden created an open transitional scene that colluded with high-handed geometrization. A garden such as that at Versailles bears rigor in the very midst of its most animated and sensuous displays. Indeed, the rigor supports and makes possible the displays themselves. Another side of the same paradox is the otherwise unexpected sensitivity to the natural setting exhibited by this garden of art and artifice—a sensitivity already apparent at Fontainebleau, about which Joseph Addison observed: "The King has humored the Genius of the place."[49]

But gradually, during the course of the seventeenth century, humoring the landscape gave way to an effort not just to dominate but to *incorporate* it. Thus landscape architecture came to claim even the landscape beyond its outermost perimeter. Artificial avenues and piercing vistas, traversing the illusory space of the garden proper, reached out into the far country in an aggressive and voracious manner. Instead of wilderness threatening to penetrate gardens, gardens now penetrated wilderness: "Here, for the first time, the pattern garden, previously cut off from a hostile world by a clear and definite edge, plunges through that edge and invades nature."[50] Invasion prepares the way for incorporation; the garden has become an advancing edge, moving into the natural world so as to take it over for its own illusory purposes. The final illusion, then, is that the environing world can be kept at a considerable distance—pushed back and out of the garden—and yet, *precisely because it is held at such a distance*, it can be included in one's lingering view down a never-ending avenue of sight.

At Versailles and elsewhere, Le Nôtre proved that he could "bring the whole countryside, wrested from the 'charmless and disorderly,' into the frame of the expanding garden."[51] For Le Nôtre, nature was very much a matter of space, the kind of space whose indefinite extension allowed for incorporation into a site, a geometrically determined and regularized site, that is. Just as the Cartesian project of mathematizing nature claimed to comprehend all of space construed as extension, so the official gardener of the Sun King attempted to encompass all of the environing land within a given site. It is thus not surprising to learn that Le Nôtre taught Descartes's *La dioptrique* to his students or that Descartes in turn consulted the great architect's plans for the Tuileries gardens.[52] The philosophical imperialism of the "father of modern philosophy" rejoined and reinforced the (e)state imperialism of the father of formal gardens in a common expropriation of the natural world.

French gardeners after Le Nôtre did not continue in anything like his grand manner. A scant half-century after Le Nôtre's death in 1700, Jean-François Blondel published *Architecture Française*, a book that praised "the beautiful disorder that produces valleys, hills, mountains."[53] By the 1780s, Jean-Joseph de Laborde was able to design a "park" such as Méréville that exhibited a pronounced Romantic sensibility. The park was filled with cascades, caves, rustic bridges, and vistas of an apparently undisturbed natural landscape. I say "apparently undisturbed" because, by an ironic twist, the appearance of the natural had to be carefully engineered: "Nature itself had to be shaped and manipulated into a picturesque composition."[54]

In other words, nature had to become more like itself or, rather, more like an idealized *image of itself.* The image came from classical literature (especially Ovid and Virgil) and from French landscape painters of the seventeenth century (primarily Claude Lorrain and Nicolas Poussin). The British, however, were most attentive to this image and first sought to put it fully into place in their outdoor gardens. Alexander Pope led the way early in the eighteenth century, believing that the aim of landscape architecture should be "the amiable simplicity of unadorned nature."[55] Trees, only one of many elements in French formal gardens, became the focal point of the British landscape-gardening school. William Kent, in a move at once egregious and revealing, planted dead trees in Kensington Gardens. "Wherever possible," writes a historian of English gardens, "mature woodland was remodelled to provide immediately the effects required."[56]

In a sense, this arborophilia represented a return to the medieval tradition of respecting nature in its pristine state. But instead of pruning nature and enclosing it behind cloistered walls, the new goal was to leave, or at least *appear to leave*, nature in an unenclosed and unaltered condition. Such an unencumbered nature was both accessible to and continuous with human habitation. The pursuit of this project of including an apparently unchanged nature within the garden proved circuitous, requiring the creation of yet another illusory space by an unprecedented alliance of gardeners and painters, each group invoking the word *landscape* in its self-description.[57] "All landscape gardening," said Pope, "is landscape painting."[58] The result was an extraordinary situation in which, for instance, the gardens of an estate such as Stourhead looked as if they had been pulled out of a painting by Claude and given three-dimensional life. And as always in illusory space, the reverse was also possible: Constable's celebrated *Winvenhoe Park, Essex* looks very much like an actual park designed by Capability Brown.[59] By the time Constable painted this scene in 1816, landscape painter and landscape architect had acquired practically the same sensibility: they were natural partners in the renaturing of nature.[60]

Most important was an assiduous cultivation of the material landscape, calculated to dissimulate itself *as cultivation.* When Brown redesigned the grounds of Blenheim Palace, he dammed the river Glyme so as to form a broad lake standing before the palace and looking as if it had been there from time immemorial. Concealing the dam and removing existing formal gardens almost entirely, he planted trees around the whole estate to create pastoral scenes that seemed to have arisen unbidden from the land—or from a painting by Constable.[61]

"At no other time in history," writes Norman Newton, "has there been such general interest in gardens and in the total physical landscape."[62] For in eighteenth-century England we observe a remarkable experiment: the *actual* inclusion of full-bodied nature within the bounds of architecture, no longer limited to incorporation by representation (as in classical Chinese gardens) or by perspectival viewing (as at Versailles). "For the first recorded time in the history of outdoor design, the landscape gardener actually *built* landscapes in presumed conformity with wild nature."[63]

Building landscape? Do we not usually build dwellings? To begin with, we need to recognize that the gardens in question were closely linked with dwelling, and not just in the pristinely delimited manner of the French formal garden, where dwelling occurred only as walking (and pausing). In contrast with Versailles or Vaux-le-Vicomte, the English garden was thought to contribute directly to dwelling-as-residing. We see this link in the prototypical garden (or "park," as it was often called) at Stowe, on which both William Kent and Capability Brown left their mark (figure 15).[64]

Notice that the house, without mediating porches, gives directly onto the lawn. Not only does the landscape go right up to the edge of the house; it entirely surrounds, literally com-prehends, the house. We are a long way from Bury, with its walled-in gardens conspicuously distinct from the château proper. Rather than the gardens being oriented in relation to the house (or château, or palace) as the vital center or source of a built place, the residence is oriented outwardly toward its environs, giving directly onto *them* as the emphatic focus of the scene.

A landscape architect such as Kent, Horace Walpole said in a celebrated *mot*, "leaped the fences, and saw that all nature was a garden."[65] Not that *all* distinction between park and field had to be erased, but anything resembling a border*line* was blurred. As might be expected, Brown hid borderlines as much as possible, sometimes digging trenches called "ha!ha!'s" that were invisible from a distance.[6] And a couplet of Pope's expressed the prevailing attitude:

He gains all ends who pleasingly confounds,
Surprises, varies, and conceals the bounds.[67]

Thus, around many of the great estates of the period, a "belt" of trees served to mark off an estate's outer limits from surrounding countryside while, at the same time, providing a view back upon the estate. In no way to be confused—even if cartographically and legally identical—with a property line, the belt is a *boundary* possessing both density and porosity.[68]

Both English and French gardeners were concerned with opening a prospective window onto a more encompassing view of the natural world than was permitted at Bury, much less in a confined medieval garden. Both kinds of gardener wished to avoid the kind of strict limit that a wall or other fixed perimeter imposes. But if the ambition of the French was "to make the domain [of the estate] so vast that no one in his senses could ever attempt to reach the term of it,"[69] the English were concerned with establishing an ac-

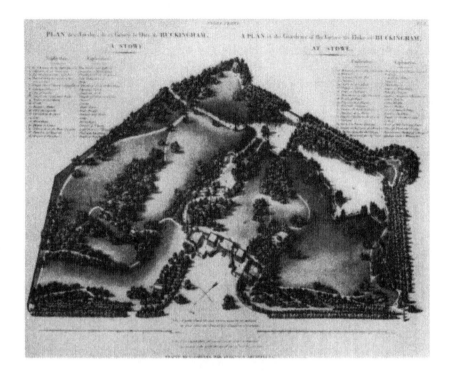

Fig. 15. Stowe, as remodeled by Capability Brown.

tual continuity between estate and nature such that the two could be said to blend indistinguishably at their respective edges:

> Like Le Nôtre in France the century before, Kent saw no further need to exclude a hostile nature. In his leap, though, he ran to embrace a congenial new partner, not, as in Le Nôtre's case, to celebrate victory over a vanquished foe.[70]

In the layout of their gardens, French formalists relied on perfectly regular lines that formed circles and triangles, and especially rectangles and squares.[71] In particular, their reliance on *straight* lines—at once hermetic and Hermetic—was unwavering. This reliance reflected the fact that a straight line, being made up of a dense series of contiguous points, is a group of determinate positions. From each position, one can gain a determinate view, a literal "stand-point," from which to look up or down a linear *allée* during a formal promenade.

British gardeners, in contrast, were advocates of what was appositely called the "wavy line." Kent even propounded the axiom that "Nature abhors a straight line."[72] More than anyone else, though, Capability Brown put the axiom into practice by insisting on the curvilinear shapes of natural objects. He envisioned nature as a realm populated by smooth and rounded forms traced out by undulating lines: "contours of green turf, mirrors of still water, a few species of tree used singly or in clumps or in loosely contrived belts—and that was all."[73] It was enough to realize a reversal in sensibility whose effects we still experience, as when we say that we prefer "unadorned nature" in private lawns and public parks.

The crucial issue is not merely that of wavy versus straight lines. Behind a commitment to the "wavy" or the "straight" lies a deeper commitment to the "natural" or "geometric" way of conceiving of gardens. Where seventeenth-century landscape architects obsessed officially about formal geometry—while being drawn *sub rosa* to its numinous aspects—the demise of this obsession in the next century, especially in England, meant that another principle of architectural design was to prevail. Recourse to nature as a primary resource of such design was a response to a growing conviction that many formal gardens—Dutch and Italian as well as French—were contrived and "artificial" precisely because they invoked Euclidean or Cartesian geometries as universal solvents. If such geometries laid claim to describing the eidetic structure of the physical world, they were nevertheless notably in-solvent as a basis for building gardens. By the mere fact that gardeners have at their disposal so many ingredients of the unbuilt and pregiven world of nature, they are in league with a world that is not fully geometrizable in a formal manner.

Philosophically expressed, it is a matter of recognizing, as Spinoza had recognized in a comparable reaction to Descartes, the inherent power of *natura naturans*, i.e., nature as ample and formative and spontaneous, in contrast with *natura naturata*, nature as parceled into determinate and inert entities. But Pope put it much more directly: "Consult the *Genius* of the *Place* in all."[74] The *genius loci* was the inspiration of Kent and Brown as master architects of the new sensibility.

But instead of simply pitting geometrism against naturalism—as is so tempting when doing intellectual history—we must realize that Brown and Kent, like Le Nôtre and Palladio before them (and like Le Corbusier and Frank Lloyd Wright after them), also offered a new synthesis of these divisive alternatives. What makes the work of these two "landscape gardeners" of such enduring interest is the fact that they did not, in contrast with those who pursued the Romantic ideal of the "picturesque," hold geometry and nature dogmatically apart from each other. If they set formal geometry aside, they also put in its place a new conception of the geometric, more in keeping with what Husserl considered a geometry of vagueness. In such a geometry, shapes such as "the notched" and the "umbelliform" count as valid objects of investigation.[75] In its kinship with topology, this nonformal geometry calls for participation rather than abstraction, soliciting the visitor to engage in the natural world made one with the garden proper, not just to meditate or promenade but to amble along winding paths and to touch the trees and flowers that diversify the scene.[76]

In articulating a new sensibility, then, Kent and Brown practiced a genuine topological-participational geometry of vagueness in their landscape designs and realized plans. The apparent simplicity of these designs and plans, relying as they do on easily perceptible tonal contrasts between light and shade (and between various basic colors and textures), instantiates the generous and spontaneous tendency of nature to set itself forth in vague yet potent shapes.

IV

I have been concentrating on gardens mainly because of their capacity to exhibit a range of relations between the naturally given and the intentionally cultivated. Gardens do so more fully and more revealingly than do domestic or institutional buildings, which, with rare exceptions, tend to exclude or ignore the natural world.[77] But beyond this basic point, gardens offer three special lessons of their own.

i. Gardens embody an unusually intimate connection between mood and built place. Whereas in other kinds of constructed place, mood is often a supervenient phenomenon, in gardens mood is an *intrinsic* feature, something that belongs to our experience of them. We go to a garden expecting to feel a certain set of emotions, and this expectation is not merely a subjective matter but is based on our perception (and memory) of the structure and tonality of the place. This *ambiance of place* was exploited in the "poetic gardens" of eighteenth- and nineteenth-century England, which were constituted from carefully arranged corners and nooks of larger estate parks.

> If "solemnity" was your wish you turned the corner to where a stone urn stood against a background of gloomy yews, or paused by a tomb inscribed "Et in Arcadia Ego." . . . If, on the other hand, the spirit of the rough northern Barbarian were uppermost, a Gothic ruin, ivy clad, with an owl and, for preference, a full moon, produced the appropriate sensations.[78]

The medieval garden in its closed-in, world-apart character was suited for melancholy and reflective moods, while the formal French garden engendered exuberant and "stately" emotions. Apart from its poetic gardens, the British park induced brisk and upbeat feelings aroused by active ambulation in the midst of flourishing arboreal life.

2. Beyond their mood-specific aspects, gardens instruct us as to the expanded building potential of certain material elements. Thomas Whately in his *Observations on Modern Gardening* (1770) identified at least four such elements: ground, wood, water, and rocks.[79] Those who build gardens work with (and within) the inherent media of the natural world. The very term *landscape architecture* suggests as much; taken literally, it means not just building *in* nature but the building *of* nature. In the tectonics of land, we build *out* (and sometimes *down* and *up* as well), shaping and reshaping for purposes that may ultimately diverge from the presumptive aims of the land itself. Such fashioning of the landscape extends to direct engagement with diverse landforms, ground covers, and such elemental factors as light and shade and color: "ecotones" as they have been called.[80]

Capability Brown, who abjured working in color for color's sake, nevertheless capitalized on the interplay of natural illumination and shadow in his landscape compositions. In these compositions, as Walpole said, "Evergreens and woods were opposed to the glare of the champain, and where the view was less fortunate, or so much exposed as to be beheld at once, he blotted out some parts by thick shades, to divide it into variety, or to make the richest scene more enchanting by reserving it to a farther advance of the spectator's step."[81] Yet light and shadow, despite their ephemerality, remain thoroughly natural phenomena.

3. Perhaps most important of all, as built places, gardens offer dwelling of some sort. But what kind of dwelling is this? It is easier to say what it is *not* than what it is. True to the liminality and transitionality of gardens, the dwelling they provide fails to fit the two archetypal forms of dwelling identified in chapter 5.

On one hand, garden-dwelling is never purely hestial. We may pause while perambulating a garden, but we do not stay on for the night. Although we certainly do make pilgrimages to gardens—e.g., the Garden of Gethsemane as well as other gardens we visit mainly for aesthetic reasons—we cannot be said to reside there.[82] Elements of hestial dwelling may, of course, be present in gardens: enclosure of walls, centration of structure, and escape upwards. But hestial dwelling itself, *in-dwelling* in the original sense of *dvelja*, does not occur here. On the other hand, elements of hermetic dwelling may also be apparent: straight avenues, distant vistas, crossing paths, outlying borders. Such elements are especially conspicuous in French formal gardens. We may be divagating from the royal axis in such gardens, yet we never wander in the *dwalde* sense of entirely aberrant straying, since our way is guided at every moment: *homo hortulanus* is not *homo viator*.

If garden experience thus deconstructs the classical dyad of hestial versus hermetic dwelling—a dichotomy already complicated by its own incestuous inbreeding—what does it offer in their place? *No one kind of dwelling proper to it.* To assume that there should be such a single kind is to fail to understand what is distinctive about gardens themselves: their refusal to be adequately grasped in the dual terms by which we construe so many other built places.

In an embowered garden, I *almost* reside, yet I *also* walk about, practicing horticulture, and talk with people who reside in the manor house. At Versailles, I dwell not just by promenading and pausing but by conversing with fellow visitors, painting pictures, and taking in the spectacle. At Blenheim, I dwell by strolling at leisure and going over the grounds; here I come close to wandering, since at times there are no discernible paths. Yet I remain aware that I am not just *anywhere*: Sir John Vanbrugh designed this extraordinary palace for the first Duke of Marlborough, its grounds were redesigned by Capability Brown, Winston Churchill was born here, and the current Duke owns the land in Oxford on which the house I once rented sits. These realizations mean that as I dwell on foot I also dwell in thought, as well as in history—and thus in language and value. At Blenheim or any comparably nuanced garden scene, I dwell in multiple modes, in several registers and on many levels. This leaves me *on the edge of dwelling*, just as gardens take me to the edge between built and natural places, or rather *are* that very edge.

V

Following "the Great Revolution of Taste" in eighteenth-century English gardens, the next stage was to be found in what, writing in the next century, Humphry Repton aptly called "appropriation":

> The views from a house, and particularly those from the drawing-room, ought rather to consist of objects which evidently belong to the place. To express this idea, I have used the word *appropriation* by which I mean, such a portion of wood and lawn as may be supposed to belong to the proprietor of the mansion, occupied by himself, not so much for the purposes of gain, as of pleasure, and convenience.[83]

We detect in this statement not only a characteristic British passion for landed *property*—a word cognate with "appropriation"—but, more particularly, the idea of possessing this property visually. In other words, one appropriates one's own property not just legally but by looking at it from the windows of one's house; one possesses it *in the gaze*. "Appropriation," adds Repton, "describe[s] that sort of command over the landscape, visible from the windows, which denotes it to be private property belonging to the place."[84]

Although the "command over the landscape" recommended by Repton is to be effected *from the place of the dwelling*, dwelling itself has here been constricted and immobilized. No longer the elastic and edgy dwelling made possible by gardens, dwelling now means living in the literal house of residence taken as the privileged viewing point from which a surveillance of one's real estate is to be made. Not only is this oculocentric sense of dwelling the converse of what is found in, say, a Zen garden—*into which* the landscape has been condensed by miniaturized symbolic representation[85]—it also differs importantly from earlier English and French models. In these latter, landscape is viewed *from the garden*, or as itself *in the garden* (or the garden as *in it*), but not from *within the house*. Repton, doubtless reflecting a growing malaise vis-à-vis nature in an increasingly industrialized England, removes the human subject from the garden and places this subject resolutely in the confinement of the house.[86] Dwelling no longer takes place in the garden's open-air "rooms"—a word strikingly applied to the planted units of the outdoor garden—but exclusively in the immured rooms of the permanent residence. We have returned to enclosure with a vengeance. Repton does not wish to banish gardens altogether, but he wants to honor the distinction between natural landscape and cultivated garden that Brown had striven to overcome in his designs for commodious park-gardens. In a fragment written with reference to the improvement of Blenden Hall, Repton states:

> In the art of landscape gardening, two things are often confounded which require to be kept perfectly distinct, viz. the landscape and the garden. To the former belong the lawns, the woods, the water, and the prospect; these may be improved by imitating nature, but a garden, as I have often repeated, is a work of art.[87]

By designating the garden, and the garden *alone*, as "a work of art," Repton intends to make up for its neglect as a circumscribed entity on the part of Brown and his epigones. "The gardens of a villa," he adds, "should be the principal object of attention."[88] A buffer between the enforced orderliness of the residence (where nature is properly possessed and subdued) and the messy disorderliness of nature (where wildness, abhorrent to Repton and his contemporaries, proliferates), the garden retains its position as the domain of the between, but now at the price of being strictly discontinuous with nature. A garden so conceived is situated between the sophisticated French garden and its rusticated English rival. At the same time, it takes us back to a strangely familiar point of origin. As at Amboise and Blois and Bury, the

Reptonian garden keeps *in* only the aspect of nature that can be intensely cultivated, keeping the rest of nature as far *out* as possible.

By the middle of the nineteenth century in England (when Repton's counsel was widely influential), the garden had come full cycle from the middle of the sixteenth century in France: the kitchen garden of the French Renaissance reappeared, on a much more modest scale, in the decorative house garden of the Victorian era. What Repton says of such a garden might have been said of the more ambitious gardens attached to capacious châteaux four hundred years before: "The delight of a garden, highly cultivated, and neatly kept, is amongst the purest pleasures which man can enjoy on earth."[89]

If Repton is right, gardens are cultivated places par excellence. But these paradises on earth have become factitious and secular and shallow. They cling to the bungalows to which they are attached as the last line of defense against an encroaching natural world, their primary function being to keep nature at bay. The irony is that by the time Repton made his recommendation, nature had already retreated to a position from which it could no longer pose a serious threat.

VI

No occupation is so delightful to me as the culture of the earth, and no culture [is] comparable to that of the garden.
—Thomas Jefferson, letter of 1811 to Charles Wilson Peale

Everyone has a garden inside of them. But you have to find your garden. Some people never do. Life doesn't offer it to them.
—Gailard Seamon, supervisor of the Jimmy Jarvis garden in Harlem (cited in *New York Times*, November 17, 1991)

Humphry Repton's claim that "the delight of a garden" is dependent on its being "highly cultivated" should give us pause, not just because many delightful gardens are *not* highly cultivated (keeping in mind that the appearance of noncultivation may itself be highly cultivated), but because the very idea of cultivation cannot be taken for granted. Do we really know what *cultivation* means? "Allons mes amis, il faut cultiver nos jardins." Even this celebrated concluding sentence of *Candide* conceals a telling ambiguity. Does Voltaire intend the literal cultivation of gardens, in accordance with the original meaning of *cultivatus*, "tilled"? Or does he mean something hortatory, such as "attend to your own affairs"? More likely the latter, we presume. But could this latter sense obtain without the former, earthbound sense? And what are we to make of still another extended sense of the word, whereby *cultivated* signifies highly (perhaps over-) educated? Repton is surely drawing on this last sense, as was Voltaire, himself an epitome of the high cultivation of the *philosophes* of the French Enlightenment. Such a strictly cultural connotation seems quite divorced from "breaking the sod," as does the sense in which we can be said to cultivate or "decorate" the interiors of houses. This latter sense, too, is a matter of cultivation, for if we cultivate gardens outside and around the house, why can we not cultivate what is inside as well?

Confronted with the polysemy of *cultivation*—while remaining convinced of its considerable pertinence with regard to the construction and enhancement of built places—we need to find a connecting thread running through the diverse senses of this notion. The thread is to be found in the oldest root of the English word *cultivate*: i.e., the Latin verb *colere*, one of whose basic meanings is "to care for." In tilling the soil, we care for it by ploughing and planting in ways useful to the growing of food. In attending to our affairs, we care for ourselves as creatures who require a certain independence and privacy in relation to other human beings. In pursuing educational aims, we care for our minds, much as we care for our bodies when we exercise or undertake athletic activities. Similarly, in cultivating friendships we care for the social dimension of our existence, a dimension also at stake when we directly "care for" others and "take care" of them.

Cultivation as caring-for extends to the architectural realm as well. Here we cultivate the many ways in which we can dwell in built places: not only in formal and informal gardens but also in institutions and residences, in neighborhoods and entire cities, even in overnight places to stay (inns, hotels, campsites). We cultivate the concrete forms in which we dwell, and we begin by cultivating the construction of places. In former times and in diverse locales (e.g., Bhutan, Rumania, Burma), construction rituals inaugurated the cultivation even before building began.[90] But even without these rites, building remains a form of cultivating.

We must question the presumption that building is an exclusively Promethean activity of brawny aggression and forceful imposition. This is not to deny that wresting and restructuring of materials may be needed in the concrete praxis of building; we encounter prototypes of such praxis as early as Marduk's ziggurat in Babylon and as recently as the Sears Tower in Chicago. But building is also, and just as crucially, *Epimethean*: a matter of attentive "after-thought" (the literal meaning of "Epi-metheus," brother of Prometheus and husband of Pandora). In this latter capacity building is most effectively cultivational in character, for it seeks not to exploit materials but to care for them. In building-as-cultivating, the builder respects the already present properties of that from which building begins.[91] Think, for example, of the care lavished on the creation of building materials by such cultures as the Minoans at Knossos, and which is still evident in the ongoing construc-

174 *Built Places*

tion of Arcosanti in Arizona, where each building block is carefully crafted and made on the building location.[92]

That from which building starts includes not only the actual construction materials—adobe or wood, concrete or metal—but the immediate locus of building and, indeed, the entire surrounding landscape.[93] The builder also starts from the intentions and wishes and practical purposes of those who are to live in the dwelling. Instead of being unquestioned, all of these initial elements of building, including those that are nonmaterial, are *there to be cultivated* by the builder who constructs in an Epimethean way. Cultivation construed as caring-for thus includes all of the following: matching precise grains of wood, finding that a certain column goes well with a given balustrade, realizing that one building design suits the location better than another, discovering that the same design also opens up a dialogue among those who are going to reside in the building it projects, as well as among friends, neighbors, and others who will be affected by this eventual building in some significant way.

Places destined for dwelling are neither merely presented to us as *already made*—*prefabricated* is here a non sequitur—nor can they be built instantly or ex nihilo. Even caves that possess habitable caverns call for cultivation, e.g., by painting animal icons on the walls. In modern dwelling places, the arrangement and rearrangement of furniture, memorabilia, and paintings (i.e., modern secular icons) are essential to achieving a sense of settled-in living. To dwell is to exercise patience-of-place; it requires willingness to cultivate, often seemingly endlessly, the inhabitational possibilities of a particular residence. Such willingness shows that we care about *how* we live in that residence and that we care about it as a place for living well, not merely as a "machine for living" (in Le Corbusier's revealing phrase).

The "on-site" pursuit of cultivation includes the continuation of building by other means than those realized by blueprints and bulldozers. If gardens call for cultivation from without, "interior decoration" represents cultivation from within. But just as the cultivation of a domicile is not limited to decoration in the literal sense of applying décor to the walls, so the interior under cultivation is not limited to the inside walls, floors, or hallways of the abode. To cultivate *its* interior we must cultivate *our* interior; it is a matter of letting one interior speak to another. Thus the particular configuration of a room may evoke resonant reveries on the part of the inhabitant of that room. These reveries, whether imaginative or memorial, *are part of the building as well as the dwelling*. As elicited by built structures and as contributing to ongoing dwelling, they cannot be considered merely "subjective" experiences.

Accomplished painters of domestic interiors such as de Witte and Vermeer convey scenes in which people are seen in moments of profound reverie.

A careful look at, for example, Vermeer's *Lady Reading a Letter at an Open Window* demonstrates that these moments are not accidentally engendered but *issue from the cultivation of the place in which they occur*. Moreover, the reveries in question may be occasioned by the merest object suddenly perceived, such as a mirror or a map on the wall, or even by a nonobject, such as a ray of the sun entering through a window. Part of the logic of interior cultivation is that the size or weight of an entity may be inversely related to its transformative potential. Secondary qualities (e.g., color, light, taste) may be even more important than primary qualities of motion, shape, size, etc. As Proust demonstrates, an entire world awaits us in a single tea-soaked madeleine, provided that the ingestion is part of a scene of intense interior cultivation.

The most intense interior cultivation—in both senses of *interior*—is found in the *home*. Without such intimate cultivation, a house or apartment or hut remains a bare habitation, a built place in which inhabitation has not yet occurred and home has not arisen. But this transformation from building to dwelling cannot occur until cultivation of several sorts, interior and exterior, has taken place. If Bachelard is right in claiming that "all really inhabited space bears the essence of the notion of home" and that home itself is "a real cosmos in every sense of the word,"[94] then home and cosmos alike— home *as* cosmos—result from practices of cultivation. As "our first universe,"[95] home has already been cultivated within and without.

When we think of buildings from the standpoint of cultivation, we release ourselves from a Promethean fixation on greatness of magnitude or boldness of design—"grandomania" in Wright's apposite term[96]—or on sheer efficiency of function (as in the modernist cult that proclaimed "form follows function"), or even on historical irony (as in mannerist and postmodern architecture). We then come to appreciate more fully what Bachelard calls the "intimate immensity" of dwelling places, their capacity to move us even in their most minute details.[97]

Building, construed in this cultivational-Epimethean manner, transforms pregiven places—"building sites"[98]—into places for inhabitation. (Another meaning of the *colere* root of *cultivate* is "to inhabit.") Not only does such building identify the potential for dwelling found in certain unbuilt places; it also realizes this potential itself in the activity of construction, and it carries this potential into new ranges by an attentiveness to the micro-features as well as the macro-features of a given edifice.

We get back into place—dwelling place—by the cultivation of built places. Such cultivation *localizes caring*. What is for Heidegger a global feature of existent human being—namely, "care" (*Sorge*)—is here given a local habitation and not just a name.[99] We care about places as well as people, so much so that we can say that *caring belongs to places*. We care about places in many

ways, but in building on them—*building with them*, indeed, *building them*—
they become the ongoing "stars of our life,"[100] that to which we turn when
we travel and to which we return when we come back home.

<h2 style="text-align:center">VII</h2>

And Jacob went out from Be'er-sheva, and went toward Havan. And he
lighted on a certain place (*Makom*), and tarried there all night, because the
sun was set; and he took of the stones of the place (*Hamakom*), and put
them under his head, and lay down in the place to sleep.

—Genesis 28

Building in a genuinely cultivational manner not only *leads to* dwelling
but, as Heidegger has emphasized, is already part of dwelling. Heidegger
would doubtless be pleased to know that the English word *building* stems
from Old English *bold*, a dwelling. *To build* means, then, both to "construct
a dwelling" and "to take up one's abode, to dwell."[101] Building, in other
words, is not only a *making*, a constructing or fabricating, but is itself a
mode of *dwelling*. Building is not merely the production of a "fabrick" separate from the act of making but is a form of living with and in the very
abode it creates.[102]

Building is already dwelling and belongs to it from the start. This distinctive approach to building was first articulated by Heidegger in his 1951
essay "Building Dwelling Thinking,"[103] and it is tempting to extend this approach still further by asserting that dwelling may even *precede* building. Indeed, Plato suggests just this thesis in the *Timaeus*. In claiming that Space
(*chōra*) makes room for the location of everything determinate (beginning
with the location of mere sensible qualities), Plato proposes that the pre-
geometrized world is *already* a dwelling place on a grand scale:

Space . . . is everlasting, not admitting destruction; providing a situation for
all things that come into being . . . [for] anything that is must needs be in
some place and occupy some room. . . .[104]

What is most striking in this claim is that space is credited with "providing
a situation for all things that come into being." *Hedra*, which is here translated as "situation," connotes place, seat, residence, place of dwelling. What
is there in the beginning is a dwelling place for all that becomes. Such a
place precedes the construction that the Demiurge, the divine architect, will
undertake in the form of geometrically informed building. Thus, given the
Platonic equation between Space and Necessity, dwelling place, as the concrete form assumed by Space, is less the result than the presupposition of
cosmogonic construction. By his sly insertion of the Archytian axiom—"any-

thing that is must needs be in some place"—Plato suggests that the same precedence obtains in more mundane contexts as well.

But if the Heideggerian point may be thus strengthened, the priority of dwelling to building holds *only if building itself is cultivational in character*. Building may presuppose dwelling inasmuch as to build at all may require a world already sufficiently accommodating to be a place *for* building, but not any or every act of building is able to convert this preexisting situation into a scene of inhabitation. Only fully cultivational acts of building will carry cosmic dwelling into the focused dwelling that we call "houses" and above all "homes." We may grant, then, the truth of Heidegger's dictum, "Only if we are capable of dwelling, only then can we build,"[105] so long as we are willing to supplement it to the following effect: only if we are capable of the cultivation building can bring with it, only then are we able to inhabit a built place that has become a dwelling place.

Heidegger is by no means the only contemporary philosopher to promote the primacy of dwelling. Emmanuel Levinas, in many ways Heidegger's most trenchant critic, holds that "the subject contemplating a world presupposes the event of dwelling."[106] Dwelling comes first, and in Levinas's view it precedes both building and the determination of objects of any kind:

> Every consideration of objects, *and of buildings too*, is produced out of a dwelling. Concretely speaking, the dwelling is not situated in the objective world, but the objective world is situated by relation to my dwelling.[107]

Otherwise put—in my own preferred way of speaking—*place precedes site*. For dwelling (in either of its two primal senses of residing or wandering) entails place, just as the world of objects—determinate, physical objects positioned in an extended, homogeneous space—is the basis of site. The building of "dwellings" is thus the realization of a power inherent in place itself, its architectonic and cultural concrescence as it were.

Once more we must resist the temptation to think of building as nothing more than literal construction, i.e., the fabrication of objects and of sites. And we must resist just as strongly the temptation to think of building as inherently guided by the postulates and shapes of plane and solid geometry. The Demiurge may be so guided, but human beings submit to these postulates and shapes only to their inhabitational peril. For his part, Levinas espouses the priority of dwelling over the geometric fixation of entities: "The *somewhere* of dwelling is produced as a primordial event relative to which the event of the unfolding of physico-geometrical extension must be understood—and not the reverse."[108] The reverse, of course, is precisely what Galileo and Descartes had maintained, namely, that the primary qualities of *res extensa* are geometrically specifiable, while the secondary or tertiary qualities (among which "the somewhere of dwelling" would have to figure, along with color, texture, etc.) are not thus specifiable.[109] To agree with Descartes and Galileo is to denude both the natural world *and* geometry of much of their own expansive significance. It is to deny the blatant fact—especially blatant in the case of cliff-dwellings—that the world of nature can facilitate human dwelling, while overlooking the possibility of alternative informal geometries and topologies of the sort elicited by the design and experience of gardens.

Levinas's point is that, in spite of the Cartesian-Galilean attempt at reversal, when I exist in a dwelling I *am somewhere*. The ambiguity of "somewhere" (*quelque part*) is revealing. On one hand, its intrinsic vagueness leads us to attribute to it an amorphous, merely floating quality that threatens to undermine its locatory power, especially if this power is predicated on the unquestioned predominance of simple location in Whitehead's sense of the term. On the other hand, to say that I am, indeed, *somewhere*—somewhere *in particular*—is to emphasize that I am concretely situated. In Plato's language, it is to say that I have a discrete place (*topos*) in occupied space (*chōra*) and am not hanging in the void of empty space (*kenon*). In my own way of putting it, this means that I have assumed a proto-place and am not merely positioned or pinpointed at an indifferent site.

The somewhere of being-in-place is therefore to be contrasted with the nowhere of being-in-site. Frank Lloyd Wright said of the modern mass-produced houses he abhorred that they "[do] not belong anywhere."[110] Instead of being somewhere in place, they could be anywhere in space. Or let us say that they have nowhere to *be*—to be dwelling places where building and cultivating combine in making inhabitation possible.

VIII

... So haben wir dennoch nicht die Räume versäumt, diese gewährenden,
diese *unseren* Räume.

—Rainer Maria Rilke, Seventh *Duino Elegy*

I emphasized in part two the way the lived body brings us into the somewhere of corporeal implacement. In the present part I have been exploring how built places return us, immeasurably enriched, to the same implacement. Just as the lived body refuses to be reduced to a sheerly physical fact or object, so built places (into and out of which the same body moves us) cannot be confined to their purely physicalistic predicates. Buildings as places cultivated for dwelling—to start with, for the in-dwelling of our own lived bodies—resist construal as sheerly constructed things. They exceed their own construction by giving rise to familiarity and reverie alike. As physical and yet other-than-physical, buildings furnish to our implacement a multiplicity of constructed environments within which mini-worlds of imagination and memory can exfoliate at leisure.

To be engaged bodily in a built place is already to dwell in that place. This is so even if we do not stay there for any considerable time: quantity of duration is no more the critical issue than is quantity of material or volume. We can feel at home right away in certain built places, while in other such places a lifetime of residence will not lead to any comparable sense of at-homeness. The "somewhen" is as radically indeterminate as the "somewhere," and both escape the confinement of purely quantitative determination. In discovering our whereabouts and whenabouts in built places, we begin to experience the "felicitous space" of habitational being-in-place.[111] Within such space, we find ourselves somewhere and somewhen in a situation that is not simply laid out in extensive space but lived out in intensive place. This place is the place of dwelling. In being bodily in built places, we enter that cultivational place-world in which imagining and remembering, self and other, primary and secondary qualities, inside and outside, house and city, garden and nature—and finally, building and dwelling themselves—are no longer exclusionary entities but have become compossible presences.

The home may well be our first universe, but it is far from being our only world. We travel to and inhabit other *cosmoi*: on hot summer days in Kansas I journeyed to the felicitous space of the Jayhawk arcade. Just as places are built in innumerable ways—built out and up, built over and overbuilt, even built down (as in the deconstructionist architecture of Gehry)—so we relate to them in multiple manners. If we do start from home and eventually return there (to my study, for example), we also go out into a larger world of interrelated places; as Rilke has it, a world of "generous spaces" (*gewährenden Räume*). For the individual human being, the core of this more encompassing world may remain the home-place, out from which so much energy and so many memories and reveries proceed. But other places and groups of places draw us out of the intimate isolation of the home. What do we encounter when we walk out of the house and into the capacious world of places that are no longer "our spaces" (*unseren Räume*)?

We walk into a world that is as much characterized by exteriority as the home is qualified by interiority. If we live in a city, we walk or drive on open sidewalks, streets, highways, covered walkways, and other public thoroughfares. We encounter edifices that exhibit complicated combinations of internal and external spaces, post offices, city halls, churches, libraries, schools, shopping malls. These public buildings are pocketed with places designed to enhance "commerce" in the broadest sense of the word. Transitional spaces of many kinds also abound in the aroundness of the urban environment: street corners, "roundabouts," even a park reminiscent of more expansive natural realms outside the city limits. If we are fortunate, we come upon an inviting and welcoming place such as the Piazza San Marco in Venice or the Jimmy Jarvis garden in Harlem, where people pause and reflect in the midst of their frenetic lives.

Moving about in a city draws us away from the interior depth of a home and into the exterior breadth of a wider urban world. It is hardly surprising that we find homelessness mainly located *in cities*, which are in many respects the antipodes of homes. Cities certainly contain homes, but in their capacity to demand and distract they are continually luring us into the streets. They take us out of our homes and into a more precarious and sometimes hostile extra-domestic world.[112]

If it is true that gardens of all kinds entice the lived body out of its self-stultified stationariness, cities also act to animate this same body. They move it out not toward a circumambient nature but toward a more extended social space that finds its most fitting expressions on stoops of apartments, in meetinghouses, and in other urban places where groups of people gather. In these places of congregation, distinctive forms of cultivation occur, ways of caring in common that range from how people greet and talk with one another to how they work and disport and are affectionate together. (And ways of *not* caring: being aggressive and indifferent and cruel toward one another.) Often the most significant unit is the "block" or neighborhood or district, that is, a middle-range region of acquaintance and friendship situated somewhere in between the home and the city.

Even the barest allusion to city places indicates what a daunting task it would be to give anything like a comprehensive account of built places. Their kinds, their history, their exact modes of situatedness, their precise forms of inhabitation, their particular styles of construction (and destruction) are so manifold as to defy complete, or even adequate, description. I shall not even begin to attempt such a *catalogue raisonnée*.

In this chapter my aim has been much more limited. I have traced out just two basic movements: a movement *back*—back into the prehistory of built places—and a movement *out*: out into the natural world toward which gardens gesture. I have not searched for formal structures of the sort exemplified by those oppositional dyads of bodily orientation or pairs of prepositional postures on the agenda in preceding chapters. Although I have noted in passing certain triads—e.g., "out–in–up" and "way–over–there"—my primary effort has been to pursue more substantive and suggestive series of terms.

The main such series has been house–garden–nature. A subsidiary series, to which I have briefly pointed just above, is that of house–city–region. If we consider that "house" appears in both series, we may be led to think of it as some kind of anchor term. In fact, it is tempting to posit the house as a prototypical built place, and on this basis to conclude that "the world is a house." But just as we have seen that there are many worlds of built places, so we should not take the house to be foundational in any strict sense. It is not the module or unit of gardens or cities or regions, much less of the natural world, which has its own quite different modules. We may start from the home, but we need not begin with the house. Other kinds of built place can be of exceeding importance, if not for residence proper then for many forms of nonresidential experience. The fact is that one can begin with any one term in the two series in question and move from there to any other term, proceeding forward or backward, and still find among the various terms "a unity of mutual implication."[113]

Implicit in the implication—enfolded in it at every step—is the lived body. If this body is more obviously active in the first substantive series (i.e., in the perambulations and synesthesias that gardens and houses and nature so often solicit), it is no less indispensable to the second. Indeed, the lived body enlivens and connects all five forms of implacement at stake in both series of terms: houses, gardens, nature, cities, and regions. To this body's active agency we owe "the liveliness and evocative power of placement."[114] Not only does it locate us in houses and gardens, homes and cities, nature and region; it also allows us to experience each of these in ever-new possibilities of building and dwelling.

If it is true that "the house, the body, and the city are the places where we are born or reborn and from which we step into a larger world,"[115] the home, the garden, and surrounding regions are likewise worlds of birth and rebirth in human experience. All of these are distinctive place-worlds that offer ways into a continually enriched implacement. Everywhere we turn when we build and dwell—and we always turn with and upon our lived bodies—we find ourselves turning in the places we have elicited or encountered by our own actions and motions.

PART IV

Wild Places

Once in his life a man ought to concentrate his mind upon the remembered earth. He ought to give himself up to a particular landscape in his experience; to look at it from as many angles as he can, to wonder upon it, to dwell upon it.

—N. Scott Momaday, as cited by Barry Lopez in *Arctic Dreams*

Our relation to the natural world takes place in a *place*.

—Gary Snyder, *The Practice of the Wild*

7

The Arc of Desolation and the Array of Description

He . . . to the border comes / Of Eden, where delicious Paradise . . . Crowns with her enclosure green . . . the champain head / Of a steep wilderness.

—John Milton, *Paradise Lost*

Nature is still elsewhere.

—Ralph Waldo Emerson, "Nature"

I

BEYOND THE cared-for garden lies insouciant wilderness; beyond the open field is the dark forest; beyond the flat floor of the desert distant mountains rise shimmering at the horizon; and beyond the halcyon harbor there is the savage sea. Thus we return to the wilderness with which we began.

Even if we often move by indirection, we always move into wilderness with our own lived bodies, whose directionality and dimensionality serve to situate us in the near and far spheres that encircle us. In particular, the body's arclike gestures adumbrate in advance certain basic structures inherent in the environing wild world—structures we shall discern in this new part. These gestures, acting as anticipatory a priori of the body, forecast the very structures they also manage to rejoin. Lying between the body as "the natural subject of perception" and the natural world it perceives is a pact already in place, a com-pact such that each entity shares in a common integumentation.[1] The compact itself is delineated by various forms of arc, some of which (such as the arc of reachability) belong mainly to the body, while others (such as the horizonal arc) inhere primarily in the natural world. In between, and belonging equally to both, are the articulatory and tensional arcs that intensify the bodily experience of built and natural places.

Yet this general movement is far from unproblematic in character. One set of problems stems from a continual dichotomization to which my own examination has been subject. Ironically, the very term I introduced at the

beginning of the preceding chapter in order to counter this dualizing trend—
i.e., *nature*—has itself fallen prey to the same trend. I refer to the emergence
of contrasts between the built and the unbuilt, architecture and nature,
building and dwelling, and especially the cultivated garden and the uncultivated natural world. In this chapter and the next we shall encounter certain
other dyadic pairs, most notably culture–nature, word–image, representation–experience, civilization–wilderness. Yet we cannot lay all the blame at
the feet of such paired terms: unpaired or multiply linked terms bring with
them their own problems. What is most important is to interpret these terms
in ways that are descriptively rich and philosophically productive.

Another set of problems is in fact more grave; these bear less on language or method than on matters of substance. Is the natural world really
something we *edge toward*? Is this world to be conceived as nothing but a
border or perimeter? The very idea of edging *out* from built places into the
wild world beyond presumes the primacy of a humanocentric starting point:
the hearth, the home, the house, the city. We have just seen that these centers
cannot hold; capacious as they are, they cannot contain the diversities and
vicissitudes of the place-world. Must we always begin then with an anthropocentric *Anlage*? Or, if we have already so started, need we stay there? Are
there not other places to go, as well as other places to start from? Just as we
have questioned the somatocentrism that lurks in approaching places from
the body alone, so now we must question the anthropocentric (or more exactly, the domocentric) belief that the most significant motion is from built
places into the natural world, as though this latter were some secondary
realm, a mere outpost of human experience to be entered belatedly and on
tenterhooks.

One thing is certain: the very act of putting the nonhuman world at the
periphery of what is cultivated marginalizes Nature. But what if Nature
(which I shall henceforth capitalize when stressing its sovereign stature as an
unassimilable Other) is the primary term, not to be held in abeyance on the
periphery of civilization? What if the supposed margin is itself a center? In
other words, what if Nature is the true a priori, that which was there first,
that from which we come, that which sustains us even as we cultivate and
construct? "I heard the earth singing beneath the street," writes Wendell
Berry.[2] Nature is not just *around* us; or rather, there is *no getting around*
Nature, which is at all times *under* us, indeed *in* us. In this regard, Nature
can be considered the Encompassing, not just in Jaspers's sense of the all-in-
clusive (*das Umgreifende*), but also in the literal sense of the word, "to be
within the compass of."[3] In this en-compassing capacity, Nature resists dichotomizing, even as it submits to analysis and reflection.

At the same time, we must recognize that Nature, too, possesses interiority, having its own depth and its own domesticity. It is not purely exterior or separate, despite Hegel's earnest effort to conceive it as the pure "outside-itself" of Spirit.[4] Nature also has its own time, rhythmic and seasonal in ways that at once eclipse and undermine chronometric time. The sea's own seasons surpass and continue to challenge the magnetic compass and the marine chronometer alike. Just as knowing where we are does not preclude shipwreck in a tempest, so knowing *when* we are somewhere in particular does not suffice to save us from tempestuous times.

In the end, humanocentrism and temporocentrism are close philosophical bedfellows. The presumptuousness of the former—arising from the *superbia* of the High Renaissance—is linked with the obsessiveness of the latter, which tries to enframe events in precise clock time. In both cases, the unquestioned premise is that what matters most is what happens in the human realm. (Not surprisingly, Western European nations enlisted Harrison's correct chronometric determination of longitude in colonialist and imperialist enterprises during the eighteenth and nineteenth centuries.)

It is time to respect Nature in its own terms, to take our lead from *it* rather than from our own inwrought personal selves and ingrown social structures. I have gestured intermittently in this direction by referring to the importance of landmarks, the horizonal arc, and three-termed eco-variables. My discussion of "region" in chapter 4 opened up the conceptual space for a consideration of Nature as the most encompassing of regions known to us, a region of regions. Furthermore, "cultivation" implies an uncultivated region in which no protective shelter or predelineated pathways may be proffered to us, where we may not only become lost in space and time but may lose any effective control of the situation.

I concluded the preceding chapter by saying that we cannot confine places to those "elicited or encountered by our own actions and motions." Now it is time to underline the word *encountered*. Given that *encounter* is a linguistic cousin of *country*, our encounter with Nature ought to take account of the countryside, a landed region no longer regarded as at the margin of our existence but at its very center.[5] An outright geocentrism—or perhaps better, an engaged ecocentrism—is the most efficacious antidote to centuries of un-self-questioning anthropocentrism and subjectivism (i.e., the two essential components of humanocentrism).

Paradoxically, only with the recognition of the primacy of wilderness will a deeper commonality of the human and natural worlds become evident. Only if earth—the wild earth that includes uncultivated land as well as unregenerate sea—is put first will the human and the natural conjoin in a common world, a *koinos kosmos* whose content and character we must now attempt to discern.

II

I wasn't lost, I just didn't know where I was for a few weeks.
—Jim Bridger, as reported by Gretel Ehrlich, *The Solace of Open Spaces*

What, then, are "wild places"?

In part three we took a concerted look at places cultivated mainly for human residence and delectation. But what of places not yet subjected to cultivation, much less to cults and cultures? Such places are genuinely "wild," that is, they have not been brought under the modifying and restraining that civilized, settled human existence brings in its train. This is not to say, however, that the distinction between cultivated and wild places is something simple or perduring. Indeed, the distinction itself may not apply during that era of prehistory when human beings were hunters and gatherers, for at that time movements from place to place were such that no hard-and-fast difference between dwelling-as-residing and dwelling-as-wandering could yet be made. This early epoch of presettlement came to an end when increasingly stable agrarian societies arose about ten millennia ago. With the advent of repetitive and adaptive agricultural practices came lasting settlements, i.e., "steads," homesteads and farmsteads, places of reliable and cyclical cultivation.[6] Such places, whether created from already existing clearings or carved out from a rebarbative Nature, stood steadfast against the uncleared natural world, in other words, against wilderness.

The idea of wilderness, then, is a comparatively late by-product of human social aggregation. Even if in historical fact wilderness came first, *as a concept* it is the outcome, not the starting point, of the deferred action of culture, in particular of agriculture. By the same token, we would be mistaken to believe that wilderness has always been an object of veneration—far from it. By the time of the Middles Ages in Europe, *wild(d)éornes* (Old English) was regarded as the place (*nes*) of wild deer (*wil(d)déor*). It was also the domain of be-wildered members of the human species, such as hermits, mad people, wanderers, and "savages," who threatened to undo the fragile fabric human civilization had begun to weave. (*Savage* derives from *silva*, woods, forest.) No wonder that throughout Europe, especially in the north, wilderness became a haunt for ghosts and ghouls, witches and werewolves. Such eerie presences undercut any tendency to romanticize or sentimentalize the wild realms of forests and mountains. This tendency would arise much later, when wilderness had lost a considerable portion of its deeply threatening character, when wilderness to fear had long since become land to cultivate, even landscape to appreciate.[7]

By that time—i.e., the end of the eighteenth century in the West—a genuinely Romantic tie to wilderness had arisen and taken elaborate shapes in painting and poetry, as well as in the antiformal gardens and parks discussed in the preceding chapter. In their transformative influence, all such works of art promoted an expanded and often impassioned relationship with wilderness. Not only did they connect the wildness of nature with the artifice of building; on many occasions they *stood in for wilderness itself*. As we have seen in the case of gardens, such standing-in occurred when parts of undomesticated nature were allowed to intrude into their midst, when a garden was located within a partially cleared wilderness area, or when wild regions were represented in fantastic mazelike patterns. In these three basic ways, gardens managed to connect the cultivated and the wild without confusing one with the other, even if "the wild" in question was often wilderness *as perceived* rather than something experienced on its own terms.

In the Old World of the Near East, gardens were linked not just to pleasure and privilege but to redemption and salvation, in fact to Paradise. The Garden of Eden, after all, was a park from which human beings were abruptly expelled. Eden was in no way the result of human cultivation, since it was thought to have existed full-grown from the beginning of time. As in the period of primeval hunting and gathering, no meaningful distinction can here be made between garden and wilderness. The garden, being wholly natural, was wilderness; and wilderness, not yet separate from human habitation, was paradisiacal.

But, as is all too well known, human beings could not persist for long in this state of unconflicted and uncontaminated bliss, any more than they could endure indefinitely as hunters and gatherers. They moved on to a postlapsarian, postnomadic state in which wilderness was no longer integral to human happiness and well-being but was instead experienced as disturbed and disturbing, alienated and alienating. In short, and by a curious return to a very different Near Eastern tradition, that of Abraham's, wilderness came to be regarded as there to be conquered and dominated.[8]

The early settlers of the New World felt the foreignness of wilderness quite acutely. Many had been lured to America in particular by reports of a new paradise, as in Robert Beverley's celebrated early description of Virginia as

> so delightful, and desirable; so pleasant, and plentiful; the Climate, and Air, so temperate, sweet, and wholesome; the Woods, and Soil, so charming, and fruitful; and all other Things so agreeable, that Paradice it self seem'd to be there, in its first Native Lustre.[9]

Beverley published these words in 1705, when Virginia could still be characterized as an "Edenic land of primitive splendor inhabited by noble savages."[10] But by 1782, J. Hector St. John de Crèvecoeur, in his widely circulated "Letters from an American Farmer," underlined the presence of a wilderness harboring human beings who were "ferocious, gloomy, and unsociable."[11] Crèvecoeur was a gentleman farmer of French aristocratic origins who, like many other Colonial Americans, had been forced to clear land for farming. In his "Letters" he spoke disparagingly of "those meadows which, in my youth, were a hideous wilderness."[12] Not even the comely views of wilderness offered by the "landskip" painters decorating the mantels and walls of Colonial houses were able to soften such a harsh judgment.

But in post-Colonial times a new mystique of the Promised Land to be found farther west in America brought with it a decided change of attitude. The trans-Mississippi region in particular was regarded as the scene for the regaining of Paradise from late in the eighteenth century up to the end of the nineteenth century, a period exactly contemporary with the seaward expansion of colonialism made possible by Harrison's marine chronometer. By 1882, a century after the publication of Crèvecoeur's text, the gazetteer Linus P. Brockett proclaimed that the entire region between the Mississippi River and the Rocky Mountains was "destined to be the garden of the world."[13] *Destined* is the crucial word. Although some found the Great Plains a virtual desert, many undaunted homesteaders felt that even the most arid land could be transformed into a new paradise—if not into the world's garden, at least into "the breadbasket of the world."[14] Even this optimism, however, was comparatively short-lived. The lament of an early homesteader in Ohio could also be heard in places farther west: "Instead of a garden I found a wilderness."[15]

After this second round of disenchantment, Americans pursued two opposed strategies. On one hand, the appellation *wilderness* was extended to ever more remote regions: following the Great Plains, to the land of the Far West (e.g., the Rocky Mountains, the vast salt desert, the Sierra Nevadas). On the other hand, by resisting this idealizing projection and staying closer to home, sedentary Americans espoused the option of cultivating wilderness in their own midst. This "middle-state" strategy—midway between casting one's lot with altogether uncultivated wilderness and confining oneself to overcultivated cities—was pursued by farmers who remained at home and cultivated their fields on their own stead. Those who stayed in place (including Crèvecoeur, at least until he fled west from fear of American Indian reprisals) sought a "landscape of reconciliation, a mild, agricultural, semi-primitive terrain."[16]

I do not wish to suggest that the American case should hold our exclusive attention when it comes to the question of wild places. But it does highlight two features found wherever uncultivated wildlands abound: allure and complexity. The allure is such as to draw human beings across entire oceans and continents, leading them to posit the existence of a seductive wild paradise in the next farther region if they did not find it where it was first imagined to be. (The "greener grass" is originally that of an idealized wilderness.) The complexity derives from the fact that the very notion of wilderness is an amalgam of the real and the imagined, the actual and the idealized; its types are manifold, ranging from Edenic to chaotic, the Paradisiacal to the perverse, not to mention the monotonous and the uninspiring. How shall we understand such a bewildering congeries of terms? How can we come to terms with something so radically resistant to conventional cultural categories as "steep wilderness"? Is "wilderness" a cultural category or an abiding independent reality? Does it make sense to speak of "wild places," or is this phrase an unwarranted oxymoron? We may begin to answer these questions by attending to two phenomena known all too well by American colonists and pioneers: *displacement* and *desolation*.

III

My home in Topeka, a mere sixty miles distant, seemed infinitely far away that summer. I had just turned ten, and I was left alone in the hostile hillocks and hollows of Camp Wood, a spartan YMCA facility in a forlorn stretch of central Kansas. I was especially conscious of the sun's merciless assault upon the dry land, heating it up to the point of being bleached. The land itself was wild, virtually untouched since the days of the great bison. The native grasses had grown on the hardened earth from time immemorial, or at least since the great inland sea evaporated some sixty million years before. At night, instead of relief from the scorching sun (and in the absence of anything as cool and comforting as the Jayhawk Theater), I experienced terror: the ground gave way to an abyss of non-being. In this parched place, I felt deeply desolate. I was also acutely displaced, so much so that my anxiety prevented me from participating in the normal activities of the camp. Perhaps the single most poignant moment of my distress occurred when camp members would play war games in the dark. Not knowing the terrain and fearing possible violence, I would slink away from the games and return mortified to my cabin. Never had I felt so desperately alone as during these nocturnal games, which combined elements of nonvisibility, unknownness, isolation, and disorientation. My most fervent wish was for deliverance from this infernal circumstance, and for a rapid return home.

What was happening in this early traumatic experience? Certainly something more than merely missing my home, my parents and sister, or my dog Daisy. All of these things certainly *were* missed and were quite consciously on my mind. But something other than homesickness was at stake. I was feeling a profound sense of emptiness, a vacuum of human affection, a sus-

picion that no one really cared whether I lived or died and that I had been
been abandoned on the windswept plains, deposited there like an indifferent,
subhuman thing.

My painfully memorable experience at Camp Wood was not altogether
unlike that of the early American colonists. Despite the obvious difference
that whereas they wished to settle in the wilderness, I wanted only to flee
it, in both cases the experience of the wild world occurred in youth—that
of a person in one instance, that of a people in the other. In each case as
well, human beings were thrust into circumstances for which they were notably ill-prepared, having come from sheltered lives somewhere farther east.
Most important, all parties were confronted by places, *wild* places, where any
previously claimed humanocentric privilege vanished in a situation whose
terms were dictated by a pitiless Nature.

The word *desolation* signifies an intensified solitariness. To be desolate is
not only to be without hope—dis-consolate—but to feel that one is entirely
alone, without the resources normally offered by friends and family in a familiar dwelling place. (The Latin root, *desolare*, means to abandon.) Desolation is a special form of despair, but a form that has everything to do with
displacement from one's usual habitat. We say with equal facility that a landscape or a person is "desolate," an ambiguity of reference shared by only a
few other words in English (e.g, "beautiful," "gorgeous," "handsome," and
their common converse, "ugly"). This transferability of sense between human
beings and landscapes is heightened by as well as mirrored in the physiognomic character of a given stretch of wilderness.[17] It was not accidental that
I found myself feeling forsaken in an arid and brittle landscape. That landscape embodied my own existential desolation, reflecting it back to me with
augmented force: the land was as solitary under the unrelenting summer sun
as I was solitary in its midst.

The desolate is not just one more sharable trait among others. It is an
emphatic and revealing trait, which allows us to grasp an entire dimension
of wild land that might otherwise be closed to us. Indeed, desolation is not
just a way into the experience of wilderness but is itself a dimension of wilderness, part of its very being.

For instance: we would readily say that much of the landscape in Tibet,
in fact almost the entire central and northwestern region of this enormous
and altitudinous country, which I once visited for almost a month, is quite
desolate. What do we mean when we say this? At the descriptive minimum,
we mean that this landscape is empty, open, and unable to support vegetative
life except in its most limited forms. Such wilderness also resists the spontaneous projection onto it of such reassuring qualities as amiability and in-
vitingness. Thus it is felt to be forbidding or at least unaccommodating to
human designs. At the same time, the desolation implies a failure to fit the

human scale: in the case of Tibet, to be "outsized," exceeding the human scale in such a way as to discourage climbing, building, and residential dwelling. A desolate landscape such as this one aggressively discourages settled habitation of any kind, with the result that nomads alone seem to feel "at home" in its midst. Here, if anywhere on earth, we encounter a landscape that calls for dwelling-as-wandering.

In the forlorn landscape of Tibet I felt abandoned *to myself.* Thrown back onto my solitary self, I looked onto an empty vista that discourages settling or even sojourning in it. One forlornness induced another, keeping in mind that *forlorn* originally signified "lost" (as *verloren* still means in German). One feels lost indeed in a wild country that seems so actively antiresidential. *Its* emptiness, instead of inviting me to enter and live in it, threw me back on *my* emptiness, my own solitude. I became akin to Stevens's "Snow Man," who, "nothing himself, beholds / Nothing that is not there and the nothing that is."[18] The void without was rejoined by the void within. By another twist of the same implacable landscape logic, an acute lack of habitable place led me to experience myself as deeply displaced, as not belonging there at all. Desolation and displacement intertwine and intensify each other.

A desolate landscape may also, paradoxically, give rise to a peculiar sense of *consolation.* In *The Solace of Open Spaces,* Gretel Ehrlich states: "Despite the desolate look, there's a coziness to living in this state [of Wyoming]."[19] The "despite" is meant ironically, since the "coziness" more than compensates for the rigors of the situation. The same holds true of those who live in central Kansas, where drought constantly lurks.[20] *Solace* does not derive from *solus,* "alone" (as does *desolate*), but from *solari,* to console, comfort, or soothe. The desolate landscape can comfort the human heart and console it, giving to the solitary human being in its forbidding midst a sense of genuine (if nonhuman) companionship, of not being entirely alone, of being-with the land's own austere presence. Although alone with respect to other human beings, the isolated figure in the empty landscape finds *in wilderness itself* a con-soling partner. The lonely individual and the desolate landscape form a silent but powerful pact.

This pact was present in the strange alliance between early Christian anchorites and the deserts they inhabited in such precarious ways. Not only did desolation remove temptation, but in the harsh conditions of the wilderness each party sustained the other.[21] Such extraordinary community between desolate human beings and equally desolate surroundings stands in contrast with situations in which people settle easily into fecund and verdant landscapes that seem to welcome them openly: for example, at many points in the Connecticut River valley as it stretches between Canada and Long Island Sound.[22] In cases of this latter sort, the partnership between person and land is based on manifest affordances of dwelling, of new life, of the New World in its green grandeur. Amid such settings as these, "all the greenery abridges space."[23]

IV

In a memorable passage from *The Seven Lamps of Architecture*, John Ruskin hints at the close tie between displacement and desolation:

> The author well remembers the sudden blankness and chill which were cast upon [a scene he was perceiving in the Jura Mountains] when he endeavoured, in order more strictly to arrive at the sources of its impressiveness, to imagine it, for a moment, [as] a scene in some aboriginal forest of the New Continent. The flowers in an instant lost their light, the river its music; the hills became oppressively desolate; a heaviness in the boughs of the darkened forest showed how much of their former power had been dependent on a life which was not theirs.[24]

What had been, just moments before, gloriously unproblematic—a matter of "deep and majestic concord"[25]—was now suddenly transformed into an "oppressively desolate" scene by its imagined *transposition*, i.e., its displacement, into the New World. Indeed, whenever a significant displacement from one landscape to another occurs, whether this be in fact or in fantasy, one risks falling into a state of desolation.

Desolation signifies not merely an effect within a dissociated psyche but something common to psyche and to wilderness alike. At Camp Wood, the displaced campsite and my miserably out-of-place psyche were continuous with the desolation of the scene and my equally desolate psyche. In this unhappy experience, as in Ruskin's thought-experiment, we observe the peculiar power of displacement, physical or psychical, to generate desolation both physical *and* psychical.[26]

The desolating action of displacement consists, I believe, in an exterocentric movement from a real or imagined place of familiarity into unknown marginal areas where desolation is prone to be found and experienced. The familiar place is prototypically a home-place. In the case of my camp experience in Kansas as in Ehrlich's arrival in Wyoming from her native state of California, the central known place was in fact a home, from which displacement had occurred by transposition into new and strange regions. The initial effect of such displacements from a home-place is a primary desolation, one of whose main modes is homesickness. But the place from which departure is made may *itself be displaced*, and then—from its new location—serve as a basis for a further displacement that induces an experience of secondary desolation. Such was the case with Ruskin's *Gedankenexperimente* in the Jura Mountains in southeastern France. The highly cultivated Victorian was already away from his place of birth and education in England, as well as from Venice, his adored "second home." Doubly displaced geographically, he paused on a hiking trail in the lower Alps and projected what the actually perceived scene would be like were it to be set somewhere in North America. Displacement in imagination arose from displacement in fact, and the ensuing desolation embodied and reflected this compounded displacement.

Still, we cannot help but wonder: where exactly does the desolation, Ruskin's or Ehrlich's or my own, stem from? I would suggest that it comes from the confluence of at least two factors. First, there is the *loss of an accustomed center* as the traveler or emigrant moves from the outright domesticity of a place of residence—whether this be California or England, Venice or Topeka—to the uncentered insecurity of a new place, e.g., Camp Wood or Wyoming, the Jura Mountains or the mountains of Tibet. Each of these latter "dis-places" lacks the abiding familiarity that makes the customary place such a supportive scene of bodily movement, visual perception, or active imagination (or all three at once, as in Ruskin's case). Such far-out places are not always frightening or threatening, but they fail to furnish the kind of reassurance that any given center-place, and certainly any domicile, abundantly provides. For this reason, a given dis-place is especially vulnerable to the incursions of desolation. The stable ground of one's primary place of inhabitation and orientation gives way to the uncertain soil of an unknown region, ec-centric in relation to the center of one's habitual experience. To remove oneself from the proto-place of such a center (or, in Ruskin's case, a second such center) is to move into a region of counter-places likely to feel forlorn at first.

Second, *the look of the land (or sea) itself* actively contributes to the experience of desolation. This look or physiognomy of the dis-place conspires with the decentered subject's own psychophysical displacement by proffering itself in four characteristic forms.

1. *Barrenness.* This trait alludes to the look of a landscape empty of generative or life-sustaining features, especially vegetation but also animals and concrete bases for human habitation (e.g., timber for dwellings). The barren is not merely the featureless; it involves the presence of features that exclude or at least discourage the organic life that belongs to the realm of Gaia. The more extensive the exclusion, the greater the sense of desolation. Cases in point are the Barren Grounds of northern Canada or, once again, many parts of Tibet, where the combination of high altitude, lack of rainfall, and dearth of human dwellings, of animals, and of visible plant life creates a forbidding impression of a lifeless world. That there are still minimal forms of life even in this extreme case—i.e., lichens and miniature flowers—does not diminish the desolating force of the barren.

2. *Vastness.* One can perceive barren land or sea in small increments and

find it nondesolate, but when it seems to continue without end, desolation begins to loom. A desolate landscape stretches out so extensively that one cannot tell just where its precise perimeter lies or even how its horizon is to be delineated. Vastness also includes an element of the empty, a sense of being unpopulated or (as in the Barren Grounds or much of Tibet and central Kansas) only sparsely populated. It is not surprising to discover that the earliest meaning of the verb *to desolate* is to depopulate, to deprive of inhabitants. A vast emptiness in the landform answers to and exacerbates a seemingly endless emptiness of emotion, memory, and thought within the person stationed in its midst. But just as such, the vast is still an aspect of place—wild place—not to be assimilated to a placeless vacuum. "The void within ourselves, the loneliness," writes Paul Gruchow, is "the surviving heart of wilderness, [what] binds us to all the living earth."[27]

3. *Impenetrability.* In Tibet, one experiences not only the barren and the vast in the dry steep land but also its unending rock-strewn surface. Everywhere there are loose (and sometimes randomly moving) boulders and smaller stones of varied descriptions. Rarely on earth does one encounter such a prospect of sheer stony essence. The result is an augmented recalcitrance or "hard-heeled" land resistant to cultivation of any kind. Tibetans consider the mining of mountains to be a sacrilege. At most, one is permitted to pile up rocks so as to form *icons* of mountains. The surface should not be penetrated but left intact. What is for the native Tibetan a matter of awe and sacred duty is for the newly arrived foreigner a scene of unremitting forlornness. No need to imagine this scene *elsewhere* in order to appreciate the desolation that arises from its grim impenetrability; it already possesses a maximal "coefficient of adversity."[28]

4. *Isolation.* "The desolate person or place gives a feeling or impression of isolation or of being deprived of human consolation, relationships, or presence."[29] Striking in this formulation is the hendiadys "person or place." As with desolation itself, indeed as a constituent part of it, isolation is not limited to what human beings experience as solitary subjects. It extends as well to the physiognomy of an entire landscape. In a place such as Tibet one senses that *the landscape itself is isolated*; hence its epithet, "the roof of the world," existing alone and aloof from its neighboring countries of Bhutan, Nepal, India, and China. As to what lies beyond a particular group of mountains, one may know absolutely nothing. A glacier, a very deep valley, other mountains of a quite different description, camps of nomads, *almost anything* might be found there. By its fiercely isolated and isolating character, the Tibetan wilderness heightens the desolation the visitor is likely to experience in its barren and impenetrable vastness.

Barrenness, vastness, impenetrability, and isolation: these name only the most conspicuous features composing the desolate look (and feel) of wild land or sea. Taken together, they collaborate closely with the state of being displaced in such regions. The result is an effect of displaced desolation located as much in the contortions of the land or water as in the convolutions of the psyche.[30]

V

The desolate physiognomy of wilderness is doubtless felt most poignantly in circumstances of isolation. Indeed, a vicious circle of isolation and desolation may ensue. The more I feel myself to be isolated (not only geographically but also socially, culturally, linguistically, etc.), the more I will tend to find my surroundings desolate; and the more I perceive these surroundings to be themselves desolate, the more I will feel isolated in various ways. And if I am displaced at the same time—as is often the case—any escape from this circle of the desolated-isolated self will be only that much more difficult to achieve, leaving the entrapped self discouraged and disconsolate.

If I am not entering a previously unknown wilderness area but *leaving* a wild place to which I have become accustomed, different considerations apply. If I have not prepared myself for leaving, or if I am peremptorily forced to leave, then I may well find myself desolated once again. *This* sense of desolation, all too common to those who are impressed into continual exile, consists in an especially dolorous mixture of some of the factors already identified. First, I feel abruptly *displaced from* my current haunts, even if I am not yet fully familiar with them. This in turn leads to a feeling of forlornness, along with the fear that no one, and in particular *no place*, will harbor me any longer. As a consequence, I experience myself as isolated from others, from place, *and from myself in place*.

Because of this triple place-bind, I may cling desperately to my companions (if I have any) and to the wild place itself even as I make my exit. I feel all the more isolated as I realize that I am about to enter yet another situation of unaccustomed challenge and demand while still remaining cathected to the place I am leaving, an attachment that may soon prove to be an obstacle in the new circumstance. No wonder that I feel so despairingly desolate! I am abandoned without adequate resources, poised on a precarious edge between two placescapes, one of which is beginning to lose its presentness just as the other is starting to descend upon me in my unprepared state. Displacement and desolation combine forces once more—this time in a potentially quite paralyzing way. What am I to do in this extremity?

The truth is that no panacea exists for the perplexity just described. While I *can* do something about my desolation on a first encounter with a new landscape—namely, start to become better acquainted with the land by exploration, habituation, and habitation—no such concretely practicable steps are yet available to me at the moment of transition from one place to another. When I am in the process of departure, the main task is to realize an effective detachment from the place I am now leaving, thus clearing the way for attachment to the new place I am about to enter. But such decathexis from place is rarely in my conscious control.

Decathexis is a major part of the work of mourning. *We mourn places as well as people*, and as part of the process we must decathect from both. Freud's model of mourning, although devised to deal with situations of death and other forms of interpersonal abandonment, may be extended to apply to the abandonment of places with which we have become bonded and which we have been forced to leave, often so abruptly that we have not been able to anticipate the consequences in any salutary way. Indeed, as in the case of the displaced Navajo (and still earlier at Betatakin), the consequences may prove so formidable as to defy constructive action.

Freud's instructive model indicates that we only slowly and quite unconsciously decathect our attachment to someone, even as we incorporate that same person into our psyche:

> When it happens that a person has to give up a sexual object, there quite often ensues an alteration of his ego which can only be described as a setting up of the object inside the ego. . . . It may be that by this introjection, which is a kind of regression to the mechanism of the oral phase, the ego makes it easier for the object to be given up or renders that process possible. It may be that this identification is the sole condition under which the id can give up its objects. At any rate the process, especially in the early phases of development, is a very frequent one, and it makes it possible to suppose that *the character of the ego is a precipitate of abandoned object-cathexes and that it contains the history of those object-choices.*[31]

Replacing *object* with *place* in this passage induces quite suggestive results. Could it be that the desolated self comes to terms with a place it is leaving by a place-precipitation comparable to that by which its own character is formed? Is it possible that the reconciled self holds within itself a precipitate of abandoned *place*-cathexes; indeed, that it also contains the history of those *place*-choices? If human beings incorporate not only abandoned loved ones but also totem animals (as Freud adds in a footnote to the same text),[32] is it not plausible to presume that we interiorize places and identify with them as well? And if such internalization of places does indeed occur, is this not itself an effective, albeit unwitting, way of coping with the desolating loss of place brought about by expulsion, deportation, and other forms of peremptory displacement? And is it not also a commemorating of abandoned places within the place-bereft psyche?

By extending Freud's model of mourning to place, we begin to trace the intimate tie between displacement and desolation as it occurs at an unconscious level. What happens at this level is no less important for being altogether unnoticed. Indeed, it can be all the more important for having happened outside the conscious mind. In the end (and mourning always concerns endings),[33] the effect of grieving over lost places can be beneficial and constructive. Instead of being devastated by a rapid or forced departure—as we might well be if we have no recourse to such a mourning process—we may manage to achieve an ultimate reconciliation with our ill-starred fate, learning to live with displacement and desolation even if not to triumph over them. In this subterranean way, displacement can give way to re-implacement in a new landscape. At the same time, the desolation occasioned by displacement may be superseded by an authentic consolation that no longer leaves us isolated from others, from place, or from our own divided selves.[34]

VI

The desert only *appears* uncultivated.
—Jean Baudrillard, *America*

The humanocentrism to which I pointed in opening this chapter is a special peril when it comes to Nature and wilderness, both of which are continually subject to the threat of reappropriation for human purposes. This threat arises, for example, when the arc of desolation—as we might call the desolating-desolated syndrome—is interpreted as a merely psychological matter, as something we human beings *suffer* that has nothing to do with the natural world itself. Even the construal of this arc as having "psychophysical" aspects runs the risk of anthropocentric absorption, especially if we presume that human beings are paradigmatic for all psychophysically specifiable creatures.[35] For the arc of desolation points elsewhere than to human subjectivity and suffering. It points to a Nature that resists appropriation by human interests and concerns and to a wilderness whose natural places are not easily reduced to cultivated places, not even in the covert manner hinted at by Baudrillard. In their autonomy—or more exactly, their autochthony—such a Nature and such a wilderness are "sublime."

Nature is sublime: so runs the Romantic theme that dominates Western art and philosophy of the nineteenth century. In his *Critique of Judgment* (a book without which Romanticism is unthinkable), Kant distinguished the "mathematical" from the "dynamical" sublime. The *mathematical* sublime is summed up in this formula: "That is sublime in comparison with which all else is small."[36] The sublime is here "the absolutely great," that which is beyond all comparison with objects of determinate magnitude.[37] It is hardly surprising, then, that wilderness was regarded by the Romantics as a natural seat of the mathematical sublime. Wilderness gives itself to us as something surpassing what any determinate set of sensations could convey—and as defying exact measurement by the sheer fact of its constantly changing appearances. Of any given wild landscape we could say that it possesses "a greatness comparable to itself alone," thus "transcending every standard of sense."[38] Yielding to survey only with difficulty, wilderness regarded as sublime calls up the idea of infinity, i.e., that which exceeds the efforts of human understanding to grasp it intuitively as a single object with definite limits.[39]

Construed as *dynamical*, sublime wilderness outstrips us still further. Now its sublimity consists in its "might" (*Macht*), before which we perceive ourselves to be powerless and thus "fearful" (*furchtbar*).[40] Although Kant holds that we may set aside such fearfulness by realizing our own ultimate independence of nature as noumenal or spiritual beings, his own examples of the dynamically sublime (e.g., "bold, overhanging, and, as it were, threatening rocks, thunderclouds piled up [in] the vault of heaven . . . volcanoes in all their violence of destruction") point instead to the judgment that "the irresistibility of the might of nature forces upon us the recognition of our physical helplessness as beings of nature" who are subject to constant "humiliation" at the hands of an overpowering natural world.[41] Wilderness is here unleashed in its dynamical wildness, not only too great to measure but also too forceful to contain.

Kant does not speak expressly of "displacement" in his discussion of the sublime in the *Critique of Judgment*. But the realization of human inadequacy in representing sublimity in its mathematical aspect nevertheless effects a psychical displacement, a demotion downward in our self-esteem as cognizing creatures. For we have to admit that however considerable our efforts may be, we cannot measure up to the mathematical sublime. Similarly, the fearfulness and humiliation occasioned by the dynamically sublime displace us from the presumptuousness of believing that we can control nature and are free from its destructive power. When confronting "the high waterfall of some mighty river,"[42] we cannot help but feel displaced in the midst of Nature, unable to accomplish ambitious aims of understanding or of domination. Indeed, "our power of resistance," as Kant avers, is "of trifling moment in comparison with [Nature's] might."[43] Before Nature in its double sublimity and far from any secure home-place, we find ourselves dispossessed of any commensurate natural powers of our own. The result is a state of mind properly designated as "desolated."

Kant twice mentions "desolation" (*Verwüstung*) in his discussion of the sublime. The first mention occurs in the phrase "hurricanes leaving desolation in their track."[44] Here desolation connotes physical devastation, laying waste, making the land barren by depopulating it. The second passage is still more pertinent:

> But in what we are wont to call sublime in nature there is such an absence of anything leading to particular objective principles and corresponding forms of nature, that it is rather in its chaos, or in its wildest and most irregular disorder and desolation, provided it gives signs of magnitude and power (*Macht*), that nature chiefly excites the ideas of the sublime.[45]

Here desolation means something other than material destruction. It connotes Nature in its "disorder" (*Unordnung*) and also signifies Nature as indomitable, wild beyond measure. Thus, when we face nature in its double sublimity, we are not only displaced before it—dislodged, and accordingly dismayed at being unable to function with our usual cognitive and practical efficiency—but also desolated by the prospect of such a deeply disordered scene. We are desolated at being so fearfully dominated by a brute Nature uncontrolled (perhaps even untouched) by *eidos* or *logos*, a Nature, rather, to be grasped as *anankē* and *chōra*.

It is not the void but wilderness that here presents itself as chaos, that is, a disorderly realm fiercely resistant to what Kant calls "ideas involving higher finality."[46] Without the systematic order bestowed by such ideas, Nature is "beyond our reach,"[47] and we as its human witnesses, displaced in relation to it, cannot be anything but desolated. (And sometimes, of course, *exhilarated*, as the Romantics presumed we *should* be. But this presumption is itself presumptuous, being contingent on the attainment of ideal conditions much more difficult to realize than the Romantic poets and *Naturphilosophen* were willing to admit.)

Landscape regarded as an object of aesthetic pleasure, of a distinctly disinterested interest—of "beauty" in Kant's strict sense of that which inheres in "the *form* of the object"[48]—is thereby challenged by landscape regarded as sublime. In its sublimity, a landscape possesses an inherent power of its own that can no longer be contained within coherent eidetic form. It has become wilderness.

Otherwise put, *landscape has become wildscape*. Of wildscape we can say, as Kant says of Nature in its dynamical sublimity, that it is "an object even *devoid of form*."[49] As formless, a wildscape is displacing and desolating in its very being and not just in its presentation and effects upon us as its perceivers. The "limitlessness"[50] of a wildscape exceeds our immediate—in fact, even our ultimate—powers of comprehension, which cannot pass "beyond the narrow confines of sensibility."[51] The most grandiose prospects of Nature, its wildest reaches, throw us back upon the limited resources of merely human cognition.

VII

The Astronomers,
The Philosophers,
The Crowd, of them,
Things, These dangerous feelers, for understanding,
now that I am alone so much I can manage to
hear another thing
singing through my face
describing the arc
and the constant
return . . .
   way out now,
   describing its own voice
   its
   reason

      —Imamu Amiri Baraka, "Evil Nigger Waits for Lightnin' "

In the landscape I am somewhere.
—Erwin Straus, *The Primary World of Senses*

But *are* wild places "devoid of form"? So it may appear, especially when we first enter their midst and find a realm that is, if not chaotic outright, at least confusing in its inaugural appearance. My first apprehension of Camp Wood and its environing hills found something so formless that I could project onto it all of my homesick anxiety. The same amorphousness characterized the wildscape of Tibet as I perceived it during my stay there. Hills, mountains, and valleys were juxtaposed in no recognizable pattern: where I expected vegetation, it was *not*; where I did not expect animals, they *were*. The effect was not just disconcerting but deeply disturbing.

Appearances can be deceptive, and nowhere more so than in the midst of wilderness. Had I not been so homesick at Camp Wood or had I lingered longer in Tibet, I most likely would have detected an inherent design in the confusing appearances. This design would have been found both at the microscale—e.g., that of grass, moss, rock formation, etc.—and at the much larger scale of whole mountain ranges, hill shapes, valley forms, etc. Since it is a matter of the natural world, we can be assured that no matter how wild it is, an immanent order (or, more likely, several orders) will be present, and if this is not evident to us then it will be transparent to a longtime resident or a naturalist standing in our place.

But order also arises at another level, more pertinent for the descriptive analysis I am undertaking in this book. I refer to the order inherent in certain leading traits that characterize wild places. I have already identified several such traits, e.g., barrenness, isolation, impenetrability, and vastness. But grasped as they were on the *via negativa* of displacement and desolation, these features cannot be held to characterize every wild place. Now it is time to consider several traits that apply to all wild places.

Before we can undertake this emotionally and descriptively more positive path, we need to make a basic distinction between wilderness and landscape. Wilderness is not just the detotalized totality of wild places; it is the undespoiled natural realm, Nature in its aboriginal independence. Wilderness is the natural world *not on view*, and especially not on view for human beings' enjoyment or exploitation. Landscape, on the other hand, is the natural world as collected in coherent clusters and *placed on view*. The most prominent instances of such collecting and displaying are found in landscape painting and landscape photography, both of which regard landscape as an object of aesthetic enjoyment. The suffix *-scape* connotes an amassed grouping of entities of the same type:

> [*Scape*] is essentially the same [word] as *shape*, except that it once meant a composition of *similar* objects, as when we speak of a fellowship or a membership. . . . The word *scape* could also indicate something like an organization or a system. . . . If *housescape* meant the organization of the personnel of a house, if *township* eventually came to mean an administrative unit, then *landscape* could well have meant something like an organization, a system of rural farm spaces.[52]

Given the considerable scope of *-scape*, it follows that there are at least as many *placescapes* as there are kinds of place: seascapes, housescapes, cityscapes, aeroscapes, dreamscapes, wildscapes, even thoughtscapes (as in systematic presentations of philosophical concepts, e.g., an "architectonic of pure reason"). But among -scaped notions, "landscape" enjoys a distinctive position. In common parlance, it signifies not just a literal stretch of land-in-view but, by extension, any coherent vista, whether the vista gives onto land or city or self. Hence we say such things as "the landscape of his memories," "the landscape of dreams," "the landscape of my mind," etc. Despite the range of its application, I shall attempt wherever possible to respect the elemental origin of *landscape* in the flora, soil, and other concretions and configurations of the land. In this part, it will refer primarily to the physiognomy of the land, the manner in which the land appears and is taken in. Construed in this more restricted sense, a landscape is not to be confused with, say, a seascape, which connotes the specific ways in which oceans, seas, lakes, and other bodies of water come to appearance.

But a tumultuous sea is a paradigm of wild place. In its overflow and undertow, a roiling sea is a palmary instance of recalcitrance to human shaping. As we know from the difficulty of determining longitude, the unruliness and protean mutability of the sea actively resists measurement. Thanks to the virtual uncontrollability, and sometimes the elemental fury, of tides, ocean currents, and other such implacable phenomena, the sea epitomizes wilderness. In contrast, land more often lends itself to being civilized: if not domesticated, at least cultivated. Its formations are frequently lasting and massive, thus fostering close scrutiny and ambitious building. Nevertheless, land can be evasive and obscure, and the earth itself "continually self-secluding."[53]

The wild places of sea and land alike challenge us to reflect on their inherent forms. Can we discern these forms, despite their resistance to specification?

The forms of wild places can be considered *moments of Nature*, where "moment" is not to be confused with "part."[54] A part or a piece is separable from that to which it is attached, while a moment is intrinsic to a given phenomenon, part of its essential being. In the case of wild places, six such moments stand out: surrounding array, sensuous surface, ground, things, arc, and atmosphere.

Before considering the leading moments of wild places *seriatim*, let us regard them first as forming one simultaneous grouping, as in this diagram:

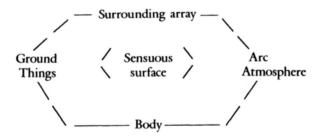

The clustering within this highly schematic (and strictly synchronic) representation suggests a first interpretation. Ground and things are matters of weight, which links them in an indissociable bond. Things relate to each other, and, constellated in various groupings within a wildscape, they come to rest on the ground (typically, but not exclusively, on the topsoil of the earth). Ground and things share in a downward pull ultimately rooted in the force of gravity but felt and perceived as more or less "heavy" (along with associated attributes of bulk, density, girth, volume, etc.). Here we are dealing with the *grave* end of the spectrum of wild places, their densest and most massive aspects. For the most part, these aspects are held immobile within wilderness and contribute to its impassive and stationary visage.

But every wild scene, even the most stolid and unmoving heath, presents us with another face, which takes us toward the *ethereal* end of the spectrum. I refer to the arc and the atmosphere, which, taken together, account for most of what is moving and changing in wild places. If the ground and the things upon it are the settled denizens of the surrounding array, the arc and atmosphere actively animate this array, furnishing it with transitory aspects. These aspects are "light" in both senses of the word: at once weightless (or seemingly so in our perception) and luminous (whether by natural luminescence or by contrived illumination). Color, for example, is conveyed mainly by the arc and the atmosphere in coordination with each other. It is not accidental that we speak of "the play of colors" or that painters find color to be at once elusive and seductive. Nor is it a matter of chance that the rainbow—that most colorful combination of arc and atmosphere ("rainbow" in French is *arc-en-ciel*)—possesses talismanic significance in many cultures. Its brief duration and comparative rarity only enhance its value as a manifestation of the natural world in its diffuse and polychromatic character.

Poised precisely between the grave and ethereal extremes constituted by ground and things and arc and atmosphere is the sensuous surface of wild places. In this surface, or better *on* it, are proffered a number of "secondary qualities." These include not only shape and size but also again color, construed now as adhering to the surface of things, as an identifying characteristic, rather than as something simply evanescent. Whatever qualifies this surface can also qualify the surface of the ground as well. In this way we reach a level of sheer immediacy in which we attend to the sensuous surface *for its own sake*, regarding it with a seemingly disinterested interest. This surface serves as the interface between the two pairs of features clustered at the left and right ends of the diagram. Acting as a bidirectionally porous membrane, it brings these four features together. Without such a commonly contiguous surface, wild places might fall into dispersion, as happens when we perceive these places in certain hallucinatory modes or represent them in the manner of Soutine or De Kooning (both of whom make the sensuous surface independent of the very things it would otherwise connect).

The diagram also shows the subjacent presence of the body and the superordinate presence—the "surpresence"—of the surrounding array. From here *below*, my lived body conducts itself in the midst of the middle realm of things on the ground, above which arc and atmosphere are situated. My body is an insistent interloper in wild places. It transforms the kaleidoscopic presentations of the surrounding array into a readable text of qualities and forms. From *above* and *around* my body this array disposes itself in ever varying patterns that nevertheless help to compose the scene as one identifiable whole. Acting in concert, body and surrounding array effect a double enclosure, creating a (more or less) coherent connection throughout.

The schema intimates that the basic features of a given wild place exist in a state of at least provisional equipoise among themselves. Such equipoise may be the source for the solace and serenity that sojourning in wilderness can bring in its train. This profound pacification, involving the integration of otherwise disparate elements, could not come either from the beautiful alone (it is too decorous to constitute the appropriate depth) or from the sublime alone (for this, in and by itself, can be quite disturbing). To realize the sonority of wilderness, a broader base is required, one in which ground and things, arc and atmosphere, are interinvolved with the mezzo-soprano of the surrounding array and the basso profundo of bodily being.

The same schematism of the wild implies that the lack or dissolution of such equipoise amounts to a structural displacement whose disorder may deeply disconcert us and occasion actual displacements in the life-world. Losing the ground under their feet, the Navajo lost the equilibrium of their landed life. The disequilibrium of a disrupted experience in which ground and things are lacking, or arc and atmosphere remote, or the surrounding array awry, disturbs bodily existence in wild places and consigns its victims to a condition of desolation. Desolating indeed is the effect of wilderness when its felt features have become errant causes, and no longer accommodating signs, of immersion in its midst.

The six moments, or "leading traits" (as we can also call them), are thus not randomly selected. They have a pattern of their own. Moreover, they belong to their own regions. Thus ground and sensuous surface form part of the *earth*, that is, land and landscape, sea and seascape. Arc and atmosphere pertain to the overarching region of the *sky*. Material things are found in between the archaic (and still extant) regions of earth and sky. They pin down and populate this middle zone of existence and experience. The surrounding array does just the opposite; diffused throughout all of the regions and interregions, it acts to connect what material things serve to separate.

We should not be surprised that the six leading traits under description here coalesce around an earth–sky axis. Many of the world's peoples, among them the Navajo, have long recognized the cosmological importance of this *axis terrae*:

> The Navajo world or universe consists of a shallow, flat disk in the form of a dish, topped by a similar form which covers it like a lid. The lower part is the Earth, while the upper part (the lid, so to speak) is the Sky. Neither of these forms can be conceived of as genuinely round, dishlike forms, since both are represented as human or anthropomorphic forms, lying down in an arching stretched manner, one on top of the other. The lower one is Mother Earth, nahasdzáán shimá, lying from east to west, while the upper one is Father Heaven, yá' shitaa', lying in the same direction, on top of and above the Earth.[55]

But we need not have recourse to cosmology to realize how powerfully structuring the earth—sky dimension can be. We need only step outside and look
around. What do we see? At the very least, we see some aspect of the earth
and catch some glimpse of the sky. However covered over—and, in particular, built over—the earth's surface may be, and however much the sky is
occluded from view, we cannot help but sense their vertically arranged, almost columnar co-presence. Nor can we avoid noticing the things on the
ground around us and underfoot that, in their comparative solidity, distinguish themselves from the ethereal entities of the atmospheric upper world.
Nowhere do we find a complete lack of things, that is, anything like a strict
void. *Everywhere there is something*, even though the something itself can belong to any of several elemental regions.[56]

When we venture still farther outside the sanctuary of our domicile,
moving into an increasingly undisturbed natural realm, the situation just described becomes ever more compelling. For then the earth and sky seem to
step forward of their own accord. They begin to set the terms, such that we
act and experience through them and even at their behest. In Heidegger's
words, they "take the measure."[57] Earth reveals itself as an abiding yet ever-
proliferating ground with a densely textured surface, sky shows itself to be
a constantly changing yet inherently orderly atmosphere, things manifest
themselves as coagulations of matter, an array of teeming landforms and life-
forms and airforms surrounds us on all sides, and an arc encloses ground
and things from the beyond of the sky.

The wild places that come forward in this way not only lend themselves
to description, they *solicit it*. I shall take up this solicitation in the remainder
of this chapter, discussing the several moment-traits I have just distinguished.

VIII

The place is offered to itself.
—Gary Snyder, *The Practice of the Wild*

One of the most salient yet rarely discussed features of being in wild
places is the way in which we are constantly surrounded by natural life and
inorganic matter, sometimes to a frightening degree (when we feel invaded)
but also sometimes quite reassuringly (when we feel sustained). This feature,
the *surrounding array*, has a solid basis in ordinary perception. In *The Ecological Approach to Visual Perception*, J. J. Gibson sets forth the view that
optical and other sensory cues surround us at all times and are apperceived
massively and spontaneously by the central body trunk and especially by the
pivoting head.[58] On the Gibsonian model, we are always in the midst of a
field of perceptual "affordances" that embody and transmit information concerning the immediate physical environment. As perceivers, we continually

pick up this information from the "ambient array" (concentrated mainly but not exclusively in the available light) to which our active bodies give us access. Thus, for example, we gain information about depth by attending to various felt and seen "gradients" immanent in the spread-out, receding field of sensory awareness. Many other aspects of the sensory world are also present and directly grasped in the ambient array.

Taking a cue from Gibson's pioneering work, let us say that wilderness presents itself to us as *the circumambience of the ambient array*. A conspicuous instance is a mountain chain that heightens and rings a low-lying valley or a large inland lake that extends our perceptions outward indefinitely. Even in less conspicuous cases, however, a circumambient world surrounds the immediate array of perceptions, e.g., in the midst of the gently rolling hills of Sonoma County, California, or in the hill-less but still rolling prairie of western Nebraska. In each case, the perceived land surrounds in two basic ways. On one hand, it *encircles* a particular place (e.g., a field or a pond), helping to delimit it as just that place and no other, while also, as a corollary, facilitating the pictorial representation of this same place (the painterly representation in effect enframes the initially afforded encirclement).[59] On the other hand, the land *fills out* that place; by no means an empty frame, the land provides detail, indeed unending detail, by which our perceptions are (in Husserl's word) "fulfilled." Think only of how an entire valley of wild flowers acts to fill in what might, at first glance, be grasped only in terms of a few contours and colors.

The twofold operation of encircling and filling-out is enacted by the sky as well as by the land. The sky encircles the earth from above, endowing the latter with illumination and shadows that fill out its sensuous surface. When earth and sky both enact this double operation, the result is an intensified and deepened circumambience. The initially afforded sensory array, the first circumambience (that of the near sphere), is set within a second array, that provided by earthscape and skyscape as these are set in turn within the far sphere. The insertion of the initial array within a still more comprehensive array is no merely mechanical matter. The nesting of one array in another is gradual and subtle, proceeding as much by sensory quality as by perceived quantity. Nevertheless, the surrounding array remains distinguishable from what is immediately present in the near sphere. We realize this every time we gaze at a photograph of a scene we have once perceived. Rarely does the photograph retain the complex interplay of initial and surrounding arrays. Instead, it tends to give us one or the other in a representation that artificially separates two arrays continuous with each other in ongoing sensory experience.

Sensed together, these two arrays furnish an *arc of abundance* for a given wilderness scene in which we find ourselves. By means of this doubly arrayed

arc, the wild scene surrounds particular objects while supplying an indefinitely fine-grained backdrop. That backdrop consists of a sensuous sea of
open-ended qualities and structures that serve to deepen what, in the initial
sensory affordances, is flattened out by its sheer proximity to the sensing
body.[60] A given wild place thus serves to *draw out depth*, that is, to take it
toward, up to, and sometimes seemingly beyond, the horizon, which is a
boundary for depth itself, closing the circle of that place's own encircling
structure.

To suspend the continual encirclement and plenary presence of the surrounding array is to suspend our most intimate connection with the wild
world; it is to undermine what Santayana called "animal faith" in this world.
No wonder that, caught up in such a circumstance (e.g., in a steep canyon
that offers no vista and no egress), we feel cut off as we encounter a scene
deprived of extended sensory presence arrayed around us. A living wildscape
has become a momentary stillscape. Where before we may have sensed *too
much* to inventory, or to represent pictorially in any adequate way (even the
photograph fails us), now we grasp *too little* to satisfy our insatiable souls,
thriving as we do on the nurture provided by the open-ended raiment of the
environing earth.

IX

> For my own part I am pleased enough with surfaces—in fact they alone seem
> to me to be of much importance. Such things for example as . . . the bark of
> a tree, the abrasion of granite and sand, the plunge of clear water into a
> pool, the face of the wind—what else is there? What else do we need?
>
> —Edward Abbey, *Desert Solitaire*

The *sensuous surface* is an aspect of the surrounding array that stands out
in our first encounter with a particular wild place. The surface is the moment
of impingement, what my sensing body first notices.[61] The "local character"
of a wild place is conveyed to us by the sensuous qualities of the surfaces it
turns toward us. The sensuous qualities themselves are of many sorts—as
many as our own sensory systems, working singly or together, can apprehend. They include classically determined primary and secondary qualities,
such as motion, shape, and color, as well as such less familiar variables as
density, luminosity, and especially texture.

Neglected by almost all philosophers and psychologists of perception
(again with the notable exception of Gibson),[62] texture is of decisive importance in the determination of the surfaces of wild places. Texture is a crucial
component of depth perception, for instance. The finer the granulation of
the sensed surface, the farther away we perceive the surface to be from us.

But texture also embodies the peculiar tangibility, or "feel," of wilderness. This last point calls for emphasis. What is at stake in the texturality of a wild place's sensuous surface is above all its inherent *palpability*, which is a most effective basis for coming to know that place's distinctive configuration, its physiognomy. If we are about to walk into this place, we need to know what sort of terrain our body will experience, how its surface is organized, and how it would feel to traverse it. At this preliminary moment, we learn a great deal merely from gazing at the surface texture arrayed before us, or from lightly touching or stroking it, or from simply stepping on it. Palpation and vision and kinesthesia often combine synesthetically, to be joined, perhaps, by audition and olfaction: we sense sounds as emanating from certain surfaces, and odors as clinging to them. Only by means of surface texture can the full sensuousness of a wildscape, its abundant changing-environing appearing, come into our ken.

Given what has just been said, it is tempting to assimilate the sensuous surface to *flesh*. Flesh, too, is primarily tactile, and it presents the surface of our body in a snug, yet entirely revealing manner. But unlike epidermal skin, flesh goes deeper into the corporeal self. More than "skin deep," it mediates between the inner self and the surrounding world. Neither matter nor mind, flesh is more like a common "element," a "general thing" that exists "midway between the spatio-temporal individual and the idea."[63] Flesh is not only *my* flesh. It also belongs to my circumambient setting experienced as a "landscape world" (in the phrase of Erwin Straus).[64] When this world is wild in character, it has its own fleshlike character. Its flesh intertwines with my flesh, and each is continuous with the other.[65]

The sensuous surface of wild places can be construed as an exemplary instance of the flesh of the world. This surface is bound to wilderness not as a loosely fitting outer garment but as at one with its basic configurations. As fleshlike, it sinks below the seen surface as such, and for this reason vision must be supplemented by other senses for the surface to be fully experienced. More than a merely visible pellicle, it is *the most manifest way wilderness presents itself to us on its own terms*. As Gibson pithily remarks, "The surface is where most of the action is."[66] Moreover, as the *felt* surface of land (or sea), it links up with my own bodily surface. The two porous surfaces, one belonging to the circumambient world and the other to my *corps propre*, intertwine and become at once co-experiential and co-essential. My lived body rejoins a wild place—this free-standing grove of trees, that unruly patch of sea—as the flesh of one takes in the flesh of the other. As I come to know it from within, such a place, despite its wildness (or rather, just because of it) becomes "flesh of my flesh."

To be convinced of the significance of the sensuous surface in the experience of wild places, we might recall cases in which this surface has been occluded from direct perception, e.g., when a very dense fog settled over the Scilly Islands onto which Admiral Shovel and his fleet crashed so resoundingly. Not only is our determination of depth then disturbed, but we also apprehend various sensuous qualities imperfectly or not at all. The entire wildscape is obfuscated in its natural luminosity, blocking its ambient light. The sensuousness of the surface, its translucent flesh, becomes literally overcast, and as a direct consequence, our perception of wilderness is compromised. Nowhere is the dictum *obscurum per obscurius* more appropriately applied, for the obscurity of wild places here becomes our own obscurity.

X

> What angels invented these splendid ornaments, these rich conveniences, this
> ocean of air above, this ocean of water beneath, this firmament of earth
> between?
> —Ralph Waldo Emerson, *Nature*

The surface is not *only* surface, but the surface *of a ground*. The surface is not a separate layer or strip that can be peeled off so as to reveal the ground below. On the contrary, the ground presents itself *as surface*. Thus ground is not depth if *depth* signifies something lying concealed beneath or behind the terrestrial or aqueous surface and disconnected from that surface as its unknown underlayer. The ground of an earth or sea surface is at once continuous with such a surface and known as such; the "groundswell" is known by and at the surface on which it appears. "The depths," said Wittgenstein, "are on the surface."[67] We might even say that the ground is *the other side* of the sensuous surface of wilderness, its closely clinging subsurface aura. It is the extension of the depth of the surface itself rather than a separate depth. But what, then, is ground?

Minimally, *ground* signifies something firm underfoot: *terra firma*. As such, ground is not to be confined to soil, which is a detachable layer *on* the surface of the earth. Thus water is a ground for vessels that float on it and count on it for support. Ground offers support on two bases: itself more or less *level*, i.e., perpendicular to the vertical vector of gravity, it is also comparatively *flat* (or at least flat enough so that things poised on it do not continually topple over).[68]

Greek mythology suggests that we need to distinguish between three levels of ground. A first level is the outer layer of the earth, Demeter's realm of fertile fields or tillable "topsoil." This is the earth's outer crust, its earthy-loamy cuticle, as it were. Beneath this crust is a second level, that of Gē or Gaia, the "dark earth," the source of fertility considered to be the realm of an Earth Mother whose "governing maternal principle . . . makes material fertility [on the earth's surface] possible."[69] As the fecund underground, Gē is the subsoil of the earth's topsoil, the dark underbelly of the land. Still deeper than Gē, however, lies Chthōn, the deep ground that subtends both of the two previous levels: "*Chthōn* with its derivatives refers in origin to the cold, dead depths, and has nothing to do with fertility."[70] The chthonic level underlies arable land and all vegetation on that land. As the deepest level of ground, it extends downward into the bowels of the earth. In contrast with the earth's exposed outer ground, the chthonic realm is one of concealment, of utter dark and night. It is the realm not just of the underground but also of the *underworld*, the domain of Hades and of dreams.[71]

We need not adhere dogmatically to this particular trilevel schema as it was set forth by the ancient Greeks. Even to their lucid minds, the levels were by no means perfectly distinct from one another—"Demeter-Gē-Chthōn frequently merge in epithet and cult"[72]—and it would be misleading to invoke this mythological model as an exclusive guide for our own investigations. What matters in any case is not the exact number of levels but, rather, the important implication that *ground* has more than one kind of depth: "Deep ground," says James Hillman, "is not the same as the dark earth."[73]

Beyond its express association with earth and land, *ground* means such things as justifying reason, decisive evidence, supporting structure—all of which imply firm stability, "something to stand on," "being well-grounded," "having a sound basis."[74] To be "aground," on the other hand, means to be fixed-in-place, unable to move. The term *underground* indicates both a firmly supportive under-level and something distinctly subversive (i.e., literally turning over from below). Heidegger has proposed that the very idea of *Grund* is deeply allied with *Abgrund*: "ground" signifies "abyss."[75] Despite such nuances, the primary sense of the word *ground* is underlying support. Antaeus, another Greek deity, regains strength from the archetypal act of touching the ground, an act whose significance is preserved in English phrases such as "touching ground," "landing with your feet on the ground," "getting back to ground level" (or to "ground zero"), etc. Thoreau remarks that "the most clear and ethereal ideas (Antaeus-like) readily ally themselves to the earth, to the primal womb of things."[76]

Ground as undergirding support is a basic feature of wilderness. Whenever we find ourselves in a wild place, we seek to be positively grounded there. It is both *from* the ground and *by* it that we come to know the place; and it is *in* the ground and *on* it that we grasp its fleshlike sensuous surface, and begin to explore it. Without a sense of stable ground—when ground has become a literally sub-versive presence—we are lost: abandoned, desolated, and prevented from proceeding further. At Camp Wood, for instance, I lacked a sense of secure grounding; the sun-baked soil was rock-hard, but it seemed to "open up beneath me" as I wandered, dazed and disconsolate, on the groundless ground, an abyss indeed.

By saying that it is "from" and "by," "in" and "on" the ground that we experience wilderness, I have two things in mind. First, the ground serves as an anchoring point, a *stabilitas loci*, for motion and perception. In Husserl's telling term, it is the "basis-place" from which we gain a sense of stability, the sure-footed space underneath our standing bodies. When the same bodies move about, the various places they traverse relate to each other through the common ground that connects them. As Husserl puts it, "A plurality of basis-places, of home-places, is unified into a [single] basis-place."[77] This latter, encompassing basis-place is the ground proper, the very basis for our experience of particular wild places. Second, through such a unified basis-place (typically a region we have come to know), we gain orientation in and toward a given wilderness area. Thus the ground assures us of being able to assume a directed stance on the earth. Its various levels, arranged in order of comparative depth, imply a vertical dimensionality, an implicit earth-axis proceeding from deep below the sensuous surface and projecting upward into the encompassing sky. In being laid out beneath our feet, the ground also extends in a horizontal direction (though just how far depends on the particular wild place or region we are in), thereby invoking a second such axis, one that is perpendicular to the vertical and swept out across the land.[78]

The ground therefore provides an enduring basis-place for our embodied implacement in a landscape scene of wilderness. As "the world's body" (in John Crowe Ransom's phrase), it is the geogonic counterpart of our own lived body, just as the same ground is also the basis for our perception of whatever lies on its sensuous surface. Subtending our body and lending it telluric powers of density and situatedness, the ground furnishes the material basis for its own perception as a wildscape. As we have seen, the material texturality of the environing world is critical for this perception. In fact, the grasping of sensuous surface would not be possible in the first place unless this surface was the surface of the very ground on which it is set. When I gaze at the side of a mountain, I see not simply the mountain's external edges but also the way these edges express the abiding presence of its internal ground. I see not just one thing (i.e., the surface alone) or two things in distinction (surface vs. ground) but two-in-one: the ground-surfacing, the surface deepening into ground.

Ground, then, is that aspect of earth that seeps into the sensuous surface of wild places while also extending that surface downward. It is thus the earth-basis of the world's body, its very flesh. Ground presents itself (and can only present itself) through surface; even when we dig into the ground, we still confront nothing but new surfaces of earth. Whereas the sensuous surface is the earth as turned outward—hence as "telling" in its display, its visibility—ground is the same earth turned inward, kept out of sight, the unseen inseam of the land. Far from being a merely contingent feature of the earth, the ground is indispensable in its invisibilizing role: "The earth," as Rilke says, "has no other refuge except to become invisible."[79]

XI

The Six Grandfathers have placed in this world many things, all of which should be happy. Every little thing is sent for something, and in that thing there should be happiness and the power to make happy.
—Black Elk, *Black Elk Speaks*

It might be thought odd to include *things* among leading features of wilderness. But it is odd only because it is so obvious: is not some*thing* always present? "Our first truth—which prejudges nothing and cannot be contested—will be that there is presence, that 'something' is there."[80] This axiomatic statement of Merleau-Ponty's is difficult to deny. It fits with the fact that the notion of a strict void, even when posited as cosmogonically necessary, withers away upon analysis. Place is found just where no-place was supposed to be, and if there are places from the start, there are also (some) *things* that occupy these ur-places. The idea of no-thing at the origin is unsustainable. On the contrary, nothing is not at the origin. *At the origin are things in places.* The things in question can be as large as oceans or as diminutive as plankton. Just as places are everywhere in the beginning, so things are also there, all over the place. This continues to be true in the human experience of wilderness; here, too, we come across nothing but things-in-places. Other animals doubtless have much the same experience. Indeed, for all animals (and presumably also plants), the wild world is as thing-rich as it is place-replete.

Things configure a given wildscape in many different patterns. Sometimes they crowd it with their multitudinous presence. Sometimes they give the appearance of a dearth of things themselves. Upon scrutiny, however, even the most barren wasteland displays a considerable variety of things. The Great Plains are carpeted with a remarkable range of native grasses and weeds and other scrubby vegetation. The valleys and hillsides of Switzerland feature myriad rocks and stones, anything from boulders to pebbles. Even the floor of Death Valley is fissured into thinglike "plates" of dried mud, and it features distinctive wild flowers. Although there may be far fewer things in a given wildscape than we might wish when we hunger after plenitude, nowhere is there nothing to be found. Things are *all around us*. But what is a thing?

A thing is *whatever is profiled on the sensuous surface of the ground*. In order to accommodate birds and clouds (whose profile appears on the sky), let us say more generally that a thing is something *with a distinctive contour*. But a thing is more than its own profile; it is also densely material, a condensation of matter, thus something literally palpable. As dense and material, things need a ground. The ground subtends not only my body as moving on (and sensing) its surface but also the very things that obtrude on this surface, providing for them a "primitive home-place."[81] Things need the grounding of the earth (or water) as the "root-basis" without which they would be merely detachable objects.[82] A sign of this rootedness is found in the fact that things are "gravid," pregnant with their own weight. Things not only fit onto the ground but are pulled down *into* it at all times, settling back there as if by a primitive rite of natural re-inhabitation.

Things, then, are physical entities that stand out in the natural domain. They are objects *in* and *of* this domain, material moments of it. Rather than detachable parts, they are aspects intrinsic to the very structure of Nature. "Things," said Merleau-Ponty, "are structures, frameworks, the stars of our life."[83] Their gravity is matched by their ability to punctuate the natural world, much as stars paint a pointillism of the dark sky.

The profiling, condensing, and punctuating powers of things are realized nowhere else but in place. Boulders on a mountainside are not merely located on the mountain; they *make their place* there. Their crushing weight acts to define the mountain's sensuous surface as beset, craggy, pockmarked, rock-strewn. Such megalithic things populate the mountainside, their abiding ground, as in an unplanned but complementary preoccupation. Their (spatially) discontinuous implacement calls for the mountain's own (temporally) perduring presence, and the converse is also the case. Even if not literally coeval, boulder-things and the ground-cum-surface to which they cling combine in a most con-natural embrace.

Things belonging to a given wild place are consistent and persistent items that are numerable in principle, even if often difficult to enumerate in fact (e.g., can we really count *all* the rocks on that mountainside?); collectible into groups (mainly by spontaneously formed Gestalten: I can perceive coherent collections of rocks on that overpopulated mountainside); and obdurate to sight, touch, motion, etc., thus possessing what Peirce calls "Secondness," i.e., causally efficacious properties that human beings cannot easily assimilate to their all-too-human cognitive states.[84] Taken together, these three general traits signify that things act to *diversify* a particular wildscape. In doing so, they help to guarantee that it will not be altogether denuded of denizens.

They ensure that the ground, the surface, and the sky are not experienced as merely planiform features in an indifferent Flatland.

The proper language or idiolect of wilderness is that of natural things. By "natural things" I mean not just things whose genesis and formation have occurred independently of human technologies but things that *bespeak Nature*. For the most part, such things are pregiven physical objects, matters of *physis* in its primal configurations: tree, bush, flower, reed, rock, boulder. Each of these natural things is "some simple thing, remoulded by age after age."[85]

Things taken in this primordial sense are as much places as they are discrete objects, and finally both at once. Take a mountain: is it a thing or a place? It is an elemental thing-place. The mountain looms before us as a massive place for things and as itself a thing. It looms as a Thing of things, just as stones and lichen on stones are in turn things of this Thing. Furthermore, just as such determinate things as rocks have and make their own determinate places, so a monumental mountain-Thing is a place of its own, albeit a nondeterminate place: where exactly does a mountain begin or end? This place is "non-thetic" since we cannot fix its limits precisely. Its place is not (to be) a site. Its implacement is "subdued."[86]

XII

The entire physical perceptual field as a constituted manifold of things that appear in perspectives is a harmonious unity of perspectivity.

—Edmund Husserl, "The World of the Living Present and the Constitution of the Surrounding World External to the Organism"

By *arc* I here mean the part of a wild place that continually fades from explicit presentation. In distinction from previous senses of the term, *arc* now refers to the *area of vanishing*, a zone of indeterminacy in which the sensuous surfaces of things no longer hold our attention and we find ourselves "gazing into the distance." What we gaze *at* when we gaze into the distance is not some discrete object, not even the ground on which such an object rests. It is an entire fading band of the land or sea. The obscurity of this band—its essential vagueness—signifies not only distance and depth but a quite special phenomenon rarely remarked upon in philosophical or psychological studies of perception: the self-obscuring of a given place, its lapsing into the indeterminate, its de-phenomenalization.

An arc is something that has the appearance of being virtually nothing. Along with atmosphere, it is quintessentially insubstantial.[87] Yet this non-thing helps to hold everything together in a given wild place, including the dense material things just discussed. Thanks to the embrace of arc, "the hold is held."[88] Arc is a mode of landscape *synthesis*; it is a "harmonious unity of perspectivity" that occurs with an upward directionality. By contrast with the downward pull of ground and of things situated on the ground, in following the arc we move decisively *up* and *out* into an alleviated region, e.g., the lower sky. This sense of arc is already at play in the *Enuma Elish*; when Marduk split Tiamat apart "like a cockle-shell," he "constructed the arc of sky" from the upper half of her carcass.[89] Less dramatically, my own body, stationed on earth and passing over the sensuous surfaces of the earth or sea, is drawn upward and outward by the arc that beckons beyond.

Let us not confuse arc with horizon. Unlike the arc, the horizon typically presents itself as *linear*; hence the idea of the "horizon line," as this has emerged in the practice of post-Renaissance artists. Leaving aside the question of whether such a line is adequate to our experience of the horizon—do we ever really experience a sheer line at, much less *as*, the horizon?—we need only remark that the arc is rarely, if ever, reducible to a linear format. The arc is not a line but a *domain*; it is a region rather than an object or a thing. Thus, even though it is essentially curved in structure, it is not accurate to speak of it as "curv*ilinear*." As exhibiting curvature (albeit curvature in torsion), the arc is more like an *arch* than a horizon. As an arch is set within a work of architecture—within the nave of a cathedral or within a monument (e.g., the Arc de Triomphe in Paris)—so the arc is set deeply within an open vista.

Furthermore, the horizon is restricted to just one sector of land or sea, i.e., where earth meets sky. Arc is not so constricted. Even if it often draws our gaze upward into the sky, in the end arc is the pervasive vanishing of land or sea as a whole, not of its constituents taken separately. A horizon encircles discrete objects and is the outer limit of the ground. The arc encloses the horizon and all that lies within it, including material things and their sensuous surfaces. It is the outer limit not just of the ground but of the entire surrounding array.

A poet closely attuned to the natural world, Wallace Stevens, observed that "the sky [is] acutest at its vanishing."[90] The mention of "acutest" reminds us that perceptual obscuration should not be equated with inefficacious existence. *The very vanishing of the arc is the source of its unsuspected, its "arcane," power.*[91] If ground derives its strength from the densely fused and slowly compacted, arc lives from what is fleeting and dispersed.

Despite its evanescence, the arc does not lack graspable character or structure. In addition to its penchant for vanishing, the arc has two readily discernible traits. First, it acts to *encompass* the scene of which it is such an integral part. To encompass is not to enframe. A frame implies a tight, uninterrupted delineation of that which is framed, a limit or perimeter rather than a boundary. While a given landscape can certainly be enframed—as when one enters eastern Colorado from the Great Plains and witnesses the massive framing effected by the Rocky Mountains to the west—such enframement is by no means always present. The arc, however, *is* always present, and it is present precisely in its capacity of encompassing the contents of any given wild scene, mountainous or flat: com-prehending these contents without forming a distinct border around them. Such inclusion is even more capacious than the encirclement effected by the surrounding array.

In its geometric acceptation, the word *arc* signifies a segment of a continuous line traced out by a compass. But the arc at stake in wilderness cannot be confined to the area traced out by a continuous closed curve. Instead of effecting an inclusion from without—as does the geometric arc—it realizes an inclusion from within. For the arc of a wild place acts not only to include its far sphere but also to situate its near sphere, where it wraps itself around the acting-moving body. Even if we rarely pause to attend to it, we experience the arc's close embrace every time we are in the midst of wilderness.

A second trait of the arc is its *bowed* character. Strictly construed, *arc* means "anything bow-shaped."[92] The most striking instance of the bowedness of the wilderness arc appears in the vault of the nighttime sky, that enormous domelike structure constellated by stars.[93] Similarly, even if less strikingly, the dome of the sky also appears when we gaze up during the day at a group of clouds, which are, in physical fact, parallel to the earth's surface. Indeed, when we look down upon an ordinary landscape from an aerie high above, we perceive a saucer-shaped arc, now facing *up* and subtending the salient ground and surface features. In none of these cases is the arc perfectly circular; it tends to be somewhat flattened out at the apex or nadir. But that does not lessen the significance of the arc's presence in the vista. The significance is such that the whole scene—not only the sky but also the earth below—is taken to be bow-shaped. As an immediately given moment of the scene's presentation, the arc-structure is deeply immanent in it.

The arc's bowed and flattened immanence is underlined in Navajo cosmogony, which represents Father Sky as arched over Mother Earth. Still earlier, the Egyptians thought of Nut, goddess of the sky, and Geb, god of the earth, as curving respectively over and under the constituents of the world.[94]

Arc is the ultimate disappearing act of any given wild place. In and through its encompassing and bowed arc, the ground, the surface, and the various things situated in the surrounding array of that place begin to enter into erasure, to become not so much invisible presences (as occurs when things go literally underground) as presences leading into, indeed *becoming*, their own dis-appearance.[95]

XIII

Obscurity spreads to the perceived world in its entirety.
—Maurice Merleau-Ponty, *Phenomenology of Perception*

The *atmosphere* is more thoroughly pervasive of wilderness than any other factor, more so even than arc or surrounding array. It is the wildwise equivalent of what Heidegger calls "moodwise situatedness" (*Befindlichkeit*).[96] Atmosphere embodies the emotional *tonality* of a wild place, its predominant mood. When we are in such a place, we sense it not only as continuous with our own feeling—or as reflecting that feeling—but also as *itself containing feeling*:

> The mood of a landscape appears to us to be objectively given with it as one of its attributes, belonging to it just like any other attribute we perceive it to have. . . . We never think of regarding the landscape as a sentient being whose outward aspect "expresses" the mood that it contains subjectively. The landscape does not express the the mood, but *has* it.[97]

As all-pervasive, atmosphere might seem to deserve first mention in an analysis of leading traits of wild places. For what we *focus on first* in our encounter with a wild place—typically, the sensuous surfaces of things on its ground—is not necessarily *first in the order of importance* in making that encounter itself possible.[98] First in pervasive power in any case is the atmosphere in which we find ourselves immersed from the very start. But precisely because we are so immersed in it and thus have little or no distance from it, the atmosphere is often the *last* factor to be grasped lucidly, if it is grasped at all. First in the order of experiencing is here last in the order of knowing. Hence my own belated treatment of atmosphere, that vaguest and yet in certain ways most formative of wilderness features.

Rather than a bowed band *through* which we begin to see a wildscape or *into* which it vanishes, the atmosphere is that which exists *in* and *around* everything in the landscape. By "everything" I mean just that: the ground, its presented surface, the things that inhabit the ground, the surrounding array, even the ephemeral arc. *The atmosphere permeates everything.* What else would we expect from something whose very name means "sphere of vapor or smoke" and which shares with the Sanskrit *atman* (soul, self) a root in *an*, breath? As breath, smoke, and vapor move not only between bodies but inside them, so the atmosphere of a wild place animates all that we experience in its presence. It is as essential to that place as breath is to our bodily being. In sharing the same atmosphere, body and place realize a common essence as well as their own most intimate unity.

No wonder the Egyptians placed Shu, august and lithe god of the atmosphere, in the very center of the cosmogonic account to which I alluded above: Shu touches his daughter Nut with his hands and his son Geb with his feet, and every other major figure touches him in turn. The atmosphere of a wildscape is not dissimilar to the figure of Shu. Thanks to the atmosphere's pan-pervasiveness, each moment of the wild scene is in touch with all the others, intertwining with them by means of the englobing sphere (*sphaira*) of the indwelling vapor (*atmos*) they inhale on equal terms.

The atmosphere is doubly pervasive of a wildscape. On one hand, it pervades *from without*, existing between various moments. In this role, it serves as something of an envelopment for these moments.[99] Atmospheric envelopment is not just a matter of scientific fact but is a felt presence, as when we sense ourselves surrounded by a moist and closely fitting mass of air. To this air we often ascribe special "atmospheric effects," such as the diffusion of light manifested in a dense fog. Indeed, an atmosphere can come to characterize an entire region. When we think of the luminous atmosphere of landscapes in southern France or on the southeastern shore of Long Island, we realize that in its enveloping role the atmosphere has become "the air of a given place or locality, especially as affected by a particular characteristic (e.g., heat, moisture, wholesomeness, unwholesomeness)."[100] In many instances, we both identify and remember a region in terms of its endemic "air," that is to say, its enveloping-pervading atmosphere. When we walk in that region, we "take the air." We *take it in* from without.

On the other hand, a wild place's atmosphere is also a matter of permeation *from within*. The atmosphere not only envelops but literally per-vades by going *through* whatever is situated in it, much as a mood utterly pervades both a given situation and the people embroiled in it. Atmosphere is here found less *between* basic features than *inside* each, being in-stilled there. We feel this immanence, for example, in a clearing in a forest on a crystal-clear day. The lucidity of the atmosphere permeates each surface and each thing, seemingly even the ground itself. In realizing such immanence, atmosphere is unique among the moments of a wildscape, since no other moment can be said to be an interior presence located *within all other moments* (even the arc holds together from without). As an inherent presence, atmosphere is invigorating and has as its most palpable expression the actual "breath" of a living creature, though it is also at play as the air that penetrates and moves through inorganic substances. The overall effect is to alleviate and animate any given wildscape: to bestow upon it an *élan vital* that vivifies the whole scene and not just the literally alive beings in it.

Anaximines of Miletus (circa 550–500 B.C.) was alert to this double aspect of atmosphere: "Just as our soul, being air, holds us together, so do breath and air encompass the whole world."[101] Anaximines is here building on the linguistic fact that the Greek word for soul, *psychē*, is cognate with *psychein*, to breathe. *Breath (pneuma)* and *air (aer)* are in turn connected by the fact that for the Greeks *aer* signifies the lower atmosphere, the immediate envelope of life on earth and thus the source of breath for all land animals.[102]

Anaximines, who held that everything is ultimately composed of air (via processes of condensation and rarefaction), is by no means alone in attributing special powers to the atmosphere. The Navajo also consider air to be sacred in its significance.[103] What is most important, however, is to notice that the aeriform atmosphere is not as characterless as we might think in being aware of its apparent invisibility. As Theophrastus wrote in reference to Anaximines's notion of *aer*:

> [For Anaximines] the underlying substance was one and infinite. He did not, however, say it was indeterminate, like Anaximander [i.e., as in the latter's conception of the Boundless, *to apeiron*], but determinate. For he said it was Air.[104]

Paradoxically, air is determinate in its very *changeability*. Anaximines, the first philosopher of air, observes that air is not at all times, or even uniformly, invisible: "Where it is most even, it is invisible to our sight; but cold and heat, moisture and motion, make it visible."[105] In other words, atmospheric effects change their very appearance as they impinge on our senses, with the result that a given landscape will present itself to us as quite different in its aerial character from season to season, day to day, even minute to minute. Think only of how one and the same spot on a beach can alter aspect drastically as an early morning mantle of mist gives way to the dazzling brightness of high noon, ceding place in turn to the velvetine languor of twilight and finally to somber darkness. At each stage, the atmosphere is part and parcel of the cycle of changes that deliver the spot to us in its manifold guises.

Closely linked with change is *motion*. Air, said Anaximines, "is always in motion; for, if it were not, it would not change so much as it does."[106] The motions in question are those of air currents and air masses. If we do not *see* these motions directly, we smell them or feel their immediate impact quite tangibly on the surface of our bodies, or we read them off in the sensuous surfaces of the surrounding array: the way the clouds move, or how the breeze is blowing through the trees. In the latter cases, motion is reflected in change of shape, e.g., in the altering configuration of a single cloud or in the fluttering pattern of leaves on a single limb.

Anaximines was on the verge of discovering that the atmosphere is the major component of what would today be called the "biosphere." The biosphere is the larger whole of which life on the surface of the earth and deep in its oceans forms an integral part. Not only breath but many other organic (and inorganic) processes are interinvolved in the biosphere. James Lovelock, the propounder of the Gaia hypothesis, has this to say about the biosphere:

> The entire range of living matter on Earth, from whales to viruses and from oaks to algae, could be regarded as constituting a single living entity, capable of manipulating the Earth's atmosphere to suit its overall needs and endowed with faculties and powers far beyond those of its constituent parts.[107]

We apprehend the biosphere *through* the atmosphere. Not only is "the atmosphere in which we live and think . . . a dynamic extension of the planetary surface, a functioning organ of the Earth"—here the intimate link between atmosphere and ground is asserted—but, in addition, the atmosphere is itself part of a vast alive entity and essential to it: "myriad forms of biotic experience, human and non-human, may collectively constitute a coherent global experience, or life, that is not without its own creativity and sentience."[108] "Experience" and "sentience" name features of the atmosphere in which we live and breathe and have our being.

Atmosphere, that seemingly most elusive and vaporous of wilderness features, shows itself to be highly structured. Conterminous with the earth's biosphere, it is changeable and motile, shapeful and emotionally toned—and alive. In particular, it is immanent to the experience of wild places as their common and altogether pervasive medium. Atmosphere is the mediatrix of the wild world. It is not just a third term but a constant (albeit a constantly changing constant) found throughout this world in its many and varied avatars. Both in the beginning and at every subsequent point, it permeates the surrounding array, bringing together the arc and the ground, the things and the sensuous surfaces that characterize the wilderness scenes into which we venture or suddenly fall.

XIV

Place and the scale of space must be measured against our bodies
and their capabilities.

—Gary Snyder, *The Practice of the Wild*

And the place of body in all this? It is present throughout. Each of the six main traits of wild places brings with it its own characteristic bodily ingression and action. This is most evident in the case of arc and ground, both of which call for a quite manifest corporeal contribution: a receptive spreading-out and taking-in in one case, a determined being-stationed or striding-forth in the other. But we could not experience the ground's own sensuous surface or the surrounding array, either, without the agency of our moving-perceiving bodies, whose considerable synesthetic powers put us in touch with this surface and array. Nor could we enter fully into the domain of things and atmosphere, those epicenters of wildscape, without the intervention of our bodily being, whether by way of dealing with particular material objects or by breathing the circumambient air. In each instance, the effects of the living body are indispensable, even if they often go unrecognized in official epistemologies of space.

Yet any sailor at sea knows of these effects at first hand. If he is attending to the immediate tasks of sailing, he will not perceive or think that he is sailing "uphill," but if he turns away from the near sphere of his actual nautical praxis to look into the distance he will see the surrounding ocean as bowl-shaped—as an aqueous arc—and will sense himself sailing *upward* into its rim.[109] In view of this uphill struggle, we should not be surprised to learn of the extent to which Puluwat navigators, who must direct themselves over an immense open sea, often prefer to attend to their concrete bodily sensations rather than to what is perceptible on the horizon. Not only in sailing but in countless other engagements with wild places, the effects of bodily bearing and practice upon the perception and use of basic wilderness features is at once powerful and subtle.

But the reverse also obtains, in that wild places *put the body into action*. Whereas many built places serve to bring the body to rest—indeed, to bring it to a virtual stasis in the case of living rooms and bathrooms and bedrooms—a wild place calls for alert apprehension, adroit exploration, and resourceful action. "Action" here includes observation, especially in the form of a literal circumspection, a "seeing-around," that takes account of the multifarious qualities and shapes of the surrounding array. It also means outright climbing, walking, and sometimes sprinting (getting away from that rattlesnake just ahead on the trail). Some wild areas call for circumambulation. Instead of walking straight toward a destination, we must often *walk around* it (an action ritualized in the approach to a holy mountain such as Mount Kailash in western Tibet). At times, we cannot even find a way to get around a natural object but must backtrack and take elaborate byways that lead us into a number of peripheral places. Insofar as bodily movement through a wildscape takes us into these by-places, the movement can be considered a *parergon*, literally a "by-work." Such was the movement of Odysseus on his circuitous and deferred return to Ithaca.

Beyond the indirection of the body's movement—and the resulting proliferation of places-on-the-way and out-of-the-way—*disorientation* is another quite pervasive effect of wild places on the human body. We have seen that built places serve to direct, support, and sustain the dyadic relations of up–down, front–back, and right–left, orienting us ever more securely in these dimensional terms. Domiciles build on—and out from—the already existing

bodily directionality such terms specify, hence the uncanny resemblance between many buildings and the human body itself. But when we come to land
and sea in their wild extensions, we cannot count on any such reassuring
resemblances. Instead of structures that mimic the body even as they protect
it, the structures of natural things and of array and atmosphere, ground and
arc, are often radically independent of human corporeal intentionality, to the
point of challenging and undermining this intentionality. For example,
climbing in rugged mountain terrain can lead to disequilibrium in terms of
up versus down, so that the climber's basic sense of level may be set askew.
The same confusion can arise with regard to the other dyads first singled
out by the Pythagoreans. As we wend our way through a heavily forested
region, the sequence of right versus left turns may become a bewildering
maze (perhaps this possibility underlies our fear of being lost in a forest,
engendering "place-panic"). Even the seemingly infrangible difference between front and back is subject to confusion when we inhabit wilderness in
the dark: was that strange sound directly in front of me or just slightly to
the right?

At other moments, however, I am quite well oriented and at home in
the wild, enjoying a lucid and heightened sense of *how I am where I am*.
Moreover, the more I perceive or come to know wilderness as an orderly
scene—"that which appears to be chaotic in nature," says Gary Snyder, "is
only a more complex kind of order"[110]—the better are my chances of finding
my way around and feeling secure there. Yet in certain wild places my sense
of security may be altogether undone; Oliver Sacks reports that, suddenly
confronted by an angry bull on a Norwegian mountain trail, he was thrown
into a maelstrom of confused reactions, ending in a disastrous fall that suspended any stable sense of up and down.[111] The always lurking possibility
of being undone at some unpredictable moment—of being disarrayed in the
surrounding array—distinguishes wild from domesticated places. This is why
we feel so "exposed" in wilderness, always at risk there to some degree.

The other dyads besides up–down examined in part two are also at stake
in the experience of wilderness, though often in less dramatically disorienting
ways. When I experience wild places in terms of the near and the far, I find
myself enmeshed in a lived tension between what is directly underfoot or
close by and what is remote from me. The "far" presents itself as the domain
where the arc of the wildscape vanishes from my sight or touch. What is far
disappears at (and sometimes over) the horizon, which surrounds land or sea
laterally as surely as the ground on which I stand or move delimits my near
sphere from below. If my moving body is often mainly concerned with near
things and surfaces—e.g., with how to move just over there to the next turn
on the trail—it also enters into relationship with more distantly situated
theres: say, that summit toward which the same trail leads. When I am bod-

ily engaged in the here—there dialectic of wilderness, Husserl's notion of the "absolute here" as a "null point" of orientation is continually contested. Not only does my corporeal implacement in wild places resist formal geometrization—to conceive of my body as a mere *point* is to indulge in "morbid geometrism"[112]—but, still more important, the orientation is given *primarily by the places* and not by my own body (much less by my mind) in separation from them. It is from place itself that my body finds its way in place.

The dyadic relation of in—out is also critical in wilderness settings. When we reside somewhere, we are preoccupied with the dynamics of being *inside* buildings; if we are not already inside, then we are making motions to get there. Dwelling qua residing is always in-dwelling. In the realm of unbuilt and uncultivated places, however, we are situated *outside*, "on the outs" and thus exposed to the elements. Yet the contrast between built and wild realms is not always as stark as this. We may be outside in the inside (e.g., in inner courtyards) as well as inside in the outside (e.g., in a clearing surrounded by dense forestation). But to be entirely inside in wilderness—to be, for example, permanently ensconced in a cave—is as exceptional for human beings as being fully exposed to the elements when inside a residence. Most often, humans are drawn to places situated between these two extremes: interplaces epitomized by gardens and parks but also found in ordinary lawns, fields, and beaches. "The margins," writes Wendell Berry, "are of the utmost importance."[113] In the broad spectrum of possibilities that the in—out dyad presents for bodily movement, the architectural end of the spectrum favors the "in" while the wilderness extreme emphasizes the "out." The challenge is how to experience both extremities while remaining somewhere in the middle, between altogether wild places (inhospitable to human presence) and overly domesticated built places (closed off from the natural world).

The paramount point is that our bodies connect with wild places by means of a pre-configuration inherent in the natural world itself. We encounter and come to know wild places as they are pre-formed, not as they are formed by us. The pre-formation arises from the conjunction of sensuous surface and arc, ground and grounded things, as well as the surrounding array and the ubiquitous atmosphere. Thanks to this conflux of simultaneously given moments, wild places manifest themselves as there to be entered and explored by our living-moving bodies. In this entry and exploration, *wild places themselves take the lead*. However active and perceptive our bodies may be, they end by following this lead, tracing out the threads the wild world weaves before and around us. In the end—indeed, from the very beginning—we find ourselves respecting "the lay of the land," or the setting of the sea, the clues and reminders belonging to *it*, including its own natural geometry. From the wild world the lived body proceeds, and to this same world it is always in course of returning.

Following out this last line of thought, we reach an antipode in relation to certain traditional notions of place and space. In the tradition of Western modernism, what I have been calling "site" became the controlling notion for implacement of all kinds. Site itself is virtually featureless in its sheerly diaphanous and homogeneous-isotropic nature. To be a site is to be the mere occasion for the positioning of those obdurate material objects or "substances" upon which so much philosophical (and scientific) concern was focused in early modern times. Thus it is hardly surprising that Descartes attempted to equate *res extensa* and "space," since space on his view is constituted by the extended substances that occupy it without remainder. Nor is it surprising that Kant could locate the origin of space (construed as the order of coexisting substances) in a form of pure a priori intuition possessed by the human subject: here the lead, the transcendental source, is sought in this subject, who constitutes the phenomenal world from within its solitary domain.

The experience of wilderness, however, leads in a very different direction. For it is the character of the land or sea itself, its own distinctive place-setting, that determines how we discover and perceive what lies within its bounds. Wild things are not positioned in space as in a neutral medium; they are not confined to the simple locations that form the absolute presupposition of modern physical science. Instead, the basic traits of wild places configure in advance the way our body finds itself located in their domain. An a priori of the (known or unknown) wild world precedes—and thus supersedes—the a priori of the (knowing and unwild) subject.

The a priori of Nature is not merely a matter of what Aristotle took to be the close match between the snugly fitting surfaces of material objects. It arises instead from the complex conformation of all the already given constituents of wilderness itself. These constituents inhere in Nature *from the start*, often in supreme indifference to human interests and concerns. Only their full complexion, their intimate interleaving, decides the character and structure of wild places in their very wildness.

8

Going Wild in the Land

Gilgamesh struck the serpent who could not be charmed.
The *Anzu*-bird flew with his young to the mountains;
And Lilith smashed her home and fled to the wild, uninhabited places.

—From *Inanna: Queen of Heaven and Earth*

Here is non home, here nys but wyldernesse.

—Geoffrey Chaucer, "Truth"

The universe flows in infinite wild streams, related
In rhythms too big and too small for us to know.

—D. H. Lawrence, "The Universe Flows"

I

WE USUALLY ASSOCIATE the words *wilderness* and *wild* without pausing to consider their nuanced differences, even though it is evident that they do not have exactly the same range of connotation. The wild can occur anywhere (e.g., in the "wild weeds" of a vacant lot in the South Bronx), while wilderness is presumed to exist only in an undomesticated, altogether "natural" place, which presents itself to us as a wildscape. In the city, no wilderness exists, except by metaphorical extension; yet much wildness is there, in criminal violence as well as in a spirited street carnival.

The word *wildness* is not only an uncommon word but is strictly dependent on *wild* for its meaning. In the laconic formulation of the *Oxford English Dictionary*, wildness is "the quality or condition of being wild, in various senses." Only one of these senses (i.e., an "uncultivated state of a place or region") relates to the natural world, and even within this single sense, it only rarely signifies "a wild place, a wilderness." Otherwise, like *wild* itself, *wildness* mainly concerns distinctively *human* states of mind or body.[1]

But the matter is not quite as straightforward as this first glance at the history of words might suggest. Some philologists trace *wild* to the Latin *ferus*, wild beast, and hence to a denizen of wild places. *Wild* may also derive from Old English words such as *weald, wald, wold,* all of which signify woods or forested regions (as survives in the toponymic term *Cotswolds* and in the pleonastic expression *wild woods*). In drawing us in these two directions—i.e., toward undomesticated animals and savage woods—*wild* (and thus also *wildness*) therefore takes us back to matters of wilderness rather than to human states. In this light, *wilderness* emerges as the more encompassing term, even if its actual appearance as a word in English is historically later than *wild* and *wildness*.

Not that *wilderness* is a recent word. It was originally indistinguishable from Middle English *wilderne*, and its first usages have been traced back to the beginning of the thirteenth century.[2] As I hinted in chapter 7, the word may have come from Old English *wild(d)déor* (literally, "wild deer" but also meaning "wild beasts" collectively) and so, as in the case of *wild* itself, from what Bachelard calls "the need to animalize."[3] But it is even more likely that *wilderness* stems from *wild(d)éornes* by the addition to *wild* of *héahnes*, summit, or *smépnes*, flat lands.[4] *Wilderness* is thus, taken literally, "the place of wild beasts."[5] Considered still more completely, the word *wilderness* derives from a compound origin at once animalistic (via *déor*), humanly perceived (i.e., inasmuch as it is *experienced* as "wild"), and land-based (i.e., as summit or plain). Regarding this triadic source, the land factor, especially when it is supplemented by the sea, is the most important. For land or sea acts to contain unconstrained animal and human wildness by situating it and converting it into "wilderness." In this settled sense, which the word has come to assume in modern English, *wilderness* is itself based predominantly on aspects of the land or sea. In fact, three of the five main definitions of *wilderness* given in the *Oxford English Dictionary* draw directly on such aspects:

1. Wild or uncultivated land; a wild or uncultivated region or tract of land, uninhabited, or inhabited only by wild animals; a piece of ground in a large garden or park, planted with trees, and laid out in an ornamental or fantastic style, often in the form of a maze or labyrinth.

2. A waste or desolate region of any kind, e.g., of open sea, of air.

3. Something figured as a region of a wild or desolate character, or in which one wanders or loses one's way; in religious use applied to the present world or life as contrasted with heaven or the future life; rhetorically applied to a place (e.g., a building or town) which one finds "desolate," or in which one is lonely or "lost."

The phrases "waste or desolate region" and "wild or desolate character" remind us of the affinity between desolation and wild places. Although wilderness is not always desolate in itself, we easily imagine (and sometimes experience) it as a scene of intense desolation. Hence the seemingly natural link between wilderness and the arid desert regions described in the Old and New Testaments; ever since Wycliffe's first English translation of the Latin Bible in the late fourteenth century, *wilderness* has connoted for Judeo-Christian readers the dry, trackless lands of the Near East and, by extension, one's entire life regarded as a journey across a "waste land" of secular temptations.[6]

Apart from such a specifically religious and ethical employment of the term, *wilderness* has come to mean that kind of place or region (land or sea) in which one readily loses one's way, goes astray, and becomes literally bewildered.[7] In this aberrant action, one loses contact with one's home-place—whether as literal domicile, as religious center, or even as a place of temporary but safe sojourn—and begins to find the situation increasingly desolate in the very senses discussed in the preceding chapter. In Husserl's language, "home-world" (*Heimwelt*) gives way to "alien world" (*Fremdwelt*).[8]

But such bewildered wildness—such desolate lostness in the alien otherness of Nature—does not have to mean that wilderness is altogether inimical to human presence. The wandering at issue remains an action *of* human beings *in* the wilderness. We wander in wilderness as in a maze, but a maze is a human construction. Can it be accidental that just after wilderness has been defined as a "wild or uncultivated region or tract of land, uninhabited, or inhabited only by wild animals," it is *also* said to be "a piece of ground in a large garden or park . . . often in the form of a maze or labyrinth"? Such a wilderness is not found but *made*: it is "*planted* with trees, and *laid out* in an ornamental or fantastic style." What does this juxtaposition of the artfully shaped with the naturally wild portend for the problematic place of human beings within the wildness of wilderness?

Otherwise put: how do "culture" and "nature" relate, or fail to relate, in the unsettling setting of wild places?

II

On the rudest surface of English earth, there is seen the effect of centuries
of civilization, so that you do not quite get at naked Nature anywhere.
And then every point of beauty is so well known, and has been described
so much, that one must needs look through other people's eyes, and feel as if
he were seeing a picture rather than a reality.

—Nathaniel Hawthorne, letter written on visiting
the Lake District of England, 1855

Everything is cultural in us (our *Lebenswelt* is "subjective") (our perception is
cultural-historical) and everything is natural in us (even the cultural rests on
the polymorphism of wild Being).

—Maurice Merleau-Ponty, Working Note of May 1960,
The Visible and the Invisible

Culture and *cultivation* were synonymous in Middle English, a reflection of the fact that both words derive from the Latin *cultus*, worship. *Cultus* in turn stems from *colere*, to take care of, till, occupy, dwell. The mention of "dwell" forewarns us of a curious twist in the history of the word *culture*. Despite its current connotation of "higher" learning, this word has profound roots in the land and the soil. *Colonia*, farm, landed estate, and *colonus*, tiller, cultivator, settler, are cousins once removed from the common stem of *colere*. Colonists are settlers and tillers and dwellers in new lands, usually after having crossed high seas. *Agriculture*, a first cousin of *culture*, explicitly brings together cultivation and land (*ager* in Latin signifies "field"). In fact, the English word *culture* at first meant a piece of tilled land; its meaning evolved from this early, fifteenth-century sense to that of "manners" in the sixteenth century. Only in the nineteenth century did *culture* come to connote what is acquired by advanced artistic and intellectual education.[9] But the biological term *tissue culture* acts to remind us of the continuing rootedness of culture in nature. At the very least, these vicissitudes indicate that the cultural and the natural are not nearly as disparate as we, by this late point in twentieth-century civilization, often imagine them to be.

The same vicissitudes—in tandem with those of the words *wild* and *wilderness*—bring us face to face with a basic dilemma. On one hand, the epigenesis of words signifies that the cultural leads us inexorably back to the natural. To be cultured is to be cultivated; but to cultivate is to plough the land—if not the topsoil of the actual earth, then the topsoil of pregiven syntactical structures. On the other hand, to pursue nature into its own lair—its wild places—is still to adhere to culture. Even stationed squarely in the midst of the wilds of nature, *we cannot get away from, or around, the cultural*. Hawthorne, in the above epigram, points to the ineluctable contribution of culture, a contribution not just to the literal landscape but to our very manner of perceiving this landscape. The truth of Hawthorne's remark comes home to us whenever we gaze upon a wild scene and see, instead of untutored Nature, a landscape informed by our acquaintance with the paintings of Constable or Cézanne. We see the scene through, or rather *with*, the eyes of these painters.

Both sides of this dilemma point toward the recognition of the deep imbrication of culture and nature in the land, including its wildest reaches. (The same imbrication is found in cultural artifacts: to speak of cultivating a writing style is to mix together what might otherwise be considered separate things, tilling and text.) But we still do not know the exact relationship of the cultural and the natural within wilderness; how do these two factors help to constitute, indeed to co-constitute, the appearance and structure of wild places?

We can begin to answer this question only if we manage to avoid espousing two extreme positions—"utter wilderness" and "culture in the wild"—each of which nevertheless offers certain temptations.

1. *Utter wilderness.* In this view, the only truly wild places are those altogether untouched and untracked by human presence. Not only do such places exist—at least a few of them still do—but they alone represent Nature in its fully sovereign state, which culture and its by-products cannot help but defile. We observe such a view in the rhetoric (if not always in the actual practice) of John Muir, especially in this passage from his essay "The Discovery of Glacier Bay by Its Discoverer":

> Climbing higher for a still broader outlook, I made notes and sketched, improving the precious time while sunshine streamed through the luminous fringes of the clouds, and fell on . . . the ineffably chaste and spiritual heights of the Fairweather Range, which were now hidden, now partly revealed, the whole making a picture of icy wildness unspeakably pure and sublime.[10]

If we set aside the late-Victorian tendency to spiritualize wilderness—a tendency also evident in contemporary painters of wild places such as Frederick Church and Albert Bierstadt—we notice that Muir's fascination with the mountains around Glacier Bay stems from his sense that he is the first (at least the first Anglo-American person) to lay eyes on this wilderness. This is the purport of his use of the terms *chaste* and *pure*, both of which reinforce his conviction that he has *discovered* this wild place. Unentered and unseen, such a place has awaited this moment to be dis-covered and ex-plored. But in its "icy wildness" it does not *need* to be discovered or explored. The place could have continued in a distinctly savage state for time immemorial and still have been "unspeakably pure and sublime." Muir speaks disparagingly of "the decent, deathlike apathy of weary civilized people, in whom natural curiosity has been quenched in toil and care and poor, shallow comfort."[11] Such people are out of touch with the very Nature that, were they to intrude into it, they would pollute (even though, on Muir's diagnosis, they desperately need to sojourn in it).

Muir's pronunciamentos exemplify a polar, indeed a polarizing, position in the nature–culture debate. The attitude they reveal is by no means unique to Muir. Traces of it are present in many who would consider themselves more moderate in their persuasion. For those who find the paradigmatic form of Nature to lie in its undisturbed state and who believe that *preservation* means keeping wilderness in an entirely pristine condition, only the unmarked features of a wild place belong to it truly; its proper inhabitants are its own spontaneously engendered flora and nonhuman animal species, its rocks and its earth. Human beings are literally *personae non gratis* in wild Nature.

2. *Culture in the wild.* At the opposite extreme is a resolutely culturalist position. In this second view, human beings are not only welcome but *essen-*

tial presences in wilderness. For culturalists, there can be no meaningful sense of wilderness that does not include a specifically human element: you cannot get to wild places, much less appreciate or understand them, except by cultural means. The paradigm of wild places becomes not that of raw wilderness—much less the wildness that simmers beneath and within wilderness itself—but a literary or pictorial representation *of* such places. Blount's *Glossographia* (1656) states that "all that which in a Picture is not of the Body or argument thereof is Landskip, Parergon, or By-work."[12] But "landskip" refused to be confined to the margins. As "landscape," it moved to the center of the scene of wilderness. Nature as depicted in landscape painting is Nature *as seen* by human beings. It is not surprising, then, that the very word *landscape* came to mean "a view or prospect of natural inland scenery" (*O.E.D.*). Eventually, the painted prospect was incorporated into the ordinary perceiver's prospect, which regards Nature *as* (*or like*) *a painting*. Whether the view of Nature is embedded in a painting or is subsequently taken up as "perspective" by someone in the midst of wilderness, human presence is ineluctably part of any experience of wilderness.[13]

In this light we may reconsider the passage from Muir's essay of 1895, which ends with the clause "the whole *making a picture* of icy wildness unspeakably pure and sublime." Underlining the clause "making a picture" changes things considerably. Instead of regarding the icy wildness in its unadulterated purity and sublimity, we now think of such wildness as conveyable to us mainly, or perhaps only, as a picture of some sort. "One feels," as Hawthorne says, "as if he were seeing a picture rather than a reality."[14] And if we emphasize the opening words of the same long sentence of Muir's, another nuance emerges: "Climbing higher for *a still broader outlook*, I *made notes and sketched*, improving the precious time while sunshine streamed . . . "[15] Not only does Muir engage in the explicitly cultural event of drawing (i.e., making pictures qua graphic images) and of writing (i.e., making pictures in words), he expressly adopts a viewing-point, an "outlook," from which to observe Glacier Bay. Moreover, by "improving the precious time" in an industrious twofold way, he implicates himself in the undeniably cultural action of time-binding. Thus, even in the midst of Muir's eloquent advocacy of landscape as utter wildness, we witness the intrusion of the slim but tenacious arm of culture.

In the second extreme view, then, nothing natural is untainted with the traces of culture. Not only is it the case that wilderness can *become* acculturated; it is *already*, from the very start, *cultural through and through*. Every wildscape is perforce a "culturescape," and it does not take the forces of a highly cultivated culture to invade and to reorient a natural landscape. Wallace Stevens put it this way in "Anecdote of the Jar":

I placed a jar in Tennessee,
And round it was, upon a hill.
It made the slovenly wilderness
Surround that hill.

The wilderness rose up to it,
And sprawled around, no longer wild.
The jar was round upon the ground
And tall and of a port in air.

It took dominion everywhere.
The jar was gray and bare.
It did not give of bird or bush,
Like nothing else in Tennessee.[16]

Merely placing a jar, that emblem of low technological culture, on a hill—
even a delicate poetic placing, an implacement in words alone—is enough to
alter the scene substantially, transubstantiating it into a circumstance in
which the jar takes "dominion everywhere." So much so that the very wildness of wilderness (a distinction the poet respects) is expunged at one stroke:
"the wilderness rose up to it, / And sprawled around, *no longer wild.*" An
ordinary jar does not merely reside in the natural environment or just leave
its trace there. "Like nothing else in Tennessee," the cultural object commands the presence of the wild world.

III

In order to be able to live within the order, in other words, in order to be
consciously tame or domesticated, one had to have lived in the wilderness.
One could know what *inside* meant only if one had once been *outside.*
—Hans Peter Duerr, *Dreamtime*

A little pure wildness is the one great present need, both of men and sheep.
—John Muir, "Wild Wool"

Like Scylla and Charybdis, the two positions just sketched represent extremes in thinking about wilderness. They call for our careful assessment, not
simply because they are extreme (truth is sometimes found *in extremis*) but
because they fail to reflect the full complexity of the relationship between
Nature and Culture (regarded as extremities). Nevertheless, as in the case of
the Antinomies of Pure Reason, we must first analyze the antithetical positions themselves to see how well they withstand critical scrutiny.

   1. *Wilderness as culture-free.* To posit a place or region entirely indepen-

dent of cultural connection or resonance is to conceive of something akin to a thing-in-itself, inaccessible to thought or language, even to sensing and perceiving. It is thus to bar human beings from any effective approach, much less any actual ingression. At the very least, it is to presume that even when we do enter wilderness as an autonomous and self-enclosed region, we can be no more than foreign and irrelevant presences there—"natural aliens" in Neil Evernden's term.[17] We may seem to *pass through* such sheer wilderness in fact or in fantasy, but we cannot really *touch* it, or be *touched* by it, much less make any significant difference to it.

This is an extraordinary and, indeed, excessive claim to make. Beyond the fact that statements in words and sentences concerning the acultural status of wilderness require culture itself for their own formulation and persuasive power, we must wonder whether the experience (and even the bare invocation) of wild places does not *eo ipso* entail certain culturally specific factors of history and language. Above all, we must ask: is it meaningful to speak of *any* place on earth, including the least habitable and most desolate, as altogether independent of the domain of culture? To begin with, human beings not only traverse wild places—coming into intimate contact with them at many points—but they leave their marks on them and even come to inhabit them, however precariously. The merest footpath embodies an intention to move through wilderness in a certain way and toward a certain destination, both of which are culturally determinate. A bare lean-to in a forest is a concrete symbol of the collective character and purposes of the civilization that has made it possible, and is a form of dwelling in the extended sense discussed in chapters 5 and 6.[18]

I am not saying, of course, that wild landscape requires the actual presence of human beings on any given occasion. People can be absent from a wild place or region for a very long time—perhaps no one has been there yet—and still the cultural dimension will be adumbrated in the scene, nascently or tacitly present. Even the most thoroughly "virgin" wilderness does not preclude the possible onset of human culture. The summit of Mount Everest, although resisting human intrusion for a considerable period, finally yielded in 1954 and has since yielded many more times. Certain physical features of this formidable natural object, i.e., ledges, passes, and other possible perches for intrepid sherpas and ambitious mountain climbers, long prefigured the eventual ascent. Mount Everest was "there-to-be-climbed," and this hyphenated construction is itself a cultural mark that pertained to the mountain in its unscaled state.[19]

A wild place is appropriated not just *by* culture but *to* culture. When this place has a concrete effect on the natural state of a nearby populated region—as occurs in the case of the Tibetan plateau just north of Mount Everest—it is itself influential upon various cultural habitudes, most obviously specifically agricultural ones. In such cases, wilderness is drawn into the work of culture by being assimilated to it. The fallout of the wild is taken up by culture and made intrinsic to it. On the other hand, a wild place can be appropriated by a culture and yet remain an alien presence within that culture. A photograph of Mount Everest may serve as a reminder of what is still most heterogeneous within Himalayan culture. It is an image not just of another place but of place-itself-as-Other, resisting acculturation of any obvious sort.[20]

Consider a brief thought-experiment. If a wild place you enter fails to offer any evident point of attachment or support—say, an unending stretch of desert or a wild patch of sea—how would you feel? Most likely, I would wager, quite desolate. Just when wilderness fails to furnish any obvious prefiguration of my presence or any possibility of protection, I begin to feel abandoned and forlorn, deprived of that saving remnant of place-provision on which human beings count for their continued existence. At the very least, this grim prospect illustrates how much we rely on, indeed take for granted, an ongoing collusion between the natural and the cultural: the nomad feels at home on the desert precisely on the basis of such a collusion. We depend on this collusion, moreover, whether we are in the midst of a highly civilized and technologized setting or in the thick of wilderness itself. Or more exactly, we rely on the real *possibility* of such collusion. Even when it is *now* seemingly altogether lacking, we believe that it can somehow—somewhen—take place. The most recalcitrant wild place, we presume, will someday accommodate the human. This bedrock belief betokens a basic judgment that the natural is ultimately accessible to the cultural.

Despite the cultural underbelly of untamed wilderness, there is nonetheless a residual truth in the first antinomical position. Even after acknowledging the many-sided insinuation of culture into nature, we must also acknowledge that the natural world is perfectly capable of standing on its own. It does not *need* human acculturation and enculturation in order to be what it is. It is what it is. If it is not self-creating, it is certainly self-sustaining. Thanks to its ingeniously self-regulating geohistory and its biosystems (of which the biosphere is the most comprehensive instance), it has preceded human presence on the planet and will doubtless outlast the demise of this presence.

2. *Wilderness as culture-bound.* Having just questioned a first extreme thesis, we now need to assess its equally radical counterpart, which holds that the natural world, even in its wildest parts, *requires culture.* In this view, wildness itself becomes the mere veneer on an unavoidably cultural foundation, from which there is no effective escape—just the converse of the idea

that culture itself is the mere froth on the deep waters of the wild. Tempting as this second position may be—and all the more so in the wake of the foregoing discussion—the limits of its validity must now be assayed.

These limits become evident as soon as we reconsider the basic features of wild places as identified in the preceding chapter. *None of these traits can be exhaustively analyzed in strictly culturalist terms.* Each retains an uneliminable residue of the extra- or precultural, indeed of wilderness itself. For instance, the arc of a wild place belongs to it as a perceived—or, more exactly, a *sensed*—trait that inheres in the place from the moment of our first encounter with it. Unlike the strictly linear horizon (which, as we know from the history of art, is a concerted cultural product), the arc is part of the field of affordances and, as such, is pregiven, i.e., given *before* any explicitly cultural contribution can occur. The same is true of the atmosphere, which is still more profoundly elemental in status. We need not agree with Anaximines—or with modern physics—as to its precise physical constitution in order to affirm its integral presence in the wild world, its presentation to us as *toujours déjà là*. By the same token, what I have called "ground" comes to us as preexisting any given encounter with it. We count on ground to be there in ongoing experience, so much so that Husserl called it the "earth-ark," the grounding principle of all human experience.[21] However massive or subtle cultural influence may be in a given instance, it can only be superimposed on such a ground in the form of a "garb of ideas" (*Ideenkleid*, literally, "idea-gown"). On this ground also rest the various material things (and Things) that co-constitute a particular wildscape, punctuating it and filling it up. Although these things/Things, along with their sensuous surfaces, are liable to be swept up in myriad interpretative schemes, they certainly do not present themselves as cultural in status from the start but as particulars preceding culture in any of the more highly organized formats which human discourse provides.

The surrounding array also appears to arise in comparative independence of cultural contributions. However much we feel tempted to construe this array in cultural categories, it precedes these categories in the order of experience.[22] Such precedence is just what *surrounding* connotes: we are immediately, and constantly, sur-rounded by the sensed array, just as we are immersed in whatever landscape we happen to find ourselves in. In contrast with Stevens's contention, however, no cultural object *makes* the "slovenly wilderness" surround us. Moreover, the changes in this array are so complex and so continual that they elude even the most sophisticated conceptual grid. Any such grid is, as it were, *always too late* to capture (or, rather, recapture) the many sensory arrays that wash over and around and through us in the course of experiencing even the most straightforwardly presented wild place.[23]

Indeed, the land or the sea in its wildness actively *resists* our efforts to colonize it with cultural means. It is recalcitrant to these efforts, taking *recalcitrant* literally as "kicking back against" the constraints and restraints of culture. Once again, wild places exhibit "Secondness" in Peirce's sense: the refractory facticity of objects set over against us. As Peirce says of sheer Secondness, it "jabs you perpetually in the ribs."[24] The Second is what ex-ists—i.e., stands out against—and is thus powerfully reactive.[25] "Outer objects," writes Peirce, "are hard facts that no man can make to be other than they are."[26] Such facts are at once "blind" and "brute," and they induce in us a distinct "sense of shock [that] is as much a sense of resisting as of being acted upon."[27] Peirce intended this last sentence to be a description of lightning, a paradigmatic phenomenon of Nature in its wild indifference to humankind. An unanticipated stroke of lightning, disruptively illuminating the land or sea over which it breaks, puts an entire culture on notice.[28]

A wild place is a Second to culture—its very Other—insofar as its very existence constitutes a challenge to cultural hegemony. Each experience of a wild place jabs us in the ribs and takes us by surprise, if we are truly open to the experience. But the shock value of wilderness is precisely what makes it valuable to those immersed in what Thoreau calls a "culture merely civil."[29] In its rebarbative sting, wilderness reminds us of what precedes and exceeds the comforts of culture. Precisely as resisting complete captivation by cultural constructs, it retains an instructive impenetrability, a permanent impassivity, an obdurate outsideness.[30]

Yet the wild world, for all its independence and resistance, remains, if not culture-bound, at least culture-permeable. It lends itself to expression and representation in culturally specific objects, not only in words and images but also in bodily and institutional practices. The Secondness of wilderness invites the Thirdness of its symbolization.[31] Indeed, we cannot identify a first place of wilderness not already marked by such symbolization. I say that "*we* cannot identify" such a first acultural place. To detect, even to imagine, a pristine place of wilderness is already to project our own presence *in that place*, if not in fact then in mind.

There is no first wild place not already in the second place of culture. There is no abyss of wilderness not already papered over (or under or around) with the text of culture. This text is a contexture: at once a texture—something closely woven—and a context. Culture contextualizes every corner of nature, including the wildest ones. The wild texture of these corners is already frayed by the domesticating f(r)iction of acculturating and enculturating processes. Even "the polymorphism of wild Being" is as tied to the cultural world as Prometheus—the first bearer of cultural life—was tied to the desolate rock on which he was exposed.

Just as there is no strict void (i.e., a spatial void devoid of things-in-place), so there is no absolute wilderness, a wilderness altogether devoid of, or impervious to, cultural categories. Even if these categories are invoked post hoc, this does not prevent their *pervasion* of wilderness.[32] The jar in Tennessee, though an ordinary object, is extraordinarily engaged with its wild surroundings. It permeates them much as a category permeates the things it categorizes, subtly and yet pervasively. The same is true of any cultural object that engages wilderness. The at least partial truth of culturalism is that some such object is always already stationed in wilderness: if not a jar, a jug; if not a jug, a path; if not a path, a bridge; if not an actual bridge, an imagined bridge.[33]

The abyss of wilderness, its fearsome unknownness, may be the generative force lying behind both the antinomical positions I have been examining. Each position can be seen as a response to abyssal wildness. Each would be a distinctive way of dealing with the place-panic occasioned by wilderness-as-void, exemplified in the recurring image of wilderness-as-desert. Still another response to such an abyss—which could be considered the ultimate displacement—is desolation. All three responses deal with the abyss of Nature by fleeing into the arms of extremity. Any such reactive flight reflects the perception that even if Nature is not *causa sui*, or self-caused, in its very wildness it is a cause to be reckoned with. It calls for extreme measures. This is so even if the two measures at stake in this section and the last have shown themselves to be inadequate as bases for understanding wilderness on its own forceful terms, culture in its immanence and pervasion, and (above all) nature and culture themselves in their intimate intertwining.

The root of the problem is not just the antagonism of thesis and antithesis. It is also, and more fundamentally, to be found in a hidebound exclusivity, a common (but inverse) attempt to keep the Other, whether as Nature or as Culture, entirely outside the self-enclosed orbit each takes as an exclusive starting-point. The natural and the cultural pervade each other utterly, however. Everything is (incipiently) cultural *in nature* and everything is (ultimately) natural *in culture*.

IV

Nature is so pervaded with human life that there is something of humanity
in all, and in every particular.
—Ralph Waldo Emerson, *Nature*

Despite the manifest disparities between the two contrary (but not contradictory) positions I have just analyzed, in the end *les extrêmes se touchent*. Thesis and antithesis converge not just in their dogmatic all-or-nothing attitude but also—as I have just intimated—in a shared stance of mutual exclusion. Yet each, in attempting to exclude its Other, ends by covertly incorporating this Other into itself. In this chiasmatic cross-back, we witness the unanticipated return of the repressed and thus a counter-dialectic that can be considered a species of auto-deconstruction. In the instance of position 1, that of "wilderness only," cultural factors subtend its own statement and condition its very possibility. Culture returns, whether in the form of a felt need to sketch and make notes upon witnessing wilderness or merely on an ordinary hike in the woods in which we realize how the natural world allows for human presence (on the trail) even as it discourages it (in dense underbrush off the trail). In the case of position 2, "culture everywhere," wildness, that alien renegade factor, returns to cultural settings, including that described in "Anecdote of the Jar." For the poet has no choice but to place the jar in an *already existing* wilderness. In its precedence, as well as by its continuing recalcitrance, this wilderness cannot be altogether excluded. The hill in Tennessee proves resistant to cultural dissolution in the form of poetic sublimation. The return of the repressed is here the return of native ground, and this return is as insistent as the return of a reinforced cultural category. Each otherness reenters the other. In this scene of mutual invasion, not only *can* the two alterities coexist; they *must* do so.

The ultimate compatibility of the natural and the cultural within wild places has already been hinted at in my assessments of positions 1 and 2. What does *prefiguration* mean but a situation in which wilderness itself makes room for culture in advance, that is, a priori? Rather than a model of culture as superimposed, a model of predisposed (but not preestablished or predictable) harmony suggests itself as a way out of the impasse implied in antinomical positions. By *harmony* I do not mean balance or equilibrium. In place of the ideal of equipoise between dwelling places and environing world often at stake in part three, here nature assumes the leading role. This role is evident in the relationship between lightning and the lightning rod. Lightning strikes first. But thanks to the lightning rod—whose verticality echoes the directionality of lightning itself—lightning can be tamed and even made useful. Conversely, we observe a bending-back of culture into nature when we read Muir's account of his discovery of Glacier Bay: the rhetoric, the wordiness, the "picture" this account sets forth brings us into a new (or renewed) proximity to the ice-bound wildness it so movingly describes.

The Other certainly does return, not only as repressed but as expressed. The lion lies down with the lamb in ever-new versions of "The Peaceable Kingdom" (the title of Edward Hicks's remarkable paintings of an innocent child in the congenial company of wild beasts). Nature rejoins culture and culture nature, on terms not just fitting but mutually enlivening, achieving what Wendell Berry calls "a continuous harmony." Such harmony does not exclude disharmony, any more than the same, in Heidegger's account, excludes the different. Nature and culture, while not equal or identical, differ within a sameness to which they both, precisely as differing, belong.[34]

Perhaps this is what John Ruskin had in mind when he wrote that "above the village of Champagnole . . . is a spot which has all the solemnity, with none of the savageness, of the Alps; where there is a sense of a great power beginning to be manifested in the earth, and of a deep and majestic concord in the rise of the long low lines of piny hills."[35] These words suggest that even short of "savageness," a wild place can possess its own "great power." But this power, "manifested in the earth," need not attain the sublime, which Ruskin deliberately plays down; the lower Alps exhibit, he adds, a "strength [that] is as yet restrained."[36] Instead of the dramatic discord inherent in the sublime—a discord, according to Kant, between imagination and under-standing—there is "a deep and majestic concord." This concord, I propose, exists not just between the outlines of hills but also between the cultural and the natural.

Ruskin concludes his description: "The deep crests of the sable hills that rose against the evening received a deeper worship, because their far shadows fell eastward over the iron wall of Joux, and the four-square keep of Gran-son."[37] We have seen that "worship" is the root sense of *cultus*, the etymon of *culture* as well as *cultivate*. Ruskin espies the cultural in the scene of the natural, most explicitly in the form of the abandoned French fortresses of Joux and Granson. Culture connects closely with Nature in the format of architecture. But the interlacing can take place in many other formats as well, some of which are not architectural at all. One of these formats is the written word, which both Ruskin and Muir (himself influenced by Ruskin)[38] employ with exquisite effectiveness in conveying an alive sense of wilderness to their readers. Nature Alive in language! In this acculturating act, the wildness of the land is recaptured and redeemed in the wilderness of the word.

V

In Wildness is the preservation of the World.
—Henry David Thoreau, "Walking"

But I retained the landscape.
—Thoreau, *Walden*

The fates of Nature and Culture are intertangled, and have been ever since human beings began to roam and settle the earth. Even to indicate bounds *around* an impenetrable wilderness area—in fact or in imagination— is to invoke a cultural practice, i.e., boundary-setting, in the delimitation of the area. Indeed, the very idea of delimiting and "preserving" wild places is culturally charged and historically specific. One form of preservation occurred in the protection of copses, or small forests, in medieval England. Another form arose in the decision to set aside Yosemite as a state park in 1864. The thinking behind this latter decision had been formulated by Thoreau in 1858: "Why should we not . . . have our national preserves . . . in which the bear and the panther, and some even of the hunter race, may still exist, and not be 'civilized off the face of the earth'?"[39] Rather than thinking of Nature and Culture as antipodes between which we must make a forced choice, we ought to regard them as coexisting in various forms of commixture within a *middle realm*, a genuine "multifarious between," in which the partners are in a relation of "consanguinity."[40]

Thoreau's words already strike the theme of the middle ground between culture and nature (words I shall de-capitalize whenever their putative antagonism has been mitigated). Thoreau's idea of "national preserves," for instance, combines the cultural entity of the "nation" with the natural region of the "preserve"; and "preserve" is in turn both cultural (as a matter of delimiting and protecting) and natural (as *what* is delimited and protected). In such preserves bear and panther (emblematic denizens of wild places) can coexist peaceably with human beings of "the hunter race," i.e., Native Americans. In a journal entry of 1859, Thoreau urged: "Let us keep the New World *new*, [and] preserve all the advantages of living in the country."[41] Preservation of wilderness, far from excluding the compresence of the human, is consonant with "living in the country," a phrase that betokens the merging of the cultural with the natural. Thoreau invites us to think of wilderness preservation as con-servation, culture serving *with* nature, staying within its bounds instead of merely setting bounds on it.

Keeping "the New World *new*" does not mean, then, that wild places must be kept entirely free from every effect of enculturation, only the destructive and disrespectful ones. It is a premise of Thoreau's thought that wilderness is not chaos but a world: its very "Wildness," in the words of the above epigraph, allows for "the preservation of the World."[42] The world thus preserved is conjoint in character, natural-cum-cultural.

Living in the country and creating a world there is just what Thoreau undertook in his experiment at Walden. He sought to live in this wild place and on it, that is, *on its terms*; but at the same time, he wished to make a coherent world out of his experience. In the end, the two intentions coalesced: "Life consists with wildness."[43] The consistency is exemplified in Thoreau's basic project of persistent inhabitation. To inhabit a wild place is to make it increasingly familiar, so much so that the true wildness of the place (not to be confused with a veneer of violence) can be fully savored. The savoring is to be done "every where,"[44] in cultivated as in uncultivated regions, nearby as well as far away, not only outside in the forest but within the mind as well.

Walden is Thoreau's lasting tribute to his two-year sojourn in a single wild place only a mile and a half south of Concord. This place did not harbor panthers or even bears. Its claim to wildness consisted merely in the fact that it was a hilly tract of land, populated largely by birds and fish, and containing a central pond and surrounding forests (some of which had been cleared by an earlier generation). Otherwise, the place was virtually uninhabited, except for occasional transients and workers on a railroad at its edge. In comparison with the overcultivated and overstuffed parlors of Concord, however, it was quite wild enough for Thoreau's purposes.

Thoreau's first major action at Walden—when "first I took up my abode in the woods"[45] on July 4, 1845—was to build a small and as yet roofless house. Comparing this shack both to a boat and a tent, he remarks that "with this more substantial shelter about me, I had made some progress toward settling in the world."[46] Boat, tent, and shack are members of a distinctive middle realm. Each of these fragile constructions, in being partly enclosed, provides protection while, as also partially open, allowing its incumbent to remain in direct communication with the surrounding wild place. In building his hut, Thoreau was able to settle into the wider natural world of the woods by carpentering his own human world near the pond. Thus he writes: "I have, as it were, my own sun and moon and stars, *and* a little world all to myself."[47] The conjunctive "and" in this sentence indicates that the two worlds are continuous: the little world of human building is at one with the larger world of nonhuman nature.

As if to prove the point, Thoreau is not in any hurry to cover over his shelter with a roof:

> This frame, so slightly clad, was a sort of crystallization around me, and reacted on the builder. It was suggestive somewhat as a picture in outlines. I did not need to go out doors to take the air, for the atmosphere within had lost none of its freshness. It was not so much within doors as behind a door where I sat, even in the rainiest weather.[48]

The porous frame—also compared to a bird cage[49]—"reacted on the builder" insofar as it brought nature into his immediate ambit instead of keeping it at bay. It was not necessary to leave the structure to get fresh air, to "take the air." Even the rain was welcomed in the intermediate space, the semi-domestic place, of the half-built structure. No wonder that Thoreau compares the situation to that of "a picture in outlines." The comparison is not casual: the perspectivism of landscape painting, with its "views," is an epitome of the cultivation of nature. At Walden, nature was literally en-cultured by entering *into* the literal out-lines, the standing walls, of Thoreau's roofless cabin.

But by the same token, the hut and its builder are in turn encompassed in the greater world of nature. It is a matter of double incorporation: nature is brought within the shelter, but this within is also brought within the larger circumambience of the natural setting.[50] By this chiasmatic action, the natural world can be considered as something like a *house*. To inhabit the hut is to inhabit the house of nature. Put otherwise: the hut is the between in which the cultural and the natural are co-inhabitants. "If we name this multifarious between the world," says Heidegger, "then the world is the house where mortals dwell."[51]

Thanks to his building, Thoreau finds himself "seated by the shore of a small pond."[52] To be *seated* is to sit on something constructed to support the human frame and to let it linger for a comfortable while. Not just pieces of furniture but entire houses serve as seats. Thus Thoreau asks himself: "What is a house but a *sedes*, a seat?—better if a country seat."[53] A "country seat" makes "living in the country" possible, and is an epitome of the middle realm between nature and culture. At Walden Thoreau not merely *enters* this realm; he *constitutes* the realm itself by building a residence near the shore of a pond. In building his cabin, he re-seats himself in the house of nature: *re-sidēre* means to settle back.

No sooner has Thoreau built his cabin and finally put a roof over it than he describes gleefully putting his possessions onto the ground outside in order to scrub the floor inside:

> It was pleasant to see my whole household effects out on the grass, making a little pile like a gypsey's pack. . . . They seemed glad to get out themselves, and as if unwilling to be brought in. I was sometimes tempted to stretch an awning over them and take my seat there. It was worth the while to see the sun shine on these things, and hear the free wind blow on them; so much more interesting most familiar objects look out of doors than in the house.[54]

Another cross-over is here realized: domestic items that usually belong inside are brought outside, where Thoreau takes up a momentary *un*built seat. But more than contingent reversal of position is at stake. The household effects welcome their place in the sun, and their appearance becomes distinctly "more interesting." What matters, then, is not customary position but con-geniality of place. In a truly con-genial place such as the natural world furnishes to furniture, there can be a free exchange of properties, made possible precisely by the loss of the usual cloistered and possessive sense of *property* and *propriety*. The molded wood of furniture merges with the wood from which it came in the first place:

> . . . life-everlasting grows under the table, and blackberry vines run round its legs; pine cones, chestnut burs, and strawberry leaves are strewn about. It looked as if this was the way these forms came to be transferred to our furniture, to tables, chairs, and bedsteads—because they once stood in their midst.[55]

In this enactment of the middle realm, culture rejoins nature by an act of counter-transference. Furniture reconnects with that from which it had become alienated in the very process of its own construction.

We find much the same chiasmatic logic of reconnection—so definitively different from the antinomical logic of disconnection—in another scene at Walden. The celebrated chapter bearing the title "Reading" appears immediately after the chapter entitled "Where I Lived, and What I Lived For," from which I have been drawing the above vignettes. It is as if Thoreau were saying that only once *situ*ated, being seated some*where*—"*where it was* then that I lived"[56]—can one begin to practice culture in its more advanced forms. Far from being antithetical to such practice, the natural setting of Walden is ideal for it: "My residence was more favorable, not only to thought, but to serious reading, than a university."[57] It was certainly more favorable than Concord: "Consider how little this village does for its own culture."[58]

The point, however, is not that Walden is a quiet and solitary place in which to read books. As the author remarks laconically in the next chapter, "I did not read books the first summer; I hoed beans."[59] Another kind of reading, reading nature, is at stake. In a celebrated passage, Thoreau writes:

> But while we are confined to books, though the most select and classic, and read only particular written languages, which are themselves but dialects and provincial, we are in danger of forgetting the language which all things and events speak without metaphor, which alone is copious and standard. [In that language] much is published, but little printed.[60]

Thus reading, the epitome of high culture, crosses back upon itself. At Walden the best use of reading is not for continually higher cultivation but for cultivating a different kind of perusal, one that takes the natural world as its text. In this way reading returns to its origin in natural things; it becomes an enhanced and heightened *seeing* that involves "the discipline of looking always at what is to be seen."[61]

Building, cleaning, reading (and writing: equally important)[62]—prototypical cultural activities—all point to one end, which is sympathy. *Sympathy* is a richly resonant term for Thoreau, connoting both the basis for inhabiting a wild place (without a minimal initial sympathetic feeling for the place, settling there is risky) *and* the result of the inhabitation itself (i.e., as the fruit of continual inhabitation). In sympathetic bonding with a wild place, the unknown is made known, the desolate becomes delicious, the Dismal Swamp is sanctified.[63] But, by the same token, the known becomes unknown, dismal and desolate, strange to us, in the very midst of the familiar. The wildness of a wild place consists in this two-way intercourse between known and unknown, self and other, culture and nature.[64] For such a multifarious between to be realized, sympathy must exist between the principles thereby brought into connection, or rather, brought *back* into a chiasmatic reconnection which their consanguinity has prepared in advance but which highfalutin cultivation has all but exsanguinated.

While empathy is one-sided—in being em-pathic, I feel *in myself* how the other feels, the two of us remaining distinct entities—sym-pathy is a reciprocal affair in which each party feels *with* the other. In sympathetic bonding, the parties themselves dissolve as separate entities. Such bonding is presumed in Thoreau's otherwise seemingly exaggerated claim that "I go and come with a strange liberty in Nature, *a part of herself.*"[65] The participation inherent in sympathetic reconnection is also evident in a pronouncement made near the end of the chapter on "Solitude":

> The indescribable innocence and beneficence of Nature—of sun and wind and rain, of summer and winter—such health, such cheer, they afford forever! and *such sympathy have they ever with our race*, that all Nature would be affected, and the sun's brightness fade, and the winds would sigh humanely, and the clouds rain tears, and the woods shed their leaves and put on mourning in midsummer, if any man should ever for a just cause grieve. Shall I not have intelligence with the earth? Am I not partly leaves and vegetable mould myself?[66]

Sympathy in nature is bivalent action and reaction between the human and the wild. On one hand, natural phenomena have sympathy *for us*, to the point of seeming to reflect our emotional states back to us in "moods" of the season or the weather. On the other hand, we have sympathy *for nature* in turn, since we have intelligence with (i.e., literally "read within") the earth itself.

In another allusion to rain—itself a concrete instance of dissolution—Thoreau becomes still more specific about the double bonding of natural sympathy:

> In the midst of a gentle rain . . . I was suddenly sensible of such sweet and beneficent society in Nature, in the very pattering of the drops, and in every sound and sight around my house, an infinite and unaccountable friendliness all at once like an atmosphere sustaining me, as made the fancied advantages of human neighborhood insignificant. . . . Every little pine needle expanded and swelled with sympathy and befriended me. I was so distinctly made aware of the presence of something kindred to me, even in scenes which we are accustomed to call wild and dreary, and also that the nearest of blood to me and humanest was not a person nor a villager, that I thought no place could ever be strange to me again.[67]

This passage makes it clear that Thoreau feels *welcomed* as already a member of the society of nature. His world is part of its world. At the same time, he himself assumes an active attitude of *welcoming*. Feeling no longer welcome in civil society—or, perhaps more accurately, being *over*welcomed there—Thoreau moves to wild places in an effort to welcome these places into himself. Nature's "friendliness" responds in kind, welcoming his welcome. This mutual welcoming is accompanied by an equally mutual *witnessing*: just as Thoreau is a willing witness of nature's welcome, so that welcome is itself a witnessing of his alert presence in its midst.

Such redoubled welcoming and witnessing betoken *kinship,* leading Thoreau to consider himself more akin to animate and inanimate natural things than to other human beings. The relation of kinship thus realized is again two-way: "The presence of something kindred to me" is matched by the thought of "my being kindred to the presence of nature." Robert Bly cites a journal entry of 1857 in which Thoreau says that "all nature is my bride," and remarks that Thoreau was once so taken by a tree that he considered marrying it.[68] More than attraction is here at issue. Between the reader of nature and the nature he reads, between welcoming and being welcomed, between witnessing and being witnessed, there is a profound sympathy. The sympathy goes so deep that the usual distinctions between the wild and the civilized disintegrate, and this happens precisely in places "which we are accustomed to call *wild and dreary.*" The desolation of the wild, far from undermining sympathetic reconnection, reminds us of it. Moreover, rather than inducing displacement—as is all too often the case with unsympathetic souls—such scenes help make Thoreau feel all the more at home. They inspire in him the radical idea that "no place," however wild, "could ever be strange to me again." The strangeness of a wild place disappears not just because I have become familiar with it but because I realize that I am bonded to it—and it to me—at the most primordial level. If it is true that "we can never have enough of Nature"[69]—as Thoreau says toward the end of *Walden*—this is because we are already at one with nature itself through a luminous wildness held in common.

VI

Some do not walk at all; others walk in the highways; a few walk across lots.
—Henry David Thoreau, "Walking"

I was the world in which I walked.
—Wallace Stevens, "Tea at the Palaz of Hoon"

Beyond domestic and intellectual ways of negotiating the middle realm between culture and nature—i.e., the ways of building and cleaning, reading and writing respectively—there are other intermediate activities that connect wild with cultivated places. In this section I shall concentrate on two of these activities: walking and guiding. Each serves to connect the cultivated with the uncultivated world. Regarding these activities, Thoreau and Muir are our surest guides. These nineteenth-century giants in the earth will help us to reappreciate and reapproach wild places in a manner that is not dependent on being transported to wilderness areas in vans and planes in the expectation that experiences in these areas will somehow redeem and redress our technologically overwrought (and philosophically underthought) lives.

For Muir and Thoreau alike, the archetypal act was not to be transported technologically but simply to *walk* out of a domestic and local culture, one which both found unduly stifling. For Muir, it was a matter of leaving the late-Victorian mansion in Martinez which his wife had inherited (and whose extensive orchards he superintended when not hiking) and heading for the high Sierras on foot. In walking to the Sierras, as in sailing to Glacier Bay, Muir sought the sublime, which is to say, a cultural ideal *within* wilderness. Walking, which for Muir came closer to striding, effected the reconnection between the natural and the cultural worlds that were otherwise so separate in late-Victorian times. His actively ambulatory body was the third term that connected civilization with wilderness: "natural" itself (or as natural as Muir's soaring spirits could imagine it to be), this body bore the brunt of culture while also holding out the promise of disburdenment from it. The sublimity of the wild places to which the walking body gave him access was at once (in its loftiness) a displaced expression of the high culture he left behind so defiantly *and* (in its wild remoteness) the most telling refutation of this culture. In and through walking, embodiment and disembodiment, as well as the natural and the cultural themselves, interlaced. "When we emerged into the bright landscapes of the sun," writes Muir, "everything looked brighter, and we felt our faith in Nature's beauty strengthened, and saw more clearly that beauty is universal and immortal, above, beneath, on land and sea, mountain and plain, in heat and cold, light and darkness."[70]

Thoreau's walking was less embodied—we rarely receive a direct description of his bodily states—but it was no less concerted in leaving cultivated circles for the natural society he craved. In his posthumously published essay "Walking," he declares: "Let me live where I will, on this side is the city, on that the wilderness, and ever I am leaving the city more and more, and withdrawing into the wilderness."[71] By walking, he could leave the very city onto which he could then gain a proper perspective from the distance of wild places:

> From many a hill I can see civilization and the abodes of man afar. . . . Man and his affairs, church and state and school, trade and commerce, and manufactures and agriculture, even politics, the most alarming of them all—I am pleased to see how little space they occupy in the landscape.[72]

Walking, then, allows for the literal dis-cerning of culture, its encirclement and limitation, from a wild place that is a lookout upon cultural space. In this regard, walking opens up *panoramas*, a favorite term of mid-nineteenth-century discourse applied both to artistic and to technologically produced "grand views."[73]

But Thoreau's purpose in walking out of Concord is not just to survey, or to look down upon, local culture. The point is not only to put jejune culture behind him but to "begin, having a *point d'appui*, below freshet and frost and fire, a place where you might found a wall or a state."[74] The mode of walking to such a beginning-place must suit the project to which it will be put, as well as the setting in which it will occur. Thoreau opts for *sauntering* in his earnest effort to determine "the art of Walking, that is, of taking walks,"[75] and he discusses two somewhat fanciful origins of the verb *to saunter*; the word stems either from *sans terre*, landless but "at home everywhere" (which is said to be "the secret of successful sauntering") or from *Sainte-Terrer*, someone who walks to the Holy Land or at least pretends to do so. Thoreau professes to prefer the latter signification, since he would like to think of walking into wild places as "a sort of crusade, preached by Peter the Hermit in us, to go forth and reconquer this Holy Land from the hands of the Infidels."[76] The Holy Land, of course, is wilderness itself, and the Infidels are those who ignore or exploit it.

Sauntering implies a certain leisurely insouciance that allows the walker to be more thoughtful and more open to the land than if he or she were to rush over it with a Muirian eye to discovery or exploration.[77] Consequently, sauntering not only better *exemplifies* the middle kingdom between nature and culture—since it combines walking with reflecting—but it *extends* this kingdom by encouraging the walker to take continual note of what he or she comes across. In contrast with a mere survey, this close scrutiny involves an intense interinvolvement between cultural and natural factors.

Such is this intensity that Thoreau urges would-be walkers to think of themselves as leaving home forever. The author of *Walden* is at his most scathing in discouraging the prospect of return:

> . . . we are but faint-hearted crusaders. . . . Our expeditions are but tours, and come round again at evening to the old hearth-side from which we set out. Half the walk is but retracing our steps. We should go forth on the shortest walk . . . in the spirit of undying adventure, never to return. . . . If you are ready to leave father and mother, and brother and sister, and wife and child and friends, and never see them again . . . then you are ready for a walk.[78]

Thoreau here anticipates Levinas's critique of nostalgic homecoming—e.g., in the paradigmatic case of the *Odyssey*—as a concerted return-to-the-same. The Odyssean project privileges culture, i.e., the *cultus* of the hearth, by guaranteeing a safe return to the home-place from adventures in the Mediterranean world. The circuit proceeds from home-culture to nature and back again to home-culture. John Muir, in always returning to a familial and familiar Martinez, is an exemplary modern Odysseus. In comparison, Henry David Thoreau is anti-Odyssean in his stern counsel never to go back home. Although he did not follow his own advice, Thoreau intended the experiment at Walden to demonstrate the real possibility of setting up an anti-home, a dis-habitation by way of re-inhabitation in the wild. Only by abandoning the assurances and reassurances of the home-place can one begin to settle into a wild place and start to live on *its* demanding terms. Thoreau's point is not so much that "the achievement of the human requires not inhabitation and settlement but abandonment, leaving"[79] as that abandonment or leaving— walking out of settled scenes—is the precondition of resettlement in still unsettled wild places.

The walking-out accomplished by sauntering away from home is no random movement. It may lack the reliable orientation inherent in the home-place, but it cannot afford to be un-oriented. But how does orientation occur in the middle realm between one's domicile and the Dismal Swamp? What form does guidance take? One model is implicit in Muir's maneuvers in the wild. His motions are at once directed by himself and directed toward something other-than-self. They are self-directed insofar as they proceed in an intentional and willful way, following a carefully conceived travel plan; but they are also directed by something other, namely, by that sublime otherness he sought in the natural world. Muir's directionality, then, takes place in between the personal ego and the metaphysical Other.

Thoreau walked to a different drummer. On one hand, he was not self-directed in any resolute way. Often he would spend considerable time spinning his body in circles before deciding in which direction to set out on a walk: "I turn round and round irresolute sometimes for a quarter of an hour, until I decide."[80] On the other hand, Thoreau ultimately respects the direction that the land—the quite physical, nonmetaphysical land—indicates to him. After his spinning exercise, for example, he found that he invariably walked toward the west or southwest. From this repeated experience, he concluded that "there is a subtle magnetism in Nature, which, if we unconsciously yield to it, will direct us aright."[81]

The Thoreauvian between, then, is not that of finite ego and infinite Other—both being abstractions—but that of the walking self and the wild-scape that lures it onward in certain definite directions. Such a self and such a scape are quite concrete in character. So too are the very directions the ambulatory self takes. These directions are not bare positions on a compass but telltale vectors of actual movement. For example, "east" is not merely a quadrant to the right of magnetic north but where Thoreau's body-self goes "only by force," while "west" is where "I go free."[82] Just as definite is the alliance between west and wilderness, and between east and culture: "We go eastward to realize history and study the works of art and literature, retracing the steps of the race; we go westward as into the future, with a spirit of enterprise and adventure."[83] To walk into wild places is to walk away from cultivated ones, but the "away" retains elements of that from which it proceeds. (To be adequate to this situation, one would have to say that one walks *away with* eastern/culture as one *saunters into* western/wilderness. Conversely, if there *is* a return trip, the wilderness will be incorporated into the cultural world one rejoins.)

Muir and Thoreau might both agree with Wallace Stevens's late-Romantic notion that "I was the *world* in which I walked." Each would also insist that the *earth* on which I walk is not of my making. Yet my own activity does make a significant difference in the kind of world and earth I inhabit or traverse, whether this activity be in the form of building (as in Thoreau's case), naming (as in Muir's: he named an entire glacier, the biggest, after himself in his voyage to Glacier Bay), or simply walking in a certain way. In any event, the merging of cultural and wild worlds is such that I have a lot to do with the particular world and earth—the life-world—I come to experience. But neither naturalist would concur with Stevens's further statement that "what I saw or heard or felt came *not but from myself.*"[84] Muir's egoistic walker is in the end overwhelmed with the sublime prospect he confronts, while Thoreau's attuned ambulator is in touch with something much more than his own self can account for. In both cases, we are led to the important notion of *being-guided.*

To be guided is not merely to guide oneself. It is to be led by something or someone else. The something is ultimately the natural world, its particular configuration, the lay of the land. But short of this (and just because the land's lay may not be evident or may be quite confusing), human beings rely on intermediary presences. One such intermediary is the map; another is the local guide, the someone else who knows the way.

Muir, approaching the *terra incognita* of glaciers in western Canada, relied on the only existing map, made in an earlier expedition by the explorer George Vancouver. At an inlet near Glacier Bay, Muir reports, "I could see nothing that could give me a clue, while Vancouver's chart, hitherto a faithful guide, here failed us altogether."[85] When maps fail and perceptual clues are lacking or ambiguous, one must have recourse to other means of guidance. Even Muir's otherwise reliable general guide, Sitka Charlie, "now seemed lost."[86] To learn *what kind of place* one is in when one is thus adrift— "*villr,*" as Norse explorers would have called it—one must turn elsewhere. Fortuitously, Muir's forlorn band suddenly spotted a faint trail of smoke in the distance. Rowing in its direction, they discovered a group of Hoona seal hunters who knew the Glacier Bay region well. One of these hunters joined Muir's expedition as its local guide.

Neither Muir nor Thoreau, despite a steady exemplification of Emerson-
ian self-reliance by both, hesitated to let himself be led by Native American
guides. Thoreau needed neither map nor local guide in the Concord area,
where he preferred to be led by the land he had known all his life (a trip to
Walden in early childhood left an indelible impression). But once out of his
native region, he relied heavily on maps and especially on Indian guides. This
is most evident in his extended account of travels in the Maine woods. On
his first trip to Maine, he was so anxious for cartographic guidance that he
elaborately traced Greenleaf's map of Maine on oil cloth, only to discover
that the map was "a labyrinth of errors."[87] Even if it is true that a map is
the most graphic and economic expression of the way in which one comes
to terms with (and measures) wilderness, after this disillusioning experience
with the Greenleaf map Thoreau turned to native guides, who rarely used
maps. One such guide told Thoreau that even after going in the most circuitous route through the Maine woods he could unfailingly return to the
point of origin on a virtually straight line. " 'How do you do that?' asked I.
'O, I can't tell *you*,' he replied. 'Great difference between me and white
man.' "[88]

What is the difference? Thoreau claims that the native guide "guided
himself in the woods."[89] But the more complete answer is that the Native
American—who is referred to only as "the Indian" in Thoreau's text—did
not so much *guide himself* as let himself be *guided by the woods*. In response
to Thoreau's insistent questioning, he began to unpack his secrets:

> "Sometimes I lookum side-hill," and he glanced toward a high hill or
> mountain on the eastern shore, "great difference between the north and
> south, see where the sun has shone most. So trees—the large limbs bend
> toward south. Sometimes I lookum locks [i.e., rocks]." . . . "Bare locks on
> lake shore—great difference between N.S.E.W. side—can tell what the sun
> has shone on."[90]

What guides the guide, then, is the interaction between certain lasting landscape features (e.g., rocks, hills, and trees) and the changing trajectory of the
sun. As in the case of steering by the wind or stars, the guidance is *from
without*. Even memory cedes place to such exterocentric being-guided. It is a
matter of a *local knowledge* based on an extreme sensitivity to precise features
of the vicinity. It follows that the best guide is a local guide, someone attuned to the distinctive features of the natural environment. As Thoreau remarks,

> Often, when an Indian says, "I don't know," in regard to the route he is to
> take, he does not mean what a white man would by those words, for his
> Indian instinct may tell him still as much as the most confident white man

knows. He does not carry things in his head, nor remember the route exactly, like a white man, but relies on himself at the moment. Not having experienced the need of the other sort of knowledge, all labelled and arranged, he has not acquired it.[91]

Despite its dubious invocation of "Indian instinct," this passage from *The Maine Woods* has the merit of positing two kinds of knowledge, local and systematic. Local knowledge of the sort most pertinent to orientation in wilderness is knowledge of particular wild places operative "at the moment"—and thus does not call for long-term systematic surveys that find expression in maps, where everything is "labelled and arranged." The difference between the two kinds of knowledge is the same as that between "landscape" and "geography," which are Erwin Straus's terms for the objective correlates of "sensing" and "perceiving" respectively. As if he were commenting on Thoreau's observation just quoted, Straus writes that "sensory space stands to perceptual space as landscape to geography."[92] The native guide—"native" in the literal sense of "born-in" the region—guides from a local knowledge that stems from sensing the landscape close up. To guide, and above all to be guided, is to draw on this sensory basis for knowing where one is. And to know where one is is to know where one is located in relation to the local landscape, on its terms and in its way.

It becomes evident that walking and being-guided are not just means of getting into (or out of) wild places; they are more even than means of orientation in these places. Profoundly human as they are, they reflect the lay of the land. Local knowledge arises, finally, from the locale itself. Walking as we do (and our very gait is an enculturated skill) and being guided as we are (whether by the pictorial images of maps or by the deictic words of guides), we are taken to a place that draws us into its own wild drama.

VII

> The thickness of the body, far from rivaling that of the world, is on the
> contrary the sole means I have to go unto the heart of things, by making
> myself a world and by making them flesh.
>
> —Maurice Merleau-Ponty, *The Visible and the Invisible*

Our tour of the middle world has borne out the truth of Merleau-Ponty's controversial claim: "Everything is cultural in us . . . and everything is natural in us." To this we need only add: everything is at once natural and cultural, not only "in us" but *in the natural world* as well.

More than continual commixture is at stake. The conjoining of culture and nature is not just a combination, much less a compromise or a mere synthesis. Something is gained, something *emerges* from the conjunction itself that is not present when the factors are held apart. Let us call the process of this emergence "thickening." By this I mean the dense coalescence of cultural practices and natural givens. In undergoing a mutual thickening, these practices and givens sediment and interfuse. The merging eventuates in an emergent thickening. Such thickening contrasts both with coarsening and with thinning. Unlike coarsening, it does not end in the production of obdurate obstacles to the further interaction of culture and nature. Unlike thinning, it is not a matter of etherealizing what has been gained, e.g., in the form of a discourse of disconnected sublimity. If coarsening is the coagulation of matter, thinning is the sublimation of the material world into disincarnate words and ideas. In the former, nature withdraws into itself; in the latter, culture tries to live from its own internal resources.

Thickening occurs when each party to the interaction gains in concert with the other. Wendell Berry cites the instance of small-scale farming. He observes that a plowed field on the edge of wilderness attracts animals, e.g., the red-tailed hawk, which would not otherwise be drawn out of its wild habitat. Meanwhile, the cultivation of this same field, if carefully accomplished, falls in with and enhances natural cycles. The field's marginal position augments the interaction of the agriculturalist with the wild life beyond, furnishing a common arena for both.[93]

Such thickening of the plot also happens in nonmarginal places. When Thoreau ambles into the surrounding wildscape, he thickens the scene into which he walks. Not only does he leave distinctive marks in the form of footprints and tracks, but his ambulatory activity subtly reshapes the natural world through which he moves. As he saunters through an uncultivated field or an uncut forest, he creates an "information trail"[94] that announces his presence to seen and unseen wild beings. Even as he watches the natural circumambience, *it* watches him. Once more we encounter a circumstance of double witnessing. Merleau-Ponty remarks that "I feel myself looked at by the things," and a contemporary Australian Aborigine narrator observes that in a certain wild place it is as if the "tree is watching you."[95]

Much the same pattern of bivalent thickening has been evident in the other middle-domain phenomena to which I have drawn attention. The crux of the pattern is the two-way traffic between primary terms: not just witnessing/being-witnessed but also welcoming/being-welcomed, guiding/being-guided, (human) knowing/(landscape) known, etc. *The thickening occurs by means of this reciprocal movement*, this circular coming-and-going. Where antinomical contraposition *draws out*—and thus thins out—bidirectional circulation *draws in*. It also *keeps in*; keeps the components in continuing interplay. This interplay is particularly evident in the early phases of Thoreau's experience at Walden. Thanks to the literally open-ended character of his half-built cabin, there is at once an insinuation of the natural environment into the built structure *and* an alteration of this environment by the very existence of the cabin. Because of the resulting concourse between the natural and the cultural, each undergoes an "augmentation of being."[96] Nature becomes more and other than it was before the building of the hut, and the hut is enhanced by its implacement in the woods.

If walking and building are thickenings, so is writing, or any cultural act that constitutes a *work*. As a cultural artifact, a work is a working-through of its elements and thus a thickening of them. In Heidegger's conception of the art work, these elements are earth and world, which enter into a struggle tantamount to a thickening of each by the other in a final commonality: "in the struggle, each opponent carries the other beyond itself . . . into the intimacy of simple belonging to one another."[97] Thus, in Heidegger's paradigm case, a Greek temple brings together earth and world in a mutual embroilment that enhances both. But even when the elements are not those of earth and world, the working of the work remains a thickening. The very elements rejected by Heidegger as merely metaphysical, i.e., "form" and "matter," are made mutually dense by their interaction, as we see most vividly in the case of literary works. Everywhere we look in the realm of cultural works—whether the work be Heidegger's exalted temple, Thoreau's humble hut, or the writing both authors accomplish in reflecting on building—there is a thickening that betokens the common sedimentation of factors drawn from the supposedly separate realms of Nature and Culture.

Thinning, on the other hand, occurs in the failure of working-through. In the case of literature, thinning happens when the density of the text as *Dicht-ung*, literally a "thick-ing," is attenuated by abstraction from the concrete connotations of the words, resulting in an un- or anti-work. Other unworked things include buildings that are sheerly functional or imitative ("done in the style of") and thoughtless "public works." An instance of the latter is a contemporary turnpike that, in contrast with a gracefully sinuous trail or path, takes no account of the surrounding country but forces its way through the land. This belabored and unimaginative structure is in effect nothing but a flat and straight site that *fails to thicken into a genuine work*.

An ordinary experience brings home this last direction of thought. Stopping at a rest area on I-91 north of Middletown, Connecticut, I notice a snow-bound scene. I pause to look at it in its unexpected thickness. The scene itself consists merely in several rocks, a few small bushes, three trees, a flagpole. A marginal spot, offering only a modest prospect. What is going on here? Certainly not an experience of the Sublime; but also not a mere scattering of miscellaneous objects such as one might find in a razed building site. I am presented instead with an arrangement of material things that cohere as in a single composition. Nature has become connatural with culture in this obscure corner of the siteful world of the modern turnpike. Contributing to the connaturality is my own vision, which belongs to my "natural endowment." On this occasion, as on so many others when I glimpse my environs, I find myself actively forming and framing the scene around me, constituting a landscape out of the demi-wilderness or the site given to me in perception. No less than my walking style, my looking is culturally informed: I look as a Westerner, one who is informed by several centuries of landscape painting in a tradition that stretches from Ruysdael to Inness, and from Monet to Soutine. Both the *way*—i.e., the minute gesture, the particular manner in which I focus and squint and roll my eyes—and the *effect* of looking, that is, the resulting "prospect," embody and exemplify this enculturation. How could it be otherwise? But the reverse is also true and could not be otherwise: the paintings in the tradition I have mentioned *and my looking as it has been influenced by this tradition* incorporate and reflect the wildness of the natural world itself. Even in their most sophisticated reaches—even in their most remote Sublimity—the art works and the looking they encourage are never wholly un-wild, never altogether sublimated.

Either way, then, whether we start with what is pristinely natural (e.g., rocks and bushes) or with what is presumed to be only cultural (paintings, flagpoles, manners of seeing), we find ourselves in the thick of things, in that middle region where the natural and the cultural are co-implicatory and com-present. Another name for this region is "flesh," or, more exactly, "the flesh of the world." This latter phrase is Merleau-Ponty's, and it points to the very situation into which our considerations have been leading us with quiet force. In this encompassing circumstance, there is a co-implacement of the natural and the cultural such that each can be said to *flesh out* the other or to give the other consistency and substance. Or more exactly, each is a phase or region of a more encompassing flesh. If "the world is universal flesh," such flesh is neither matter alone nor mind alone but something running through both, a common "element," as it were.[98]

Given the axiom of universal flesh, it follows that my body and natural things are not just conterminous but continuous with each other. Speaking of the body—a body we know to be cultural through and through—Merleau-Ponty remarks that natural things "even enter its enclosure, they are within it, they line its looks and its hands inside and outside."[99] Conversely, the body is "of their family . . . it uses its own being as a means to participate in theirs, because each of the two beings is an archetype for the other."[100] In this two-way participation in universal flesh, we recognize the situation of sympathy in which all of nature is akin: "The flesh of the world (the 'quale') is indivision of this sensible Being that I am and all the rest which feels itself (*se sent*) in me."[101]

Just as Merleau-Ponty discovers thickening in the elemental flesh of body-cum-world, so we have encountered thickening in the common flesh of the cultural-cum-natural. In such flesh, the fibers of culture and nature compose one continuous fabric. Interwoven thus, these fibers are inseparable in experience even if they are distinguishable upon analysis or reflection. Human beings cannot help but reflect, but when they construe the result of reflection as the direct deliverance of experience they commit the Fallacy of Misplaced Concreteness, as Whitehead calls the logicist propensity that fails to be true to concrete lived experience and that segregates this experience into separate points and sites. Yet as Whitehead reminds us in his own version of universal flesh, "in a certain sense, everything is everywhere at all times."[102] In the cosmic tapestry, discrete threads may be discernible on close scrutiny, but the overall pattern presents itself as a single Gestalt. The pattern emerges from the ongoing intimacy between the warp of culture and the woof of nature. The effect of such dense co-immanence of components is a palpable thickness of the felt fabric.

Unlike the thick autonomy of memory, the thickness here at stake is not nomological. The law of naturo-cultural density is not human alone, hence it cannot be subsumed exclusively under the sign of *nomos*, human law or management (both of which entail specific memorial powers). By the same token, this thickness cannot be forced underground into the realm of *chthōn*, the deep earth. As with culture and nature themselves, autonomy and autochthony conjoin in a common ground and a common law. If the ground is earth, the law is language. In the end, however, the earth speaks its own language, and instituted language articulates a wildness to be found in self and nature alike.

VIII

We will not come to any deep understanding of our place in nature except as we delve into its basic documents, and these documents are our wild places.
—Paul Gruchow, *The Necessity of Empty Places*

I am back on I-91, this time driving south from Northampton, Massachusetts, to Hartford, Connecticut. As I proceed, I confront a remarkable variety of vistas. The first thing to catch my eye is Mount Holyoke, a sizable mountain on top of which is perched a restaurant. The positioning of this building at the very top of the mountain might well have been disruptive, an ugly intrusion of the commercial into the natural. Instead, the restaurant is discreetly placed in a small clearing among a group of trees. It is barely visible from the highway; in fact, I had not noticed it on previous trips to this area of New England. Not entirely unlike the iron wall of Joux or the stone keep of Granson, the restaurant serves to embellish the landscape in which it is set rather than to detract from it.

Only a few miles farther down the road, I stop to gaze at the Connecticut River and its immediately surrounding areas. The outlook is close to the viewpoint Thomas Cole assumed in his famous landscape painting *The Oxbow*. But in place of the idyllic combination of river, hills, and farmland as seen from Mount Holyoke in Cole's painting (finished in 1836, the same year in which Emerson's *Nature* was published), there is now a dispiriting scene of urban encroachment. A gargantuan water tower seems to be walking on stupendous stilts toward the river (presumably to replenish itself!). This excrescence upon the land is not so much unsightly as vastly out of scale. The natural and the cultural, though coexisting for perfectly practical reasons, here enter into an uneasy alliance in which disproportion triumphs over the elegant equilibrium I had just admired in the implacement of the mountain-top restaurant.

As I head farther south toward Hartford, I come into an area of extensive construction on the turnpike itself. In one stretch of this construction, concrete walls have been erected on both sides of the road; they are of such a height as to eliminate any view whatsoever of the surrounding landscape. Here the incursion of the cultural has acted to eliminate any effective access to the natural world; not only can I not *see* or *hear* behind these walls, but their length is such that I could not *walk* around them either. In another phase of the construction, extensive disruption of the land has taken place in preparation for a broadening of the turnpike. In this case, the vista is not blocked; but the earth has been torn up, trees uprooted, and a previously tranquil scene has become a scene of confusion. Landscape has become anti-scape.

By the time I reach Hartford itself, I find myself in a complex scene of modern and postmodern buildings. These buildings are so closely packed together that not even the barest trace of open land remains. On the northern outskirts of the city, the earth is being reshaped into what will become the new margins of a highway. But in downtown Hartford the very possibility of such reshaping has been eliminated. The cityscape has taken over the landscape completely. In this cityscape I witness the antipode of an unassailed wildscape, since *nothing in what was once wilderness has here been untouched.*

One way to understand this all-too-common disenfranchisement from the land is in terms of the basic features discussed in the preceding chapter. The very first stage of my journey was one in which these features were intact and fully represented. Significant exemplars of sensuous surface (i.e., the forested hillside) and of ground (i.e., the surrounding plains out of which the nearby mountain arose) were present in the vista of Mount Holyoke. So too were various material things (trees, the restaurant among them, etc.), an arc (the sweep of the scene as forming one coherent vista), and an atmosphere (upward-tending, lucid, and continuous). These features became progressively less fully represented in the course of my trip until a zero point of exhaustion was reached in the final stage. The turning point lay midway, in my perception of the ungainly water tower—that gigantic *thing* dominating an entire landscape, thrusting the surface and ground, the arc and atmosphere, into merely peripheral positions. By the time I reached the site of recent construction on the turnpike, these last four factors were almost altogether excluded from my perception, put out of sight by the walls along the highway, or else so radically altered in the course of construction as not to be recognizable as such. In this truncated scene, I was most acutely aware of the absence of arc, within both the near sphere and the far sphere. The same absence plagued my close-up view of the city of Hartford.

My journey from Northampton to Hartford—on the thinned-out "super" highway whose only identifying label is the empty toponym "I-91"—is a fable of the progressive denudation of a primal wilderness. It is a characteristically modernist tale. In the course of this brief trip, basic traits of what was at least partially wild to begin with were progressively eliminated until the landscape itself became, if not lifeless, *featureless*. The landscape became before my very eyes just what Descartes had posited prophetically as "Nature": a monolith of Space. If Matter and Space are identical, then Nature can have no "secondary qualities" of its own. There are no appearances to be saved, since the only appearances are identical with our own subjective representations. In the current context, this means that we have only our own memories or fantasies of what the landscape was or could be like. During my journey south on I-91, open and accommodating places in the land gave way with frightening rapidity to straitened sites for the massive storage of water or for efficient transportation, and finally to literal building sites in downtown Hartford.

I offer this example not just to lament the dire straits to which Western, and more especially American, culture in its postindustrial period has brought us in its passion for possessing and reshaping the wilderness. More pertinent to the present discussion are two aspects of the contemporary vernacular landscape. First, this landscape affords a concrete demonstration that there is indeed no preestablished harmony between culture and nature, so that the equilibrium of these two factors is everywhere precarious and all too easily disrupted. Second, this same circumstance of *via rupta* helps to explain why it is that Americans at this point in history turn with such relish and relief to wilderness in whatever form it can be found—or packaged. If we fail to find it in the stretches of actual wilderness that are allowed to survive in nature preserves and national parks (or in scattered "green belt" developments),[103] we seek it avidly in blatantly artificial and constructed sites such as Disney World, Marine World, Safari Park. The capitalization of these latter place names (itself perhaps reflecting their considerable monetary capitalization) betrays a paradoxical circumstance in which the wild is presented, and represented, not on its own terms and by its own means but by a technologically contrived support system. The rationale seems to be: if we are willing to create artificial flowers, why not construct artificial places? But where have all the real flowers and the actual wild places gone?

We are not likely to find satisfactory answers to these questions in our present historical predicament, in which we are strung out between wilderness and site. Wilderness may be what we want (or at least *imagine ourselves wanting*; it is not clear how much actual wilderness we can tolerate, or for how long), but site is what we are getting, and getting increasingly.

By "strung out between wilderness and site" I mean that we drastically lack viable and significant intermediate positions between these two extremities. Such alternative middle-range options were available in abundance at the time Thomas Cole painted *The Oxbow*, and they are even given explicit representation in his painting: farms that are not strictly rectilinear, smoke rising not from satanic mills and factories but from industries constructed on a human scale, a ferry boat crossing the Connecticut River, limited clear-cutting of forests on distant mountain slopes, a winding road that respects the contours of the land, etc. By and large, we lack contemporary equivalents of such alternatives, and for this reason we believe that the only meaningful choice is that between wild and sited existence. But is this so?

Here we should notice that wilderness and site, despite their antithetical status, possess a similar resistance to memory and history. Only rarely does wilderness yield to history—e.g., during Ruskin's epiphany in the Jura, or Muir's ecstasy at Glacier Bay—and it only infrequently serves as a setting for remembering. Sites resist memory and history even more fiercely. Their erection often means the destruction of local history, and their facile replacement by other sites (or by new, "improved" buildings on the same site) induces a radical forgetfulness.

But one group of crucial differences between wilderness and site remains: those bearing on the lived body. Wilderness actively solicits bodily movement. Indeed, wild places *require* the body's intervention, sometimes for the sake of sheer survival. We cannot doubt that *the lived body gets fully engaged by wilderness*. This body becomes the world in which it walks. The same is not true for sites, which act to disengage bodily activity and presence. Sites discourage corporeal activity by confining human beings to simple locations. Their constructed—and often literally overconstructed—"nature" does manage to alleviate any concern as to physical survival. But such construction ends by being a constriction. The waywardness of world is reduced to the pinpointing of site.

A site leaves precious little room for a living-moving-perceiving body. Sometimes, as in stretches of construction along I-91, a site will preclude

even the bare perception of an environing landscape. Plain walking is mini-
mized, as when automated walkways provide movement while rendering oti-
ose the motion itself of walking. Often walking is not even a consideration,
as when one drives to Hartford to work, or to ponder the cityscape as I did
in my car. According to the landscape logic of Wallace Stevens (a long-time
resident of Hartford), no walking means no world. Such is the price we pay
for a site-saturated existence that has lost touch with wild places: *atrophy of
the body-in-place*.

IX

Each place is its own place, forever (eventually) wild.
—Gary Snyder, "The Place, the Region, the Commons"

Such sited but unplaced lives, dissevered from wilderness as they are,
might as well be pursued underground, an idea explicitly proposed by Jules
Verne. Apart from science fiction, however, is there a way out, into a richer,
wider world? If there is, it lies through reconnection with the earth. Such
reconnection is not limited to literal incursions into nature. Even if I am not
walking in the wilderness but driving through it, I can be attentive to it. My
bare glance can take it in, and I can ruminate on what I have seen. What
matters most is not *my* precise mode of movement—how or by what means
I move—but what my moving body lets me experience. What matters is *letting the land take the lead*. Instead of taking the lead myself, i.e., as guided
by my own egological interests, I need to let the earth be the guiding force,
the first voice, the primary presence. Instead of imposing myself *on* the
earth—realizing my personal (and all too often Promethean) plans there—I
need to seek out, from within the cues offered by the earth itself, certain
decisive directions to be taken. The right direction is to be found less in
myself and in other human beings conceived as humanocentric agents than
in the land (or sea) that lies before and around me. If the modern predicament stems in large part from the egocentrism that underlies humanocentrism—often disguised in the unquestioned meliorism of a technological
existence—the form of a possible solution may well be *ecocentric* in character.[104]

An ecocentric direction has emerged spontaneously at several points in
this part. Take, for example, the twin phenomena of displacement and desolation as discussed in the preceding chapter. Although we would be mistaken
to hold that they belong intrinsically more to wild places than to the individuals afflicted by them, the basic pattern of a displacement between particular places—e.g., as occasioned by a forced emigration—followed by an
experience of desolation was telling. The desolation concerns both the place

being left and the new place to which one is going. Thus we were not surprised to find that "desolation in the land" is a basic phenomenon that brings in its train connotations of "desert," "wasteland," and "wilderness" itself. The "errand into the wilderness" undertaken by the New England colonists was a journey into a land they found dismally desolate to start with.[105] Displacement and desolation of this sort may therefore be considered primarily, even if not exclusively, phenomena of wilderness. Their psychical expressions reflect a sense that the immediate landscape is barren and unyielding. They start with—and often continue as—an experience of the environing world as alien and hostile, a place unfit for inhabitation. Or rather, as no place at all but a site for suffering. To say "site" is to extend the field of displacement and desolation to contemporary New England as well. My experience of approaching Hartford and of Hartford itself—in the heart of New England— was one of the "sitification" of a comparatively unmarred landscape. I sensed (and not only perceived) that the land itself had become displaced—in the case of the massive highway construction, literally so—and was rendered desolate. I felt displaced myself as I drove through this scarified scene. Even here, the land, albeit a lacerated landscape buried beneath the cicatrix of site, took the lead.

In Muir's account of his exploration of Glacier Bay, Thoreau's encomium of walking, and Ruskin's elegaic description of the Champagnole landscape, we witness the individual subject drawn out of any putative "egological" center and thrust, quite willingly, into the environing world. The adventuresome, walking subject finds himself already caught up in the contour of the wild land. In their peregrinations, Ruskin and Muir and Thoreau let the land speak to them—to their moving bodies—even as they articulated its presence in their writings. None of these nineteenth-century naturalists would agree with Robert Frost: "The land was ours before we were the land's."[106] From their point of view, Frost has it the wrong way around. We are in the land's hands first of all; it becomes *ours* only afterward, when possessive egocentric life takes over.

Another case in point is found in my own peri-phenomenological description of the fundamental features of wild places.[107] Each of these features stems from, and is primarily situated in, the wildscape that surrounds us. Material things, for example, act as cynosures for our attention and interest. Things are densely ecocentric, drawing us out of our egological confinement and into the environing world they serve to diversify and populate. That world itself is decidedly outside our ego, extra-epidermal. It has its *own skin*: the sensuous surface of things. This surface, deepened into the flesh of the world, attracts us by its qualitative richness, especially in the form of its manifest palpability. We constantly *go out* to touch it. The movement is ecstatic. We also go out of ourselves into the arc of the land—or the sea—as

we find ourselves swept up in its embrace. The ancient and still surviving
wish to find the end of a rainbow entails a desire to leave the confinement
of our egocentric predicament so as to discover a treasure *out there*, at the
place where the *arc-en-ciel* touches the ground. Further, the very ground directly under our stationary or walking feet is certainly extra-egological. It
takes us out of our locked-in, in-sited selves; it takes us *down under*. The
atmosphere, in contrast, takes us *up and out*: we draw our breath *from it*, not
from ourselves. In this way as well, and reinforced by the atmosphere's multifarious luminosity, we become exterocentric to ourselves.

All these foregoing features appear to us by means of a qualitative array
environing our lived bodies. In sensing and perceiving wild places, we take
our lead from this array, which is no mere set of representations but an entire
world-sphere. In this sphere, we are already outside of ourselves, beside ourselves, as it were. We are most fully beside ourselves in wilderness, which
calls for heightened alertness and attunement. In wild places, the surrounding
array finds its deepest source and resource. A wild place is both the *terminus
a quo* and the *terminus ad quem* of our sensing and perceiving lives. From
it, presentational immediacies derive, and to it they revert. In between, they
pass through the circuit of the self thanks to the concrete intermediacy of
the body.

Even the body is outside the ego. By this I mean not just that "the ego
is first and foremost a body ego,"[108] but that the self is already outside itself,
transcending itself in its immersion in the natural world. Far from being an
inert support for egoic mind, the lived body takes us out of our own skin
into the world's flesh. At the same time and by the same action, the lived
body takes us back into place. My body is a body-in-place. It is embedded
in a place-world. Place is where we are (when we are) bodily. To be in place
is to be beyond ourselves as egocentric site-setting selves. Even being *here* is
to be other than a self-centered self. It is to be already on the verge of being
out *there*, in various places. Many of these are socially specified places, i.e.,
places that reflect our historical and political being-with-others. But some are
predominantly natural places, wild in their being there.[109] Into these latter
our body moves us, sometimes preceded by our imagination and language.
Wild places lead our bodies out of themselves and into the natural world.

The sited self, in contrast, is at once bodiless and placeless—and one
because the other. This is as much as to say that it lacks wildness.

But every self remains delineated by culture in its many forms. Culture,
however, eventually returns us to nature. Even if the scars of the site-specified self have replaced furrows on the soil, these same scars lead us back again
to the earth. A main meaning of *scarify* is to "loosen the surface of the soil."
Even time-lines and horizon-lines—those primary scar-lines of modernity—

are finally wrinkles in the flesh of the very wilderness they serve so relent-
lessly to repress.

Holmes Rolston puts the point thus: "Every culture remains resident in
some environment."[110] That is to say, every culture *has its place in some natural region*, however much that region has been devastated and leveled into
a scene of sites. Culture, that last fastness of the collective ego, reconnects,
despite itself, with a wild realm of natural places. In order to sustain and
renew itself, it must touch base with the wild earth from which it arises.

Hartford, the cultural center of its region, is situated alongside the Connecticut River, whose occasional violent flooding reminds the city dwellers
of their proximity to virtually uncontrollable natural forces. Beneath and beyond the all-too-fragile surface of a site such as Hartford is a residual wildness, even if wilderness as such is difficult to locate in this oversited city.
Wild weeds grow in its gutters. The paved-over surfaces crack open to reveal
the earth subtending the acute angles of the architecture overhead.

X

It is therefore essential to look again at the whole question of our conception
of place, both in order to pass on to another age of difference (since each
intellectual age corresponds to a new mediation of difference), and in order
to construct an ethics. . . .
—Luce Irigaray, "Sexual Difference"

If following the lead of the land leads us to ecocentrism, ecocentrism
leads in turn to *lococentrism*. And one because the other: to be other and
outer in the direction of the eco- (from Greek *oikos*, house, household) is to
be other and outer as implaced. For what is finally in first place is place itself,
locus. Even the natural places that underlie contemporary sites have been preceded by still earlier wild places in the course of the earth's prolonged evolution. Nothing is unimplaced in nature, even if many places have become
the denuded sites of our citified/sitified selves.[111]

A stance of ecocentrism does not, however, signify that the only genuinely *ecological* issue is whether we can save or preserve the land, especially
wild land. We can and should and must do just this. But the more pressing
question from a lococentric perspective is whether we will *let the land save
us*. Taking the lead from landscape means letting its intrinsic sagacity and
value become *our* sagacity and value. We must "value Earth because it is
valuable, and not the other way around."[112] This means being willing to
learn lessons from the natural world—lessons, for instance, concerning the
wisest use of natural resources—instead of wreaking our violence on it, ex-

pecting it to be obedient and to yield to our aggressive designs. Rather than seeing nature as mere "standing-reserve" to be exploited by the frame-up, or *Gestell*, of technology,[113] it is a matter of allowing the land to guide us in action and thought by its own deep structures. Concentrating on what we can get out of it—its "natural resources" as source of efficient energy—must give way to a recognition of its inherent causal efficacy. *Its* power, not ours in relation to it, is what is at stake. And this power is none other than the power of place: *dynamis topou*, in Aristotle's fortuitous formula. Land power is lococentric through and through; it is found in and among places, not in space and not in time.

In this lococentric light, an alternative reading of Frost's evocative poetic line suggests itself. That the land was *ours* before we were the land's may mean that, at first, in their New World fever, Americans tended to expropriate the land, managing and marshaling it for their own selfish and short-sighted purposes. It was a matter of pushing back a dreaded, unknown wilderness by making radical invasions into it (e.g., in the destructive technique of clear-cutting forests).[114] But more recently a quite different approach has emerged: permitting large tracts of the land to remain in their original state (i.e., in designated "wilderness areas") or letting the land return to a wild state (as is now happening here and there in the Great Plains). Each of these latter-day developments expresses a growing conviction that the land is no longer ours to exploit but that, if anything, we are the land's subjects: we belong to *it*, and not it to us.

The land, i.e., cultivated and uncultivated earth alike, must be allowed to stand on its own and to repossess its own rectitude. *Rectitude* is closely related to *right*. Essential to rectifying the status of land is to recognize its intrinsic rights. Not only a person but *land* also has rights. To speak of land rights—not rights *to* land but rights *of* land, including what the land has a right to expect from us—is to turn ethics in a new direction: away from a sanctioning source in God, society, or the individuated or collectivized self and back toward the natural world and its own proper denizens. John Muir grasped this direction in a journal entry of 1867: "How narrow we selfish, conceited creatures are in our sympathies! How blind to the rights of all the rest of creation!"[115] Judged by traditional criteria, such an ecocentric direction is decidedly eccentric. It may have little to do with rationally justified rules of conduct and nothing whatsoever to do with instrumental values (which are all too often values aimed at the exclusive benefit of humankind). An ecocentric ethics recognizes the inherent value of the natural world itself. It insists that we *respond* to this value. A new sense of responsibility emerges in which human beings have an abiding commitment to respect the earth— i.e., its landed (and aqueous) places—as well as members of other species. Even our responsibility to humans is ultimately to *people in places*, not to unplaced persons existing in a void. When it comes to being ethical, there is no escaping the imperative of place. Lococentrism prevails here as well, for those who will let landscape back into their lives.

Aldo Leopold was perhaps the first person to argue explicitly for a land-based ethics. Observing that "there is as yet no ethic dealing with man's relation to land," he proposed an extension of ethical precepts to the earth itself.[116] The most basic of these precepts is that "a thing is right when it tends to preserve the integrity, stability, and beauty of the biotic community. It is wrong when it tends otherwise."[117] It only needs to be added that such integrity, stability, and beauty belong not just to the indwelling inhabitants but *to the places inhabited by the biotic community*. Places, as well as the flora and fauna that occupy them, can be integral, stable, and beautiful. Indeed, in the biotic community, place and occupant-of-place belong together indissolubly. As a result, both particular places and their natural denizens call for our respectful nurturance as entities valuable in their own right. Places embody values; better yet, they *situate* them. If the values themselves are generic—i.e., characterize many sorts of things, including buildings and paintings and people—their instantiation in particular places is always unique, "idiolocal," as it were.

An ecocentric ethics, an *eco-ethics* of the sort Muir envisaged and Leopold spelled out, returns ethics to its place(s) of origin. The word *ethics* itself stems from *ēthea*, which in Homeric Greek signified the habitats of wild animals. Such abodes are the rightful places of these animals, who are fully justified in living in them and thereby moving in the various ways characteristic of them as natural species. Human beings have no right to dislodge them, much less to impose their own peculiar way of life on them. As Levinas puts it, it is a matter of "recognizing in the Other a right over [our] egoism."[118] The lead is *from the Other to us*, from animality to humanity. But this is as much as to say that guidance is to be found *in the land (or sky or sea) first*, since animals (including ourselves as animals) are endemic creatures of the earth. What is right for earth—for its ecosystem as a whole—is right for the creatures who live on it and in it.

When we allow the earth to come first, we are in effect enacting an ancient myth of origin that stems from pre-Hesiodic times in Greece. In Apollodorus's version of this myth, "Ouranos was first king of the ordered world; he married Gaia."[119] Gaia, goddess of earth, was there first, there as telluric Chaos before her marriage to the cosmic procreator Ouranos, god of the Heavens. In their elemental compact, these two deities prefigured the partnership of ground and arc in everyday experiences of wilderness. The primacy of earth extends from the mythical to the mundane.

The ecocentricity for which I am arguing must allow room for a poly-centered earth, i.e., for a "polymorphism of wild Being." Nothing would be gained from merely replacing the monocentrism of egocentric life with a monocentrism of Nature as reified into a gigantic Monolith, a colossus of Space defying a nonspatial Self or spiritualized Soul.[120] We have seen how misleading such an oppositional model can be in the closely related case of Nature versus Culture. Just as the latter dichotomy is at once bridged and undermined by the multiplex role of the human body, so any monocentric view of Nature is placed in question by reference to the diversity of its inhabitants.

And of its places: diverse inhabitation of the earth means diversity of ecobiotic niches, manyness of biotopes and biochores. Ecocentrism entails a multilocular earth. In this light, the term *ecology* might seem to be ill-chosen. For the *logos* buried within the word connotes a rationally unified structure, a conceptual monocentrism. But if we trace *logos* back to the active verb *legein*, we soon reach *gather* and *lay*, suggesting that what is crucial in ecology is how the earth is gathered together, disposed, laid out: how the lay of the land is configured.[121] "Ecology" is sanctioned by its concern with the disposition, the lay-out of the earth construed as diversely alive and polycentrically implaced.

If eco-ethics teaches us to let the earth *be* in its living (and nonliving) variety amid multifarious habitats and locales, this does not mean that we are forbidden to alter anything whatsoever on the planet. We may be called upon to change things on earth *on behalf of the earth*, as solicited by the plight of its endangered denizens or regions. To prevent the earth's despoliation requires concerted intervention, e.g., for the sake of saving deeply threatened rain forests.[122] But the need for such locally specific counter-action does not mean that the ethical role of humans is to become "stewards" of the earth.[123] The role is better conceived as that of *selective husbandry*. In its oldest acceptation, husbandry does not consist in mastery—as the association of *husband* and *master* might suggest—but in the careful and caring pursuit of household economy: *oikonomia* signifies "house management." Given that *oikos* is embedded in *ecology*, *economy*, and *ecocentricity*, it follows that the natural world as conceived from an eco-perspective, far from being antithetical to dwelling-as-residing, invites it and makes it possible. But this does not mean that the earth is nothing but "the house *where mortals dwell*."[124] The earth's destiny is not to be the site for human habitation alone; nor does the idea of the earth as a house need to be conceived by analogy with a human house. It might well be the other way around: *our* dwelling places may draw their most telling inspiration from *its* dwelling places. This is certainly the case if the earth is indeed the primary place of residence for all species, the world's first housing agency, as it were. Regarding such housing, we are enjoined to practice economy, *its* economy, "nature's economy," the Great Economy of Nature itself.[125]

Natural eco*nomy* is also rooted in *nemein*, to graze, pasture, spread, apportion, dispense. This heritage gives to *nomos* a different nuance than is evident in the abstract term *nomological*:

> *Nomos* is Greek for "pasture," and the "Nomad" is a chief or clan elder who presides over the allocation of pastures. *Nomos* thus came to mean "law," "fair distribution," "that which is allotted by custom"—and so the basis of all Western law.[126]

It is important to distinguish, however, between *distribution* and *allocation*. *Allocation* implies human intervention in the form of apportionment by custom or law. In traditional Tibet, lands in the Lagyab Lhojang area of the Northern Plateau were allocated to nomadic households by the Panchen Lama. Every three years a reallocation occurred based on the amount of livestock owned by a given household. This household (itself often composed of several families) was allowed access to a number of pastures to be used in different seasons. Even though they were not fenced off, boundaries were staked out by the Panchen Lama and strictly observed.[127] In nonallocative *distribution*, in contrast, a nomadic pastoralist allowed his flocks to range freely over an open terrain, typically when en route to allocated pasturelands. The oldest root of *nomad*—older even than *nomos*, which is associated with allocation and thus with law—is *nem-*, which refers to the free distribution of animals in places not bound by legal decree: "The occupation of shepherd, in the Homeric age, had nothing to do with a parcelling of land; when the agrarian question came to the foreground, in the time of Solon, it was expressed in an entirely different vocabulary."[128] After Solon, *nomos* and *logos* joined forces inside the city walls (foreshadowing the eventual hegemony of site-space), leaving the extramural world to fend for itself. Such fending—the word means shifting or venturing—meant letting animals graze in areas unrestricted by law. Thus the nomadic trajectory became one that "distributes people (and animals) in an open space, one that is indefinite and noncommunicating."[129]

But even the freest-ranging nomads still follow the land's lead. They do not roam entirely at random over the land but "cling to the smooth space left by the receding forest, where the steppe or the desert advance."[130] Such economizing remains true to its *nem-* root by first respecting the disposition of the land in its natural state—e.g., by acting at "specific locations" in accordance with the "divagation of local climates"[131]—and only then fitting into regimes of allocation. In this sense, the land's dis-position, its lay-out, precedes both distribution and allocation. In the austere economy of pastoral nomadism, nature's disposing regulates the proposing of human beings. In this Great Economy, *nem-* takes the lead over *nomos* and *legein* over *logos*, just as place takes precedence over site. Lococentrism prevails.

What would be desolate wilderness for the city-dweller is welcome terrain for the nomad, who feels *oikoi*, at home, even in the most forbidding desert or steppe. Just such unlikely places as these provide dwelling for nomadic populations: that is, dwelling-as-wandering, within which the primary domicile is the tent.[132] As Toynbee remarks, nomads characteristically "fling themselves upon the Steppe, not to escape beyond its bounds but *to make themselves at home on it.*"[133] The economy practiced in such a seemingly unpropitious location is decidedly ecocentric. In letting grazing animals lead the way and in respecting the seasons, the pastoral nomad perforce follows the land's lead. Open-ended pastures rather than fenced-in fields are the functional units of implacement. Not unlike gardens in this respect, pastures are way-stations between civilization and wilderness; they are also middle grounds between the high mountains (where grazing is not possible) and the city (the site of the allocative actions of law and justice). In a pasture, as in many gardens, one can gaze into the depths of the local landscape.[134] The surrounding array is unoccluded, and the basic landscape features are disclosed in stark lucidity. In such an outward-tending middle realm, one is not inclined to possess, to territorialize, the land. Husbandry replaces mastery, shepherding being the only form of allowable stewardship. A genuinely pastoral economy is thereby realized—one which, regulated by the configuration and character of the wild land, guides animals and humans alike in a common ecocentric venture.

Wild places can be found anywhere on earth. They do not exclude the presence of human beings. They may even include a jar that is left thoughtlessly on a hill along with other debris. But it remains necessary to get to the hill, if only to see how the wilderness surrounds the jar. Then one will view the composite scene, at once natural and cultural, in its own depth.[135] As it is, in the contemporary world, serious sojourns into wilderness are all too rarely undertaken. In their stead are pointless and endless errands, not into wild places but into the supermarket and the shopping mall. The *mall*, a term that stems from the British Mall (a walkway bordered by trees in Saint James Park in London), is what the wilderness has become. Not only has it taken the place of an aboriginal wilderness—being constructed on the very spot that once was wild—but it is itself a wilderness in the perjorative sense familiar to the early American colonists: chaotic, unproductive, and unlocated. For it is literally true that a shopping mall yields few places but many sites.

A site is no place to be, much less to remain. It is not even worth a postmodern nomadic journey to get there. Once there, moreover, where are we? We are in the midst of a desert of shops, a waste land of services, a chaos of commerce. If not nowhere, we are in an extremely shallow somewhere. No depth, not even any significant perceptual depth, is found here. The depth of nature—what Levinas calls "depth in distance"—has ceded place to a purely "synthetic" depth, depth in the shallows of human experience, depth bottomed out.[136] As soon as I attempt to look into the horizontal distance, my gaze is cut off by the busy bodies of other shoppers. If I try to look *up* or *out*, my view is blocked altogether. Earlier arcades, such as those located in Milan and Paris, at least allowed a glimpse of the sky, thanks to their transparent glass roofs.[137] The transparency has for the most part become occluded by opaque building materials that keep the natural world out of view and out of touch.

To feel the ultimate desolation and the equally ultimate displacement that characterize this scene, imagine yourself locked in a mall overnight, empty of people and featuring only shadowy shops whose windows contain unmoving and unspeaking mannikins. Nothing alive here, much less anything "unspeakably pure and sublime." Nothing but the comedy—or the tragedy—of plastic and metallic objects and forms. Everything, including the site, is artificial. Certainly no "fit place for life."[138] One could not survive for long in such a hard-edged circumstance. The desolation stems not just from the arid architecture or the monotony of the building complex as a whole. It also stems from a sense that in being here one has been deprived of place itself, cast into a placeless realm. One knows instantly that a better implacement exists elsewhere, whether in one's own home or in the wilderness. Even if the mall is a wilderness of sorts, it is not a household. No natural economy, no husbandry is practiced on its premises; here the economy is demand-based industrial economy, the "little economy" of commerce.[139] Although reminiscent of a desert, there is nothing pastoral here, there is no *nem* in this hulking lonely structure. Distribution of animals and land has given way to the allocation of materials and monies. The disposition of natural place has yielded to the imposition of artificial site.

The mall is not only desolate but *desolated* for its lack of deep ecology. Ecocentricity is out of place here. Even if the mall is filled with plants and other reminders of the natural world, this world itself remains *outside*, somewhere else on earth. "Nature is still elsewhere."[140] True place is elsewhere. Real life is missing, *"la vraie vie est absente."*[141] At best, real life and true place are *represented* in the mall, e.g., by photographs of wild places or by recorded sounds of animal or human voices. The three-dimensionality of place and voice—their distinctive depth, their life—has been replaced by the two-dimensionality of lifeless visual and auditory icons. Time and space come together in such a site and its attenuated images, but neither life nor place appear in this flattened-out, homogeneous scene.

The clear sight of open landscape has given way to the clear-cut dimensions of a rectilinear and self-enclosed building complex. Depth, the elusive basis of all dimensions, indeed the "first dimension,"[142] has been eliminated in favor of shallowness of affect and image, a flatness reinforced by glossy walls and sleek floors. Walking is still allowed but is actively discouraged by the escalators that transport one's inert body upward from floor to floor until, at the top, one views the empty–full prospect of an infernal and unreal non-scape full of sound and sight, signifying "nothing that is not there and the nothing that is" (Wallace Stevens).

It is to this estranged scene that I traveled as I completed my trip to Hartford. Earlier on the same journey, I had glimpsed another world, obscurely but impressively present. Even as viewed from I-91, that world, the natural world, was seen to possess its own inalienable configuration and depth. From within my speeding automobile, I could not help but notice an alluring set of places, indeed an entire region exhibiting its own landform features, arc and atmosphere, things and ground, all connected by shimmering sensuous surfaces. I was given a landscape even as I was driving toward a sitescape.

What more could I ask for? All I have to do now is to drive back to that beckoning region, leave my car, and start walking. Then an unmalled world of wild places not visible from, much less touchable in, the urban scene will open up. Emerson was right: "Cities give not the human senses room enough."[143] To get the right room, I need only saunter out of the mall and return to whatever unwalled wilderness remains. If I do this, I will find myself in agreement with Thoreau: "When we walk, we naturally go to the fields and woods: what would become of us, if we walked only in a garden or a mall?"[144]

PART V

Moving between Places

We shall not cease from exploration
And the end of all our exploring
Will be to arrive where we started
And know the place for the first time.

—T. S. Eliot, "Little Gidding"

9

Homeward Bound: Ending (in) the Journey

> We would like only, for once, to get to where we are already.
>
> —Martin Heidegger, "Language"

I

THE BOOK YOU have been reading constitutes a twofold journey. It has taken us, author and reader alike, on a conceptual journey concerning place—concerning its character and the manifold ways in which we come to know a given place—as well as on a lived and remembered journey between particular places: between Kansas and Tibet, Vicenza and Venice, Vaux-le-Vicomte and Versailles, Glacier Bay and Walden Pond, Northampton and Hartford. Despite manifest differences, the travel in concepts has been continuous with the experiential trips; indeed, each form of voyage has called for the other. Kant's basic rule that concepts without intuitions are empty, intuitions without concepts blind, remains valid in the place-world. To do a philosophy of place requires recourse both to the luminosity of conceptual distinctions and to the felt density of actual occasions. In both regards and often in quite parallel ways, this text has represented a journey back into place: a virtual re-installation in place itself.

But does not the very idea of *journey* take us back instead to the putative primacy of *time*? To give a quasi-narrative recounting of the varieties and vicissitudes of place as I have done in successive chapters of this book suggests that I have myself fallen into some sort of temporocentrism. Have I not given a running (if not altogether breathless) account *in sequence* of aspects of orientation and direction, of certain basic bodily contributions to implacement, of two ways of dwelling, and of fundamental features of wilderness places? Have I not been telling a *story* of place and thereby translating place itself into temporal terms? Does not explicitly invoking the theme of journey at the end only return us to the very position I attempted to abandon in the beginning? Must we not then concede priority to time after all?

A close scrutiny of the notion of journey shows, however, that even such an ostensibly temporal idea as this (the French cognate *journée* means "day-

long") harbors a commitment to place. Much as narratives of many kinds
(including those of journeys) cannot help but allude to place in the form of
"settings," so journeys themselves—whether migrations seriously undertaken
or mere pleasure trips—are place-bound and place-specific. Place would not
matter so much if journeys consisted merely in returning to a precise point
in Space or Time conceived in terms of simple location. Such exact spatio-
temporal pointillism means reverting to the identical, to *just this* spot on a
map or a calendar (ideally, both at once)—a spot that is no place at all but
a site. Yet the effect, if not the express purpose, of most journeys is to get
us back into an accommodating, nonpunctiform place, not excluding a place
defined mainly in temporal terms (e.g., "the beginning place"). In fact, when
we journey back to the same place, the place itself need not be strictly the
same; it would even be bizarre for the place to be altogether unchanged. We
know it as different even as we return to it as identifiably (but not identically)
the same. And this is so because of the inherent plasticity and porosity of
place itself, its nonconfinement to precise spatial or temporal parameters, its
continual capacity to overflow (and sometimes to undermine) these limits.
More than mere backdrop, places provide the changing but indispensable material medium of journeys, furnishing way stations as well as origins and
destinations of these same journeys.

    Homecoming presents an especially striking instance of the difference
that place makes in a journey. When Odysseus comes back to his home kingdom of Ithaca, he is as struck by the changes he observes as by the con-
tinuities: persevering Penelope is ostensibly self-identical, but life at court has
become insubordinate and unruly. (By hanging slave-girls and killing
Penelope's suitors, however, Odysseus evinces an unwillingness to live with
such disturbing differences and an insistent desire to return to the *status quo
ante*.)[1] Much the same circumstance obtains whenever I return to my own
hometown, which is at once recognizably the same and yet disarmingly different each time I come back. To be sure, both kinds of journey, epic and
personal, are ineluctably *in* space and *in* time, as becomes evident when we
focus on the determinate events narrated in an epic or an autobiography. Yet
these very events, which form the foci of narration, are not without placeful
properties. The allure of my childhood home even includes its address at
"3210 West 17th St.," for me an almost talismanic place-marker. However distant in space and time it has become for me, the house at this address is still
a place, a most significant place, as I return to it. "Home is where one starts
from,"[2] and it is also where one returns to in a journey of homecoming. In
between, life's journey offers a set of scenes as place-rich and place-varied as
Odysseus experienced in his eventful circumnavigation of the Mediterranean
world.

Not only is a journey replete with the lore of place, but it adds a crucial dimension to our understanding of what place is all about. When I take a journey, I *move from place to place*. In migrating, I move from one determinate place in a given region, a place-of-origin, to another equally determinate place, the place-of-destination, in a geographically separate region, say, from Buchs, Switzerland, to Turkey Creek, Kansas. On a pilgrimage, I also move between a definite starting place and an equally definite ending place, each located in a different region; but now the destination is valorized as having sacred and not only biographical or practical significance. In nomadic life, in contrast with both migration and pilgrimage, my movement between places, although frequent and diverse, remains *within* a given region, usually a region claimed or reclaimed at the outer fringes of civilization (e.g., in deserts, on steppes, on oceans).[3] This is not to mention an insidious nomadism endemic to modern times, in which the individual, afflicted with disorientation and anomie, drifts within the indifferent spaces of housing developments and shopping centers and superhighways.

On every kind of journey, one moves between heterogeneous places. A beginning-place and an end-place may stand out as the most conspicuous parts of a journey—they delimit the diurnal aspect, the daily duration, the *diēs*, of the journey—but the in-between places are just as interesting, and sometimes more so. Whereas the starting- and ending-places are often the same—paradigmatically so in the case of homecoming—the interplaces are intrinsically diverse, sometimes to the point of being distracting, as in the picaresque manner of *Don Quixote*. But they may also be highly structured among themselves, as in epic journeys of many descriptions, including the *Odyssey* and the *Divine Comedy*. These latter journeys exhibit an essentially disparate spatiality, an irrecusable otherness of intermediate places visited by the epic hero. Not only are there nine circles in Dante's vision of Hell, but every given circle is itself further diversified: the eighth circle, for example, has ten subdivisions, each with its own peculiar placiality.

A journey of the kind undertaken by Don Quixote or Dante or Odysseus is a journey through what Deleuze and Guattari call the "Dispars"—that is, a divergent and heterotopic spatiality—in contrast with the "Compars," a homogeneous and metrically determinate space. The Dispars, which is also (somewhat paradoxically) called "smooth space," is described thus:

> Smooth space is precisely the space of the smallest deviation: therefore it has no homogeneity, except between infinitely proximate points, and the linking of proximities is effected independently of any determined path. It is a space of contact, of small tactile or manual actions of contact, rather than a visual space like Euclid's striated space. . . . A field, a heterogeneous

smooth space, is wedded to a very particular type of multiplicity: non-met-
ric, acentered, rhizomatic multiplicities which occupy space without "count-
ing" it and [which] can "only be explored by legwork."[4]

In the cases cited just above, legwork is the main means by which a journey
is accomplished. Whether on a long-legged horse (e.g., Don Quixote and
Sancho Panza, or the legendary Crusaders) or literally on foot (e.g., Dante
and Virgil), the journey is made by maintaining bodily contact with the underlying earth. Even Odysseus, the intrepid sailor, must explore on foot the
coasts and islands he comes upon; and in *Ulysses*, Joyce's retelling of the
Homeric epic, the protagonists continually walk from place to place in and
around Dublin. In such perambulations, particular places are linked "independently of any determined path." A potent factor of the undetermined,
often of distinct danger, attends the journeyer and eliminates the security of
a predetermined trajectory, as is expressly signaled at the beginning of the
Inferno in Dante's immersion in "a dark forest" (*una selva oscura*) and in his
frightening encounters with several savage beasts. Moreover, what matters on
such heroic (or, in the case of *Don Quixote* and *Ulysses*, mock-heroic) journeys
is an immediate, unpremeditated engagement with a particular place rather
than a survey, i.e., a distanced visual perception of the scene. The "rhizomatic multiplicities" constitutive of such journeys are found in unsurvey-
able places whose idiolocal peculiarities are experienced in the first person by
means of touch and sound as well as sight. Disparateness of place reigns over
the self-identity of space and the punctuality of time.

Journeys thus not only take us to places but embroil us in them. For this
reason they cannot be reduced to superficial visitations, or "day trips," in
which we career or cruise between places considered as arbitrary stopping-
points. Don Quixote, for all his bizarre antics, gets deeply involved in the
places he encounters. To be sure, the cartographer and the topographical
landscape painter—along with the historian of a region—legitimately avoid
complete immersion in the places with which they are concerned. But where
they assume a certain distance from places (indeed, the very idea of "landscape" implies this distance), the journeying person is caught inescapably in
a placeful net of the Dispars. Only in the strictly homogeneous space of the
Compars can we imagine ourselves gliding between places in a frictionless
fashion.

The *Odyssey*, that ur-epic of Western tradition, is densely place-beset in
its structure. The names of its primary episodes are place-names or surrogates
of place-names: toponyms or eponyms.[5] Moreover, "the essential rhythm of
the *Odyssey* is set up in the *spatial* alternation of its episodes."[6] Beyond the
fact that the very notion of "episode" cannot be grasped except in spatial
terms (*episodic* derives from *epeisodos*, coming in besides), the *Odyssey*'s epi-

sodes are the very episodes *of* particular places. The narrative of these same episodes is less a means of linking them together in a common stream of time than of intertwining them in space—and, more particularly, in place. "Much of the action of the narrative," writes Michael Seidel, "connects place and process for Odysseus."[7] Indeed, the essential unit of Homer's *epos* is the *ethos*, i.e., the natural locale, the particular region signified by such place-names as "Hades," "Wandering Rocks," "Pylos," "Scheria," etc. Homer "speaks with names"—with local place-names—and in his epic the land and sea are at once sources of names and ethical preserves, realms of values and virtues as well as mnemonic resources. For archaic Greek bards as for contemporary Western Apache storytellers, places provide permanence, a bedrock basis for situating stories in scenes that possess moral tenor.[8]

The *Odyssey* is therefore at least as much a narrative of place as it is a narrative of events. It is a narrative of *events in place*. Such a narrative is inherently "chronotopic" in the Bakhtinian sense of offering an indissoluble mixture of spatio-temporal happenings.[9] Chronotopism is all the more evident in the *Divine Comedy* and *Ulysses*, where a co-determination of date and place is continually effected. Dante's epic takes place at Eastertide, A.D. 1300, between the night of Maundy Thursday and Wednesday noon after Easter, with visits to particular places dated even more exactly: e.g., Dante's arrival at the gate of Hell at 7:00 P.M. on Good Friday. Joyce's masterpiece takes place entirely on the *journée* of June 16, 1904, when the myriad events narrated in the text are given locations in places that correspond to actual street addresses in a reconstructed map of Dublin.[10]

In a notebook preparatory to *Ulysses*, Joyce wrote: "Topical History: places remember events."[11] The initial spatio-temporal equipoise of the phrase "topical history" is subverted by the claim that the active agent is place and not historical events, the former actively remembering the latter. Joyce calls into question the characteristically modern conception of viewing memory as exclusively time-bound, i.e., as recollection of the past. The inherent localism of memory also obtains for narration, in which places, instead of being merely settings or scenes, are active agents of commemoration. Nick Thompson, a Western Apache storyteller, puts it this way: "All these places have stories." The topotropism of Homer and Joyce, Cervantes and Dante, also appears in the earth epics of the Western Apaches, not to mention the Australian Aborigines, the Navajo, the Salteaux, and the Lakota Sioux. In these diverse epical traditions, Western and non-Western alike, memorable journeys consist of events in places. Hearing of such journeys, we come to know places with as much right and as much insight as we know the time in which they have transpired. Narration hereby lives up to its own origin in *gnarus*, knowing. In learning of narrated times and places—times-of-places and places-in-times—we acquire a distinctive form of local knowledge.

II

But what of *our own* journeys, the travelings of our (so-called "ordinary") selves, the trips of those who are *not* classical heroes, folk heroes, even mock- or anti-heroes? A quite basic, yet seldom noticed, structure of mundane journeys is a phenomenon I shall call "double-tracking." As I journey from place to place in the everyday life-world, two parallel and simultaneous processes are likely to occur without premeditation. On one hand, I find myself attending closely to the immediate perceptual environs, the "near sphere" or "focal field" (as I called it in part two) with its usually less than Odyssean lures and dangers. I must make my way safely across or around whatever obstacles lie before me in this close world if I am to reach my destination successfully. Here most of my cues stem from the unaided perception of whatever presents itself to the naked eye (and to the equally unadorned ear and the direct senses of touch, taste, and smell). I notice *this* looming person or *that* oncoming car in my path. On the other hand, I am also aware of a more encompassing circumambient field within which the focal field itself is set. Although this larger field is mappable (it would constitute a district or region on a map), I do not take it as metrically determinate or even as laid out in a regular way. Instead, I grasp it as a diversely configurated, multidimensional environment with its own inherent directionality. Thus my sense of the "cardinal directions" arises from such comparatively remote natural phenomena as the rising and setting of the sun, the path of the moon, the constellations of the stars, the disposition of hills and mountains that surround me. Less direct cues include the relative speed and height of clouds coming from over the horizon, allowing me to infer that the ocean is located "over there." On a journey, I attend to these indices of the far sphere, whether they are in the direction of my destination or not. For they inform me of what lies before and around me, even (and especially) when a given destination is out of the normal range of my direct perception.

As I pursue my everyday journey, e.g., from my home to the service station where my car is to be fixed, it is crucial that I relate both kinds of information—that coming from from the focal field and that from the circumambient world—to each other. Not only do I *keep track* of my journey, I *double-track* it, heeding not just two separate sets of cues but their continuing interrelationship as well. A particular perception in the here of my proto-place takes on its full significance only as it links up with what is in the there of an oncoming com-place or counter-place. Conversely, I cannot grasp what is there in the next stage of my journey except in relation to the here of where I am just now. My journey, in other words, is not simply from here to there but from here to here to here, or more precisely from the here-in-view-of-there to the there-reached-from-here. A dialectic of place ensues in which I go not just between discrete and preestablished points but find myself within an evolving nexus of ever-changing places, all of which can be characterized by hereness as well as thereness. Even if each of the places of my journey remains recognizably the same, a given place is what it is only in relation to the other places.[12]

The dialectic of an everyday journey is temporal as well as placial. It is a matter of now and then as well as here and there. The here of my journey is at the same time a now (though not necessarily a strictly momentary now), and a given there is also the then of my arrival at the next stage and eventually at my destination "there in the future" (as Alkinoös says to Odysseus).[13] To the essential heterogeneity of place, its heterotopism, is conjoined a multiplicity of times, a heterochronism. Right now, as I walk about my near sphere, I notice the unfolding of several disparate temporal phenomena: that other walker accomplishing his "legwork" at a certain pace, those oncoming cars bearing down upon me at high speed, that lupine dog advancing toward me at an alarming rate. So, too, I experience the day of my journeying as possessing its own polyrhythm, its diurnal "parts" (morning, high noon, afternoon, dusk, evening) succeeding each other in a manner that may not be chronometrically determinate but is nonetheless not shapeless either, each of its unique events having its own tempo. When the remoteness that lies beyond the visible horizon is taken into account, the complexity becomes chronic indeed. For the then of the there may include such ever-shifting *temporalia* as weeks, months, entire seasons of the year, and even sometimes phases of my life. These I also take into account, however indefinite they may be. Even if I do not perceive them as such, I have to be alert to cues concerning their incoming or outgoing presence: those March winds ushering in spring, as well as the heavy Friday afternoon traffic signaling the onset of the weekend. All of this needs to be noticed, and is usually noticed, albeit subliminally.

It would be more accurate to say, then, that as a journeyer I perform a *double* double-tracking. Not only do I relate the near to the far in terms of place. I also tie together the double placial ambit thus achieved with the double temporal outlay just described. To move forward at all on my daily rounds, to "advance" toward the service station—which for me now in the present is at once a place (for repair) and a time (a close future)—is to reckon with the intricate intertwining of all of the pertinent placial and temporal parameters of my mundane voyage. It is to enter into a highly ramified network of places and times.

I accomplish the redoubled tracking by traversing various particular way stations on my journey. These way stations serve as condensed reminders and retainers of my journey's placio-temporality. As such, they (along with beginning- and end-places) are designated by extremely economic toponyms. When someone asks me *where* I am *now* in my journey, I almost always answer by giving a discrete place-name: "Quogue," "Atlanta," "Amherst," "New Haven," etc. Similarly, if I am asked where I am *going*, I tend to respond by offering still other toponyms: "Santa Barbara," "Stony Brook," "Fairfield." The use of such place-names is no contingent matter, something I could do without. They are the locatory units of everyday journeys, indices of attachment to the land (or sea or air) through which such journeys are made. Signs of literal progress in one sense, these "local signs" are also insignia of just where and when we are and have been in the place-world.

Even on mundane journeys, places are areas of possible *immersion*. Far from being superficial "positions"—which, having no dimensionality, can offer no room for immersion[14]—they are loci of and for involvement. But such multilocular involvement requires motion on my part: motion in/between places. I effect the motion of a journey by linking places in significant propinquity to each other on a more or less coherent (if not always definite) path. At any given moment, my motion also immerses me in the where of the place I am in. Paradoxically, it is precisely from (and in) such immersion, such motionless motion in place, that I am able to move to the other way stations of the journey, and eventually to my destination. *Movement is therefore intrinsic to place*—thus to what is often taken to be the very paradigm of the lasting and the *un*moving in human experience. As holding and marking the stages of a journey, places exhibit notably stationary virtues. But as the loci of engaged motion—both the more conspicuous motion of moving-between-places and the more subtle motion of being-in-place—places show themselves to be remarkably nonstatic. They are the foci of flow on the pathway of the journey.

III

The doubling and redoubled structure of ordinary journeys is forcefully inscribed in an extraordinary narrative account written by Matsuo Bashō in the late seventeenth century. Neither heroic nor mock-heroic, neither comic nor tragic, this is the journey of a poet who, having achieved worldly success as a genius of haiku, decided to give up material and social attachments and to travel to places famous for their inspirational beauty or historical significance, from Edo (ancient Tokyo) in eastern Japan to Ogaki in the west, passing through many locations in northern Japan, without returning to his place of origin. Bashō wrote several autobiographical accounts of his journey, one of which has the intriguing title "The Narrow Road to the Deep North."[15] This title combines the two primary domains at stake in the double-tracking discussed in the last section: "the narrow road" is the immediate focal field of the traveler, while "the deep north" alludes to the remote sphere sought in his travels. A coordinate double-tracking of time is also suggested, since the now of each successive way station is correlated with the then of more encompassing temporal units, such as months and seasons. Precision of place (in the form of place-names) concatenates with a commensurate exactitude of time: "It was early on the morning of March the twenty-seventh that I took to the road," he writes, adding at the end of the text that his journey was completed by the early summer of "1694," five years later.[16] And yet he makes it clear that he is offering the reader something other than a mere compendium of his daily travels.[17] What, then, does he offer?

One important clue is given by Bashō's own haiku as found throughout the text. The poet composed these seventeen-syllable poems (sometimes on the spot) as he traveled, and each of them presents a condensed image of an experience in a particular place. In fact, every such image can be said to "clot" the experience of that place.[18] For example, after remarking that by climbing around the deserted temple of Ryushakuhi he "felt the purifying power of this holy environment pervading my whole being," Bashō adds this haiku:

In the utter silence
Of a temple,
A cicada's voice alone
Penetrates the rocks.[19]

This distinctly chronotopic utterance offers the prospect of a heterogeneous scene of rocks, temple, and cicada—all brought together in the extended present of an "utter silence." The silence signifies the poet's immersion in this scene, his arrested motion at the place of the temple (the here) and his equally arrested attention at the sudden sounding of the cicada's voice (the now). As the cicada's voice "penetrates" the rocks, so do place and time penetrate each other in the poem, meeting in the center place of the temple. Despite the intensity of his engagement, the poet declares his awareness of wishing to move on to the next stage of his journey: "I wanted to sail down the River Mogami."[20] As the *there* that will be reached *then*, the Mogami River beckons beyond the horizon of the current scene at the temple.

Quite apart from its descriptive merits, such an episode illustrates Bashō's commitment to the Buddhist doctrine of *mujo*, according to which all things are impermanent, fleeting, and empty. His decision to undertake an arduous journey when he was in ill health and getting on in years reflects this same commitment. The traveler's inns in which he often stayed are themselves concrete symbols of *mujo*, bringing together impermanence in time (the overnight stay) and merely momentary stability in space (the rented room).

William LaFleur observes that "as a place that houses transients, [such an inn] articulates transience."[21] The inn thus contrasts both with the comparatively stable identity of the home and with the even greater stability of the hermit's hut.[22] An inn is the transitory halting-place of the ambulatory journeyer whose ongoing motion assures that no place, not even the place of destination, will be a scene of complete arrest. Thus Bashō, soon after reaching his goal of Ogaki, decides to depart once again; his very destination is no more than a place of departure:

> Everybody [in Ogaki] was overjoyed to see me as if I had returned unexpectedly from the dead. On September the sixth, however, I left for the Ise Shrine, though the fatigue of the long journey was still with me, for I wanted to see the dedication of a new shrine there. As I stepped into a boat, I wrote:
>
> As firmly cemented clam-shells
> Fall apart in autumn,
> So I must take to the road again,
> Farewell, my friends.[23]

Like human life itself, Bashō's bold journey consists in a continual alternation of staying put and moving on. His sojourn is a liminal state with no lasting stopping places. He pauses at an inn or temple only to leave again right away; no sooner is one journey finished and its adventures shared with friends than he begins another journey. The alternation need not be frenetic or manic or distracted. If known and savored as such, it can be the source of a special sense of significance not otherwise accessible. Whitehead has written that "contrast elicits depth, and only shallow experience is possible when there is a lack of patterned contrast."[24] Journeys may be considered systematic pursuits of patterned contrasts difficult to obtain in an entirely sedentary existence. The formal patterns of these contrasts are precisely those of the here versus the there, the near versus the far, the now versus the then, stopping versus starting, the permanent versus the impermanent, and complex combinations of all of these (including seasonal variations). But on any given occasion during a journey, the contrasting pattern is concretely experienced, as we see in this recounting of Bashō's visit to the ancient stone monument of Tsubo-no-ishibumi:

> In this ever-changing world where mountains crumble, rivers change their courses, roads are deserted, rocks are buried, and old trees yield to young shoots, it was nothing short of a miracle that this monument alone had

survived the battering of a thousand years to be the living memory of the ancients. I felt as if I were in the presence of the ancients themselves, and, forgetting all the troubles I had suffered on the road, rejoiced in the utter happiness of this joyful moment, not without tears in my eyes.[25]

An awareness of sameness within change is here thrown into relief by a recognition of the mutability of all things. Although the experience itself belongs entirely to the present now "of this joyful moment" and to the present place of Tsubo-no-ishibumi, it bears on a past *then* that has survived for a millennium. Moreover, the bearer of this past of an ancient culture is itself a spatially determinate object, a monument situated specifically in the here of the poet's experience. Paradoxically, the very stolidity of this monument allows it to elicit the "living memory" and even the "presence" of "the ancients themselves." Stopping Bashō in place, the monument transports him in time. A contesseration of place and time—their configuration as parts of a larger puzzle—makes possible the coexistence of alteration and stabilization. A last vignette vividly exemplifies this coexistence:

As we turn every corner of the Narrow Road to the Deep North, we sometimes stand up unawares to applaud and we sometimes fall flat to resist the agonizing pains we feel in the depths of our hearts. There are also times when we feel like taking to the road ourselves, seizing the raincoat lying near by, or times when we feel like sitting down till our legs take root, enjoying the scene we picture before our eyes.[26]

What matters is not the journey as such, much less its value as an incursion into the heroic or the exotic, the natural or the supernatural. What matters is its ability to present a contrast between the virtues of lastingness and the values of transience, between remaining in place and moving among places, and to do both in ways that realize an intricate dialectic of space and time.

IV

It comes as something of a shock to realize that Bashō lived and wrote during the same century when quite fateful developments were occurring in the Western world. These developments in the seventeenth century, "the century of genius," were such as to forcibly remove the idea of place from respectable philosophical and scientific parlance and to replace it with the "great narratives" of Space and Time.[27] These meta-narratives were as journeyless as they were joyless. At best, they stand as cautionary or explanatory tales, one of whose primary effects was to suppress any concerted consideration of place. Thus Newton condescendingly distinguished "relative Place" from "absolute Place," distinctly implying that to be merely a relative place is to be beneath contempt (and, in any case, outside of serious scientific concern). And yet it was precisely as relative, as a matter of internal and external relations of distance and position, that place was mainly treated—when it was treated at all—by Descartes and Locke and above all Leibniz.

How different is the case of Bashō⁻, who was as unabashedly place-attuned as his contemporaries in Western Europe were unremittingly place-purblind! At stake here is not just a contingent divergence between Japanese and European sensibilities in a given historical period. Bashō's eagerness to feature place prominently in the narration of a journey—in a descriptively rich *petit récit*—betrays an entire way of being-in-the-world in which places are more crucial constituents than are space and time. While even absolute Place is subordinate to absolute Space in Newton's great narrative of modern physics, places count in Bashō's text not despite but *because of* their relativity to each other. This very relativity allows them to be the ultimate units, the "contact-loci," not just of mobility but of stability as well, and thus to be the epicenters of every journey. The same relativity also enables places to be the most revealing arenas in which to experience the dialectic of here–there, near–far, now–then, beginning–halting, and permanent–transitory, a dialectic that subtends the progress of any given journey, and of any given life.

Japan, unlike Western Europe, did not undergo a violent rupture between a premodern or medieval period and an identifiably modern epoch. In place of radical scission, a gradual and slow modification of perception and thought occurred "pianissimo" (in Robert Bellah's word).[28] Bashō, as a representative figure of the seventeenth century in Japan, drew inspiration from such medieval figures as Gyogi (eighth century) and Saigyo (twelfth century) without feeling any disruptive discontinuity between himself and these illustrious predecessors. In fact, he was engaged in a poetic project that carried forward their pioneering ventures—ventures that were already acutely place-sensitive. Although anchored in a period one cannot help but call "modern," Bashō was deeply continuous with a period which the tyranny of historical periodicity forces us to label "medieval."

Bashō's sensibilities sit athwart the modernist thinking of his near (but far-flung) contemporaries Descartes and Locke, Newton and Leibniz. But the fact that his sensibilities connect with much earlier perceptions of place in Japanese culture suggests that it is concretely possible for those who exist in a *post*modern era in the West to take inspiration from premodern as well as nonmodern instances of place-appreciation.[29] In this vein we should not hesitate to appropriate insights from Bashō himself, despite his historical embeddedness in the seventeenth century and his geographical locus in Japan, and we can do so with much the same inspiration he took from the inaugural work of Gyogi and Saigyo. At the same time, we can forestall any charge that we have merely *regressed* to the premodern, since Bashō's life and work call the very distinction between modern and premodern into question.

Perhaps the most basic thing to be learned from Bashō's journey is that a fundamental distinction can be made between *fixity* and *stability* when it comes to matters of place. By "fixity" I mean two things. On one hand, I refer to the assumption that only what is *observed from a fixed position or "perspective"* in external space is to be accorded objectivity as a phenomenon.[30] On the other hand, fixity implies a strict determinacy in the *position of the object* thus viewed: e.g., the center of a perfect circle in Euclidean space, or any point at which the coordinates on a Cartesian grid intersect in expressing the value of a given variable (including the location of a site on a map by means of comparable coordinates: Flagstaff, say, at "G-4" on a road map). Fixity of position is an instance of simple location, i.e., the presumption that a given object taken as an independent individual thing possesses one (and only one) determinate site.[31] Both simple location and fixed, one-point perspective are important chapters in the modernist grand narrative of Space. In this metastory, they stand in close proximity to claims that all space is homogeneous, isotropic, and infinite and that, nevertheless, *for us* no object in space is experienced directly but must be represented in our minds as the specific content of an "idea" or a "perception."

"Stability" is quite another matter. From Bashō we learn that it signifies a way of being in space that suspends fixation on fixity itself in both of the senses just distinguished. One concrete sign of this double suspension is the fact that Bashō employs *paintings as maps* for his journey rather than using official maps, which, by the latter half of the seventeenth century in Japan, were already drawn from a fixed vantage point above the landscape.[32] Another sign is the continual creation of expressly chronotopic haiku, which may be taken as spontaneous poetic deconstructions of simple locations. For example:

> Behind this door
> Now buried in deep grass,
> A different generation will celebrate
> The Festival of Dolls.[33]

Not only is the door not simply located in space in the present (any such punctate localization is here dissolved by its immersion in "deep grass"), but its implacement is diversified by its role in a future when it will be a door *for others*. In neither way is the door considered the kind of individual substance that is strictly separable in space (and in time) from other substances. Instead of simple location, it possesses "multilocularity."[34] As in the case of the rhizome (which sports roots at multiple locations underground), a given place in the force field of Bashō's poetic vision is multilocular, and yet retains its own stability.

A striking instance of this rhizomatic stability appears in a final pair of haiku, both written by Bashō's traveling companion, Sora:

A thicket of summer grass
Is all that remains
Of the dreams and ambitions
Of ancient warriors.

I caught a glimpse
Of the frosty hair of Kanefusa
Wavering among
The white blossoms of *unohana*.[35]

Here one and the same place is the occasion for two different localizations. In the first haiku, the place evokes the *absence* of the world of ancient warriors, who exist only in memory. In the second, this world is rendered momentarily *present* by the poet's imagination of the gray hair of the aged warrior Kanefusa. Memory and imagination complicate and diversify the self-same place, which keeps its *stabilitas loci* throughout these variations. In such a place as this (as in the haiku's own textual place) we realize that whereas strict fixity of position and perspective is incompatible with the movement between places essential to a journey, stability proves to be such movement's constant companion. Stability and movement are complementary, each enhancing the other in the course of a journey that is as placeful as it is eventful.

V

From time to time, a man lifts his head, sniffs, listens, considers, recognizes his position: he thinks, he sighs, and, drawing his watch from the pocket lodged against his chest, looks at the time. *Where am I?* and *What time is it?* Such are the inexhaustible questions turning from us to the world. . . .
—Paul Claudel, *Art poétique*

The ongoing alliance of stability and movement in the progress of a journey entails an entangling of space and time in the particular places and pathways of that journey. The detailed narrative of this intertwined space and time, being place-bound and place-reflective, is not to be confused with the great (and greatly confining) narrative of Space and Time. In the modern Western world, and very much thanks to the *grand récit* of Space and Time with which this world was inaugurated (and by which it has continued to be sustained down to the present day), we have little choice but to regard time and space as rivalrous opponents, since time is considered to be strictly ever-altering and sequential and space simultaneous and unchanging. In the modern myth, each encroaches on the territory of the other, threatening it with usurpation and even annihilation. No wonder that so many have come to suffer from this dire competition (dire because there is no prospect of an irenic resolution), and that entire pathologies, both social and psychological, have issued from distortions of temporal and spatial experiences in agonistic relations with one another.[36] As Kant showed in the *Critique of Pure Reason*, the antinomy that results from taking space and time as separate parameters is unresolvable, especially when the antinomy is stated in terms of whether the world has a determinate beginning (or ending) in space or time.[37] And yet the merest daily journey brings space and time together in the event of place. In such a journey—and all the more so in an epic journey—the merging of motion and stability replaces the separate dimensionalities of time and space.

In chapter 1, I traced out two sources of the modern predicament as engendered by the *gigantomachia* of Space and Time: an overriding concern for the exact measurement of time (symbolized by the desperate search for a reliable marine chronometer) and an obsession with the idea of mental representations (according to which nothing can count as an experience unless it is represented within the mind regarded as the "mirror of nature"). This concern and this obsession have set the scene of modernity askew. They have led, for example, to a view of memory as having to do mainly with the precise representation of the past in quasi-visual "recollections."[38] More generally, they have produced the frenzied sense that there is never "world enough and time" to linger in the leisurely pursuit of our most cherished projects, or even for the fulfillment of our most mundane goals. But, as I have indicated at many subsequent points in this book, we also suffer greatly from deficient modes of spatiality. With space shrunken to mere site in accordance with a paradigm of isometric extension, we find ourselves in leveled-down landscapes, dreary tractscapes where the Identical triumphs over the Different and the Same, the Compars over the Dispars. Even if we are less personally preoccupied with spatial imprisonment than we are with temporal displacement, we are no less the victims of modernist conceptions of space than we are of "modern times." Our building, our daily living, our mapping, our social relations, and our political (dis)empowerments all reflect our captivation in site-specified spaces. Much as we would like to make time more expansive, it only seems to vanish, while space, on the other hand, appears to be altogether too extensive—too empty and infinite—for concrete undertakings. If time has become all too "ecstatic," disintegrating before our very eyes, space stands stock-still, offering no adequate basis for our stabilities and instabilities.

The dual dominance of Space and Time is an expression, as well as an original and continuing cause, of the neglect of Place in human experience. Once more, this dominance and its effects are easier to detect in the case of time. As Vine Deloria puts it, "If time becomes our primary consideration, we never seem to arrive at the reality of our existence in places."[39] The Hopi, however, know better; for them, "if it does not happen 'at this place,' it does not happen 'at this time'; it happens at 'that' place *and* at 'that' time."[40] In other words, time and place are as inseparable in the end as they are in the beginning (a beginning in which we ask ourselves Claudel's questions: "Where am I?" "What time is it?"). But it is equally true that preoccupation with space obscures our immersion in concrete places. If something does not happen *at these places*, it also will not happen in the encompassing but abstract spatial extent in which they are located. It—an "it" best rendered as an "event" (Heidegger) or as an "actual occasion" (Whitehead)—happens at that place *and* in that space, as well as *in that time*: in all three together, *totum simul*.

Or let us say that time and space, rather than existing before place and independently of each other, *both inhere in place to start with*. Another redoubling occurs just here—and now—as we follow the double helix of space and time as enmeshed in particular places. Chronotopism runs deep; it characterizes the very depths of Tiamat, the depths of primordial Place as it exists before the superimposition of Mardukian or Demiurgic geometrism and the eventual modernist scission of Time and Space. The spatio-temporal matrix, instead of preceding places, is part of their very stability, ingredient in their very permanence. The permanent itself is not only a temporal category (e.g., "everlasting," "sempiternal") situated somewhere between the unchangingness of eternity and the everchangingness of time. It is also and equally a placial category. What Kant sought to prove regarding time—that it "presupposes something permanent in perception"[41]—we may assert of space as well. They both presuppose the *permanent in place*. Just as there can be no experience of time except as the time of events in places, so there can be no sense of space that is not anchored, finally if not immediately, in particular places. The ultimate "Refutation of Idealism" lies in the permanence of place.

The Navajo, who suffer so acutely from displacement, are prescient in their belief that their land is something "persisting through eventual change."[42] Dinétah (Navajo Land) is something permanent, and this means something lasting indefinitely in space and time—or, more exactly, enduring in a space indissociable from a time, both together being inextricably engaged in a particular place. It is thanks to the intimate interlacing of space-and-time-in-place that anything like permanence, not to mention stability, is possible. But the same intertwining also gives rise to movement, including the kind of movement that is constitutive of journeys.

VI

I know I'm not here to explore vacuousness at the heart of America. I'm only in search of what *is* here, here in the middle of the Flint Hills of Kansas. I'm in quest of the land and what informs it.
— William Least Heat-Moon, *PrairyErth (A Deep Map)*

Journeys, then, are not just travels in time or across space. They engage us ineluctably in place—often in many places (and not just in succession but also all-at-once, as in the dialectic of the here–there). But we can say just as well that places engage us in journeys. This is so to the extent that there is nothing like a completely static place, a place involving no movement, no change, no transiency. If places introduce permanency into journeys—since they are where we can *remain* as we move about—journeys bring out what is impermanent and continuously changing when we are in place itself. To be in a place is to be somewhere in which movement in the local landscape and thus journeying in that landscape becomes possible. In a site, by contrast, we are stuck in space (as well as frozen in time) such that we can move effectively only insofar as we overcome distance at various rates of acceleration—the higher the rate, supposedly the better. In this circumstance, site-stasis sets in, and journeys become mere travels or trips. In contrast, being-in-place brings with it actualities and virtualities of motion that have little if anything to do with speed and everything to do with exploration and inhabitation, with depth instead of distance, horizon rather than border, arc and not perimeter.

Therefore, just as places make journeys possible by situating bodily movement and giving more or less tenacious support to this movement, places themselves engender and encourage journeys in their midst. If being on a journey is to be in or among places, to be in a place is to be capable of journeying. Between places and journeys there is a relationship of mutual implication.

Eventful and placeful as it can be, every journey, including that undertaken in this book, must come to an end. *This end is in place itself.* In this regard it does not matter if the journey moves continually in one place (e.g., philosophizing while walking within an ancient stoa, or reading the chapters of this same book) or manages to move between numerous places. What matters is the movement itself as well as the fact that all movement, short of a *perpetuum mobile*, knows a terminus. Implaced and continually re-implaced, journeying comes to term eventually. It finds its way back to place.

The place to which a journey comes need not be a single spot. We can come to a set of places and consider *that* the end of the voyage. This happens, for example, when we return to an academic community we left many years ago. The journey ends in several places on the campus: a dormitory, the library, several classrooms we still remember. Nor need the end of the journey consist in a place we have known before. I can journey to Topolobampo, Mexico, somewhere I have never been. Nevertheless, unless I am emigrating to this exotic place (or am caught there in a political revolution), I will return to my homeland, which will be a second and familiar destination of the same total journey.

Ends of journeys fall into two extreme exemplars: homesteading and homecoming. In *homesteading*, I journey to a new place that will become my future home-place. The homesteading place is typically unknown to me, or known only from accounts given by others who have preceded me. But I am determined to settle down for the long term in this novel place. For instance, my Swiss ancestors homesteaded in Kansas, whose flatlands were utterly alien to their Alpine home-worlds. They settled in for the long term—which did not prevent them from gazing nostalgically at paintings of the mountains and valleys they had left behind. Only the milling they pursued in the new land served to link them with the old country. Homesteading need not be as literal or as land-based as this, however—given that a stead is any place in which one can take up continuous occupancy.[43] I can homestead in a city where I have accepted a new position. All that matters is that I commit myself to remaining in the new place for a stretch of time sufficient for building a significant future life there, sometimes for several generations. In homesteading, then, we witness once more the deep alliance that can be effected between time and place.

In *homecoming*, the duration of this alliance is no longer of major importance. What matters most now is the fact of return to *the same place*.[44] My great-grandfather revisited his Swiss village of origin several decades after homesteading in America. He stayed for two weeks, repaid those who had lent him money to come to the New World, then abruptly left, never to return. Brief as his return journey was, it was long enough to accomplish homecoming. If time is thus not primarily at stake in homecoming, neither is space. Once more, the issue is that of returning not to the identical spot in space but to a place that may itself have changed in the meanwhile. As we have seen, this was precisely Odysseus's fate in coming home to Ithaca. But it is also everyone's destiny who has returned home only to discover striking differences, e.g., that one's childhood home is much more diminutive than one had remembered it to be.

Homesteading and homecoming possess two features in common. On one hand, they both involve *re-implacement*. An initial implacement is succeeded by a displacement elsewhere as a journey is undertaken; the displacement, which may itself be multiple, in turn gives way to a last implacement at the end of the journey that is comparatively conclusive and stable. The difference, of course, is that the re-implacing realized in homesteading is conspicuously "steady," not just long-lasting but such as to involve dwelling-as-residing.[45] In homecoming, the re-implacing may be momentary and need not include residing or re-residing. Indeed, homecoming may be followed by yet another journey, e.g., back to one's *contemporary* home, whereas the intention in homesteading is to remain in one's newly adopted home-place. But homecoming is no less poignant for lacking longevity.

On the other hand, both homesteading and homecoming can achieve *co-habitancy*. I borrow this word from Thoreau, for whom it signifies a special kind of settled coexistence between humans and the land, between the natural and the cultural, and between one's contemporaries and one's ancestors.[46] In homesteading (at least that of an ecologically sensitive sort), one seeks to attain an ongoing co-habitancy with one's new home-place and its denizens. Indeed, only by a concerted and prolonged co-habitation between the homesteader and the land can homesteading become something more than forced exploitation of the region. Co-habitancy thus construed is difficult to achieve. My Swiss forebears did not accomplish it during nearly two decades of assiduous effort on the "prairyerth,"[47] whereupon they turned back to milling and to co-habitancy with the Smoky Hill River. Despite its frequent failures, homesteading flourishes when it attains the equipoise of co-habitancy. Indeed, without the realization of a certain minimal co-habitancy, homesteading becomes abortive or even self-defeating. For it then fails to come to terms with what the land calls for by way of an abiding partnership.

In homecoming, by contrast, the co-habitancy is distinctively different. By coming home, I effect a series of special alliances: with those who still remain there; with those who were once there but are now dead or departed; with my own memories; with my own current self, disparate as it doubtless is from the self who once lived in this same place; and above all with the home-place I once left.[48] The co-habiting is not now with a new place and an open future—both of which demand prolonged effort—but with a known place and a past remembered in that place, as well as a past *of that place* in the present. What counts is not a continuing investment in a place but the intensity and quality of my current experience in returning there.

Re-implacement and co-habitancy are on the agenda at the ends of journeys. They are at stake in all getting back in/to place: *in* place in homecoming and *to* place in the case of homesteading. Their active ingrediency does not occur as an end-*point*, a strict *terminus ad quem*. Instead, they contribute to the endings of journeys as nonpunctiform ways in which these journeys fade and phase out. Precisely as end*ings*, ie., as durational processes, co-habitancy and re-implacement are temporal in character. Yet their temporality remains inseparable from their placiality, quite expressly so in the case of re-implacement yet no less importantly so in co-habitancy. In becoming re-implaced, I am either entering a new place (in homesteading) or a place anew (in homecoming), whereas in experiencing co-habitancy I am making my peace with place (as homesteading requires) or reconnecting with place (as happens in homecoming). Every journey starts with/in place and moves between places; every journey, even one that is truncated, also finds itself ending in or with place—whether or not this final place is identically the same as the starting-place from which the journey began.

Ending-places exhibit one last generic structure: that of *habitat–habitus*. By the time we end and linger in a certain place, that place has become a habitat for us, a familiar place we have come to know (or to re-know). As a habitat, a place is something sufficiently settled to exhibit the requisite density for ending a journey: for being a genuine "stopping-place." A habitat-place embraces and supports the ending itself, and as such is a paradigm of that placial permanence which we have seen to be a condition of possibility for all journeying. As in the case of habitats of other species, we find ourselves at ease and at home in this kind of place; here we can be "ethical" in the originary sense of this word, which implies a community of like-minded (but not necessarily like-bodied) creatures. Co-habitancy fosters such a literally co-in*habitat*ional community, as Thoreau foresaw in his parable of Spaulding Farm:

> I took a walk on Spaulding's Farm the other afternoon. I was impressed as if some ancient and altogether admirable and shining family had settled there in that part of the land called Concord, unknown to me. . . . I saw their park, their pleasure-ground, beyond the wood, in Spaulding's cranberry-meadow.[49]

It is not accidental that Thoreau visited this habitat on an ambulatory journey. By his legwork he found a place of/for co-habitation. Walking out from Concord, he re-implaced himself on a farm that was once homesteaded by the Spauldings; but it was also, and much longer ago, homesteaded by a community of creatures more deeply and unself-consciously ethical than their human successors. Thoreau's own journey to Spaulding's Farm was a homecoming to a place where, though he had never lived there, he knew co-habitancy to thrive.

To enter and reenter a habitat in homesteading and homecoming, the proper habitus is also called for: the right set of skills for inhabiting or re-inhabiting that ending-place. As Thoreau's walking demonstrates, such skills are mainly bodily in character. They include powers of orientation that help to direct us to the habitat we seek, along with habitual body memories that allow us to return to the same place if we so desire. But other habitual abilities are brought to bear as well, notably those of being able to conceive of places in certain ways, to articulate thoughts about them, and to express such thoughts to others who find themselves on similar journeys. Cultural comportments rejoin and relay corporeal habitudes in the co-constitution of a place in which a journey ends—and from which it may begin again (as continually happened in the case of Thoreau). The way a journey finishes is a function of the natural-cum-cultural habitus that brings us to the place where it ends and that enables us to regard this place as a habitat in which the ending itself becomes possible.

On the basis of the habitat–habitus cycle we may infer that the ending here in question is also always a matter of *beginning*, and in two senses. First, this ending is what it is only as an ending *of* a beginning to which we have later access through sedimented habitualities of thought and action. In this capacity, the habitual looks *back* to the beginning of any given ending, a beginning we reexperience in homecoming. But a second beginning is implied insofar as in ending we also look *forward* to what is to come, as is exemplified in homesteading or the continuation of a journey (or even in its mere repetition). For such forward movement—sometimes beyond any known destination or trajectory—habitual skills are also requisite.

"In my end is my beginning."[50] The double truth of T. S. Eliot's formula is nowhere more fatefully inscribed than in the homecoming or homesteading with which many of the most significant journeys end. In these two ways of ending, both of which depend on the interfusion of habitats with habits in the accomplishment of co-habitational re-implacement, places figure as the presupposition as well as the precipitate.

VII

Homecoming and homesteading generate two special paradoxes that call for our attention. First, in homecoming I can find myself in the extraordinary situation where I return to a place which I can be said to know *for the first time*, even though in fact I have been there before and still retain intact memories of my earlier experiences there. Eliot points to this paradox expressly when he writes that "the end of all our exploring"—that is to say, the end of our journeys—is to arrive in a familiar place and "know the place for the first time." Heidegger hints at a closely similar circumstance: "we would like only, for once, to get to where we are already." In ending a journey in homecoming, I get to where I have been already—an extant or previous home—but I now experience it as if it were a new place. This new/old place seems to present itself to me this time for the first time.

Here we are at the antipode of the extreme view that homecoming requires the strict self-identity of the home, a view we have found to be questionable in a number of cases. But we are also on the far side of the more moderate view that calls only for a sameness of the home-place that is compatible with minor changes in its mere presentation. For now the changes seem to amount to a "transformation into another kind of thing," a sea-change, or rather a change into another kind of place. And yet, despite the radical changes, the place in question is still recognizably the *same* place. It is the same place I remember having inhabited in quite particular ways and at diverse times. Far from being a rare experience, this happens whenever I return to a previously familiar place—paradigmatically, but not exclusively, a home-place—and suddenly find myself deeply alienated from it, experiencing that place for the first time as off-putting, as "a very different kind of place."

The issue is not whether in this new perception we thereby come to a true, or truer, grasp of what is in fact the case. The issue is how we can come to such a disparate perception of what is unquestionably the same place. The basis for this disparity is twofold. First, a given home-place is always sufficiently ambiguous to accommodate a radical revision of its appearance and significance as we reencounter it. Part of the very meaning of "home" is that it is able to give rise to quite divergent perceptions and significations. A home can be experienced at one time as perfectly amicable, at another time as hostile; yet it remains one and the same place *through* these vicissitudes and not just despite them. If it is indeed true that "all really inhabited space bears the essence of the notion of home,"[51] home as inhabited bears multiple meanings, a number of which diverge markedly from each other. Second, the journey that has intervened between my leaving home in the first place and the present moment of return has led me to other experiences in other places, thereby tempting me to regard a given place, and most notably a home-place, as quite different from what I first took it to be. I know it for the first time upon return in that I am now sensitive to aspects unappreciated when I was first living there. The home-place I knew then was not the whole, or even the essence, of the place to which I now return. It is as if I had to leave my home to become acquainted with a more capacious world, which in turn allows me to grasp more of the home to which I return. The movement of such a journey of departure and homecoming is from part to whole and back to part. But the second "part" is a part that directly reflects the whole, for I now know my home in the light of the larger place-world through which I have traveled. Had I remained at home and not left, I would never have come to see it in such a different and more complete light. The longest way around is the shortest way home.

The second paradox generated by homecoming and homesteading is complementary to the first. It consists in the fact that I can come to a place I have never before visited and yet have the distinct sense that I know it *for a second time*. The place seems familiar to me even though I am certain that I have not encountered it before. Inhabiting is here tantamount to re-inhabiting; and I know that I have never been in the very place I am *re*-inhabiting. How are we to understand this puzzling situation, a species not just of *déjà vu* but of *déjà vécu*? To understand it is not only to resolve a paradox but to contribute to the de-literalization of place itself.

Gary Snyder speaks of himself as "re-inhabiting" a certain region of the western slope of the Sierra Nevada, the San Juan Ridge, although, before moving there, he had never lived in that place. Snyder is quite aware that the same region had been inhabited by Native Americans, Washo and Miwok and Maidu, who long ago opened up certain basic and promising inhabitational possibilities, including exemplary forms of co-habitancy. Even if none of the native residents remain and even if Snyder is altogether "new to the place," he still regards himself (and others who have since joined him) as re-inhabiting the region. Such re-inhabitation obtains on two conditions. First, the re-inhabitants must take up life in the region in a manner that echoes (though it need not imitate) the "placeways"[52] of the original occupants. Such place-sensitive mores include a dextrous pursuit of agriculture, a caring relationship to animals, a special respect for plant life, etc. Here what matters most is the adoption of the appropriate habitus, the right set of local practices, the special skills that make not just bare inhabitation but co-habitancy possible. Second, the land itself has to hold open the opportunity to pursue these placeways and practices in its very midst. The habitat determines what kind of life is viable there. In Snyder's case, the San Juan Ridge affords limited agriculture and is "better as forest,"[53] yet it allows Snyder and others to live there gratefully.

Both conditions support the real possibility not of inhabitation and co-habitancy but of re-inhabitation. They do so by drawing on "a past which has never been a present."[54] The habitus comes from a local tradition that preexists the present moment of its habitation, and the habitat contains the geo- and bio-history of the place. To inhabit a place in terms of the habitat and habitus is thus to re-inhabit it by living there on preestablished terms laid down long before the actual advent of current homesteaders. In re-inhabiting the place in these ancient terms, new settlers return to what already exists even as they prepare for a future in which novel forms of inhabitation will doubtless emerge. Between habitus and habitat, lore and land, the re-inhabiters, "showing solidarity with a region,"[55] become re-inhabit*ants*. They put themselves back on a land they see at once for a first *and* for a second time. Their homesteading is in effect a homecoming, a coming home to the habitualities of the place and the habitudes of its history.

In the end—precisely at journey's end—both homesteading and homecoming are first-and second-time in status. But a divergent emphasis remains within a shared structure of sameness. In homecoming, I am in fact return- ing for a second—at least a second—time to a home-place; but thanks to the manifoldness of the home-place itself and to the multifarious between of the intervening journey, I see it with new eyes, as if for the first time. In homesteading (especially in the form of re-inhabitation), in fact I am coming to a place for the first time, but it is as if I am there for a second time, thanks to my appreciation of the natural history of the habitat and to my employment of habitual practices of settlement. Each circumstance is two- fold: at once "in fact" and "as if," yet with differential and reversed valence.

The two paradoxes at issue in this section are thus mirror images of one another. Each is the reverse of the other in a common matrix of double timing. In homecoming, I expect to experience the home-place to which I return to be something merely undergone for a second time, but I am sur- prised to discover that I grasp it for the first time in certain basic regards. In homesteading, I anticipate a first-time experience, but I end up with some- thing strikingly second-time in status.

VIII

> The dialectic of repetition is easy; for what is repeated has been, otherwise it
> could not be repeated, but precisely the fact that it has been gives to
> repetition the character of novelty. . . . when one says that life is a repetition
> one affirms that existence which has been now becomes.
>
> —Sören Kierkegaard, *Repetition*

> What is inside is also outside.
>
> —Johann Wolfgang von Goethe, cited by Maurice Merleau-Ponty,
> "Eye and Mind"

Other dual structures, closely related to those just analyzed, obtrude at every journey's end. The *re* of *re-inhabitation* and *re-implacement*, for instance, is both the *re-* of *repetition* (i.e., another form of two-timing) and the *re-* of *moving back*. The "back" at stake in the latter is that of going back to an origin—hence to a first-time event. But the origin is less a unique event or thing or place than a new start, a second chance, a moment of renewal. The single origin of the first time is complicated from the beginning; already at the origin are adumbrations of a succession of second times. First timing is second timing. The "re-" proliferates from the start, something we realize fully only at the end. Similarly, the structure of the "in" is at least double throughout a journey, where we find ourselves in a series of way stations—*in* each, contained there, even (momentarily) located there. Aristotle's obsession

with the "in" of containment finds its proper place in this pinpointed lo-
catedness, whose symbolic expression is the street address. But in pursuing
a journey we also discover ourselves to be *in* in quite another sense: "in" as
immanent, immersed, and implaced. In such an in, we are not just contained
or located but undergo the more radical experience of merging with the place
we are in, losing our separate selves as travelers and becoming one with the
landscape we travel through. This is the "in" at stake in re-*in*-habitation,
which aims not merely to find a place in which to subsist but to make living
there intrinsically valuable and memorable, so that someday we can say *"there
we have been."*

Ostensibly, *re-* is a temporal term and *in* a spatial word. In fact, each is
spatial *and* temporal. To move back is to regress both in space and in time.
To in-habit or re-inhabit is to enter a place temporally—with the right
rhythms—while merging with it spatially: "co-habitancy" here takes on yet
another dimension. Ultimately, however, the re/in pair is itself placial in character. This is evident in "getting back/into/place." What we get *back into* is
a place where the journey can come to an end in space and time, enabling
us to experience it on its own merits as the place that it is.

Just as we must acknowledge a past that was never a present, so we must
aver a place that is no position, much less a physically or metaphysically *first*
position. It is to this place, an end-place, that we get back on journeys of
homesteading and homecoming. Such a place is in effect *nowhere* inasmuch
as it is not literally *somewhere*. It is this unpositioned place—not to be confused with the void, a strict *non*-place—that gives rise to the paradoxical fate
of being known both for the first time (even when it has been known before)
and for the second time (even when it has never been encountered at all).

If we are to get back into place in this nonprimary and nonsimple sense,
we must take our time. A retarded movement back, a motion *in ritardando*,
is prescribed. In exploring and discovering altogether new places, the tempo
tends to be accelerated. But in the return to the nonorigin of an end-place,
the proper rhythm is slow rather than swift, a matter of *gravitas* rather than
celeritas. The habitus ensconced in re-inhabitation signifies just such slowed-
down speed: the need for the gradual re-acquisition of the right habits, the
sedimentation of the appropriate habitudes, the growth of effective habitua-
tions. All of these latter are matters of memory, and of body memory in
particular. For it is the remembering body that, concluding a time-consuming
but timely and well-timed journey, brings us back into place.

When we are brought back into a place at the end of a journey, we also
find ourselves imagining other possibilities than our body may have experienced before. We come to live in this old/new place in altered corporeal
comportments. The "re" and "in" are transformed—*transplaced*—beyond expectation. The normal retainers of time such as clocks and calendars are sud-

denly insufficient, even irrelevant, to the experience of being in this ac-
customed/unaccustomed place. The usual containers of space such as city limits, map lines, or the grids of the National Survey of 1785, spring leaks as an
entire new world floods into the place where our journey has put us back
down. Just when we are in imminent danger of being overwhelmed by the
strangeness of the end-place (whether previously known or not), we are able
to accomplish re-implacement and co-habitancy. We are back into place in a
nonbackward way. And, as the exemplary place of Walden has taught us, what
we are now in is something equally without, just as the without we are in
is itself ultimately within that encompassing wild place called "earth."

Journeying on earth itself, we move in and between places. Whether on
land or sea, the way out is the way in. Even though the earth surrounds and
sustains us—is way out around us—virtually every part of it is a potential
home-place into which we might move. Almost any place, even on the high
sea, offers "a home-base on earth."[56] Moving on earth we are always *in this
very place*, in a "local absolute,"[57] in the midst of a close world, and all within
an encompassing arc. Going out into the earth's arc is always a coming back
into it, a homecoming into a homeland whose limits cannot be captured by
cartographic borderlines. But the way in is also the way out: truly to go into
a place on earth, to homestead there, is to be released from the *limes*, the
wall, and at last the mall.

IX

A house is a machine for living in.
—Le Corbusier, *Towards a New Architecture*

You could walk out of the house, but you always returned home.
—Witold Rybczynski, *Home: A Short History of an Idea*

To speak of homesteading and homecoming is to invoke the issue of
home, a topic first discussed in part three. Now, at the close of this book,
questions concerning home rise again. What is it to return home? Can we
return at all? Is home ever the same place it was (in either sense of *ever*)?
Or is it true that "you can't go home again"? Kierkegaard, with Thomas
Wolfe, argues that you cannot return home, for it is *never the same place* you
left; witness Kierkegaard's own ill-starred effort to return to his former lodg-
ings in Berlin.[58]

But we need not be so discouraged as were Kierkegaard and Wolfe, who
tended to confuse the identical with the same in reaching their skeptical judgments. Surely we *can* come back to a home as recognizably the same. Is this

not what I did in revisiting my childhood home in Topeka? But *what* then did I revisit? Certainly a place and certainly a house, indeed a house-in-a-place. But this implaced house is no longer my home. I have a home elsewhere; and even if I did not, *this house*, now occupied by another family, cannot count as "home" any more. The same homelessness obtains in homesteading, where there is no home *as yet*. If in homecoming I come back to a home that *was*, in homesteading I come to a home *to be*. In the present in which I am engaged in both experiences, I find myself in a limbo between a past and a future home.

If I cannot, strictly speaking, return to a former home, much less come to a future home, do I simply come (back) to a house? But can we keep *home* strictly separate from *house*? The common and recurrent phrase "house and home," if no mere hendiadys (i.e., one concept expressed by two words), nevertheless suggests that the two terms are closely related. Both are collective and, in particular, familial in their application and use. Each connotes something more than mere shelter, and both are basic to dwelling-as-residing and especially to what I have called "full-fledged" dwelling-places: each allows for repeated return and each bears felt familiarity with it.[59] But the two notions begin to diverge upon closer inspection. In chapter 5 I said that a home is "something more than a house." Yet in a certain sense a home is also something *less* than a house, since a house has to be constructed while a home need not be built: "Home could just be a hearth, a fire on the bare ground by any human lair. That may well be the one thing that nobody can quite do without: a fireplace, some focus."[60] To allude to the hearth, however, is to land immediately in another elusive binary pair: "hearth and home." Even in Romance languages that do not have different words for "house" and "home," hearth is a metonymy for home, e.g., *le foyer familial* or *focolare domestico*.[61] But just as we must deliteralize "home"—this is the primary point of distinguishing "home" from "house" in the first place—so we must not confine hearth to fireplace alone. Any number of things can provide sufficient focus to serve as a hearth: a group of memorabilia, a coffee table, a television set, a stereo set, a Japanese tokonoma, a Greek iconostassi, etc. The focal thing must be material, presumably in order to act as an adequate support for all the paraphernalia of the home and thus to bear the weight of what I have called "localized caring."

A home, even if not built, is always *somewhere in particular*—or, more exactly, *somewhere in*. A house could be *anywhere out*, that is, out there in mapped and sited space. This is why we do not hesitate to move houses from one location to another, as when a neighbor's house in Topeka was once moved across the street to make way for a new elementary school. This was a memorable event for me, partly because I did not then distinguish between house-as-built-object and home-as-hearth. Once the distinction is made, however, the move becomes a mere engineering feat, while my neighbors, hopefully, preserved the same sense of home in their new location. Similarly, the burning of my great-uncle's home in Enterprise represented the annihilation of his physical house, yet the place where the house had been remained to hold my memories of his home. Houses are displaceable from their sites and subject to destruction, even to literal re-placement, but homes are undetachable from the places to which they belong.

Homes, then, are not physical locations but situations for living: "It takes a heap o' living to make a house a home." This is why homes can be "somewhere in" places: deeply ensconced there, yet at no definite point or position. No wonder that the hearth can stand in for home, since it is the feature deepest within a house and a place we literally *in*habit. From this focal center domestic energy radiates outward, exceeding the very house that is the material frame of the home.

The inwardizing tendency of dwelling in a domicile also obtains for homecoming, in which we return to a house in order to refind a home. The paradox of homecoming, whereby we *come home* to what may no longer *be* a home for us, is resolved by the sheer fact that we re-enter the very structure that once housed a home only to discover that the identical structure no longer encloses the same domesticity.

Human beings are, in Pascal's observation, restless creatures; they cannot remain stationary in one room for more than twenty-four hours without going stir crazy. The problem is the stationariness, not the singleness, of the room. For if we only move about the room, we can bestir ourselves sufficiently to avoid the *taedium vitae* with which Pascal was concerned. In this regard, the home is a paradigmatic kind of end-place. We not only journey back *to* it but also move around *in* it once back. The dialectic of the "re" (qua back) and the "in" is once again critical:

> Home is the place where, when you have to go there,
> They have to take you *in* . . . [62]

Having to go home is having to go back to where you will be taken in—in a place in which you can move about with ease and familiarity. To be taken in you don't have to have proved yourself in any particular way, or have gained merit in the world at large, much less be a Prodigal Son. You just need to be a member of a household whose journeys have taken you elsewhere, to other places than the home-place to which you now return. Here, in this now, you are received as a person who belongs to this place, a home-person who calls for being welcomed back.[63]

X

Oh! that feeling of safety, of arrival, of homecoming when we finally reached
the edges of her yard, when we could see the soot black face of our
grandfather, Daddy Gus, sitting in his chair on the porch, smell his cigar, and
rest on his lap. Such a contrast, that feeling of arrival, of homecoming, the
sweetness and the bitterness of that journey, that constant reminder of white
power and control.

—bell hooks, "Homeplace: A Site of Resistance"

The autobiographical account by bell hooks of her difficult journey across
town reminds us that homecoming, however much we may desire it, is not
simply sweet but is often achieved with the most strenuous effort across the
most daunting obstacles. Odysseus had to escape or evade the many lures and
traps along his way, and even after arriving at Ithaca he had to contend with
disarray in his home-place. bell hooks and her siblings had to walk through
a frightening, hostile environment in order to visit her grandparents in the
poor white part of town: "I remember the fear, being scared to walk to Bab's
(our grandmother's house) because we would have to pass that terrifying
whiteness—those white faces on the porches staring us down with hate."[64]
The white faces stared down from their porches on the young black woman
no less menacingly than Polyphemus stared down at Ulysses and his men
from his cyclopean height. hook's journey across town, not entirely unlike
the journey across Dublin of the modern Ulysses, Leopold Bloom, was one
of her "most intriguing experiences."[65] But it was also one of the most fearful moments of her childhood. Not surprisingly, she preferred "the segregated blackness of our community" to the neighborhood of whites, whose
porches, "even when empty or vacant . . . seemed to say 'danger,' 'you do not
belong here,' 'you are not safe.' "[66]
    While bell hooks's account warns us against any false idealization of the
homecoming experience, it also conveys the paradox of coming home to a
place fraught with more peril than the place from which one has come. Still
more important, it shows how, when viewed in certain political and social
contexts, places can reverse roles. hooks's grandparents, wishing to move
"up" in a society dominated by whites, ended by making themselves more
vulnerable to the very whites they were emulating socioeconomically. hooks's
mother, Rosa Bell, stayed in the segregated part of town and created there
a home-place that nurtured bell hooks and her siblings. Not only this, but
the protective posture of staying-put allowed the home-place to be what
hooks calls a "site of resistance" vis-à-vis the surrounding society in general

and white racism in particular. In such a circumstance, "the task of making homeplace was not simply a matter of black women providing service [i.e., as they did when working as 'nannies' in white households]; it was about the construction of a safe place where black people could affirm one another and by so doing heal many of the wounds inflicted by racist domination."[67] hooks invokes racial apartheid in South Africa, where the effort to deny any significant sense of home-place is part and parcel of a strategy of racist domination quite aware of "the subversive value of homeplace."[68] The subversiveness is based, paradoxically, on the very privacy of place that might seem, from another perspective, to be a turning away from social and political reality. "The primacy of domesticity," writes hooks, is "a site for subversion and resistance."[69] Turning and staying within—an in-version central to human in-habitation—ends by being a source of strength, capable of engendering a potent presence without.

The African-American predicament is revealing in another regard. Black people in America live in a state of permanent exile. Forcibly and perhaps forever, they have been displaced from their homeland. As hooks also says in *Yearning: Race, Gender, and Cultural Politics,*

> If we fall prey to the contemporary ahistorical mood, we will forget that we have not stayed in one place, that we have journeyed away from home, away from our roots, that we have lived drylongso and learned to make a new history. We have not gone the distance, but we can never turn back.[70]

As we have seen in the case of the Navajo, any significant displacement of a people has potentially disastrous consequences. The most dangerous displacement is doubtless that from the homeland. If return to this land of origin is barred—as it is both for Navajos and for blacks—more than homesickness ensues; a profound sense of placelessness in the new society may lead to profound despair. With literal re-inhabitation of the homeland precluded, the only way out is through re-inhabitation of another sort. This is what hooks in effect recommends: *re-inhabit the home-place*, even if it is located in a land of exile.

Saint Augustine advised: "Do not wish to go out; go back into yourself; truth dwells in the inner man."[71] This introverting counsel, seemingly so apolitical, can be suitably expanded to fit the circumstance of displaced peoples. The turn within can be a re-turn to the domesticity of place, a re-occupation of the domicile, though the re-entry must be done differently and more deeply this time, keeping in mind the memories of where one has been.[72] At the same time, one must be mindful of a larger world without—not only the wider political realm but, behind or around it, the domain of nature. The point is to practice "home economics," while staying aware of the Great Economy of the natural world of which the domestic and political worlds are finally only parts. In the end, we must be ecocentric in both senses of this term: re-centered in the home-place (the *oikos*) and the political arena (the *polis*), while also de-centered in the wild places that compose the natural environment. The going in and the going out are co-requisite and finally co-terminous.

The de-centering, the way out, is a response to the undeniable tyranny of the home-place, for, as Mary Douglas puts it, "even its most altruistic and successful versions exert a tyrannous control over mind and body."[73] The same is true of all comparatively closed-in social or political units, including neighborhoods, towns, cities, and the modern state itself. The larger the unit, at least in eras of industrialism and high technology, the more tyrannical the control can be. The greater also the possibility of construing a given region or the homeland itself as superior to all other regions or homelands: the homeland becomes a "fatherland" that arrogates to itself the right to subdue its neighboring countries. Missing from this monstrous perversion of im-placement—this massive conversion of the particularity of places into the totalism of one privileged state-site—is a sense of the values and virtues of the home-place to which hooks appeals. These values and virtues have every-thing to do with the closeness and familiarity of the place that is home. The home-place fosters dialogue as well as nonverbal exchanges of many kinds, and thus nurtures interpersonal reciprocity. The domestic scene may indeed be tyrannous in certain insidious ways, but it can also be the place of most effective and lasting resistance to the tyranny of sites.

XI

If the day ever comes when they know who
They are, they may know better where they are.
            —Robert Frost, "A Cabin in the Clearing"

Where you have been, including where you have traveled, has a great deal to do with who and what you are, although the determination is by no means simple. Just as we have had to reject models of simple location — models based on the primacy of point and position—so we must also eschew any model of simple causation of character or temperament by implacement. Nevertheless, as D. H. Lawrence and Lawrence Durrell both insisted, there is such a thing as "spirit of place." Many centuries ago, Servius wrote, "*Nullus enim locus sine genio est*" (for no place is without its genius). But the genius, i.e., the unique Gestalt of traits that make a place *this* place, is not simple in itself; nor is its working ever simple. William Least Heat-Moon devotes over six hundred pages in his *PrairyErth* to the thick description of Chase County, Kansas, while admitting that he has not fathomed the place.

The usual parameters fail to fit. Yet everyone knows what it is like to live *in* a place and to be *from* a place: little ambiguity there. The complexity arises when we ask ourselves just what kind of personal or collective character emerges from a place, what sort of "who" reflects it, and how the reflection is accomplished. People in Marion County, which borders on Chase County, claim to be able to tell at a glance whether a stranger is from Chase or not. But they are hard-pressed to say in what the Chase-character consists, often falling back on particular episodes or incidents in the history of their neighbors.[74] By the same token, people from Missouri are regarded as "stubborn" by people from Kansas—hence the epithet "Show Me State"—and yet it would be difficult to say precisely how this stubbornness is to be defined.

People and place come together most insistently in "regional character," which is based on noticeable dialects, gestural styles, and whole ways of thinking. Even if one could analyze differences of comportment or speech or thought with precision, however, one would still be hard put to list the exact ingredients of such regional identity insofar as it is independent of various expressive vehicles. And rightly so, given that a place, even the seemingly most desolate windswept prairie place (such as is found in Chase County; Least Heat-Moon devotes an entire chapter to the tiny town of Saffordville, with a population of five people and no stores left), yields complex descriptions. Given also that persons are themselves dauntingly complex, the relationship between persons and places cannot be one of "objective succession" (in Kant's definition of causality).

Granting that there is no unidirectional causality coming from place to person, we might be tempted to maintain the very opposite, namely, that places take on their character from the people who live in them. A recent study of the aboriginal Pintupi people of northwestern Australia appears to claim as much:

> Places are imbued with the identity of those who live there. In other words, the Pintupi can discuss a country and thereby also refer to the people associated with it, who typically camp there. . . . To hear mention of a place is, for the Pintupi, to identify the persons associated with it, and to hear of people is to think of their places.[75]

But for a place to be "imbued" with the identity of its inhabitants is not to be caused to assume this identity in any straightforward way. The last sentence just quoted hints at a two-way influence: if places reflect the people who live in them, the very same people equally suggest the places they are from. One suspects that Kant's alternative category of "community," which operates by a principle of reciprocity, is here being tacitly invoked. As if to confirm this suspicion, the author goes on to speak of "persons and country as mutually embedded" and of the "inseparability of people and place."[76]

Instead of thinking of places as *causing* people to have certain individual and social characteristics, or simply the reverse, we should concentrate instead on the single complex unit, "persons-in-places." Persons who live in places—who inhabit or re-inhabit them—come to share features with the local landscape; but equally so, they make a difference to, perhaps indelibly mark, the land in which they dwell.

"Dwell," I say, keeping in mind that there are many ways of dwelling, two of which I have emphasized. Like land and character themselves, these two forms of dwelling often coexist and in their very reciprocity give rise to the further expression of character. William Least Heat-Moon (who lives in Missouri) is a sojourner in the Kansas county whose longtime citizens he has interviewed and come to know. His form of dwelling (i.e., as wandering) complements theirs (dwelling-as-residing). On another pilgrimage in another country, Bashō peregrinated between settled places. But in both cases the genius of the places the authors visited becomes evident in the kind of writing they do. Whether in the brevity of haiku or in a voluminous quasi-autobiographical account, the character of Matsushima and Mount Gassan, of Saffordville and Cottonwood Falls, comes through in the genre and style of the texts that describe them.

Character will out, and this is as true of the character of places as of people's character in those same places. Western Apache "stalking stories" draw upon much the same expressive qualities of a particular place. Such stories *convey the character of the place*. Much as Thoreau "retained the landscape" in the language of *Walden*, so these stories retain the landscape of western Arizona as the uniquely appropriate scene for tales of poignant moral import. The ethical point they make is by words but, like character (i.e., *ethos*), the ethics is ultimately rooted in the land. As one of Basso's informants, Benson Lewis, a contemporary Apache, says:

> I think of that mountain called "white rocks lie above in a compact cluster" as if it were my maternal grandmother. I recall stories of how it once was at that mountain. The stories told to me were like arrows. Elsewhere, hearing that mountain's name, I see it. Its name is like a picture. Stories make you live right. Stories make you replace yourself.[77]

The ethical energy, the earth character, flows from land to words and back again to land, as "you replace yourself" in the earth that is the source of character and story alike. Between land and language stands the speaker or writer as their common "sustaining medium."[78] It is precisely as such a medium, as a moving mediatrix *between* people and places, that itinerant authors such as Bashō, Thoreau, and Least Heat-Moon can express the elusive but fateful link between place and character.

We must be careful, however, not to be drawn back into literalization.

The prerequisite peregrination need not be between geographically identifiable places, any more than homecoming requires a strictly identical home-place to which to return. This is not to deny that journeys can be mapped, and usefully so. Nobuyuki Yuasa, the translator of *The Narrow Road to the Deep North*, appends three maps of Bashō's itineraries. Anthropologist Fred Myers presents eight maps of his Pintupi informant Maantja tjungurrayi's nomadic excursions in the Lake Macdonald region.[79] But the exact trajectories, even the precise destinations, are not always known; nor need they be. We do not know precisely where Thoreau went on his afternoon walks out of Concord, and we often do not know just how Least Heat-Moon moved across Chase County despite his copious descriptions and detailed maps of the Kansas landscape. Although Victor Bérard tried to map Odysseus's actual movements in the Mediterranean, we no more have to know exactly what the Greek hero's movements were in cartographic space than we have to know just how bell hooks crossed her hometown to get to her grandparents' home. What is important in all these cases is *the course and direction of the journey itself*, its tenor and import, whatever its precise path may be. To demand literalism of the path, whether in word or in image, is to convert the plasticity of places into the rigidity of sites.

The same de-literalization applies to the movement inherent in journeys. Even though most journeys involve actual movement between places, one may journey while remaining in a single place. Each of us does something like this, as I suggested earlier, within our own home-place. A friend of mine likes to walk around the same piece of land she lives on, sometimes sticking to the surrounding lawn, sometimes going to the mail box at the end of a half-mile lane, sometimes strolling to a nearby cliff and beach that lie on the western side of the same plot of land. Making a journey-in-place, she visits various way stations within the circuit of the place as a whole. Even when the trajectory remains the same, the variations introduced by time of day, season, her own mood, her dog's pace, etc., suffice to make the perambulation a distinctively different journey every time.

What matters on a journey is not movement as such but the *form of motion*. At the limit, one can travel without moving. Toynbee says of desert nomads that, strictly speaking, "they do not move."[80] Or rather, *they move in place*, that is, in a seasonally determined cycle of places within the region they inhabit on the edge of the desert. Nor does one need the desert to be nomadic in this manner, for there are urban nomads, nomads of the sea, nomads of the mind.[81] One can even be altogether "stuck in place," as are the main characters in Beckett's "Happy Days," and still experience a vivid sense of journeying in that place. Distinguishing between a "tree travel" exemplified by Goethe's *Italienreise* and a "rhizome travel" illustrated by Kleist's *Marionettentheater*, Deleuze and Guattari remark that "what distinguishes the two kinds of voyages is neither a measurable quantity of movement, nor something that would be only in the mind, but the *mode of spatialization*, the manner of being in space, of being for space."⁸² But when we de-literalize movement by focusing on the form or mode of motion, we are no longer restricted to two kinds of voyages: not only arborescent trips of tourism (Goethe or Ruskin or Edith Wharton, all in Italy) or rhizomatic underground voyages (Odysseus in the underworld; Dante in Hell; Kafka's K beneath the hotel, in *The Castle*) but also voyages of exploration (e.g., Sir Walter Raleigh on the Orinoco) and of scientific discovery (Darwin in the Galápagos), not to mention pilgrimages, which fall into a complex fascicle of different types and subtypes that range from religious to secular and from having fixed routes (e.g., to the shrine at Santiago de Compostela) to possessing varying approaches (e.g., to Banares, City of Light). In each instance, close inspection would reveal its own "mode of spatialization," or, rather, its own kind of placialization, its own way of getting back into place.

XII

Knowing where and who are intimately linked.
—Gary Snyder, "Re-Inhabitation"

Where we are has a great deal to do with who and what we are—this continuing leitmotif has its converse in Whitehead's proposition that "the actual entity, in virtue of being *what* it is, is also *where* it is."⁸³ Where something or someone is, far from being a casual qualification, is one of its determining properties. As to the *who*, it is evident that our innermost sense of personal identity (and not only our overt, public character) deeply reflects our implacement. It follows that threats to this implacement are also threats to our entire sense of well-being. As Proust avers, "not knowing where I was, I could not even be sure at first who I was."⁸⁴ Concerning instances of "place-alienation" in which a place has become something quite other than one remembers it as being, Sven Birkerts can write: "No matter what plea or adjustment I make, I cannot catch hold of the peculiar magic of those places. It is less that *they* are gone than that *I* am."⁸⁵ When places change aspect or fade in significance, I change or fade with them: *their* alteration is *my* alteration. But my own changes may be funded back into the very places that have been so formative of my identity in the first place.

Given this reciprocity of person and place, place-alienation is itself two-way: I from it, it from me. When caught up in this double-sided otherness, I feel, almost literally, "beside myself." I feel myself to be other than myself and not just somewhere other than where I am in world-space (e.g., my exact address, my cartographic location, etc.). Even though I am literally here in a particular place, my place is not *this* place. By the same token, this place is no longer *my* place: indeed, my place has become other to (and other than) me. The entire situation, and not just my psyche, is schizoid.

Most of the time, we deny the mutual determination of person and place. We tend to blame either the person or the place for what has gone wrong in our lives. If we don't blame another human being, we single out the place we are in. Under the sway of an angry mood, we become outspokenly critical of our place's malevolent powers, its "illth."[86] We experience what Aristotle called the "active influence" of a place as an influence for the worst, and our alienation may become obsessive as we ruminate on the baneful effects of the place. Our animus is directed against this place precisely because (and in proportion to) our conviction that the place has been at least the primary occasion, if not the exclusive cause, of our current distress.

An extreme form of place-alienation occurs when human beings (not to mention other animals) are forced out of a place. Yet displacement as involuntary relocation is the unfortunate fate of many peoples on earth, including the vast majority of Native Americans. The Navajo experience a sense of *place-deprivation* with special acuity because of their conviction that the land on which they have lived for many generations was given to them as a permanent residence from their critical moment of emergence in this, the fifth and last world. Not only was everything given its proper place at that aboriginal moment, but they, the Dinéh, were granted an entire region of places they were meant to occupy indefinitely: "They were placed in a Holy Way."[87] Living in this Way, "persisting through eventual change," allows no room for displacement.[88] Hence there arises a circumstance in which anger (at the displacers) combines with incredulity (at being displaced) as well as with intense longing for the place vacated. Much the same combination of outrage, unbelief, and nostalgia exists among those everywhere—from America to Europe to Palestine to Tibet—for whom displacement has meant unwanted expulsion from a native land or region.

The longing for return to a home-place and a home-territory is the curious converse of the circumstance of many journeys. On a journey, a traveler often *seeks displacement*, whether in the adventuresome pursuit of the disparate or in order to reach a definite destination. This is why so many journeys (including the inns at which one stays on journeys) are apt expressions of the doctrine of *mujo*, the mutability of all things. For an adherent of *mujo* such as Bashō, not to keep moving on, responsive to change at every step, is to risk being bound to a false and delimited ego-self that is the personal expression of being stuck-in-place. As Saigyo put it in a haiku that comments on his own decision to leave a secure position as a guard in the retinue of a retired emperor,

So loath to lose
What really should be loathed:
   One's vain place in life,
We maybe rescue best the self
   Just by throwing it away.[89]

To throw away the finite egoic self, then, it is important to *change place* and above all to leave "one's vain place." The endorsement of mutability and the effort to live in a manner appropriate to it—e.g., by continually traveling from place to place—stands in stark contrast with the Navajo desire to remain in one stable ancestral place. For the Navajo, not to stay in that ultimate place of residence, that resting-place, is to lose not only one's personal identity but the Great Self that provides the collective identity of an entire people. In one regard, however, the Navajo themselves might not disagree with Saigyo's counsel. If the particular place in which one exists is just serving one's vanity—if it is a question of a shallow place, a mere site—then one should exchange it for a more authentic and engaging venue. But if one's place is not merely self-serving, the Navajo would insist that one can move— and move meaningfully—while still remaining in that same place. There is something overlooked by the *mujo* adept: a sense of abiding place tied to a selfhood exceeding anything that can be experienced by the isolated, ego-fixated individual. Alienation from any such larger sense of place—exemplified by the whole region of Dinétah—is tantamount to alienation from the Great Self.

But what of those in a displaced, secular, and postmodern age who lack any sense of a perduring place of collective self-belonging, much less a Great Self that is the counterpart of such a place? What also of those who are not only displaced from a particular region but who have in effect *nowhere to go*? Such a nowhere is, as it were, the existential equivalent of the no-place of cosmogonic accounts of creation. By "nowhere to go" I mean not so much literal homelessness as the pervasive fact that no single place or group of places seems any longer to offer an abode for a more capacious selfhood. This is not, however, to posit or presuppose some hypostatized ideal place—a Shangri-la of the Self—that could resolve postmodern perplexities. Rather than any such delusory topomania, it would be better to follow the desultory and modest path of Bashō, placing and re-placing ourselves on narrow roads as we pursue our own contemporary journeys.

Such journeys need not consist of aimless wandering between places, salutary as that might be as a first stage. Whatever the value of sheer vagabondage, something else is at stake, namely, *getting back into place itself*: back into the very idea, indeed the very experience, of place. Here we might take inspiration from landscape painters, who get back into the place-of-origin from which they begin—e.g., the Connecticut River Oxbow as painted by Thomas Cole from the heights of Mount Holyoke—and transmute it into the pictorial content (at once *Gehalt* and *Gestalt*), the sublimated substance, of their completed work. In this way, landscape painters manage to make the most of a place, giving it an allure and a direction that may not have been noticed in its initial discernment. Such a place is re-placed from its sedentary existence in the perceived landscape to the aesthetically vivid placiality of a finished painting. The result is redemptive, not only of the place-of-origin as it finds new pictorial depths and of the artist who has effected the transformation but also of ourselves as the spectators of the art work. Thanks to the work and even short of actual travel, we get back into place. As Bashō indicates in the postscript to *The Narrow Road to the Deep North*, we need not undertake a literal journey in order to appreciate the virtues of being back in place. We can find our way back to place on the basis of the guiding and instaurative work of others.

Alienated we are in many ways—so lost in space and time as to be displaced from place itself—but the existence of pictorial and narrational journeys to and between places reminds us that we are not altogether without resources in our placelessness. When the resources of re-implacement and co-habitancy are drawn upon as well, we find ourselves back on the road to a resolute return to place. The road itself is a route of renewed sensitivity to place, affording a refreshed sense of its continuing importance in our lives and those of others. The sense and the sensitivity offer a viable alternative to being and feeling out-of-place. By taking up the pathway of place anew, we can discover the riches of the place-world again. At the end of this journey, we shall know once more, perhaps for the very first time, what it means to get back into place.

XIII

To make an end is to make a beginning.
The end is where we start from.
                    —T. S. Eliot, "Little Gidding"

As abiding and expansive presence, place outlasts much that vanishes, including many of the events that happen in its midst and the dwellings built on it. It was the shock of seeing the complete destruction of my great-uncle's home in Enterprise that first brought me, abruptly, to an awareness of the significance of place. Staring at the razed scene, my only consolation was to reflect that although his much-loved house was gone, *the place remained*. In that place, empty though it was, I could begin to put back together the shards of my shattered experience: to re-place myself in the present. I realized this re-placing by means of rumination and writing, but I might have done it differently. Had I continued to live in Kansas, I might have tried to rebuild the physical house, as a form of literal "replacement." Had I been a historian or a biographer rather than a philosopher, I might have attempted to compose a history of Enterprise in which this house would figure prominently, thereby giving to it a commemorative re-presence in words. Had I become a painter, I doubtless would have tried to re-create, by purely pictorial means, the structure in its former glory. Exactly which form my effort took does not matter greatly. What matters is that I was moved to action in the first place *by place itself*, and with whatever means were at my disposal.

Here we must ask finally: what goes on when I (or anyone else deprived of place) undertake such concerted actions of re-placement, actions having so little ostensible utilitarian significance? The answer is: a re-creation of the self who inhabits (or will re-inhabit) the place in question. Another statement of Sven Birkerts is to be remembered: "My best, truest . . . self is vitally connected to a few square miles of land."[90] This points to the situation I have in mind, although its terms are difficult to pin down. While many may resonate with Birkerts's experience, they would be hard-pressed to say exactly *which* self, or aspect of self, is "vitally connected" with a particular place. And they would be harder pressed still to say *how* such a connection occurs, and in what exactly it consists: here we circle back to the intriguing issue of the link between character and place. But *that* the connection occurs—and that it has something very basic to do with the formation and eventual identity of the self, personal or collective, or even Great—is indisputable. What we need to find at this concluding point is a means for understanding the close link between self and place.

Gaston Bachelard proposes such a method in the form of "topoanalysis," which he presents as an alternative to psychoanalysis. Bachelard defines topoanalysis as "the systematic psychological study of the sites of our intimate lives."[91] If we substitute "places" for "sites"—in keeping with the root sense of *topoi*—we have the engaging idea that we should look for the efficacy of places within "our intimate lives." These are the lives we live *from within, in ourselves* (*intimus* means "inmost," *intus* is "within"). The alliance between place and the "in"—first explored in the West by Aristotle[92]—runs deep. Indeed, the alliance takes us precisely into the interiority of the self, that is, into a psychical depth that cannot be determined by any objective measurement, spatial or temporal. Not that the places of our intimacy are dateless, but dating constitutes a comparatively superficial superimposition on a more profound durational placescape within our experience, much as the metric mapping of landscape constitutes a homogeneous spatial overlay on a heterogeneous landform.[93] Beneath chronometry and cartography alike there is a primordial topography—a *chorography*, a "tracing of place"—at one with the most intimate layers of our psychical lives. Topoanalysis is designed to fathom and describe these layers.

Does this mean that we must ensconce ourselves in psychical interiority in order to re-connect with places as experienced and remembered? Is re-placing a matter of re-minding? Does getting back into place mean getting back into mind? Tempting as it may be to think in this direction, especially in the rhetorically alluring form of "raising consciousness" about place, we must resist the lure. Intimacy need not be mental but can be found in our body and in the places around us: in the houses and gardens, fields and forests, in which our bodies live and move. The introspection of self-contained mind, its "inwit" in Shakespeare's word, must be supplemented, and in many cases supplanted, by the exteroception of the environing place-world and by the intermediation of the body. Topoanalysis looks *without* as much as, and finally more than, it seeks within. The secret of places, the source of their continual alchemical influence on our lives, is borne bodily by "the rays of the world" (in Husserl's phrase) more completely than by the inner rays of a mind closed in upon itself.

Robert Burton wrote in *The Anatomy of Melancholy* that " 'Tis the mind, not the place, causeth tranquility, and that gives true peace and content."[94] This statement is as revealing for the time in which it was written—the early seventeenth century, a time of science and witchcraft—as for its substantive claim. For it was written at the very moment when the modern era was emerging, an era that brought with it the suppression of place as a central category of human experience. Place was marginalized, becoming a matter of closeted concern in the work of Burton's contemporaries, Descartes and Locke. The emphasis shifted to the all-consuming container of Mind, a representational machine whose only solvent was found in diaphanous "ideas." Within the machinations of this mental machine, place was reduced to what could be represented by icons, indices, or symbols: it became place-in-mind.

It is one thing to claim that we keep the *past* in mind. Indeed, we pay linguistic lip service to the notion even today.[95] To keep *places* in mind is something else again, yet this is just what was proposed by "the new way of ideas" inaugurated in the early modern epoch, and it is what we continue to believe whenever we allow ourselves to slide down the slippery path of subjective (and eventually transcendental) idealism. But we need only look around us to realize that places themselves put an end to any such philosophical fantasy. We are always, at all times, *out there in places*: most prominently on journeys but even, and sometimes most especially, when we summon up places in mind and memory. The net of Place encompasses the maw of Mind.

It is less a question of what gives "true peace and content" than of comparative priority. On my interpretation—as ancient as the Pythagoreans and as contemporary as postmodernism—the priority belongs to Place, not to Mind. Place comes first: before Space and Time (those fellow travelers of Mind) and before Mind and Body (the other regnant modern pair). Yet the priority of place is neither logical nor metaphysical. It is descriptive and phenomenological. It is felt: felt bodily first of all. For we feel the presence of places by and in our bodies even more than we see or think or recollect them. Places are not so much the direct objects of sight or thought or recollection as what we feel *with* and *around*, *under* and *above*, *before* and *behind* our lived bodies. They are the ad-verbial and pre-positional contents of our usually tacit corporeal awareness, at work as the pre-positions of our bodily lives, underlying every determinate bodily action or position, every static posture of our *corpus*, every coagulation of living experience in thought or word, sensation or memory, image or gesture.

The priority of places is also ontological. My treatment of place began with the Archytian axiom that to be is to be in place. There is no being except being in place. Put the other way around, there is no utterly placeless existing, even if there are beings deeply alienated in and from place who suffer from the dire state of being out of their native places. To be a sentient bodily being at all is to *be* place-bound, bound to be in a place, bonded and bound therein.

Reversal, however, is only the first step of any decisive deconstruction. It will not do merely to assert the priority of Place *over* Mind or Body or Time or Space. More decisive still is indicating that place is prior only as subsisting *under* these most influential modern instances of the binary oppositions Western metaphysics has posited at every step of its imperialistic course. Despite their hegemony, could it be that place, the neglected third term that is either repressed or merely taken for granted, is the effective undoing of these dyads? Or more exactly, their *under*doing?

This is where the apparently innocent preposition *in* reenters the scene. For it should be manifest by now, especially after our analysis of such terms as *depth*, *distance*, *region*, and *horizon*, that Time and Space, Body and Mind, reside *in* place and are resumed there. Let us turn around Reid's claim (cited as an epigraph to part one) that "created things [have] their particular place in space, and their particular place in time" and say instead that created things in space and time *have their abode in place*. So, too, my lived body and the mind with which it is sometimes so continuous (and so alien at other times) are ineluctably implaced: I could not make use of them, much less know them, unless they were always already in place.

This is not to claim, however, that to be in place is to be situated on some determinate physical or metaphysical substrate. We should not posit yet another foundational term. The place that subtends the modern metaphysical dyads is itself so particular, so phenomenally unique, that it withstands any attempt to reify it into an opaque noumenal reality. To stand under—to be under-standing in the manner of place, not in the "understanding" manner of mind—is not to undergird or underlie as offering the sturdiness of definite support, that is, as a (conceptual or physical) foundation. It is to be an underling or understudy that turns out to be surprisingly subversive, not by overturning but by *turning under* the dominant terms of philosophical discourse, thus undermining their hegemony.

We get a more positive sense of the insurrectional power of place when we reflect on the familiar phrase "spirit of place," *genius loci*. Like the congeneric terms *soul* and *feeling*, *spirit* signifies that which refuses to submit to dichotomizing. To get into the spirit of a place is to enter into what makes that place such a special spot, into what is concentrated there like a fully saturated color. But the spirit of a place is also expansive. Moving out, entering not just the area lying before and around me but entering myself and others as its witnesses or occupants, this genial spirit sweeps the binarism of Self and Other (yet another of the great modernist dichotomies) into the embracing folds, the literal im-plications, of implacement. Such a spirit, like the souls and feelings with which it naturally allies itself, submerges all the established metaphysical limits and many of the physical borders as well.

Jaspers writes that "the soul of a landscape, the spirits of the elements, the genius of every place will be revealed to a loving view of nature."[96] In the end, it is not a matter of having to choose between introspection and exteroception, Mind and Body, Time and Space, Self and Other, or even Place and Site. Thanks to the congenial matrix uncovered by topoanalysis, we may affirm both members of all these divisive dyads and thereby live our lives in an intimacy neither simply mental nor merely physical but altogether placial. The *in* of intimacy resides in place *before* it resides in the more determinate modes of in-hood that inhere in being-in-the-world, a term which we have every right by now to replace with *being-in-place*.

Getting back into place, the homecoming that matters most, is an ongoing task that calls for continual journeying between and among places. Just as there is no limit to the ways in which we may get back into places, there is no effective end to how we may continue our ingression into their indefinite future. Only a perfected present or a projected future perfect would foreclose our voyaging with them in a perpetually ramifying manner. As travelers on such a voyage, we can resume the direction, and regain the depth, of our individual and collective life once again—and know it for the first time.

New Work on Place:
Space, Time, and History

How to Get from Space to Place in a Fairly Short Stretch of Time

PHENOMENOLOGICAL PROLEGOMENA

All existing things are either in place or not without place.

—Archytas, as cited by Simplicius

The power of place will be remarkable.

—Aristotle, *Physics*, Book 4

Space is a society of named places.

—Claude Lévi-Strauss, *The Savage Mind*

Nothing could extinguish the fact and claim of estate.

—W. E. H. Stanner, "Aboriginal Territorial Organization"

I

IT IS SENSIBLE, perhaps even irresistible, to assume that human experience begins with space and time and then proceeds to place. Are not space and time universal in scope, and place merely particular? Can place do anything but specify what is already the case in space and time? Or might it be that place is something special, with its own essential structures and modes of experience, even something universal in its own way?

Phenomenology began as a critique of what Husserl called the "natural attitude," that is, what is taken for granted in a culture that has been influenced predominantly by modern science—or, more precisely, by scientism and its many offshoots in materialism, naturalism, psychologism, and so forth. One belief endemic to the natural attitude concerns the way places relate to what is commonly called "space." Once it is assumed (after Newton and Kant) that space is absolute and infinite as well as empty and a priori in status, places become the mere apportionings of space, its compartmentalizations.

Indeed, that places are the determinations of an already existing monolith of Space has become an article of scientific faith, so much so that two books in anthropology that bear expressly on place—both quite valuable works in many regards—espouse the view that place is something *posterior to space,* even *made from space.* By "space" is meant a neutral, pre-given medium, a tabula rasa onto which the particularities of culture and history come to be inscribed, with place as the presumed result. We find this view, for example, in James F. Weiner's richly suggestive ethnography of the Foi of Papua New Guinea, *The Empty Place:* "A society's place names schematically image a people's intentional transformation of their habitat from a sheer physical terrain into a pattern of historically experienced and constituted space and time. . . . The bestowing of place names constitutes Foi existential space out of a blank environment."[1]

The idea of transformation from a "sheer physical terrain" and the making of "existential space"—which is to say, place—out of a "blank environment" entails that to begin with there is some empty and innocent spatial spread, waiting, as it were, for cultural configurations to render it placeful. But when does this "to begin with" exist? And where is it located? Answers to both questions will generate a vicious regress of the kind at stake in Kant's first antinomy: to search for a first moment in either time or space is to incur shipwreck on the shoals of Pure Reason.[2]

Or consider the following claim from Fred R. Myers's otherwise remarkable ethnography of desert aboriginal people of Central Australia, *Pintupi Country, Pintupi Self:* "The process by which space becomes 'country', by which a story gets attached to an object, is part of the Pintupi habit of mind that looks behind objects to events and sees in objects a sign of something else."[3] Here we are led to ask, What are these "objects" behind which events lurk and to which stories get attached? The neutrality of the term "object" suggests that the first-order items in the universe are denuded things—denuded of the very "secondary qualities" (in the demeaning term of Galilean-Cartesian-Lockian discourse) that would make them fit subjects of events and stories. We wonder, further, what is this "process by which space becomes 'country,'" by which space is "culturalized," and by which "impersonal geography" becomes "a home, a *ngurra.*"[4]

Myers intimates that all such transformations are a matter of the "projection"—or, alternatively, of the "reproduction"—of determinate social actions and structures. "Country" is the system of significant places as specified by the Dreaming, which represents "a projection into symbolic space of various social processes."[5] And the structure of the Dreaming in turn—a structure isomorphic with the landscape of the country—is "a product of the way Pintupi society reproduces itself in space and time."[6] The phrase "in space and time" is telling: the reproduction is in some preexisting medium. Having no inherent configurations of its own, this presumptively empty medium must be populated after the fact (but the fact of what? what fact?) by processes that impute to empty space the particularities that belong to the Dreaming. Generality, albeit empty, belongs to space; particularity, albeit mythic, belongs to place; and the twain meet only by an appeal to a procedure of superimposition that is invoked ex post facto.

But the Pintupi themselves think otherwise, as Myers himself avers: "To the Pintupi, then, a place itself with its multiple features is logically prior or central."[7] Whom are we to believe? The theorizing anthropologist, the arsenal of his natural attitude bristling with explanatory projectiles that go off into space? Or the aborigine on the ground who finds this ground itself to be a coherent collocation of pre-given places—pre-given at once in his experience and in the Dreaming that sanctions this experience? For the anthropologist, Space comes first; for the native, Place; and the difference is by no means trivial.

It is not, of course, simply a matter of choosing between the anthropologist's vantage point and that of the natives—as if the Pintupi had chosen to participate in a debate on the comparative primacy of space versus place. Nor is any such primacy Myers's own express concern. As an anthropologist in the field, he has the task not to argue for space over against place but to set forth as accurately as possible what being-in-place means to the Pintupi. Just there, however, is the rub: even when treating a culture for which place is manifestly paramount, the anthropologist leans on a concept that obscures what is peculiar to place and that (by an implicit cultural fiat) even implies its secondariness. The anthropologist's theoretical discourse—in which the priority of space over place is virtually axiomatic—runs athwart his descriptive commitment.

The question is not so much *whom* we are to believe—both anthropologist and natives are trustworthy enough—but *what* we are to believe. Are we to believe that human experience starts from a mute and blank "space" to which placial modifiers such as "near," "over there," "along that way," and "just here" are added, sooner or later: presumably sooner in perception and later in culture? Or are we to believe that the world comes configured in odd protuberances, in runs, rills, and flats, in *fele* and *do:m*, as the Kaluli might put it[8]—all of which are traits of places? (Ironically, in this view flatness and, more generally, "featurelessness" belong to place to begin with.)

I take the second view as just stated to be both more accurate as a description and more valuable as a heuristic in the understanding of place. In doing so, I join not only the Pintupi and the Kaluli but also certain early and late figures in Western thought. Both Archytas and Aristotle proclaimed that place is prior to space, and, more recently, Bachelard and Heidegger have re-embraced the conviction. All four thinkers subscribe to what I have called the Archytian Axiom: "Place is the first of all things."[9] In between the ancients and the postmoderns there was a period of preoccupation with space—as well as with time, conceived of as space's cosmic partner. But how may we retrieve a sense of the priority of place by means other than arguing from authority (as I have just done in citing certain congenial Western thinkers) or arguing against authority (as occurs when modern science is pilloried, which Husserl does in attacking the natural attitude)?

My suggestion is that we can retrieve such a sense by considering what a phenomenological approach to place might tell us. Even if such an approach is not without its own prejudicial commitments and ethnocentric stances, it is an approach that, in its devotion to concrete description, has the advantage of honoring the actual experience of those who practice it. In this regard it rejoins not only the anthropologist in the field but the native on the land: both have no choice but to begin with experience. As Kant insisted, "there can be no doubt that all our knowledge begins with experience."[10]

For Kant, "to begin with" means *to be instigated by*. Thus he must add the qualification that "though all our knowledge begins with experience, it does not follow that it all arises out of experience."[11] Knowledge of any rigorous sort does not derive from experience. Kant makes this perfectly clear in his *Anthropology from a Pragmatic Point of View*, arguably the first theoretical treatise on anthropology in the West: "General knowledge must always precede local knowledge . . . [because] without [general knowledge], all acquired knowledge can only be a fragmentary experiment and not a science."[12] This paradigmatic Enlightenment statement sets the stage—indeed, still holds the stage in many ways—for the idea that space precedes place. Space, being the most pervasive of cosmic media, is considered that about which we must have general knowledge, whereas we possess merely local knowledge about place.

But what if things are the other way around? What if the very idea of space is posterior to that of place, perhaps even derived from it? What if local knowledge—which, in Geertz's appropriately pleonastic locution, "presents locally to locals a local turn of mind" —precedes knowledge of space?[13] Could place be general and "space" particular? Phenomenology not only moves us to ask these impertinent anti-Enlightenment questions but also provides reasons for believing that the answers to them are affirmative.

In a phenomenological account, the crux in matters of place is the role of perception. Is it the case, as Kant believes (along with most modern epistemologists), that perception provides those bare starting points called variously "sensations," "sense data," "impressions," and so forth? Or is something else at work in perception that conveys more about place than mere sensory signals can ever effect? It is certainly true—and this is what Kant emphasizes in the idea of "to begin with"— that sensory inputs are the *occasions* of the perception (eventually the knowledge) of concrete places. These impingements—as connoted in the term *Empfindungen*, Kant's word for "sensations"—alert us to the fact that we are perceiving, and they convey certain of the very qualities (including the secondary qualities) of the surfaces of what we perceive. But their pointillistic character ill equips them for supplying anything like the sense of being in a place. Yet we do always find ourselves in places. We find ourselves in them, however different the places themselves may be and however differently we construe and exploit them. But how do we grasp this "in" of being in a particular place: this preposition which is quite literally a "pre-position" inasmuch as we are always already in a place, never not implaced in one way or another?[14]

If perception is "primary" (as both Husserl and Merleau-Ponty insist), then a significant part of its primariness must be its ability to give to us more than bits of information about the phenomenal and epiphenomenal surfaces of things—and more, too, than a conviction that we are merely in the presence of these surfaces. Beyond what Husserl calls the "hyletic" factor, and Merleau-Ponty "sensing," there must be, as an ingredient in perception from the start, a conveyance of what being in places is all about. Merleau-Ponty considers this conveyance to be *depth*—a "primordial depth" that, far from being imputed to sensations (as Berkeley, for example, had held),[15] already situates them in a scene of which we ourselves form part. Husserl's way of putting it is that "every experience has its own horizon" and that we continually find ourselves in the midst of perceptual horizons, both the "internal" horizons of particular things (i.e., given by their successive sides) and the "external" horizons that encompass a given scene as a whole.[16]

But precisely as surrounded by depths and horizons, the perceiver finds herself in the midst of an entire teeming place-world rather than in a confusing kaleido-scope of free-floating sensory data. The coherence of perception at the primary level is supplied by the depth and horizons of the very place we occupy as sentient subjects. That is why we can trust this coherence with what Santayana called "ani-mal faith," and Husserl, "primal belief (*protodoxa*)."[17] We come to the world—we come into it and keep returning to it—already placed there. Places are not added to sensations any more than they are imposed on spaces. Both sensations and spaces are themselves implaced from the very first moment, and at every subsequent mo-ment as well.

There is no knowing or sensing a place except by being in that place, and to be in a place is to be in a position to perceive it. Knowledge of place is not, then, subsequent to perception—as Kant dogmatically assumed—but is ingredient in perception itself. Such knowledge, genuinely local knowledge, is itself experien-tial in the manner of *Erlebnis*, "lived experience," rather than of *Erfahrung*, the already elapsed experience that is the object of analytical or abstract knowledge. (Kant, significantly, speaks only of *Erfahrung*.) Local knowledge is at one with lived experience if it is indeed true that this knowledge is of the localities in which the knowing subject lives. To live is to live locally, and to know is first of all to know the places one is in.

I am not proposing a merely mute level of experience that passively receives simple and senseless data of place. Perception at the primary level is synesthetic—an affair of the whole body sensing and moving. Thanks to its inherent complexity, bodily perceiving is directed at (and is adequate to) things and places that come configured, often in highly complicated ways. Moreover, the configuration and complication are already meaningful and not something internally registered as sensory givens that lack any sense of their own: the sensory is senseful. Nor does the inherent meaningfulness of what we perceive require the infusion of determinate concepts located higher up the epistemic ladder. The perceived possesses a core of immanent sense, a "noematic nucleus" in Husserl's technical term.[18] Because this senseful core is actively grasped, it follows that perception is never entirely a matter of what Kant calls "receptivity," as if the perceiving subject were merely passive. Not only is primary perception inseparable from myriad modes of concrete action, but it is itself "a kind of *passivity in activity*."[19] To perceive synesthetically is to be actively passive; it is to be absorptive yet constitutive, both at once.

It is also to be constituted: constituted by cultural and social structures that sediment themselves into the deepest level of perception. The primacy of percep-tion does not mean that human sensing and moving are precultural or presocial. No more than perception is built up from atomic sensations is it constructed from brute givens unaffected by cultural practices and social institutions. On the con-trary: these practices and institutions pervade every level of perception, from the quite implicit (e.g., tacitly grasped outer horizons) to the extremely explicit (e.g., the thematic thing perceived). The permeation occurs even—indeed, especially— when a given perception is preconceptual and prediscursive. To be not yet articu-lated in concept or word is not to be nonculturally constituted, much less free from social constraints. Hence, the primacy of perception does not entail the priority of perception to the givens of culture or society, as if the latter were separable contents of our being and experience: these givens become infusions into the infrastructures of perception itself. The primacy of perception is ultimately a primacy of the lived body—a body that, as we shall see in more detail later, is a creature of habitual cultural and social processes.

But perception remains as constitutive as it is constituted. This is especially evident when we perceive places: our immersion in them is not subjection to them, since we may modify their influence even as we submit to it. This influ-ence is as meaningful as it is sensuous. Not only is the sensuous senseful, it is also *placeful*. As Steven Feld puts it, "as place is sensed, senses are placed; as places make sense, senses make place."[20] The dialectic of perception and place (and of both with meaning) is as intricate as it is profound, and it is never-ending.

Given that we are never without perception, the existence of this dialectic means that we are never without implaced experiences. It signifies as well that we are not only *in* places but *of* them. Human beings—along with other entities on earth—are ineluctably place-bound. More even than earthlings, we are place-lings, and our very perceptual apparatus, our sensing body, reflects the kinds of places we inhabit. The ongoing reliability and general veracity of perception (a reliability and veracity that countenance considerable experiential vicissitudes) entail a continual attunement to place (also experienced in open-ended variation). But if this is true, it suggests that place, rather than being a mere product or portion of space, is as primary as the perception that gives access to it. Also suggested is the heretical—and quite ancient—thought that place, far from being something sheerly singular, is something general, perhaps even universal: a thought to which we shall return.

II

Nature makes itself specific.

—Kant, *The Critique of Judgment*

It is characteristic of the modern Western mind to conceive of space in terms of its formal essence—hence the insistent search for mathematical expressions of pure spatial relations. For Newton, More, Gassendi, Descartes, and Galileo, space was homogeneous, isotropic, isometric, and infinitely (or, at least, indefinitely) extended. Within the supremely indifferent and formal scene of space, local differences did not matter. Place itself did not matter. It was not for nothing that Descartes proposed in his *Principles of Philosophy* that matter and space were the same thing—which meant that space had no qualities not present in matter, whose own primary property was a metrically determinable pure extension. Place was simply a creature of such extension, either its mere subdivision ("internal place" or volume) or a relationally specified location in it ("position").[21] In his *Mathematical Principles of Natural Philosophy*, Newton still recognized "absolute" and "relative" places, but both kinds of places were only "portions" of absolute *space*, which was where all the action (e.g., gravitational action) was to be found. On the basis of absolute space, places were apportioned and mapped out: just there is the conceptual root of the paralogism I detect in certain recent anthropological treatments of place and space.

In this early modern paradigm shift, there was little space for place as a valid concept in its own right. As a result, place was disempowered: all the power now resided in space—and in time, the second colossal concern of modern thought. Although time was held to have direction, it was as essentially devoid of content as was space. A century after Newton described space and time as "God's infinite sensoria," Kant considered them to be "pure forms of intuition" located within the finite human subject. By this act of internalization, Kant sealed the fate of place even more drastically: at most, the human subject had "position" in the space and time of its own making. But place was of almost no concern in the *Critique of Pure Reason* (1781).[22]

One way to avoid the high road of modernism as it stretches from the abstract physics of Newton to the critical philosophy of Kant and beyond is to reoccupy the low land of place. For place can be considered either premodern or postmodern; it serves to connect these two far sides of modernity. To reinstate place in the wake of its demise in modern Western thought—where space and time have held such triumphant and exclusive sway—one can equally well go to the premodern moments described in ethnographic accounts of traditional societies or to the postmodern moment of the increasingly nontraditional present, where place has been returning as a reinvigorated *revenant* in the writings of ecologists and landscape theorists, geographers and historians, sociologists and political thinkers—and anthropologists themselves.

III

> Do we not sense from the outset a certain difference, by virtue of which locality belongs to me somewhat more essentially [than, for example, size and weight]? . . . Men and animals are spatially localized; and even what is psychic about them, at least in virtue of its essential foundedness in what is bodily, partakes of the spatial order.
>
> —Husserl, *Ideas Pertaining to a Pure Phenomenology and to a Phenomenological Philosophy*, Second Book

How, then, do we get back into place? In the very way by which we are always already there—by our own lived body. Ironically, Kant was the first Western thinker to point to the importance of bodily structure for implacement. In his remarkable precritical essay of 1768, "On the First Ground of the Distinction of Material Regions in Space," he argued that the two-sidedness—especially the two-handedness—of the human body is essential for orientation in "cosmic regions" of surrounding sky or earth:

> Even our judgments about the cosmic regions are subordinated to the concept we have of regions in general, insofar as they are determined in relation to the sides of the body. . . . However well I know the order of the cardinal points, I can determine regions according to that order only insofar as I know towards which hand this order proceeds. . . . Similarly, our geographical knowledge, and even our commonest knowledge of the position of places, would be of no aid to us if we could not, by reference to the sides of our bodies, assign to regions the things so ordered and the whole system of mutually relative positions.[23]

The bilateral body is singled out, then, just when it is a question of orientation in regions (*Gegenden*), where places are concatenated in formations that resist the ascription of pinpointed location. Could it be that the body is essentially, and not just contingently, involved in matters of implacement?

Kant's prescient observations about the body in its basic bilaterality anticipated and complemented Robert Hertz's brilliant speculations on the cultural significance of right- versus left-handedness.[24] Both Kant and Hertz subscribed, tacitly if not explicitly, to a more general principle: that the human body's brachiated and multiply articulated structure renders it a uniquely valuable vehicle in the establishment of place. Precisely by allowing us to make a diverse entry into a given place—through hands and feet, knees and hips, elbows and shoulders—the body insinuates itself subtly and multiply into encompassing regions. If the body were an inert and intact thing with no moving parts, a fleshly monolith, it could be grasped as something sheerly physical that is punctually located at a given position in space and does not reach out farther. This is how Galileo construed *all* bodies: as inert, non-self-moving entities submitting to the laws of gravitation and motion. But once a *Körper* (body as physical object) has become a *Leib* (body as lived)—once there is resurrection in the body, as it were—more than merely punctiform positioning in empty space (and at an equally stigmatic moment in time) is at stake. This is what Kant discovered—and then quickly forgot. It is also what Husserl and Hertz rediscovered a century and a half later.

The several members of a lived body move not randomly but by what Merleau-Ponty calls "corporeal intentionality." Thanks to this intentionality, the lived body integrates itself with its immediate environment, that is to say, its concrete place. The integration is effected by various "intentional threads" that bind body and place in a common complex of relations.[25] But none of this pervasive integumentation between body and place would be possible without the freely moving members of the body as it situates itself in a particular place, remembers itself in that place, and so forth. The lived body—the body living (in) a place—is thus "the natural subject of perception."[26] The experience of perceiving that I discussed earlier requires a corporeal subject who lives *in* a place *through* perception. It also requires a place that is amenable to this body-subject and that extends its own influence back onto this subject. A place, we might even say, has its own "operative intentionality" that elicits and responds to the corporeal intentionality of the perceiving subject. Thus place integrates with body as much as body with place. It is a matter of what Keith Basso calls "interanimation."[27]

Other aspects of the lived body are at stake in being-in-place, each of them specifying further what first caught Kant's keen eye. First, various kinesthesias and synesthesias—as well as sonesthesias, as Feld insists[28]—allow bodily self-motion to be registered and enriched, ultimately constituting what Husserl terms the "aesthesiological body." This body itself serves as a "field of localization" for the manifold sensuous presentations (including sonorous ones) that stem from a particular place but are registered by (or with) a lived body that finds itself in that place.[29] Second, immanent bodily dimensionalities of up/down, front/back, right/left—explicitly recognized by Kant, who was inclined, however, to reduce them to the three Cartesian coordinates—help to connect body with the placial settings of these same three dyads.[30]

Third, the concreteness of a lived body, its density and mass, answers to the thick concreteness of a given place, but the difference between the two concretions is just as critical because it sets up a "coefficient of adversity" that makes ordinary perception itself possible.[31] Fourth, a given lived body and a given experienced place tend to present themselves as particular: as just this body in just this place. Each thus actively partakes in the "this-here"—which does not, however, exclude significant variations, ranging from bi-gendered to bi-located bodies.[32] And fifth, the porosity of the skin of an organic body rejoins, even as it mimics, the openness of the boundaries of places; there is a resilient, pneumatic structure shared in a common "flesh of the world."[33] Were the body a window-less monad, it could neither negotiate the varieties nor grasp the valences of the places in which it finds itself. And these same places have to have their own windows if the body is to enter them in turn.

In addition to these five factors, we need to recognize the crucial interaction between body, place, and *motion*. A given place may certainly be perduring and consistent, but this does not mean that it is simply something inactive and at rest—as is all too often assumed. Part of the power of place, its very dynamism, is found in its encouragement of motion in its midst, its "e-motive" (and often explicitly emotional) thrust. Indeed, we may distinguish among three kinds of bodily motion pertinent to place. The first and most limited case is *staying in place*. Here the body remains in place, in one single place. Yet such a body in such a situation is never entirely stationary except in extreme circumstances of paralysis or rigor mortis. Even when staying in place, the body changes the position of some of its parts, however modestly: moving its limbs, rotating its head, twiddling its thumbs. The body twitches in place. Moreover, an unmoving body may still move if it is transported by another moving body: the driver of a car, the rider on horseback. Toynbee remarks that Bedouins riding on horses "move by not moving."[34] We might say that the body of the Bedouin stays in one position, yet the locus of this position—where "locus" signifies a position in its capacity to change places in space—itself changes as the mount moves between different places.[35]

The second case, *moving within a place*, is the circumstance in which I move my whole body about a given place while still remaining in it. Insofar as I am typing this manuscript, I am in one position; but when I get up to pace, I move around in the room I am in. I move within a circumscribed "space" defined by the walls of the room. The whole body moves in the whole room. Similarly, much ceremonial action is taken by bodies moving in set ways within entire prescribed places: kivas, plazas, longhouses, temples.

Finally, *moving between places* denotes the circumstance in which bodies travel between different places. No longer is movement circumscribed by the restrictions of a single position or one place; now it ranges among a number of places. In this case, the motion is a genuine transition and not just a trans-portation.[36] The most salient instance is the journey, and cases in point are em-igrations, pilgrimages, voyages of exchange, and nomadic circulations. In all of these, the bodies of the journeyers follow more or less preordained routes between particular places: for example, the pilgrimage route to Santiago de Compostela as it connects various interim places throughout western Europe. The body's active role is most evident in the literal legwork of circumambulations and other forms of movement, but it is no less present in the building of homesteads in the land of emigration or in the setting up of temporary nomadic encampments. Just as staying in place corresponds to position, and moving the whole body within one locus answers to place proper, so moving between places corresponds to an entire region, that is, an area concatenated by peregrinations between the places it connects.

There is much more to be said about the role of the body in place, especially about how places actively solicit bodily motions. At the very least, we can agree that the living-moving body is essential to the process of implacement: *lived bodies belong to places* and help to constitute them. Even if such bodies may be displaced in certain respects, they are never placeless; they are never only at discrete positions in world time or space, though they may *also* be at such positions. By the same token, however, *places belong to lived bodies* and depend on them. If it is true that "the body is our general medium for having a world,"[37] it ensues that the body is the specific medium for experiencing a place-world. The lived body is the material condition of possibility for the place-world while being itself a member of that same world. It is basic to place and part of place. Just as there are no places without the bodies that sustain and vivify them, so there are no lived bodies without the places they inhabit and traverse. (Even imaginary places bring with them virtual bodies—"subtle bodies" in an earlier nomenclature.) Bodies and places are connatural terms. They interanimate each other.

IV

We may suggest that the day will come when we will not shun the question
whether the opening, the free open, may not be that within which alone pure
space and ecstatic time and everything present and absent in them have
the place which gathers and protects everything.

—Heidegger, "The End of Philosophy and the Task of Thinking"

Places gather: this I take to be a second essential trait (i.e., beyond the role of the lived body) revealed by a phenomenological description. Minimally, places gather things in their midst—where "things" connote various animate and inanimate entities. Places also gather experiences and histories, even languages and thoughts. Think only of what it means to go back to a place you know, finding it full of memories and expectations, old things and new things, the familiar and the strange, and much more besides. What else is capable of this massively diversified holding action? Certainly not individual human subjects construed as sources of "projection" or "reproduction"—not even these subjects as they draw upon their bodily and perceptual powers. The power belongs to place itself, and it is a power of gathering.

By "gathering" I do not mean merely amassing. To gather placewise is to have a peculiar hold on what is presented (as well as represented) in a given place. Not just the contents but the very mode of containment is held by a place. "The hold is held."[38] The hold of place, its gathering action, is held in quite special ways. First, it is a holding *together* in a particular configuration: hence our sense of an ordered arrangement of things in a place even when those things are radically disparate and quite conflictual. The arrangement allows for certain things—people, ideas, and so forth—to overlap with, and sometimes to occlude, others as they recede or come forward together. Second, the hold is a holding *in* and a holding *out*. It retains the occupants of a place within its boundaries: if they were utterly to vanish and the place to be permanently empty, it would be no place at all but a void. But, equally, a place holds out, beckoning to its inhabitants and, assembling them, making them manifest (though not necessarily manifest to each other, or to the same degree). It can move place-holders toward the margins of its own presentation while, nevertheless, holding them within its own embrace.

Third, the holding at issue in the gathering of a place reflects the layout of the local landscape, its continuous contour, even as the outlines and inlines of the things held in that place are respected. The result is not confusion of container with contained but a literal *con*figuration in which the form of the place—for example, "mountain," "mesa," "gulley"—joins up with the shapes of the things in it. Being in a place is being in a configurative complex of things. Fourth, intrinsic to the holding operation of place is *keeping*. What is kept in place primarily are experiencing bodies regarded as privileged residents rather than as orchestrating forces (much less as mere registrants). My body-in-place is less the *metteur en scène* than itself a *mise en scène*—or rather, it is both at once, again a matter of "passivity in activity."[39]

And last, places also keep such unbody-like entities as thoughts and memories. When I revisit my hometown of Topeka, Kansas, I find this place more or less securely holding memories for me. In my presence, it releases these memories, which belong as much to the place as to my brain or body. This kind of keeping is especially pertinent to an intensely gathered landscape such as that of aboriginal Australia—a landscape that holds ancestral memories of the Dreaming. Yet even when I recall people and things and circumstances in an ordinary place, I have the sense that these various recollections have been kept securely in place, harbored there, as it were.[40]

Gathering gives to place its peculiar perduringness, allowing us to return to it again and again *as the same place* and not just as the same position or site.[41] For a place, in its dynamism, does not age in a systematically changing way, that is, in accordance with a preestablished schedule of growth and decline; only its tenants and visitors, enactors and witnesses (including myself and others in these various roles), age and grow old in this way. A place is generative and regenerative on its own schedule. From it, experiences are born and to it human beings (and other organisms) return for empowerment, much like Antaeus touching the earth for renewed strength. Place is the generatrix for the collection, as well as the recollection, of all that occurs in the lives of sentient beings, and even for the trajectories of inanimate things. Its power consists in gathering these lives and things, each with its own space and time, into one arena of common engagement.

V

Husserl's essences are destined to bring back all the living
relationships of experience, as the fisherman's net draws up from
the depths of the ocean quivering fish and seaweed.

—Merleau-Ponty, *Phenomenology of Perception*

It should be clear by now that I do not take place to be something simply physical. A place is not a mere patch of ground, a bare stretch of earth, a sedentary set of stones. What kind of thing is it then? The "what is" locution—Aristotle's *ti esti* question—combined with "kind of" suggests that there is some single sort of thing that place is, some archetype of Place. But whatever place is, it is *not* the kind of thing that can be subsumed under already given universal notions—for example, of space and time, substance or causality. A given place may not permit, indeed it often defies, subsumption under given categories. Instead, a place is something for which we continually have to discover or invent new forms of understanding, new concepts in the literal sense of ways of "grasping-together."

A place is more an *event* than a *thing* to be assimilated to known categories. As an event, it is unique, idiolocal. Its peculiarity calls not for assumption into the already known—that way lies site, which lends itself to predefined predications, uses, and interpretations—but for the imaginative constitution of terms respecting its idiolocality (these range from place-names to whole discourses). The "kind" at stake in "kind of" is neither a genus nor a species, that is, a determinate concept that rules over its instances, but something operating *across* margins, laterally, by means of homology or similitude. Yet place qua kind remains something specific inasmuch as it alters in keeping with its own changing constituents. The kind in question, the answer pertinent to the "what is" question, is more a type or a style than a pure concept or formal universal. While such a concept or universal is fixed in definition (if not always in application), a *type* or *style* connotes an open manifoldness, a unity-in-diversity, and not a self-identical unity. Further, a type or style admits of degrees—so sensitively that a change of a few degrees may bring with it a change in identity, as when analytical Cubism gave way imperceptibly but still decisively to synthetic Cubism.

In the case of place, then, the kind is itself kind of something, rather than a definite sort of something. This is why we speak of places in phrases like "a clean well-lit place," "a place for recovering one's sanity," "a Southwestern landscape," or "a Southern plantation." The indefinite article employed in these locutions bespeaks the indefiniteness of the kind of thing a place or region is. Such indefiniteness—not to be confused with indeterminacy, much less with chaos—is in no way incompatible with the ostensive definiteness of demonstrative pronouns and adverbial locatives, that is, those "essentially occasional expressions" that are so frequently used to refer to particular places or regions: "just here," "in this place," and so forth. I would even say that the open-endedness of place, its typological status as morphologically vague, its de-finition, creates the semantic space within which definite demonstrations and exact localizations can arise.[42]

Rather than being one definite sort of thing—for example, physical, spiritual, cultural, social—a given place takes on the qualities of its occupants, reflecting these qualities in its own constitution and description and expressing them in its occurrence as an event: places not only are, they happen. (And it is because they happen that they lend themselves so well to narration, whether as history or as story.) Just as a particular place is at least several kinds of things, so there are many sorts of places and not one basic kind only—one supposedly supreme genus. Sorts of places depend on the kinds of things, as well as the actual things, that make them up. A biochore or biotope directly reflects the character of its constituents, that is, its soils and flora and fauna; an agora is qualified by the people who pass through it or linger there; a dwelling is characterized less by its architecture than by the quality of the life that is sustained in it. If, as Wallace Stevens put it, "a mythology reflects its region," then a region reflects both what is held together there (its "contents," its co-tenants) and how it is so held.[43]

A place or region is metaphysically neutral inasmuch as it does not possess some given substrate, a "ground" that would be metaphysically definite enough to determine the place or region as just one kind of entity. And if there is no such preexisting ground, then the model of adding successive strata of meaning (added by cultures or minds, actions or words) is of dubious application.[44] Even to call such a putative ground "the earth" is already to regionalize, or rather to geologize, at the most basic level. The fact is that there is not any "most basic level" to be presumed as simply there, "*einfach da*," as Husserl says of objects that are posited by the positivism of the natural attitude.[45] Stripping away cultural or linguistic accretions, we shall never find a pure place lying underneath—and still less an even purer Space or Time. What we will find are continuous and changing qualifications of particular places: places qualified by their own contents, and qualified as well by the various ways these contents are articulated (denoted, described, discussed, narrated, and so forth) in a given culture. We designate particular places by the place terms of the culture to which we as place designators and place dwellers belong, but the places we designate are not bare substrates to which these terms are attached as if to an unadorned bedrock. They are named or namable parts of the landscape of a region, its condensed and lived physiognomy.[46]

The power of place consists in its nontendentious ability to reflect the most diverse items that constitute its "midst." In many regards, a place *is* its midst, being in the midst of its own detailed contents; it is what lies most deeply amid its own constituents, gathering them together in the expressive landscape of that place. No mind could effect such gathering, and the body, though necessary to its attainment, requires the holding and keeping actions native to the place it is in.[47]

VI

> Truths involve universals, and all knowledge of truths
> involves acquaintance with universals.
>
> —Bertrand Russell, *The Problems of Philosophy*

Thus we are led back to a question that was posed at the beginning of this essay: Is place a universal? Here we are inclined to ask in a skeptical vein, How can the epitome of the local be a matter of the general? What kind of generality can place possess? What sort of universal might it be? Indeed, how could it be a universal at all in face of the enormous diversity of places which anthropology, more than any other discipline, brings to our attention? Does not all this diversity make the search for sameness a futile and misguided effort?

In *Aspects of the Theory of Syntax*, Chomsky distinguishes between "formal" and "substantive" universals. Substantive universals are fixed in character and delimited in number: for example, Jakobson's list of the distinctive features whose various combinations determine the phonological component of given natural languages, or the Port-Royal syntactic categories of Noun, Verb, and so forth. Formal universals, in contrast, specify the abstract conditions of possibility for the pervasive structures of any and every natural language: for example, the condition that proper names must designate objects that are spatiotemporally contiguous or that color words have to divide up the color spectrum into continuous parts with no gaps.[48]

The choice here proffered by Chomsky is pertinent to place, but only by dint of calling the choice itself into question. On the one hand, place is something like a formal universal in that it functions like a general feature, even a

condition of possibility, of all human (and doubtless all animal and plant) experience—however expansive the term "experience" is taken to be. On the other
hand, place is also a quite distinctive feature of such experience. Place is not a
purely formal operator empty of content but is always contentful, always specifiable as this particular place or that one. And if *both* things are true of place, if it
is both formally true of every experience and true to each particular experience,
then any rigid distinction between formal and substantive universals will dissolve before our very eyes. The deconstruction of this distinction will already be
effected by the character of place itself, by its inherent generative force. For in
the end, place is neither formal (place is not a condition of but a force for) nor
substantive (there is not a fixed number of places in the universe, or of particular
features or kinds of places).

This allows us to ask: Is the only choice that between "bloodless universals"
and "substantive identities"?[49] Is not the aim, in anthropology as in any philosophy that is sensitive to the differences different cultures make, to discover
genuine concrete universals, that is, structures that are at once elastic enough to
be exemplified in disparate cultures yet also taut enough to be discernibly different from each other in content or definition? An example would be funeral
practices, which are observed by all known cultures yet which differ dramatically
from culture to culture. The marking of death and the remarking of the life that
preceded it is concretely universal, though the modes of marking and remarking
are tangibly diverse. A concrete universal of this sort is neither so adamantine as
to be indifferent to its instantiations nor so purely reflective as to be the indifferent mirroring of any and every cultural difference: neither form of indifference
does justice to the actual difference that the embodiment of a concrete universal
introduces. As Hegel insisted, a concrete universal is operative in contingent
circumstances and has no life apart from those circumstances. Let us say that
it is endoskeletal to what happens in a given time and place and yet sufficiently
generic to be immanent to occurrences in other times and places (not just by
homology but by actual ingredience).

Does this mean that the kind of universal at stake in place is nothing but
an "empirical commonality," that which just happens to be the case in several
or even many times and places?[50] No: the empirically common comes down to
statistical frequency or contingent overlap and fails to capture what is shared
by members of a class of things that all possess some genuinely generic trait
(whether this be an action, a quality, a relation, or some other characteristic).
While manifested in the "special world" (*idios kosmos,* as the ancient Greeks
would say) of a particular place and time, the shared trait nevertheless belongs
to the "common world" (*koinos kosmos*) of authentic concrete universals. Such
a bivalent universal, belonging both to special worlds and to a common world,
serves to relate items that would otherwise be a mere congeries of terms that,

at most, resemble each other. It is thus a relational universal that consists in its very capacity to assemble things as well as kinds of things.

Thus we might well agree with Bertrand Russell that a relational universal is "neither in space nor in time, neither material nor mental," yet "it is [still] something."[51] But what kind of something is it? If it manages not to be in space or time, can it nevertheless be in place? I would hazard that the kind of universal most relevant to a philosophically informed anthropology of place is at once concrete and relational—concrete as relational (and vice versa)—and serves to connect disparate data across cultures, yet not emptily and in name only. Such a universal proceeds *laterally,* by assimilating phenomena of the same level of abstraction, rather than vertically (by subsuming concrete phenomena under more abstract terms).[52] Lateral universals are especially pertinent to the anthropology and phenomenology of place. For in their very concreteness, particular places do not form hierarchies of increasing abstraction. Instead, they fall into various groupings of comparably concrete terms: home places, workplaces, way stations, and so forth. The constitution of such places is at once concrete-relational and lateral in scope and is effected *by places themselves* (much more so than by times, which serve to separate more than to connect). Minds may note the sameness shared by different places, but they do not make this sameness. The sameness is the work of places in interaction with bodies that find themselves engaged with them.

But what does sameness of place signify? Certainly not identity of position—a much more delimited concept. Places are significantly (though not literally) the same when they are members of the same material *region.* Places concatenate with each other to form regions of things. A region, as Husserl conceives it, holds together things that share the same "material essence" (*sachhaltiges Wesen*), which—unlike a formal essence—has its own positive content. This content affiliates things in such a way that we may consider them as belonging to the same overall region. Thus physical things qua physical belong to the region of Nature. Psychological phenomena—for example, memories and thoughts—belong to Psyche, regarded as a distinctively different region (yet one that is commensurate with that of things).[53] Similarly, placial phenomena such as location and situation belong to the region Place. Within Place as a generic region, particular kinds of places abound: wild places and built places at one level, kitchens and bedrooms at another, and so on.

A given place, like anything else characterized by material essences, is inseparable from the concrete region in which it is found and instantiates qualities and relations found in that region. This is true not just of physical places but of other sorts of places as well: just as, say, the Grand Canyon is qualified by properties that are regional in a geological sense (e.g., the presence of arroyos, colored sandstone rock layering, certain effects of seasonal weather), so the place of the Grand Canyon in my memory of it occupies a region of my psyche (roughly, that of "memories-of-traveling-in-the-American-Southwest"). From this simple example it is evident, once again, that place is not one kind of thing: it can be psychical as well as physical, and doubtless also cultural and historical and social. But as a coherent region in Husserl's sense of the term, it holds these kinds—and much else besides—together.[54]

If place is indeed regional in any such sense as this, it cannot be universal in traditional Western acceptations of this term. In particular, it cannot be a substantive or a formal universal. The universality of place is too complex—or too loose—to be captured by these classical forms of universality, one of which reduces to strict sameness of content and the other to identity of form. Place is more complicated than this, and its universality is at once concrete, relational, lateral, and regional. Of these traits, "regional" is the most comprehensive and can be regarded as containing *in nuce* the other traits. For as a regional universal, place is defined by a material essence or set of such essences, each of which is concrete and relational and each of which also operates by lateral inclusion. In its regionality, a place cannot superintend objects *in general* (i.e., abstract objects such as numbers) in the manner of a formal domain. A given place such as the Grand Canyon bears only on its own actual occupants, which are structured by the same material essences by which the place itself is to be construed. The things and localities, the people and animals, in the canyon, are held together not just by their literal location in the same piece of geography but, more significantly, by the fact that they are *part of the same place*—a place exhibiting various material-essential features possessed or reflected by everything in that place (aridity, verticality, rough textures, etc.).

As a regional universal, place cannot be tucked away in cross-cultural area files as just another "common-denominator of culture," that is, something possessing only empirical commonality.[55] The commonality of the regional is determined by material essentialities and not by empirical congruencies. But it would be equally mistaken to assume that place, not being built on such mere congruencies, is too idiosyncratic to be discussed intelligibly, that is, too singular to be the subject of any investigation sensitive to the possibility of essential structure. Place is again in the middle, situated between the Charybdis of sheer singularity and the Scylla of contingent commonality. It occupies an intermediate area in what Collingwood calls the "scale of forms" that defines human knowledge.[56] Neither the most abstract member of this scale (a leading candidate for which is doubtless "object in general") nor the most concrete (this is the utter "individual," Aristotle's *tode ti,* the bare "this-here"), place is nevertheless sufficiently general to be coherently discussed as a guiding or regulative notion—for instance, in this very essay—and yet sufficiently particular not to be fully subsumable under formal essences. In Husserl's oxymoronic language, place is an "eidetic singularity," singular enough to be unique to a given occasion and yet wide-ranging enough to exceed what is peculiar to it alone on that same occasion.[57]

Even if place does not function as a formally or substantively universal concept, it is nonetheless a concrete and relational general term that contributes to the constitution of an entire region. The many ways in which place figures into the discourse and life of native (as well as contemporary Western) peoples—in fact, never does *not* figure in some significant manner—point to its status as genuinely general, that is, pervasive in its very particularity. Construed in this light, indeed, the local is the general. Particular places tell us how a region is—how it disposes itself. They are that region's condensed contents and are indispensable for conceiving what is regionally the same in the very face of the manifold descriptive and explanatory, gestural and linguistic, historical and social, ethical and political, differences that distinguish the life-worlds of diverse peoples.

Precisely in their comparative sameness, places prove to be universal: they are the necessary basis for regional specification. Without places, regions would be vacuous and thus all too easy to collapse into each other—ultimately, into abstract space. As it is the essence of a place to be regional, so it is equally essential to a region to be anchored in particular places. If this were not the case, if place were after all merely contingent or common—merely empirical—and if it did not involve something of the order of essence, it would not possess the "power" ascribed to it by Aristotle over two millennia ago.

VII

Just as nature finds its way to the core of my personal life and becomes
inextricably linked with it, so behavior patterns settle into that nature,
being deposited in the form of a cultural world.

—Merleau-Ponty, *Phenomenology of Perception*

Now we must, finally, *put culture back in place*. This is not, of course, to locate it anywhere other than where it already is. Yet the abiding implacement of cultural practices has often gone unacknowledged. All too frequently, late modern Eurocentric thinking has located culture in two extremes—either in overt behavioral patterns (in "positivisms" of many sorts, sedimented in the *natürliche Einstellung* that so disturbed Husserl) or in symbol systems (e.g., in structuralist accounts of verbal language and transverbal symbols). Culture is situated either in something strictly observable or in something sheerly diaphanous: the perceived and recorded action or the evanescing sign.

These radical measures, taken respectively by psychology and semiology, may have been justified at the time they were proposed, and all the more so as a reaction to the unremitting mentalism and historicism so prevalent in eighteenth- and nineteenth-century thought. If Culture is not located in Mind—mind as representational (Locke) or mind as Objective Spirit (Hegel)—it is also not positioned in History (least of all in a teleologically ordered model of history considered as a series of progressively superior stages). Although behaviorism took us altogether out of our minds and synchronically based semiologies lured us out of diachronic history, each enterprise flung itself into an extreme epicenter of overreaction. More recently, counter-countermeasures have set in: cognitive psychology has brought behaviorism back to a more subtle look at mind, and hermeneutical theories of meaning have drawn the theory of symbols into a richer sense of the dense interpretive matrix from which language and other sign systems spring.

Yet within this largely salutary return to the specificities of mind and sign, the inherent implacement of culture has been missed. Braudel pointed toward this implacement in his monumental study of the geographical basis of history in the age of Phillip II, but this bold direction has not been taken up in other disciplines.[58] In fact, no systematic effort has been made to account for the indispensability of place in the evolution and presentation of cultural institutions, beginning with the fact that the very cultivation at stake in culture has to occur *somewhere*. "Everyone supposes," remarks Aristotle nonchalantly, "that things that are are somewhere, because what is not is nowhere."[59] Given that culture manifestly exists, it must exist somewhere, and it exists more concretely and completely in places than in minds or signs. The very word *culture* means "place tilled" in Middle English, and the same word goes back to Latin *colere*, "to inhabit, care for, till, worship." To be cultural, to have a culture, is to inhabit a place sufficiently intensely to cultivate it—to be responsible for it, to respond to it, to attend to it caringly. Where else but in particular places can culture take root? Certainly not in the thin air above these places, much less in the even thinner air of pure speculation about them.

To be located, culture also has to be *embodied*. Culture is carried into places by bodies. To be encultured is to be embodied to begin with. This is the common lesson of Merleau-Ponty and of Bourdieu, both of whom insist on the capital importance of the "customary body"—the body that has incorporated cultural patterns into its basic actions. These actions depend on *habitus*, "history turned into nature," a second nature that brings culture to bear in its very movements.[60] Moreover, just as the body is basic to enculturation, so the body is itself always already encultured. No more than space is prior to place is the body prior to culture. Rather than being a passive recipient or mere vehicle of cultural enactments, the body is itself enactive of cultural practices by virtue of its considerable powers of incorporation, habituation, and expression. And as a creature of habitus, the same body necessarily *inhabits* places that are themselves culturally informed. (It also inhabits places by rising to the challenge of the novel circumstance.) Far from being dumb or diffuse, the lived body is as intelligent about the cultural specificities of a place as it is aesthesiologically sensitive to the perceptual particularities of that same place. Such a body is at once encultured and implaced and enculturating and implacing—while being massively sentient all the while.

Basic to local knowledge, therefore, is knowledge of place by means of the body: such knowledge is "knowledge by acquaintance," in Russell's memorable phrase.[61] Bodies not only perceive but know places. Perceiving bodies are *knowing bodies,* and inseparable from what they know is culture as it imbues and shapes particular places. It is by bodies that places become cultural in character. It is all too easy to suppose that what is cultural represents an articulated separate stratum laid down on a mute perceptual ground. In fact, even the most primordial level of perceiving is inlaid with cultural categories in the form of differential patterns of recognition, ways of organizing the perceptual field and acting in it, and manners of designating and naming items in this field. Thus culture pervades the way that places are perceived and the fact that they are perceived, as well as how we act in their midst. As Merleau-Ponty puts it, "the distinction between the two planes (natural and cultural) is abstract: everything is cultural in us (our *Lebenswelt* is "subjective") (our perception is cultural-historical) and everything is natural in us (even the cultural rests on the polymorphism of wild Being)."[62]

In other words, the endemic status of culture—pervading bodies and places and bodies-in-places—is matched by the equally endemic insinuation of "wild Being" into the body/place matrix. Even the most culturally saturated place retains a factor of wildness, that is, of the radically amorphous and unaccounted for, something that is not so much immune to culture as alien to it in its very midst, disparate from it from within. We sense this wildness explicitly in moments of absurdity—and of "surdity," sheer "thisness." But it is immanent in every perceptual experience and thus in every bodily insertion into the perceived places anchoring each such experience. This ontological wildness—not to be confused with literal wilderness, much less with mere lack of cultivation—ensures that cultural analysis never exhausts a given place. Just as we should not fall into a perceptualism that leaves no room for expressivity and language, so we ought not to espouse a culturalism that accords no autochthonous being to bodies and places. In the very heart of the most sophisticated circumstance is a wildness that no culture can contain or explain, much less reduce. The wildness exceeds the scope of the most subtle set of signifiers, despite the efforts of painters to capture it in images and of storytellers to depict it in words.[63]

Precisely because of the ubiquity of such wildness in body, place, and culture, the temptation to espouse the idea of a primary "precultural" level of experience is difficult to overcome. Perhaps no serious Western thinker, including Husserl and Merleau-Ponty, has altogether resisted the charisma of the precultural—especially when it accompanies a preoccupation with uncovering the foundations of experience and knowledge. But the passion for epistemic (and other) origins is itself culturally specific and stems from an epistemophilic proclivity that is not ingrained or instinctual, Aristotle's and Freud's claims notwithstanding. All human beings may desire to know, but they do not always desire to know in the foundationalist manner that is an obsessive concern of European civilization. Moreover, whatever people may wish to know, they are already doing at the bilateral level of knowing bodies and known places. As knowing and known, bodies and places are not precultural—even if they are prediscursive as directly experienced. Their very wildness contains culture in their midst, but culture itself is wild in its intensity and force.

This is a lesson to be taken back into place. Despite the inherent wildness of all places (including urban places), there are no first-order places, no First Places that altogether withstand cultural pervasion and specification. But we can continue to endorse the Archytian Axiom of place's primacy—to be is still to be in place—provided only that we recognize that places are at once cultural and perceptual as well as tame and wild. And provided, too, that we realize that the place-world defies division into two distinct domains of Nature and Culture. If it is equally true that "everything is natural in us" and that "everything is cultural in us," this is so primarily within the concrete and complex arena of place, where the compenetration of the natural and the cultural arises in every experience and every event—and in every expression thereof.

VIII

I can only say, there we have been: but I cannot say where.
And I cannot say, how long, for that is to place it in time.

—T. S. Eliot, "Burnt Norton"

Place is not only compenetrative but also (as I have already hinted) deconstructive—deconstructive of oppositions that it brings and holds together within its own ambience. These oppositions include binary pairs of terms that have enjoyed hegemonic power in Western epistemology and metaphysics. I am thinking of such dichotomies as subject and object, self and other, formal and substantive, mind and body, inner and outer, perception and imagination (or memory), and nature and culture themselves. It is always from a particular place that a person, considered as a knowing "subject," seizes upon a world of things presumed to be "objects." The reduction of persons to subjects—and, still more extremely, to minds—and of things to objects could not occur anywhere other than in place. Yet to be fully in a place is to know—to know by direct acquaintance as well as by cultural habitus—that such a double reduction delivers only the shadowy simulacrum of the experiences we have in that place. (It is also to know that the mere representation of objects by minds, or of places by maps, is a further reduction.) Similarly, to be implaced is to know the hollowness of any strict distinction between what is inside one's mind or body and what is outside, or between what is perceived and what is remembered or imagined, or between what is natural and what is cultural. When viewed from the stance of place, these various divisions enter into a deconstructive meltdown—or more exactly, they are seen to have been nondiscontinuous to begin with: merged, "esemplastic" in Coleridge's word.

One very important dichotomy subject to the deconstructive power of place is that of space and time, which we have seen to be twin preoccupations of modern thinking in the West. But the phenomenological fact of the matter is that *space and time come together in place*. Indeed, they arise from the experience of place itself. Rather than being separate but equal cosmic parameters—as we believe when we say (with Leibniz) that space is "the order of co-existence" and time "the order of succession"—space and time are themselves coordinated and co-specified in the common matrix provided by place.[64] We realize the essential posteriority of space and time to place whenever we catch ourselves apprehending spatial relations or temporal occurrences *in a particular place*. Now I am in a room in Atlanta, and it is here that I am composing this essay. Not only the punctiform here and now, but also relations and occurrences of much more considerable scope collect around and in a single place. My quarters are an integral part of a house in a certain neighborhood and city, themselves set within an entire region called "the South," all of which have their own dense historicities as well as geographies. Even these extensive geo-histories I grasp from within my delimited room-place.[65]

Space and time, then, are found precisely in place—the very place that was declared by Newton to be merely "a part of space which a body takes up."[66] As we have seen, Newton considered space to be "absolute." But in a self-undermining aside, Newton himself wrote that "times and spaces are, as it were, the *places of themselves* as of all other things."[67] Not only do imperial space and time require recourse to lowly places in their very definition (rather than conversely), but also the status of space and time as equal but opposite terms is put into question by their common implacement. The binarist dogma stretching from Newton and Leibniz to Kant and Schopenhauer is undone by the basic perception that we experience space and time *together* in place—in the locus of a continuous "space-time" that is proclaimed alike in twentieth-century physics, philosophy, and anthropology.

To speak of space-time is to speak once more of event. For an event is at once spatial and temporal, indeed indissolubly both: its spatial qualities and relations happen at a particular time. But the happening itself occurs in a place that is equally particular. Thus "event" can be considered the spatiotemporalization of a place, and the way it happens as spatiotemporally specified. It is revealing that we speak of an event as having "a date and a place," replacing "space" by "place." This is in keeping with Heidegger's observation that "spaces receive their essential being from particular localities and not from 'space' itself."[68] Even if we cannot replace "date" by "place," we can observe that there is no such thing as a pure date, a sheer occurrence that occurs nowhere. Every date is an implaced happening. And since every date, every *time,* is indissociably linked with space, it is ultimately, or rather first of all, situated in a particular locality.

When we say that something "happens in space and time," this way of putting it not only reinforces the putative primacy (as well as the equally putative equiprimordiality) of space and time but also fosters the impression that for something to happen it must occur at a precise point or moment. Punctiformity is the very basis of specification by calendars, clocks, and maps and is thus a matter of "simple location," in Whitehead's term for isolated punctate positions in space and time.[69] The poet, along with the ordinary person, knows better: to say "there we have been" is not the same thing as to say precisely "where" we have been in geographical space, and if we are to express the duration of an event we "cannot say, how long, for that is to place it in time." In the modern Western era, to place in time or in space is ultimately to situate in site, that is, on a planiform surface of point-moments. A site is an exsanguinated place—precisely the sort of scene in which space and time seem to triumph over place. But what if matters are the other way around? What if time, space, and their projections and reductions as sites are non-simply located *in places?* Then place would no longer be the mere occasion for happenings positioned in an infinitely capacious space and time. Place itself would be the happening, and space and time what it occasions, specifying them in determinate and measurable sites.

The "eventmental" character of places, their capacity for co-locating space and time (even as they deconstruct this very dyad), can be considered a final form of gathering. This form is not the gathering-out of particular persons and things in a configured place or region, or the in-gathering effected by the body as the crux of nature and culture, but a still more general and pervasive gathering-with that occurs by virtue of the very power of implacement to bring space and time together in the event. Such comprehensive gathering is the turning point of space and time, the pivot where space and time conjoin in place. Just as this most inclusive and momentous gathering is the undermining of space and time construed as independent and preexisting dimensions, it is also the basis for any theory of space and time taken as absolute or relative, simultaneous or successive, intuitive or conceptual. The deconstruction of space and time by place clears the way for their conjoint reconstruction. But the two dimensions remain, first and last, dimensions of place, and they are experienced and expressed *in place by the event of place.*[70]

IX

As native concepts and beliefs find external purchase on
specific features of the local topography, the entire landscape seems to
acquire a crisp new dimension that moves it more surely
into view. . . . In native discourse, the local landscape
falls neatly and repeatedly into places.

—Keith Basso, "'Speaking with Names':
Language and Landscape among the Western Apache"

The gathering power of place works in many ways and at many levels. At the mundane level of everyday life, we are continually confronted with circumstances in which places provide the scene for action and thought, feeling and expression. Think only of where you are as you read these words: the place you are in right now actively supports (or at least allows for) the act of reading this text. Just as I write these words in my Atlanta room, you read them in yours— somewhere. Of course, I could write in a different place and you could read in another place. But the loci you and I are in nevertheless influence, sometimes quite considerably, overt actions such as reading and writing, and they influence still more what Malinowski called "the imponderabilia of actual life," such things as emotional tonality, degree of impatience, the understanding of a text, relations with consociates, and so forth.[71]

If this is true of our immediate locus—of what Husserl called the "near sphere"—it is just as true of more generous placial units such as the house we inhabit or the building in which we work.[72] Both Bachelard and Heidegger insist that it is in dwellings that we are most acutely sensitive to the effects of places upon our lives. Their "intimate immensity" allows them to condense the duration and historicity of inhabitation in one architecturally structured place.[73] What happens in such "domestic space" is an event in the sense discussed in the last section. Equally eventful, however, are the journeys we take between the dwellings in which we reside, for we also dwell in the intermediate places, the *interplaces*, of travel—places that, even when briefly visited or merely traversed, are never uneventful, never not full of spatiotemporal specificities that reflect particular modes and moods of implacement. Even on the hoof, we remain in place. We are never anywhere, anywhen, but in place.

Midway between staying at home and making a journey is the arena of *ceremonial action*. When ceremonial action concerns rites of passage (a term redolent with the idea of "the passing of time"), however, it is all too tempting to consider this action a matter of sheer diachronic development—"stages on life's way," in Kierkegaard's timely phrase. Thus it is all the more striking that van Gennep, whose *Rites of Passage* was first published in 1909 (the same year in which Hertz's "The Pre-Eminence of the Right Hand" appeared), refused this temptation and insisted on describing the threefold process of separation, transition, and incorporation in resolutely spatial, or, more exactly, *placial,* terms. Van Gennep insisted, for example, that "territorial passage" provides the proper framework for an understanding of ritualized passage in the social sphere:

> The passage from one social position to another is identified with a *territorial passage,* such as the entrance into a village or a house, the movement from one room to another, or the crossing of streets and squares. This identification explains why the passage from one group to another is so often ritually expressed by passage under a portal, or by an "opening of the doors."[74]

Under the heading of territorial passage itself, van Gennep discusses such notions as frontiers, borders, crossroads, and landmarks. Most important of all, however, is the concept of threshold, in which movement from one place to another is effected. A threshold is the concrete inter-place of an important transition. Van Gennep emphasizes the particularity of the threshold; only as *this* place can it serve as the support for a rite of passage:

> The door is the boundary between the foreign and domestic worlds in the case of an ordinary dwelling, between the profane and sacred worlds in the case of a temple. Therefore to cross the threshold is to unite oneself with a new world. It is thus an important act in marriage, adoption, ordination, and funeral ceremonies.[75]

The very transition effected by passing through a threshold is inextricably place-bound, and its description requires an entire paraphernalia of place predicates (e.g., "boundary," "edge," and "zone").

But precisely at this critical juncture, van Gennep disappoints us. Ignoring the manifest place-situatedness of his own descriptions, he asserts that "the symbolic and *spatial area of transition* may be found in more or less pronounced form in all the ceremonies which accompany the passage from one social and magico-religious position to another," concluding that "the *spatial separation* of distinct groups is an aspect of social organization."[76] Here van Gennep, like Durkheim, relies on the language of space and spatiality as if it were the only alternative to talk of time and temporality. Van Gennep recognizes what Bourdieu calls a "theoretical space"—and this is a significant move beyond the temporocentrism implicit in the very idea of passage—but missing is an explicit acknowledgment of the concrete place-specific character of his own examples and primary terms of description. In company with so many other modern thinkers, van Gennep suffers from what Freud calls "the blindness of the seeing eye."[77] Place is there to be seen if only we have the vision to behold it.

A decisive step beyond van Gennep's is taken by Nancy Munn in her discerning analysis of *kula* exchange, a highly ritualistic action that, like a rite of passage, is subject to misconstrual from the start. In this case, however, the primary misprision has to do with space rather than with time: if "passage" leads us to think primarily of time, *kula* "exchange," especially in its inter-island form, tempts us to think mainly in terms of transactions across geographical space. As Munn demonstrates, nothing could be farther from the truth.

Although Munn's *The Fame of Gawa* opens with a cartographically accurate map of the Massim region of Papua New Guinea, her discussion of *kula* exchange soon posits a realm of intersubjective "spacetime" that is much closer to landscape than to geography. She shows that *kula* participants are indissolubly linked to local and extralocal places and to the pathways between them. Gawan acts of hospitality, for instance, "constitute a mode of spacetime formed through the dynamics of action (notably giving and traveling) *connecting persons and places.*"[78] Gifts of food (as well as other items of hospitality) occur in particular places of exchange, either on one's home island or on an island to which one has traveled by canoe. These gifts precede *kula* exchange proper and are the "dynamic base" of such exchange by virtue of ushering in the event of exchange itself, which takes place in an extensive area all too easily conceived in terms of objective space. But Munn rightly refuses this temptation:

> Although kula shell transactions also entail dyadic exchange units [i.e., as in hospitality relations] . . . these transactions are not restricted exchanges or closed spacetimes. The shells that the two men transact travel beyond them. . . . The travels of kula shells create an emergent spacetime of their own that transcends that of specific, immediate transactions. This spacetime may be thought of as that of circulation.[79]

Implicit here is a distinction between what I have called "place proper"— instanced in the concrete transactions of hospitality and shell exchange—and "region" (i.e., a collocation of internally related places), in which the defining unit is that of the *kula* shell in its circulatory journey. At every stage of this journey, the shell requires new transactions to relay it. Each such transaction can be said to constitute a spacetime and not merely to fit into an already existing framework of space and time. The framework is created and recreated with each successive transaction.[80]

Perhaps the most persuasive instance of such a constitution of space-time is the construction and launching of the canoes that are requisite to *kula* exchange while also being objects of a special exchange themselves. To build canoes is both to engage in a specific spatiotemporal event of making—a bodily action calling for a particular place of construction—and to facilitate the reaching of other islands by a specific pathway (*keda*) between them. No wonder the launching of such canoes is a major event: "The canoe is finally launched," writes Malinowski, "after the long series of mingled work and ceremony, technical effort and magical rite."[81] This series of events is itself a rite of passage in which (as Munn observes) "transition takes place across spatiotemporal zones" as wood is located and stowed above the beach, then made into finished vessels that are launched into the sea. The beach is a threshold and as such has many "medial qualities," above all its location as if between island and ocean.[82]

Canoes thus connect one set of liminal rituals, intra-island (i.e., what happens in a given place), with another set, specifically inter-island (*kula* and canoe exchange proper, i.e., what happens between places in a region). In the end, both sorts of rituals are bound to place, whether to one and the same place or to different places connected by a sea route. In all these places, space and time combine forces. The sea voyage itself, adds Malinowski, "is not done on the spur of the moment, but happens periodically, at dates settled in advance, and it is carried on along definite trade routes, which must lead to fixed trysting places."[83] Here space (in the form of "definite trade routes") and time (in terms of periodical journeys) come together in place—in places of exchange connected by regional pathways—just as space and time combine in the initial making of canoes. Place and region gather space and time in emergent events of construction and exchange.

For this gathering to happen, the place and region in which it occurs must possess a property alluded to earlier in this essay: porosity of boundaries. An important aspect of being in a place or region is that one is not limited altogether by determinate borders (i.e., legal limits) or perimeters (i.e., those established by geography). For a place or region to be an event, for it to involve the change and movement that are so characteristic of *kula* exchange, there must be permeable margins of transition. The permeability occurs in numerous forms. A beach, at the edge of the sea and subject to tidal encroachments, is certainly exemplary of a porous boundary, but even in a land-locked situation such as that of the Western Desert of Australia, places and regions can retain a remarkable permeability. As W. E. H. Stanner notes:

> The known facts of inter-group relations [in aboriginal Australia] simply do not sort with the idea of precise, rigid boundaries jealously upheld in all circumstances. And the idea that a region was cut up, as it were without remainder, into exclusive but contiguous descent-group estates, could not have sufficed for the dynamic aboriginal life we know to have existed. . . . The conception which most nearly accommodates the facts . . . is that of *spaced estates* with overlapping ranges, and, thus, *partially interpenetrative domains and life-spaces.*[84]

Distinct and impenetrable borders may belong to sites as legally and geographically controlled entities, and hence ultimately to "space," but they need not (and often do not) play a significant role in the experience and knowledge of places and regions—of "estates" and "ranges" in Stanner's nomenclature.[85]

Whether in the waters of the Massim region of Papua New Guinea or on the dry land of the Western Desert in Australia—or anywhere else where place and region, rather than position and site, are of determinative import—we find that porousness of boundaries is essential to place. A place could not gather bodies in the diverse spatiotemporal ways it does without the permeability of its own limits. The sieve-like character of places might well be regarded as another essential structure of place, one that could be called "elasticity." But I prefer to regard it as a corollary property of that perceptual structure earlier identified as "external horizon." For the very nature of such a horizon is to *open out* even as it encloses. It is intrinsic to perceptual fields to possess bleeding boundaries; the lack of such boundaries converts these fields to delimited and closed-off sites such as prison cells or jury boxes.

By returning to horizons we have come full circle, and we need only add that the horizons that form the perceptual basis of boundaries are themselves spatiotemporal in status. To be in a perceptual field is to be encompassed by edges that are neither strictly spatial—we cannot map a horizon (even if we can draw it)—nor strictly temporal: just when does a horizon happen? A given horizon is at once spatial and temporal, and it belongs to a field that is the perceptual scene of the place whose horizon it is. Once again, but now coming in from the margins, we discover that place includes space and time as part of its own generative power. Rather than being the minion of an absolute space and time, place is in charge of their shared matrix.

X

The old meaning of the word "end" means the same as place:
"from one end to the other" means: from one place to the other. The end
of philosophy is the place, that place in which the whole of philosophy's
history is gathered in its most extreme possibility.

—Heidegger, "The End of Philosophy and the Task of Thinking"

I started with an uneasiness occasioned by recent anthropological treatments of place as something supposedly made up from space—something factitious carved out of space or superimposed on space (in the end, it doesn't matter which, given the unquestioned premise of space's primacy). From there, a consideration of the perceptual basis of being-in-place revealed that human beings are implaced *ab origine,* thanks to the presence of depths and horizons in the perceptual field and thanks also to the cores of sense that anchor this same field. The world comes bedecked in places; it is a place-world to begin with.

It was precisely the resonance of "to begin with" that then led me to reflect on the kind of universality possessed by place. Rejecting the standard choice between formal and substantive universals—as well as the related and equally standard choice between a priori and empirical universals—I explored the idea

of a specifically regional universal that is concrete-cum-relational and that operates laterally, across cases and not above or under them. Such a universal, which
could also be called a "general," is metaphysically neutral in that its instantiation
is directly reflective of the particular entities in a given place and their mode of
configuration. The instantiation itself occurs by means of essential structures
that pervade places as we know them. I singled out two structures of special
pertinence: the lived body's active ingredience in implacement (i.e., getting
into, staying in, and moving between places) and the gathering power of place
itself. Gathering is an event, and an exploration of place-as-event allowed us to
see how places, far from being inert and static sites, are themselves continually
changing in accordance with their own proper dynamism. Places are at once
elastic—for example, in regard to their outer edges and internal paths—and yet
sufficiently coherent to be considered as the same (hence to be remembered,
returned to, etc.) as well as to be classified as places of certain types (e.g., home
place, workplace, visiting place).

Moreover, the eventful potency of places includes their cultural specificity.
Time and history, the diachronic media of culture, are so deeply inscribed in
places as to be inseparable from them—as inseparable as the bodies that sustain
these same places and carry the culture located in them. But inseparability and
inscription are not tantamount to exhaustion; a factor of brute being, concealed
within the locative phrase "this-here," always accrues to a given place, rendering it wild in its very idiolocality, and wild as well in its most highly cultured
manifestations.

On this basis I was able to draw the heretical inference that space and time
are contained in places rather than places in them. Whether we are concerned
with dwelling places or places on a journey, with places in a landscape or in a
story (or in a story itself indissociable from a landscape), we witness a concrete
topo-logic, an experiential topology, in which time and space are operative in
places and are not autonomous presences or spheres of their own. Proceeding
in this direction, we arrived at the opposite side of the mountain of Western
modernity, which had assumed (and often still assumes, at the level of "common
sense") that time and space, in their impassive absoluteness, are prior to place.
Instead, as Archytas had foretold, place is prior to all things—even if the very
idea of priority needs to be bracketed along with the binary logic so effectively
deconstructed by place itself.

Something else to be garnered from our considerations is that if we are to
take the idea of local knowledge seriously, we have to rethink both "locality" and
"knowledge." "Locality" must be rethought in terms of, first, the triple distinction between position, place, and region; second, the idea of porous boundaries;
and third, the role of the lived body as the mediatrix between enculturation and
implacement—their localizing agent, as it were. Above all, what is local must be
allowed to take the lead, in keeping with the Archytian Axiom: place sets the
pace with regard to its configurative arrangements, its landscape logic, its per-

ceptual peculiarities, its regional universality, and its metaphysical neutrality. By the same token, "knowledge" needs to be reconstrued as specifically placial, as a matter of acquaintance with places, knowing them by means of our knowing bodies. Such knowledge—neither propositional nor systematic, and not classifiable as simply subjective or objective, natural or cultural—is knowledge appropriate to the particularities of places in keeping with their felt properties and cultural specificities. It entails an understanding of places, where "understanding" is taken literally as standing under the ample aegis of place (and pointedly not under the protective precision of concepts).

Merleau-Ponty suggests that the anthropologist has "a new organ of understanding at his disposal."[86] Is this organ not an understanding of *place*? After all, the ethnographer stands in the field and takes note of the places he or she is in, getting into what is going on in their midst. The ensuing understanding reflects the reciprocity of body and place—and of both with culture—that is as descriptive of the experience of the anthropologist as of the native. It also reflects both parties' grasp of a concrete universality, a generality immanent in place thanks to the lateral homologies and sidewise resemblances between things and peoples in places. The understanding of place activates universals that are as impure as they are singular.

Local knowledge, then, comes down to an intimate understanding of what is generally true in the locally obvious; it concerns what is true about place in general as manifested *in this place*. Standing in this place thanks to the absolute here of my body, I understand what is true of other places over *there* precisely because of what I comprehend to be the case for this place under and around me. This does not mean that I understand what is true of all places, but my grasp of one place does allow me to grasp what holds, for the most part, in other places of the same region. My ongoing understanding of surrounding and like places is characterized by essential structures manifested in my own local place and illuminating other places as well. That anything like this induction of place is possible exhibits place's special power to embrace and support even as it bounds and locates.

To insist thus on the considerable outreach of local knowledge in this manner is necessarily to argue against what might be called, modifying a celebrated phrase of Whitehead's, the Fallacy of Misplaced Abstractness. By this is meant the tendency to posit a plane of abstract perfection and purity onto which complexities and dirty details come crowding. The fallacy consists in believing the plane to be a priori and settled, the complications a posteriori and changing. The abstractness of this plane is misplaced in that its status as prior is the reverse of what actually obtains: the plane is itself an abstraction from what is concrete, that is, from that which is supposedly only secondary and epiphenomenal and yet is in fact phenomenally given as primary.

A conspicuous instance of this fallacy is the presumption that space furnishes just such a perfected plane, in relation to which mere places are nothing but parts or constructs, decorations, or projections. Here the misplacement is of place itself, which is shoved into a minority position (or, which comes to the same thing, reduced to position per se). Time also exemplifies the fallacy, especially when it is conceived (as it was by Locke) as "the length of one straight line, extended in infinitum."[87] In both cases, it is a matter of showing that the true concreteness belongs to place—plain old place, the place under our feet and around our eyes and in our ears.

It is undeniable that the concreteness of place has its own mode of abstractness: that is, in its relationality (there is never a single place existing in utter isolation) and in its inherent regionality (whereby a plurality of places are grouped together). We can admit such relating and regioning and still avert the danger of a misplaced abstractness proper to place itself. This danger consists in making place, or its components, into a new plane of perfection, a new tabula rasa, onto which all that matters in human experience comes to be written. Spatiocentrism and temporocentrism would then give way to an equally spurious topocentrism!

In order to prevent this mere reversal of priority, I have maintained that place is no empty substratum to which cultural predicates come to be attached; it is an already plenary presence permeated with culturally constituted institutions and practices. As the basis of collective as well as individual habitus, these institutions and practices pervade the bodies of sensing subjects in a given place as well as the gathering power of the place itself: even when prediscursively given (and prereflectively experienced), neither body nor place is precultural. Just as place invades space from the bottom up, so culture penetrates place from the top down, as it were. But only *as it were,* for the very directionalities of "up" and "down" are legacies of bodily orientation in places (as Kant reminds us) and are elicited by powers inherent in places themselves (as Aristotle affirms). It would be more accurate to say simply, and in conclusion, that as places gather bodies in their midst in deeply enculturated ways, so cultures conjoin bodies in concrete circumstances of implacement.

Smooth Spaces and Rough-Edged Places:
The Hidden History of Place

Every body must be in a place.

—Philoponus, in *Aristotelis Physicorum:*
Libros Quinque Posteriores Commentaria

If there is no place thought about,
there is no thought at all—no intelligible
proposition will have been entertained.

—Gareth Evans, *The Varieties of Reference*

I

TIME IS ONE; space is two—at least two. Time comes always already unified, one time. Thus we say, "What time is it now?" and not "Which time is it now?" We do not ask, "What space is it?" Yet we might ask: "Which space are we in?" (and we certainly do ask "Which place am I in?"). Any supposed symmetry of time and space is skewed from the start.

If time is self-consolidating—constantly gathering itself together in coherent units such as years or hours or semesters or seasons—space is self-proliferating. Take, for example, the dimensionality of space. One dimension in space is represented by a point or a line, whose radically reduced format mocks the extensiveness of cosmic space. Two dimensions, as in a plane figure, also falls far short of our sense that space spreads out indefinitely far beyond the perceiving subject. Only with three dimensions do we begin to approach an adequation between the structure and the sense of space. For then the subject is surrounded by something sufficiently roomy in which to live and move. (English "room" and German *Raum* are distant linguistic cousins.) Indeed, as Aristotle, Kant, and Merleau-Ponty all remark, the three-dimensionality of space directly reflects our bodily state, that is, the fact that because we are upright beings, three perpendicular planes implicitly meet and intersect in us. Even here, proliferation abounds: our bilateral symmetry means that each dimension is doubled: one vertical plane bifurcates into "up" and "down," the other vertical plane into "front" and "back," and the horizontal plane into "right" and "left." Thus subject-centered space is triple, only to be redoubled. Further, if we think of spatiality not as body-based but as locatory—as determined by landmarks and other locales in the environment—the proliferation is more striking still. There are the four cardinal directions, which themselves split easily into the thirty-two points of a compass. Nor need we be so arithmetically well-rounded. Even apart from fancy mathematical models of *n*-dimensional space, and recent techno- logical instantiations of virtual space, there is no end to the number or ways in which we can be oriented in space—in accordance with what Deleuze and Guattari call "the variability, the polyvocity of directions" by which we can move in any given spatial scene.[1] Beyond (or rather underlying) direction, however, is *place*. Heidegger remarks that "space has been split up into places."[2] The fact is that we continually find ourselves immersed in a multiplex spatial network whose nodal points are supplied by particular places. If space is infinitely large, place is indefinitely many.

This suggests that the ultimate source of spatial self-proliferation is not the body or the way the world is but the placialization of space itself. If so, the dis- tinction between space and place is not derivative but generative. That is why I began by saying that "space is two—at least two." Space is a doublet composed of itself (whatever that is) and place.

You may well respond: time, too, is always different, not the same as it was even a moment ago, indeed never the same as itself, self-split at its origin (as Derrida might put it), while space abides through the before and after of time. If I pitch a tent on a mountain in northern Maine just as the sun is going down, night comes on, bringing with it an ever-changing array of nocturnal sounds and sights, the scene never exactly alike from moment to moment. I fall asleep eventually in this evanescent world, and when I awaken in the morning I find myself reassuringly in the same circumambient landscape—the same "space." Here space seems permanent and time fleeting. Is it not time that is the dis- persive element? Time qua change "disperses subsistence," says Aristotle in the *Physics,* while place in contrast is said merely to "contain" things.[3]

Yet even if time is thus ever self-differing, the very medium of change, this does not mean that there is more than one kind of time operative in any given cir- cumstance. When we ask, "What is today's date?" and (more generally), "What time is it?" we are not asking about which of several sorts of time now obtains. Aristotle himself remarks that "time is everywhere the same."[4] Even when one distinguishes between a felt or "phenomenological" time and an "objective" time—as do Bergson, James, and Husserl—one will manage, sooner or later, to reunify these times so as to obviate incoherence. We witness such reunification, for example, in Husserl's celebrated "time diagram," which maps objective time (as represented by successive points on a horizontal line) onto experienced or durational time, in the form of vertical and diagonal lines stemming from the first line. Even the three main modes of time we call "past," "present," and "future" are finally aspects of one temporal sweep, one continuous display of time, however jarring their juxtaposition may be in a given case. Every time we feel time's passing or coming, we cannot help but think of the coming or passing as parts of one encompassing time. Doubtless this is why Kant argued in the Transcendental Aesthetic that time, not space, is the truly universal form of intuition, within which all appearances, inner and outer alike, are forcibly included. It would be altogether Kantian to say that the *unio mentalis* is effected by an *unio temporalis*. In time, as in mind, the *disjunta membra* of our experience come together. The vanishing of moments in temporal succession proves thus to be only one aspect of the larger picture of time: as Kant reminds us, the schema of succession is flanked by those of permanence and coexistence, both of which are totalizing in their distinctly different ways.

Space, of course, is also totalizing—which is why Kant paired it with time in the Aesthetic (as a coordinate form of intuition) and in the Antinomies of Pure Reason (where the totalizing tendencies of both create insuperable metaphysical problems). However, we do not need Kant to tell us of the encompassingness of space: camping in Maine, I was reassuringly surrounded by the spatial spread of the open landscape at all times. Yet as I lingered in that landscape, I noticed something else happening, something that did not belong simply to the order of space as sheer extension. This was my momentary camp itself, the place I created on the modest mountain where I pitched my tent, built a fire, talked with friends, and gazed out onto the landscape itself. This place was not just an aspect or part of the total space of the situation—even if it is true that it was located in that world-space. (On a topographic map, my camp would certainly have a precise position, but this position in cartographic space does not begin to capture, much less exhaust, my sense of being in a particular mountain-place.) The place was unique: I could pitch the same tent, talk with the same fellow campers, and even (perhaps) have the same thoughts, but if all this occurred on a neighboring and even quite similar mountain, the place would be quite different. Further, it would be different even if the sense of surrounding space stayed much the same. Thus we are back to the divergence between space and place, that puzzling doublet.

To mark this divergence, many languages—certainly most European languages—distinguish between "place" and "space" (for example, *locus* versus *spatium, lieu* or *endroit* versus *espace, luogo* versus *spazio, Platz* or *Ort* versus *Raum,* and so on). These same languages do not make a comparably decisive distinction between two senses or types of time. We have to strain words to talk consistently of a difference between, say, "temporality" and "time" or "duration" and "time" (in Heidegger's and Bergson's terms, respectively). Philosophers may remark the difference, but common sense and ordinary experience are largely oblivious of it. Time insists on its own oneness, whereas space tends toward twoness in its disparity from place, its fateful other.

II

The difference between space and place is one of the best-kept secrets in philosophy. Above all in modern Western philosophy, where the very distinction came to be questioned and then discredited: one way of understanding modernity, as I shall suggest, is by its very neglect of this distinction. The ancient world, however, knew otherwise—knew better. Indeed, the premodern and the postmodern join forces in a common recognition of the importance of place as something essentially other than space, something one cannot afford to ignore in its very difference from space.

Let me only remind you that Plato in the *Timaeus* draws on the difference between *chora* and *topos*. Conventionally translated as "land," "area," or "space," *chora* is the realm of Necessity, *ananke*, and is said to be "the Receptacle—as it were, the nurse—of all Becoming."[5] *Chora* is the ultimate "in which" (*en ho*) for changeable and changing entities, their "seat" (*hedra*): "by nature it is there as a matrix (*ekmageion*) for everything."[6] *Chora* is space-like in two ways: first, it provides "room" (that is, space to be occupied) for what becomes; second, it is homogeneous or neutral in constitution: "that which is to receive in itself all kinds must be free from all characters [of its own]."[7] This last characterization may well look ahead, as Heidegger intimates, to the modern idea of a homogeneous space,[8] but it also anticipates Deleuze and Guattari's conception of a "smooth space" composed of a nonhomogeneous "space of contact, of small tactile and manual actions"—typified in a steppe, a desert, or the open sea—a field of flux that resists the "striation" effected by parallel lines of force (especially those traced out by gravity).[9] Yet the very action of *chora*—its violent thrashing motion—has the effect of grouping the four elementary "kinds" or "powers" into four "regions" (*chorai*) within which particular "places" (*topoi*) arise:

> Because it was filled with powers that were neither alike nor evenly balanced, there was [at first] no equipoise in any region of it; but it was everywhere swayed unevenly and shaken by these things, and by its motion shook them in turn. And they, being thus moved, were perpetually being separated and carried in different directions; just as when things are shaken and winnowed by means of winnowing baskets and other instruments for cleaning corn, the dense and heavy things go one way, while the rare and light are carried to another place and settle there.[10]

"Place" in the last sentence translates *topos*, that is, the settled spot where bodies (*somata*) come to reside once they have been thrown together with like bodies in the same region.

What is the end of the tale for Plato—the sedate outcome of a tumultuous cosmogony—is the beginning of the story for Aristotle, who makes *topos* and not *chora* his primary concern. In book 4 of his *Physics,* Aristotle, commenting on Plato, identifies *chora* with *hule,* and makes the revealing claim that in his esoteric teachings, Plato "declared that place and space were the same thing."[11] The claim reveals more about Aristotle than about Plato, since it betrays Aristotle's own belief that *chora* does not precede or encompass *topos.* The same claim also looks forward to the characteristically modern notion that place and space differ from each other only trivially. However, while the modernists want to dissolve place into space, Aristotle attempts to reduce space to place. What, then, does Aristotle mean by "place"?

The Stagirite defines place as "the first unchangeable limit of that which surrounds."[12] For Aristotle, the exemplary case of place is that of a stationary vessel that contains a combination of air and water. "Just as the vessel is a place which can be carried around, so place is a vessel which cannot be moved about."[13] Notice that this delimited and delimiting idea of place brings with it the supposition that place is primarily locatory and that what it locates is a physical thing: "Not everything that is, is in a place, but [only] changeable body."[14] Place is where a thing is—where the locative adverb "where" (*pou*) has the status of a universal category. However, beyond locating (or, more exactly, as locating), place is something surrounding, with the result that a given place is coextensive with what it contains: its inner surface and the outer surface of the thing contained are strictly contiguous: "The limits are together with what is limited."[15] Just here problems arise—problems that were to preoccupy commentators on Aristotle for at least a millennium, and still do. For example, on Aristotle's account the place of a boat moored in a river will continually change since the surface of the water in immediate contact with the boat will alter constantly as the water flows past the boat. However, if the appropriate surrounder is itself located in something "unchangeable," such as the solid bank of the river, then two boats equidistant from the same bank will occupy the same place despite being in different locations in the water itself.[16]

In my view, these problems, all of them stemming from Aristotle's constrictive sense of place as locating and (especially) surrounding, are more grave than those arising from his doctrine of "natural place," according to which "each thing moves to its own place."[17] On closer inspection, it becomes clear that this controversial doctrine commits Aristotle to a particular physicalist model only of region, not of place proper.

> [T]he locomotions of the natural simple bodies (such as fire and earth and the like) not only show that place is something but also that it has some power, since each body, if not impeded moves to its own place, some above and some below. These are the parts and kinds of place: above, below, and the rest of the six dimensions

[that is, three times two] . . . in nature each is distinct and separate. "Above" is not anything you like, but where fire, and what is light move [to]. Likewise, "below" is not anything you like, but where heavy and earth-like things move [to].[18]

"Above" and "below" as just invoked are not simply places, much less positions, but whole territories to which "natural simple bodies" belong by physical birthright, as it were. This shows in turn that place "has some power" (*echei tina dunamin*) and is "not just relative to us."[19] Relative to us—that is, to our body as pivot—are position and direction, but Aristotle is clear that these latter do not exhaust implacement; he says expressly that places "differ not by position alone but in power too."[20] This last observation is prescient: it foresees the difference between locatory and subject-centered spatiality with which recent work in linguistics and philosophy has been concerned.[21] It is also remarkable for setting the terms for the debate about place that was to ensue in Western philosophy during the next two thousand years.

Regarding this debate—which stretches from Strato and the Stoics to Patrizi and Gassendi—two general remarks are in order. First, it was Aristotle's unswerving commitment to the power of place that upheld a conversation that is surely one of the most concerted and fruitful in the history of philosophy: had place not been accorded such *dunamis,* it would not have been worth the effort of so much discussion concerning its exact nature. Second, despite its considerable dynamism, place gradually lost out to space in the course of the two millennia in question. For many ancient Greeks, what I like to call the Archytian Axiom was taken to be unquestionably true: to be is to be in place; conversely, to be without place is not to be.[22] Plato and Aristotle alike, their differences concerning place versus space notwithstanding, both cite versions of this axiom—as do such disparate thinkers as Gorgias and Zeno. Aristotle's endorsement is most to the point: "Everyone supposes that things that are are somewhere, because what is not is nowhere—where for instance is a goat-stag or a sphinx?"[23] However, beginning with Philoponus, who in the sixth century AD posited an empty spatial extension, and continuing through Crescas and Bradwardine (both of whom insisted, seven centuries later, on the spatial infinity of God), we reach a point in the Renaissance when a quite different axiom captivated philosophical (as well as scientific and theological) minds: to be is now to be *in space,* where "space" means something nonlocal and nonparticular, something having little to do with close containment and everything to do with an outright infinity. Koyré has aptly described this radical transformation of thought, this triumph of space over place, as a movement "from the closed world to the infinite universe."[24]

III

Before coming to the modern epoch itself, I want to dwell for a moment on a fascinating but neglected chapter of the ancient era in its Hellenistic and more particularly its Neoplatonic course. I shall single out only two figures from a galaxy of philosophers who devoted themselves to thinking about place and space after Aristotle: Iamblichus and Philoponus. Both were critics and creative transformers of Aristotle. Iamblichus (who lived in the fourth century AD and was an important influence on seventeenth-century views of space)[25] concedes the importance of the surrounding limit in the determination of place, but he refuses to conceive of this limit as a mere "surface" (*epiphaneia*) that is geometrically structured. Instead, place should be conceived in terms of "boundary" (*horos*), which is an active power—so active that it is even said to be "the primary cause (*archegos*)" of bodies.[26] However, for it to be such a cause, that is, a cause both as defining a body and as the source of the body's existence,[27] place qua boundary has to be more than corporeal, given Iamblichus's premise (doubtless derived from Plotinus) that "everywhere the incorporeal reality ranks as prior to the corporeal one. Thus place, being incorporeal, is superior to the things that exist in it."[28] Precisely as incorporeal, the power of place consists in more than its encompassingness. In one of the most extraordinary statements of placial power ever made in the West, Iamblichus proclaims that this power consists in "[s]ustaining and supporting bodies, raising up the falling ones and gathering together the scattered ones, filling them up as well as encompassing them from every side."[29]

"Sustaining and supporting," as well as "raising up," refer to the way that a given place holds bodies in certain postures, forestalling their falling freely in space, while "gathering together" suggests that these postures are held in a single coherent pattern in relation to each other. "Filling up," on the other hand, implies that place, far from being a mere "termination" or "last extremity" of bodies—or even their "common limit"—insinuates itself into these very bodies and acts as their dynamic indwelling agent: "Regarded thus, place will not only encompass bodies from outside, but will fill them totally with a power which raises them up."[30] Moreover, such an indwelling and upholding power applies to nonmaterial as well as to material things—to anything that is "contained" in anything else.[31] With the mention of "contained" (*periechomenen*), we have come full cycle from an Aristotelian starting-point. "Containment" remains a sine qua non for being in place; yet now it is only a minimal criterion, inasmuch as true placial power is found in actions of sustaining and upholding, gathering and filling things. Rather than things defining places—as occurs on any strict container model, since the container has to take its cue from the contained— places empower things from (and as) their boundaries.

If Iamblichus looks back to Aristotle—only to radically revise him—Philoponus looks forward to the modern age, parlaying Plato into the present. If Plato's conception of *chora* can be considered the precursor of modernist notions of space, this is even more true of Philoponus's treatment of the same term. Take, for instance, Philoponus's claim that "we do not maintain that extension is a body, but that it is the room of a body and [is] only empty dimensions without any substance and matter [to fill it up]."[32] As the room of a body (*chora somatos*), place or space cannot be defined, much less confined, by body alone. However, rather than being a power that connects and fills bodies—it is even said to be without any power of its own[33]—*chora* is held to be a pure dimensional entity, a matter of "only empty dimensions" (*diastaseis monas kenas*). Indeed, Philoponus's most telling critique of Aristotle's surrounder view is that surface qua surface is two-dimensional, while bodies in place are three-dimensional. Thus place (*topos*) is said to be "cubic in the sense of three-dimensionally extended (*triche diastaton*)."[34]

Philoponus, the discoverer of impetus in physics, is parachronistically modern in two ways when it comes to matters of place and space. First, *diastaseis,* the word for "dimension," is closely akin to *diastema,* Greek for "interval" or "extension," and in their affinity both terms anticipate Descartes's insistence on the three-dimensional character of *res extensa:* to be extended is to be three-dimensional and vice versa. Second, the more Philoponus pursues the difference between "corporeal" and "spatial" extension—that is, the extension of a given body and that of the place or "room" in which that body is located—the more he envisions, contra Descartes, an open space that is at once empty and immense. Spatial extension is empty in the manner of a void: "There exists an extension different from the bodies which happen to be in it, a void (*kenon*) in its proper sense, and this is also precisely place."[35] Such a void, however, though in principle always present, is in fact always filled with bodies, resulting in a universe as plenary as Descartes and Aristotle (both fierce critics of the void) might have wished.[36] Spatial extension is also immense: Philoponus thus speaks of a "cosmic extension" (*to kosmikon diastema*) that is "the room and the place of the universe."[37] An extension that is coextensive with the universe (*to pan*)—which is what results from pushing the idea of spatial extension to its cosmological limit—is clearly heading toward the idea of a spatial infinity that knows no end. At least this is so once it is assumed that the universe itself is no closed whole (as it certainly still was for Aristotle) and has no effective limits. This idea was explored extensively by such medieval thinkers as Walter Burleigh and Richard of Middleton, and by such a Renaissance figure as Giordano Bruno, who drew out the full consequences of Philoponus's notion of a cosmically vast spatial extension. We do not have to wait for medieval theology or for Renaissance science, however, to appreciate the increasingly powerful attraction of an unlimited, indeed an undelimited, spatiality. The attraction, one could almost say the fatal attraction, is already evident in Philoponus.

In the allure of this burgeoning infinity, there is little room left for place. The slippery slope of its eventual demise has already been broached in the sixth century AD. It is especially telling that Philoponus lumps together the two terms *chora* and *topos* in the indifferent hendiadys "room and place," or "space and place," as if to signify that the struggle to keep these terms distinct from each other is no longer worth the candle. When Philoponus adds that the universe at large "does not have in itself any differences," this lack of differences (*diapho-rai*) entails that there are no intrinsic configurations within cosmical extension, thus nothing like particular places that possess an autonomy and power of their own.[38]

IV

A thousand years later and we find ourselves in the dense imbroglio of the seventeenth century. If I leap this far ahead,[39] it is largely due to my conviction that a late Neoplatonist such as Philoponus already espoused models verging on a distinctively modern idea of space as absolute and infinite. This idea is decidedly ancient in origin, despite the received wisdom that it is comparatively recent: received and revived, for example, by Michel Foucault, who considers the medieval conception of space to be restricted to "the space of implace-ment," to "a hierarchic ensemble of places" without any significant sense of infinite space.[40] Even Alexandre Koyré, otherwise such a sure-footed guide in these matters, intimates that only in the seventeenth century do we find the substitution for the conception of the world as a finite and well-ordered whole, in which the spatial structure embodied a hierarchy of perfection and value, of an indefinite or even infinite universe no longer united by natural subordination, but unified only by the identity of its ultimate and basic components and laws; and the replacement of the Aristotelian conception of space—a differentiated set of inner-worldly places—by that of Euclidean geometry (an essentially infinite and homogeneous extension) is from now on considered as identical with the real space of the world.[41]

However, all of the elements of this supposed seventeenth-century revolu-tion were already present long before "the century of Genius." Homogeneity is suggested by the neutrality of Platonic *chora,* and Euclidean geometry is actively at work in the Philoponean model of three-dimensional spatial extension, while infinity is at least implied in the cosmical expansion of the same extension. In short, space in its supposedly "modern" format has been around for much lon-ger than three centuries, and it is time to set the record straight.[42]

I am even prepared to argue that Descartes, that arch-demon of early mo-dernity, takes several steps back compared with Philoponus and his numerous medieval and Renaissance progeny. Not only does he equivocate concerning the existence of spatial infinity (preferring to speak of the indefinite instead), but he retains a remarkably Aristotelian conception of "external place" as "the surface immediately surrounding what is in the place."[43] As such a surface, external place encloses the "internal place" or volume of a physical body, delineating its exact size and shape. Thus we are taken right back to a physicalistic model of place. If internal place is equivalent to corporeal extension in the Philoponean sense, the "space" it occupies is tantamount to Philoponus's notion of spatial extension. Significantly, Descartes refuses to generalize such extension to the point of something "cosmic": at most it possesses a "generic unity" that allows different bodies of the same volume to occupy it.[44] On the familiar Cartesian formula, space is matter: there is no space without the matter that occupies it, and no matter that is not extended three-dimensionally as a volume in space. In its full characterization, however, *res extensa* comprehends not only the volume of physical bodies but also the positions of these bodies—which is to say, their places. For in the end Descartes ascribes position to place and volume to space:

> The difference between the terms "place" and "space" is that the former desig-
> nates more explicitly the position, as opposed to the size or shape [that is, the
> volume], while it is the size and shape that we are concentrating on when we talk
> of space. . . . When we say that a thing is in a given place, all we mean is that it oc-
> cupies such and such a position relative to other things; but when we go on to say
> that it fills up a given space or place, we mean in addition that it has precisely the
> size and shape of the space in question.[45]

This seemingly innocent remark—including its telltale expression "space or place"—harbors momentous consequences. For in singling out position as intrinsic to place (and thus as extrinsic to space qua volume), Descartes is departing from Aristotle and Philoponus and proposing something that will preoccupy the entire early modern period. This is the notion of what Whitehead calls "simple location," construed as "the very foundation of the seventeenth-century scheme of nature."[46] Simple location encompasses both place and space—in whatever acceptation these terms assume during this century—just as it bridges over the celebrated differences between absolutist and relativist views of space and time. According to the doctrine of simple location, any "bit of matter"—that is, any physical body—"is where it is, in a definite region of space, and throughout a definite finite duration of time, apart from any essential reference of the relations of that bit of matter to other regions of space and to other durations of time."[47] Put in the terms just discussed by Descartes, simple location is the view that position matters most in questions of place. A simple location is a position in a determinate region and thus a position relative to other occupants of that region—even if, as Whitehead stresses, that region itself is considered without reference to other regions. Others in the history of philosophy, most notably Theophrastus and Aquinas, had certainly noticed the crucial role of relative position in the determination of place. However, position as such began to become thematic, and not exceptional, only in the second half of the seventeenth century, that is, after the publication of *Principles of Philosophy* in 1644. Still in equipoise with volume in the *Principles,* position was soon to become an obsessive concern of thinkers as diverse as Locke and Newton and Leibniz.

John Locke thinks of place and space alike in terms of measurable distance: "[E]ach different distance is a different modification of space; and each idea of any different distance, or space, is a simple mode of this idea."[48] By compounding particular distances, we reach the idea of "immensity" or, more vividly put, "the undistinguishable inane of infinite space."[49] Yet Locke is no more committed to infinite space than is Descartes. His concern is with finite relations of distance between discrete positions in space. Thus his concept of place is "nothing else but [the] relative position of anything."[50] In comparison with relative position, the idea of volume or "capacity" is said to be "confused."[51] What matters is not extension as such—a term Locke attempts to avoid[52]—but the measurable aspects of extension, and these aspects all depend on determinate positions. So powerful is the idea of relative position that it comes to dominate what Locke has to say about both space and place. Although officially place is said to be "but a particular limited consideration" of space, in the end the determination of each is exactly the same: "as in simple space, we consider the relation of distance between any two bodies or points; so in our idea of place, we consider the relation of distance betwixt anything and any two or more points, which are considered as keeping the same distance one with another, and so considered as at rest."[53] The difference between space and place—a difference respected, even if continually contested, for two millennia in Western thought—begins to dissolve in the acidic solution of purely relational positions. In this important regard, Locke is more consummately modern than is Descartes.

Everyone knows that Newton considered space and time to be absolute entities, the "infinite sensoria" of God Himself. The absolutism is undoubtedly there, although it is likely to be more the mark of Gassendi and More than of Newton's own proclivities. A close look at the text of the *Mathematical Principles of Natural Philosophy,* published only shortly before Locke's *Essay,* shows that, despite the rhetoric of "absolute space," there is an undercurrent of relativism that brings the two Englishmen much closer than one might have guessed is possible. Even if Newton denies that place consists in "situation" and at least once defines place as a "a part of space which a body takes up"—the Cartesian notion of internal place so resolutely rejected by Locke—he describes "relative space" as "some movable dimension or measure of the absolute *spaces;* which our senses determine by its position to bodies."[54] By this last phrase, Newton means the simple locations of physical bodies in relation to each other. Indeed, "all places" are said to be defined "from the positions and distances of things from any body considered as immovable."[55] Not only is Newton extremely close to Locke in this last claim, but he espouses place-relativism even more fiercely than his compatriot by positing that "immovable places" are "those that, from infinity to infinity, do all retain the same given position one to another."[56] The physical universe itself, in other words, is composed of fixed places—"primary" or "absolute" places—a significant part of whose very absolutism consists in their unchanging relation to each other.[57] No wonder, then, that Whitehead can say that "simple location holds whether we look on a region of space-time as determined absolutely or relatively."[58]

Put otherwise, Kant's effort to contrast Newton and Leibniz as offering strictly incompatible models of space is misleading at the very least. Just as there is much more respect for placial and spatial relativism in Newton than Kant admits, so there is in Leibniz a lingering shadow of absolutism—as when Leibniz defines space as "that which comprehends all those places."[59] Nevertheless, the shadow is only a trace of the primary phenomenon of space conceived as "something merely (*purement*) relative,"[60] words that directly echo Locke. For space is officially defined as "an order of coexistences."[61] Such an order is interpreted as "situation or distance,"[62] where situation is equivalent to relative position or, more exactly, to sameness of place: "place is that, which is the same in different moments to different existent things, when their relations of co-existence with certain other existents, which are supposed to continue fixed from one of those moments to the other, agree entirely together."[63] Thus Leibniz can boast that "in order to explain what place is, I have been content to define what is the same place."[64] In making this move, Leibniz has accomplished two things: he has reduced place to relative position (for it is into the same relative position that "different existent things" are put) and he has conflated place with space. A sign of this conflation—the same we find in Philoponus and in Locke—is found in Leibniz's casual but concerted use of the same phrase so revealingly employed by Descartes as well, namely, "place and space."[65]

V

In the remainder of this essay, I want to address two major issues: first, the effect of the triumph of the relational view of place, including the effect of assimilating place to space; second, the consequences of this assimilation for the emergence of the "modern subject." In both cases, we shall be considering the larger stakes in a story that may have struck you so far as a mere matter of curiosity. Whatever intrinsic interest this story has, you may be asking yourself: fine, but so what? Let me try to say what this *what* amounts to, and in two stages.

First, to the degree that the relational view of place/space won out in the modern period, the West witnessed less the apotheosis of infinite space than the demise of place as an independent and viable concept. In large part, place was absorbed into space; insofar as it survived at all, it was in the denuded form that I shall call, for lack of a better term, "site." It is my view that, contra Koyré, the advent of the infinity of space was to begin with (and perhaps most enduringly) the creation of the late Neoplatonic period of Hellenistic philosophy. The idea of such infinity was available ever since Philoponus espoused a truly "cosmical extension." In this light, later and more celebrated thinkers such as Giordano Bruno and Nicolas of Cusa only pursued the idea to its bitter end—for instance, in the extreme notion that there is not just infinite space but an infinite number of worlds in such space. This latter was an idea for which Bruno was burned at the stake in 1600, suggesting that the seventeenth century opened with the effort to suppress infinite space. Leading thinkers of this century continued to dispute such space, especially insofar as it entailed the void, concerning which Locke and

Newton were supportive, and Descartes and Leibniz virulently opposed—their very variance on this issue exhibiting the uncertain destiny of infinite space during the century.

At the same time, and for many of the same reasons, the idea of place was beginning to disappear from philosophical and scientific treatment. Prominent minds of the time felt compelled to consider it—to give *some* account of it, however convoluted such an account might be. This is exactly what we witness in Descartes, whose discussion of "internal" versus "external" place is ultimately more confusing than clarifying. Place remains on Newton's list of master predicables: "time, space, place, and motion";[66] but his treatment of it raises more questions than it answers: above all, how is "place" finally distinct from "space" (both are ultimately immovable and static; both are homogeneous in constitution and isometric in measurability; and so on)? We have seen how both Locke and Leibniz are driven to assimilate place to space under the common heading of relative position or situation. Despite the lip service still paid to the term "place," by the end of the century (or, more exactly, by 1715–16, the date of the Leibniz-Clarke correspondence) in fact place has been indifferently merged with space and is no longer deemed worthy of separate treatment—as it still was for Gassendi and Descartes. When Pascal wrote that "the silence of these infinite *spaces* terrifies me,"[67] he was commenting as much on the increasing absence of place as an anchor from which to view such spaces as he was on any new cosmology or physics of space itself.

A century later, place is no longer discussed at all, much less missed, in philosophy. With the single exception of Kant's remarkable pre-Critical essay of 1768, "Concerning the Ultimate Ground of the Differentiation of Regions in Space," it is difficult to find any significant treatment of place from the death of Leibniz in 1716 until Bergson's Latin dissertation of 1888, whose topic is Aristotle's notion of place—as if Bergson realized that to take up the topic again one has to return to this most sober and thorough of ancient analyses. (The irony, of course, is that Bergson's *Time and Free Will*, published the very next year, asserts the primacy of durational time in human experience, thereby reinforcing the temporocentrism that had been regnant since the publication of *The Critique of Pure Reason* in 1781 and that reached an apogee in the evolutionism and historicism of the nineteenth century.)

My interpretation of this extraordinary circumstance—in which one of the indispensable topics of ancient, medieval, and even early modern philosophy came to be so deeply neglected—is twofold. First, "place" was dissolved into "space" as the dominant term of Eurocentric discourse; compared with the unbounded extent and even distribution of space, place came to seem merely parochial, a matter indeed of "particular limited consideration." The increasing ease with which the very word "place" became exchangeable with "space" is a leading symptom of this absorptive hegemony of the spatial world. Second, a progressive disenchantment with the idea of spatial infinity set in after the intoxication—and the terror—of late Renaissance and early modern vistas of "the undistinguishable inane of infinite space." If place was taken up into space (becoming merely "a part of space" in Newton's phrase again), its ghostly remnant was transmuted into site. By this latter term, I mean the leveled-down, emptied-out planiform residuum of place deprived of its actual and virtual "powers" (the very powers on which Aristotle and Iamblichus laid such eloquent stress).

The result is "striated space," defined by Deleuze and Guattari in *A Thousand Plateaus* as "the *relative global:* it is limited in its parts, which are assigned constant directions, are oriented in relation to one another, divisible by boundaries, and can be fit together."[68] I take Leibniz (influenced decisively by Locke) to be the primary culprit in this dire development: his notion of space as "something merely relative" led him to propose a new discipline of "site analysis" (*analysis situs,* a rigorous analytic-geometric discipline). If space and place are both utterly relational, a sheer order of coexisting points, then they will not retain any of the inherent properties ascribed to place by ancient and early modern philosophers: properties of encompassing, holding, sustaining, gathering, situating ("situation" in Leibniz does not situate at all; it merely positions in a nexus of relations). So as not to incriminate Leibniz unduly, let me simply say that he brought to its logical term the full implications of the stranglehold of simple location in which so many of his immediate predecessors were also ensnared. As Whitehead points out, the direct result of simple location in philosophy as in physics is the Fallacy of Misplaced Concreteness. For our purposes, this means a loss of the concrete particularity of place as well as the august absoluteness of infinite space—and the dissolution of both in the emptiness of sites.

The supremacy of site is the great theme of Foucault's examination of eighteenth-century disciplinary and institutional spaces. At the beginning of *The Birth of the Clinic,* he speaks of "the flat surface of perpetual simultaneity"[69] that characterizes medical perception and practice in the century of Enlightenment. This surface, traversed by the gaze of the examining physician, is at once homogeneous and segmented: homogeneous as the sheer display of a given medical syndrome, segmented as located in the actual physical body of a patient. The first is the basis for what Foucault calls the "configuration" of knowledge, the second for the "localization" of that same knowledge, these two terms being shrunken residues of space and place respectively. However, they are no more than relics of a previous discourse now overtaken by the discourse of site—the site, the exact location, of a disease in a particular part of the afflicted body. In *Discipline and Punish,* Foucault extends this *analysis situs*—no longer geometric but fully historical and political in his deft hands—to entire institutional settings, including the architecture of these settings. Now the surface of simultaneity (notice the presence of the Leibnizian criterion of coexistence surviving in Foucault's locution) is embodied in the structure of prisons, hospitals, factories, barracks, reformatories, asylums, and so on. Both in architectural plan and in disciplinary regime, each of these institutions combines seriality with carcerality.

In their built reality, each is in effect a line of cells, a set of segmented but contiguous and isomorphic subsites within the major site of the institution itself.

The result is a "space of domination" in which surveillance prevails at every possible panoptical point[70] and in which space and place alike (assuming these terms are still somehow distinguishable) are fixed: "it is a segmented, immobile, frozen space. Each individual is fixed in his place."[71] Everything in site-space is "constantly located."[72] What was a matter of simple location in seventeenth-century physics and philosophy has become the constant location of the "disciplinary individual," of "calculable man," in the course of the eighteenth century.[73] The act of "elementary location or partitioning" is tantamount to the suppression of active place and space—not to mention time, now strictly regulated by chronometric means in the workplace.[74] "The rule of functional sites" has taken over space, time, and place in a veritable "laboratory of power" whose aim is to bring about a rigid "location of bodies in space."[75] Thanks to the micro-practices of disciplinary power, such bodies become "docile bodies" in Foucault's memorable term[76]—bodies that exist only in sites and as a function of sites.[77] These bodies are disembodied precisely to the extent that they have become disimplaced.

A second thing that matters is the fate of the human subject in all this. If Foucault is right in claiming that the very idea of "Man," as *homo universalis,* is the creation of the eighteenth century, we can also say that long before twentieth-century deconstructions of the generically human, the plight of the subject was becoming extreme. Literally so: as Hannah Arendt remarks, alienation in the modern world consists in a "twofold flight from the earth into the universe and from the world into the self."[78] The modern subject finds himself caught between the extremes of universe and self—which is to say, between the infinite exteriority of the spatial universe and the infinitesimal interiority of the Cartesian cogito. "Nothing," says Pascal, "can fix the finite between the two infinites which enclose it and which escape its grasp."[79] In between is a vacuum, one of whose main expressions is a lack of the "public realm," to use Arendt's term for the primary privation of modernity. I would prefer to call this dearth of the public realm a lack of public place—an absence of concrete, perceptible locales that allow for bodily ingression as well as for shared historicity.

One absolute, entirely external, rejoins the other, wholly internal, calling for a place of certainty—which is to say, calling for place itself—in the face of the abyss opened up by the absence of place. Pascal's anguished outcries issue from the lack of any such place-certainty. The anguish, felt as intolerable, cannot last for long. This is doubtless why site (qua relative position) quickly emerged to paper over the abyss of no-place. The very attributes of sites—their homogeneity, isotropism, isometrism, unidirectionality, and monolinearity—conspired to act as tranquilizing forces in the generation of empty, planiform surfaces of simultaneity. Yet these same attributes can scarcely hide the fact that site, though the successor to place, is also its antithesis, its antidote, indeed its *pharmakon*—

the remedy that is the undoing. If infinite space can still be considered as place in extremis (that is, as the place of the universe as a whole: which is why Newton, concerned with just such a super-place, cannot dispense with the language of place altogether and can even call it "absolute"), site is no longer placelike in any significant respect. Further, if infinite space can be considered as place taken to its limit, site is the dismantling of place itself, its delimitation. Site is anti-place dancing on the abyss of no-place.

It is emblematic that Kant, who brings modernity to its most rigorous and systematic point, finally has no room for place in his conception of the human subject. By this I mean not just that the very term "place" drops out of his discourse regarding the subject (it remains only as "position" [*Stelle*] in his discussion of physical movement), but that the phenomenal self, the only self we can know, is radically unimplaced. The only effective unity of this self is the unity of consciousness, the "I think" that accompanies cognition. Beyond this frail and formal unity there is nothing more lasting to grasp—nothing substantial, nothing simple, nothing of the nature of an abiding self. Even "in inner intuition," says Kant, "there is nothing permanent, for the 'I' is merely the consciousness of my thought."[80] As the *Paralogisms of Pure Reason* make clear, we cannot know the human subject as a subject: "we do not have, and cannot have, any knowledge whatsoever of any such subject."[81] Of course, for Kant there is a deep subject, the noumenal self, but this "subject of our thoughts"[82] and of moral action is not the object of any possible knowledge. Nor is this transphenomenal subject situated in space or time—nor, a fortiori, in place. Indeed, it is doubtful whether the phenomenal self itself is so situated. In his discussion of the *Paralogisms,* Kant says that "neither space nor time, however, is to be found save in us."[83] If so, it would follow that the phenomenal subject is not in space and time (since they are in this subject) and thus that this same subject is also not in place.

With Kant, then, we reach an extremity that was already nascent in Descartes: the modern subject is a placeless subject. This subject, living only in the flattened-out sites it itself projects or constructs, cannot count on any abiding place in the world. The Fallacy of Misplaced Concreteness brings in its train the Fallacy of a Displaced Self—a purely phenomenal Self displaced into merely epiphenomenal Sites. The simple location of things ends in the positioning of human beings in a succession of sheer sites, thereby engendering docile bodies to occupy these sites. These bodies and sites are indifferent to one another and to the placeless selves they are supposed to subserve.

VI

We do not have to agree with Arendt that the primary kind of place lacking in modernity is the public scene of open political debate, the place of the agora and the agon.[84] Nevertheless it is difficult to deny some significant connection between the demise of place as a viable philosophical category and the rise of the alienated modern subject. The alienation first articulated by Pascal and then codified and rationalized by Kant is, I would suggest, an alienation from place at least as much as it is an alienation from abiding metaphysical and religious ideas and ideals. The turn to the "juridical" subject of human rights in the latter part of the eighteenth century was not accidentally inspired by John Locke's liberalism—the abstractness and universality of these rights are consonant with, indeed reflective of, the lack of concrete implacement for subjects who lived in the wake of Cromwell (and, more than a century later in France, of the Revolution). Just as Foucault argues that the putatively free individual of modern liberal society is a product of the disciplinary technology of power—"the 'Enlightenment,' which discovered the liberties, also invented the disciplines"[85]—so I would argue that the same individual is a creature of lack of location. The modern subject is radically unlocated, someone who does not know the difference between place and space, or even the difference between either of these and the sites to which he or she is confined in the pseudo-voluntarism that thinks that such a subject can go anyplace. However, belief in global nomadism is a delusion, since to be able to go anywhere is to be located nowhere.

In place of the false "global absolute" that is the proper realm of infinite, homogeneous, and striated space, we need to rediscover the "local absolute" that is the domain of true nomadism. The latter absolute is "an absolute that is manifested locally, and [it is] engendered in a series of local operations of varying orientations."[86] Local operations are actions taken in particular places, that is to say, in "smooth spaces," about which Deleuze and Guattari have this to say:

> Smooth space is precisely the space of the smallest deviation: therefore it has no homogeneity, except between infinitely proximate points, and the linking of proximities is effected independently of any determined path. . . . Smooth space is a field without conduits or channels. A field, a heterogeneous smooth space, is wedded to a very particular type of multiplicity: non-metric, acentered, rhizomatic multiplicities which occupy space without "counting" it and [which] can "only be explored by legwork."[87]

Such a distinctively postmodern space may offer a way of getting back into place—a place where the human subject can pursue once again a *vita activa* that has become smothered in the sites of an unimplaced modernity, and thereby regain an anchor in the known world. The names for such a renewed sense of place are various: "region" in late-Heideggerian thought, "enclave" in Lyotard's work, "earth" in the case of ecology, and so on. Of course, these same names are also ancient: "region" translates *chora*, "enclave" carries forward *chorion* and *choridion* (still other variations on Platonic *chora*), and "earth" is central to Aristotle's cosmology as well as to Iamblichus's imaginative extension of that cosmology.[88]

In this way, we might begin to realize that "topoanalysis" which Bachelard sketched in *The Poetics of Space*—and to which Heidegger's equally sketchy "Topology of Being" seems strangely to correspond.[89] We might also start to reinstate place itself within our lives, philosophical and otherwise, and to take these lives beyond liberties and disciplines, carceral cells and sheer series, docile bodies and equally docile minds. The untethered subject might begin to repossess itself in and around particular places. At the very least, to smooth spaces we need to add rough-edged places if the postmodern subject is to be reattached to the concrete life-world (or rather we should now say: "place-world"). To do so would be to reconnect place and space themselves as members of a new indefinite dyad that challenges the all-too-definite monads of time and site. It would be to tell a new tale of two cities—of place and space, neither of these being beholden to site or tied to time.

In starting, I said that time is one and space is two. We have seen, if mostly by indirection, how this is so—how time, for example, tends toward the hegemonic and monistic (most evidently in nineteenth-century thought) or simply the self-unified (in the transcendental subject, or even in the sense that in reading this essay you have been immersed in one continuous stretch of time). Space, on the other hand, is two—at least two, though not merely because there are in fact several sorts of space, such as hyperspaces or virtual spaces (these being the concern of the topologically minded mathematician). Rather, space forms a twosome, an uneven doublet, with place as its odd and incongruous other. The twoness is not that of two things, or even of two of a kind, but instead that of two quite variant kinds—which nevertheless coexist in all their disparity and cannot seem to do otherwise. Hence the ongoing saga of the uneasy alliances, the ambivalent togethernesses, of place and space.

Aristotle proclaimed that "the minimum number, strictly speaking, is two."[90] I have focused on the minimal dyad of place and space. If we were to find ourselves in a more generous mood, however, we might imagine an indefinite tetrad in which new notions of place, space, site, and time could reengage philosophical thought. From this tetrad would emerge differing (but not altogether different) ideas of what it means to be in a place, how it is to be encompassed by endless space, by what means sites can be reinstated in non-debilitating ways, and how time may appear otherwise. The sardonic unsettling effected by the postmodern period might thereby give way to the rethinking of terms whose continuing importance will be reaffirmed but whose effective significance will, at the same time, be radically altered in direction and force.

Notes

Preface

1. *Devastate* derives from Latin *vāstare*, to lay waste. *Vāstus* means "waste, desert, unoccupied land." *Văstus*, affiliated but not precisely the same word, means "void, empty, immense, extensive"; as a noun, it signifies "a vast or immense space." *Waste* and *vast* thereby meet in the composite word *devastate*.

2. "Le silence éternel de ces espaces infinis m'effraie" (Blaise Pascal, *Pensées*, ed. L. Lafuma [Paris: Editions de Luxembourg, 1951], fragment no. 201).

3. T. S. Eliot, "The Waste Land," sec. 1, ll. 60–64.

4. Cf. Aristotle, *De Anima*, 429a, 25–26: "Those who say, then, that the soul is a place of forms speak well." On place as container, see Aristotle, *Physics*, bk. 4. For Aristotle's critique of the Atomistic void, see *Physics*, bks. 6–9.

5. Friedrich Nietzsche, *A Genealogy of Morals*, Third Essay, sec. 28.

6. Hans Jonas, "To Move and to Feel: On the Animal Soul," *The Phenomenon of Life: Toward a Philosophical Biology* (Chicago: University of Chicago Press, 1966), p. 104. Jonas traces the immobility of plants to the photosynthesizing mechanisms of leaves and roots: "Possessing them, the plant is relieved of the necessity (as it is also deprived of the possibility) of movement" (p. 103). On the other hand, "the great secret of animal life lies precisely in the gap which it is able to maintain between immediate concern and mediate satisfaction, i.e., in the loss of immediacy corresponding to the gain in scope" (p. 102). Scope entails movement between places, and gap is the distance that such movement must traverse.

7. "Tout le malheur des hommes vient d'une seule chose, qui est de *ne savoir pas demeurer en repos dans une chambre*" (Pascal, *Pensées*, fragment no. 136; my italics).

8. On the concept of "biotope," or living place—in distinction from "biochore," or habitat—see H. Hediger, *Wild Animals in Captivity: An Outline of the Biology of Zoological Gardens*, trans. G. Sircom (New York: Dover, 1964), pp. 6ff. Hediger makes it clear that territory, strictly speaking, is defined by the social grouping of animals, especially by dominant members of a given group. For a treatment of human territoriality that builds on the earlier work of Konrad Lorenz, see Robert D. Sack, *Human Territoriality: Its Theory and History* (Cambridge: Cambridge University Press, 1986).

9. The *im-* of *implacement* stresses the action of getting in or into, and it carries connotations of *im*manence that are appropriate to the inhabitation of places.

10. That is true even of this present preface. Not only are you reading it *in* a given place, but it is itself a place: a textual place of sentences and propositions. Or more exactly, it is a pre-place, a place in advance of the place of the book. It pre-positions the book it opens; it is a pre-text for getting placed in this book. We could even say that it *takes the place* of the book it precedes. On the peculiarity of prefaces, see Jacques Derrida, "Outwork, prefacing," *Dissemination*, trans. Barbara Johnson (Chicago: University of Chicago Press, 1981), pp. 3–59.

11. On the "dromocratic society"—a society obsessed with speed—see Paul Virilio, *Speed and Politics,* trans. M. Pollizotti (New York: Semiotext[e], 1986).

12. See Georg W. F. Hegel, *The Philosophy of History,* trans. J. Sibree (New York: Dover, 1956), pp. 79–102; *The Philosophy of Right,* trans. T. M. Knox (Oxford: Oxford University Press, 1967), pp. 216ff.; and Fernand Braudel, *The Mediterranean and the Mediterranean World in the Age of Phillip II,* vols. 1 and 2. Maurice Merleau-Ponty writes that "there is no essence, no idea, that does not adhere to a domain of history and of geography" (*The Visible and the Invisible,* trans. A. Lingis [Evanston, Ill.: Northwestern University Press, 1968], p. 115; see also pp. 258–90). For an impassioned defense of the notion that particular places determine human character and destiny, see D. H. Lawrence, "The Spirit of Place," *The Symbolic Meaning* (New York: Viking, 1961), pp. 20ff.

13. I have in mind such essays of Heidegger's as "Conversation on a Country Path" (composed in 1944–45, first published in 1959, and translated into English by J. M. Anderson and E. H. Freund in *Discourse on Thinking* [New York: Harper, 1966], pp. 58–90) and "Building Dwelling Thinking" (first given as a talk in 1951; trans. A. Hofstadter in *Poetry, Language, Thought* [New York: Harper, 1971], pp. 145–61). The first essay treats "region" (*Gegend*), while the second singles out "location" (*Ort*). "The Origin of the Work of Art" (first delivered in 1935), which I discuss in chap. 5, already concerns itself with the "place of conflict" (*Streitraum*) in which earth and world come into strife, but it does not concentrate on place as such. I have given a systematic treatment of Heidegger's idea of place in "Heidegger In and Out of Place," in *Heidegger: A Centenary Appraisal* (Pittsburgh: Silverman Phenomenology Center, 1990), pp. 62–98.

14. See, for example, Yi-Fu Tuan, *Topophilia* (Englewood Cliffs, N.J.: Prentice-Hall, 1974), and *Space and Place* (Minneapolis: University of Minnesota Press, 1977); Edward Relph, *Place and Placelessness* (London: Pion, 1976); D. W. Meinig, ed., *The Interpretation of Ordinary Landscapes* (Oxford: Oxford University Press, 1979); David Seamon and Robert Mugerauer, eds., *Dwelling, Place, and Environment* (Dordrecht: Nijhoff, 1985; reissued by Columbia University Press, 1989); J. N. Entrikin, *The Betweenness of Place* (Baltimore: Johns Hopkins, 1991. Still earlier, J. B. Jackson, W. G. Hoskins, and David Lowenthal all pointed to the importance of landscape in the study of history, geography, and urban planning. Jackson's influential journal *Landscape* began publication in 1951; Hoskins's *Making of the English Landscape* was published in 1955; and Lowenthal's seminal article, "Geography, Experience, and Imagination: Towards a Geographical Epistemology," appeared in 1961.

15. For instance, Jonathan Z. Smith, *To Take Place: Toward Theory in Ritual* (Chicago: University of Chicago Press, 1987); E. V. Walter, *Placeways: A Theory of the Human Environment* (Chapel Hill: University of North Carolina Press, 1988); Stanley Tigerman, *The Architecture of Exile* (New York: Rizzoli, 1988); Tony Hiss, *The Experience of Place* (New York: Knopf, 1990); Christopher Lasch, *The True and Only Heaven: Progress and Its Critics* (New York: Norton, 1990); James F. Weiner, *The Empty Place: Poetry, Space, and Being among the Foi of Papua New Guinea* (Bloomington: Indiana University Press, 1991); Fred R. Myers, *Pintupi Country, Pintupi Self: Sentiment, Place, and Politics among Western Desert Aborigines* (Berkeley: University of California Press, 1991); Michael Jackson, *Paths toward a Clearing: Radical Empiricism and Ethnographic Inquiry* (Bloomington: Indiana University Press, 1989); Peggy Brook, ed., *Women, Rites and Sites: Aboriginal Women's Cultural Knowledge* (London: Allen & Unwin, 1989); and Daphne Spain, *Gendered Spaces* (Chapel Hill: University of North Carolina Press, 1992). Ethical aspects of place are treated in M. A. C. Otto's *Der Ort: Phänomenologische Variationen* (Freiburg/Munchen: Alber, 1992).

16. See Gaston Bachelard, *The Poetics of Space,* trans. M. Jolas (Boston: Beacon Press, 1958), pp. xxxiiff. Heidegger speaks of a "topology of Being" in *Aus der Erfahrung des*

Denkens (Pfullingen: Neske, 1954), p. 23: "poetizing that thinks is in truth the topology of Being (*die Topologie des Seyns*)."

Introduction to the Second Edition

1. See, notably, Martin Heidegger, "Building Dwelling Thinking," in *Poetry, Language, Thought*, trans. A. Hofstadter (New York: Harper, 1971), pp. 143–62; "Die Kunst und der Raum," in Heidegger, *Gesamtausgabe*, vol. 13 (Frankfurt: Klostermann, 1983). See my assessment of his treatment of space and place in *The Fate of Place: A Philosophical History* (Berkeley and Los Angeles: University of California Press, 1997), chap. 11; and, especially, Jeff Malpas's magisterial book *Heidegger's Topology: Being, Place, World* (Cambridge, Mass.: MIT Press, 2006). For Sartre's discussion of place, considered as belonging to "situation," see his *Being and Nothingness*, trans. H. Barnes (New York: Washington Square Press, 1972), pp. 629–37. See also Gaston Bachelard, *Poetics of Space*, trans. M. Jolas (New York: Orion, 1964). Others who acknowledge place include Gabriel Marcel, as well as Henry Bugbee in *The Inward Morning: A Philosophical Exploration in Journal Form* (Athens: University of Georgia Press, 1999). Outside philosophy, the cultural geographer Yi-Fu Tuan had written *Space and Place: The Perspective of Experience* (Minneapolis: University of Minnesota Press, 1977).

2. See Edward S. Casey, *Remembering: A Phenomenological Study* (Bloomington: Indiana University Press, 1987), chap. 9. See also my earlier essay, "Keeping the Past in Mind," *Review of Metaphysics* (September 1983), first delivered as an invited address to the Society for Phenomenology and Existential Philosophy in 1982.

3. Among many publications since the first edition was published, see Doreen Massey, *Space, Place, and Gender* (Minneapolis: University of Minnesota Press, 1994), esp. chaps. 12–14; Doreen Massey, *For Space* (London: Sage, 2005); Robert D. Sack, *Homo Geographicus: A Framework for Action, Awareness, and Moral Concern* (Baltimore, Md.: Johns Hopkins University Press, 1997); John Agnew, "Space: Place," in *Spaces of Geographical Thought: Deconstructing Human Geography's Binaries*, ed. P. Cloke and R. Johnston (London: Sage, 2005); Michael R. Curry, "'Hereness' and the Normativity of Place," in *Geography and Ethics: Journeys in a Moral Terrain*, ed. J. D. Proctor and D. M. Smith (London: Routledge, 1999); Lynn A. Staehli, "Place," in *A Companion to Political Geography*, ed. K. Mitchell and G. Toal (Oxford: Blackwell, 2003); Nigel Thrift, "Steps to an Ecology of Place," in *Human Geography Today*, ed. D. Massey, J. Allen, and P. Sarre (Cambridge: Polity Press, 1999).

4. See J. E. Malpas, *Place and Experience* (Cambridge: Cambridge University Press, 1999).

5. See Keith Basso and Steven Feld, *Senses of Place* (Santa Fe, N.Mex.: School of American Research Press, 1996). My essay "How to Get from Space to Place in a Fairly Short Stretch of Time," reprinted in this volume, formed the introductory essay to this collection. Henri Lefebvre's *The Production of Space* (trans. D. Nicholson-Smith [Oxford: Blackwell, 1991]), a neo-Marxist analysis of spatial relations, has wrought a revolution in the social sciences: in this book, place is everywhere implied even if only rarely thematized.

6. See Jessop et al., "Theorizing Socio-Spatial Relations," *Society and Space* 26, no. 3 (July 2008), and my commentary "Questioning Socio-Spatial Relations" in the same issue: there I argue that place is *primus inter pares* among the four models proposed by Jessop.

7. A recent meeting, "Place '08," held in September 2008 at Park City, Utah, announced its agenda as surveying "the recent discovery of the topic of place in more formal and computational directions of research, among them location-based services,

gaming, human computer interface design, ontology, robotics and localization, social networks, gazetteers and georeferencing, vernacular geography, tagging and text miming, geographic information retrieval, qualitative modeling of environments, modeling affordance, and modeling uncertainty" (First Call for Papers, International Workshop on Computational Models of Place).

8. For my later thinking on the relation of time and place, see the epilogue to this volume as well as *Representing Place: Landscape Painting and Maps* (Minneapolis: University of Minnesota Press, 2002), especially pp. 265–66, 274–75. I return to the model of event just below, in section II.

9. For an engaging account of globalization that emphasizes that it is not simply one single phenomenon, see Eduardo Mendieta, *Global Fragments: Globalizations, Latinamericanisms, and Critical Theory* (Albany: State University of New York Press, 2007), esp. p. 189: "There are 'only globalizations'—if only because there are so many ways of trying to make sense, to organize our ways of knowing this globalized world."

10. See the introduction and especially chap. 7, "The Arc of Desolation and the Array of Description."

11. Speaking of nomadic movements, Deleuze and Guattari say that the nomad "is in a *local absolute,* an absolute that is manifested locally, and engendered in a series of local operations of varying orientations: desert, steppe, ice, sea. Making the absolute appear in a particular place" (*A Thousand Plateaus,* trans. Brian Massumi [Minneapolis: University of Minnesota Press, 1987], p. 382; their italics). I return to this theme in the epilogue below, p. 365.

12. Mary Watkins, "Psyches and Cities of Hospitality in an Era of Forced Migrations: The Shadows of Slavery and Conquest on the 'Immigration' Debate," in *Politics and the American Soul* 77 (Spring 2007): 9–10. Watkins refers to a document of the National Immigration Law Center entitled "Same Language for Policies Limiting the Enforcement of Immigration Law by Local Authorities," dated November 2004 (National Immigration Law Center).

13. It is notable that MoveOn, remarkably successful in reaching millions of citizens by electronic transmissions, also encourages face-to-face public demonstrations and gatherings in members' apartments.

14. For the concept of the multi-voiced body, see Fred Evans, *The Multi-Voiced Body: Society and Communication in the Age of Diversity* (New York: Columbia University Press, 2008).

15. On this atmosphere, see my paper "Public Memory in Place and Time," in *Framing Public Memory,* ed. Kendall Phillips (Tuscaloosa: University of Alabama Press, 2004).

16. On this part of Manhattan, see Pete Hamill, *Downtown: My Manhattan* (New York: Little Brown, 2004).

17. See especially this book, pp. 29–32, 229–41, 252–53, 262–63.

18. To be "territorial" is to seek to extend the borders of an original home territory so as to include nearby states and regions. "Territoriality" includes both defensive and aggressive aspects of inhabiting a territory. See Robert Ardrey's classic book, *The Territorial Imperative: A Personal Inquiry into the Animal Origins of Property and Nations* (New York: Kodansha America, 1997), which pursues the biological and ethological basis of territoriality, in contrast with an approach that emphasizes the role of social drive, as in Robert D. Sack, *Human Territoriality: Its Theory and History* (Cambridge: University of Cambridge Press, 1986).

19. For an argument that territory in a stricter sense than I here outline is a creation of the modern period, thanks to its conception of spatial distribution and measurement, see Stuart Elden, "Missing the Point: Globalization, Deterritorialization, and the Space

of the World," *Transactions of the British Institute of Geography* 30 (2005): 8–19. In this same excellent essay, Elden argues that territory in the modern calculable and quantitative sense remains an uneliminable element in contemporary globalization. At the same time, he points to the fact that territory itself has yet to be rigorously discussed in contemporary political geography and political science (see ibid., 10, 16).

20. Gary Snyder points out that native peoples may not have a written constitution (with certain notable exceptions, e.g., the Iroquois), but they have the experiential equivalent of the homogenizing effect of a constitution: "In the hunting and gathering way of life, the whole territory of a given group is fairly equally experienced by everyone" (Gary Snyder, *The Practice of the Wild* [Washington, D.C.: Shoemaker and Hoard, 1990], p. 87).

21. Deleuze and Guattari, *A Thousand Plateaus,* p. 314. These authors are notable for their insistence on the power of "deterritorialization" and "reterritorialization," both of which undo the implicit fixity of an established territory: see ibid., 282, 312, 315ff., 388. Stuart Elden remarks, however, that these two latter concepts cannot take the place of territory itself, which remains pivotal to their own conception: see Elden, "Missing the Point," pp. 9–10.

22. These phrases are found at pp. 73–74 in the first edition of this book.

23. Edward S. Casey, *Representing Place: Landscape Painting and Maps,* p. 74. For further discussion of region, see the first essay in the epilogue of the current volume, "How to Get from Space to Place in a Fairly Short Stretch of Time."

24. See Snyder's description of watershed as "a kind of familial branching, a chart of relationship, and a definition of place. The watershed is the first and last nation whose boundaries, though subtly shifting, are unarguable" ("Coming into the Watershed," in *A Place in Space* [New York: Counterpoint, 1995], p. 229).

25. Gary Snyder, "The Place, The Region, and The Commons," in *The Practice of the Wild,* p. 30. Snyder adds that "[t]he regional boundaries were roughly drawn by climate, which is what sets the plant-type zones—plus soil types and landforms" (ibid.).

26. For further discussion of material essence as "essential to the identity of just [this] region," see *Representing Place: Landscape Painting and Maps,* pp. 74–75, 89–91.

27. See Rachel Carson, *The Edge of the Sea* (New York: Houghton Mifflin, 1955).

28. On reciprocal presupposition, see Deleuze and Guattari, *A Thousand Plateaus,* pp. 89–91, 108, 140–41, 145, 146.

29. Gérard Barbeau, from the National Institute of Agronomical Research close to Angers, France, states that "the quality of the [soil] is of paramount importance. . . . The variability induced by the physical characteristics of the *terroirs* is much more important than everything else" (cited in "The World of Wine," *Science News* 157 [Jan. 1, 2000]: 12). Damaris Christensen, the author of this article, adds that "wines made from the same kind of grapes, grown in the same region using identical practices but in a slightly different *terroir,* harvested at exactly the same time, and made into wine in exactly the same ways, still can be remarkably different. . . . These underlying differences must be due to the *terroir*" (ibid., 13). I am grateful to James Hillman for bringing this testimony to my attention.

30. Maurice Merleau-Ponty, *The Visible and the Invisible,* trans. A. Lingis (Evanston, Ill.: Northwestern University Press, 1968), p. 253. Merleau-Ponty adds: "Moreover the distinction between the two planes (natural and cultural) is abstract" (ibid.).

31. See Sylvia Rodríguez, *Acequia: Water Sharing, Sanctity, and Place* (Santa Fe, N.Mex.: School for Advanced Research Press, 2007).

32. Gary Snyder, *The Practice of the Wild,* p. 40. He adds: "The commons is a curious and elegant social institution within which human beings once lived free political lives while weaving through natural systems. . . . The level above the local commons is the

bioregion. Understanding the commons and its role within the larger regional culture is one more step toward integrating ecology with economy" (ibid.).

33. See Snyder's *The Old Ways* (San Francisco: City Lights, 1977).

34. *The Practice of the Wild*, p. 40; his italics.

35. "The culture areas of the major native groups of North American overlapped, as one would expect, almost exactly with broadly defined major bioregions. . . . Biota, watersheds, landforms and elevation are just a few of the facets that define a region. Culture areas, *in the same way*, have subsets such as dialects, religions, sorts of arrow-release, types of tools, myth motifs, musical scales, art styles" (ibid., 40–41; my italics).

36. For a compressed account of the history of place, see my essay "Smooth Spaces and Rough-Edged Places: The Hidden History of Place," reprinted in this volume.

1. Implacement

1. James Joyce, *Finnegans Wake* (New York: Viking Press, 1939), p. 558. Michel Foucault has this to say about being lost at sea: "the ship is a floating piece of space . . . a place without a place that exists by itself and that is closed in on itself and at the same time is given over to the infinity of the sea . . . the ship is the heterotopia *par excellence*" ("Of Other Spaces," *Diacritics* 16 [1986], p. 27).

2. Simplicius, *In Aristotelis Categorias Commentarium*, as translated (in part) in Shmuel Sambursky, ed., *The Concept of Place in Late Neoplatonism* (Jerusalem: Israel Academy of Sciences and Humanities, 1982), p. 171.

3. The remark is cited in *American Practical Navigator: An Epitome of Navigation*, originally by Nathaniel Bowditch (Washington, D.C.: Government Printing Office, 1966), p. 44. Latitude, i.e., position north or south of the equator, is comparatively easily determined by measuring the height of the sun or the pole star above the place of observation. The determination of latitude has been known for at least two millennia in the West. Hipparchus (second century B.C.) had speculated that one could determine longitude by comparing the exact time of a solar eclipse at one place with the time it occurred at a second place. But this brilliant and prescient idea is applicable only to small regions of the earth and requires the rare event of an eclipse, and in any case is unfeasible on sea voyages.

4. Quoted in ibid., p. 44.

5. Columbus's claim that he knew where he was in terms of longitude was "due to a pious fraud, prepared, like the falsified reckonings of the outward voyage, for his [crew members'] encouragement, and in sober truth he [was] as helpless as any of them" (Rupert T. Gould, *The Marine Chronometer: Its History and Development* [London: Holland, 1923], p. 1).

6. Richard Eden, "Epistle Dedicatory," in his translation of John Taisnier, *A very necessarie and profitable book concerning navigation . . .* (London: 1579), cited by Lloyd A. Brown, *The Story of Maps* (New York: Dover, 1977), p. 208.

7. For Galileo's observations, undertaken from 1612 until his death, see his *Opere*, ed. Eugenio Alberi (Florence, 1842–56), vol. 3, pp. 59–99. Another unwieldy clock, equipped with two balances and two spiral springs, was proposed by Leibniz in 1675. A historian of marine chronometry has written that this machine "illustrated his fatal propensity for writing upon subjects whose principles he had imperfectly mastered" (Gould, *Marine Chronometer*, p. 31, with reference to fig. 7).

8. The French Académie Royale des Sciences, under the patronage of Louis XIV and the scientific inspiration of the transplanted Italian Jean Dominique Cassini, proved by 1676 that the accurate determination of longitude by reference to the eclipses of Jupiter's

satellites was indeed possible. One of Cassini's colleagues was reported to have said, "Si ce n'est pas-là le veritable secret des Longitudes, au-moins en approche-t-il de bien près." But as Brown remarks, "the fact remained that the sea was too boisterous and unpredictable for astronomers and their apparatus" (*Story of Maps*, p. 225).

9. Cited in ibid., p. 234.

10. Ibid.

11. Max Jammer, *Concepts of Space: The History of Theories of Space in Physics*, 2d ed. (Cambridge, Mass.: Harvard University Press, 1969), p. 4. Even so, Koyré makes it clear that space remained for Galileo and Descartes the preferred parameter, to the point of impeding scientific progress; see Alexandre Koyré, *Galileo Studies*, trans. J. Megham (Atlantic Highlands, N.J.: Humanities Press, 1978), esp. chaps. 1 and 2. On p. 82, Koyré writes that "thorough-going geometrization, spatialization, the elimination of time . . . lead Descartes, as they had previously led Galileo, . . . to conceive of uniformly accelerated motion as motion in which the speed increases in proportion to the path covered, and not in proportion to the time elapsed."

12. Note that the gradual perfection of the marine chronometer occurred precisely in the interval between the death of Descartes in 1650 and the publication of Kant's *Critique of Pure Reason* in 1781. The career of this chronometer is coextensive with the emergence of philosophical modernity.

13. "O Grief! O Grief! Time eats away our lives, / And the dark Enemy that gnaws the heart / Drains the blood from us on which he thrives!" (Baudelaire, "L'Ennemi," in *Les Fleurs du Mal*).

14. Cf. T. S. Eliot, "The Waste Land," sec. 2 ("A Game of Chess"), ll. 152–69. "Closing Time" in the previous sentence refers to Norman O. Brown's *Closing Time* (New York: Random House, 1973).

15. "Had we but world enough, and time, / This coyness, lady, were no crime" (Andrew Marvell, "To His Coy Mistress" [1650–52]).

16. Immanuel Kant, for example, says that "we represent the time-sequence by a line progressing to infinity" (*Critique of Pure Reason*, sec. 5); this line reappears in Husserl's famous "diagram of time" in his 1905 lectures on inner time-consciousness.

17. "Time will not fail; for it is always at a beginning" (Aristotle, *Physics*, 222b, 3–4, Hardie and Gaye translation; elsewhere I mainly cite the recent translation of Edward Hussey, *Aristotle's Physics* [Oxford: Oxford University Press, 1983]). Aristotle's model of time, like that of Plato, is resolutely circular and cyclical.

18. I say "of our own making" because one could argue that modern scheduled time is itself a creation of late-eighteenth-century industrialist society, whose origins coincide with Harrison's success of 1761. On this point, see E. P. Thompson, *The Making of the English Working Class* (New York: Vintage, 1963), esp. pt. 2.

19. This is the title of Carnap's article in *Kantstudien* 30 (1925), pp. 331–45: "Uber die Abhängigkeit des Eigenschaften des Raumes von denen der Zeit."

20. Hans Reichenbach, *The Philosophy of Space and Time* (New York: Dover, 1958), p. 169.

21. I take the term *absolute presupposition* from R. G. Collingwood, *An Essay on Metaphysics* (Oxford: Oxford University Press, 1940), pp. 20ff.

22. Locke also points explicitly to the origin of the linearity of time in the inward succession of ideas. If "fleeting extension" is "but as it were the length of one straight line, extended *in infinitum*," the subjective source of this extended time-line is found by "reflection on the train of ideas, which we find to appear one after another in our own minds." (From John Locke, *An Essay concerning Human Understanding*, ed. P. H. Nidditch [Oxford: Clarendon Press, 1975], bk. 2, chaps. 15 and 14, respectively.) If Descartes

and Locke were the first to linearize time so decisively, the temptation does not end with seventeenth-century thinkers. Kant continues the tradition late into the eighteenth century, and it is still evident in a twentieth-century philosopher such as C. D. Broad: "Every experience has some duration. It is, in this respect, like a finite straight line and not like a geometrical point" (*An Examination of McTaggart's Philosophy* [Cambridge: Cambridge University Press, 1938], vol. 2, pt. 1, p. 38).

23. Alfred North Whitehead, *Prows and Reality*, ed. D. R. Griffin and D. W. Sherburne (New York: Free Press, 1978), p. 129.

24. Henri Bergson says tellingly: "We set our states of consciousness side by side in such a way as to perceive them simultaneously, no longer in one another, but alongside one another; in a word, we project time into space . . . and succession thus takes the form of a continuous line or chain, the parts of which touch without penetrating one another" (*Time and Free Will: An Essay on the Immediate Data of Consciousness* [*Essai Sur le données immédiates de la conscience*], trans. F. L. Podgson [New York: Harper, 1960], p. 101). See also pp. 102 and 129–30.

25. Ibid., p. 102. My italics.

26. Simplicius, *In Aristotelis Categorias Commentarium*, p. 173.

27. "Even if it is dark and we are not acted upon through the body, but there is some change in the soul, it immediately seems to us that some time has passed together with the change" (*Physics*, 219a, 3–6; Hussey translation).

28. James Hillman, *Re-Visioning Psychology* (New York: Harper & Row, 1975), p. 130.

29. Bergson, *Time and Free Will*, p. 104. The phrase *the profit and loss* is from Eliot's "Waste Land": "A fortnight dead, he forgot the profit and loss, / A current under sea / Picked his bones in whispers" (sec. 4, "Death by Water," ll. 312–16).

30. Bergson, *La pensée et le mouvant* (Paris: Presses Universitaires de France, 1934), p. 167.

31. This insensitivity is doubly ironic: first, insofar as one might have expected a more nuanced appreciation of "lived space" (which would certainly include a description of place) from the person who taught us so much about lived time; second, because Bergson wrote a thesis in Latin, in the same year *Time and Free Will* first appeared, entitled "The Idea of Place in Aristotle" (*Quid Aristoteles de Loco Senserit*). Did he therefore believe that given the difficulties in Aristotle's notion of *topos* to which he pointed in this thesis, there could not be a more constructive assessment of place?

32. On the role of place in Heidegger's thought, see Joseph P. Fell, *Heidegger and Sartre: An Essay on Being and Place* (New York: Columbia University Press, 1979), and Otto Pöggeler, *Der Denkweg Martin Heideggers* (Pfullingen: Neske, 1963), esp. 280–99 ("Topologie des Seins"). Bachelard's "topoanalysis," to which I referred in the preface, converges with Heidegger's "topology of Being," but Bachelard fails to distinguish between "space" (*espace*) and "place" (*lieu*) in his otherwise remarkable *Poetics of Space*.

33. Cf. *inter alia* Max Jammer's remark that "qualifications of time, as 'short,' or 'long,' are taken from the vocabulary of spatial concepts" (*Concepts of Space*, p. 3). I owe several of my examples to Jammer's discussion. Ernst Cassirer has discussed the predominance of spatial images in linguistic expression in his *Philosophy of Symbolic Forms*, trans. R. Manheim (New Haven, Conn.: Yale University Press, 1953), vol. 1, pp. 198–214. But temporal terms can also qualify spatial phenomena. Karl Marx remarks that "among the ancient Germans the size of a piece of land was measured according to the labour of a day; hence the acre was called *Tagwerk, Tagwanne* (*jurnale*, or *terra jurnalis*, or *diornalis*)" (*Capital: A Critique of Political Economy*, trans. Ben Fowkes [New York: Penguin, 1976], vol. 1, p. 164, n.).

34. Aristotle, *Physics*, 2192, 15. In the end, Aristotle ascribes the origin of before—after to "magnitude," but magnitude is itself an aspect of place; see 219a, 12–13.

35. T. S. Eliot, "Burnt Norton," sec. 3, *Four Quartets.* Notice that Eliot embeds the temporal before and after in a setting designated expressly as a "place." Aristotle adds that "in time, too, the before and after is present" (*Physics,* 219a, 19). The derivation just performed is not merely a function of the Greek language or of Greek thought. The Hebrew word for "before" (in the temporal sense) is *lifney,* which means literally "to the face of," "to the front of."

36. The misrepresentation is that time can only be characterized in terms of before and after; the false inference is that time is *inherently* so characterized or structured.

37. Saint Augustine, *Confessions,* trans. R. S. Pine-Coffin (New York: Penguin, 1961, bk. ii, chap. 15.

38. Isaac Newton, Scholium to the Definitions of *Mathematical Principles of Natural Philosophy* (1687).

39. Saint Augustine, *Confessions,* bk. ii, chap. 26: "I begin to wonder whether time is an extendedness of the soul itself" (I here slightly modify Pine-Coffin's translation).

40. Ibid.

41. This is not to deny that time may be *coeval* with place, as when we say that it "takes time to get to know a place." If place is something more than a mere point, it is time-saturated. But this fact does not alter the further fact that models of time, including that offered by Saint Augustine, tacitly *borrow* traits from place in various subreptive manners.

42. Simplicius, *In Aristotelis Categorias Commentarium,* p. 175.

43. Ibid. Simplicius adds that place and time are basic to generation, "one in respect of mass and the other in respect of the extension of existence, and both simultaneously and together representing as by an image the contracted indivisibility of eternity."

44. Aristole, *Physics,* 208b, 34–35.

45. Ibid., 208b, 34.

46. "Those who assert that there is void say that there is place; for the void would be place deprived of body" (Aristotle, *Physics,* 208b, 26–27). This observation helps to explain the difficulty involved in successfully carrying out the thought experiment with which the preface opens. Even if we manage to imagine a void, there is still some sort of place.

47. Ibid., 28–33. My italics.

48. As cited by Simplicius, *In Aristotelis Categorias Commentarium,* and translated in Sambursky, *The Concept of Place in Late Neoplatonism,* p. 37. Sambursky holds that this fragment, along with another (cited below), is to be attributed to "Pseudo-Archytas," who is "an unknown Neopythagorean philosopher" (p. 14). Whether one agrees with this attribution or not, there is no doubt that the fragments in question reflect the views of the historical Archytas, and for this reason I shall not bother to distinguish between the latter and his hypothetical successor and stand-in.

49. Aristotle, *Physics,* 208b, 35–209a, 2.

50. Saint Augustine, *Confessions,* bk. II, chap. 14.

51. See Edmund Husserl, *The Phenomenology of Internal Time-Consciousness,* pt. i, Introduction (lectures from the year 1905), and Friedrich Waismann, "Analytic Synthetic," *Analysis* 2–3 (1950–51), reprinted in R. M. Gale, ed., *The Philosophy of Time* (New York: Anchor, 1967), p. 55. Gale obligingly entitles the entire first section of his anthology "What, then, is Time?" I owe my awareness of the ritualistic repetition of Augustine's question to my colleague Peter Manchester.

52. An entire school of late Neoplatonists reiterated the gesture. Sambursky's *Concept of Place in Late Neoplatonism* is an eloquent testimonial to this fact. It contains selections from (among others) Theophrastus, Damascius, Archytas, Plotinus, Iamblichus, Proclus, and Simplicius. Reading these thinkers of place allows us to realize to what

degree Western philosophy has lost touch with an ancient insight, which Archytas first articulated in so many words and which these Neoplatonic thinkers carried forward.

53. In Sambursky, *The Concept of Place in Late Neoplatonism*, p. 37. For other versions of this argument, as given by Zeno and Gorgias and repeated by Plato in *Parmenides*, 145d–e, see F. M. Cornford, *Plato and Parmenides* (Indianapolis: Bobbs-Merrill, n.d.), pp. 149–50.

54. On the concept of the "absolute edge," see D. G. Leahy, "To Create the Absolute Edge," *Journal of the American Academy of Religion* 57 (1990), pp. 779–89. Concerning the universe, Aristotle remarks that "there is nothing besides the universe (*to pan*) and the sum of things (*holon*), nothing which is outside the universe; and this is why everything is in the world (*ouranos*)" (*Physics*, 212b, 16-19).

55. Simplicius, *Corollarium de Loco* (part of his commentary on Aristotle's *Physics*; Simplicius is commenting on the Pythagorean position), as translated in Sambursky, *The Concept of Place in Late Neoplatonism*, p. 141. See also Aristotle, *Metaphysics*, 1080b, 33, on the Pythagorean implacement of numbers.

56. Bergson, *Time and Free Will*, pp. 84–85. Indirect evidence for the inherent spatiality of number is provided by the "number-forms" Francis Galton discovered to be held tacitly by subjects he investigated in the late nineteenth century (*Inquiries into Human Faculty* [London: Dent, 1907], pp. 72ff).

57. John Milton, *Paradise Lost*, bk. 1, ll. 253–55. Satan is speaking after his fall. He presents himself to Beelzebub as "one who brings a mind not to be changed by place or time" (ll. 251–52) precisely because *his* mind is its own place.

58. Aristotle, *De Anima*, 429a, 27.

59. This is not to deny that my mind, by means of its own intentionality, is also capable of transcending its own place, as we signify when we say that "my mind is somewhere else." On the subject of mindful memory, see my essay "Remembering Resumed: Pursuing Buddhism and Phenomenology in Practice," in J. Gyatso, ed., *In the Mirror of Memory: Reflections on Mindfulness and Remembrance in Indian and Tibetan Buddhism* (Albany: State University of New York Press, 1992).

60. Simplicius, *Corollarium de Loco*, in Sambursky, *The Concept of Place in Late Neoplatonism*, p. 141.

61. On this point, see ibid., p. 140, n. 14.

62. Sambursky, *The Concept of Place in Late Neoplatonism*, p. 15. Jammer adds that "it seems reasonable to assume that originally the term 'place' [*makom*] was used only as an abbreviation for 'holy place' (*makom kadosh*), the place of the 'Shekinah'" (Jammer, *Concepts of Space*, p. 27). This is not to deny that as Judaic theology became more abstract, the concrete metonymy was less insistently intended: God's omnipresence, not his Place, was the dominant theme of many subsequent speculations, as is evident in Psalm 139. Saint Augustine inquires into God's placelike properties in the *Confessions:* "When you have filled heaven and earth, does that part of you which remains flow over into some other place?" (bk. 1, chap. 3).

63. Cited in Sambursky, *The Concept of Place in Late Neoplatonism*, p. 15.

64. Cited in ibid., p. 35, from Philo's treatise *De Somnis*.

65. Cited from Henry More's *Enchiridium metaphysicum*, chap. 8, by Alexander Koyré, *From the Closed World to the Infinite Universe* (Baltimore: Johns Hopkins University Press, 1957), p. 148.

66. The depersonalization of God and his conception as a Place is hinted at by Plotinus: "the place of the intelligible world [i.e., the place of God] is the place of life and the very principle and source of the Soul and the Intellect" (*Enneads*, II, 5, 3, 39; cited in Sambursky, *The Concept of Place in Late Neoplatonism*, p. 39).

67. Nor does it matter if the identity of God is singular or plural. Simplicius reminds us that the name of the Syrian goddess "Atargatis" (probably the Phoenician goddess Astarte) means "the place of gods" (*Corollarium de Loco*, as cited in ibid., p. 141).

68. *Holy Bible: Revised Standard Verson* (New York: Nelson, 1953), p. 1. I have capitalized "Deep" for the sake of emphasis.

69. I cite the translation of Hesiod's *Theogony*, ll. 116–34, in G. S. Kirk, J. E. Raven, and M. Schofield, *The Presocratic Philosophers* (Cambridge: Cambridge University Press, 1983), p. 35.

70. *Chaos* derives from the same Greek root as does *chasm: cha-*, as in *chaskein, chain-ein*, to gape, yawn, open wide. To open wide is to create a place, however indefinite, within the boundaries of the opening itself. On the inherent logic in chaos, see Gary Mar and Patrick Grim, "Pattern and Chaos: New Images in the Semantics of Paradox," *Nous* 25 (1991), pp. 659–94.

71. Aristotle, *Physics*, 208b, 31–32.

72. Ibid., 209b, 16–17. But Aristotle is surely not correct in his view that "in the *Timaeus*, [Plato] still declared that place and space (*ton topon kai ton chōran*) were the same thing" (209b, 15–16). The *Timaeus* delineates precisely how specific places (*topoi*) become differentiated from general regions. Such places are the immediate loci of the material *things* that result from the Demiurge's intervention into the primordial scene of the Receptacle.

73. Cited by Charles Long, *Alpha: Myths of Creation* (New York: Braziller, 1963), p. 126.

74. Cited from D. A. MacKensie, *Myths of China and Japan* (London: Allen & Unwin, 1923), p. 261.

75. "Of old, Heaven and Earth were not yet separated, and the In and Yo [feminine and masculine principles] not yet divided. They formed a chaotic mass like an egg which was of obscurely defined limits and contained germs. The purer and clearer part was thinly drawn out, and formed Heaven, while the heavier and grosser element settled down and became Earth" (from the *Nihoni* [ca. A.D. 720] as cited in *The Nihonigi*, trans. W. G. Aston [London: Allen & Unwin, 1956], p. 1). "In the begining Earth and Heaven were great World-giants. . . . The Heaven in those days lay upon the Earth" (John Rhys, *Lectures on the Origin and Growth of Religion as Illustrated by Celtic Heathendum* [London: Williams and Norgate, 1862], p. 669).

76. A line is made up of points, and it is of related interest that Husserl conceives of the now as a point expressly described as a "limit" and as a "source." (See Husserl, *Phenomenology of Internal Time-Consciousness*, secs. 13, 28–29, 31). As such, the now-point may be the secular equivalent, here below, of God-as-Place. The point of human time and the place of the universe are epicenters in extremis. No wonder, then, that Husserl could ascribe such cosmic power to time at the level of absolute flux, to which the now-point offers direct access. For further discussion of Husserl's model of time, see Paul Ricoeur, *Time and Narrative*, trans. K. Blamey and D. Pellauer (Chicago: University of Chicago Press, 1988), vol. 3, pp. 23–44, esp. pp. 28–30 on the tension between the now as limit and as source.

77. Plato, *Timaeus*, 37d.

78. Saint Augustine, *Confessions*, bk. II, chaps. 18 and 21. My italics. As Ricoeur remarks, the where question "consists in seeking a *location* for future and past things" (*Time and Narrative*, vol. 1, p. 10).

79. For Saint Augustine, the place of time is to be found in the mind: "All different times do exist *in the mind* [and] nowhere else that I can see" (*Confessions*, bk. 11, chap. 20; my italics). But to say "in the mind" is *not* to say passively contained there. On the

contrary. It is the mind's inherent dynamism that "regulates this process [of temporal transition]" (bk. ii, chap. 28). Only the mind "performs [the] three functions . . . of expectation, attention, and memory" (ibid.). Ricoeur, citing this same passage, observes that even in this mental activism "the quasi-spatial [i.e., placial] imagery of a movement from the future toward the past through the future has not been eliminated. . . . The vocabulary here continues to oscillate between activity and passivity" (*Time and Narrative,* vol. i, p. 19).

80. For an enumeration of such descriptions, see D. C. Williams, "The Myth of Passage," in Gale, ed., *The Philosophy of Time,* p. 103.

81. See Saint Augustine, *Confessions,* bk. ii, chap. 28. This represents more than a mere example because, like the allied instance of melody, it shows that there is no such thing as a *pure* passage of time, i.e., a passage that does not pass *from* one place *to* another. To pass is to pass through a place. The place itself can be as diaphanous as a note or a word or even as ontologically slim as a "quality" (in Aristotle's sense of the term) and yet still count as a place-from-which or to-which temporal passage is made. Passing, like moving (of which it is a species), is a transition between places. Ricoeur, discussing the celebrated passage about the psalm, says that the place-language "has its ultimate justification in the passivity that accompanies the entire process"—even if we should be "no longer misled by the representation of two places [i.e., past and future], one of which is filled up as the other is emptied, as soon as we have ascribed dynamic character to this representation [by the invocation of the mind's active role in *distentio animi*]" (*Time and Narrative,* vol. i, p. 19).

82. J. M. E. McTaggart, "Time," as reprinted in Gale, ed., *The Philosophy of Time,* p. 87.

83. Ibid., p. 88, n. He adds: "But spatial movement in which direction?" This is precisely the right question, since in my estimate space (qua homogeneous and isotropic) offers no *directional* indication. Only place is intrinsically orienting.

84. Ibid., p. 93; my italics. Elsewhere in his celebrated and much-controverted article, McTaggart offers a veritable cornucopia of place prepositions. Thus *into, along, out of, towards* are all drawn upon in his description of "the movement of time" (p. 88, n.).

85. "The locomotions of the natural simple bodies . . . not only show that place is something but also that it has some power, since each body, if not impeded, moves to its own place" (*Physics,* 208b, 8–13). In this statement Aristotle suggests that locomotion is a dependent variable of the places between which it moves.

2. Displacement

1. John Locke, *An Essay concerning Human Understanding,* ed. P. H. Nidditch (Oxford: Clarendon Press, 1975), bk. 2, chap. 13, sec. 10. The sentence in which this phrase is embedded commences with a virtual reiteration of the Archytian axiom: "For to say that the world is somewhere, means no more than that it does exist; this, though a phrase borrowed from place, signifying only its existence, not location; and when one can find out, and frame in his mind, clearly and distinctly, the place of the universe, he will be able to tell us whether it moves or stands still in the undistinguishable inane of infinite space." In the very next paragraph of the *Essay,* however, Locke makes the characteristic modern reduction of place to the position of a subordinate part of space: "The idea, therefore, of place we have by the same means that we get the idea of space (whereof this is *but a particular limited consideration*)" (my italics).

2. Isaac Newton, Scholium to the Definitions of *Mathematical Principles of Natural Philosophy,* sec. 2.

3. Heidegger parodies the container model, which is ultimately derived from Aristotle, in a passage from his 1925 lectures on time: "The desk in the classroom, the classroom in the university building, the building in the city of Marburg, Marburg in Hessen, in Germany, in Europe, on Earth, in a solar system, in world-space, in the world—a uniform relation of being which is in principle no different in all of these connections" (M. Heidegger, *History of the Concept of Time*, trans. T. Kisiel [Bloomington: Indiana University Press, 1985], p. 158). Such a model, Heidegger adds, only touches on "outward appearance" and is dominated by the metaphysics of the "present-at-hand" (*Vorhandensein*).

4. An adequate autobiography, or a thorough biography, if it is to be "true of a [person's] whole life" (Saint Augustine, *Confessions*, bk. 11, chap. 28), must discuss, or at least allude to, the most significant place-names experienced in that life—even if by way of pseudo-toponyms!

5. Georg W. F. Hegel, *Phenomenology of Spirit*, trans. A. V. Miller (New York: Oxford University Press, 1977), chap. 1 ("Sense Certainty"), pp. 58–66. I return briefly to the status of locative expressions at the beginning of chap. 4.

6. The full statement, itself a rewrite of Archytas, is "For everyone supposes that things that exist are somewhere, because what is not is nowhere—where for instance is a goat-stag or a sphinx?" (Aristotle, *Physics*, 208a, 29–31).

7. Carl O. Sauer, the eminent American geographer, remarks that "the subject matter of geography begins with the distinction between proper names and common nouns, which is perhaps as old as the faculty of language. The proper name given to a particular place identifies its uniqueness and location and also calls attention to the need of such identification in a cultural context, as a place providing food, water, or shelter, perhaps as one to be avoided, as a landmark in getting from one place to another, as noted for a memorable event, or as having ritual significance. Place name is location in cultural connotation" ("On the Background of Geography in the United States," *Selected Essays 1963–1975* [Berkeley, Calif.: Turtle Island Foundation, 1981], p. 242). For a detailed analysis of particular place-names, see Adrian Room, *Place-Names of the World: A Dictionary of Their Origins and Backgrounds* (London: Angus & Robertson, 1987).

8. Jean-François Lyotard, "Scapeland," in *The Lyotard Reader*, ed. A. Benjamin (Oxford: Blackwell, 1989), p. 212. Notice that Lyotard in effect collapses the distinction between physical and psychological place: "state" and "state of mind" are conterminous concepts.

9. Ibid., p. 213. Lyotard adds the qualification "if place is cognate with destination," and he invokes Aristotle's notion of *topos* as "a place without a DESTINY." In fact, however, an Aristotelian *topos* has a distinct destiny, even a destination: to act as the natural repository for the bodies that belong to it.

10. I might call a *painting* of the landscape view "Grand Tetons," but this reflects the fact that the painting, unlike my own view, is framed, and thus a determinately bounded entity that can bear a proper name. The painting singles out the initial perceptual determinacy of a landscape and gives to it the added determinacy of an image-in-a-frame.

11. Vilhjálmur Stefánsson, *My Life with the Eskimos* (New York: Macmillan, 1913), pp. 148–49. A similar incident is reported on pp. 146–47. I owe this reference to J. Melvin Woody.

12. "A white hunter who goes seven miles south, then three miles east, then four miles southwest, and two miles northwest, will have a fairly definite idea of how to draw a line that will take him thence to his original starting point" (ibid., p. 148). Stefánsson adds condescendingly that "the Indian or Eskimo in my experience will have no such notion, and instead of going straight home will go back over the route by which he came, unless

there are some landmarks in sight which he recognized earlier in the day." He holds that an Eskimo lacks "the general principles to guide him that are clear in the mind of the average white man." But Stefánsson nevertheless rejects the idea of "instinctive" abilities supposedly possessed by "primitive" peoples and attributes significant differences in preferred forms of orientation to "the environment under which they have grown up from childhood" (p. 149).

13. It is a curious fact that "deadlines" are interpreted almost entirely in temporal terms in the modern world. Yet to meet a deadline in time one has to deliver a product somewhere in space: e.g., the post office, the bank, the publishing house. In the end, the two lines coincide; the critical time is to be realized *at* a particular point in space.

14. "Most white men, even those of slight education, have a knowledge of the properties of angles" (*My Life with the Eskimos*, p. 148). The truth of this dubious claim depends on the meaning of the ambiguous phrase "slight education."

15. Landmarks require (a) conspicuous appearance such that they can be viewed (or heard, or smelled) from afar; (b) memory, individual or collective, of previous experiences with them; (c) knowledge of how they relate to other objects in their natural settings. None of these conditions was met in the situation narrated by Stefánsson in *My Life with the Eskimos*.

16. The legend of Tupaia is recounted in David Lewis, *We, the Navigators* (Honolulu: University of Hawaii Press, 1972), pp. 17–18.

17. On the notion of "seamark," see Thomas Gladwin, *East Is a Big Bird* (Cambridge, Mass.: Harvard University Press, 1970), pp. 162ff. For the most part I have followed Gladwin's account, with supplementation from Lewis, *We, the Navigators*, and R. Robin Baker, *Human Navigation and the Sixth Sense* (New York: Simon & Schuster, 1981).

18. For a helpful diagram that explains the etak system, see Gladwin, *East Is a Big Bird*, p. 184. Gladwin explains that "when the navigator envisions in his mind's eye that the reference island is passing under a particular star he notes that a certain number of segments have been completed and a certain proportion of the voyage has therefore been accomplished." Gladwin also remarks that "the contribution of etak is not to generate new primary information, but to provide a framework into which the navigator's knowledge of rate, time, geography, and astronomy can be integrated to provide a conveniently expressed and comprehended statement of distance traveled" (p. 186). For a critique of Gladwin's reliance on units of spatial distance and for an alternative model, see Edwin Hutchins, "Understanding Micronesian Navigation," in D. Genter and A. L. Stevens, eds., *Mental Models* (Hillsdale, N.J.: Erlbaum, 1983), pp. 209ff.

19. On the feature of "high imageability" as crucial to landmarks—and to all important public places—see Edward Relph, *Place and Placelessness* (London: Pion, 1976), p. 35. On the idea of a landmark as a "special configuration in the landscape," see Yi-Fu Tuan, *Space and Place: The Perspective of Experience* (Minneapolis: University of Minnesota Press, 1977), p. 72.

20. Gladwin, *East Is a Big Bird*, p. 184.

21. But for a detailed discussion of certain senses in which dead reckoning, on which Colombus relied for the most part, is validly employed by the Puluwatans, see Lewis, *We, the Navigators*, chap. 4, and Hutchins, "Understanding Micronesian Navigation," p. 202, n. 2.

22. Gladwin, *East Is a Big Bird*, p. 171. Lewis remarks similarly that "holding course by swells seems always to be a matter more of feel than sight" (*We, the Navigators*, p. 87).

23. Spoken by the Santa Cruz navigator Tevake as cited in Lewis, *We, the Navigators*, p. 87. The speaker is from the Society Islands, but the technique he describes is also used by Puluwat navigators.

24. "I have heard from several sources that the most sensitive balance was a man's testicles, and that when at night or when the horizon was obscured, or inside the cabin, this was the method used to find the focus of the swells off an island" (communication from Captain V. Ward cited in Lewis, *We, the Navigators,* p. 87). This is surely navigating by the short hairs!

25. Baker, *Human Navigation,* p. 101. Certain birds use a quite similar technique. The "general area" might most naturally be termed a "region."

26. I discuss horizons and regions more fully in chap. 4. Let me only say now that the horizon of a landscape at once delimits the region of which it is the outer limit and adumbrates what is outside that region, invisible yet accessible (if only we can locomote sufficiently to get there). As such, a horizon can no more be constrained by—or even represented by—map-lines than can lived duration be captured and condensed in time-lines. Just as duration in Bergson's ramified sense is "the time of your life" (and not of the clock), so the landscape is *the space of your life* (and not of the map). Both belong ultimately to place: time as place-dependent and landscape as place-creating.

27. A contemporary investigator of the navigational sense in animals and human beings writes that orientation is "concerned solely with direction and not with destination" (Baker, *Human Navigators,* p. 4). Extrapolating, we might say that destination spells out the deadly and death-dealing fate of modern Westerners: getting to the right place *at the right time.* Direction signifies the enlivening path of the pre- and the postmodern.

28. Tuan, *Space and Place,* pp. 72–73. Tuan also observes that "all people undertake to change amorphous space into articulated geography" (p. 83).

29. Nonetheless, a member of the comparatively stationary Temne tribe of Sierra Leone has "no need to make a conscious effort to structure space, since the space he moves in is so much a part of his routine life that it is in fact his 'place.' The Temne has his place, knows his place, and is rarely challenged by unstructured space" (ibid., p. 79).

30. By speaking of "moving bodies" I do not want to suggest that literal movement of the body is required for the generation of placescapes. What matters is how the body bears on landscape. As I look at the mountains before me, I may be standing still and moving only my eyes; and even if I do not move my eyes but focus steadily on one particular point in the landscape, say a distant cliff, I am actively organizing and interpreting what I see. I am making the landscape a place-for-me (or a place-for-us if I am perceiving in the company of others). As is the case with the Puluwat navigator who lies supine in his canoe sensing the ocean swells, I am shaping an interspace that will be a place for experiences present and to come. Such a placescape is not a given, much less a pregiven, entity. It is coaxed into existence by my actually or virtually moving body, a body that is nevertheless drawn out, *moved,* by particular landscape features. (Landscapes suggest many possible movements, including the movement of not-moving.) A placescape is the joint product of the interaction of my body and the landscape upon which it bears; or we might say that it is the quotient of their difference.

31. By "double horizon" I have in mind the analogue of what Edmund Husserl distinguishes as "internal" vs. "external" horizons in his *Experience and Judgment,* trans. J. S. Churchill and K. Ameriks (Evanston, Ill.: Northwestern University Press, 1973), pp. 360–61: "What comes to self-possession as a *thing* is surrounded by a presumptive horizon, an internal horizon and an external horizon" (his italics). Husserl makes perceptual horizons paradigmatic for his analysis.

32. While I am not proposing that place involves what Husserl calls an *"absolute* flux," I am suggesting that the overflowingness just discussed is the placial analogue of time's deep-going fluency. Compare Martin Heidegger on this point: "All things of earth, and the earth itself as a whole, flow together into a reciprocal accord" ("The Origin of the

Work of Art," *Poetry, Language, Thought,* trans. A. Hofstadter [New York: Harper, 1971], p. 47).

33. On the cultural diversity and specificity of the human body, see the evocative collection of articles on this subject in *Fragments for a History of the Human Body,* ed. M. Feher, with R. Nadaff and M. Tazi (New York: Zone, 1989), 3 vols.

34. In Greek, *ex-* signifies "out of," while *peira* means "attempt, trial, test." *Empirical* also derives from *peira.*

35. This is not to say that there cannot be improvement in the *instrumentation* by which a theoretical posit is determined and utilized. Thus Pierre Le Roy constructed a marine chronometer in 1766, which, because of its combination of efficiency and simplicity, soon became the standard worldwide. Eventually Thomas Earnshaw constructed an inexpensive sea clock that was widely adopted because it sold for one-tenth the going price of a duplicate of John Harrison's No. 4.

36. If places were absolute metaphysical posits, they would not require navigation to reach them. Navigation is an inherently experimental—indeed, a risky—procedure that occurs only in *un*familiar terrain or waters. Thus navigation is to be distinguished from mere pilotage, which is "the method of determining the direction of a familiar goal across familiar terrain" (Baker, *Human Navigators,* p. 4; cf. pp. 5–6, 24–25).

37. Since these ingredients are always *already* cultural in status to some degree, it would be more correct to say that implacement *re*-acculturates the items that have already become *en*-culturated in the natural world. I shall return to the issue of culturation in chap. 8.

38. The sociality of place is preserved in such place-words as *plaza, piazza, place, Plaza,* and *plein,* all of which connote a communal urban space set aside specifically for socializing of various sorts.

39. Vincent Scully, *The Earth, the Temple, and the Gods: Greek Sacred Architecture* (New Haven, Conn.: Yale University Press, 1962), pp. 2–4. See also p. 6: "In that architecture the action of buildings and landscape was fully reciprocal in meaning as in form." Martin Heidegger also analyzes early Greek temples in relation to their surrounding landscape; see his "Origin of the Work of Art" (cited in n. 32), pp. 40–44, esp. p. 42: "The temple-work, standing there, opens up a world and at the same time sets this world back again on earth, which itself thus emerges as native ground."

40. Scully, *The Earth, the Temple, and the Gods,* p. 5. Scully claims that in noncultural contexts "the landscape is normally a constant." But is landscape ever *constant*? Is it not ever-changing, both in physiognomy and in meaning?

41. Ibid., p. 2; my italics.

42. *Orient* originally meant "east," one of the cardinal directions on earth and an especially privileged direction because it is in the east that (as Hemingway put it) the sun also rises—and so does Venus, as the morning star. Similarly, places orient us by illuminating daily the Saturnian darkness of our obsessions and obligations. They do so not by proposing determinate goals but by giving guidance in the guise of direction. Thanks to place, the sun also rises—within.

43. On the earth-sky axis as a "Dimension," see M. Heidegger, "Poetically Man Dwells . . . ," *Poetry, Language, Thought,* pp. 220–22.

44. Concerning cardinality in the formation of an ancient Chinese city, see Paul Wheatley, *The Pivot of the Four Quarters: A Preliminary Enquiry into the Origins and Character of the Ancient Chinese City* (Chicago: Aldine, 1971). For diagrams of the cardinal directions and their diverse connotations in Chinese, Maya, and Pueblo cultures, see Tuan, *Space and Place,* p. 94, fig. 9. On the general importance of cardinal directions for a premodern sense of orientation and for an insightful treatment of non-Western notions

of space, see Ernst Cassirer, *The Philosophy of Symbolic Forms,* trans. R. Manheim (New Haven, Conn.: Yale University Press, 1975), vol. 2, pp. 83–94.

45. Tuan, *Space and Place,* p. 92.

46. Much the same cautionary statement can be made regarding a phenomenon that is, structurally speaking, the converse of the Nazca markings: the Holy of Holies in the Jewish tabernacle. In the latter, it is the enclosing and withholding of space *within* the temple rather than its open-air manifestation that constitutes the creation of a sacred place. Both the built-up interiority of the tabernacle and the built-out exteriority of the Nazca figures illustrate a deep continuity between nature and culture. The post-Exodus temple was situated specifically in the low-lying desert of the Promised Land, its self-seclusion reflecting the harshness of that particular place, while the Nazca earthworks are located in the highlands of Peru in which the sky seems to be an almost tangible presence. In both cases, cultural place has been carved out of natural terrain in such a way as to mirror the latter even as it is transformed. On the Nazca figures, see Thomas Bridges, "The Nazca Markings," *Parabola* 2 (1978), pp. 48–53. In "The Mysterious Markings of Nazca" (*Natural History* 56 [1947], pp. 200–38), Paul Kosok and Maria Reiche speculate that the markings were used as aids to astronomical observations that were in turn employed for calendrical purposes. On the structure of the Jewish tabernacle, see Irving Friedman, "The Sacred Space of Judaism," *Parabola* 2 (1978), pp. 20–23, and Jonathan Z. Smith, *To Take Place* (Chicago: University of Chicago Press, 1987), pp. 43–73, 83–86, 108–12.

47. A more complete treatment would also point to aspects of body, region, and horizon in the cultural constitution of place: e.g., the procession of bodies in the Panathenaea on the Acropolis, the grouping of sacred buildings in the region of the *temenos* (precinct of the temple), and the function of specifically cultural horizons (for instance, in Gadamer's conception of *Horizontsverschmelzung,* according to which cultural horizons both establish a radical otherness and submit to mutual "fusing" upon adequate comprehension). By the same token, consideration of narrative aspects of place-as-encultured is called for. A suggestive start has been made by Stephen Crites, "The Spatial Dimensions of Narrative Truthtelling," in G. Green, ed., *Scriptural Authority and Narrative Interpretation* (Philadelphia: Fortress Press, 1987), pp. 97–118. On "horizon-fusing," see H.-G. Gadamer, *Truth and Method* (New York: Seabury, 1975), pp. 269ff. For a clarifying philosophical discussion of culture as such, see Joseph Margolis, *Culture and Cultural Entities: Toward a New Unity of Science* (Dordrecht: Reidel, 1984).

48. Notably multidimensional is the Maya model of time: "There, a curiously distinctive conception of time as multidimensional and eternally recurrent led to the creation of two intermeshing time counts, which in combination permitted the numbering of years in terms of a cycle of fifty-two" (Wheatley, *Pivot of the Four Quarters,* p. 384). As having several dimensions and being cyclical, such a conception is the exact converse of the monolinear model of early modern thought.

49. An account of such a circumstance—one that turned out well in the end—is given by Vilhjálmur Stefánsson in *Hunters of the Great North* (New York: Harcourt Brace, 1922), pp. 78–88. For a sensitive treatment of the "ice desert," especially its effect of deemphasizing vision in favor of other sensory systems, see E. S. Carpenter, R. Flaherty, and F. Varley, *Eskimo* (Toronto: University of Toronto Press, 1959), and Barry Lopez, *Arctic Dreams: Imagination and Desire in a Northern Landscape* (New York: Bantam, 1987).

50. Lyotard, in *The Lyotard Reader,* p. 212. "Estrangement" is in capital letters in the original statement.

51. On uncanniness, see Sigmund Freud, "The Uncanny," *Standard Edition of the Complete Psychological Works,* vol. 17; Martin Heidegger, *Being and Time,* trans. J.

Macquarrie and E. Robinson (New York: Harper, 1962), secs. 40, 57. For a challenging discussion of being out-of-place as at once a curse (e.g., as homelessness) and a blessing (from an evolutionary perspective), see Neil Evernden, *The Natural Alien: Humankind and Environment* (Toronto: University of Toronto Press, 1985), chap. 5.

52. Thayer Scudder et al., *Expected Impacts of Compulsory Relocation on Navajos* (Philadelphia: Institute for the Study of Human Issues, 1979), p. 62. Not only rural peoples but also seminomadic hunters and gatherers such as the Ik of eastern Africa have suffered greatly from forced confinement to a single area that had formerly been only a resting place in an annual nomadic cycle. In the case of the Ik, the symptoms of displacement were even more extreme than among the Navajo and included indifference and savagery toward their own people. A detailed and moving account of the Ik is Colin M. Turnbull, *The Mountain People* (New York: Simon & Schuster, 1972).

53. From a statement by a Dinéh chief in the brochure "Big Mountain Dinéh Resist Relocation," issued by the Big Mountain Support Group, New York, 1987.

54. Cisco Lassiter, "Relocation and Illness: The Plight of the Navajo," in David Michael Levin, ed., *Pathologies of the Modern Self: Postmodern Studies on Narcissism, Schizophrenia, and Depression* (New York: New York University Press, 1987), p. 228.

55. Cited in ibid., p. 224.

56. Ibid.

57. Ibid., p. 227.

58. Paul Shepard, *Nature and Madness* (San Francisco: Sierra Club Books, 1982), p. 24. Shepard adds: "They are mnemonic: integrated components of a sacred history and the remembered and unconsciously felt past. The whole of the region or home range becomes a hierophantic map, a repository of the first creation that parallels and overlies history." Shepard is here alluding to the Australian Aborigines, but his statements are equally pertinent to the Dinéh. For accounts of the Australian Aborigines, see R. M. Berndt and C. H. Berndt, *The Speaking Land: Myth and Story in Aboriginal Australia* (New York: Penguin, 1989), and Bruce Chatwin, *The Songlines* (New York: Penguin, 1987).

59. Lassiter, "Relocation and Illness," p. 228. Cf. Novalis: "Nature is everywhere the ground on which history grows, season after season" (from his notebooks as cited in Thomas Frick, ed., *The Sacred Theory of the Earth* [Berkeley, Calif.: North Atlantic, 1986], p. 78). But the very idea of natural ground, far from being prehistorical, is itself historical through and through.

60. "The Dinéh's ancestral land is their most important source of cultural knowledge. Virtually all learning in traditional Dinéh culture is experiential; it occurs in the process of raising livestock and making prayers in a particular ancestral place. It involves becoming a part of that place" (Lassiter, "Relocation and Illness," p. 228).

61. Memory loss is a frequently reported symptom among displaced Navajo; it is often associated with disorientation (see ibid., pp. 225–26). In other words, displacement is tantamount to disorientation, in perception and memory as well as in culture.

62. Cited in "Big Mountain Dinéh Resist Relocation." A number of relocated Navajos, after an unsuccessful attempt at adjustment, have vanished. See Lassiter, "Relocation and Illness," p. 223, on the issue of disappearance.

63. See Milton L. Miller, *Nostalgia: A Psychoanalytic Study of Marcel Proust* (Port Washington, N.Y.: Kennikat Press, 1969).

64. For this interpretation of nostalgia, see my essay "The World of Nostalgia," *Man and World* 20 (1987), pp. 361–84.

65. Sven Birkerts, "Place: A Fragment," in Frick, ed., *The Sacred Theory of the Earth*, p. 54.

66. Lawrence Durrell in his *Alexandria Quartet,* cited in ibid., p. 225. Cf. the saying of Edward Weston: "The landscape of a people is the greatest factor in molding their habits, their looks, their physical and spiritual attributes" (ibid.). And see Durrell's collection of travel writings, *Spirit of Place: Letters and Essays on Travel* (New York: Dutton, 1969).

67. Lassiter, "Relocation and Illness," p. 226; my italics.

68. Birkerts, "Place: A Fragment," p. 54.

69. See M. Heidegger, "The Age of the World Picture," *The Question concerning Technology and Other Essays,* trans. W. Lovitt (New York: Harper, 1977), pp. 115–54.

70. Mark Schoepfle et al., "The Human Impact of the Navajo-Hopi Land Dispute," Navajo Community College, Shiprock, Ariz., November 1980. Although the 1974 partition of 1.8 million acres remains deadlocked, in November 1992 the Hopi were given 400,000 acres of public land located elsewhere. In exchange, the Hopi will grant seventy-five-year leases to 150 Navajo families who still live on Hopi territory—on the understanding that the Navajo will eventually transfer the land thus leased back to the Hopi. Meanwhile, the grief continues. For a detailed assessment of the overall situation, see Emily Benedek, *The Wind Won't Know Me: A History of the Navajo-Hopi Land Dispute* (New York: Knopf, 1992).

3. Directions

1. *Enuma Elish,* stanzas one and two, as translated by N. K. Sanders in *Poems of Heaven and Hell from Ancient Mesopotamia* (Baltimore: Penguin, 1970, p. 73. Although I have consulted the standard translation by Alexander Heidel in *The Babylonian Genesis: The Story of Creation,* 2d ed. (Chicago: University of Chicago Press, 1963), I prefer that of Sanders for its poetic eloquence and philosophical appositeness.

2. *Poems of Heaven and Hell,* p. 87.

3. Ibid., p. 90.

4. Ibid., p. 92. In the Heidel translation the second sentence reads: "He split her open like a mussel into two [parts]; half of her he *set in place,* and formed the sky [therewith] as a roof; he fixed the crossbar [and] posted guards; he commanded them not to let her waters escape" (*Babylonian Genesis,* p. 42; my italics).

5. *Poems of Heaven and Hell,* p. 93. On p. 92, Nebiru, "zenith" or the central band of the heavens (as well as Marduk's astral name), is set up as an ultimate ground of direction from on high. Also concerning Nebiru, see p. 102: "Nebiru, at the still center, is the god they adore." On the theme of directions as places, with copious evidence from other cultures, see Yi-Fu Tuan, *Space and Place* (Minneapolis: University of Minnesota Press, 1976), chaps. 6–7, and chap. 4. in this book.

6. *Poems of Heaven and Hell,* pp. 93—94. In other creation myths, a male body serves as the material of creation: e.g., in the southern Chinese myth cycle of Fan Ku (ca. third century A.D.): "From his skull was shaped the dome of the sky, and from his flesh was formed the soil of the fields; from his bones came the rocks, from his blood the rivers and seas; from his hair came all vegetation" (cited in Barbara C. Sproul, ed., *Primal Myths: Creating the World* [New York: Harper & Row, 1979], p. 202).

7. Nevertheless, the aboriginal state of Plato's Receptacle is one of *elemental* confusion—i.e., a confusion of four sorts of elements—and is thus not altogether different from the initial scene in the Mesopotamian epic, in which two kinds of water lie "mingled together." Furthermore, Plato describes the Receptacle as a "matrix": "By nature it is there as a matrix for everything" (*Timaeus,* 50c; "matrix" is Cornford's translation of *exmageion,* a soft mass in which impressions are made). The basic elements are said to be "bodies" with "depth": "In the first place, then, it is of course obvious to anyone

that fire, earth, water, and air are bodies; and all body has depth" (53c). But such bodies, existing in such a matrix, exist only to be transformed by geometric regularization. The very next sentence in the text reads: "Depth, moreover, must be bounded by surface; and every surface that is rectilinear is composed of triangles."

8. By "body" I mean not an inert material thing but the animate, self-moving, self-aware body of a living organism. Examples of inert material things include the stereo-metrically fashioned physical bodies as crafted by the Demiurge in the *Timaeus* or the extended bodies with which Descartes identifies space itself.

9. Aristotle, *Physics*, 208b, 15–16; my italics.

10. Ibid., 208b, 14-18.

11. On this problem and its consequences, see Max Jammer, *Concepts of Space*, 2d ed. (Cambridge, Mass.: Harvard University Press, 1969), pp. 76ff., and Richard Sorabji, *Matter, Space, and Motion* (Ithaca, N.Y.: Cornell University Press, 1988), pp. 125ff.

12. A notable exception is George Berkeley, who makes bodily motion (along with touch and vision) intrinsic to the estimation of distance: "What [one] sees only suggests to his understanding, that after having passed a certain distance, to be measured by the motion of his body, which is perceivable by touch, he shall come to perceive such and such tangible ideas which have been usually connected with such and such visible ideas" (*An Essay towards a New Theory of Vision* [London: Dent, 1934], p. 33).

13. Hellenistic and especially Neoplatonic authors do treat "body" in relation to place, but long in advance of Descartes the body in question has become the sheerly physical body. The specifically lived, and still more specifically human, body is not recognized for its unique role in the constitution of place. For representative statements, see Shmuel Sambursky, *The Concept of Place in Late Neoplatonism* (Jerusalem: Israel Academy of Sciences and Humanities, 1982), pp. 25, 45, 51, 99.

14. Simplicius, *Collarium de Loco*, part of which is translated in ibid., pp. 123ff.

15. A paradox worth pondering is the fact that *place* and body are just as much identified in mythical thought as are *space* and body in Cartesian reflection. But in one case the identity is through an *image*—e.g., "body-of-Tiamat"—while in the other it is through a *concept*, i.e., the essence of body and space as "extension." The result of this variant form of identity is that place is enhanced and validated in the Sumerian epic while it is brought close to extinction in the early modern account. On the ascendancy of the infinite in late medieval, Renaissance, and early modern thinking, see Alexandre Koyré, *From the Closed World to the Infinite Universe* (Baltimore: Johns Hopkins University Press, 1957). The body–place alliance has been given insightful inspection by Ernst Cassirer in *The Philosophy of Symbolic Forms*, trans. R. Manheim (New Haven, Conn.: Yale University Press, 1955), vol. 2, pp. 79–108, 140–43. True to his inspiration by the modernism of the Enlightenment, Cassirer prefers to speak of the body's role in the generation of "space" rather than of "place," even though many of his claims are in fact more applicable to the latter than to the former; e.g., "Because all existence is articulated in the form of *space* and all change in the rhythm and periodicity of time, every attribute which adheres to a specific spatiotemporal *place* is immediately transferred to the content that is given in it" (p. 81; my italics). The uninterrupted transition from "space" to "place" within one and the same sentence is symptomatic of the nonchalance with which Cassirer regards place per se.

16. Immanuel Kant, *Critique of Pure Reason*, trans. N. K. Smith (New York: Macmillan, 1950), B1. Kant adds immediately that "it does not follow that [all our knowledge] *arises out* of experience" (my italics). To start in experience is not to derive from that experience. We can say by extension that all our experience starts with being-in-place, even though it does not follow that all experience derives from place.

17. On these proclivities, see Martin Gardner, *The Ambidextrous Universe: Left, Right, and the Fall of Parity* (New York: Mentor, 1969). In the preceding sentence in the text, I am employing *ambidextrous* in an extended, nonliteral sense. I will return to the subject of bifurcation in discussing the here–there.

18. The resulting lived binarism is not to be confused with the linguistic and metaphysical binarism subject to deconstructive attack on the part of Derrida and others. Where dyads such as /p/ vs. /t/, mind vs. body, self vs. others, offer us only *forced options*, i.e., limited choices determined in advance by preexisting frameworks, no such predetermination normally obtains when I am bodily in place. In a situation of the sort I have described in the text, the way lies quite radically open.

19. The full statement is "neither/nor, that is, *simultaneously* either or" (Jacques Derrida, *Positions*, trans. A. Bass [Chicago: University of Chicago Press, 1981], p. 43; his italics).

20. Even the precise designation of a given dyad remains open; what is front or back for me may be designated as right or left for someone else viewing my body from its side. Not only may the individual members of a given corporeal dyad be exchanged, then, but (as this example shows) entire dyads may be interchanged with one another.

21. We witness the view's persistence in this representative statement: "Although space itself is otherwise isotropic, the earth's gravitational field determines a locally unique upright direction and, also, a prevailing solid surface that (on a suitable scale) is approximately flat, orthogonal to the local upright direction, and hence bounds the local space of free mobility from 'below'" (R. Shepard and S. Hurwitz, "Upward Direction, Mental Rotation, and Discrimination of Left and Right Turns in Maps," in S. Pinker, ed., *Visual Cognition* [Cambridge, Mass.: MIT Press, 1983], p. 162).

22. "This [three] dimensionality of space is still veiled in the spatiality of the ready-to-hand" (M. Heidegger, *Being and Time*, trans. J. Macquarrie and E. Robinson [New York: Harper, 1962], p. 136). Elisabeth Ströker suggests how dimensionality arises from directionality: "By dimension we understand a continuum of possible transitions of *orientational oppositions*" (*Investigations in Philosophy of Space*, trans. A. Mickunas [Athens: Ohio University Press, 1987], p. 63, n.; her italics). "Orientational oppositions" can be taken to refer to the three dyads discussed in this chapter, each of which involves an oppositional pairing of terms. Out of these binaries of corporeal directionality the dimensions of the life-world—and perhaps ultimately of pure space—emerge.

23. For Maurice Merleau-Ponty's distinction, see *Phenomenology of Perception*, trans. C. Smith (New York: Humanities Press, 1962), p. 244. For Heidegger's comparable distinction, see *Being and Time*, pp. 418–24 where there is, however, no mention of the lived body. Edmund Husserl's discussion of spatial idealization is found paradigmatically in *The Crisis of European Sciences and Transcendental Phenomenology*, trans. D. Carr (Evanston, Ill.: Northwestern University Press, 1970), sec. 9 ("Galileo's Mathematization of Nature") and the much-discussed appendix, "The Origin of Geometry."

24. I borrow the phrase from Kant: "There are two stems of human knowledge, namely, sensibility and understanding, which perhaps spring from a common, but to us unknown, root" (Kant, *Critique of Pure Reason*, A15 B29, p. 61).

25. "Ich finde so auch 'meinen Leib' vor, ich nehme ihn beständig wahr aus *Träger der Hier*" (Edmund Husserl, *Zur Phänomenologie der Intersubjectivität*, ed. Iso Kern [The Hague: Nijhoff, 1973], vol. 1, p. 236; my italics). On p. 237 Husserl says simply that "mein Leib ist für mich da durch meinen Leib."

26. "All worldly things there for me continue to appear to me to be oriented about my phenomenally stationary, resting organism. That is, they are oriented with respect to here and there, right and left, etc., whereby a firm zero of orientation persists, so

388 Notes to pages 51–53

to speak, as absolute here" (E. Husserl, "The World of the Living Present and the Constitution of the Surrounding World External to the Organism," trans. F. D. Elliston and L. Langsdorf, in *Husserl: Shorter Writings*, ed. P. McCormick and F. Elliston [Notre Dame, Ind.: University of Notre Dame Press, 1981], p. 250). On the identification of the absolute here with the body as null-point, see E. Husserl, *Cartesian Meditations*, trans. D. Cairns (The Hague: Nijhoff, 1960), p. 123: "[My Nature] is constituted as an identical unity of my manifold modes of givenness—an identical unity in changing orientations around my animate organism (the zero body, the body in the absolute Here)."

27. On attuned space, see Ströker, *Investigations in Philosophy of Space*, pt. 1, chap. 1, esp. the statement on p. 27: "My phenomenal place in attuned space is not ascertainable. As an attuned being, I have no determinable location in this space. . . . Attuned space has no center of reference from which it would be possible to order and separate the experienced things and determine them as there in relationship to a fixed here." In Ströker's view, the lived body becomes a center of reference—hence a bearer of the here—only in what she calls "the space of action" and "the space of intuition." (On these latter two kinds of space, see her chaps. 2 and 3 respectively, particularly pp. 89ff.) My own view is that attuned space, while it certainly exists, is much more exceptional than Ströker supposes and that therefore it cannot be taken as exemplary when it comes to the dimension of the here–there.

28. Among Brenda Milner's classic studies of H. M., see especially "The Memory Defect in Bilateral Hippocampal Lesions," *Psychiatric Research Reports* 11 (1959), pp. 43–58. On the general question of temporal lobe epilepsy, see D. Blumer and A. E. Walker, "Memory in Temporal Lobe Epileptics," in G. A. Talland and N. C. Waugh, eds., *The Pathology of Memory* (New York: Academic Press, 1969), pp. 65–74.

29. On the notion of the "knowing body," *le corps connaissant*, see Merleau-Ponty, *Phenomenology of Perception*, pp. 283 and 309, n.

30. By making this dual claim, I am maintaining no more than that the body is a *sufficient* condition of being implaced. That the body is also a *necessary* condition will be demonstrated in the course of this chapter and the next.

31. On the *Zentralkörper*, see *inter alia* Husserl, *Cartesian Meditations*, p. 123.

32. Concerning this particular localization, see Husserl's remarks on the "*Hinterkopf*" in *Ding und Raum* (The Hague: Nijhoff), sec. 64, pp. 227–28. (I owe this reference to Elizabeth Behnke.)

33. On this migration, see Erwin Straus, "The Forms of Spatiality," *Phenomenological Psychology*, trans. E. Eng (New York: Basic Books, 1966), p. 26: "The 'I' of the awake, active person is centered in the region at the base of the nose, between the eyes; in the dance it descends into the trunk."

34. For this example, see Husserl's amusing (and instructive) analysis of the "infinitely distant foot," which nevertheless remains bound up with my *Ich-Zentrum* located in my upper body; *Ding und Raum*, p. 280. Elizabeth Behnke suggests (in a private communication) that at this level of analysis the body becomes a "where-house" of here–there oppositions.

35. Despite his recognition of the here in sense 1, Husserl appears to adopt this second sense when he writes that "I am *here* somatically, the center of a primordial 'world' oriented around me. Consequently my *entire primordial ownness*, proper to me as a monad, has the content of the Here" (*Cartesian Meditations*, p. 119; Husserl italicizes "here"; the rest of the italics are mine).

36. Standing, moreover, allows us to oppose our body to the bodies of others, further reinforcing our sense that we are *here* in possession of our place, our own body-place. The idea of a "standing army" comes to mind: "Standing army, stand down: you are crushing

the people you are supposed to protect" (William Safire, "The Great Panhandler," *New York Times,* July 15, 1991, p. A15).

37. Range is restricted to "reach" when my body ceases to move as a total entity; even as stationary, I can reach out with my arms and explore a place that exceeds the perimeter of my body proper. On the notion of reach, especially as it extends to our entire "world within reach," see A. Schutz and Th. Luckmann, *The Structures of the Life-World,* trans. T. Engelhardt and R. Zaner (Evanston, Ill.: Northwestern University Press, 1973), pp. 41ff. The authors draw on G. H. Mead's idea of the "manipulative zone."

38. For further discussions of region, see chap. 4, sec. 1.

39. Husserl, *Cartesian Meditations,* p. 117; his italics.

40. As Husserl puts it, "Each of these contents [i.e., my here vs. the other's here] excludes the other; they cannot both exist in my sphere of ownness at the same time." Ibid., p. 119.

41. I say "at least" the five forms in question, since other forms may exist. For example, existing bodily on the earth brings with it a special sense of terrestrial hereness —*being here on this plane*—which is not just another regional here but sui generis. Such a planetary here is so embedded in the lives of human beings that photographs of the earth taken from the moon—from a place that had always been regarded as "out there"—were quite shocking to behold. What had been taken to be a permanent Here was suddenly represented as There. This reversal of locatory status had the effect, however, of helping humans to appreciate their earth-bound here all the more fully. Further reinforcing the status of the Earth Here (as we may call it) is Husserl's claim that even if we were to colonize another planet—or live in outer space on space ships—we would simply reestablish another earthly here *there.* (Cf. Husserl's late essay, "Foundational Investigations of the Phenomenological Origin of the Spatiality of Nature," in *Husserl: Shorter Writings,* pp. 224–28.)

42. A. N. Whitehead, *Process and Reality,* ed. D. R. Griffin and D. W. Sherburne (New York: Free Press, 1978), p. 170. Whitehead adds that the lost traveler "has got his own body, but he has lost [the 'other places']." In Husserl's language, he has secure possession of his "absolute Here," but he lacks a precise sense of the corresponding theres of that here.

43. Erwin Straus, *The Primary World of Senses,* trans. J. Needleman (Glencoe, Ill.: Free Press, 1963), p. 202.

44. By the same token, the there, in its very manyness, calls for the oneness of the here. This is not to deny, of course, that in numerous instances my here is in fact paired with an equally singular there—e.g., when I pursue a single goal to be realized in one there-place only (that bookcase, that kitchen).

45. Husserl writes: "These two primordial spheres, mine which is for me the original sphere, and his which is for me an appresented sphere—are they not separated by an abyss I cannot actually cross, since crossing it would mean, after all, that I acquired an original (rather than an appresenting) experience of someone else?" (*Cartesian Meditations,* p. 121; Husserl underlines "separated"). For Emmanuel Levinas's conception of separation, see his *Totality and Infinity,* trans. A. Lingis (Pittsburgh: Duquesne University Press, 1969), pp. 53–91, 102–105.

46. We may feel counter-places in less dramatic situations as well. Even as I settle into my "easy chair," I am aware of the difference between being just here, in this cozy spot, and being over there at the piano, which to play would require a certain definite effort. Despite its generally welcome presence, the piano as *there* still stands over against me, *countering* me, as it were.

47. The primary status of the here–there, its status as a paradigm of the pre-phenom-

enality of body-in-place, entails its nonreducibility to metric determination. An indefinite dyad indeed! Whenever we experience ourselves in the here–there axis—and we never fail to experience ourselves in it insofar as we feel ourselves to be embodied beings—we find ourselves in a circumstance of the nonmeasured. Thus as I sit in my own living room and gaze across at the wall opposite, I apperceive the difference between my here *here* and the wall over *there* as a felt and adverbial, not as a measurable, distance. The point is not that I could not measure the distance from my chair to the wall—I certainly could; but in so measuring it I would not have specified the felt distance, the "*Ab-stand*," between my hereness and the wall's thereness. Nor can I even traverse this distance in any merely metrical manner; I move *between* the here and the there not as between two points in space but as between two places whose loci are continually changing.

48. The geographical independence of the near–far dimension is also realized in relation to the here–there. Throughout my journey, I experience myself as here in a very particular car-place. This zonal here (itself centered on the absolute here of my lived body) is in turn located in a regional here: being here in Connecticut and then (as I cross the state border) being here in Massachusetts. At each point of my trip corresponding theres arise in the form of counter- and com-places, restricted as well as regional. But this dialectic of the here and the there happens on its own, largely unaffected by the changing melodrama of my sense of the near and the far, even when this sense reflects the reality of geographical distance. It is as if the phenomenal bi-presence of the here and the there—despite its own complexity of form—subtends the less reliably constant ratio of the near and the far.

49. The (t)here is not a case of simultaneous commixture but of variation by situation: what is now there for me is here for someone else (or for myself at a subsequent point). The exclusivity and opposition of the here–there dyad is maintained even when both members of the dyad are invoked in order to do justice to a particular circumstance. The phenomenon of commixture implies that the far and the near differ by degrees, otherwise they could not intermingle so thoroughly. Thus I cannot agree with Ströker when she claims that "the difference between [nearness and remoteness] is not a mere matter of degree; nearness and remoteness differ qualitatively" (*Investigations in Philosophy of Space*, p. 29).

50. Straus, *The Primary World of Senses*, p. 385.

51. Ströker hints at this last point when she writes that "it is only where nearness and remoteness are *abolished*—i.e., in metric space—that space and time are sundered" (*Investigations in Philosophy of Space*, p. 30; my italics).

52. Here I must disagree with Straus when he writes that "Here and There are not purely spatial determinations; they are spatio-temporal phenomena" (*The Primary World of Senses*, p. 385). They may not be *purely* spatial in connotation, but they are *mainly* so, and precisely in contrast with the near and the far, which, as Straus himself insists, are "spatio-temporal forms of sensing."

53. On the spatio-temporality of the life-world, see E. Husserl, *The Crisis of European Sciences and Transcendental Phenomenology*, trans. D. Carr (Evanston, Ill.: Northwestern University Press, 1970), pp. 210, 375, and esp. 168: "The [life-]world is a spatio-temporal world."

54. Straus, *The Primary World of Senses*, p. 384.

55. My notion of near sphere is closely related to but not identical with Patrick Heelan's "near zone" of hyperbolic visual space; see the insightful treatment in his *Space-Perception and the Philosophy of Science* (Berkeley: University of California Press, 1983), pp. 28–35, 62–77, 158–70. The term *near sphere* (*Nähsphäre*) occurs in Husserl's later writings, e.g., in the phrase "primarily familiar near sphere, the core-sphere (*Kernsphäre*)" ("The

World of the Living Present," p. 249). In an appendix to *The Crisis of European Sciences* (p. 324), Husserl uses the expressions "near world" (*Nahwelt*) and "far world" (*Fernvelt*), where near world is made equivalent to "domestic world" (*Heimwelt*). I remain indebted to Elizabeth Behnke for help in tracking down these references in the labyrinth of Husserl's published and unpublished writings.

56. I borrow the notion of advertability from Schutz and Luckmann: the world within actual reach "embraces not only actually perceived objects but also objects that can be perceived through attentive advertence" (*The Structures of the Life-World*, p. 37). Schutz and Luckmann's acute analysis of reach is flawed only by their view that "the world in my actual reach, the sector of the world that is accessible in immediate experience, has a *fixed structure in a coordinate system*" (p. 37; my italics). What guarantees the presence of such a structure? What exact purpose does it serve?

57. As Schutz and Luckmann express this point, "I am to various degrees familiar with the world within attainable reach. I am in any case familiar with the set of applicable types from my previous experiences that have sedimented in my stock of knowledge" (ibid., p. 39).

58. Indeed, a chronic debilitating illness such as multiple sclerosis can alter significantly the entire infrastructure of the near sphere, to the point that virtually nothing but one's own sensations are felt to be genuinely near. For observations on this phenomenon, I am indebted to Kay Toombs.

59. By distinguishing between pathway and (reachable) nodal point, I do not wish to imply that any such "point" is limited to a fixed position or a settled substance. My reachable point may be itself a pathway, e.g., when I am trying to find my *way out* of a room. Here various bodily actions direct me to a particular pathway as their common aim. For a discussion of the implications of reach for domestic spaces, see Anne Buttimer, "Home, Reach, and the Sense of Place," in A. Buttimer and D. Seamon, eds., *The Human Experience of Space and Place* (London: Croom & Helm, 1980), pp. 166–86.

60. On this point, see Heelan, *Space-Perception and the Philosophy of Science*, pp. 76–77 and chap. 16 ("Retrospective"). It therefore follows that "being in the near visual zone then is a sufficient condition for belonging to the zone of actual or potential reach of a subject. It is not, however, any longer necessary" (p. 76). It is not necessary insofar as an object remotely located in terms of physical space can also inhabit my near sphere via technological transmission. But this effect is by no means dependent on modern technology: ancient Gaelic *farnan* signifies "at a distance in a little while."

61. I can also range in depth. Coming into Boston from its outlying areas, I attempt to get into the heart of the city, into its depths. Depth is here the far as it is traversed toward a destination situated in its very midst. But depth in the far sphere need not be so definitely structured as this; it can occur merely as a fading fringe of my perceptual field. Indeed, it need not be located at the same level on which I myself am currently situated; it may also be downward-turning into an abyss or upward-tilted into the sky. Yet to be far away in depth—or on another plane in relation to my near sphere—is still to lie within the orbit of my virtual movement. Thus objects in the far sphere frequently appear with a telephoto effect, i.e., as foreshortened and yet strangely "close."

62. The attraction of the linear model of the horizon is persistent. In his classic essay "The Horizon," Cornelius van Peursen is torn both ways. On one hand, he avers that "the horizon is more than a simple physical line, a fixed border of the world"; yet he also claims that "as a directly given phenomenon, the horizon presents itself as a line which recedes as we advance" (trans. F. Elliston and P. McCormick, in Elliston and McCormick, eds., *Husserl: Expositions and Appraisals*, pp. 185 and 183 respectively). Heelan, on the other hand, speaks expressly of the "horizon sphere"; see his *Space-*

Perception and the Philosophy of Science, pp. 59ff., esp. the statement on p. 59: The horizon sphere is "the spherical surface with the viewer at its center. . . . Objects on the horizon sphere are infinitely far away in physical space."

63. Both citations are from Aaron Gurwitsch, *The Field of Consciousness* (Pittsburgh: Duquesne University Press, 1964), p. 406.

64. Van Peursen, "The Horizon," p. 182.

65. "The horizon, in adding nothing to the world, is for that reason precisely all the more indispensable" (ibid., p. 184). On the horizon's unreality, see p. 183.

66. Jacques Derrida, *Edmund Husserl's Origin of Geometry: An Introduction,* trans. J. Leavy (Stony Brook, N.Y.: Nicolas Hays, 1978), p. 117.

67. The horizon as we experience it via our moving bodies is an outermost boundary in time as in space. To move toward it along multiple routes takes not just time but, thanks to its strict unreachability, an indefinitely large amount of time. Moreover, in view of its status as continually open and incomplete, the future is of special importance in the case of the horizon: "Horizon is the always-already-there of a future which keeps the indetermination of its infinite openness intact" (ibid., p. 117). At the same time, however, the horizon is subject to sedimentations from the past history of its perception. Nothing in the present (since it has purely phenomenal presence), the horizon beckons both from its past and future appearings. In this bivalent capacity, it exhibits a specifically social status, since the horizon is not only what *I* take it to be but what entire groups of people have taken it to be and will continue to take it to be; *we* act in terms of the horizon we have shared and (presumptively) will share. On social typification as it impinges on "spatial arrangements," see Schutz and Luckmann, *The Structures of the Life-World,* pp. 37, 40–41, and 229–43.

68. "Measurants" are bodily and are comparable to "dimensions": "we have with our body, our senses, our look, our power to understand speech and to speak, *measurants* for Being, dimensions to which we can refer it, but not a relation of adequation or of immanence" (M. Merleau-Ponty, *The Visible and the Invisible,* trans. A. Lingis [Evanston, Ill.: Northwestern University Press, 1968], p. 103; his italics). On p. 152 Merleau-Ponty argues that the lived body is the *measurant* of the things around it, and on p. 260 he calls it a "universal *measurant.*"

69. This phrase is the title of chap. 7, pt. 2, of Karl Bühler's *Sprachtheorie: Die Darstullungsfunction der Spache* as translated (in part) in R. J. Jarvella and W. Klein, eds., *Speech, Place, and Action* (New York: Wiley, 1982), pp. 13ff. "Here" is designated as a "place marker" on p. 14. Bühler discusses the role of the "body feeling representation" (*Körpertastbild*) in deixis at p. 25. Baler's pioneering work, first published in 1934, has given rise to an entire field of linguistics, "deictics," one of whose leading American practitioners, Charles J. Fillmore, has written that "a Locating Expression, then, is an expression by which a Figure is said to be at a Place identified with Reference to a Ground. In the particular case of *deictic* Locating Expressions, the Ground is the Speaker's (or in some cases the Hearer's) body" ("Towards a Descriptive Framework for Spatial Deixis," in ibid., p. 43; his italics). I am indebted to Henry Tylbor for these references.

70. On the notion of the "carpentered environment," see Heelan, *Space-Perception and the Philosophy of Science,* pp. 1, 19, 58, 144, 164, 172, 248, 250–51. Heelan considers the space of the near sphere—e.g., when interpreted as Euclidean visual space—to be culturally conditioned but not conventionally determined; see pp. 147, 157–58, 170, 172.

71. On the difference between *Heimwelt* and *Fremdwelt,* see Husserl, *Zur Phänomenologie der Intersubjektivität,* vol. 3. The same cultural specificity obtains for here–there, only less dramatically so, as we would expect since here and there are less directly reflective of their immediate surroundings than near and far. I thank Anthony Steinbock

for bringing the importance of home-world vs. alien-world in Husserl's writings to my attention.

72. Place, says Locke, is "made by Men, for their common use, that by it they might be able to design the particular Position of Things" (*An Essay concerning Human Understanding*, ed. P. H. Nidditch [Oxford: Clarendon Press, 1975], p. 170). "Common use" refers to manual labor, and I take "the particular Position of Things" to imply place that has become private property. For Locke's views of property and value, see his *Second Treatise on Government*. I have benefited from discussion with James E. Donelan and especially from reading his unpublished paper "Locke, Place, and Property."

73. Alfred North Whitehead, *Science and the Modern World* (New York: Free Press, 1953), p. 52. A more technical definition is as follows: "To say that a bit of matter has *simple location* means that, in expressing its spatio-temporal relations, it is adequate to state that it is where it is, in a definite finite region of space, and throughout a definite finite duration of time, apart from any essential reference of the relations of that bit of matter to other regions of space and to other durations of time" (p. 58; his italics).

74. Ibid., p. 39; my italics.

75. T. S. Eliot, "Burnt Norton," second stanza; his italics. As Heidegger observes, the same distinction obtains between "here" and "where": "The 'here' does not mean the 'where' of something present-at-hand" (Heidegger, *Being and Time*, p. 142).

76. I plan to trace out the history of the reduction of place to site in a separate monograph on the vicissitudes of the concept of place in Western thought. It is this same reduction that motivated the search for exact longitude on which I focused in chap. 1; longitude, after all, is nothing but simple location at a determinate meridian.

77. Whitehead, *Science and the Modern World*, p. 51. The phrase "fundamental assumption" is used on p. 52. It is an instance of what R. G. Collingwood, in *An Essay on Metaphysics* (Oxford: Oxford University Press, 1940), chap. 5, would term an "absolute presupposition."

78. Whitehead, *Science and the Modern World*, p. 58.

79. Ibid., p. 91.

80. Ibid., p. 93. His italics. On the body as a total event, see p. 73. On the withness of the body, see Whitehead's *Process and Reality*, ed. D. R. Griffin and D. W. Sherburne (New York: Free Press, 1979), p. 311.

81. Whitehead, *Science and the Modern World*, p. 70.

82. On modal location, see ibid., p. 71. The phrase "location elsewhere" occurs there. On "prehensive unification of modal presences of entities beyond itself," see p. 73.

83. Whitehead, *Process and Reality*, p. 7.

84. The formulation is by M. Merleau-Ponty, *Phenomenology of Perception*, p. 255. I cite it for its conciseness. Berkeley himself declared depth to be nothing but distance as measured in "paces or miles" (*Essay toward a New Theory of Vision* [1709] in *The Works of George Berkeley*, ed. A. A. Luce and T. E. Jessop [London: Nelson, 1948], vol. I, p. 171).

85. Merleau-Ponty, *Phenomenology of Perception*, p. 255.

86. G. W. F. Hegel, *Philosophy of Nature*, trans. M. J. Petrey (London: Allen & Unwin, 1970), vol. 1, p. 256. Descartes laid the ground for this indifferentist position when he claimed that "there is a merely nominal difference between the three dimensions of body—length, breadth, and depth; for in any given solid it is quite immaterial which aspects of its extension we take as its length, which as its breadth, etc." (René Descartes, *Rules for the Direction of the Mind*, in *The Philosophical Writings of Descartes*, ed. J. Cottingham, R. Stoothoff, and D. Murdoch [Cambridge: Cambridge University Press, 1985], vol. 2, p. 63). J. J. Gibson remarks that "the notion of space of three dimensions with three axes for Cartesian coordinates was a great convenience for mathematics . . . but an

abstraction that had very little to do with actual perception" (*The Ecological Approach to Visual Perception* [Hillsdale, N.J.: Erlbaum, 1986], p. 148).

87. Merleau-Ponty, *Phenomenology of Perception*, p. 256. Merleau-Ponty's indictment extends to all modern philosophers, from Descartes to Bergson.

88. Ibid., p. 266.

89. Ibid., pp. 256, 257. Another definition of primordial depth is "a level of distances and sizes" (p. 266). Such a level "defines the far and the near, the great and the small, before any object arises to provide us with a standard for comparison." On level, see pp. 248–54.

90. Ibid., p. 266. "Thickness" translates *épaisseur*. Construed in this way, depth is like void—"place bereft of things" in Aristotle's classical definition (*Physics*, 213b, 32)—except that depth is not empty but always already full.

91. Merleau-Ponty, *Phenomenology of Perception*, p. 266.

92. Ibid., p. 265. The attribution of "originality" occurs in the preceding sentence: "This being simultaneously present in experiences which are nevertheless mutually exclusive, this implication of one in the other, this contraction into one perceptual act of a whole perceptual process, constitutes the originality of [primordial] depth" (pp. 264–65).

93. The quoted phrase is Heidegger's: "We call the first, original, literally incipient extending in which the unity of true time consists 'nearing nearness' (*nähernde Nähe*). . . ." ("Time and Being" in *On Time and Being*, trans. J. Stambaugh [New York: Harper, 1972], p. 15).

94. Merleau-Ponty, *Phenomenology of Perception*, p. 262.

95. Maurice Merleau-Ponty, "Eye and Mind," trans. C. Dallery, in *The Primacy of Perception*, ed. J. Edie (Evanston, Ill.: Northwestern University Press, 1964), p. 180. J. J. Gibson, also a critic of the view of depth as an indifferent "third dimension," comes up with a similar model of depth as envelopment-by-occlusion. For Gibson, depth arises from "an array of adjoining surfaces" in which an occlusion of the edges of these surfaces is a critical factor. See Gibson's *Ecological Approach to Visual Perception*, pp. 286, 308, and Gibson's earlier treatment in *The Perception of the Visual World* (Cambridge, Mass.: Houghton Mifflin, 1950), pp. 6ff. I have compared Merleau-Ponty and Gibson at greater length and developed my own thoughts about the relation between depth and place in "'The Element of Voluminousness': Depth and Place Re-examined," in M. Dillon, ed., *Merleau-Ponty Vivant* (Albany: State University of New York Press, 1990), pp. 1–29.

96. Working note of April 1960, in Merleau-Ponty, *The Visible and the Invisible*, p. 242; my italics.

97. Merleau-Ponty, "Eye and Mind," p. 180; his italics. Merleau-Ponty adds: "Once depth is understood in this way, we can no longer call it a third dimension. In the first place, if it were a dimension, it would be the *first* one; there are forms and definite planes only if it is stipulated how *far from me* their different parts are" (his italics).

98. Whitehead, *Science and the Modern World*, p. 91.

99. This line is also from "Burnt Norton," second stanza.

4. Dimensions

1. Shakespeare, *Hamlet*, act 1, scene 2.

2. On shifters—a form of syncategorematic expression (i.e., Husserl's term for words whose meanings are context-dependent)—in the form of deictic and anaphoric verbal signs, see U. Eco, *A Theory of Semiotics* (Bloomington: Indiana University Press, 1976), pp. 115–21. Part of the meaning of a shifter is that what it names may not exist or has never

existed. Yet its designation is "rigid" (in Kripke's term) in that the expression designates the same individual in any possible world no matter whether that individual exists or not. (See Saul A. Kripke, *Naming and Necessity* [Cambridge, Mass.: Harvard University Press, 1980], pp. 48–49; 10, n; and 49, n.) David Kaplan distinguishes between "pure indexicals" such as *I* and "demonstratives" such as *that* and *he*, arguing that "the referent of a pure indexical depends on the context, and the referent of a demonstrative depends on the associated demonstration" ("Demonstratives: An Essay on the Semantics, Logic, Metaphysics, and Epistemology of Demonstratives and Other Indexicals," in J. Almog, J. Perry, and H. Wettstein, eds., *Themes from Kaplan* [Oxford: Oxford University Press, 1989], p. 492; see also pp. 481ff.). *All* indexicals are rigid designators; they are, in Kaplan's preferred phrase, "directly referential" (see p. 493).

3. As Karl Bühler says, "the words *I* and *you* refer to the role holders in the on-going speech drama, in the speech action. . . . The main and original function of personal pronouns like *I* and *you* is not to *denote* sender and receiver, just as names *denote*, but only to refer to these role holders" (from *Sprachtheorie*, pt. 2, chap. 7, sec. 4, as translated in R. Jarvella and W. Klein, *Speech, Place, and Action: Studies in Deixis and Related Topics* [New York: Wiley, 1982], p. 19; his italics).

4. Merleau-Ponty, *Phenomenology of Perception*, p. 267; my italics.

5. On "bi-presence," see L. Lévy-Bruhl, *The Notebooks on Primitive Mentality*, trans. P. Rivère (New York: Harper, 1978), pp. 4–8, 18, 38, 67, 74–76, 179.

6. Elisabeth Ströker suggests that the orientations given by the dimensional dyads "are neither corporeal nor in or of things. They are relationships of the lived body toward the thing; these relationships are neither causal nor telic, but primarily functional relationships first constituting themselves in the interplay between the acting body and the world to be acted upon. And they are given to the subject in no other way than in the subject's dealing with the world" (*Investigations in Philosophy of Space*, p. 64). In modern attempts to find the simple location of space and time, one set of thinkers—Descartes, Galileo, Gassendi, and Newton most prominently—plant them firmly in the outer physical world, while another group, led by Kant, puts space and time resolutely inside the human subject. Is not this antinomy of origin to be resolved by admitting bi-location in the manner of Spinoza and Leibniz, Hegel and Whitehead?

7. A number of writers on whom I have drawn in this part—most notably Kant, Whitehead, and Heidegger—have suggested the need for a more encompassing term than *place*. Heidegger, for example, insists on the necessity of positing a region as that "out of which what is de-severed brings itself close, so that one can come across it with regard to its place" (*Being and Time*, p. 143). In the perspective of *Being and Time*, places are in every case places *within* regions, which nevertheless give themselves to us as "ready-to-hand already in individual places" (p. 137). Even regions which are not ready-to-hand, such as those provided by the sun's daily trajectory (i.e., sunrise, noon, sunset, etc.), count as fully regional and thus provide the "whithers" for particular places. A given whither organizes a region as a "totality of places" within which in turn given things can be said to "belong somewhere" (both phrases in this sentence are on p. 136). For further treatment of Heidegger's view of place, see my essay "Heidegger In and Out of Place," *Heidegger: A Centennial Appraisal* (Pittsburgh: Silverman Phenomenology Center, 1990), pp. 62–98.

8. Aristotle, *Physics*, 212a, 20–22.

9. Merleau-Ponty, *Phenomenology of Perception*, p. 146.

10. On the *Timaeus* as anticipating modernist conceptions of space, see M. Heidegger, *Introduction to Metaphysics*, trans. R. Manheim (New Haven, Conn.: Yale University Press, 1959), p. 66: "the transformation of the barely apprehended essence of place (*topos*)

and of *chōra* into a 'space' defined by extension was initiated by the Platonic philosophy."

11. Plato, *Timaeus*, 43b (Cornford translation). Such motions, adds Plato, are "unregulated, now reversed, now side-long, now inverted" (43e).

12. "These are the parts and kinds of place: above, below, and the rest of the six dimensions" (Aristotle, *Physics*, 208b, 12–14).

13. Ibid., 18. At 208b 10 Aristotle says that place "has a certain power" (*echei tina dunamin*).

14. Ibid., 14–18.

15. Only the places of mathematical objects—e.g., points—can be said to be *determined* by our bodily position and thus to have no inherent position of their own: such objects "are not in place, but still have right and left according to their position relatively to us, with 'right' and 'left' in a sense merely relative to position, since they do not have either of these by nature" (ibid., 23–25).

16. See René Descartes, *Optics*, trans. and ed. J. Cottingham, R. Stoothof, and D. Murdoch (Cambridge: Cambridge University Press, 1983), vol. 1, pp. 169–70. Descartes, who is often assumed to be an unremitting oculocentrist, remarks on p. 169 that "as regards position, i.e., the orientation of each part of an object relative to our body, we perceive it by means of our eyes *exactly as we do by means of our hands*" (my italics).

17. "The threefold dimension [of space] seems to arise from the fact that substances in the existing world so act upon one another that the strength of the action holds inversely as the square of the distances [between these substances]" (I. Kant, "Thoughts on the True Estimation of Living Forces" [1747], trans. J. Handyside, in *Kant's Inaugural Dissertation and Early Writings on Space* [Chicago: Open Court, 1929], p. 11; in bold face in the text). But in this same essay, Kant's allegiance lies with Leibniz, not with Newton, since Kant agrees with Leibniz that there could be no space at all without dynamic substances possessing intrinsic "force" (*Kraft*) of their own. Twenty years later, Kant still tried to derive dimensionality from the nature of physical space, but then he introduced a new determinant: the *body*. N. K. Smith remarks that in Kant's essay "On the First Ground of the Distinction of Regions in Space" (1768) "the three dimensions of space are primarily distinguishable by us only through the relation in which they stand to our body" (*A Commentary to Kant's "Critique of Pure Reason"* [New York: Humanities Press, 1962], p. 162). This new approach continued to bear fruit in Husserl and Whitehead, Merleau-Ponty and Mach. Mach, for example, found "the physiological basis for our familiarity with the three dimensions of geometric space" to lie in the fact that "the system of space-sensations is in the main very similar, though unequally developed, in all animals which, like man, have three cardinal directions *distinctly marked on their bodies*" (*Space and Geometry*, trans. T. J. McCormack [Chicago: Open Court, 1906], p. 18; my italics).

18. Clifford Hill, "Up/Down, Front/Back, Left/Right: A Contrastive Study of Hausa and English," in J. Weissenborn and W. Klein, eds., *Here and There: Cross-Linguistic Studies on Deixis and Demonstration* [Philadelphia: Benjamins, 1983], p. 13).

19. Aristotle, *Physics*, 208b, 12–21.

20. "What I want to do is to restore the world as a meaning of Being absolutely different from the 'represented,' that is, as the vertical Being which none of the 'representations' exhaust and which all 'reach,' the wild Being" (working note of May 1960 in Merleau-Ponty, *The Visible and the Invisible*, p. 253; see also pp. 234, 244, 268, 271–73). Vertical being is also implicit in Heidegger's statement that "the upward glance passes aloft toward the sky, and yet it remains below on the earth. The upward glance spans the between of sky and earth. . . ." ("Poetically Man Dwells . . . ," in *Poetry, Language,*

Thought, trans. A. Hofstadter [New York: Harper, 1971], p. 220). Not only the Greek world view that inspires Heidegger but many other cosmologies, e.g., that of Buddhism, regard up and down as defining the primary dimension of the universe, while right–left and ahead–behind possess no such embracing significance.

21. Hill, "Up/Down, Front/Back, Left/Right," p. 38, n. 4. Hill adds that "this continuous adaptation to the force of gravity leads to highly developed sensations of vertical orientation. . . . There is no similar force that the body must push against in order to maintain a 'frontward' position."

22. The paradox of up–down predominance in a visually and practically horizontal field is noted by Roger Shepard and Shelley Hurwitz: "The terrain on which we have mostly had to find our way about is to a rough approximation horizontal; its ups and downs are usually quite small compared with the horizontal distances we must traverse to get from one significant location to another. However, as a consequence of its gravitational basis, the upright direction has always been the most salient, constant, and unique direction in our world" ("Upward Direction, Mental Rotation, and Discrimination of Left and Right Turns in Maps," in S. Pinker, ed., *Visual Cognition* [Cambridge, Mass: MIT Press, 1983], p. 190). One sign of the predominance of the upright direction is seen in a recent study by Nancy Franklin and Barbara Tversky in which efforts to locate objects said to be situated in the vertical plane were consistently favored over attempts to situate objects described as situated in the horizontal plane: "In searching imagined scenes, subjects were fastest to locate objects above or below the observer, slower to locate objects in front of the observer and then behind, and slowest to locate objects to the left or right" ("Searching Imagined Environments," *Journal of Experimental Psychology: General* 119 [1990], p. 67; see also pp. 63–77).

23. George Lakoff and Mark Johnson, *Metaphors We Live By* (Chicago: University of Chicago Press, 1980), pp. 14–21. In their treatment of metaphors such as "happy is up; sad is down," the authors provide an analysis of the "physical basis": "drooping posture typically goes along with sadness and depression, erect posture with a positive emotional state" (p. 15).

24. Hill, "Up/Down, Front/Back, Left/Right," p. 14.

25. For purposes of simplification, in what follows I do not distinguish between up–down and above–below. Strictly speaking, however, the distinction between above and below applies to the relative *location* of objects, places, and regions, while that between up and down refers to two different directions of *movement*. A related distinction is that between "high" and "low," which involve reference to a standard *ground level* and whose meaning differs depending on the kind of object or situation present. On this last point, see Herbert H. Clark, "Space, Time, Semantics and the Child," *Cognitive Development and the Acquisition of Language* (Albany: SUNY Research Foundation, 1973), p. 36. However, *pace* Plato in the *Timaeus* (where the difference between "motion" and "dimension" is moot), I shall not attempt any systematic differentiation between these three pairs of related terms so as not to foreclose the full richness of the phenomena with which they are associated. Similarly, and for much the same reason, I will not distinguish rigorously between ahead–behind and before–after or forward–backward. Nor will I even seek to rigorously separate "dimension" from "direction," or either of these from "orientation," to which they both contribute.

26. For an elegant, if ultimately unconvincing, explanation of this circumstance, see Shepard and Hurwitz, "Upward Direction," pp. 161–93.

27. On the phenomenon of "you are here" maps and their potentially misguiding effects, see M. Levine, I. N. Jankovic, and M. Paliji, "Principles of Spatial Problem Solving," *Journal of Experimental Psychology: General* 111 (1982), pp. 157–75.

28. Heidegger remarks that "the nature of the Dimension is a meting out. Meting out (*die Zumessung*) is not yet measurement" ("Poetically Man Dwells . . . , p. 220). He adds: "We now call the span thus meted out the Dimension."

29. Merleau-Ponty, *Phenomenology of Perception*, p. 244.

30. Erwin Straus, "The Upright Posture," *Phenomenological Psychology*, trans. E. Eng (New York: Basic Books, 1966), p. 142. A comparable importance of vertical hierarchy in Nietzsche's *Genealogy of Morals*—and precisely as stemming from the active–passive body—is emphasized by Gilles Deleuze in his "Active and Reactive," trans. R. Cohen, in D. Allison, ed., *The New Nietzsche* (New York: Delta, 1977), pp. 80ff.

31. On the inversion of the perceived world, see G. M. Stratton, "Vision without Inversion of the Retinal Image," *Psychological Review* (1897); discussed by Merleau-Ponty in *Phenomenology of Perception*, pp. 244–50. Concerning the room seen obliquely in a mirror, see Max Wertheimer, "Experimentelle Studien über das Sehen von Bewegung," *Zeitschrift für Psychologie* (1912), discussed by Merleau-Ponty, ibid., pp. 248–50.

32. Also active are the "vestibular sacs," which maintain a frame of reference sensitive to the least change in bodily position or movement as measured against gravitational forces.

33. This phrase is found in ibid., p. 206. Spatial level is discussed on pp. 244–54.

34. Oliver Sacks reports a patient with Parkinson's disease who did not realize that he was walking in an extremely bent-over, "Tower of Pisa" way until he was shown a videotape of his actual posture. "Mr. MacGregor" addressed this distressing situation by inventing a pair of spectacles which reinstated a sense of level that allowed him to walk in a nontilted fashion. See Sacks, "On the Level," *The Man Who Mistook His Wife for a Hat* (New York: Summit, 1985), pp. 67–72. As in the case of the Stratton experiment, a distinct gradualism was evident: Mr. MacGregor's "spirit spectacles" (as he called them) "worked, in a fashion—at least he stopped tilting; but it was a continuous, exhausting exercise. And then, over the ensuing weeks, it got easier and easier." Mr. MacGregor had an unimpaired physiological system of equilibrium—including a normal (and literal) level of fluid in his semicircular canals—but his neurological deficit, introduced by Parkinson's disease, meant that the problem lay rather in "his ability to *use* his balance organs, in conjunction with the body's sense of itself and with its visual picture of the world." Sacks's emphasis on the active use of the body rejoins Merleau-Ponty's stress on the body as responsible actor: "as a mass of tactile, labyrinthine and kinesthetic data, the body has no more definite orientation than the other contents of experience . . . nevertheless, *as an agent,* it plays an essential part in the establishment of level" (*Phenomenology of Perception*, p. 249; my italics).

35. Merleau-Ponty, *Phenomenology of Perception*, p. 248. He italicizes "spatial level."

36. On the constancy phenomenon (not to be confused with the "constancy effect"), see Straus, "The Upright Posture," pp. 145, 147.

37. "What all of these Gnostic traditions have in common is the theme that the ability to stand upright is a human feature which the archons were unable to imitate when they created their own human [being]. The created body came to possess this uniquely human ability only by divine gift" (Michael A. Williams, "Divine Image—Prison of Flesh: Perceptions of the Body in Ancient Gnosticism," in *Fragments for a History of the Human Body*, ed. M. Feher, with R. Nadaff and N. Tazi [New York: Zone, 1989], vol. 1, p. 139).

38. Heidegger, *Being and Time*, p. 138. In another passage Heidegger underlines how above–below distinctions can be experienced as inhering in particular places: "The 'above' is what is 'on the ceiling'; the 'below' is what is 'on the floor'; the 'behind' is what is 'at the door'" (pp. 136–37).

39. According to the *Corpus Hermeticum*, "the head corresponds to the sky, a place inhabited by the spirit and by higher intelligences, while man's lower half—'the genital

parts, the origin of generation, are in the lower part' says Pico della Mirandola—corresponds to that part of the universe which is located under the Moon, an area where, 'as everyone knows,' says Pico, 'generation and corruption are born'" (Patrizia Magli, "The Face and the Soul," in *Fragments for a History of the Human Body*, vol. 2, p. 109). But there is an implicit hierarchy even in this correspondential view. On one hand, the upright posture represents an extension of the radius of the earth; on the other hand, the same posture is "*the one and only original and absolute vertical direction*" (cited and italicized by Magli, p. 110, from H. de Superville, *Essai sur les signes inconditionnels dans l'art* [Leyden, 1827]). The latter claim would seem to make the upright body the source of the verticality of the cosmos.

40. On the distinction between "ethereal world" and "tomb world," see Ludwig Binswanger, "The Case of Ellen West," trans. W. M. Mendel and J. Lyons, in R. May, E. Angel, and H. Ellenberger, eds., *Existence* (New York: Basic Books, 1958), pp. 303–12. A more technical way to put the distinction is to say that "upward from ground level is unmarked, or positive, and downward is marked, or negative" (Clark, "Space, Time, Semantics," p. 39), where a marked term is more complex, or more problematic, than an unmarked term taken for granted or as a positive standard.

41. The quoted phrase is from Magli, "The Face and Soul," p. 110.

42. Erwin Straus remarks that "isotropy holds only for purely geometric, and not for physical space," and he gives as an example the case of "verticals" in the "space of the observer": "While horizontal parallels appear to converge, the verticals do not follow this transformation—an indication of the role that gravity and its overcoming play in the formation of sensory space" (*Man, Time, and World*, trans. D. Moss [Pittsburgh: Duquesne University Press, 1982], p. 149).

43. The logic of "beyond" or "over" is of special interest. Clark ("Space, Time, Semantics," p. 46) argues that the use of "beyond" in a sentence such as "A is beyond B" entails two points of reference: "A is on the far side of B from the point of view of C," where C is precisely the bodily position of the speaker.

44. A psychological study of orienting behavior in both actual and imagined perceptual situations has demonstrated that when asked to indicate where local landmarks are, subjects hesitate far less if these landmarks are thought to be located in front of rather than behind them: "people can point to landmarks that are in front of them, but hidden from view, faster than landmarks behind them" (M. Jeanne Sholl, "Cognitive Maps as Orienting Schemata," *Journal of Experimental Psychology: Learning, Memory, and Cognition* 13 [1987], p. 622). Another study discovered that "the only consistent effect on response profiles [in an experiment that tested ability to locate target objects on a circle around subjects] was the tendency to make Front and Back responses more quickly and accurately than the others" (D. L. Hintzman, C. S. O'Dell, and D. R. Arndt, "Orientation in Cognitive Maps," *Cognitive Psychology* 13 [1981], p. 156). This finding implies that the entire dyad of ahead–behind possesses an orientational advantage in comparison with the other two-dimensional dyads. One suspects, however, that this generic advantage only carries forward the particular strength of the forward direction in orientation to *local* landmarks. This advantage is far from absolute. I have cited the Franklin and Tversky study in which up–down reaction times were consistently favored over front–back. In the same study, it was also shown that the privileged position of front vs. back locations is quickly suspended when subjects are asked to imagine themselves reclining, in which case response times for objects located ahead of or behind the observer were equivalent, while up–down reaction times lost their usual advantage ("Searching Imagined Environments," pp. 70–71, 74–75).

45. Franklin and Tversky, "Searching Imagined Environments," p. 74.

46. Anatomy and language are here closely related. Hill remarks on the striking

fact that "the back" in several languages names both the entire region behind us *and* a particular part of our backside, while there is no comparable semantic spread in regard to "the front": "That back and *baya* [in Hausa] actually refer to a portion of the body, unlike front and *gaba*, suggests the seminal role that human anatomy plays in determining referential functions for these lexical items; for referential asymmetry is apparently related to this anatomical asymmetry; that is to say, the greater differentiation of the anterior part of the body leads to a variety of specific names, which usurp, as it were, the naming function of the more general term" ("Up/Down, Front/Back, Left/Right," p. 13).

47. Clark, "Space, Time, Semantics," p. 43; his italics.

48. Aristotle first explictly endorsed the privilege of vision: "We prefer sight to almost anything else. The reason is that this, most of all the senses, makes us know and *brings to light many differences between things*" (*Metaphysics*, 980a, 25–28; my italics). On the primacy of vision, see also Hans Jonas, "The Nobility of Sight: A Study in the Phenomenology of the Senses," *The Phenomenon of Life: Towards a Philosophical Biology* (Chicago: University of Chicago Press, 1982), pp. 135–51.

49. Straus, "The Upright Posture," p. 162; my italics.

50. The quote is from ibid.

51. Or do crabs move sideways? Clark observes that "the front is normally the end of the object containing the perceptual apparatus (e.g., dogs, fish, crabs, etc.), or the end that leads when the object is in typical motion (e.g., *in front of the rocket in outer space*), but in some cases these two criteria conflict and one must be chosen as primary (as in *crabs move sideways*)" ("Space, Time, Semantics," p. 42; his italics).

52. Here a purely linguistic analysis is misleading, since it suggests that the front of a person and the front of an object are of equal value; and the same holds for the back dimension. Thus Clark maintains that "in English, therefore, there are two fronts and backs: (1) an inherent front and back, as of a car, person, rocket, or whatever; and (2) an egocentric front and back, that defined by the canonical encounter [i.e., an encounter between my body and an object]" (ibid., p. 46). Clark himself admits that "these two uses do not always coincide," but he does not go on to attribute the incongruity to anything inherent in the bodily basis of the anomalous situation. The asymmetry in question, far from being anomalous, is, in my view, just what we would expect in the circumstance.

53. Ströker, *Investigations in Philosophy of Space*, p. 92. Ströker adds: "Strictly speaking, seeing 'toward the back' is *functionally* impossible. Even if we were to turn our head around, considered functionally, we would still be oriented forward" (her italics).

54. The first phrase cited is from Eliot, "The Dry Salvages": "The backward look behind the assurance / Of recorded history, the backward half-look / Over the shoulder, towards the primitive terror." The second phrase is from Shakespeare, *The Tempest*, act 1, scene 2, where the "Abysme" is said to be "of Time."

55. This is not to say that my back-field is entirely a domain of ignorance. F. Attenave and P. Farrar studied people's sense of what is behind them and found that many subjects felt as if they had "eyes in the back of their heads" and could at least visually imagine what lay behind their backs. But the images they conjured up were significantly less clear than the images of objects hidden in places in front of them, and attempts to specify where objects behind them were located took more time to determine—and were less accurate—than efforts to locate unseen objects before them ("The Visual World behind the Head," *American Journal of Psychology* 80 [1997], pp. 549–63).

56. The use of the rearview mirror when driving in a forward direction is revealing and somewhat paradoxical. I look *forward* into a mirror that allows me to see *back*, by opening up a momentary corridor of space in the region I have just traversed. Whenever I move on a predelineated path, it acts as a slate onto which the footprints, or tireprints, of my moving body *have been* inscribed. Indeed, I am bound to my path's sequentiality

and hence tend to remember it step by step, diachronically, rather than synchronically by means of a synoptic look backward.

57. Aristotle, *Physics*, 208b, 14–18.

58. In this regard, the scope of deixis is considerably larger than a leading deictic linguist such as Fillmore is willing to grant. What Fillmore regards as exceptional instances of "deixis by default" (e.g., "they're up front") are more the rule than the exception. In deixis by default, a sentence such as "they're up front" stands in for a somatocentric judgment such as "they're ahead of where we are now standing." For this analysis, see Charles J. Fillmore, "Towards A Descriptive Framework for Spatial Deixis," in R. Jarvella and W. Klein, *Speech, Place, and Action* (New York: Wiley, 1982), pp. 39–40. Fillmore regards such related cases as "the child is in front of the tree" (which he parses as "the child is near the tree, on the side of the tree *closest to me*") as implicitly egocentric. Even Hill's subtle distinction between "ego-aligned" and "ego-opposed" deixis (cited by Fillmore on p. 41 still draws covertly on the central position of the human body. On these issues, see also Clark, "Space, Time, Semantics," p. 47, table 3, where a distinction between "nonegocentric, nonintrinsic," "nonegocentric, intrinsic," and "egocentric, nonintrinsic" prepositions is maintained. In my view, all three categories are made possible by the pivotal position of the body throughout.

59. "The left/right orientation . . . is possible for an object only if that object has *both* a vertical or up/down orientation *and* a front/back orientation" (Charles J. Fillmore, "Santa Cruz Lectures on Deixis" [Bloomington: Indiana University Linguistics Club, 1975], cited in Hill, "Up/Down, Front/Back, Left/Right," p. 38; Fillmore's italics). Hill comments on this passage that "the left/right axis is, in effect, derived from an intersection of the other two" (p. 39, n. 6). Indirect evidence for this priority comes from the phenomenon of left–right reversal in mirrors. Close analysis of this reversal reveals that it is in fact dependent on a prior front–back reversal of the body of the person who is viewing herself in the mirror. (See Gardner, *The Ambidextrous Universe*, pp. 29–32, esp. p. 30: "In a strict mathematical sense, the mirror has not reversed left and right at all, it has reversed front and back." The "strict mathematical sense" here in question refers to the fact that the mirror reverses only the axis that is perpendicular to its surface—and this is the front–back axis as one stands facing the mirror. But we identify ourselves with the image of the person *in the mirror* and thus assume that a right–left reversal has occurred: "It is only because you imagine yourself standing behind the glass, facing the other way, that you speak of it as a left–right reversal.")

60. "The confusion of left and right occurs . . . with regard to figures that have no motor, but only a purely optical (for example, ornamental) interest" (E. Mach, *The Analysis of Sensations* [New York: Dover, 1959], p. 111). For more recent studies of the phenomenon, see W. S. Farrell, Jr., "Coding Left and Right," *Journal of Experimental Psychology: Human Perception and Performance* (1979), pp. 42–51. Farrell speculates that the difference between right–left and up–down discrimination may be based on the basic physical fact that distinctions in vertical direction rely upon a "natural referent" (i.e., the earth as a "ground plane") and a "natural direction away from that referent" (i.e., upward), while there is no such built-in asymmetry in the horizontal direction and thus no physical basis for consistently marked differences between right and left. Hence, any distinction between right and left must invoke what Clark calls "fairly arbitrary criteria" ("Space, Time, Semantics," p. 47). See also R. H. Maki, C. A. Grandy, and G. Hauge, "Why Is Telling Right from Left More Difficult Than Telling Above from Below?" *Journal of Experimental Psychology: Human Perception and Performance* (1979), pp. 52–67.

61. See M. C. Corballis and I. L. Beale, "Bilateral Symmetry and Behavior," *Psychological Review* 77 (1970), pp. 452–54.

62. Hemi-attention, or (as it is also called) "unilateral neglect," is thus a bizarre neu-

rological syndrome in which "patients neglect the left side of the world and of their bodies, denying that their own left arm belongs to them and forgetting to put it into its sleeve; confronting a group of four people, they speak and act as if only the two on the right existed; asked to bisect a line, they make a mark ¾ of the way to the right side. Bisiach asked some Italian patients with this syndrome to imagine they were in the Piazza del Duomo of Milan, facing the cathedral, and asked what they would see; they described only the buildings in the right half of the Square. Then he asked them to imagine that they were on the steps of the cathedral, facing away from it, and describe the square again: now they imagined and described the other half of the Piazza!" (communication from Ulric Neisser, June 1989). See also Sacks, "Eyes Right!" *The Man Who Mistook His Wife for a Hat*, esp. pp. 73ff.

63. Rodney Needham, introduction to Needham, ed., *Right & Left: Essays on Dual Symbolic Classification* (Chicago: University of Chicago Press, 1973), p. xxii. See also pp. xxv, xxvii. Needham is here speaking not only of the perceptual and physical domains of the right and left but also of the manifold cultural extensions of the same distinction.

64. Robert Hertz, "The Pre-eminence of the Right Hand: A Study in Religious Polarity," trans. Needham, in *Right & Left*, p. 4. For a thorough treatment of the neurological and psychological bases of the right–left differentiation, see M. C. Corballis and I. L. Beale, *The Psychology of Right and Left* (Hillsdale, N.J: Erlbaum, 1976); and Vilma Fritsch, *Left and Right in Science and Life* (London: Barrie and Rockcliff, 1968).

65. Hertz, "The Pre-eminence of the Right Hand," p. 21.

66. Ibid., p. 14.

67. Ibid., p. 3. His italics.

68. See Geoffrey Lloyd, "Right and Left in Greek Philosophy," in Needham, ed., *Right & Left*, p. 170. E. Steir has speculated that in pre-Homeric times shields were held with the left hand to cover the heart more adequately, leaving the right hand to be dominant in military action (*Untersuchungen über Linkshändigkeit* [Jena: Fischer, 1911], as cited by G. von Bonin, "Anatomical Asymmetries of the Cerebral Hemispheres," in V. B. Mountcastle, ed., *Interhemispheric Relations and Cerebral Dominance* [Baltimore: Johns Hopkins, 1962], p. 1).

69. Aristotle, *Parts of Animals*, 665a, 22ff. Aristotle is forced to admit important exceptions; e.g., the heart as located on the left side (665b, 11–18) and the indeterminate locus of males vs. females in the womb (*History of Animals*, 583b, 2ff.). Lloyd comments (with reference to *De Caelo* 284b, 24ff.) that for Aristotle "right, above, and front are said to be the *archai*, the starting-points or principles, not only of the three dimensions, breadth, length, and depth, respectively . . . but also of the three types of change, locomotion, growth, and sensation in living beings" (Lloyd, "Right and Left in Greek Philosophy," p. 173).

70. Adapted from Rodney Needham, "Right and Left in Nyoro Symbolic Classification," in Needham, ed., *Right & Left*, p. 328. Even if the ascription of auspicious vs. inauspicious symbolic values to right and left respectively is not as straightforward as this list suggests, it certainly does bring with it certain practical consequences. Thus the afterbirth of male babies is always buried to the right side of the door to the house, that of girls to the left, while men are buried lying on their right side, women on their left. (On the problems of such ascription, see Needham's introduction, esp. xix–xxx.) According to the Nyoro, God himself points upward with his right hand and proclaims, "This is heaven," meanwhile pointing down with his left hand in order to say, "This is earth" (p. xxii). Concerning the Chinese attitude toward right and left, see Marcel Granet, "Right and Left in China," in Needham, pp. 43ff. On the Zuni, *see* E. E. Evans-Pritchard, introduction to R. Hertz, *Death and the Right Hand*, trans. R. and C. Needham (London: 1960), p. 22.

71. Other instances of the complementary values attached to right and left are less transparent. Thus the left hand is the most sacred member of the Mugwe, a priestly caste of the Meru people. It alone possesses ritual power. Even so, if a table of associated values is constructed for the Meru, we find the following (adapated from R. Needham, "The Left Hand of the Mugwe," in Needham, ed., *Right & Left,* p. 116):

Right	Left
day	night
north	south
east	west
senior	junior
man	woman/child
sunrise	sunset
light	darkness
older	younger
elders	Mugwe
political power	religious authority

Here a reversal of values is posited specifically—and only—for those who, like the Mugwe, have religious authority. In other cultures, exceptions are recognized only for extraordinary states such as sleep and death. Thus for the Temne the left hand becomes stronger than the right and communicates with God after death, even though the same hand is considered inferior during a person's lifetime. (On this example, see James Littlejohn, "Temne Right and Left," in ibid., pp. 294ff.)

72. Cited by Lloyd, "Right and Left in Greek Philosophy," p. 180, from "Dualism and Symbolic Antithesis in Indonesian Society," by J. M. van der Keoef, *American Anthropologist* 56 (1954), pp. 847ff.

73. E. E. Evans-Pritchard, *Nuer Religion* (Oxford: Oxford University Press, 1956), p. 234.

74. Francis La Flesche, "Right and Left in Osage Ceremonies," in Needham, ed., *Right & Left,* pp. 39–40. The Osage imagine this symbolic man as having motion: as he moves, so the entire tribe (with both of its divisions) moves.

75. "The Chief holds his reception standing on a dais with his back to the north and his face to the south, i.e., facing the light or the Yang. . . . when the Chief stands facing the south he receives the full rays of the sun; he thus assimilates the Yang, the luminous principle" (Grant, "Right and Left in China," p. 49). To this observation, we need only add that the sun *rises* at the chief's (i.e., emperor's) left side, which is thus favored.

76. Littlejohn, "Temne Right and Left," p. 291. It is tempting to speculate that the critical factor is less the *east* as such than whatever direction is perceived as generative of light and heat. Thus the primacy of the south in China—and in the Atoni and Arab cultures—would be only a variant on a common theme: i.e., our "primary orientation" is toward whatever direction provides daylight most readily and reliably. Such speculation rejoins the provocative critique of Hertz offered by J. Chelhod, "A Contribution to the Problem of the Pre-Eminence of the Right, Based upon Arabic Evidence," in Needham, ed., *Right & Left,* pp. 239–55. Instead of proposing sacred vs. profane as the most primitive opposition—as did Hertz—Chelhod argues, on the basis of Arabian sources, that light and shadow, hot and cold, and thus south and north may be even more determinative of right-hand predominance. (On the Atoni predilection for the north–south axis as aligning right–left distinctions, see Charles Frake, "Order in the Atoni House," in ibid., pp. 203–38.)

77. Our head, although a single entity, has a right vs. left side, as concretized in the case of ears and eyes. In certain contexts, the head is used to point out right and left directions. (The same principle applies to *parts* of the head; Tibetans point out directions with their lips.)

78. "Symmetry probably has survival value at different levels. [In evolution from stationary sea organisms to moving creatures] radial symmetry probably gave way to bilateral symmetry as organisms evolved the capacity to move, since linear movement is most efficiently accomplished by a system that is bilaterally symmetrical" (Corballis and Beale, "Bilateral Symmetry and Behavior," p. 461, drawing on the early work of Herman Weyl, *Symmetry* [Princeton: Princeton University Press, 1953]).

79. Jerome Bruner points to the possible connection between holding and acting with two hands and topic and comment in language ("Up from Helplessness," *Psychology Today* 2 (1969), p. 30. Corballis and Beale, who cite Bruner on this point, observe that "asymmetry in intermanual functions may therefore have set the stage for the cortical asymmetry of function that is characteristic of language representation in the human brain" ("Bilateral Symmetry and Behavior," p. 462).

80. Both *maintaining* and *manipulation* stem from Latin *manus*, hand.

81. Immanuel Kant, "On the First Ground of the Distinction of Regions in Space," trans. J. Handyside, in J. Handyside, ed., *Kant's Inaugural Dissertation and Early Writings on Space* (Chicago: Open Court, 1929), p. 23. A contemporary geographer bears out the truth of Kant's observation: "Anyone who is used to working with maps will know how true this [observation] is. . . . once one has located the north pointer, one orients oneself to the map by automatically associating east with the right hand and west with the left hand" (J. A. May, *Kant's Concept of Geography and Its Relation to Recent Geographical Thought* [University of Toronto: Department of Geography Research Publications no. 4, 1970], p. 71). From Kant's description of using a map, it is also clear that north as implicitly opposite the head of the map reader is associated with "up"—the "north pointer" points resolutely *up*—just as we would expect from the upward position of the head in relation to the rest of the body. As a result, to walk due north as indicated by the map is to walk *ahead*.

82. Kant, "On the First Ground," p. 23; my italics.

83. Ibid., pp. 22–23. In *Being and Time*, pp. 143–44, Heidegger criticizes Kant's reliance on feeling in this same passage. The phrase "inner difference" is from this critical sentence: "From the common example of the two hands, it is already clear that the shape of one body can be completely similar to that of another, and the magnitude of their extension exactly the same, while yet there remains an inner difference, namely, that the surface which bounds the one cannot possibly bound the other" ("On the First Ground," p. 27). For an assessment of Kant's critique of Leibniz, see Fritsch, *Left and Right in Science and Life*, pp. 158ff.

84. Hertz, "The Pre-eminence of the Right Hand," p. 20.

85. Ibid.

86. Ibid., p. 21.

87. Ibid., p. 10.

88. Kant, "On the First Ground," pp. 22–23; my italics.

89. Hertz, "The Pre-eminence of the Right Hand," p. 13.

90. Ibid., p. 16. My italics.

91. It can be argued that the distinction between right and left calls for a more precise and rigid axial line than do above–below or front–back (both of which are often separated by a zone rather than by a line). Thus Littlejohn states that the necessary "ground of distinction" between right and left "must be a fixed, in a sense absolute, and directed

straight line. It must be fixed, for otherwise there could be almost no end to the subdivisions of left and right" ("Temne Right and Left," p. 289). But I use the qualifying
phrase "roughly perpendicular" to indicate that the situation is not strictly comparable
to that of Cartesian coordinates.

92. M. Heidegger, *On Time and Being,* trans. J. Stambaugh (New York: Harper,
1972), p. 15.

93. E. E. Evans-Pritchard, "Nuer Spear Symbolism," in Needham, ed., *Right & Left,*
p. 94. Evans-Pritchard vacillates between attributing the source of this animation to the
right hand and to the right arm. On one hand, "it is an extension of the right *hand,*
which stands for the strength, vitality, and virtue of the person" (my italics). On the
other hand, he affirms that "for the Nuer also the right *arm* stands for what is strong,
virile, and vital and consequently for masculinity and hence for the paternal kind and
the lineage" (p. 95; my italics). This is not a question of contradiction (not all languages
distinguish between "arm" and "hand"), but a matter of noticing that both hand and
arm—and ultimately the entirety of the lived body—count as places in their own right.

94. For insightful remarks on the minimal dimensionality of the three dyads, see
Clark, "Space, Time, Semantics," pp. 42–43. Clark remarks that only a relation such as
"beside" calls for *two* dimensions. He adds that front–back—and I would say, left–right
as well—can *also* be predicated on three-dimensional reference objects. (The term *reference object* is Clark's, as is *ground level,* which should not be mistaken for Fillmore's and
Talmy's more general notion of "Ground": the latter is the speaker's body in the case
of deictic locating expressions and is the reference object in nondeictic locating expressions.)

95. In three of Franklin and Tversky's five reported experiments, feet-related objects
were located more readily on imagined searches than were head-related objects. The
authors speculate that "the feet are canonically located *on the ground,* whereas the head
has a more variable location, so the feet may serve as a better anchor in the world than
the head" ("Searching Imagined Environments," pp. 74–75; my italics).

96. Kant, "On the First Ground," p. 21. The derivation itself is stated thus: "the plane
to which the length of our body stands perpendicular is called, in reference to us, horizontal; it gives rise to the distinction of the regions we indicate by *above* and *below.* Two
other planes, also intersecting at right angles, can stand perpendicular to this horizontal
plane, in such manner that the length of the human body is conceived as lying in the line
of their intersection. One of these vertical planes divides the body into two outwardly
similar parts and supplies the ground for the distinction between *right* and *left;* the other,
which is perpendicular to it, makes it possible for us to have the concept of *before* and
after" (p. 22; his italics). Notice, however, that the human body continues to be invoked
in this otherwise formal statement.

97. The full statement is: "Is not the space between heaven and earth like a bellows?
It is empty without being exhausted: the more it works the more comes out" (Lao Tzu,
Tao Te Ching, trans. D. C. Lau [New York: Penguin, 1963], p. 61). Nancy Franklin (private communication) has pointed out to me the asymmetry that we more readily imagine
the vertical column as closed from below (e.g., in the bowels of the earth) than from
above.

98. The phrase "the flesh of the world" occurs in Merleau-Ponty, *The Visible and the
Invisible,* pp. 248–51. This is not to deny that left–right may be determined by "intrinsic"
relations among external objects rather than by "egocentric" criteria: "The chair is to the
left of the couch." But notice that in a case such as this there is a residual ambiguity that
may require reference to *my* bodily position for complete disambiguation: *in what exact
respect* is the chair to the left of the couch? Which left, that determined by the couch as

reference object or that determined by myself as Ground? I doubt if the former alternative can make coherent sense without at least implicitly drawing on the latter: the *couch's* left is not simply that belonging to this piece of furniture but left as it would be experienced *if I were to be seated on it.* For a detailed consideration of this and related questions, see V. Ullmer-Ehrich, "The Structure of Living Space Descriptions," in Jarvella and Klein, *Speech, Place, and Action,* pp. 219–48, and W. J. M. Levelt, "Cognitive Styles in the Use of Spatial Direction Terms," in ibid., pp. 258–66.

99. Franklin and Tversky, "Searching Imagined Environments," p. 76. My italics.

100. Henry David Thoreau, "Walking," reprinted in Thoreau, *Natural History Essays* (Salt Lake City: Peregrine Smith Press, 1980), pp. 104–106. Thoreau always took walks in a direction between west and south-southwest from his home in Concord and yet never repeated a walk. Moreover, just as a map must be aligned with the two hands of the map reader, so a compass is useless unless employed in conjunction with landmarks and other natural phenomena: "The points of the compass are not available to humans in the absence of familiar landmarks, clear sky, and knowledge of time of day and year" (Shepard and Hurwitz, "Upward Direction," p. 163).

101. For recent studies of landmarks in situations of orientation, see A. A. Merril and J. C. Baird, "Semantic and Spatial Factors in Environmental Memory," *Memory and Cognition* 5 (1987), pp. 101-108; T. G. Garling, E. Lindberg, M. Carreiras, and A. Book, "Reference Systems in Cognitive Maps," *Journal of Environmental Psychology* 6 (1986), pp. 1–18; and E. K. Sadalla, L. J. Staplin, and W. J. Burroughs, "Retrieval Processes in Distance Cognition," *Memory and Cognition* 7 (1980), pp. 291–96. On Eskimo orientation, see E. Carpenter, *Eskimo Realities* (New York: Holt, 1973). On Saharan nomads' orientational behavior, see K. Lynch, "Some References to Orientation," in R. M. Downs and D. Stea, eds., *Image and Environment* (Chicago: Aldine, 1973).

102. Franklin and Tversky, "Searching Imagined Environments," p. 74. I find myself in agreement with virtually all of Franklin and Tversky's remarkable analysis and would only insist on including the here–there and near–far dyads in a more complete consideration.

103. On body memory, see my *Remembering: A Phenomenological Study* (Bloomington: Indiana University Press, 1987), chaps. 8 and 9. Concerning cognitive maps, see esp. P. Gould and R. White, *Mental Maps* (Baltimore: Penguin, 1974); P. Johnson-Laird, *Mental Models* (Cambridge, Mass.: Harvard University Press, 1983); and J. C. Baird and M. Wagner, "Modelling the Creation of Cognitive Maps," in Pick and Acredelo, *Spatial Orientation,* pp. 321–44.

104. "Place is a part of space which a body takes up" (sec. 3 of the Scholium to the Definitions in Newton's *Mathematical Principles of Natural Philosophy.* Newtonian space is unfit for human habitation; in it there can be no lived bodies and thus no places for these bodies. Heidegger, perhaps with Newton in mind, observes that "'the' space, 'space,' contains no spaces *and no places*" ("Building Dwelling Thinking," in *Poetry, Language, Thought,* p. 155; my italics).

105. Aristotle, *Physics* 222b, 8 (Ross translation). Hussey translates: "time will not give out, for it is always at a beginning."

5. Two Ways to Dwell

1. I am construing the notion of the a priori primarily in a nontemporal sense, but what I have said in these opening paragraphs also holds in temporal terms. Thus the child experiences the world mainly as a set of places felt by his or her body, places that endure as internalized within this body. William James has this to say on the matter: "The places thus first sensibly known are elements of the child's space-world which remain with him all his life . . . to the end of time certain places of the world remain defined for him as the

places *where those [bodily] sensations were*" (*The Principles of Psychology* [New York: Dover, 1950], vol. 2, p. 35; his italics).

2. On these two stages of deconstruction, see Jacques Derrida, *Dissemination,* trans. B. Johnson (Chicago: University of Chicago Press, 1981), pp. 6–7, where Derrida insists that the stages are enacted "in a kind of disconcerting *simul.*" See also Derrida, *Positions,* trans. A. Bass (Chicago: University of Chicago Press, 1981), pp. 65–66, where the stage of "overturning" is contrasted with that of "a positively displacing, transgressive" deconstruction.

3. On the social a priori—and on the considerable array of other a priori structures—see Mikel Dufrenne, *The Notion of the A Priori,* trans. E. Casey (Evanston, Ill.: Northwestern University Press, 1967), and *L'inventaire des a priori: recherche de l'originaire* (Paris: Bourgois, 1981), pp. 208–20.

4. *Enuma Elish,* trans. N. K. Sandars, in B. Sproul, ed., *Primal Myths* (New York: Harper, 1979), p. 104.

5. An engaging treatment of the theme of the hotel as a modern dwelling place par excellence is James Clifford's "Traveling Selves, Traveling Others," a talk delivered at the conference entitled "Cultural Studies Then and Now," University of Illinois, Urbana, April 1990.

6. I say "apparently antithetical" because the kindred term *dwale,* which meant "error" or "delusion" as well as "stupefying drink," may be a bridge between the two otherwise separate ur-senses of *dwell.* To be stupefied (which is the meaning of the Middle Dutch *dwellen*) is to be hindered or delayed in one's course, made to tarry in a way that begins to resemble residing somewhere. On this question, see Eric Partridge's entry under "dwell," especially his statement that this word "comes from OE *dwellan,* to wander, to linger, to tarry, akin to OE *dwalian,* OFris *dwalia,* to wander, be in error, OE *dwala,* error, OFris *dwalinge,* OE *dwolung,* doubt, and ON *dvelja,* to linger, delay, tarry" (*Origins: A Short Etymological Dictionary of Modern English* [New York: Macmillan, 1959], p. 172).

7. "Alles Räumliche dehnt sich aus" (Theodor Lipps, *Raumaesthetik und geometrisch-optische Täuschungen,* in *Schriften der Gesellschaft für psychologische Forschung,* vol. 2, 1897; cited by Rudolf Arnheim, *The Dynamics of Architectural Form* [Berkeley: University of California Press, 1977], p. 86). On the complex cultural and social significance of arcades, see Susan Buck-Morss, *The Dialectics of Seeing: Walter Benjamin and the Arcades Project* (Cambridge, Mass.: MIT Press, 1989). Benjamin saw arcades—first constructed in Paris in the early nineteenth century—as paradigmatic modern phenomena. The word *arcade* derives from the Latin *arcus,* bow, hence the bowed ceilings and skylights and the serpentine winding of corridors.

8. What matters here is not the sheer calendrical length of our acquaintance with a given dwelling; the familiarity may emerge rapidly and may bear on the *kind* of dwelling rather than on a particular building. Thus we need not have literally inhabited a given dwelling to find it familiar in its ambiance or structure. "I find this familiar," I may say to myself, settling into a cabin on the north rim of the Grand Canyon, even though I have never stayed there before. I recognize the form of dwelling at stake and thus feel "at home" immediately.

9. On the interiority of dwelling places, see Edward Relph, *Place and Placelessness* (London: Pion, 1976), pp. 52–56. Even if "it is the insideness that most people experience when they are at home and in their own town or region" (p. 35), this still does not mean that such insideness is a *sine qua non* of all significant dwelling, as is implied in Emmanuel Levinas's claim that the home possesses an "essential interiority" (*Totality and Infinity,* trans. A. Lingis [Pittsburgh: Duquesne University Press, 1968], p. 157).

10. I am indebted to David Seamon for suggesting in conversation that between

journeying and dwelling there is a continuum of cases. On this point, see Bernd Jager, "Theorizing, Journeying, Dwelling," *Duquesne Studies in Phenomenological Psychology* (1975), pp. 235–60. I return to the issue of the journey in chap. 9.

11. On the body as *Leib* (vs. *Körper*), see E. Husserl, *The Crisis of European Sciences,* trans. D. Carr (Evanston, Ill.: Northwestern University Press, 1975), p. 50; on holding sway, see ibid., pp. 217–18.

12. By "dwelling places of a distinctly residential character"—i.e., a "residence"—I mean any place, from the barest but or pit-house to the most elaborate palace, that encourages and facilitates staying for an appreciable period. More than a mere stopping-point but less than a "final resting place," a residence allows for sojourns lasting from overnight (e.g., in the case of inns) to decades of continuous residence. For an illuminating discussion of huts and other "primitive" forms of residence, see Joseph Rykwert, *On Adam's House in Paradise: The Idea of the Primitive Hut in Architectural History* (Cambridge, Mass.: MIT Press, 1981).

13. For closely related considerations, see David Seamon, *Geography of the Lifeworld: Movement, Rest, and Encounter* (New York: St. Martin's Press, 1979).

14. Andrea Palladio, *The Four Books of Architecture* (New York: Dover, 1965; originally published in 1570), bk. 1, chap. 23. Chap. 22 treats ceilings, and chap. 24 considers vaults.

15. E. Straus, "The Upright Posture," in *Phenomenological Psychology*, ed. E. Eng (New York: Basic Books, 1966), p. 143.

16. The word *estate* has the same ultimate root—Latin *stare*, Greek *histanai*—as does *standing*. Along with a host of cognate words (*state, status, constant, statute, stature, establish,* even *distance*), both *estate* and *standing* "refer to something that is instituted, erected, constructed, and, in its dangerous equilibrium, threatened by fall and collapse" (Straus, ibid., p. 143). Heidegger points out that *parousia* in Greek and *Anwesen* in German mean at once "being" (or "presence") and estate qua homestead (see Martin Heidegger, *An Introduction to Metaphysics,* trans. R. Manheim [New Haven, Conn.: Yale University Press, 1959], p. 61).

17. Michelangelo, letter of 1560; cited in Rudolf Wittkower, *Architectural Principles in the Age of Humanism* (New York: Norton, 1971), p. 101, n. 1.

18. Vitruvius, *Ten Books on Architecture*, bk. 2, chap. 1, in the English translation of M. H. Morgan (Cambridge, Mass.: Harvard University Press, 1914), p. 73.

19. Leon Battista Alberti, *De re aedificatoria*, bk. 1, chap. 1 (cited by Wittkower, *Architectural Principles*, pp. 21–22). My italics. As Leonardo's friend Luca Pacioli put it, "After having considered the right arrangement of the human body, the ancients proportioned all their work, particularly the temples, in accordance with it" (cited from Pacioli's *Divina proportione* by Wittkower, p. 15). What guarantees the parallelism between the proportions of the body and those of the building is the existence of what Wittkower calls "cosmic ratios," i.e., proportions that are common to both: "As man is the image of God and the proportions of his body are produced by divine will, so the proportions in architecture have to embrace and express the cosmic order" (p. 101). But the human body remains the concrete basis of proportionality. Alberti proposed a system of architectural measurement which he called "exempeda" (literally, "out of feet") and which is based on human feet (*pedes*) as basic units. (On this system, see Erwin Panofsky, "The History of the Theory of Human Proportions as a Reflection of the History of Styles," reprinted in Panofsky's *Meaning in the Visual Arts* [New York: Doubleday, 1955], pp. 95–96.)

20. Fig. 1 is from Wittkower, *Architectural Principles*, pl. 1a. This view in plan (i.e., from on top) has the paradoxical effect of making the body contained in the church appear to be both standing and prone.

21. For a nuanced discussion of such resemblances, see Kent C. Bloomer and Charles

W. Moore, *Body, Memory, and Architecture* (New Haven, Conn.: Yale University Press, 1977), pp. 2–5, 46–49. I am indebted to Bloomer for a series of illuminating discussions that have clarified and expanded on his pioneering work.

22. Palladio, *The Four Books of Architecture*, bk. 2, chap. 2. Commenting on this passage, George Hersey remarks that "a palace is in fact metaphorically a clothed body. . . . The purpose of the clothes is to show off beautiful organs and hide ugly ones" (*Pythagorean Palaces: Magic and Architecture in the Italian Renaissance* [Ithaca, N.Y.: Cornell University Press, 1976], p. 114).

23. M. Heidegger, *Hebel der Hausfreund* (Pfullingen: Neske, 1957), p. 13. I shall return to this important passage in chap. 8.

24. Cited from Jane Austen, *Emma*, by Witold Rybczynski, *Home: A Short History of an Idea* (New York: Penguin, 1986), p. 101.

25. For Freud's metaphor, see his "Formulations on the Two Principles of Mental Functioning" (1911), *Standard Edition of the Complete Psychological Works*, trans. J. Strachey (London: Hogarth, 1958), vol. 12, p. 222: "In the same way [i.e., as in the provision for a child's fantasying], a nation whose wealth rests on the exploitation of its soil will yet set aside certain areas for reservation in their original state and for protection from the changes brought about by civilization (e.g., Yellowstone Park.)." On transitional space, see D. W. Winnicott, "Transitional Objects and Transitional Phenomena," *International Journal of Psychoanalysis* 34 (1953). Winnicott sometimes refers to this space specifically as "place," for example in the following passage from another paper: "[such space is] the only place where play can start, a place that is at the continuity-contiguity moment, where transitional phenomena originate" ("The Location of Cultural Experience," *International Journal of Psychoanalysis* 48 [1967], p. 372).

26. One approaches the Audience Hall along a linear central axis that runs straight north through the Gate of Heavenly Peace and the Gate of the Noon Sun before reaching the Forbidden City within. See Nelson I. Wu, *Chinese and Indian Architecture* (New York: Braziller, 1963), fig. 136, as cited in Yi-Fu Tuan, *Space and Place: The Perspective of Experience* (Minneapolis: University of Minnesota Press, 1977), p. 39.

27. On this point, see Bloomer and Moore, *Body, Memory, and Architecture*, pp. 46–47.

28. I refer to Aristotle's discussion of the various "ways one thing is said to be *in* another," *Physics*, 210a, 15–25, and to Heidegger's treatment of "Being-in" (*In-sein*) in *Being and Time*, trans. J. Macquarrie and E. Robinson (New York: Harper, 1962), sec. 12, pp. 78–86. At one earlier point, Heidegger mentions, only to dismiss as mere "outward appearance," the relationship of "the desk in the classroom, the classroom in the university building, the building in the city of Marburg. . . ." (*The History of the Concept of Time*, trans. T. Kisiel [Bloomington: Indiana University Press, 1985], pp. 157–58).

29. This is Arnheim's phrasing of Zucker's position; see Rudolf Arnheim, *The Dynamics of Architectural Form* (Berkeley: University of California Press, 1971), p. 92, with reference to Zucker's article in a symposium on "Inside and Outside in Architecture," *Journal of Aesthetics and Art Criticism* 17 (1966), pp. 3–15. For a set of cross-cultural studies of boundaries, see J.-P. Bourdieu and N. Alsayyad, eds., *Dwellings, Settlements and Tradition: Cross-Cultural Perspectives* (Lanham, Md.: University Press of America, 1989), pt. 2, "Questions of Boundaries."

30. We are "cut out" of such places. Ernst Cassirer notes that "*templum* (Greek *temnos*) goes back to the root *tem*, 'to cut,' and thus signifies that which is cut out, delimited. It first designates the sacred precinct belonging to the god and consecrated to the god and then, by extension, every marked-off piece of land, every bounded field or orchard, whether it belongs to a god, king, or hero" (*The Philosophy of Symbolic Forms*, trans. R.

Manheim [New Haven, Conn.: Yale University Press, 1955], vol. 2, p. 100). On the same sharp "cut" between two basic kinds of space, see M. Eliade, *The Sacred and the Profane: The Nature of Religion,* trans. W. Trask (New York: Harcourt, 1959), introduction and chap. 1, and Jean-Claude Galey, ed., *L'espace du temple,* vol. 2 (Paris, 1986). *Profane* itself is a place term since it means literally "*before* the apparition," i.e., before the apparition of the numinous being belonging to the inner depth of the temple.

31. Robert Venturi, *Complexity and Contradiction in Architecture* (New York: Museum of Modern Art, 1966), p. 86.

32. Gaston Bachelard, *The Poetics of Space,* trans. M. Jolas (Boston: Beacon Press, 1964), pp. 217–18.

33. Arnheim, *The Dynamic of Architectural Form,* p. 92.

34. Edmund Husserl, "Foundational Investigations of the Phenomenological Origin of the Spatiality of Nature," trans. F. Kersten, in P. McCormick and F. Elliston, eds., *Husserl: Shorter Writings* (Notre Dame, Ind.: University of Notre Dame Press, 1981), pp. 225–26.

35. For a developmental view of the pre-thetic position, see Julia Kristeva, *Revolution in Poetic Language,* trans. M. Waller (New York: Columbia University Press, 1984), pp. 43–67. Kristeva herself speaks only of "thetic," but I am interpreting her notion of "semiotic *chōra*" as equivalent to pre-thetic, even though Kristeva herself insists that conceptually (even if not developmentally) the thetic qua "symbolic" is presupposed by the semiotic. I thank Tom Brockelman for useful discussions of Kristeva's work as it bears on architecture.

36. The plan is from Palladio, *The Four Books of Architecture,* bk. 2, pl. 2.

37. James S. Ackerman, *Palladio* (New York: Penguin, 1966), p. 164. The employment of "along" and "alongside" in this statement is revealing. Ackerman adds that "this duality was recognized by the client, Girolamo Chiericati," citing the latter's petition of March 1551 for a building permit: "I have been advised by expert architects and by many revered citizens to make a portico along the facade of my house on the Isola for greater convenience *to me* and for the convenience and ornamentation *of the entire city*" (my italics).

38. From Palladio, *The Four Books of Architecture,* bk. 2, pl. 2.

39. Henri Bergson, *Matter and Memory,* trans. N. M. Paul and W. S. Palmer (New York: Doubleday, 1959), p. 145. In italics in the original.

40. Aldo van Eyck in *Architectural Design* 32 (1962), cited by Venturi, *Complexity and Contradiction,* p. 84. Van Eyck adds: "The transition [between inside and outside] must be articulated by means of defined in-between places which induce simultaneous awareness of what is significant on either side." These "in-between places" are what answer architecturally to the intermediation of the body as an ongoing *metaxu* in human experience.

41. This is Heidegger's phrase from *Hebel der Hausfreund,* p. 13: "The single houses . . . the villages, the cities are works of architecture, which in and around themselves gather the multifarious between."

42. On aura in memory, see my *Remembering: A Phenomenological Study* (Bloomington: Indiana University Press, 1987), pp. 76–78, 204. Concerning aura as "unique existence at the place where [a work of art] happens to be," see Walter Benjamin, "The Work of Art in the Age of Mechanical Reproduction," *Illuminations,* trans. H. Zohn (New York: Schocken, 1969), pp. 220ff.

43. Ackerman, *Palladio,* p. 165; my italics. Thus, for example, "the smallest [room in the palazzo] is 12′ × 18′, its neighbor 18′ × 18′, [the next] 18′ × 30′." In this sequence, the larger dimension of one room becomes the smaller (or the equal) in the next room. Each

of the numbers is a multiple of 6, thereby resulting in the proportions 2:3, 3:3 [=1:1], 3:5. Palladio must have been aware that this last series corresponds to the fifth, unison, and major sixth as measured by distances on a monochord. Here the harmony between architecture and music—a Pythagorean notion reintroduced by Alberti—becomes evident. Palladio went further than Alberti, however, in unifying his building by such cosmic harmonies in all *three* dimensions: "What differentiates Palladio's proportions from Alberti's is that they are used in integrated systems that bind plan and elevation, interior and exterior, room and room, giving a sense of the pervasiveness of the architect's control" (p. 167). On the relation between music and architecture in Renaissance architecture, see Wittkower, *Architectural Principles,* pp. 107–26.

44. See James, *Principles of Psychology,* vol. 2, pp. 134–44.

45. M. Heidegger, "The Origin of the Work of Art," in *Poetry, Language, Thought,* pp. 63–64: "Truth establishes itself as a strife within a being that is to be brought forth in such a way that the conflict opens up in this being, that is, this being is itself brought into the rift-design (*Riss*). The rift-design is the drawing-together, into a unity, of sketch and basic design, breach and outline (*Umriss*). This strife that is brought into the rift and thus set back into the earth and thus *fixed in place* (*festgestellte*) is figure, shape, Gestalt" (my italics). For an extended critical assessment of Heidegger's evolving notion of place, consult my "Heidegger In and Out of Place," *Heidegger: A Centenary Appraisal* (Pittsburgh: Silverman Phenomenology Center, 1990), pp. 62–98. Indebted as I am to Heidegger's pioneering writings on place and region, I find that nowhere does he account for the active agency of the human body in issues of implacement. Also, he does not attempt to determine what place itself is, proposing only a family of related terms (*location, site, spaces vs. space*) that cannot be subsumed under space qua Greek *stadion* (distance, interval), Roman *spatium,* or Cartesian *extensio.* How this family of place-terms is itself configurated—and how it has an autonomy of its own—is never established.

46. For the contrast between *Streitraum* and *Spielraum,* see Heidegger, "The Origin of the Work of Art," p. 61.

47. The Greek temple at Paestum is first mentioned in ibid. on p. 40 and is under close analysis for the next four pages of the text. The only "common ground" (*einige Grunde*) between earth and world identified by Heidegger is the intimacy effected by the rift (*Riss*) between these two factors themselves: "This rift carries the opponents into the source of their unity by virtue of their common ground" (p. 63). Ironically, "rift" lends itself to a somatic interpretation never given by Heidegger. (I refer here to the "self-split *origo*" as outlined in part two.)

48. Ibid., p. 45.

49. Upright posture is a continuing condition of such action. Straus remarks that "within the totality of the new spatial dimensions acquired with upright posture, lateral space is perhaps most important" (*The Primary World of Senses,* trans. J. Needleman [Glencoe, Ill.: Free Press, 1963], p. 142). "Lateral space," the space of free movement, is closely akin to what I am here calling "leeway." In architecture, leeway gains expression in what Robert Venturi calls "poché," i.e., the residual leftover space in a built structure (see his *Complexity and Contradiction,* pp. 82–84, where both "closed" and "open" poché space are discussed as they figure into buildings and even into entire cities). I thank Tom Brockelman for this reference.

50. Palladio, *The Four Books of Architecture,* bk. 2, chap. 12. Cf. Heidegger's dictum that the architect "makes space for spaciousness" ("The Origin of the Work of Art," p. 45).

51. Concerning intimate immensity, which is close to what I am calling "opened-up implacement," see Gaston Bachelard, *The Poetics of Space,* chap. 8. For an insightful

study of the child's experience of domestic places, see M. J. Langevelt, "The Stillness of the Secret Place" and "The Secret Place in the Life of the Child," *Phenomenology and Pedagogy* 1 (1983), pp. 10–17 and 180–91.

52. The bodily basis of architecture did not escape Goethe's attention: "One would think that architecture as a fine art works solely for the eyes. Instead, it should work primarily for the sense of mechanical motion in the human body—something to which scant attention is paid. When in dance we move according to definite rules, we experience a pleasant sensation. A similar sensation should be aroused in someone who is led blindfolded through a well-built house" (from Goethe's fragment, *Baukunst*; cited by Arnheim, *The Dynamics of Architectural Form*, p. 152). We need only add that the motion of the body in dwelling places is far from "mechanical." It is altogether dynamical—as dynamical as dwelling itself may be when it is fully lived out in the ambiance and arc of an embodied existence.

53. "If we think of the verb *to dwell* in a wide and essential sense, then it denotes the way in which humans fulfill their wandering from birth to death on earth under the sky. *Everywhere the wandering remains the essence of dwelling,* as the staying between earth and sky, between birth and death, between joy and pain, between work and world" (Heidegger, *Hebel der Hausfreund*, p. 13; my italics). Christian Norberg-Schulz, who cites this passage, writes that "man, thus, finds himself when he *settles,* and his being-in-the-world is thereby determined. On the other hand, man is also a wanderer. As *homo viator,* he is always on the way" (*The Concept of Dwelling: On the Way to Figurative Architecture* [New York: Rizzoli, 1985], p. 12; his italics).

54. The proper name *Hestia* derives from *estia,* "hearth, a household or family, an altar, places which are to a country as hearth is to a home" (Liddell and Scott, *Greek-English Lexicon* [Oxford: Clarendon Press, 1925]). One scholar traces *Hestia* to Sanskrit *vas,* to inhabit (see Richard L. Farnell, *The Cults of the Greek States* [New Rochelle, N.Y.: Caratzas, 1977], p. 359).

55. "The Second Hymn to Hestia," from *The Homeric Hymns,* trans. Charles Boer (Chicago: Swallow Press, 1970), p. 141.

56. "She obtained as her sacred place the central point of the house, the hearth" (Carl Kerényi, *The Gods of the Greeks* [London: Thames and Hudson, 1951], p. 91).

57. Paola Coppola Pignatelli, "The Dialectics of Urban Architecture: Hestia and Hermes," *Spring* (1985), p. 43. Note that Rhea is Hestia's mother and Kronos is her father. On Hestia's relationship to earth, see also S. A. Demetrakopoulos, "Hestia, Goddess of the Hearth," *Spring* (1979), p. 72: "Hestia as earth means that she is the matrix, the material, the *sine qua non* of all differentiation."

58. From Wittkower, *Architectural Principles,* pls. 11a and 11b.

59. Fig. 6 is from Ackerman, *Palladio,* p. 77, fig. 32. Fig. 6 is Palladio's own design from his *Four Books of Architecture.*

60. I take this drawing of a hogan from *Webster's New Collegiate Dictionary* (Springfield, Mass.: G. & C. Merriam, 1981), p. 540.

61. On the structure and symbolism of the hogan, see Peter Nabokov and Robert Easton, *Native American Architecture* (Oxford: Oxford University Press, 1988). Concerning holy wind, consult James K. McNeley, *Holy Wind in Navajo Philosophy* (Tucson: University of Arizona Press, 1981).

62. On interior spaciousness, see Frank Lloyd Wright, "Prairie Architecture," *Frank Lloyd Wright: Writings and Buildings* (New York: Meridian, 1960), esp. p. 44: "The house became more free as 'space' and more livable, too. Interior spaciousness began to dawn." In the same text, Wright says that "the *integral* fireplace became an important part of the building itself in the buildings I was allowed to build out there on the prairie. It refreshed me to see the fire burning deep in the masonry of the house itself" (p. 42; his italics).

63. Pignatelli, "Dialectics of Urban Architecture," p. 44.

64. Rafael López-Pedraza, *Hermes and His Children* (Dallas: Spring Publications, 1977), p. 8.

65. Pignatelli, "Dialectics of Urban Architecture," p. 45. She adds: "The Greek *polis*, [once] set into a right-angle grid, is therefore the spatial translation of Hermes' distinguishing traits." Hermes is also an upright figure. "Herms" were upright stone posts that served as landmarks and house protectors. They often sported a protruding phallus as well as a head of Hermes. W. K. C. Guthrie remarks in this connection that "we are back again at our primeval upright stone from which so much of Hermes' nature seems to have taken its origin" (*The Greeks and Their Gods* [Boston: Beacon Press, 1950], p. 92).

66. Pignatelli, "Dialectics of Urban Architecture," p. 46. In a pure grid, e.g., that of Cartesian geometry, the center can be located anywhere. Thus it is effectively *nowhere*. Such a situation is to be contrasted with Nicolas of Cusa's view that in the known universe the center is everywhere and the circumference nowhere. López-Pedraza remarks that "Hermes has no need to fight for his center; he does not have one" (*Hermes and His Children*, p. 8).

67. The figure is from R. E. Wycherley, *How the Greeks Built Cities* (New York: Anchor, 1969), fig. 23. This plan, which betrays a Pythagorean isometrism, represents Miletus in the second century A.D. but stems ultimately from the scheme of Hippodamus drawn up several centuries earlier. Wycherley comments that "the Ionian architect realized and explored the possibilities of combining stoas at right angles, fitting them into the rectangular street system, and so forming effective and impressive schemes" (p. 76).

68. For a mordant critique of the International Style along these lines, see Tom Wolfe, *From Bauhaus to Our House* (London: Cape, 1982). In conversation, architect and sculptor Kent Bloomer has remarked on the paucity of buildings actually *built* in the International Style. However elegant houses in this style may be, few people wish to *live in them*. This is not to deny, however, that the hermetic organization of space can be constructively adapted to architecture, as we witness in the creative use of regular rectangular structures by architects as different as Palladio and Le Corbusier. (On Le Corbusier's use of regular figures, see Peter Blake, *Le Corbusier: Architecture and Form* [New York: Penguin, 1960].)

69. Wycherley, *How the Greeks Built Cities*, p. 88. My italics.

70. Indeed, the Heideggerian distinction of earth from world can be considered a close cousin of the mythological dichotomy: as protective and "self-seclusive," earth is reminiscent of the virtues of Hestia, while world as open and communal recalls Hermes in his communicative and connection-making capacities.

71. Pignatelli, "Dialectics of Urban Architecture," p. 47. Her italics.

72. I borrow these terms from Pignatelli's use (ibid., p. 45), even though she does not relate them to built places. By invoking Hermes and Hestia and descriptions such as these, I do not mean to imply that the two kinds of building and dwelling to which they are extended in this chapter are to be described exclusively in terms of the gender differences that inhere, all too stereotypically and tendentiously, in the original Greek conception of these gods. Thus concentricity and rectilinearity *as such*—i.e., as formal-geometric properties of building—are not based on gender, or for that matter on sexual, differences. It should also be noted that the Greek conception itself is not without certain complexities: Hermes is at once the god of communication and yet the keeper of silence (as is still signified in the English phrase *hermetic silence* and, more generally, in *hermetic* in the sense of enclosed or concealed).

73. Criticizing architecture of the previous generation in America, Wright remarks that "the 'interiors' consisted of boxes beside or inside other boxes, called *rooms*. All boxes inside a complicated boxing. Each domestic 'function' was properly box to box. I

could see little sense in this inhibition, this cellular sequestration that implied ancestors familiar with the cells of penal institutions" (*Frank Lloyd Wright*, p. 43; his italics).

74. This is not to deny the possibility of other ways of specifying site-space via alternative non-Euclidean and non-Cartesian geometries, just as there are at least several significant forms of participational-topological architectural implacement. For a sense of the considerable range of such formal possibilities, including those with esoteric roots, see Alberto Pérez-Gomez, *Architecture and the Crisis of Modern Science* (Cambridge, Mass.: MIT Press, 1983).

75. For the Piagetian model of the development of spatial perception, see Jean Piaget and Bärbel Inhelder, *The Child's Conception of Space*, trans. F. J. Langdon and J. L. Lunzer (New York: Norton, 1967). These authors insist that both Euclidean and projective geometry are derivative from the topological phase, in which the key notions are proximity and separation, order and enclosure (see part one ["Topological Space"] and pp. 13, 68, 153, 301, 451).

76. Space as *chōra*, analogized to a mirror, is amorphous and has no quality or structure of its own. In the precosmic stage, whatever is to become must participate in this vast Receptacle, the source of all becoming. Becoming itself occurs by way of "regions" (*chōran*) and "places" (*topoi*), for which the Receptacle provides a "seat" (*hedra*). This hearthlike seat furnishes a distinctively participational and topological matrix onto which the Demiurge can superimpose the geometric shapes from which solid objects are built up in a cosmic architecture strikingly homologous to the development of Euclidean geometry in the child or to land-surveying in the adult. In his constitution of a well-ordered universe, the Demiurge is simultaneously childlike (insofar as he begins with a distinctively pre-Euclidean space) and adult (as a rational world-architect for whom formal geometry is exemplary).

77. Hestia "acts as a mediator for psychological integration analogous to Hermes' mediating activities as connector and mover of soul" (Barbara Kirksey, "Hestia: A Background of Psychological Focusing," in James Hillman, ed., *Facing the Gods* [Dallas: Spring Publications, 1980], p. 107).

78. Demetrakopoulos, "Hestia," pp. 59–60. The coadunation in question is preinscribed in the curious linguistic fact that the Indo-European root *arkw-* underlies both *arch* and *arrow*. The bowed character of the arch is hestial in inspiration, while the swiftness of the (straight) arrow is a main trait of Hermes.

79. The illustration is from fig. 103 in Norman T. Newton, *Design on the Land: The Development of Landscape Architecture* (Cambridge, Mass.: Harvard University Press, 1971), p. 140.

80. I take the term *node* from Kevin Lynch, who defines *nodes* as "the strategic foci into which the observer can enter, typically either junctions of paths, or concentraions of some characteristic" (*The Image of the City* [Cambridge, Mass: MIT Press, 1960], p. 72). Lynch describes the Piazza San Marco as a node that is "highly differentiated, rich and intricate, [and that] stands in sharp contrast to the general character of the city and to the narrow, twisting spaces of its immediate approaches" (p. 78).

81. Arnheim, *The Dynamics of Architectural Form*, p. 89.

82. "People gravitate naturally toward the edge of public spaces. They do not linger out in the open. If the edge does not provide them with places where it is natural to linger, the space becomes a place to walk through, not a place to stop. It is therefore clear that a public square should be surrounded by pockets of activity . . . the edge must be scalloped" (Christopher Alexander, *A Pattern Language*, cited by M.-J. Dozio, P. Federsen, and K. Noschis, "Everyday Life on an Insignificant Public Square: Venice," *Ekistics* 50 [1983], p. 104).

83. By listing in random order the pairs of terms that have been discussed in the three

preceding chapters, I do not mean to imply that they are of indifferent significance in the human experience of place. Important differences of structure and type remain. One such difference is found in the fact that the five dyads discussed in part two (here—there, right–left, etc.) are of more general scope than those described in this chapter. For these five pairs apply to bodily being in *any* given place—built or natural—whereas the recently discussed pairs (inside–outside, with–between, etc.) are most particularly pertinent to built places and do not have commensurate relevance to natural places. Otherwise put, the previous five dyads all operate on each of the six new terms. There is a right vs. left, near vs. far, etc., option for *each* with, *each* between, etc., while the reverse operation does not obtain: there is *not* always a with or a between for a given right or left, above or below, etc.

6. Building Sites and Cultivating Places

1. James Hillman, *Re-Visioning Psychology* (New York: Harper, 1975), p. 101; my italics.

2. For a treatment of these two zones in a broader but still quite relevant context, see Mircea Eliade, *The Sacred and the Profane: The Nature of Religion* (New York: Harcourt, 1959), chap. 1.

3. Johann Wolfgang von Goethe, *Italian Journey 1786–1788*, trans. W. H. Auden and E. Mayer (San Francisco: North Point Press, 1982), p. 50.

4. Ibid., pp. 81–83.

5. This phrase is from the title of one of Wallace Stevens's late poems, "A Mythology Reflects Its Region."

6. I borrow this distinction from Spiro Kostof, *A History of Architecture: Settings and Rituals* (Oxford: Oxford University Press, 1985), pp. 21ff. For Kostof, both forms "imply a determined marking of nature. Humans impose through them their own order on nature" (p. 21).

7. A boundary is not merely a "border" or a "perimeter," i.e., a linear contour literally drawn around the edge of an object. In establishing boundaries, architecture rejoins nature, which possesses many boundaries but few borders. The boundaries of buildings, like boundaries in nature, consist of marginal regions in which tensions are played out and resolutions reached (or at least suggested). As Rudolph Arnheim puts it, "Boundaries are the precarious products of opposing forces" (*The Dynamics of Architectural Form* [Berkeley: University of California Press, 1977], p. 73). For this very reason, boundaries delimit in manifold ways, not just in the geometric or legal senses that inform borders. They display diverse dynamisms in different settings. (On this last point, see Henri Focillon, *The Life of Forms in Art*, trans. C. B. Hogan and G. Kubler [New York: Zone, 1989], chap. 2, esp. p. 66: "Even if reduced merely to a slender and sinuous line, [an ornamental boundary] is already a frontier, a highway.")

8. The drawing is from Kostof, *History of Architecture*, p. 23, fig. 2.2.

9. Ibid., p. 21.

10. Ibid. A pit house, insofar as it is found partially under the soil (e.g., "sod houses" built in Kansas and Nebraska prairies in the middle of the nineteenth century), is strictly speaking a "burrow" in Arnheim's sense of the term: a form of primitive building that reveals its function by its very shape. A "shelter" need *not* manifest its function by its outer surface. But the huts at Terra Amata seem clearly to be at once shelters and burrows, based on Arnheim's criteria. (See Arnheim, *The Dynamics of Architectural Form*, pp. 148–51.) On the artistic *representations* of such "primitive huts," see Joseph Rykwert, *On Adam's House in Paradise: The Idea of the Primitive Hut in Architectural History* (Cambridge, Mass.: MIT Press, 1981).

11. *Betatakin* means "ledge house" in Navajo. The building itself, however, is not Navajo in origin; the Anasazi, ancestors of today's Hopi and Zuni, are ethnically unrelated to the Navajo, who later settled in the region.

12. For a discerning study of horizontality vs. verticality, see Bernd Jager, "Horizontality and Verticality: A Phenomenological Exploration into Lived Space," *Duquesne Studies in Phenomenological Psychology* 1 (1971), pp. 212–35.

13. In this enlarged context, built places are the nodal points of the bidirectionality, as well as of the horizontality and verticality, in which bodies and buildings conjoin in the circumpresence of nature. As providing the immediate locus of edifices, built places are less capacious than the natural world in which these edifices are set; but as the arena of inhabitation (or as way-stations on a journey), they are more extensive than the discrete proto-places of bodily action.

14. Hegel remarks in this connection that in building, "the elements are made use of in accordance with their nature and co-operate for a product by which they become constrained. . . . Thus they fortify a structure for law and order *against* themselves" (G. W. F. Hegel, *Reason in History,* trans. R. S. Hartman [New York: Liberal Arts Press, 1954], p. 35; his italics). I owe this reference to J. Melvin Woody.

15. Vitruvius, *Ten Books on Architecture,* trans. M. H. Morgan (Cambridge, Mass.: Harvard University Press, 1914), p. 170.

16. See ibid., bk. 1, chap. 6 (on winds); p. 181 (on quarters of the sky); and pp. 15–16 (on natural light). Vitruvius thinks that architecture must also be sensitive to the characters and demands of the gods and that building sites should be chosen with deities as well as the natural setting in mind. See bk. 1, chap. 7.

17. Palladio, *The Four Books of Architecture* (New York: Dover, 1965), p. 25. For Palladio's treatment of grounds, rivers, swamps, etc., see bk. 1, chap. 7, and esp. bk. 2, chap. 12, "On the Site to Be Chosen for the Fabricks of Villas."

18. Charles W. Moore, William J. Mitchell, and William Turnbull, Jr., *The Poetics of Gardens* (Cambridge, Mass.: MIT Press, 1988), p. 6.

19. Milton draws explicitly on his early experience of Italian gardens as models for his description of Paradise as a garden. See *Paradise Lost,* bk. 4, ll. 223–63. Italian gardens had walls and doubtless were influenced by Moorish models that are in turn traceable to Middle Eastern origins. Walls create enclosure, and *garden* is derived from the Indo-European root *gher-,* which signifies enclosed space. J. B. Jackson remarks that "the earliest gardens in our history were essentially enclosures, built for defense or privacy or storage or for growing food" ("Nearer Than Eden," *The Necessity for Ruins* [Amherst: University of Massachusetts Press, 1980], p. 21).

20. I construe *liminal* in Victor Turner's sense of the term. Instead of seeking its role in ritual as he does, however, I shall take up its spatial or, more exactly, its placial aspects as these emerge in gardens. See Turner, *The Forest of Symbols: Aspects of Ndembu Ritual* (Ithaca, N.Y.: Cornell University Press, 1967), pp. 98ff.

21. Pausing for viewing—and for meditating—has been an important feature of gardens from China and Japan to western Europe. Louis XIV wrote in the guidebook he intended for visitors to the gardens of Versailles: "on fera une pause pour considérer" (cited from Louis XIV's *Manière de montrer les Jardins de Versailles* [1705] [Paris: Plon, 1951], sec. 10).

22. Robert Harbison, *Eccentric Spaces* (Boston: Godine, 1988), p. 4. As Harbison also remarks, gardens are "intermediate enough to make us think they *are* nature and not simply embellishments or enhancements of it, regions which unlike paintings let us forget there is anything beyond" (p. 5). But I shall argue that many gardens forcefully remind us of what lies beyond them.

23. Jackson, "Nearer Than Eden," p. 20. "Even within a given culture there are many versions of the garden. Yet we somehow recognize them all."

24. There are still traces of the original fields laid out in England by the Anglo-Saxons and early Scandinavian settlers. Not until the Conquest, however, can we discern an intention to set aside particular plots as pleasure gardens or "pleasances." See Trevor Rowley, "Medieval Field Systems," in Leonard Cantor, ed., *The English Medieval Landscape* (Philadelphia: University of Pennsylvania Press, 1982), pp. 25–28. On the distinction between gardens and fields, especially the encroachment of one upon the other, see Jackson, "Nearer Than Eden," pp. 25ff.

25. Cited by John Harvey, *Medieval Gardens* (London: Batsford, 1981), p. 10.

26. Cited in ibid.

27. The nourishing aspect would be questioned and removed by the French gardeners of the seventeenth century; Louis XIV expressly forbade the growing of comestible fruits in his gardens at Versailles.

28. Harvey analyzes this example in *Medieval Gardens*, p. 11.

29. On these four forms of game garden, see Leonard Cantor, "Forests, Chases, Parks, and Warrens," in his *English Medieval Landscape*, pp. 56–85.

30. On the various values of trees, see Harvey, *Mediaeval Gardens*, p. 17.

31. Ibid., p. 142.

32. This same attitude pervades the makers of the classical Chinese garden. But in the latter case nature is not so much *included* as *represented* within the enclosure of the garden itself (e.g., by miniature landscapes that imitate external models). See Edwin T. Morris, *The Gardens of China: History, Art, and Meanings* (New York: Scribners, 1983), esp. chaps. 3 and 7. See also the discussion of Chinese gardens as special places for remembering, in my *Remembering: A Phenomenological Study* (Bloomington: Indiana University Press, 1987), pp. 207–12, 260, 343–44.

33. William Howard Adams, *The French Garden 1500–1800* (New York: Braziller, 1979), p. 18. Even the allegorical character of the medieval garden, evident in such common appellations as "The Garden of Love" and "The Garden of Salvation," was still manifest in early sixteenth-century French gardens.

34. The figure is from ibid., p. 19, fig. 11.

35. Ibid., p. 21.

36. Moore, Mitchell, and Turnbull, *The Poetics of Gardens*, p. 14.

37. Figs. 13 and 14 are from Adams, *The French Garden*, p. 87, figs. 92 and 93. In the full plan, the *petit parc* is the dense, square central area just above the inverted V-shape.

38. "Unlike Vaux-le-Vicomte, the gardens at Versailles impose no particular promenade, despite an equally strong central axis which actually leads to a multitude of possible paths of *divertissement*" (Allen S. Weiss, "Anamorphosis Absconditus," *Art and Text* [1987], nos. 23–24, p. 6). At Versailles the otherwise considerable distances of the garden (the central axis alone was over eight miles long, since it also connected up with the central avenue of the city of Versailles) are experienced as reduced because of foreshortening effects.

39. Vincent Scully, *Architecture: The Natural and the Manmade* (New York: St. Martin's Press, 1991), p. 28.

40. For the design of the Château Richelieu, see fig. 78 in Adams, *The French Garden*. The plan of the château consists in essence of four squares (including the square containing the castle itself) situated on a longitudinal axis between two circles. Adams also discusses the "obsessive harmony" of the never-completed Charleval, where "nature is hypnotized by an almost totalitarian vision of a Renaissance on earth" (p. 44).

41. Ibid., p. 88.

42. Cited in ibid., p. 97.

43. For a formal analysis of these ratios, with special emphasis on their roots in Ficino and Alberti, see George Hersey's extraordinary analysis in *Pythagorean Palaces: Magic and Architecture in the Italian Renaissance* (Ithaca, N.Y.: Cornell University Press, 1976).

44. "These cadenced accents, carefully spaced, further emphasized the ceremonial itinerary or promenade which became an integral part of the experience of the French garden. The ideal world of memory, of contemplation, and of the pleasures of the senses had to be held together by a perfectly orchestrated score of rhythmic walks and stops" (Adams, *The French Garden*, p. 52). Such regulated perambulation contrasts with that "erroneous wandering" which was induced by a Baroque garden such as the Boboli in Florence. (On the Boboli, see Harbison, *Eccentric Spaces*, pp. 6–10.)

45. Moore, Mitchell, and Turnbull, *The Poetics of Gardens*, p. 199. Pointing to the same ambivalence, the authors add that a landscape architect such as Le Nôtre "uses finite formal geometries to bring us to the brink of infinity."

46. Frances Yates has established that a widespread Hermetic belief in the numinousness of number and shape, stemming from Kabbalistic and other sources in the Renaissance, lasted well into the seventeenth century. On these matters, see esp. *The Art of Memory* (London: Routledge, Kegan & Paul, 1966) and *Giordano Bruno and the Hermetic Tradition* (Chicago: University of Chicago Press, 1964). Alberto Pérez-Gómez has documented the impact of this Hermetic subculture on the architecture of the same period: "As a rule . . . the architects of the seventeenth century managed to synthesize the dimensions of qualitative, preconceptual spatiality and geometrical conceptual space" (*Architecture and the Crisis of Modern Science* [Cambridge, Mass.: MIT Press, 1983], p. 175). Given the existence of this antiformalist undercurrent, it is inadequate, though tempting, to conclude that the formal French garden of the seventeenth century was simply organized as "a powerful Cartesian grid where art and nature were bound together by mathematical regularity. The simplification of the vast, open spaces allowed no secrets, but only an idealized existence enforced by an inexorable logic" (Adams, *The French Garden*, p. 78). If it is certainly true that the invocation of mathematical regularity in the design of formal gardens pointed to an "idealized existence" in which art and nature might realize a perfect harmony, it is much less certain that this harmony "allowed no secrets."

47. The employment of perspective in theatrical representations further reinforced the illusoriness of garden space. Adams remarks that perspective had tremendous appeal to "landscape architects who were increasingly preoccupied with illusion and appearance, once the magic of the new scenery, often a garden setting, was revealed" (*The French Garden*, p. 63). Far from delineating the structure of that space itself, perspective was in fact an instance of *Ideenkleid*—irresistible insofar as it was sanctioned by Renaissance theorists such as Alberti—applied to the garden qua site. It was the creation of illusion in the name of scientific truth. As Pérez-Gómez puts it, "Perspective both revealed the truth of reality and reflected man's power to modify it; that is, it was a form of magic" (*Architecture and the Crisis of Modern Science*, p. 181). Indeed, perspective was first developed in painting and in theater, and thus as a means of producing spatial illusion in the aesthetic arena. Palladio's Teatro Olimpico at Vicenza, built in 1580, made abundant use of perspectival effects. For a nuanced description of theater at Versailles, see Naomi Miller, "The Theater in the Garden: From Artifice to Artefact," in *Theatergarden: Bestarium* (Cambridge, Mass.: MIT Press, 1990).

48. Scully, *Architecture*, p. 221.

49. Addison's remark is in his essay "The Pleasures of the Imagination," *Spectator,*

no. 411–422, June 21–July 4, 1712. But it is one thing to *humor* a given natural setting and quite another thing to *honor* it expressly. The ancient Greeks honored the setting by expressly orienting their temples toward it.

50. Moore, Mitchell, and Turnbull, *The Poetics of Gardens*, p. 198. On Versailles as *claiming* environing space, see p. 22: "The great *allées* that André Le Nôtre made for Louis XIV at Versailles are memorable perhaps even more as claims than as compositions." Adams notes that "throughout the seventeenth century one can see the garden's edge opening out, claiming more and more of surrounding nature as a part of its stage setting . . . the garden finally extended toward the furthest horizon, making the sky itself a part of the garden theater under Le Nitre's stagecraft. . . ." (*The French Garden*, p. 71).

51. Moore, Mitchell, and Turnbull, *The Poetics of Gardens*, p. 14. The phrase "charmless and disorderly" is attributed to the Moghul emperor Babur upon conquering India. To induce charm and order, he built sumptuous gardens on the Persian foursquare pattern.

52. On this point, see Weiss, "Anamorphosis Absconditus," n. 16.

53. Cited from Blondel's book (published in 1752) by Adams, *The French Garden*, p. 117. My italics. The new French style, exulted Blondel, has the aesthetic qualities of *le pittoresque, la poétique,* and *le romantique.* Romanticism here arises in three-dimensional gardens and parks as well as in literature and painting.

54. Ibid., p. 131. For engravings and photographs of Méréville, see figs. 154–62.

55. This statement of 1713 is cited in Christopher Hussey, *English Gardens and Landscapes: 1700–1750* (New York: Funk & Wagnalls, 1967), p. 14. Such simplicity is precisely *not* the geometric simplicity pursued by Le Nôtre and his contemporaries. The latter had been assimilated by the British in a slavishly imitative manner in the late seventeenth century and, thanks to an additional infusion from the Dutch, had given rise to an obsession with topiary gardens, i.e., the formal sculpting of bushes and trees into fantastic shapes: "things grown reflecting the shape of things built" (a saying of the time as cited by Derek Clifford, *A History of Garden Design* [New York: Praeger, 1966], p. 126).

56. Hussey, *English Gardens and Landscapes*, p. 12. On British landscape gardeners' masterful implacement of trees by "belting," "clumping," and "dotting," see Moore, Mitchell, and Turnbull, *The Poetics of Gardens*, pp. 62ff.

57. Humphry Repton is given credit for inventing the term *landscape gardening* in 1788: "I have adopted the term *Landscape Gardening,* as most proper, because the art can only be advanced and perfected by the united powers of the *landscape painter* and the *practical gardener.* The former must conceive a plan, which the latter may be able to execute" (cited in J. C. Loudon, *The Landscape Gardening and Landscape Architecture of the Late Humphry Repton, Esq.* [London: Longman, 1841], p. 29; Repton's italics).

58. Alexander Pope, "Epistle on Taste," cited by Moore, Mitchell, and Turnbull, *The Poetics of Gardens*, p. 141.

59. For an extensive analysis of Constable's painting, see E. H. Gombrich, *Art and Illusion* (Princeton, N.J.: Princeton University Press, 1961), pp. 33ff. On the influence of Claude at Stourhead, see Scully, *Architecture*, p. 334.

60. Both painters and gardeners "tried to eliminate nature's accidental flaws, thereby allowing an immanent beauty to emerge" (Moore, Mitchell, and Turnbull, *The Poetics of Gardens*, p. 65). The same authors observe wittily that "the watercolorists painted ideal landscapes, the gardeners then built them, and the watercolorists painted these in turn" (p. 9).

61. For a close analysis of Blenheim, see ibid., pp. 64–65.

62. Norman T. Newton, *Design on the Land: The Development of Landscape Architecture*

(Cambridge, Mass.: Harvard University Press, 1971), p. 207. Cf. Clifford's comparable statement: "In England in the third decade of the eighteenth century there began to be apparent the Great Gardening Revolution, a reversal of taste without precedent in the history of gardening and hardly to be equalled in that of any other art" (*History of Garden Design*, p. 123). For an excellent collection of texts that bear on the development of English gardens from the seventeenth to the nineteenth century, see J. D. Hunt and P. Willis, *The Genius of the Place: The English Landscape Garden 1620–1820* (Cambridge, Mass.: MIT Press, 1990).

63. Newton, *Design on the Land*, p. 220; his italics.

64. The figure is from Clifford, *History of Garden Design*, fig. 64.

65. Cited from Horace Walpole, *The History of the Modern Taste in Gardening* (1771), in Hunt and Willis, *The Genius of the Place*, p. 313.

66. The "ha!ha!" had a fence *at its bottom* (to keep wandering livestock at bay). Walpole remarked that thanks to the ha!ha! the English garden was "set free from its prim regularity, that it might assort with the wilder country without" (from *The History of the Modern Taste in Gardening*, cited in ibid.). Harbison considers the ha!ha! a characteristically British way of achieving boundlessness; for the English garden, "an un-wall had to be invented, which performs the physical functions without having the visual value of a wall. The ha-ha or sunken fence is an English joke on law and order that exercises real constraint with English deviousness" (Harbison, *Eccentric Spaces*, p. 5).

67. Cited by Moore, Mitchell, and Turnbull, *The Poetics of Gardens*, p. 46.

68. In its discontinuous clumping, a belted boundary is well suited to help realize the goal expressed by Stephen Switzer in his *Iconographia Rustica* (1742): "I would throw my Garden open to all View, to the unbounded Felicities of distant Prospect and the expansive volumes of Nature herself" (cited by Clifford, *History of Garden Design*, p. 134).

69. Ibid., p. 130. Clifford adds sarcastically: "given such a scale, a unified and appropriate ending to it all seems scarcely possible short of surrounding the entire domain with a palatial façade . . . a mountain range, or the ocean itself."

70. Moore, Mitchell, and Turnbull, *The Poetics of Gardens*, p. 21.

71. The French gardeners of the seventeenth century were by no means the first, nor were they even the most monumental, in applying such strict linearity to the landscape: the Nazca lines in Peru delineate gigantic triangles, rectangles, and trapezoids superimposed on an often rugged landscape. See Maria Reiche, "Nazca Lines, Peru," in Marilyn Bridges, ed., *Markings: Aerial Views of Sacred Landscapes* (New York: Aperture, 1986), pp. 8–31.

72. Humphry Repton said scathingly that "this favourite meandering and undulating line soon prevailed in everything . . . till, at length, it became as monotonous as the straight line" (cited in Loudon, *Landscape Gardening*, p. 521). Nevertheless, the wavy line "carried all before it," as Clifford asserts, citing Shenstone's couplet (*History of Garden Design*, p. 154):

> Show to the pupils of Design
> The triumphs of the Waving Line

73. Clifford, *History of Garden Design*, p. 159. Brown's sparseness leads Moore et al. to compare his parks with zen gardens; see *The Poetics of Gardens*, p. 51.

74. Alexander Pope, "An Epistle to Lord Burlington" (1731); his italics. The full verse runs: "To build, to plant, whatever you intend, / To rear the Column, or the Arch to bend, / To swell the Terras, or to sink the Grot; / in all, let *Nature* never be forgot. / Consult the *Genius* of the *Place* in all, / That tells the Waters or to rise, or fall."

75. Cf. Edmund Husserl, *Ideas I,* trans. W. R. B. Gibson (New York: Collier, 1956), secs. 67–70.

76. "In England a garden has never been primarily a place to sit in, or a place to debate in, or a place to act in; not for the English the *fêtes champêtres* of Fontainebleau and Chantilly . . . for the English a garden has always been a place to walk about in and to play games in" (Clifford, *History of Garden Design,* pp. 124–25).

77. It is ironic but characteristic that the domestic architecture on the very estates whose grounds Brown and Kent designed was for the most part Neoclassicist (influenced by Palladio via Inigo Jones) or Baroque in inspiration. Both of these styles discouraged intimate relationships with the surrounding natural environment, much as modernist architecture of the International Style was to do once again in the twentieth century. (Frank Lloyd Wright was exceptional in precisely this regard, since his houses and buildings were often ecologically sensitive.) But unlike buildings in the International Style, Neoclassicist and Baroque edifices contained considerable interior ornamentation, thereby introducing into their interiors what had been ignored outside them. (This last observation emerged in conversation with Kent Bloomer.)

78. Clifford, *History of Garden Design,* p. 144.

79. This claim is discussed by David Watkin, *The English Vision: The Picturesque in Architecture, Landscape, and Garden Design* (New York: Harper, 1982), p. 72. Whately also mentions "building proper" as a fifth element.

80. On ecotones, see Moore, Mitchell, and Turnbull, *The Poetics of Gardens,* p. 32.

81. Cited from Walpole's *History of the Modern Taste in Gardening,* in Hunt and Willis, *The Genius of the Place,* p. 314.

82. On the theme of pilgrimages to gardens, including eighteenth-century English parks, see Moore, Mitchell, and Turnbull, *The Poetics of Gardens,* pp. 117–57.

83. Cited in Loudon, *Landscape Gardening,* pp. 222–23; his italics. A landscape gardener at first influenced by Capability Brown, Humphry Repton rebelled against Brown and became known as a proponent of the "picturesque" style in gardens. He reveals a more austere and nonpicturesque aspect of his thought in the writings on which I am here drawing. Frederick Law Olmstead and Calvert Vaux, planners of Central Park in New York, were avid readers of Repton.

84. Ibid., p. 601. In both of Repton's statements we hear echoes of Locke's conception of property as what has become one's own (*propius*) through labor on the land, and we sense as well the ever-lengthening shadow of British colonialism and imperialism.

85. For examples of Japanese Zen gardens of the *karesansui* (dry gardening) type, see chaps. 5 and 6 of Mitchell Bing and Josse Wayembergh, Japanese *Gardens: Design and Meaning* (New York: McGraw-Hill, 1981). For a detailed structural analysis of one such garden, Ryoan-ji in Kyoto, see Moore, Mitchell, and Turnbull, *The Poetics of Gardens,* pp. 55–58. On p. 21 these authors point out that "after Kent, English gardens would become attempts (different from, but curiously parallel with the Japanese) to simulate nature, embrace it, and perfect it." (See also p. 65 on this parallel.) A comprehensive study of miniaturization in Oriental gardens is undertaken by Rolf A. Stein, *Le monde en petit* (Paris: Flammarion, 1987).

86. Repton revealingly abjures extensiveness per se as a criterion of the beauty of landscape: "Extent and beauty have ever appeared to me distinct objects; and a small place, in which the boundary is not obtrusive, may be more interesting, and more consonant to elegance and convenience, than a large tract of land" (in Loudon, *Landscape Gardening,* p. 223). Here a basic premise of Le Nôtre and Brown alike, i.e., the desirability of extensive grounds, is put into question.

87. Cited in ibid., p. 430. Repton also asserts that "all rational improvement of

grounds is, necessarily, founded on a due attention to the character and situation of *the place to be improved:* the former teaches what is advisable, the latter what is possible to be done" (H. Repton, *The Art of Landscape Gardening* [Boston: Houghton Mifflin, 1907], p. 7; my italics).

88. Cited in Loudon, *Landscape Gardening*, p. 434. Such gardens are neither formal nor informal; they are decorative and useful at once: flower gardens, fruit gardens, and vegetable gardens. Although an estate may include all three kinds of garden, a minimal organization should be maintained; all flowers or fruits or vegetables *of the same type* should be grouped together. In this way, order is realized—in contrast with the indiscriminate mixing of flora in wilderness—yet without requiring that the order be geometric in the French mode.

89. Cited in ibid.

90. For construction rituals in Burma, see Chime Wongmo, "Rituals of Bhutanese House Construction," in B. N. Ariz and M. Kapstein, eds., *Soundings in Tibetan Civilization* (New Delhi: Manohar, 1985), pp. 107–14. For Scandinavia (specifically the Scandinavian occupation of Iceland), see Mircea Eliade, *The Myth of the Eternal Return, or Cosmos and History* (Princeton, N.J.: Princeton University Press, 1974), pp. 10–11. For China, see various studies of *feng shui*, i.e., geomancy. For Rumania, see Eliade, *The Sacred and the Profane*, chap. 1. For Tibet, see Claes Corlin, "The Symbolism of the House in rGyal-Thang," in M. Aris and A. Kyi, eds., *Tibetan Studies in Honor of Hugh Richardson* (Warminster: Aris & Phillips, 1980), pp. 87–92.

91. I say "builder" here and not "architect," inasmuch as the latter word connotes, by its literal meaning, the Promethean ideal of "master maker." In fact, in many instances builder and architect combine in one person: e.g., in the case of many medieval cathedrals. The two roles become dissociated systematically, however, in highly industrialized societies.

92. On the mode of construction at Arcosanti, see Paolo Solari, *Arcosanti: An Urban Laboratory?* (San Marcos, Calif.: Slawson, 1984).

93. Perhaps the most convincing example of how buildings may be integrally related to the larger landscape is found in Greek temples of the classical period. Vincent Scully has shown how these temples are consistently oriented to particular landscape features, especially "horned" mountains in the vicinity (*The Earth, the Temple, and the Gods* [New York: Praeger, 1962]). On the general importance of the "building site"—where this latter term does not imply a merely homogenous space—see Kevin Lynch, *Site Planning*, 2d ed. (Cambridge, Mass.: MIT Press, 1971), chaps. 1–5.

94. The first claim is from Gaston Bachelard, *The Poetics of Space*, trans. M. Jolas (Boston: Beacon Press, 1958), p. 5; the second is on p. 4.

95. Ibid., p. 4. For recent discussions of the concept of home, see Witold Rybczynski, *Home: A Short History of an Idea* (New York: Viking, 1986), and a special issue of *Social Research* entitled "Home: A Place in the World" (vol. 58 [Spring 1991]), esp. the articles by Joseph Rykwert ("House and Home") and Mary Douglas ("The Idea of a Home: A Kind of Space").

96. "I hated grandomania then as much as I hate it now" (from an article of 1936 in the *Architect's Journal*, reprinted in F. L. Wright, *On Architecture* [New York: Grosset & Dunlap, 1941], p. 179). This from an architect who once designed a colossal "mile-high" building!

97. On the theme of intimate immensity, see Bachelard, *The Poetics of Space*, trans. M. Jolas (Boston: Beacon Press, 1975), chap. 8.

98. I employ this common term with some misgiving. Nevertheless, there is a nontendentious sense of *site*, as invoked in this comment by an architect pondering Heidegger's

tracing of *Ort* (site) to "tip of a lance": "infinitely small but mighty by its power to encompass and condense, [the *Ort* is] where all forces and vectors are concentrated to be liberated and released through a mysterious transformation of energy into matter, of image into built form. This transformation becomes *the history of the site as place*" (Raimound Abraham, "The Anticipation of Architecture," in *Education of an Architect*, ed. E. Diller, D. Lewis, and K. Shapich [New York: Rizzoli, 1988], p. 140; my italics). The italicized phrase, however, indicates that site alone does not suffice to capture the task of building in a cultivational manner.

99. On *Sorge*, see Martin Heidegger, *Being and Time*, trans. J. Macquarrie and E. Robinson (New York: Harper, 1962), pt. 1, div. 1, chap. 6 ("Care as the Being of Dasein"). The "care-structure" is global insofar as by its means the various "existentials" are held together in Dasein's "potentiality-for-Being-a-whole" (cf. div. 2, chap. 3). *Fürsorge*, literally "care for," means both solicitous concern for others and social welfare. Heidegger trades on this ambiguity in his discussion of care, concern (*besorgen*), and "solicitude," esp. on pp. 157–60.

100. This phrase occurs in Maurice Merleau-Ponty's working note of November 1959: "Say that the things are structures, frameworks, the stars of our life: not before us, laid out as perspective spectacles, but gravitating about us" (*The Visible and the Invisible*, trans. A. Lingis [Evanston, Ill.: Northwestern University Press, 1968], p. 220).

101. *Oxford English Dictionary*. Similarly, German *bauen*, to build, is closely tied to *beuren*, dwelling; indeed, Old English *buan is* the root of *bauen* itself and means to remain or stay in a place, in short, to dwell in one of its two primary senses. Similarly, *abode* and *abide* stem from Old English *bidan*, to stay, wait—and thus also entail dwelling-as-residing.

102. *Bheu*, the Indo-European source of *building*, is akin to the Sanskrit *bhū*, which means to be, become, arise, emerge; stay, abide; happen, occur. It is in turn related to *bhūmi*, earth, soil, ground; territory, district; place, site, situation; position, posture, attitude; floor of a house, story; area, base of a geometric figure; limit; receptacle. Notice that *bhūmi* combines the natural ("earth") with the architectural ("floor," "story") and even with the geometrical ("area," "limit") while signifying "place" and "situation" throughout. (I thank Janet Gyatso for assistance on this etymology.) Notice that in the sentence "building is dwelling" all three words are etymologically affine—given that *being* is also derived from *bheu*. (On this derivation of *being*, see M. Heidegger, *Introduction to Metaphysics*, trans. R. Manheim [New Haven, Conn.: Yale University Press, 1959], p. 71).

103. Martin Heidegger, "Building Dwelling Thinking," trans. A. Hofstadter in *Poetry, Language, Thought* (New York: Harper, 1971), esp. pp. 158ff.

104. *Timaeus*, 52a–b (Cornford translation).

105. Heidegger, "Building Dwelling Thinking," p. 160; italicized in the text and repeated (unitalicized) later on the same page. Heidegger is not claiming that building is the *only* form of letting-dwell. It is rather, as he adds, "a *distinctive* letting-dwell" (p. 159; my italics). Other ways of letting-dwell include poetic language and political action.

106. Emmanuel Levinas, *Totality and Infinity*, trans. A. Lingis (Pittsburgh: Duquesne University Press, 1969), p. 153.

107. Ibid. My italics. In saying "my dwelling," Levinas privileges the home as an archetypal dwelling place. But on Levinas's view the home itself includes a factor of "wandering" (*errance*) and of *dis*appropriation; see pp. 152–74.

108. Ibid., p. 168. His italics.

109. On the issue of the geometric specifiability of primary vs. secondary qualities—an issue first raised by Galileo, according to Husserl—see Edmund Husserl, *The Crisis*

of European Sciences and Transcendental Phenomenology, trans. D. Carr (Evanston, Ill.: Northwestern University Press, 1970), pp. 34–37 ("The Problem of the Mathematizability of the 'Plena'").

110. Frank Lloyd Wright, *On Architecture* (New York: Duell, Sloan & Pearce, 1941), p. 177. Wright nevertheless proposed his own version of mass housing: the inexpensive "Usonian" house.

111. Bachelard uses the phrase "felicitous space" in *The Poetics of Space*, p. xxxi. Such space involves a two-way movement: "the house images move in both directions: they are in us as much as we are in them" (p. xxxiii).

112. This is not to say that homes and cities are utterly disparate. Bernd Jager writes that a city is "the house of a larger secular community" ("Body, House, and City: The Intertwinings of Embodiment, Inhabitation, and Civilization," in D. Seamon and R. Mugerauer, *Dwelling, Place, and Environment* [New York: Columbia University Press, 1989], p. 216). Alberti, on the other hand, proposed that a house is to be conceived as "a small city" (cited by Christian Norberg-Schulz, *Existence, Space, and Architecture* [New York: Praeger, 1971], p. 31). Nevertheless, the criteria identified by Kevin Lynch as belonging intrinsically to all cities—i.e., paths, edges, districts, nodes, and landmarks—have no comparable presence in houses or homes (*The Image of the City* [Cambridge, Mass.: MIT Press, 1960], chap. 3, esp. pp. 47–48). In my remarks I am deliberately disregarding any distinction between a house (i.e., the built structure of a residence that provides access and protection) and a home (i.e., the house as lived-in interiority, having a familial and felt depth of its own that is unique in each case). Home can be built in many kinds of houses. I return to this theme in chap. 9.

113. Jager, "Body, House, and City," p. 215.

114. Frank Gehry, in conversation with Donlyn Lyndon, "The Loyola Forum," in *Places* 5 (1988), p. 43.

115. Jager, "Body, House, and City," p. 215.

7. The Arc of Desolation and the Array of Description

1. The phrase "natural subject of perception" is found in Maurice Merleau-Ponty, *Phenomenology of Perception*, trans. C. Smith (New York: Humanities Press, 1962), p. 206: "perceiving as we do with our body, the body is a natural self and, as it were, the subject of perception." The idea of a compact between body and world is delineated in Mikel Dufrenne, *The Notion of the A Priori*, trans. E. S. Casey (Evanston, Ill.: Northwestern University Press, 1967), pt. 3.

2. Wendell Berry, "The Mad Farmer in the City," *Collected Poems* (San Francisco: North Point Press, 1985), p. 123.

3. On the Encompassing, see Karl Jaspers, *Reason and Existenz*, trans. William Earle (Chicago: Noonday Press, 1955), pp. 51–76. *Encompass* comes from Old French *compasser*, to measure with a compass, and ultimately from Vulgar Latin *compassare*, to measure off by steps (*com*, an intensifier + *passus*, pace).

4. See G. W. F. Hegel, *Philosophy of Nature*, trans. M. J. Petrie (London: Allen & Unwin, 1970), sec. 254, pp. 223ff. Petrie translates *Aussersichsein* as self-externality.

5. *Encounter* as meeting (from French *encontrer*) is related to *country* via the etymon *contra*, against, opposite, and ultimately through the Indo-European root *kom*, which also underlies Greek *koinos*, common.

6. Concerning the transition from hunting-gathering to settled agricultural societies, see Paul Shepard, *Nature and Madness* (San Francisco: Sierra Club Press, 1982), chaps. 2 and 3. On the concept of "stead," see John R. Stilgoe, *Common Landscape of*

America: 1580–1845 (New Haven, Conn.: Yale University Press, 1982), pp. 14–16. I shall return to the concept of homestead in chap. 9.

7. Since *wild* is cognate with *will* and *ness* signifies "place," it follows that *wilderness* connotes "the will of the place"—in contrast with the will of human beings to subdue and cultivate wild places. (I owe this observation to Bruce Wilshire.) On the vexing subject of wilderness vs. civilization, see esp. Hans Peter Duerr, *Dreamtime: Concerning the Boundary between Wilderness and Civilization*, trans. F. Goodman (Oxford: Blackwell, 1985).

8. On the Abrahamic notion of wilderness, see Max Oelschlaeger, *The Idea of Wilderness: From Prehistory to the Age of Ecology* (New Haven, Conn.: Yale University Press, 1991), pp. 49–53.

9. Cited from Robert Beverley, *The History and Present State of Virginia* (1705), by Leo Marx, *The Machine in the Garden: Technology and the Pastoral Ideal in America* (New York: Oxford University Press, 1964), p. 76.

10. Marx, *The Machine in the Garden*, p. 85.

11. J. Hector St. John de Crèvecoeur, *Letters from an American Farmer* (New York: Penguin, 1986), p. 72. Crèvecoeur is, of course, referring to Native Americans, but he is repeating the medieval conviction that the wild forest is populated by unkempt and unsafe beings.

12. Ibid., p. 91. As William Cronon remarks, "In this vision, the transformation of wilderness betokened the planting of a garden, not the fall from one" (*Changes in the Land: Indians, Colonists, and the Ecology of New England* [New York: Hill & Wang, 1983], p. 5).

13. Cited from Linus P. Brockett, *Our Western Empire; or the New West Beyond the Mississippi*, by Henry Nash Smith, *Virgin Land: The American West as Symbol and Myth* (Cambridge, Mass.: Harvard University Press, 1970), p. 185.

14. "The great Interior Valley was transformed into a garden: for the imagination, the Garden of the World" (Nash, *Virgin Land*, p. 123). The epithet "breadbasket of the world" was still applied to Kansas when I was growing up there in the 1940s and 1950s.

15. The sentence cited comes from Adalard Welby, *A Visit to North America* (London, 1821), as quoted by Roderick Nash, *Wilderness and the American Mind* (New Haven, Conn.: Yale University Press, 1983), p. 26. Nash observes: "Clearly the American wilderness was not paradise. If men expected to enjoy an idyllic environment in America, they would have to *make it* by conquering wild country."

16. Marx, *The Machine in the Garden*, p. 87. The phrase "middle state" is originally that of the Scottish cleric Hugh Blair, who, in lectures on rhetoric published in 1783, remarked that "the happiest state of man is the middle state between the *savage* and the *refined*, or between the wild and the luxurious state" (cited by Marx, p. 105; Blair's italics).

17. "The land is the earth's surface or a part of the earth's surface; landscape is the physiognomy of the land, land in its effect on us" (Max Friedlander, *Landscape Portrait Still Life*, trans. R. F. C. Hull [New York: Schocken, 1963], p. 13). If this is true, then landscape will exhibit certain expressions and moods that are often first noticed in the physiognomy of the human face. But "first noticed" is not to be confused with "first given": it remains moot as to whether physiognomic expression is ultimately rooted in the land or in the person. See Glen Mazis, *Emotion and Embodiment: Fragile Ontology* (New York: Lang, 1994).

18. Wallace Stevens, "The Snow Man," in *The Collected Poems of Wallace Stevens* (Knopf, 1955), pp. 9–10, last stanza.

19. Gretel Ehrlich, *The Solace of Open Spaces* (New York: Penguin, 1985), p. 9.

20. On Kansas as a "dust bowl," see Dennis Farney, "On the Great Plains, Life Becomes a Fight for Water and Survival" (*Wall Street Journal*, Aug. 16, 1989). See also Paul Gruchow, *Journal of a Prairie Year* (Minneapolis: University of Minnesota Press, 1985).

21. It is not surprising to learn that one of the earliest meanings of *wilderness* was precisely the desert. Along with the uncharted sea, the desert was regarded as archetypally desolate. (The *Oxford English Dictionary*, abridged ed., from which I draw this fact, uses *desolate* three times in the entry for "wilderness," for example, in the phrase "a waste or desolate region of any kind, e.g., of open sea." Notice also that the German word for desolation, *Verwüstung*, contains the stem *wüst-*, the basis of *Wüste*, desert, and related to English *waste* via Latin *vāstus*, empty.) On the continuing cultural importance of the desert for the Western mind, see Shepard, *Nature and Madness*, chap. 3, "The Desert Fathers."

22. On the accommodative character of the Connecticut River valley, see J. B. Jackson, "A Puritan Looks at Scenery," *Discovering the Vernacular Landscape* (New Haven, Conn.: Yale University Press, 1984), pp. 59–64.

23. Ehrlich, *The Solace of Open Spaces*, p. 10.

24. John Ruskin, *The Seven Lamps of Architecture* (London: Dent, 1907), p. 181.

25. Ibid., p. 180.

26. By the same token, desolation can also bring on displacement, as when acute (mental) despondency leads us to change (physical) places. Many instances of emigration fit under this description. The pertinent terms of the interaction remain psychophysical and not physical only or psychical only.

27. Paul Gruchow, *The Necessity of Empty Places* (New York: St. Martin's Press, 1985), p. 127.

28. This phrase, coined by Gaston Bachelard, is extended by Jean-Paul Sartre in his *Being and Nothingness*, trans. H. Barnes (New York: Philosophical Library, 1956), pp. 482ff.

29. Entry under "desolate" in the *Random House Dictionary* (New York: Random House, 1983).

30. Three cautionary notes are in order here. First, the four features I have singled out are not *necessary* to the experience of desolation. It is perfectly possible, for example, that one might experience a very confined, *non*vast space as fully desolate—say, a prison cell or the field in which one must work daily. At most, one could say that spatial vastness *induces* and *intensifies* desolation. Second, the valorization of a given trait is *culturally specific*, varying from culture to culture and even from one period of time to another within a particular culture. Consider only the contrast between an early American assessment of open spaces and what a northern Italian might think of the same spaces. Finally, one and the same scene of wilderness is experienced quite differently by recently arrived emigrants than by those who are already habituated to this scene.

31. Sigmund Freud, *The Ego and the Id*, trans. J. Strachey (New York: Norton, 1960), p. 29; my italics. The metaphor of "precipitate," borrowed from geology, is itself redolent of place.

32. Ibid., p. 29, n. The incorporation of totem animals had first been recognized by Freud a decade earlier in *Totem and Taboo*.

33. On mourning as a complex process of ending, see my discussion in *Remembering: A Phenomenological Study* (Bloomington: Indiana University Press, 1987), pp. 255–57.

34. By what I have just said, I do not mean to imply that *every* unanticipated or unwished-for displacement is accompanied by desolation or even by ordinary distress. There are certainly circumstances in which rapid removal from our customary homeplace is experienced as alleviating: e.g., when we move without hesitation into, say, a

rented vacation home. In this latter case, a suspension of the usual responsibilities entailed by our usual center-place occurs, and we find ourselves accepting and even enjoying
the very displacement; the new ambiance seems the opposite of desolate. Nevertheless,
the foregoing discussion holds true for almost all cases in which the departure from an
abiding home-place is sudden, involuntary, and seemingly permanent. If we are convinced that we *cannot,* under any circumstances (or only the most trying ones), return
to our habitual abode, we shall be drawn into the desperate syndrome I have described,
a syndrome with which we seem able to cope only at the deeply unconscious level where
Freud's theory of mourning becomes so illuminating.

35. This presumption complicates the otherwise admirable analysis of Husserl in his
Ideas Pertaining to a Pure Phenomenology and to a Phenomenological Philosophy, bk. 3,
trans. T. E. Klein and W. E. Pohl (The Hague: Nijhoff, 1980), esp. chap. 1 and supple-
ments and 2.

36. Immanuel Kant, *Critique of Judgment,* trans. J. C. Meredith (Oxford: Clarendon
Press, 1952), p. 97.

37. Ibid., pp. 94–95.

38. The first phrase is from ibid., p. 97; the second is on p. 98.

39. Indeed, the infinity of nature transcends even what we can *imagine* of it: "Nature,
therefore, is sublime in such of its phenomena as in their intuition convey the idea of
their infinity. But this can only occur through the inadequacy of even the greatest effort
of our imagination in the estimation of the magnitude of [the sublime] object" (ibid., p.
103).

40. Ibid., pp. 109ff.

41. The first citation in this sentence is from ibid., p. 110; the others are from p. 111.
For Kant, sublimity stems *ultimately* from our own constructive psyche, not from Nature
per se. It "does not reside in any of the things of nature, but only in our own mind" (p.
114).

42. Ibid., p. 110.

43. Ibid. This sentence exists in apparent tension with the sentence cited in n. 42.
In the end, however, the two claims are reconcilable by means of a distinction between
the phenomenal world—where Nature's "might" is most apparent—and our cognitive
faculties, which are required for the actual *experience* of the sublime in either of its two
forms.

44. Ibid.

45. Ibid., p. 92.

46. Ibid.

47. Ibid., p. 119.

48. Ibid.; my italics.

49. Ibid.; my italics.

50. Ibid.

51. Ibid., p. 103.

52. Jackson, *Discovering the Vernacular Landscape,* p. 7; his italics.

53. Martin Heidegger, "The Origin of the Work of Art," trans. A. Hofstadter in *Poetry, Language, Thought* (New York: Harper, 1971), p. 48: "The earth is the spontaneous
forthcoming of that which is continually self-secluding and to that extent sheltering and
concealing."

54. On the distinction between moment and part, see Edmund Husserl, *Logical Investigations,* trans. J. N. Findlay (New York: Humanities Press, 1970), vol. 2, investigation
3 ("On the Theory of Wholes and Parts"), sec. 17, pp. 467–69.

55. R. Pinxten, I. van Dooren, and F. Harvey, *The Anthropology of Space: Explorations*

into the Natural Philosophy and Semantics of the Navajo (Philadelphia: University of Pennsylvania Press, 1983), p. 9, drawing on Berard Haile's pioneering work in L. Syman, ed., *Blessingway* (Tucson: University of Arizona Press, 1975). The authors of *The Anthropology of Space* add: "According to traditional [Navajo] beliefs, Earth and Heaven are referred to as two beings analogous to humans: they are said to have arms, legs, a head, a trunk, and so on. . . . Both are stretched out lengthwise; the Earth lies with the head to the East, with the eastern Sacred Mountain as a cushion, and with the feet against the western Sacred Mountain. . . . The male Heaven lies face down on top of her, and oriented the same way . . . the Heaven must be seen rather as a shell-like cover that tops the whole space between earth surface and stars including all living beings in between" (p. 11).

56. The Navajo also reject the cosmic void: "Earth and Heaven are such that in, under, and upon them there is always something. It is in no way possible to say that there would be nothing, emptiness, or open space within the universe or creation since then 'creation would not have been finished'" (Pinxten, van Dooren, and Harvey, *The Anthropology of Space*, p. 13).

57. M. Heidegger, "Poetically Man Dwells . . ." in *Poetry, Language, Thought*, trans. A. Hofstadter (New York: Harper, 1971), p. 220–21: "The upward glance spans the between of sky and earth. This between is measured out for the dwelling of man. . . . Only insofar as man takes the measure (*vermisst*) of his dwelling in this way is he able to *be* commensurately with his nature" (his italics). Heidegger's term for the between of sky and earth is "the dimension" (p. 220).

58. J. J. Gibson, *The Ecological Approach to Visual Perception* (Ithaca, N.Y.: Cornell University Press, 1976), particularly chaps. 4 and 5.

59. I am pursuing the question of such pictorial enframing in a separate study of the representation of place in landscape painting and in maps.

60. At this point my analysis begins to depart from that of Gibson, who claims that the entirety of sensory depth is *already given* in the near-world of the initial circumambient array. I maintain that although the rudiments of depth are certainly already present within this inner array (by "inner" I mean fully immanent to the initial set of affordances), the full presentation of depth, its literal "deepen-ing," requires supplementation by the outer, surrounding array that belongs to the full experience of a given natural place.

61. As Gibson remarks, "the terrestrial world is mostly made of surfaces, not bodies in space" (*The Ecological Approach to Visual Perception*, p. 15). The same is certainly true of the sea world. Technically regarded, surfaces "separate the substance from the medium" (p. 32). In my own preferred terms, this means that surfaces serve to separate things from the atmosphere.

62. For Gibson's account of texture as "the structure of the surface," see ibid., pp. 24–31. Gibson distinguishes between "pigment texture" and "layout texture."

63. M. Merleau-Ponty, *The Visible and the Invisible*, trans. A. Lingis (Evanston, Ill.: Northwestern University Press, 1968), p. 139. The analogy of flesh to "element" occurs on pp. 139–40. See also pp. 147–49, 248–51, 273–74. In adapting *flesh* for my own purposes, I am taking over a term whose sense in Merleau-Ponty's thinking is overtly ontological. My own more modest employment of the term is more purely descriptive or phenomenological.

64. Erwin Straus, *The Primary World of Senses*, trans. J. Needleman (Glencoe, Ill.: Free Press, 1963), pp. 317ff.

65. On the flesh of the world, see esp. Merleau-Ponty, *The Visible and the Invisible*, p. 255 (where it is said to be "indivision of this sensible Being that I am and all the rest which feels itself in me"), p. 267 ("it is a question of finding in the present, the flesh of the world"), and p. 271: "The flesh of the world = its *Horizonthaftigkeit* (interior and

exterior horizon) surrounding the thin pellicle of the strict visible between these two horizons." On intertwining, see p. 138 ("there is reciprocal insertion and intertwining of one in the other") and esp. the working note of November 16, 1960: "Chiasm [of] my body—the things, realized by the doubling up of my body into inside and outside—and the doubling up of the things (their inside and their outside)[.] It is because there are these 2 doublings-up that are possible: the insertion of the world between the two leaves of my body [and] the insertion of my body between the 2 leaves of each thing and of the world" (p. 264). Merleau-Ponty insists on the *implaced* nature of the flesh, which is "not a fact or a sum of facts, and yet [is] adherent to *location* and to the *now*" (pp. 139–40; his italics).

66. Gibson, *The Ecological Approach to Visual Perception*, p. 23. These actions include light reflectance, chemical reactions, touching, vaporization, etc.

67. Ludwig Wittgenstein, *Zettel*, trans. and ed. G. E. M. Anscombe and G. H. von Wright (Berkeley: University of California Press, 1967).

68. On the flat and level aspects of ground, see Gibson, *The Ecological Approach to Visual Perception*, p. 10 and p. 24. Concerning terminology, *ground* is closely related to *terrain*, which conveys the actual feel of a landscape in its earthiness (e.g., as is implied in a phrase such as "getting to know the terrain"). But taken in the strict sense, *terrain* refers to "a tract of country considered with regard to its natural features, configuration, etc.; in military use, e.g., as affecting its tactical advantages, fitness for maneuvering, etc.; also, an extent of ground, region, territory" (*OED*). On one hand, the meaning of *terrain* is tightly tied to surface features (as in the first two senses just cited show); on the other, construed in a broader sense (as in the third sense), *terrain* refers to an aspect of ground itself. Hence my preference for staying with *ground*, which I also prefer to *earth* or *land*. *Earth* is too extensive for present purposes insofar as it names the entire planet on which we reside; in its more restricted sense as "soil," it is too narrow. *Land* is also too restrictive when it is used in the sense of cultivated fields; and even in the larger sense of "any definite site regarded as a portion of the earth's surface" (a definition in American law), it is still too tied to the surface of the earth to take the place of *ground in* the polysemous senses in which I shall be employing this word.

69. James Hillman, *The Dream and the Underworld* (New York: Harper, 1979), p. 36. Throughout the present discussion I am indebted to Hillman's insightful treatment. Neither he nor I posit the Earth Mother, or Great Mother, as a literal figure or as an idol. But the interpretation of Gē in maternal terms is fraught with tendentious assumptions: e.g., that fertility is only female, that the woman stands *under* the earth's surface and *bears* its full weight, that she is therefore *invisible* and *unheard*, etc. Also, the association of woman with earth gives rise to a damaging disparagement: both are presumed to exist for the sake of exploitation or subordination. I am indebted to Sharon Hartline for bringing these implications to my attention.

70. Cited from Wilamowitz-Moellendorf's *Der Glaube* by Hillman, ibid., p. 35.

71. If the chthonic seems to resemble the sea's depths, we should recall that the latter are the unmediated underside of the sea's surface. Lacking the interposition of a middle realm such as that of Gē, the watery depths are at once more frightening in prospect and more unknown in content than are the depths of earth. The underworld is usually populated with sharply delineated regions and particular figures—as is manifest from Homer's *Odyssey* to Dante's *Inferno*—while the aqueous depths are characteristically left in a state of vagueness, as if to respect the dissolving capacity of water: *vague* means "wave" in French.

72. Hillman, *The Dream and the Underworld*, p. 36.

73. Ibid., p. 35.

74. "The ground is quite literally the *basis* of the behavior of land animals. And it is also the basis of their visual perception" (Gibson, *The Ecological Approach to Visual Perception*, pp. 131–32; his italics). Husserl conceives the earth as a basis by employing the suggestive term *Erdboden*, literally "earth-basis" but usually translated as "ground." (See E. Husserl, "Foundational Investigations of the Phenomenological Origin of the Spatiality of Nature," trans. F. Kersten, in P. McCormick and F. Elliston, *Husserl: Shorter Works* [South Bend, Ind.: University of Notre Dame Press, 1981], pp. 224–25: "I can always go farther on my earth-basis. . . . The 'earth' as the unitary earth-basis cannot be at rest and therefore cannot be experienced as a body.") While Gibson and Husserl emphasize the literal or physical status of ground as basis, Wendell Berry draws on the logical sense of the word: "To choose principle over community . . . is to destroy the only ground upon which principle can be enacted, and renewed" ("Discipline and Hope," *A Continuous Harmony* [New York: Harcourt Brace, 1970], p. 164).

75. See Martin Heidegger, *The Principle of Reason*, trans. R. Lilly (Bloomington: Indiana University Press, 1991).

76. Henry David Thoreau, journal entry of May 20, 1851; cited by Barbara Novak, *Nature and Culture: American Landscape and Painting 1825–1875* (New York: Oxford University Press, 1980), p. 115.

77. Husserl, "Foundational Investigations," p. 227. "Basis-place" translates *Bodenstätte*.

78. It is this horizontal axis that subdivides into the four cardinal directions, as well as into right vs. left, front vs. back, etc.

79. From the letter of November 13, 1925, to his Polish translator. In the same letter Rilke also says that "our task is to stamp this provisional, perishing earth into ourselves so deeply, so painfully and passionately, that its being may rise again, 'invisibly,' in us." Straus also discusses the intrinsic invisibility of landscape in *The Primary World of Senses*, pp. 322ff.

80. Merleau-Ponty, *The Visible and the Invisible*, p. 160.

81. Husserl, "Foundational Investigations," p. 230.

82. The term *root-basis* (*Stammboden*) is applied to the earth by Husserl, ibid., p. 227: "I must already be a human being for myself on the earth as my root-basis."

83. Merleau-Ponty, *The Visible and the Invisible*, p. 220. The full statement of this working note of November 1959 is: "Say that the things are structures, frameworks, the stars of our life: not before us, laid out as perspective spectacles, but gravitating about us."

84. On Secondness, see C. S. Peirce, *Collected Papers*, ed. C. Hartshorne and P. Weiss (Cambridge, Mass.: Harvard University Press, 1965), vol. 1, pp. 278ff. Merleau-Ponty writes in the same vein that a thing "is an ob-ject, that is, it spreads itself out before us by its own efficacy and does so precisely because it is gathered up in itself" (*The Visible and the Invisible*, p. 161). Concerning collection into groups, see Ernst Cassirer, "Group Concept and Perception Theory," *Philosophy and Phenomenological Research* [1944], vol. 5, pp. 1–35.

85. R. M. Rilke's phrase in the Ninth Elegy:

> Praise the world to the Angel, not the untellable: you
> can't impress him with the splendour you've felt; in the cosmos
> where he more feelingly feels you're only a tyro. So show him
> some simple thing, remoulded by age after age,
> till it lives in our hands and eyes as a part of ourselves.
>   Tell him *things*.

(*Duino Elegies,* trans. J. B. Leishman and Stephen Spender [New York: Norton, 1963], pp. 75–76; italics in the original.) Rilke does not, however, restrict "things" to natural things, but includes as well jugs and other crafted objects.

86. I take the word *subdued* from one of Merleau-Ponty's last working notes (November 1960): "not objects, but fields, subdued being, non-thetic being, being before being" (*The Visible and the Invisible,* p. 267). Merleau-Ponty is here discussing Bachelard's sense of "material elements." For a nuanced and insightful analysis of mountains (and other natural objects) as "things," see David Strong, *Crazy Mountains* (Albany: SUNY Press, 1995).

87. If ground and things possess "causal efficacy" and the sensuous surface and surrounding array of landscape exhibit "presentational immediacy," then arc and atmosphere present us with the intriguing phenomenon of an acausal immediacy: "acausal" in not being operative in the manner of discrete substances that influence one another, "immediate" in having effects that are directly transparent to the observer. (I am using *causal efficacy* and *presentational immediacy* in Whitehead's suggestive construals. In a relationship of causal efficacy, things "conform" to one another and the cause is "objectified" in the effect. Presentational immediacy is the directly present, phenomenal aspect of the perceived world; the term is thus close in meaning to what I have called "surrounding array." See A. N. Whitehead, *Symbolism: Its Meaning and Effect* [New York: Macmillan, 1927], chaps. 1 and 2.)

88. "The idea of *chiasm,* that is: every relation with being is *simultaneously* a taking and a being taken, the hold is held; it is *inscribed* and inscribed in the same being that it takes hold of" (Merleau-Ponty, *The Visible and the Invisible,* p. 266; his italics [working note of November 1960]). The same phrase, "the hold is held," is used by Heidegger in his analysis of memory in *What Is Called Thinking?* (New York: Harper, 1968), p. 3.

89. *Enuma Elish,* trans. N. K. Sandars, *in Poems of Heaven and Hell from Ancient Mesopotamia* (Baltimore: Penguin, 1971), p. 92.

90. From the fourth stanza of Stevens's poem "The Idea of Order at Key West": "It was her voice that made / The sky acutest at its vanishing."

91. Latin *arca,* chest, is the common root of *arch* and *arcane.* Just as the bodily chest contains and hides the heart and other organs, so arcane knowledge and arches act to hold and conceal things within a given structure.

92. *Random House Dictionary. Arc* derives from Latin *arcum,* bow, arch, curve. French *arc* means "bow."

93. Here we rejoin, by a very different route, the domed structure so important in "domestic" architecture, e.g., that inspired by Palladio's Villa Rotonda in the West or the Navajo hogan in the American Southwest. In all such cases, the *domus* of the house incorporates and mimics the dome of the heavens.

94. On the "flattened" character of the arc, especially as it appears in different settings, see Patrick Heelan, *Space-Perception and the Philosophy of Science* (Berkeley: University of California Press, 1983), pp. 59–60, 67–68: "The sky is perceived not as a sphere but as a *flattened* vaulted ceiling" (p. 60; his italics). On the Egyptian representation of the cosmos, see ibid., p. 31 and fig. 2.3. On the Navajo cosmogony, see Pinxten, van Dooren, and Harvey, *The Anthropology of Space,* p. 9.

95. By "dis-appearance" I mean "beginning not to appear" rather than "ceasing to exist." Notice that in thus dis-appearing, the arc contributes powerfully to the dynamic sublimity of a wildscape. It also contributes to the immeasurability indissociable from the sublime in its mathematical mode.

96. See M. Heidegger, *Being and Time,* trans. J. Macquarrie and E. Robinson (New York: Harper, 1962), secs. 29–30.

97. Otto Baensch, "Kunst und Gefühl," *Logos* (1923); cited by Susanne Langer, *Feeling and Form* (New York: Scribners, 1953), p. 19; his italics.

98. I owe this line of thought to Bruce Wilshire, from whose careful reading of this entire part of the book I have benefited greatly.

99. The idea of envelope is specified in the first two definitions of *atmosphere* in *Webster's Third New International Dictionary:* "1. A gaseous mass enveloping a heavenly body; the whole mass of air surrounding the earth; a gaseous envelope or medium. 2. A supposed medium around various bodies, any surrounding envelope."

100. This is the third definition of *atmosphere* in *Webster's Third*. Notice how this statement is situated on the borderline between the physical and the metaphorical meanings of the word.

101. Cited (in part) in John Burnet's translation from his *Early Greek Philosophy* (New York: Macmillan, 1958), p. 75.

102. The upper atmosphere, i.e., the supra-lunar realm, is the *aithēr*, the fifth element that is a composite of a purer form of fire and air and that glows overhead: *aithein* means "to burn, glow." In early modern physics, ether was considered to be a subtle substance permeating all space, a medium through which waves of light are propagated.

103. On this question, see esp. James K. McNeley, *Holy Wind in Navaho Philosophy* (Tucson: University of Arizona Press, 1981).

104. Theophrastus as cited by Burnet, *Early Greek Philosophy*, p. 73.

105. Quoted from Hippolytus's *Refutation of all Heresies* by Burnet, ibid.

106. Anaximines as reported by Hippolytus, ibid.

107. James E. Lovelock, *Gaia: A New Look at Life on Earth* (Oxford: Oxford University Press, 1982), p. 9. Regarding the Gaia hypothesis, I have learned much from David Abram's essay "The Perceptual Implications of Gaia," *Ecologist* (1985), and from discussions with Abram on the philosophical significance of the biosphere, especially with respect to its inner tie to atmosphere and breath.

108. Abram, "The Perceptual Implications of Gaia," pp. 96, 102.

109. I owe this last example to a conversation with David Strong.

110. Gary Snyder, *The Practice of the Wild* (San Francisco: North Point Press, 1990), p. 93.

111. See Oliver Sacks, *A Leg to Stand On* (New York: Harper, 1987), chaps. 1 and 2.

112. On morbid geometrism, see Eugene Minkowski, *Lived Time*, trans. N. Metzel (Evanston, Ill.: Northwestern University Press, 1970), pp. 277ff. On the associated notions of "null point," "absolute here," and "zero [point] of orientation," see E. Husserl, "The World of the Living Present and the Constitution of the Surrounding World External to the Organism," trans. Elliston and Langsdorf, in *Husserl: Shorter Writings*, pp. 249–50.

113. Wendell Berry, "Preserving Wildness," *Home Economics* (San Francisco: North Point Press, 1987), p. 151. Berry sees margins as "the divisions between holdings, as well as between kinds of work and kinds of land. These margins—lanes, streamsides, wooded fencerows, and the like—are always freeholds of wildness, where limits are set on human intention. . . . This is the landscape of harmony." Berry develops the same theme in "Getting Along with Nature," pp. 13ff.

8. Going Wild in the Land

1. Eight of fifteen definitions of the adjective *wild* in the *O.E.D.* relate specifically to the human condition. Only two definitions relate specifically to nonhuman nature. These latter concern nature as "tumultuous" and as "wasted"—hardly co-extensive with the full signification of wild natural places. Further reinforcing this humanocentric sense of *wild*

is its etymological origin in Swedish *villr*, bewildered, astray, lost, and in *vill*, confused or giddy; *vill*, also signifying "uncontrollable" or "willful," is cognate with English *will*.

2. The *O.E.D.* lists this (transliterated) sentence as containing the first known usage: "Weste is cleped bat londe, bat is longe tilce atleien, and wildernesse" (from the "Trin[ity] Coll[ege]. Hom.," p. 161). Roderick Nash claims that the first occurrence of the word is in the early-thirteenth-century text *Layamons Brut* (*Wilderness and the American Mind* [New Haven, Conn.: Yale University Press, 1982], p. 3, n.).

3. Gaston Bachelard, *Lautréamont* (Paris: Corti, 1939), p. 51: "*the need to animalize* . . . lies at the origin of imagination. The primary function of imagination is to make animal forms" (his italics).

4. This latter line of development was reinforced by importation of the Middle Dutch *wildernesse, wildernisse*. Recall that the very first full-scale landscape painting was done in the Lowlands, the place of origin for *wilderness* in its recognizably modern linguistic format.

5. This is Nash's formulation in *Wilderness and the American Mind*, p. 2.

6. Samuel Johnson even defined *wilderness* in his 1755 *Dictionary of the English Language* as "a desert; a tract of solitude and savageness" (cited by Nash, ibid., p. 3). To this day, the French language uses the phrase *lieu désert* to signify wilderness.

7. *Bewilder* also goes back to *villa*, to lead astray; *wilder*, "to cause to lose one's way, as in a wild or unknown place," is still listed as a verb in the *O.E.D.*

8. On the distinction between home-world and alien world, see E. Husserl, *Zur Phänomenologie der Intersubjektivität*, ed. Iso Kern (The Hague: Nijhof, 1973; vol. 15 in the Husserliana series), pp. 214–18, 622–25. I owe this reference to Anthony Steinbock.

9. I draw here on the entries "culture" and "cultivate" in *The Oxford Etymological Dictionary*, ed. C. T. Onions (Oxford: Oxford University Press, 1966).

10. John Muir, "The Discovery of Glacier Bay by Its Discoverer," *Wilderness Essays* (Salt Lake City: Peregrine Smith, 1980), p. 14.

11. Ibid., p. 23.

12. Cited in the entry under "landscape" in the *Oxford English Dictionary*. Concerning the evolution of landscape painting as it bears on wilderness, see J. B. Jackson, *Discovering the Vernacular Landscape* (New Haven, Conn.: Yale University Press, 1984), pp. 5ff. On painting as parergon, see Jacques Derrida, *Truth in Painting*, trans. G. Bennington and I. McLeod (Chicago: University of Chicago Press, 1987), pp. 37–82.

13. "Perspective" as I employ it here is not to be confused with the strict one-point perspective viewpoint that prevails in Renaissance models of representational space. The perspective now in question is that of the *embodied subject*, who always "takes up a view" on whatever is being experienced from the total stance (often a moving stance) of his or her lived body—and of a mind which, like the body itself, is influenced, if not actually constituted, by cultural categories.

14. This passage, from a letter of 1855, cited more completely in the epigraph to this chapter, is cited in Thomas Frick, ed., *The Sacred Theory of the Earth* (Berkeley, Calif.: North Atlantic, 1986), p. 37. By speaking of "seeing a picture," Hawthorne doubtless has in mind the fact that the Lake District had been previously painted and written about many times before his arrival there.

15. Ibid., p. 14. My italics.

16. Wallace Stevens, "Anecdote of the Jar," *The Palm at the End of the Mind*, ed. H. Stevens (New York: Vintage, 1972), p. 46.

17. See Neil Evernden, *The Natural Alien: Humankind and Environment* (Toronto: University of Toronto Press, 1985).

18. Recall in this connection the "construction rites" discussed by Mircea Eliade:

the existence of these rites at the moment of beginning to build signifies the enormous cultural-religious significance of the act of constructing (cf. *The Sacred and the Profane: The Nature of Religion,* trans. W. R. Trask [New York: Harcourt, Brace & World, 1959], chap. 1).

19. By "prefigure" I do not mean that such a place has been designed or intended for human use or enjoyment. I mean, rather, that a wild Thing such as Mount Everest *makes place* for the possible implacement of human beings. It does so by adumbrating in advance certain structures of access and sojourn. Although the mountain may not permit permanent dwelling, it does permit dwelling in the form of wandering. Even going astray on its slopes and failing to reach its peak introduce the culture of climbing into its midst. This culture includes such specific practices as the use of pitons and rope, the sociality of climbing groups, the following of maps, photography, etc.

20. In what follows I take *acculturation* to refer to the first phases of a given cultural process, especially those by which something "natural" or "wild" comes into the ken of human beings and begins to be assimilated to their intentions and projects. *Enculturation,* on the other hand, signifies the full process of assimilation of nature to culture: i.e., the putting *into culture* of what stems from the natural world. A just-blazed trail acculturates the wilderness in which it appears; the same trail, represented in a painting, has become enculturated.

21. On the "earth-ark" (*Arche-Erde*), see E. Husserl, "Foundational Investigations of the Phenomenological Origin of the Spatiality of Nature," trans. F. Kersten, in E. Husserl, *Shorter Writings,* ed. F. Elliston and P. McCormick (Notre Dame, Ind.: University of Notre Dame Press, 1983), pp. 228ff. I do not mean to imply that the ground is an altogether static entity. It is certainly subject to interpretation, e.g., as *chōra,* "chthonic depth," or as "Mother Earth." But being subject to interpretation is not equivalent to being nothing but the product of interpretation itself. The ground remains even as its interpretations change from culture to culture. (On the Native American interpretation of ground as Mother Earth, see Sam D. Gill, *Mother Earth: An American Story* [Chicago: University of Chicago Press, 1987]. This book is especially instructive regarding the conjoint contribution of several cultures—in this case, Anglo and Native American—in the evolution of a single basic notion.)

22. Whether the surrounding array precedes culture in the *order of being* is another question, i.e., a question of the "social construction of reality." (When I referred to "the more highly organized formats," I meant to leave room for the possibility that the effect of culture is operative in diminutive or micro-formats that influence the very first appearance and reception of the various fundamental features.) In the order of experience that phenomenology describes, such precedence is difficult to deny. But this does not mean that this precedence cannot, or should not, be disputed from an ontological—and a fortiori a historical or political—perspective.

23. For much the same reason, the objective measurability of this place is put into question—or at least deferred and suspended—by the mercurial action of the surrounding array we experience there. Indeed, a given array's inherent *im*measurability is one of the most effective and dramatic ways in which it defies culture. Every culture, though perhaps most acutely modern Western culture, has a propensity for pinpointing time and space, rendering these parameters determinate and predictable. The evanescent array of landscape—all the more evanescent in wilderness—challenges this propensity and acts to undermine it within the primary experience of the persons who generate and sustain a shared culture.

24. Charles S. Peirce, *Collected Papers* (Cambridge, Mass.: Harvard University Press, 1935), vol. 6, par. 95.

25. On Secondness as existence, see ibid., vol. 1, pars. 27ff., where it is called "fact"; on its reactiveness, see vol. 6, pars. 32, 212. On Secondness as resistance, see vol. 5, pars. 45–46. Maine de Biran's idea of things as "resistance" is closely related. Peirce was familiar with Biran's work. I owe the idea of this parallel to Jeffrey Gaines.

26. Ibid., vol. 5, par. 46.

27. See respectively ibid., vol. 2, pars. 311 and 85; and vol. 5, par. 45.

28. On the philosophical significance of lightning qua *Blitz*—especially as this emerges in the fragments of Heraclitus—see M. Heidegger and E. Fink, *Heraclitus Seminar,* trans. C. H. Seibert (University: University of Alabama Press, 1982), pp. 37ff.

29. "I wish to speak a word for Nature, for absolute freedom and wildness, as contrasted with a freedom and culture merely civil" ("Walking," in Henry David Thoreau, *Natural History Essays* [Salt Lake City: Peregrine Smith, 1980], p. 93).

30. By stressing the Secondness of wilderness, I do not mean to deny its comeliness, its amenity, its power to appeal to us. Wild places *beckon* as well as *repel.* If they did not do so, we should not be so ardent about exploring them in the first place! But the factor of appeal is much more obviously the product of a given culture's conception of wilderness than is the resistance of the latter.

31. On Thirdness construed as conceptual or linguistic mediation, see Peirce, *Collected Papers,* vol. 6, pars. 32, 69, 202, 212.

32. *Pervasion,* the action of permeating, derives from *per* (through) + *vadere,* to go, walk. In walking, then, I pervade the space of my world. (Latin *spatium,* space, and *spatiari,* to walk, stroll, are akin.)

33. I borrow these various cultural artifacts from Heidegger, who recognizes in them the same wilderness-binding power as Stevens finds in a jar. Heidegger himself prefers to speak of "gathering" rather than "binding." On the bridge, see Heidegger's essay "Building Dwelling Thinking," *in Poetry, Language, Thought,* trans. A. Hofstadter (New York: Harper, 1971), pp. 152–55; on the jug, see "The Thing," in ibid., pp. 166–74; on the path, "Conversation on a Country Path," in M. Heidegger, *Discourse on Thinking,* trans. J. M. Anderson and E. H. Freund (New York: Harper, 1966), p. 70.

34. "The same never coincides with the equal, not even in the empty indifferent oneness of what is merely identical. The equal or identical always moves toward the absence of difference, so that everything may be reduced to a common denominator. The same, by contrast, is the belonging together of what differs. . . . The same gathers what is distinct into an original being-at-one (*Einigkeit*)" (Heidegger, "Poetically Man Dwells . . ." in *Poetry, Language, Thought,* pp. 218–19). Concerning the harmony between cultural and natural, see Wendell Berry, *A Continuous Harmony: Essays Cultural and Agricultural* (New York: Harcourt Brace Jovanovich, 1970).

35. John Ruskin, *The Seven Lamps of Architecture* (London: Dent, 1907; first edition, 1849), p. 180.

36. Ibid.

37. Ibid., p. 181.

38. On the indebtedness of Muir to Ruskin, see John F. Sears, *Sacred Places: American Tourist Attractions in the Nineteenth Century* (Oxford: Oxford University Press, 1989), pp. 148ff.

39. Cited by Nash, *Wilderness and the American Mind,* p. 102, from Thoreau's 1858 article on his second trip to Maine in the *Atlantic Monthly.* On the early formation of national parks, see Sears, *Sacred Places,* and Nash, chap. 6 ("Preserve the Wilderness!"). Following Yosemite, Yellowstone was the next significant step (1872). European fascination with the idea of natural preserves is evident in Freud's use of Yellowstone as an analogy to the maintaining of an area of imaginative free play within the developing mind

(see his "Formulations On the Two Principles of Mental Functioning" [1911], *Standard Edition of the Complete Psychological Works* [London: Hogarth, 1958], vol. 12, p. 222, n.). On the whole idea of wilderness preservation, see Wendell Berry, "Preserving Wildness," *Home Economics* (San Francisco: North Point Press, 1987), pp. 137–51.

40. I borrow the word *consanguinity* from Emerson's discussion of the relationship between nature and culture in his *Nature* (Boston: Beacon Press, 1985; first edition, 1836), p. 78. The phrase "multifarious between" (*vielfältige Zwischen*), which I have cited before in chap. 5, is from M. Heidegger, *Hebel der Hausfreund* (Pfullingen: Neske, 1957), p. 13.

41. Quoted from Thoreau's journals by Nash, *Wilderness and the American Mind*, pp. 102–103; Thoreau's italics.

42. Thoreau, "Walking," *Natural History Essays* (Salt Lake City: Peregrine Smith, 1980), p. 72. Notice in this connection Thoreau's fascination with the image of Atlas: "like Atlas, to take the world on my shoulders" (p. 106). But world for Thoreau is not just something we shoulder or support; it also connotes beauty and order: "the Greeks called the world kósmos, Beauty, or Order, but we do not see clearly why they did so, and we esteem it at best only a curious philological fact" (p. 130).

43. Ibid., p. 114.

44. I take the important phrase "every where"—not merely "everywhere"—from this sentence in Thoreau's *Walden:* "Olympus is but the outside of the earth every where" (in *Thoreau*, ed. Robert F. Sayre [New York: Library of America, 1985], p. 390).

45. Ibid., p. 389.

46. Ibid., p. 390.

47. Ibid., p. 426. My italics.

48. Ibid.

49. "I found myself suddenly neighbor to the birds; not by having imprisoned one, but having caged myself near them" (ibid.)

50. Compare John Muir's remark: "I only went out for a walk, and finally concluded to stay until sundown, for going out, I discovered, was actually going in" (cited by B. Devall and G. Sessions, *Deep Ecology: Living As If Nature Mattered* [Salt Lake City: Peregrine Smith, 1985], p. 205).

51. Heidegger, *Hebel der Hausfreund*, p. 13. Heidegger italicizes the first use of "world."

52. Thoreau, *Walden*, pp. 390–91.

53. Ibid., p. 387. Thoreau continues: "I discovered many a site for a house not likely to be soon improved, which some might have thought too far from the village, but to my eyes the village was too far from it." *Site* (Latin *situs*) is an etymological cousin of *seat*.

54. Ibid., p. 412.

55. Ibid., pp. 412–13.

56. Ibid., p. 402; my italics; the "I" is in italics in the original. Thoreau also says, "I think that the richest vein is *somewhere hereabouts*" (p. 401; my italics).

57. Ibid., p. 402.

58. Ibid., p. 409. "What does our Concord culture amount to?" (p. 407).

59. Ibid., p. 411.

60. Ibid.

61. Ibid.

62. *Walden* can be construed as a book about writing or, more generally, "scripture." For this interpretation, see Stanley Cavell, *The Senses of Walden* (San Francisco: North Point Press, 1981; expanded ed.), esp. chap. 1, "Words."

63. "When I would recreate myself, I seek the darkest wood, the thickest and most interminable and, to the citizen, most dismal, swamp. I enter a swamp as a sacred place, a *sanctum sanctorum*. There is the strength, the marrow, of Nature" ("Walking," p. 116).

Thoreau prefers "a Dismal Swamp" to "the most beautiful garden that ever human art contrived" (ibid.): "I derive more of my subsistence from the swamps which surround my native town than from the cultivated gardens in the village" (p. 115). It will be noticed, however, that gardens and swamps share the common feature of marginality. If gardens are situated on the margins between fully built structures and wholly unbuilt wilderness, swamps are marginal between water and land. Because of their amphibious nature, they are often literally located on the edge of farms or fields. Thoreau remarks that at the times when he was considering purchasing a farm, "I have frequently found that I was attracted solely by a few square rods of impermeable and unfathomable bog—a natural sink *in one corner of it*" (p. 115; my italics).

64. Compare Heidegger's instructively different series of instances of the *vielfältige Zwischen:* "Between earth and sky, between birth and death, between joy and pain, between work and word" (*Hebel der Hausfreund*, p. 13).

65. *Walden*, p. 425. My italics. Compare Merleau-Ponty's claim that the seer belongs to the seen: "He who sees cannot possess the visible unless he is possessed by it, unless he *is of it*" (*The Visible and the Invisible*, pp. 134–35; his italics). I wish to thank Irene Klaver for emphasizing the importance of the theme of sympathy in *Walden*.

66. Ibid., p. 432. My italics.

67. Ibid., p. 427. See also the statement that "the gentle rain which waters my beans and keeps me in the house to-day is not drear and melancholy, but good for me too" (p. 426).

68. Bly refers to this journal entry of 1857: "There was a match found for me at last. I fell in love with a shrub oak" (Robert Bly, ed., *The Winged Life: The Poetic Voice of Henry David Thoreau* [San Francisco: Sierra Club Books, 1986], p. 114).

69. *Walden*, p. 575.

70. John Muir, *The Mountains of California* (New York: American Museum of Natural History, 1961), p. 258. The editor of this volume, Jack McCormick, remarks that "John Muir arrived in California a few days before his thirtieth birthday, in the spring of 1868. Although he was headed for Yosemite Valley, more than a hundred miles to the east, he spurned the transportation facilities of the era and set out on foot" (p. ix).

71. "Walking," p. 106.

72. Ibid., pp. 100–101.

73. Thoreau relates his fascination with having seen panoramas of the Rhine Valley and the Mississippi, "a Rhine stream of a different kind" (ibid., pp. 111–12). The importance of panoramas in the middle decades of nineteenth-century American culture is underlined by Barbara Novak in *Nature and Culture: American Landscape Painting 1825–1875* (Oxford: Oxford University Press, 1980).

74. *Walden*, p. 400. This clause follows a diatribe against "the mud and slush of opinion, and prejudice, and tradition, and delusion, and appearance" that obtains in cities and towns. The language of *place* is striking here: not only in the phrase "a place where you might found a wall or a state" but also, in the same paragraph, "till we come to a hard bottom and *rocks in place*" (my italics).

75. "Walking," p. 93.

76. Ibid., p. 94.

77. Not that John Muir always rushes over the land to get to his goal. In a charming chapter of *The Mountains of California* entitled "The Bee-Pastures" Muir describes his comparatively gentle traversing of the San Joaquin Valley by employing Thoreau's favorite walking word: "Sauntering in any direction, hundreds of these happy sun-plants brushed against my feet at every step, and closed over them as if I were wading in liquid gold" (pp. 261–62).

78. "Walking," p. 94.

79. Cavell, "Thinking of Emerson," *The Senses of Walden*, p. 138.

80. "Walking," p. 105.

81. Ibid., p. 104.

82. Ibid., p. 105. Also: "It is hard for me to believe that I shall find fair landscapes or sufficient wildness and freedom behind the eastern horizon."

83. Ibid., p. 106. For Thoreau, the future is *what you walk into:* "Read your fate, see what is before you, and walk on into futurity" (p. 411).

84. This line, like that of the epigraph to this section, is from the last stanza of Stevens's 1921 poem "Tea at the Palaz of Hoon." My italics.

85. Muir, "The Discovery of Glacier Bay," p. 6. Muir adds that "at daybreak I looked eagerly in every direction to learn what kind of place we were in; but gloomy rainclouds covered the mountains."

86. Ibid.

87. He "traced what we afterwards ascertained to be a labyrinth of errors, carefully following the outlines of the imaginary lakes which the map contains" ("Ktaadn," *The Maine Woods*, reprinted in *Thoreau*, ed. Sayre, p. 602). As Thoreau remarks at the conclusion of "Ktaadn," "the country is virtually unmapped and unexplored" (p. 655). See the group of maps reprinted as an appendix to the edition just cited.

88. Thoreau, "The Allegash and East Branch," *The Maine Woods*, p. 735.

89. Ibid., p. 734.

90. Ibid.

91. Ibid., p. 735.

92. Erwin Straus, *The Primary World of Senses*, trans. J. Needleman (Glencoe, Ill.: Free Press, 1963), p. 318. Straus adds that "to be fully in the landscape we must sacrifice, as far as possible, all temporal, spatial, and objective precision" (p. 324). It should be said, however, that Muir's and Thoreau's native guides do *not* sacrifice temporal and spatial precision. Indeed, they are *more* precise than the available "objective" representations, e.g., current cartographic representations. It remains true, however, that "in the landscape we cease to be historical beings, i.e., beings objectifiable to themselves. . . . [There] we are beyond the reach of both the objective world and ourselves" (p. 322).

93. For these points, see Wendell Berry, "Getting Along with Nature," *Home Economics*, esp. p. 13: "The hawk came because of the conjunction of the small pasture and its wooded borders. . . . This is the phenomenon of edge or margin that we know to be one of the powerful attractions of a diversified landscape, both to wildlife and to humans. . . . These margins are biologically rich, the meeting of two kinds of habitat."

94. I owe this phrase to Anthony Weston, whose reading of a penultimate draft of this entire part has been invaluable. I am also indebted to David Strong for his comments on still-earlier versions.

95. The full statement is "Feeling make you, / Out there in open space. / He coming through your body . . . / because tree just about your brother or father . . . / and tree is watching you" (Bill Neidjie, "I Give you this Story," in B. Neidjie, S. Davis, and D. Fox, eds., *Australia's Kakadu Men*, p. 51). The citation from Merleau-Ponty is in *The Visible and the Invisible*, p. 139.

96. I cite Hans-Georg Gadamer's idea of *Zuwachs an Sein* in his *Truth and Method* (New York: Seabury, 1975), pp. 124–25, 132–35.

97. Heidegger, "The Origin of the Work of Art," in *Poetry, Language, Thought*, trans. A. Hofstadter (New York: Harper, 1971), p. 49. Thickening is also implied when Heidegger adds that "thus the striving becomes ever more *intense* as striving" (my italics).

98. The first citation in this sentence is from *The Visible and the Invisible*, p. 137. At p. 139 Merleau-Ponty states that "the flesh is in this sense an 'element' of Being."

99. Ibid., p. 137.

100. Ibid.

101. Working note of May 1960, ibid., p. 255. It is not surprising that Merleau-Ponty has recourse in another working note to the notion of *Einfühlung*, a term which he construes literally as "feeling at one": "We are already in the being thus described. . . . *We are of it* . . . between it and us there is *Einfühlung* (working note of May 1960, p. 248; his italics).

102. A. N. Whitehead, *Science and the Modern World* (New York: Mentor, 1948 [1925]), p. 93.

103. On the composition of extended green belts in the New York region, see Iver Peterson, "Linking Bits of Leftover Land to Put Parks Closer to Home," *New York Times*, Jan. 8, 1992, and Anne Raver, "Endangered Species: New York City's Native Trees," *New York Times*, Jan. 11, 1992.

104. Although I came up with the term *ecocentric* in the course of my own deliberations, I find Max Oelschlaeger's recent discussion of the same term confirming and clarifying. Oelschlaeger states that "ecocentrists take natural systems as the dominant reality, such that even life itself must be set in a larger evolutionary frame of reference that contains inorganic constituents" (*The Idea of Wilderness: From Prehistory to the Age of Ecology* [New Haven, Conn.: Yale University Press, 1991], p. 293). In contrast with anthropocentrism and biocentrism, ecocentrism emphasizes the intrinsic value of the *entire* ecosystem, human and nonhuman, living and nonliving.

105. I refer to Perry Miller's classic work *Errand in the Wilderness* (Cambridge, Mass.: Harvard University Press, 1956).

106. Robert Frost, "The Gift Outright," in *Selected Poems of Robert Frost* (New York: Holt, Rinehart, 1961), pp. 299–300.

107. On "peri-phenomenology" as the description of "what has every chance of being lost sight of," see William Earle, *Evanescence: Peri-Phenomenological Essays* (Evanston, Ill.: Caxton, 1989), esp. pp. 1–4.

108. Sigmund Freud, *The Ego and the Id* (*Standard Edition of the Complete Psychological Works* [London: Hogarth, 1961], vol. 19, p. 26).

109. Some places, of course, are at once natural and social: e.g., gardens. *Every* movement into a wild place has social and political aspects (e.g., in the forms of models and motives), but this is not to say that it yields only, or ultimately, to a social or political analysis.

110. Holmes Rolston III, *Environmental Ethics* (Philadelphia: Temple University Press, 1988), p. 13. See also Rolston's statement on p. 3: "an ecology always lies in the background of culture. . . . Whatever their options, however their environments are rebuilt, humans remain residents in an ecosystem." But when Rolston says that "no culture develops in independence of the environment on which it is superimposed" (p. 15), he adopts an overlay model of culture that I find questionable.

111. Lococentrism is evident not only in ecology and exploration, perambulation and poetry, but is also found in landscape painting, geomancy, and especially in cartography, i.e., the drawing of maps, an endeavor once called "chorology." Ernst Haeckel, the first person to use *ecology* in a systematic sense, linked the term to *chorology* (i.e., the science of place) in *The History of Creation* (1873; English translation, 1892). Mapping is a graphic determination of *chōra*, Plato's term for a wild cosmogonic matrix of places. A map— whether a mere sketch map made as a reminder or an elaborate world-map of the sort that became important in the Age of Exploration—puts three-dimensional geographical places into the two-dimensional format of cartographic space. Even though many maps (with the notable exception of "contour maps") do not represent such landscape elements as hills or lakes, they are nevertheless lococentric in their aim of providing an exact and nonmisleading representation of particular places on the surface of the earth.

Since maps are usually based on actual visits to places (or on aerial photography of the same places), they have their genesis in the localized world of landscape—the degree of localization depending on the scale of a given map.

112. Rolston, *Environmental Ethics*, p. 4. Rolston insists on the intrinsic value of nature, speaking of nature as an "objective value carrier." For a discussion of the issue of intrinsic values, see Oelschlaeger, *The Idea of Wilderness,* pp. 199, 208–10, 293–95.

113. On *Gestell* (usually translated as "enframing" or "skeletal framework") and the idea of "standing-reserve" (*Bestand*), see M. Heidegger, *The Question concerning Technology,* trans. W. Lovitt (New York: Harper & Row, 1977), pp. 17f.

114. The American case was itself only a striking instance of a much more pervasive attitude of exploiting nature that came to the fore in seventeenth-century Europe. On this theme, see Carolyn Merchant, *The Death of Nature: Women, Ecology, and the Scientific Revolution* (New York: Harper, 1980).

115. Cited by Roderick Nash, *The Rights of Nature: A History of Environmental Ethics* (Madison: University of Wisconsin Press, 1989), p. 39. Nash argues that despite his precocity on the question of "rights of nature," Muir did not espouse these rights consistently throughout his career; see pp. 40ff.

116. Aldo Leopold, "The Land Ethic," *A Sand County Almanac* (New York: Oxford University Press, 1988), p. 218. He also observes that "land, like Odysseus' slave-girls, is still property. The land-relation is still strictly economic, entailing privileges but not obligations." Although based on a lifetime as a naturalist, Leopold's formulation of a land ethics dates from the late 1940s. For a comprehensive history of an ecologically based ethics, see Nash, *The Rights of Nature*, pp. 63–70, and Oelschlaeger, *The Idea of Wilderness,* chap. 7, esp. pp. 209ff. ("The Evolution of Leopold's Land Ethic").

117. Leopold, *A Sand County Almanac*, p. 240.

118. Emmanuel Levinas, *Totality and Infinity,* trans. A. Lingis (Pittsburgh: Duquesne University Press, 1969), p. 40. Levinas italicizes "right." The "Other" to which Levinas refers is not Nature but another human being. However, the application of his claim to nonhuman nature is in keeping with his conception of the Other as an entity utterly transcendent to the petty concerns of the "egoism" of the I, concerns which belong to the "Same" in Levinas's nomenclature. Just as the human Other expresses itself in an unreducible face-to-face relation, so the nonhuman Other of nature expresses itself in an equally unreducible confrontation with wilderness. The "exteriority" of which Levinas speaks in this connection is to be compared with the ecocentricity under discussion.

119. From Apollodorus, *Bibliotheca,* trans. C. Doria and H. Lenowitz, in *Origins: Creation Texts from the Ancient Mediterranean* (New York: Anchor, 1976), p. 318.

120. Emerson is tempted by this dualistic model in his early essay *Nature* (Boston: Beacon Press, 1989), esp. chap. 1, which is replete with dichotomizing statements such as this: "philosophically considered, the universe is composed of Nature and Soul" (p. 7). Only in what he calls somewhat disdainfully "the common sense" does Emerson acknowledge the multiplicity of Nature: "*Nature,* in the common sense, refers to essences unchanged by man; space, the air, the river, the leaf." The corresponding danger of monocentrism is found in the emphasis on a single, whole earth, e.g., on the part of the Gaia hypothesis. Even if the earth and its atmosphere do form one ultimately unified system, *within* this system there is continual strife, struggle, terror, and as much disruption as harmony.

121. On the etymology of *legein,* with special emphasis on "gathering," see M. Heidegger, *An Introduction to Metaphysics,* trans. R. Manheim (New Haven, Conn.: Yale University Press, 1959), pp. 123ff. See also David Michael Levin, *The Listening Self* (London: Routledge, 1989), pp. 207–208, 246–55. Greek *legein* is the root of Latin *legere,*

itself the source of "*in-telligence.*" To have "intelligence with the earth" is thus a supremely ecological act.

122. For a detailed account of the crisis in rain forests in Brazil, see Catherine Caufield, *In the Rainforest: Report from a Strange, Beautiful, Imperilled World* (Chicago: University of Chicago Press, 1984).

123. On stewardship as an ecological imperative in the thought of René Dubos, Joseph Sittler, and others, see Nash, *The Rights of Nature,* pp. 95–99. The critique of stewardship by deep ecologists is treated on pp. 149–50.

124. Heidegger, *Hebel der Hausfreund,* p. 13. My italics. In this statement, Heidegger comes dangerously close to endorsing the view I am here contesting, namely, that the earth is a place *meant* or *destined* for human dwelling.

125. On these questions, see the informative book by Donald Worster, *Nature's Economy: A History of Ecological Ideas* (Cambridge: Cambridge University Press, 1977). On nature's "Great Economy," see Wendell Berry, "Two Economies," *Home Economics,* pp. 56ff., esp. p. 57: "There is no human accounting for the Great Economy." Berry contrasts the Great Economy of nature as a whole with the "little economy" by which human beings live and thrive, all too often at the expense of the Great Economy that is its irreplaceable source.

126. Bruce Chatwin, *The Songlines* (New York: Penguin, 1987), p. 184.

127. For an excellent recent study of Tibetan nomadism in this western area of the Northern Plateau (Changtang), see M. C. Goldstein and C. M. Beall, *Nomads of Western Tibet: The Survival of a Way of Life* (Berkeley: University of California Press, 1990). The allocation is at present determined by the Chinese government. For a more general study, see Pierre Hubac, *Les nomades* (Paris: La Renaissance du Livre, 1948).

128. Cited from Emmanual Laroche, *Histoire de la racine "Nem" en grec ancien* (Paris: Klincksieck, 1949) by Gilles Deleuze and Félix Guattari in their "Treatise on Nomadology—the War Machine," in *A Thousand Plateaus: Capitalism and Schizophrenia,* trans. B. Massumi (Minneapolis: University of Minnesota, 1987), p. 557, n. 51. Deleuze and Guattari comment that "*to take to pasture (nemō)* does not refer to a parcelling out, but to a scattering, to a repartition of animals" (their italics). *Nomos* became the abstract principle behind both justice or right (*dikē*) and laws (*thesmoi*), all of which are distinctively urban phenomena.

129. Ibid., p. 380. I have substituted "and" for "or." The first eight words in the text are italicized. The authors add that we have to do with "a very special kind of distribution, one without division into shares, in a space without borders or enclosure." Allocation, by contrast, involves precisely such division by means of definite borders.

130. Ibid., p. 381. Even the nomad who lives within legally allocated lands also follows the land's lead. The periodic *re*-allocation of the traditional Tibetan nomadic system reflects this lead by "maintaining a balance between livestock numbers and the carrying capacity of the pastureland." On this point, see Goldstein and Beall, *Nomads of Western Tibet,* p. 69. The authors also claim that "the long-term viability of *all* pastoral groups requires that their system of livestock management prevent overgrazing and destruction of their resource base—the vegetation." They show that even at the present time an ecologically feasible balance has been achieved by the nomads of the Northern Plateau, despite efforts by the Chinese government to reduce their herds significantly (pp. 174ff.). In contrast with the overgrazing that has ruined the land in many areas of the U.S. Middle West and Southwest (where the demands and interests of a selfishly human economy have been predominant), the Tibetan method has husbanded the local environment in ecologically sensitive ways.

131. Pierre Hubac, *Les nomades* (Paris: La Renaissance du Livre, 1948), p. 26. The

phrase "specific locations"—not to be confused with Whitehead's "simple locations"—is used in *A Thousand Plateaus*, p. 381: "the earth does not become deterritorialized [by distributive nomads] in its global and relative movement, but at specific locations."

132. In this light, dwelling-as-residing is dwelling within the nomological walls of the *polis:* walls from which Socrates rarely exits in his obsessive search for *logos* as rational structure. Only when discussing Beauty in the *Phaedrus* does he make a concerted effort to pursue dialectic extra-murally.

133. Arnold Toynbee, *A Study of History* (New York: Oxford University Press, 1947), abridged ed., vol. 1, p. 168. My italics.

134. I do not mean to suggest that gardens and pastures are parallel at every point. For one thing, formal gardens act to delimit one's trajectory and may—as in the lesser *allées* at Versailles—obstruct vision of the landscape. For another, the role of animals in the two settings is very different. Where animals lead the way in pastoral life—"a nomad's migration," remarks Chatwin, "is a guided tour of animals" (*The Songlines*, p. 184)—in gardens they are either excluded or carefully contained in confined "paradises."

135. John R. Stilgoe cites Stevens's "Anecdote of the Jar" and comments that "because [the jar] is an artificial construct it makes apparent the previously unrealized wilderness. *Without the artifact, the wilderness is formless,* the hill is indistinguishable, and chaos does not exist because it is everywhere" (*Common Landscape of America: 1580 to 1845* [New Haven, Conn.: Yale University Press, 1982], p. 51; my italics). To this, we need only add that it is not the artifact alone but the artifact as constituting a *place* that gives form to the chaos of wilderness.

136. On the distinction between these two kinds of depth, see Levinas, *Totality and Infinity*, p. 39: the face-to-face relation involves "a distance in depth—that of conversation, of goodness, of Desire—irreducible to the distance the synthetic activity of the understanding establishes between the diverse terms, other with respect to one another, that lend themselves to its synoptic operation." Levinas's discussion, though applying specifically to the interhuman realm, is uncannily pertinent to the question of place, especially natural place. In the shopping mall, conversation, goodness, and Desire are notably absent, their place being taken by chatter, banality, and the satisfaction of physical and social needs.

137. On this point, consult Walter Benjamin's Arcades Project as discussed by Susan Buck-Morss, *The Dialectics of Seeing: Walter Benjamin and the Arcades Project* (Cambridge, Mass.: MIT Press, 1989).

138. I take this phrase from James Lovelock, *Gaia: A New Look at Life on Earth* (Oxford: Oxford University Press, 1987), p. x: "The Earth's living matter, air, oceans, and land surface form a complex system which can be seen as a single organism and which has the capacity to keep our planet a fit place for life." This single organism is the aptly named "biosphere."

139. On the stringency and wastefulness of "little economy," see Berry, "Two Economies," pp. 60ff.

140. R. W. Emerson, "Nature," in *Essays: Second Series*, as reprinted in *The Complete Essays and Other Writings of Ralph Waldo Emerson*, ed. B. Atkinson (New York: Modern Library, 1950), p. 419.

141. Levinas, *Totality and Infinity*, p. 33. Levinas is here citing Rimbaud's celebrated *mot*, which was quoted by André Breton at the conclusion of his first *Surrealist Manifesto*. The same apothegm is taken over as the title of a novel by Milan Kundera, *Life Is Elsewhere*, trans. P. Kussi (New York: Knopf, 1974).

142. M. Merleau-Ponty, *L'Oeil et l'esprit* (Paris: Gallimard, 1964), p. 65.

143. Emerson, "Nature," p. 407. Emerson adds: "We go out daily and nightly to feed

the eyes on the horizon, and require so much scope, just as we need water for our bath."

144. "Walking," pp. 98–99.

9. Homeward Bound

1. Hence Levinas's interpretation of Odysseus's homecoming as a return to the Same and a failure to confront the Other in his own home. See E. Levinas, "On the Trail of the Other," trans. D. J. Hoy, *in Philosophy Today* 10 (1966), pp. 43–44.

2. T. S. Eliot, "East Coker," sec. 5.

3. For a discussion of fundamental differences between migration and nomadic life, see Gilles Deleuze and Felix Guattari, "Treatise on Nomadology—the War Machine," *A Thousand Plateaus: Capitalism and Schizophrenia*, trans. B. Massumi (Minneapolis: University of Minnesota Press, 1987), pp. 380 ff. In Deleuze and Guattari's description, "the migrant goes principally from one point to another, even if the second point is uncertain, unforeseen, and is not well localized" (p. 380), while the nomad "distributes himself in a smooth space; he occupies, inhabits, holds that space" (p. 381). Put another way, in migration the intermediate places are comparatively indifferent, while in nomadic life they are as important as the beginning and ending places: for the pastoral nomad all the places count as integral parts of the same cycle of movement. In this respect, pilgrimage fits between migration and nomadism, since the intermediate places on a *via sacra* may have their own special interest, e.g., inns and monasteries in which to sojourn on the way to Santiago de Compostella.

4. Ibid., p. 371.

5. Commenting on a leading French scholar of the *Odyssey*, Michael Seidel says: "[Victor] Bérard sees the structure of the narrative [to lie] in its place names" (*Epic Geography: James Joyce's Ulysses* [Princeton, N.J.: Princeton University Press, 1976], p. 5).

6. Ibid., p. 12; my italics.

7. Ibid., p. 13.

8. On Western Apache place names as they figure into "speaking with names" or storytelling, see Keith Basso, "'Stalking with Stories': Names, Places, and Moral Narratives among the Western Apache," in E. Bruner, ed., *Text, Play, and Story* (New York: American Ethnological Society, 1984), pp. 24ff. (Basso's essay is reprinted in K. Basso, *Western Apache Language and Culture: Essays in Linguistic Anthropology* [Tucson: University of Arizona Press, 1990].)

9. Mikhail Bakhtin, *The Dialogical Imagination*, ed. M. Holquist and trans. C. Emerson and M. Holquist (Austin: University of lixas Press, 1981), esp. pp. 84ff., 97, 104, 250ff. By invoking the chronotope, I do not deny or question the temporality of narrative, its inherently chronological commitments. After all, these commitments are ultimately founded in embedded structures of the human life-world. (On this embeddedness, see David Carr, *Time, Narrative, and History* [Bloomington: Indiana University Press, 1986].) But I do want to assert the equiprimordiality of place in the face of its characteristic relegation to mere setting in literary theory (a relegation reflecting the modernist preoccupation with linear time).

10. On the exact placement of episodes in *Ulysses,* see Seidel, *Epic Geography,* pp. 131–32 ("The Dublin of *Ulysses*"), and Don Gifford with R. S. Seidman, *Ulysses Annotated* (Berkeley: University of California Press, 1988). Also chronotopic is the *periplus,* the ancient Mediterranean navigational guide used by Phoenician sailors to guide them from place to place along a coast or between islands. Indeed, the very conception of "circumnavigation"—the literal meaning of *"peri-plus"*—brings with it both place-sen-

sitivity (i.e., to particular coasts and islands) and time-awareness (i.e., in the form of the guide's fixed sequence of places to be visited). To go "around" (*peri*) coasts or islands in the manner of Odysseus is to engage in an activity at once temporal and spatial. Thus it is not surprising to learn that Homer, sometimes referred to as "the father of Greek geography," may have made extensive use of existing Phoenician *periploi*, which "filter through the Homeric rhapsodist's ear to the tip of his Greek tongue" (Seidel, p. 4). The use of *periploi* by Homer was first explored in depth by Victor Bérard in *Les Phéniciens et l'Odyssée*, a book that decisively influenced Joyce. If it is true that (as Bérard claims) "the Greeks have their *nostoi;* the Semites . . . their *periploi*" (quoted by Seidel, p. 4), in Homer's colossal tale the homecoming of *nostos* is combined with the roundabout sailing guided by a *periplus*. As a consequence, the epic narrative of the *Odyssey* often has the character of a travelogue, narrating *seriatim* places visited by Odysseus and his crew. *Periploi* also lie at the origin of the "portolan charts" used in the Age of Discovery. Thanks to their peculiar iconography of figures oriented to the natural borders of the landscape, these charts encouraged the participation of the map reader, who circulated around the map table in the course of a sea voyage. Such rotational movement is itself a form of journey and shares with other journeys the factor of immersion in successive places.

11. In Phillip F. Herring, ed., *Joyce's Ulysses Notesheets in the British Museum* (Charlottesville, Va.: University of Virginia Press, 1972), p. 119. On Joyce as resuming his predecessors in the epic tradition, see Thomas J. J. Altizer, *History as Apocalypse* (Albany: SUNY Press, 1985), chap. 9 ("Joyce and the End of History").

12. Strictly speaking, then, the double-tracking of places is always a *multiple* tracking. At any interim moment of my journey, my current place is related to several other places, not only beginning and ending places but intermediate places as well. As the tracking becomes more multiple, however, it also becomes less concerted and intentional, i.e., closer to *noticing*. (I wish to thank Irene Klaver for a clarifying discussion of the phenomenon of multiple tracking.)

13. *Odyssey*, bk. 7, l. 196 (Lattimore translation).

14. William James remarks that position "has nothing intrinsic about it; it can only obtain between a spot, line, or other figure and *extraneous co-ordinates*" (*The Principles of Psychology* [New York: Dover, 1950], vol. 2, p. 149; his italics).

15. "*Oku-No-Hosomichi*" may also be rendered as "Back Roads to Far Towns," as in the translation by Cid Corman and Kamaike Susumu (Buffalo, N.Y.: White Pine Press, 1986).

16. The citation is from Matsuo Bashō, "The Narrow Road to the Deep North," trans. N. Yuasa, in Bashō, *The Narrow Road to the Deep North and Other Travel Sketches* (London: Penguin, 1966), p. 98. A detailed map of the journey in question is provided by the translator on p. 147. I put the year "1694" in quotes to indicate that this designation is that of the Western calendar. For a general study of Japanese pilgrimage, see Oliver Statler, *Japanese Pilgrimage* (New York: Morrow, 1983).

17. Bashō asks his friend Tosai near the end of his trip to "make a summary of the day's happenings and leave it at the temple as a souvenir" (ibid., p. 141). But his own text is something other than any such summary. For Bashō's critique of travel diaries, see "The Records of a Travel-worn Satchel," in ibid., pp. 73–74, esp. the remark that most things in such diaries "are not even worth mentioning unless there are fresh and arresting elements in them" (p. 73).

18. I take the notion of "clot" from Corman and Susumu's preface to *Back Roads to Far Towns*.

19. Bashō, *The Narrow Road to the Deep North*, p. 123. The prose remark is on p. 122.

20. Ibid., p. 123.

21. William R. LaFleur, *The Karma of Words: Buddhism and the Literary Arts in Medieval Japan* (Berkeley: University of California Press, 1983), p. 76.

22. For a discussion of these contrasts, see ibid., pp. 76–79.

23. Bashō, *The Narrow Road to the Deep North*, p. 142.

24. A. N. Whitehead, *Process and Reality*, ed. D. R. Griffin and D. W. Sherburne (Glencoe, Ill.: Free Press, 1978), p. 114.

25. Bashō, *The Narrow Road to the Deep North*, p. 113.

26. Ibid., p. 143.

27. I borrow the term "great narratives" (*grands recits*) from Jean-François Lyotard, *The Postmodern Condition: A Report on Knowledge*, trans. G. Bennington and B. Massumi (Minneapolis: University of Minnesota Press, 1984), pp. 32–37, 48–49. Lyotard identifies the essence of modernity with the temptation to offer great narratives—e.g., Hegelian or Marxist views of history—and for him it becomes the task of postmodernity to question the privileged status of such narratives.

28. See Robert N. Bellah, "To Kill and Survive or to Die and Become: The Active Life and the Contemplative Life as Ways of Being Adult," *Daedalus* (Spring 1976), pp. 57–76; cited by LaFleur, *The Karma of Words*, p. 182. Bellah points to the same gradual transition in China as in Japan.

29. We need to distinguish the increasingly convincing critique of the modern at the level of theory—notably in the case of Heidegger, Lyotard, or Habermas—from the fact that, at a practical level, we remain thoroughly enmeshed in modernity, largely because of the stranglehold that technology, the stepchild of modernity, has on our daily lives.

30. Such a position is "the point of view of Sirius" of which the French speak and which is explicitly singled out for critique by M. Merleau-Ponty in the *Phenomenology of Perception* (preface and introduction) and by Deleuze and Guattari in *A Thousand Plateaus* (pp. 371ff.).

31. On the Fallacy of Simple Location, see A. N. Whitehead, *Science and the Modern World* (New York: Macmillan, 1925), chap. 3, esp. pp. 50ff., and *Process and Reality*, p. 137. Cf. *Process and Reality*, p. 59, where Descartes's doctrine that any existing substance "requires nothing but itself in order to exist" is indicted as the metaphysical basis of simple location.

32. "Relying solely on the drawings of Kaemon which served as a guide, I pushed along the Narrow Road to the Deep North" (Bashō), *The Narrow Road to the Deep North*, p. 112). As the context of this remark makes clear, the "drawings" were paintings by Kaemon (1665–1746), who was a painter, sculptor, and poet.

33. Ibid., p. 98. Even the very different translation of Corman and Susumu retains the chronotopism of this haiku: "the grass door also / turning and turning into / a doll's household" (*Back Roads to Far Towns*, sec. 1).

34. Freud describes ego defenses as "multilocular" in their ability to change location to meet fresh challenges stemming from external reality. See Draft N (sent to Fliess, May 31, 1897), in *Standard Edition of the Complete Psychological Works*, vol. 1, p. 256: "Defence too becomes *multilocular*" (his italics).

35. Bashō, *The Narrow Road to the Deep North*, pp. 118–19. Kanefusa (1127–1189) was renowned as someone who fought bravely in his old age.

36. For accounts of the pathologies of space and time, see, for example, E. Minkowski, *Lived Time*, trans. N. Metzel (Evanston, Ill.: Northwestern University Press, 1970); M. Boss, *Grundriss der Medizin* (Bern: Huber, 1971]; L. Binswanger, *Ausgewählte Vorträge und Aufsätze* (Bern: Francke, 1942–55), 2 vols.

37. See Immanuel Kant, *Critique of Pure Reason*, trans. N. K. Smith (New York: St.

Martin's Press, 1950), A430 B458–A434 B462. Ever since Spinoza (summing up the nisus of seventeen-century philosophy and physics) declared space and time to be two independent—albeit closely coordinated—aspects of Substance, philosophers have assumed that each dimension of the universe pursues its separate course in accordance with its own laws, its own special effects, and its own unique modes of involvement. This assumption is still present in Kant's treatment of space and time as utterly distinct forms of pure sensible intuition, and it is not seriously questioned until Alexander and Whitehead, both attempting to take account of Einsteinian physics, place space and time in an intimate cosmological commerce with each other. Heidegger, arguing on very different grounds, also arrived at a conception of space-time in his last major essay, "Time and Being."

38. I have examined this assumption at length in *Remembering: A Phenomenological Study* (Bloomington: Indiana University Press, 1987), pts. 3 and 4.

39. Vine Deloria, *God Is Red* (New York: Grosset & Dunlap, 1973), p. 85.

40. Benjamin Lee Whorf, "An American Indian Model of the Universe," reprinted in D. Tedlock and B. Tedlock, eds., *Teachings from the American Earth* (New York: Liveright, 1975), p. 128; my italics.

41. Kant, "The Refutation of Idealism," *Critique of Pure Reason*, B275. At B277 Kant speaks of "the permanent in space" as what is required by the consciousness and determination of time. I am grateful to Melvin Woody for suggesting this line of thought.

42. R. Pinxten, I. van Dooren, and F. Harvey, *The Anthropology of Space: Explorations into the Natural Philosophy and Semantics of the Navajo* (Philadelphia: University of Pennsylvania Press, 1983), p. 17. The full sentence is "This general dynamic feature of created things cannot be understood as actual movement or displacement; rather it is a much less specific and more general persisting through eventual change." When Keith Basso points to the Western Apache belief that "grandmothers and uncles must perish, but *the landscape endures*" (Basso, "'Stalking with Stories,'" p. 43; my italics), he is alluding to the kind of place-permanence I here have in mind.

43. Strictly speaking, a homestead is any land (usually including the buildings on it) that is immune from legal seizure and that stays in the same family for a number of generations. In the United States, the Homestead Act of 1862 allowed any citizen (or alien who intended to become a citizen) the right to occupy 160 acres with a commitment to farm on it. In what follows, I am extending the concept to include any prolonged settlement of a new place, urban as well as rural.

44. The return effected in homecoming need not be to one's actual former home per se—that is, the literal house. One can return as well to a certain neighborhood, state, or region and still experience "homecoming," whose scope is even more considerable than homesteading. I shall be employing both notions in their most extended senses.

45. As a corollary, it ensues that homesteading often brings *building* with it and, at least in the case of rural homesteading, a conversion of wild into built places.

46. For Thoreau's brief but pointed treatment of co-habitancy, see "Walking," reprinted in H. D. Thoreau, *Natural History Essays* (Salt Lake City: Peregrine Smith, 1980), pp. 131–32. I have hyphenated the word in order to emphasize the *co*. I am grateful to Irene Klaver for bringing Thoreau's notion to my attention.

47. I take the term *prairyerth* from William Least Heat-Moon, *PrairyErth: A Deep Map*. In chap. 9 ("Homestead") of this remarkable book, Moon explores a number of aspects of homesteading and re-inhabitation of the land.

48. Thoreau invokes memory specifically in his inaugural discussion of "cohabitancy": speaking of ancestral presences on a certain farm near Concord, he writes: "They fade irrevocably out of my mind even now while I speak and endeavor to recall them and recollect myself. It is only after a long and serious effort to recollect my best thoughts that I become again aware of their cohabitancy" ("Walking," p. 132).

49. "Walking," p. 131.

50. These are the last lines of T. S. Eliot's "East Coker," *Four Quartets*. Earlier in the same poem, Eliot reverses the formula: "In my beginning is my end." Either way, the habitat–habitus cycle is very much at stake.

51. Gaston Bachelard, *The Poetics of Space*, trans. M. Jolas (New York: Orion, 1964), p. 5. I cited this same sentence in chap. 6.

52. I borrow this term from E. V. Walter, *Placeways* (Chapel Hill: University of North Carolina Press, 1988). Snyder's description of his own venture is found, *inter alia*, in his essays "The Place, the Region, and the Commons" and "Good, Wild, Sacred," *The Practice of the Wild*, pp. 25–47, 78–96. See also Snyder's essay "Re-Inhabitation," *The Old Ways* (San Francisco: City Lights, 1977), pp. 57–66.

53. "The land my family and I live on in the Sierra Nevada of California is 'barely good' from an economic standpoint. With soil amendments, much labor, and the development of ponds for holding water through the dry season, it is producing a few vegetables and some good apples. It is better as forest: through the millennia it has excelled at growing oak and pine" (*The Practice of the Wild*, p. 94).

54. The phrase "a past which has never been a present" occurs in M. Merleau-Ponty, *Phenomenology of Perception*, trans. C. Smith (New York: Humanities Press, 1962), p. 242. It is taken up by Emmanuel Levinas in *Totality and Infinity: An Essay on Exteriority*, trans. A. Lingis (Pittsburgh: Duquesne University Press, 1969), pp. 69, 130.

55. Snyder, *The Practice of the Wild*, p. 41.

56. Ibid. p. 26. This is what cliff dwellings exemplify so tellingly: the real possibility of inhabiting a wild place that is appreciated, built into, and finally left in its very wildness.

57. The nomad, say Deleuze and Guattari, "is in a *local absolute*, an absolute that is manifested locally, and engendered in a series of local operations of varying orientations: desert, steppe, ice, sea" (*A Thousand Plateaus*, p. 382; their italics). This local absolute contrasts with the "relative global" of striated space—with sites, which are always only relative to other sites.

58. S. Kierkegaard, *Repetition: An Essay in Experimental Psychology*, trans. W. Lowrie (New York: Harper, 1964), Pt. 1. Kierkegaard poses his experiment in repetition thus: "Thou canst take a trip to Berlin, where thou hast been before, and convince thyself now whether a repetition is possible and what significance it may have" (p. 33).

59. Mary Douglas argues that there is a special repeatability about *interior* furnishings that distinguishes a home from a house: in a home, "there has to be something regular about the appearance and re-appearance of its furnishings" ("The Idea of a Home: A Kind of Space," *Social Research* 58 [1991], p. 289). Douglas has in mind a phenomenon like the roll-up bed. My own idea of repeated return applies to house and home alike, since I have in mind the entire entity to which one goes back after a round-trip journey.

60. Joseph Rykwert, "House and Home," in ibid., p. 51. Rykwert here alludes to the fact that *focus* in Latin means "hearth," "fireplace." On the unbuilt character of homes, see also Douglas's comment: home "does not need bricks and mortar, it can be a wagon, a caravan, a boat, or a tent" ("The Idea of a Home," p. 289). It can also be a hollow in the ground or a cave, which are even more fully unbuilt.

61. On this point, see John Hollander, "It All Depends," *Social Research* 58 (1991), pp. 42–43. Regarding the house/home distinction, English, Dutch (*huis/heem*), German (*Haus/Heim*), and Scandinavian languages clearly mark the difference. In all of these northern European languages Old Norse *heima* is the common ancestor of their word for "home," just as their words for "house" may trace back to *hud*, Indo-European for "to hide," whereas Romance languages are notoriously vague: Is *chez lui* an allusion to "his house" or to "his home"?

62. Robert Frost, "The Death of the Hired Man"; my italics.

63. We can also be welcomed back into the household of the natural world—back to the earth itself. Homecoming as return to the (h)earth. This is surely what *Walden* proclaims to be at once eminently possible and desirable. Wild places do not have to be domesticated or even homesteaded in any strict sense to be come back to in such telluric *Heimkunft*. They only need to be places we care about. "Home is where the heart(h) is." It is also where we settle, where we rejoin our *deme* or family, *deme* being the root of the *domus* that houses us as a collective body.

64. bell hooks, "Homeplace: A Site of Resistance," *Yearning: Race, Gender, and Cultural Politics* (Boston: South End Press, 1990), p. 41. I have kept "bell hooks" in the lower case out of respect for the author's own convention.

65. Ibid.

66. Ibid.

67. Ibid., p. 42. hooks does not hyphenate "home-place." In an oppressive society, the home-place became "the one site where one could freely confront the issue of humanization, where one could resist" (ibid.). hooks also says that in her home-place "all that truly mattered in life took place—the warm and comfort of shelter, the feeding of our bodies, the nurturing of our souls. There we learned dignity, integrity of being, there we learned to have faith" (pp. 41–42). The mention of "bodies" points to the political dimension of body-in-place, a dimension whose nuanced analysis was eloquently pursued by Foucault and more recently by feminist theorists. By the same token, the act of building—an act done *by* bodies and *for* bodies—is itself an inexorably political act: "All those concerned with building must recognize that every foundation laid is always and inevitably a political act" (Rykwert, "House and Home," p. 62). Concerning aspects of domestic space as approached from specifically feminist perspectives, see Henrietta Moore, *Space, Text, and Gender* (Cambridge: Cambridge University Press, 1986) and Daphne Spain, *Gendered Spaces* (Chapel Hill: University of North Carolina Press, 1992).

68. Ibid., p. 47. "An effective means of white subjugation of black people globally has been the perpetual construction of economic and social structures that deprive many folks of the means to make homeplace. . . . For when a people no longer have the space to construct homeplace, we cannot build a meaningful community of resistance" (pp. 46–47).

69. Ibid., p. 48. hooks uses "site" and "place" interchangeably.

70. Ibid., p. 40.

71. Saint Augustine, *De vera religion*, p. 39, n. 72, cited by Husserl at the end of the Fifth *Cartesian Meditation*, trans. D. Cairns (The Hague: Nijhoff, 1960), p. 157.

72. hooks remarks à propos African origins, "memory need not be a passive reflection, a nostalgic longing for things to be as they once were; it can function as a way of knowing and learning from the past . . . it can serve as a catalyst for self-recovery. We are talking about collective black self-recovery. We need to keep alive the memory of our struggles against racism so that we can concretely chart how far we have come and where we want to go, recalling those places, those times, those people that gave a sense of direction" (hooks, *Yearning*, p. 40).

73. Douglas, "The Idea of A Home," p. 303.

74. For instance: "A man from Marion, immediately west of here . . . told me: *we used to call it Chasem County. The story there was chase'em, catch'em, kick'em* (*PrairyErth*, p. 18; his italics).

75. Fred R. Myers, *Pintupi Country, Pintupi Self: Sentiment, Place, and Politics among Western Desert Aborigines* (Berkeley: University of California Press, 1991), p. 92.

76. Ibid., p. 93. The second phrase is from this revealing sentence: "This inseparability of people and place makes territorial boundaries highly flexible if not insignificant."

Here the rejection of a strict container model of the place is manifest. It is also significant that kinship among the Pintupi is determined less by blood and genealogy than by the *places* they share, i.e., the camps they keep together: "The underlying idea is that coresidence in a camp is the spatial expression of a group of kin; shared activity constitutes people as related" (p. 92).

77. Cited in Basso, "'Stalking with Stories,'" p. 21. As Annie Peaches, another Apache, puts it, "The land makes people live right. The land looks after us. The land looks after people" (p. 21). The contemporary Laguna Pueblo author Leslie Silko affirms the deep link between land and story: "[our] stories cannot be separated from geographical locations, from actual physical places within the land. . . . There's always at least one story connected with those places" ("Language and Literature from a Pueblo Indian Perspective," in L. A. Fiedler and H. A. Baker, Jr., eds., *English Literature: Opening up the Canon* [Baltimore: Johns Hopkins University Press, 1981], p. 69). Concerning the relationship between ethics and place, see also Charles Taylor, *Sources of the Self: The Making of the Modern Identity* (Cambridge, Mass.: Harvard University Press, 1989), esp. p. 28: "To know who you are is to be oriented in moral space. I feel myself drawn here to use a spatial metaphor; but I believe this to be more than personal predilection. There are signs that the link with spatial orientation lies very deep in the human psyche."

78. This is Gadamer's phrase for the pervasive presence of language: "Language [*die Sprache*] does not really stand alongside art and law and religion, but represents the sustaining medium of all of these manifestations of the spirit" (H.-G. Gadamer, "The Nature of Things and the Language of Things," in *Philosophical Hermeneutics*, trans. D. E. Linge [Berkeley: University of California Press, 1976], p. 76).

79. See Bashō, *The Narrow Road to the Deep North*, pp. 145–47; and Myers, *Pintupi Country, Pintupi Self*, pp. 80–88. The latter maps are based on narrative accounts by Maantja tjungurrayi, which are further discussed in Myers's doctoral dissertation of 1976, "To Have and to Hold: A Study of Persistence and Change in Pintupi Social Life" (Bryn Mawr College).

80. Arnold Toynbee, *A Study of History* (New York: Oxford University Press, 1947), vol. 1, p. 168, where Toynbee also writes: "they flung themselves upon the Steppe, not to escape beyond its bounds but to make themselves at home on it." Deleuze and Guattari, who cite this last remark and the one in the text, comment that "they are nomads by dint of not moving, not migrating, of holding a smooth space that they refuse to leave, that they leave only in order to conquer and die" (*A Thousand Plateaus*, p. 48).

81. On nomadism of the sea, see José Emperaire, *Les nomades de la mer* (Paris: Gallimard, 1954).

82. Deleuze and Guattari, *A Thousand Plateaus*, p. 482. My italics. The authors can continue to use "space" instead of "place" because, as I have noted above, they make a systematic distinction between "smooth" and "striated" space. Smooth space, which is the space of the nomad, is close to what I would call "place" in this book, while striated space, which is explicitly rooted in seventeenth-century homogeneous space, is virtually identical with what I prefer to call "site." (See esp. the chapter entitled "The Smooth and the Striated," pp. 474ff.)

83. Alfred North Whitehead, *Process and Reality*, ed. D. R. Griffin and D. W. Sherburne (New York: Macmillan, 1978), p. 59. His italics.

84. Marcel Proust, *Remembrance of Things Past*, trans. C. K. S. Moncrieff and T. Kilmartin (New York: Random House, 1981), vol. 1, p. 5.

85. Sven Birkerts, "Place: A Fragment," in Thomas Frick, ed., *The Sacred Theory of the Earth* (Berkeley, Calif.: North Atlantic, 1986), p. 54; his italics.

86. I adapt this term from E. V. Walter, who uses it as the converse of "wealth"; see

his essay "Pauperism and Illth: An Archeology of Social Policy," *Sociological Analysis* 34 (1973), pp. 239–54.

87. Pinxten, van Dooren, and Harvey, *The Anthropology of Space*, p. 27.

88. The "general dynamic feature of created things cannot be understood as actual movement or displacement" (ibid., p. 17). The phrase "persisting through eventual change" is also found on p. 17.

89. Saigyo's haiku is from his *Sanka-shu;* cited and translated by LaFleur, *The Karma of Words*, p. 160.

90. Birkerts, "Place: A Fragment," p. 54.

91. Bachelard, *The Poetics of Space*, p. 8.

92. Aristotle, *Physics*, 201a, 14–24. Of eight senses of *in* distinguished by Aristotle, the last is stated thus: "as [a thing] is in a vessel and, generally, *in a place*" (210a, 23–24; my italics).

93. "For a knowledge of intimacy, localization in the spaces of our intimacy is more urgent than determination of date" (Bachelard, *The Poetics of Space*, p. 9). The temptation to associate date and place as if they were on a par with each other is seen in Bergson's discussion of these two factors in *Matter and Memory*, trans. N. M. Paul and W. S. Palmer (New York: Doubleday, 1959), pp. 13ff., 68–71, 208ff.

94. Robert Burton, *The Anatomy of Melancholy*, ed. F. Dell and P. J. Smith (New York: Tudor, 1948), p. 528. Burton is here paraphrasing Seneca.

95. I examine the notion critically in my essay "Keeping the Past in Mind," *Review of Metaphysics* 37 (1983), pp. 77–95.

96. Karl Jaspers, *Philosophy*, trans. E. B. Ashton (Chicago: University of Chicago Press, 1970), vol. 2, p. 242. *A loving view:* this is the subdominant view which the modernist emphasis on "point of view," on the externality of the objective perspective on things, "the view from nowhere," lacks. Indeed, in the perspective of modernity, it is practically oxymoronic to speak of a "loving view"; and yet it is just this view which many places ask us to take. Concerning spirit and soul in relation to place, see my essay "Getting Placed: Soul in Space," in *Spirit and Soul: Essays in Philosophical Psychology* (Dallas: Spring Publications, 1991), pp. 290–309.

How to Get from Space to Place in a Fairly Short Stretch of Time

This is an edited version of a previously published essay. Reprinted by permission from *Senses of Place,* edited by Steven Feld and Keith H. Basso. Copyright © 1996 by the School for Advanced Research, Santa Fe, New Mexico.

1. James F. Weiner, *The Empty Place: Poetry, Space, and Being among the Foi of Papua New Guinea* (Bloomington: Indiana University Press, 1991), p. 32.

2. See Immanuel Kant, *Critique of Pure Reason*, trans. N. K. Smith (New York: MacMillan, 1950 [1787]), A 426 B 454ff. In an antinomy one has compelling reasons to assert the truth of both the thesis and the antithesis of a given proposition; here, the thesis is that "the world has a beginning in time, and is also limited as regards space."

3. Fred R. Myers, *Pintupi Country, Pintupi Self: Sentiment, Place, and Politics among Western Desert Aborigines* (Berkeley and Los Angeles: University of California Press, 1991), p. 67.

4. Myers, *Pintupi Country*, p. 54. We might as well say, whereby Nature becomes Culture, since the dominant assumption in Western thought of the last three centuries is that Nature presents itself primarily as Space. *Ngurra* itself is said, significantly, to be "the place where one belongs . . . and to which one returns" (ibid., p. 55). The idea of "geography" as plain starting point is especially odd, since geography is itself a second- or even

third-order accretion to the experience of place and, more particularly, of landscape. Even a geographer as sensitive as Yi-Fu Tuan embraces it: "All people undertake to change amorphous space into articulated geography" (Tuan, *Space and Place* [Minneapolis: University of Minnesota Press, 1977], p. 83).

5. Myers, *Pintupi Country*, p. 47.

6. Ibid., p. 48.

7. Ibid., p. 59.

8. Steven Feld, "Waterfalls of Song: An Acoustemology of Place Resounding in Bosavi, Papua New Guinea," in *Senses of Place*, ed. Steven Feld and Keith H. Basso (Santa Fe, N.Mex.: School for Advanced Research, 1996).

9. The full statement is: "Perhaps [place] is the first of all things, since all existing things are either in place or not without place" (cited from Simplicius, *Commentary on Aristotle's Categories*, and translated by Samuel Sambursky in Sambursky, *The Concept of Place in Late Neoplatonism* [Jerusalem: Israel Academy of Sciences and Humanities, 1982], p. 37n). The power of the Archytian Axiom pervades the ancient Greek world. Plato cryptically quotes it in the *Timaeus* when he writes that "anything that is must needs be in some place and occupy some room, and . . . what is not somewhere in earth or heaven is nothing" (*Timaeus* 52 B, in F. M. Cornford, *Plato's Cosmology* [New York: Liberal Arts Press, 1957]). Aristotle similarly inscribes the axiom at the opening of his treatment of place in his *Physics*, Book 4, when, referring to Hesiod, he says that "he thinks as most people do that everything is somewhere and in place" (*Aristotle's Physics, Books III and IV*, trans. E. Hussey [Oxford: Clarendon Press, 1983], 208 b 32–33).

10. Kant, *Critique of Pure Reason*, B1.

11. Ibid.

12. Immanuel Kant, preface to *Anthropology from a Pragmatic Point of View*, ed. and trans. M. Gregor (The Hague: Nijhoff, 1974 [1797]); my translation. In this lecture course, Kant distinguishes between "physiological" and "pragmatic" forms of anthropology, strikingly anticipating much later distinctions between "physical" and "cultural" anthropology. In physiological anthropology, one studies "what nature makes of man," while in pragmatic anthropology the aim is to grasp "what man, as possessing free activity, can or does or must make· of himself." He also discusses the need for fieldwork, which he labels "voyages," and for avoiding an anthropological enterprise based on racial differences as such.

13. Clifford Geertz, *Local Knowledge: Further Essays in Interpretive Anthropology* (New York: Basic Books, 1983), p. 12.

14. Aristotle discusses eight senses of "in" in his treatment of place, concluding that the most pertinent sense is "as a thing is in a vessel" (*Physics* 210 a 24).

15. George Berkeley, *An Essay towards a New Theory of Vision* (London: Dent, 1934).

16. The sentence cited is from Edmund Husserl, *Experience and Judgment: Investigations in a Genealogy of Logic*, trans. J. S. Churchill and K. Ameriks (Evanston, Ill.: Northwestern University Press, 1973), p. 32; in italics in text. Internal and external horizons are discussed in ibid., section 8, "The Horizon-Structure of Experience." Maurice Merleau-Ponty discusses "primordial depth" in his *Phenomenology of Perception*, trans. C. Smith (New York: Humanities Press, 1962), pp. 254–67. The affinity of the notions of "horizon" and "depth" is close: just as every perceived thing is perceived in its own depth—that is, within the horizons provided by its own sides—so a collection of things in a given perceptual field has a depth as a whole that is limited only by the external horizon of this same field. The affinity of horizon-cum-depth to the phenomenon of "lift-up-over sounding" in Feld's descriptive term for the Kaluli experience of immersion in places of the Papua New Guinea rainforest calls for further exploration (see Feld, "Waterfalls of Sound").

17. George Santayana, *Skepticism and Animal Faith* (New York: Dover, 1955); Edmund

Husserl, *Ideas Pertaining to a Pure Phenomenology and to a Phenomenological Philosophy*, First Book, *General Introduction to a Pure Phenomenology*, trans. F. Kersten (The Hague: Nijhoff, 1982), section 103.

18. Husserl, *General Introduction to a Pure Phenomenology*, section 91.

19. Husserl, *Experience and Judgment*, trans. J. S. Churchill and K. Ameriks (Evanston, Ill.: Northwestern University Press, 1973), p. 108 (his italics).

20. Feld, "Waterfalls of Song," p. 91.

21. See René Descartes, *Principles of Philosophy*, in *The Philosophical Writings of Descartes*, vol. 1, trans. J. Cootingham, R. Stoothoff, and D. Murdoch (Cambridge: Cambridge University Press, 1985 [1644]), part 2, sections 10–20). In section 10, Descartes says that "there is no real distinction between space, or internal place, and the corporeal substance contained in it; the only difference lies in the way in which we are accustomed to conceive of them" (ibid., p. 227). As equivalent to "space," "internal place" is tantamount to three-dimensional volumetric extendedness. "External place" refers to the surface surrounding a given body in a place. For a more complete treatment of Descartes—and of other early modern thinkers— see part 3 of my book *The Fate of Place: A Philosophical History* (Berkeley: University of California Press, 1997).

22. "Almost," I say, since Kant did note in passing that motion is "alteration of place" (1950 [1787], A 32 B 48). On "position" (*Stelle*), see ibid., A 263 B 319ff.

23. Immanuel Kant, "On the First Ground of the Distinction of Regions in Space," trans. J. Handyside, in *Kant's Inaugural Dissertation and Early Writings on Space* (Chicago: Open Court, 1928 [1768]), pp. 22–23. It is not widely known that before 1772 (often taken as the moment of the "critical turn"), Kant designated his philosophical project as that of "general phenomenology." The term "phenomenology" itself was borrowed from Lambert's lectures on physics, which Kant had read in the early 1760s. Similarly, though to much different effect, Wittgenstein sometimes described his philosophical work of the 1920s as "phenomenology," but under the influence of the early Vienna Circle he came to abjure the term.

24. Robert Hertz, "The Pre-eminence of the Right Hand: A Study in Religious Polarity," in *Right and Left: Essays on Dual Symbolic Classification*, ed. R. Needham, pp. 3–31 (Chicago: University of Chicago Press, 1973 [1909]),

25. On corporeal intentionality and intentional threads, see Merleau-Ponty, *Phenomenology of Perception*, trans. C. Smith (New York: Routledge, 1962), introduction, Part 1. Merleau-Ponty rarely speaks of place as such, but on my reading it is entailed in everything he says about the lived body and its "setting" (*milieu*), "landscape" (*paysage*), or "world" (*monde*). Husserl had already singled out the voluntariness of bodily movement as a noncontingent character: "In virtue of its faculty of free mobility, the subject can now induce the flow of the system of its appearances. . . . With regard to all other things, I have the freedom to change at will my position in relation to them" (*Ideas Pertaining to a Pure Phenomenology and to a Phenomenological Philosophy*, Second Book, *Studies in the Phenomenology of Constitution*, trans. R. Rojcewicz and A. Schuwer [Dordrecht: Kluwer, 1989], pp. 166–67).

26. Merleau-Ponty, *Phenomenology of Perception*, p. 208.

27. See Keith H. Basso, "Wisdom Sits in Places," in *Senses of Place*, p. 55: "As places animate the ideas and feelings of persons who attend to them, these same ideas and feelings animate the places on which attention has been bestowed."

28. Feld, "Waterfalls of Sound," 95.

29. On the aesthesiological body, see Husserl, *Studies in the Phenomenology of Constitution*, p. 297, along with p. 163 on the body as a "physical-aesthesiological unity." On sonesthesia, see Feld, "Waterfalls of Sound." Concerning the body as a "field of localization," see Husserl, *Studies in the Phenomenology of Constitution*, section 38, esp. p. 159. The term "operative intentionality," employed in the previous paragraph, is also Husserl's and is

described by Merleau-Ponty as "that which produces the natural and antepredicative unity of the world and of our life, being apparent in our desires, our evaluations and in the landscape we see, more clearly than in objective knowledge" (Merleau-Ponty, *Phenomenology of Perception*, xviii; my italics).

30. See Kant, "On the First Ground," pp. 21–22. Aristotle had already recognized the relativity of the three dimensional dyads to bodily position: "Relatively to us, they—above, below, right, left [etc.]—are not always the same, but come to be in relation to our position [thesis], according as we turn ourselves about" (*Physics* 208 b 14–16). But this relativity to the body is for Aristotle a contingent fact, since in his view "in nature [*en to phusei*] each [dimension] is distinct and separate" (*Physics* 208 b 18). Husserl argues, on the contrary, that such bodily based dimensionality is a necessary structure: "All spatial being necessarily appears in such a way that it appears either nearer or farther, above or below, right or left. . . . The body (*Leib*) then has, for its particular ego, the unique distinction of bearing in itself the zero point of all these orientations" (Husserl, *Studies in the Phenomenology of Constitution*, p. 166; he italicizes "zero point").

31. Jean-Paul Sartre, *The Philosophy of Jean-Paul Sartre*, ed. R. Cumming (New York: Vintage Books, 1965), p. 590.

32. On the bi-gendered body, see Marilyn Strathern, *The Gender of the Gift* (Berkeley and Los Angeles: University of California Press, 1988). Concerning bi-location, see Lucien Lévy-Bruhl, *The Notebooks on Primitive Mentality*, trans. P. Riviere (New York: Harper and Row, 1978), pp. 5–17. In a striking instance of bi-location, a Chambri informant pointed to a rock in his backyard to which ancestors were believed to have moored a boat and said, "Here I am! There I am!" (Frederick Errington and Deborah Gewertz, personal communication, 1993).

33. On the flesh of the world, see Maurice Merleau-Ponty, *The Visible and the Invisible*, trans. A. Lingis (Evanston, Ill.: Northwestern University Press, 1968), pp. 123, 267.

34. "Toynbee is profoundly right to suggest that the nomad is . . . *he who does not move*. . . . Of course, the nomad moves, but while seated, and he is only seated while moving (the Bedouin galloping, knees on the saddle, sitting on the soles of his upturned feet, 'a feat of balance')" (Deleuze and Guattari, *Nomadology*, 51, their italics, with reference to Arnold Toynbee, *A Study of History*, vol. 1 [New York: Oxford University Press, 1947], pp. 164–86).

35. On a different but related sense of locus, see Husserl, *Studies in the Phenomenology of Constitution*, p. 35; on changing place in space, see ibid., p. 213: "I, the person, am in space at this place. Others are over there, where their bodies are. They go for a walk, they pay a visit, and so forth, whereby indeed their spirits, along with their bodies, change their place in space." The difficulty with this formulation, however, is that it subordinates place to space, conceived of as "the space of the one objective surrounding world" (ibid., p. 213), and thus fails to acknowledge the priority of place.

36. In transportation, I am passively carried by an animal or machine whose purposes are independent of my own; in transition, I move in order to pursue my own purposes, purposes that can be attained only in the new place to which I move. Of course, I may choose to effect a transition by means of transportation, but then I bend the animal or mechanical purposes to suit the realization of my own aims. The difference, starkly put, is between letting the horse roam where it wants to go and steering it to my own destination. For further discussion of moving between places, see Edward S. Casey, *Getting Back into Place*, chap. 9.

37. Merleau-Ponty, *Phenomenology of Perception*, 146.

38. So say both Martin Heidegger, *What Is Called Thinking?* trans. J. Glenn Gray (New York: Harper and Row, 1972), p. 17 and Maurice Merleau-Ponty, *The Visible and the Invisible*, p. 266, neither knowing the other had so spoken.

39. Husserl, *Experience and Judgment*.

40. On the special aptitude of places for holding memories, see Casey, *Remembering: A Phenomenological Study* (Bloomington: Indiana University Press, 2000, 2d ed.), chap. 9.

41. Such sameness of place contrasts strikingly with that posited by Leibniz in his Fifth Letter to Clarke (1716). For Leibniz, to be in the same place signifies merely to be in a position or "site" (*situs*) that can in principle be occupied by any other object and that stays unchanged by the fact of occupation. See Gottfried Wilhelm Leibniz, *Philosophical Papers and Letters*, ed. L. E. Loemaker, vol. 2 (Chicago: University of Chicago Press, 1956), pp. 1145–48.

42. On "morphological concepts of vague configurational types," see Husserl, *General Introduction to a Pure Phenomenology*, section 74. Concerning "essentially occasional expressions," see Husserl, *Logical Investigations*, vol. 1, trans. J. N. Findlay (New York: Humanities Press, 1970), section 36. In an essentially occasional expression, "it is essential to orient actual meaning to the occasion, the speaker and the situation" (ibid., p. 315). Husserl gives the example of "here," which "designates the speaker's vaguely bounded spatial environment. . . . The genuine meaning of the word is first constituted in the variable presentation of this place" (ibid., p. 317). For contemporary treatments of these same matters in analytical philosophy, see Gareth Matthews, *The Varieties of Reference* (Oxford: Oxford University Press, 1982), especially chap. 6, "Demonstrative Identification," which includes a discerning assessment of "here" (see pp. 151–69); and Saul Kripke, *Naming and Necessity* (Cambridge, Mass.: Harvard University Press, 1980), especially his brief discussion of demonstratives as "rigid designators" on pages 10n and 49n. Notice that the use of the definite article to refer to a place, though perfectly permissible in English, is often uninformative as to location: "the garage," "the grocery store," "the lake." In such cases, the location is presumed to be known in advance, as when we say, "Meet me at the library."

43. "A Mythology Reflects Its Region," in Stevens, *Opus Posthumous* (New York: Knopf, 1957), p. 118.

44. For a convincing critique of "stratigraphic" theories of meaning, see Clifford Geertz, *The Interpretation of Cultures* (New York: Basic Books, 1973), pp. 37–51.

45. Husserl, *General Introduction to a Pure Phenomenology*, section 27.

46. I take landscape to be distinct from geography, which is a second-order representation of a physical place or region. Except for the two-handedness that is a condition of orientation in reading a map, in geography no body need be present; indeed, disembodiment is a geographical ideal. But we are in a landscape only by grace of being bodily there. On the distinction between landscape and geography, see Erwin Straus, *The Primary World of Senses: A Vindication of Sensory Experience*, trans. J. Needleman (Glencoe, Ill.: Free Press, 1963), p. 308.

47. It will be noticed that I have been attempting to speak of place—including landscape, construed as the face of place, its expressive facies or sensuous surface—without making any reference to mind. Even if it is true that "the mind is its own place" (Milton, *Paradise Lost*) or that "the mind is the place of forms" (Aristotle, *De Anima*), such statements do not establish that the mind, even the savage mind, is essential to place. My emphasis on body is meant to dispute a mentalistic (if not overtly idealist) tendency that begins in Kant, continues with Cassirer, and is still present in contemporary speculation.

48. See Noam Chomsky, *Aspects of the Theory of Syntax* (Cambridge, Mass.: MIT Press, 1965), pp. 27–30.

49. Geertz, *The Interpretation of Cultures*, pp. 43–44.

50. I borrow the term "empirical commonality" from Geertz (ibid.), who appears to employ it as equivalent to "substantive identity." Cultural anthropology, he writes, should seek "a definition of man stressing not so much the empirical commonalities in his behavior, from place to place and time to time, but rather the mechanisms by whose agency the

breadth and indeterminateness of his inherent capacities are reduced to the narrowness and specificity of his actual accomplishments" (ibid., p. 45). In the idea of shared "mechanisms," Geertz suggests something close to what Jerome Bruner has labeled "process universals," in contrast to "product universals." Speaking of the way in which languages distinguish between marked and unmarked features, Bruner observes that this is "a way in which all languages deal with the task of alerting the attention of the recipients of messages to what needs special processing. That is a process universal" (Bruner, "Review and Prospectus," in *Universals of Human Thought: Some African Evidence,* ed. Barbara Lloyd and John Gay, 256–62 [Cambridge: Cambridge University Press, 1981], p. 256). In contrast, a product universal is found in the fact that "most languages mark the plural form and not the singular" (ibid., p. 257).

51. Bertrand Russell, *The Problems of Philosophy* (London: Home University Library, 1912), p. 152.

52. Maurice Merleau-Ponty ("From Mauss to Claude Lévi-Strauss," in *Signs,* trans. R. McCleary, 114–25 [Evanston, Ill.: Northwestern University Press, 1964], p. 120) writes that in anthropology what is at issue is "no longer the overarching universal of a strictly objective method, but a sort of lateral universal which we acquire through ethnological experience and its incessant testing of the self through the other person and the other person through the self." I wish to thank Irene Klaver for drawing my attention to the importance of this passage.

53. Concerning regional ontology, see Husserl, *General Introduction to a Pure Phenomenology,* sections 9, 10, 16. Formal ontology is "the eidetic science of any object whatever" (section 10). Notice that "material" in Husserl's usage signifies concrete content, not anything necessarily physical. On Nature versus Psyche, see especially Husserl (*Studies in the Phenomenology of Constitution,* section 2, "The Constitution of Animal Nature").

54. For Husserl, "region is nothing other than the total highest generic unity belonging to a concretum" (*General Introduction to a Pure Phenomenology,* section 16, p. 31). The relation between a region and its concreta—whether entities or events—is not just relational but *reciprocally* relational. To its concreta (i.e., its inhabitants) a region lends "generic unity" in the form of an "essentially unitary nexus," but the concreta give to this unified nexus specific positions that are indicated by deictic markers, including both toponyms and choronyms: I remember myself as having been on the "north rim" of the Grand Canyon. (Husserl's phrases are from *General Introduction to a Pure Phenomenology,* section 16, p. 31.) I resort to "choronym" as designating the name of a region proper (*chōra*) in distinction to a toponym of a place (*topos*).

55. George Peter Murdock, "World Ethnographic Sample," *American Anthropologist* 59, no. 4 (1957).

56. See R. G. Collingwood, *An Essay on Philosophical Method* (Oxford: Oxford University Press, 1932), passim.

57. On eidetic singularities, which are tantamount to the lowest specific differences, see Husserl, *General Introduction to a Pure Phenomenology,* section 12, "Genus and Species." The "object in general" is the proper content of formal ontology, while "this-here" is defined by Husserl as "a pure, syntactically formless, individual single particular" (ibid., section 12, p. 29). To interpret place as an intermediate term as I have just done is to rejoin Lévi-Strauss's opening gambit in *The Savage Mind:* just as traditional peoples do not lack abstract categories ("concepts" such as "tree" or "animal"), so they are also not precluded from employing the most intensely concrete terms (on the contrary: they are remarkably adept in just this regard, for example, in the identification and naming of botanical or animal species). But even the most concrete terms are already abstract to some degree, already climbing the scale of forms: "Words like 'oak', 'beech', 'birch', etc., are no less entitled to be considered

as abstract words than the word 'tree'; and a language possessing only the word 'tree' would be, from this point of view, less rich in concepts than one which lacked this term but contained dozens or hundreds for the individual species and varieties" (Claude Lévi-Strauss, *The Savage Mind* [Chicago: University of Chicago Press, 1966], p. 2).

58. Fernand Braudel, *The Mediterranean and the Mediterranean World in the Age of Philip II*, vol. 1, trans. S. Reynolds (New York: Harper, 1972).

59. Aristotle, *Physics* 208 a 29–30.

60. Pierre Bourdieu, *Outline of a Theory of Practice*, trans. R. Nice (Cambridge: Cambridge University Press, 1977), p. 78.

61. Russell, *The Problems of Philosophy*, chap. 5.

62. Merleau-Ponty, *The Visible and the Invisible*, p. 253. See also his statement that "there is an informing of perception by culture which enables us to say that culture is perceived—there is a dilatation of perception" (ibid., p. 212).

63. Curiously but significantly, the wildness at stake here is precisely what makes cultural anthropology possible, in Merleau-Ponty's assessment. Once having lived in another culture, the anthropologist "has regained possession of that untamed region of himself, unincorporated in his own culture, through which he communicates with other cultures" (Merleau-Ponty, "From Mauss to Claude Lévi-Strauss," p. 120). The wildness within is the condition of possibility for grasping the wildness without. For further discussion of the relation of culture and nature in the context of wild places, see Casey, *Getting Back into Place*, pp. 229–40.

64. Leibniz, *Philosophical Papers and Letters*, p. 1066.

65. German *Raum*, "space," is the etymon of English "room." Compare Merleau-Ponty's working note of June 1, 1960: "In fact it is a question of grasping the nexus—neither 'historical' nor 'geographic' of history and transcendental geology, this very time that is space, this very space that is time . . . the simultaneous Urstiftung of time and space which makes there be a historical landscape and a quasi-geographical inscription of history" (Merleau-Ponty, *The Visible and the Invisible*, p. 259).

66. Isaac Newton, *Mathematical Principles of Natural Philosophy*, Scholium to the Definitions, section 3 (London, 1687).

67. Ibid., section 4; my italics. Newton adds: "All things are placed in time as to order of succession; and in space as to order of situation. It is from their essence or nature that they are places; and that the primary places of things should be movable, is absurd" (ibid.). Leibniz similarly claimed that "every change, spiritual as well as material, has its own place (*sedes*), so to speak, in the order of time, as well as its own location in the order of coexistents, or in space" (letter to De Volder of June 20, 1703, in *Philosophical Papers and Letters*, vol. 2, p. 865).

68. Heidegger, *Poetry, Language, Thought*, p. 154.

69. For Whitehead's treatment of simple location, see his *Science and the Modern World* (New York: Macmillan, 1925), pp. 50ff. To be simply located is to be "here in space and here in time, or here in space-time, in a perfectly definite sense which does not require for its explanation any reference to other regions of space-time" (ibid., p. 50).

70. This is not to say that the status of space and time, once given a basis in place, becomes simply secure, or that their common reconstruction entails a creative, or even a productive, outcome. On many occasions, notably on many modern occasions, a thin temporality and a sheer spatiality derive from a placial matrix. Hospitals and penitentiaries of the sort analyzed by Foucault or shopping malls of the kind on which most Americans have come to depend are cases of deficient, or at the very least unaesthetic, modes of implacement. They are architectural and institutional events whose spatiotemporality is literally superficial, a matter of surfaces rather than of depths. Yet even in these inauspicious instances space and

time come paired in place, which continues to hold them together, however inauthentic or detrimental such holding may turn out to be. When implacement enriches rather than deprives, as in imaginatively place-specific architecture, the space and time that result become the very basis of expansively expressive experiences.

71. Bronislaw Malinowski, *Argonauts of the Western Pacific* (London: Routledge, 1922), p. 18.

72. On the near sphere (*Nähsphäre*), see Edmund Husserl, "The World of the Living Present and the Constitution of the Surrounding World External to the Organism," trans. F. A. Elliston and L. Langsdorf, in *Husserl: Shorter Works*, ed. F. A. Elliston and P. McCormick, 238–50 (Notre Dame, Ind.: University of Notre Dame Press, 1981), pp. 249–50. The idea is taken up by Patrick Heelan in the first chapter of his *Space-Perception and the Philosophy of Science* (Berkeley and Los Angeles: University of California Press, 1979), where the specifically hyperbolic geometry of the near sphere is developed—with interesting implications for a mathematically precise study of place.

73. On "intimate immensity," see Gaston Bachelard, *The Poetics of Space*, trans. M. Jolas (New York: Orion Press, 1964), chap. 8. The specifically social metaphoricity of the house is asserted by Arnold van Gennep: "A society is similar to a house divided into rooms and corridors" (*Rites of Passage*, trans. Monika B. Vizedom and Gabrielle L. Caffee [Chicago: University of Chicago Press, 1960], p. 26).

74. Van Gennep, *Rites of Passage*, 192; his italics.

75. Ibid., p. 20. Concerning the particularity of the threshold, van Gennep says: "The neutral zone shrinks progressively till it ceases to exist except as a simple stone, a beam, or a threshold" (ibid., p. 17). Concerning the complexities of the threshold in one particular culture, see Charles O. Frake, "How to Enter a Yakan House," in Frake, *Language and Cultural Description*, ed. A. S. Dil (Palo Alto, Calif.: Stanford University Press, 1980), pp. 214–32.

76. Van Gennep, *Rites of Passage*, 18, 192; my italics.

77. Joseph Breuer and Sigmund Freud, *Studies in Hysteria*, vol. 2 of *Standard Edition of the Complete Psychological Works of Sigmund Freud*, ed. J. Strachey (London: Hogarth, 1955), chap. 4. Concerning "theoretical space," see Bourdieu's remark that "as long as mythic-ritual space is seen as an opus operatum, that is, as a timeless order of things coexisting, it is never more than a theoretical space" (*Outline of a Theory of Practice*, p. 117). Durkheim's treatment of the collective basis of space (and time) is found in Emile Durkheim, *The Elementary Forms of the Religious Life*, trans. J. F. Swain (New York: MacMillan, 1915), pp. 23ff.

78. Nancy D. Munn, *The Fame of Gawa: A Symbolic Study of Value Transformation in a Massim (Papua New Guinea) Society* (New York: Cambridge University Press, 1986), p. 9; my italics. Munn's definition of "intersubjective spacetime" is "a multidimensional, symbolic order and process—a spacetime of self-other relations constituted in terms of and by means of specific types of practice" (10). The term "place" is rarely used by Munn. Exceptions include the following statements: a *kula* gift "will not disappear but will be retained as a potentiality within the ongoing present and at some later time (and place)" (65); "each household and house is a relatively autonomous locus" (69); gardens in Gawa "constitute an interior spacetime whose ancestral stones must be maintained in place" (10). Munn also employs the locution "spatiotemporal locus" (10).

79. Ibid., pp. 57–58.

80. Munn remarks that "sociocultural practices" of many sorts "do not simply go on in or through time and space, but [they also] . . . constitute (create) the space-time . . . in which they 'go on'" (ibid., p. 11). She adds that *kula* transactors are "concretely producing their own spacetime" (ibid.). This, in my view, applies more appropriately to place.

81. Malinowski, *Argonauts of the Western Pacific*, p. 147.

82. Munn, *The Fame of Gawa*, p. 41.

83. Malinowski, *Argonauts of the Western Pacific*, p. 85.

84. W. E. H. Stanner, "Aboriginal Territorial Organization: Estate, Range, Domain, and Regime," *Oceania* 36 (1965), pp. 1–26, at pp. 11–12; his italics.

85. Indeed, the distinction between estate (that is, the "country" as the locus of ritual ownership for patrilineal descent-groups) and range (that is, the circuit over which a given group hunts and forages) is by no means crisp. Sometimes quite distinct—for example, in times of drought—and sometimes coincident, as in times of good precipitation, their relationship is continually changing, which means that their common boundaries are always shifting. Hence Stanner proposes that the two notions, in their covariant vicissitudes, be considered a "domain": "estate and range together may be said to have constituted a domain, which was an ecological life-space" (ibid., p. 2; his italics). On the indefiniteness of aboriginal boundaries, see also Myers, *Pintupi Country,* 93: the "inseparability of people and place makes territorial boundaries highly flexible if not insignificant." Here Myers insists on a property of places that does not belong to "impersonal geography," that is, to sheer space regarded as preexisting the constitution of particular places. For an illuminating discussion of boundaries in general, see Lefebvre, *The Production of Space*, pp. 192–94. On *tok* as "path" in Kaluli culture, see Steven Feld's remark that "the concept . . . grounds the boundedness of places in the figure of their connectedness" (Feld, "Waterfalls of Sound," 111).

86. Merleau-Ponty, "From Mauss to Claude Lévi-Strauss," p. 120.

87. John Locke, *An Essay Concerning Human Understanding,* ed. A. C. Fraser, 2 vols. (New York: Dover, 1959 [1690]), book 2, chap. 15.

Smooth Spaces and Rough-Edged Places

This is an edited version of an essay of the same title that first appeared in *Review of Metaphysics* (1998). Reprinted with permission.

1. Gilles Deleuze and Felix Guattari, *Nomadology: The War Machine,* trans. Brian Massumi (New York: Semiotexte, 1986), p. 53: "The variability, the polyvocity of directions, is an essential feature of smooth spaces of the rhizome type, and it alters their cartography."

2. Martin Heidegger, *Being and Time,* trans. John Macquarrie and Edward Robinson (New York: Harper, 1962), p. 138.

3. On time as dispersive, see Aristotle, *Physics* 4.12.221b3: *existesin to huparchon.* Edward Hussey translates this phrase "removes what is present" in his *Aristotle's Physics, Books III and IV,* but I prefer my colleague Peter Manchester's translation above. On place as container, see *Physics* 4.2–5.

4. Aristotle, *Physics* 4.14.223b11; Hussey translation. Unless otherwise specified, I will use this translation as cited in the previous footnote.

5. Plato, *Timaeus* 49a, in *Plato's Cosmology* (New York: Liberal Arts Press, 1957).

6. Ibid., 50c.

7. Ibid., 50e.

8. On *chora* as an antecedent of modern notions of space, see Martin Heidegger, *Introduction to Metaphysics,* trans. Ralph Manheim (New Haven, Conn.: Yale University Press, 1959), p. 66: "the transformation of the barely apprehended essence of place (*topos*) and of *chora* into a 'space' defined by extension was initiated by the Platonic philosophy. . . . Might *chora* not mean: that which abstracts itself from every particular, that which withdraws, and in such a way precisely admits and 'makes place' for something else?"

9. On "smooth space," see Deleuze and Guattari, *Nomadology,* 18–23, 34–35, 38, 48. Plato explicitly invokes the quality of smoothness in comparing the situation of the re-

ceptacle to that of someone who makes impressions in "some soft substance [that] allows no shape to show itself there beforehand, but begins by making the surface as *smooth* and level as he can" (*Timaeus* 51a; my italics).

10. Plato, *Timaeus* 52e–53a.

11. The full statement is: "Plato, too, says in the Timaeus that matter and space are the same thing (for 'the participative' [*to metaleptikon*] and space [*ten choran*] are the same thing). Though he gave a different use to 'the participative' in what are called his 'unwritten doctrines' from that in the Timaeus, he still declared that place and space [*ton topon kai ten choran*] were the same thing. While everyone says that place is something, he alone tried to say what it is" (*Physics* 4.2.209b11–17). From this statement it is clear that the reduction of space to matter is very much Aristotle's, not Plato's, doing. Aristotle is not, however, dogmatic concerning the reduction of space to place; he hedges his bets by saying that "a body has a place and a space" (*Physics* 4.1.209a7–8).

12. Aristotle, *Physics* 4.4.212a20–1.

13. Ibid., 4.4.212a14–16.

14. Ibid., 4.5.212b27–8.

15. The full statement is: "Place is thought to be some surface (*epipedon*) and like a vessel (*aggeion*) and surrounder (*periechon*). Moreover, place is together with the object, because the limits are together with what is limited" (*Physics* 4.4.212a18–20). The surrounder itself has to be bodily: "a body is in place if, and only if, there is a body (*soma*) which surrounds it" (*Physics* 4.5.212a31–32). With this last statement, the prospect of an infinite regress begins to loom.

16. These conundra and others are explored in Richard Sorabji, *Matter, Space, and Motion* (Ithaca: Cornell University Press, 1988), pp. 186–201. Ironically, Aristotle's own example of the river might have led him to a conception of "smooth space," for which questions of exact location would be irrelevant. Instead, his concern with questions of precise "position" (*thesis*) draws him ineluctably toward a commitment to striated space, concerning which the issue is always that of "simple location"—a term of Whitehead's that we have encountered before in this book and that will again become important later in this essay.

17. Aristotle, *Physics* 4.5.212b29. Aristotle adds "and this is reasonable . . . everything remains naturally in its proper place" (4.5.212b29–30).

18. Aristotle, *Physics* 4.1.208b8–20.

19. Ibid., 4.1.208b14.

20. Ibid., 4.1.208b21–22.

21. See, for example, Gareth Evans, *The Varieties of Reference*, ed. John McDowell (Oxford: Oxford University Press, 1982), pp. 151–70.

22. I base this axiom on the statement attributed to Archytas by Simplicius: "All existing things [*ta onta panta*] are either in place [*en topo*] or not without place [*ouk aneu topou*] . . . it is necessary for other things to be in place, but for place to be in nothing." (The translation is by Sambursky, in *The Concept of Place in Late Neoplatonism* [Jerusalem: Israel Academy of Sciences and Humanities, 1982], p. 37; hereafter *The Concept of Place.*)

23. Aristotle, *Physics* 3.8.208a29–31. Plato's endorsement is at *Timaeus* 52b: "Anything that is must needs be in some place and occupy some room . . . what is not somewhere in earth and heaven is nothing." Even if Plato's and Aristotle's citations of the axiom allude to an item of common wisdom, this only reinforces the status of this axiom as an "absolute presupposition" in Collingwood's sense of the term. On Gorgias and Zeno, see Cornford, *Plato's Cosmology*, pp. 192 n. 3 and 195–97.

24. See Alexandre Koyré, *From the Closed World to the Infinite Universe* (Baltimore,

Md.: Johns Hopkins University Press, 1957). Curiously, however, Koyré only tells the last chapters of this long tale, those that bear on the Renaissance and early modern period. For a more complete account, the reader must consult such texts as Samuel Sambursky, *The Physical World of Late Antiquity* (New York: Basic Books, 1962) and Richard Sorabji, *Matter, Space, and Motion.*

25. "Iamblichus's doctrine influenced the philosophy of space in modern times" (Sambursky, introduction to *The Concept of Place,* 17). The influence appears to have come mainly through Henry More, who as the leading Platonist of his time had a decisive impact on Newton.

26. "One must not conceive place as a mere limit in the way that we conceive the mathematical surfaces as limits of mathematical bodies, but as the physical boundaries of physical bodies, and as the alive boundaries of ensouled living beings" (Sambursky, *The Concept of Place,* 47; citing Simplicius, *In Aristotelis Physicorum Libros Quattuor Priores Commentaria,* ed. Hermann Diels [Berlin: 1882]). On place as "primary cause," see Sambursky, *The Concept of Place,* p. 45.

27. Place "encompasses and defines [bodies] as deriving their existence from it, for which reason bodies possess being in place as encompassed by it and as preserving their own extension in the unextended nature" (Sambursky, *The Concept of Place,* p. 45).

28. Ibid., p. 45. Another expression of the same premise is on p. 49: "We should in general always elevate the limit to being the higher cause."

29. Ibid., p. 43; repeated twice for emphasis. The power of place is characterized as *somatoeide,* a term that according to Sambursky should be construed as corporeal in an "active," not a "material," mode; see his comment on p. 42 n. 1. A more complete statement of this same power is found on p. 47: "One has to conceive place not only as encompassing and establishing in itself the things existing in place, but as sustaining them by one single power. . . . And the bodies sustained by this power, falling down by their proper nature, but being raised up by the superiority of place, will thus exist in it."

30. Ibid., p. 47. The terms "termination," "last extremity," and "common limit" (*telein, eschaton,* and *koinon peras*) are also found on the same page, all of them being posed in contrast with the indwelling power of place. For an alternative view of "filling," compare the remark of Dilthey: "The space which my body occupies, as given in outer perception, is progressively filled, so to speak, with inner states through accumulating experience, through practice, through the establishment of a context for the feeling of life, the exertion of the will, muscular sensations, and a variety of specifically localized feelings" (Wilhelm Dilthey, *Introduction to the Historical Sciences: Selected Works,* ed. Rudolph A. Makkreel and Fritz Rodi [Princeton, N.J.: Princeton University Press, 1989], vol. 1, p. 269). It is characteristically "modern" to claim that space is filled with experiences rather than with things.

31. "One must extend the whole nature of place to all things whatsoever which exist as entities contained in entities of another kind, not speaking homonymously but applying the same statement concerning the genus. For there is one relation between things encompassed and things encompassing; it is the same everywhere, but it varies according to the different degrees of reality of the participants—for the relation is different in bodies and with incorporeals" (Sambursky, *The Concept of Place,* p. 49).

32. Philoponus, *In Aristotelis Physicorum Libros Quinque Posteriores Commentaria,* ed. H. Vitelli (Berlin, 1888); as translated in Sambursky, *The Concept of Place,* p. 115.

33. "It is absolutely ridiculous to say that place as such has a certain power . . . place has not the power to carry the bodies toward their proper places" (Sambursky, *The Concept of Place*). It follows that boundaries are also not empowering entities.

34. Ibid., 111. On Philoponus's critique of Aristotle, see p. 103: "The surface (*epiphaneia*), being two-dimensional, could not contain a three-dimensional object as such,

because it could not touch the body as a whole . . . only the boundaries (*ta perata*) of the body are indeed in the surface."

35. Ibid., p. 113. The two extensions in question are designated respectively as *somatikon* and *topikon*, for example, at 101: "It is only possible that the corporeal extension will be in the spatial extension, so that [the] two extensions will coincide." Corporeal extension is the extension of any given body and obtains for that body alone; spatial extension is the room into which any number of different bodies, albeit all of the same volume, can fit in succession. Thus, regarded by itself, it is empty, that is, to-be-occupied. Aristotle discusses spatial extension at *Physics* 4.4.211b15–28—where it is designated merely as "extension" (*diastema*)—only to reject it as an adequate model of place. Indeed, Philoponus asserts that "I mean the same thing whether I speak of the void or of the three-dimensional spatial extension" (Sambursky, *The Concept of Place*, p. 103). This results in Philoponus's second major critique of Aristotle: "No absurdity results from the assertion that place is an empty extension essentially differing from the bodies contained in it, as against what Aristotle said" (ibid.).

36. "I certainly do not maintain that this interval [spatial extension] at any time is or can be empty of any body; this is never the case . . . always other bodies enter it, while it itself remains immobile as a whole as well as in its parts" (Sambursky, *The Concept of Place*, p. 113).

37. Ibid., p. 119. See also p. 113: the cosmical extension "contains the body of the whole cosmos [and cannot] be moved."

38. The denial of intrinsic differences occurs at Sambursky, *The Concept of Place*, p. 119 n. 118. Sambursky comments: "Philoponus rejects qualitative differences of space (natural places)."

39. For a comprehensive account of the intervening millennium, see Edward Grant, *Much Ado about Nothing: Theories of Space and Vacuum from the Middle Ages to the Scientific Revolution* (Cambridge: Cambridge University Press, 1981).

40. Michel Foucault, "Of Other Spaces," *Diacritics* 16, no. 1 (1986), pp. 22–28. The growing awareness of Philoponus's prescient philosophy and science has been due largely to the efforts of Richard Sorabji. See, for example, the volume he edited, *Philoponus and the Rejection of Aristotelian Science* (Ithaca, N.Y.: Cornell University Press, 1987).

41. Koyré, *From the Closed World to the Infinite Universe*, viii.

42. In my book *The Fate of Place: A Philosophical History* (Berkeley and Los Angeles: University of California Press, 1997), I demonstrate the slow but sure emergence of infinite and absolute space from Philoponus to Newton. In fact, Philoponus denies infinite space per se, even though the logical consequence of his notion of cosmical extension, taken to its limit, ineluctably entails such space. The idea of absolute space is implied by Philoponus's idea of spatial extension as a stable, immovable dimensional framework that is not altered by that which occupies it.

43. Descartes, *Principles of Philosophy*, p. 229. Descartes specifies that such a surface does not belong, strictly speaking, to the "surrounding body" but to "the boundary between the surrounding and surrounded bodies," being in effect the "common surface" (ibid.). Concerning the question of infinity, Article 26 of the same text states that "we should never enter into arguments about the infinite. Things in which we observe no limit—such as the extension of the world, the division of the parts of matter, the number of the stars, and so on—should instead be regarded as indefinite" (ibid., p. 201). As Descartes makes clear in the next article, he prefers to reserve the term "infinite" for God, but if God is coextensive with the extended universe, then surely it, too, is infinite—a controversial consequence that Descartes prudently sidesteps.

44. "In reality the extension in length, breadth, and depth which constitutes a space is exactly the same as that which constitutes a body. The difference arises as follows: in the

case of a body, we regard the extension as something particular . . . but in the case of a space, we attribute to the extension only a generic unity, so that when a new body comes to occupy the space, the extension of the space is reckoned not to change but to remain one and the same" (Descartes, *Principles of Philosophy*, p. 227).

45. Ibid., p. 229. Note also Descartes's claim that "internal place is exactly the same as space."

46. Alfred North Whitehead, *Science and the Modern World* (New York: Macmillan, 1953), p. 58.

47. Ibid. See also p. 49 for a more elaborate alternative formulation. Whitehead remarks that "this concept of simple location is independent of the controversy between the absolutist and the relativist views of space or of time" (ibid., p. 58).

48. Locke, *An Essay Concerning Human Understanding*, vol. 1, p. 220. Locke italicizes "simple mode." The importance of distance follows from Locke's instrumentalist conception of place: "this modification of distance we call place, being made by men for their common use . . . men consider and determine of this place by reference to those adjacent things which best served to their present purpose" (ibid., p. 223).

49. Ibid., p. 224.

50. Ibid. Locke says expressly that "we can have no idea of the place of the universe, though we can of all the parts of it" (ibid.).

51. "The word place has sometimes a more confused sense, and stands for that space which any body takes up" (ibid.). Elsewhere in the *Essay*, Locke makes it clear that volume belongs properly to the idea of "solidity," not to space proper: see ibid., p. 156.

52. A brief discussion of "extension" at the beginning of chapter 13 of book 2 was dropped after the first three editions of the *Essay*. See Fraser's note on p. 220.

53. The first statement occurs at ibid., p. 225; the second is on p. 222.

54. Newton, Scholium to the Definitions, section 2; my italics. The mention of "situation" and "a part of space which a body takes up" is in section 3. In the same section, Newton also rejects, in good Philoponean fashion, the idea of place as "the external surface of the body."

55. Ibid., section 4; my italics.

56. Ibid.

57. The terms "absolute places" and "primary places" occur at ibid., section 4.

58. Whitehead, *Science and the Modern World*, 49.

59. Leibniz, "Fifth Paper," in *The Leibniz-Clarke Correspondence*, ed. H. G. Alexander (Manchester, UK: University of Manchester Press, 1956), as reprinted in J. J. C. Smart, *Problems of Space and Time* (New York: Macmillan, 1976), p. 92. See also the statement that "space is that, which results from places taken together" (ibid.).

60. Ibid., "Third Paper," p. 89. Leibniz adds that "space denotes, in terms of possibility, an order of things which exist at the same time, considered as existing together, without enquiring into their manner of existing."

61. Ibid.

62. Ibid., "Fifth Paper," 91. Leibniz underlines "situation." On p. 97, Leibniz speaks of space as "an order of situations," thereby reinforcing the relativism of place by abstracting it.

63. Ibid., "Fifth Paper," p. 92. "Fixed existents" are "those, in which there has been no cause of any change of the order of their co-existence with others; or (which is the same thing) in which there has been no motion" (ibid.). The resemblance of fixed existents to Newton's idea of "immovable places"—as well as to Locke's contention that "the parts of pure space are immovable" (Locke, *Essay*, 227)—is striking.

64. Leibniz, "Fifth Paper," pp. 93–94. Locke uses the same language: "When we find anything at the same distance now which it was yesterday, from any two or more points,

which have not since changed their distance one with another, and with which we then compared it, we say it hath kept the same place" (Locke, *Essay*, 222).

65. Thus Leibniz writes that "the mind not contented with an agreement, looks for an identity, for something that should be truly the same; and conceives it as being extrinsic to the subjects: and this is what we call place and space" ("Fifth Paper," p. 93). It follows that the identity in question, since it can never be perfectly realized in reality (individual differences between relational terms preclude it), must be "ideal": place or space so conceived is "an ideal thing, containing a certain order, wherein the mind conceives the application of relations" (ibid.; see also p. 94: "a mere ideal thing"). The ideal, in turn, is linked with the possible, and Leibniz, by stressing both, has unwittingly fallen into what Whitehead calls "the Fallacy of Misplaced Concreteness."

66. Newton, Scholium to the *Principia Mathematica*, section 4.

67. Blaise Pascal, *Pensées*, no. 206 (Brunschvicg edition). See also no. 205: "swallowed up in the infinite immensity of the spaces which I know not and which know not me, I am frightened and astonished."

68. Deleuze and Guattari, *Nomadology*, 54; their italics.

69. Michel Foucault, *The Birth of the Clinic: An Archeology of Medical Perception*, trans. A. Sheridan Smith (New York: Pantheon, 1973), p. 6.

70. On the "space of domination," see Michel Foucault, *Discipline and Punish: The Birth of the Prison*, trans. Allan Sheridan (New York: Pantheon, 1977), p. 187. On surveillance, see pp. 170–77 ("Hierarchical Observation").

71. Ibid., p. 195. The phrase "fixing in space" occurs at p. 231.

72. Ibid., p. 197. The full statement is: "this enclosed, segmented space, observed at every point, in which the individuals are inserted in a fixed place, in which the slightest movements are supervised, in which all events are recorded, in which an uninterrupted work of writing links the centre and periphery, in which power is exercised without division, according to a continuous hierarchical figure, in which each individual is constantly located, examined and distributed among the living beings, the sick and the dead—all these constitute a compact model of the disciplinary mechanism."

73. "Calculable man," that is, the subject of the newly emerging human sciences, appears at ibid., p. 193. "Disciplinary individual" is found at on p. 227.

74. On time-regulation, see ibid., p. 220, as well as the celebrated studies of E. P. Thompson concerning timetables in eighteenth-century England. The phrase "elementary location or partitioning" is at ibid., p. 143.

75. The phrase "laboratory of power" occurs at ibid., p. 204; "the rule of functional sites" is on p. 243; and the last phrase in this sentence is at p. 205.

76. On docile bodies, see ibid., pp. 135–69.

77. See Thomas R. Flynn, "Foucault and the Spaces of History," *Monist* 74 (1991), pp. 165–86.

78. Hannah Arendt, *The Human Condition* (Chicago: University of Chicago Press, 1958), p. 6.

79. Pascal, *Pensées*, no. 72.

80. Immanuel Kant, *The Critique of Pure Reason*, trans. Norman Kemp Smith (New York: St. Martins Press, 1965), B413. Kant adds: "all that I really have in thought is simply the unity of consciousness, on which, as the mere form of knowledge, all determination is based" (B427). Any further unity, like the "absolute unity" implied by the Cartesian cogito, is a transcendental illusion, and thus a paralogism of pure reason; see ibid., A405.

81. Ibid. Kant's skepticism of self-knowledge is so extreme that he even says that "I represent myself to myself neither as I am nor as I appear to myself" (B429). These words indicate the extremity of Kant's skepticism concerning the knowability of the self.

82. Ibid., A373. See also A375: "space itself, with all its appearances . . . is, indeed, only

in me"; and A378: "space itself, however, is nothing but an inner mode of representation in which certain perceptions are connected with one another."

83. Ibid., A373.

84. For this thesis, see Arendt, *The Human Condition*, pp. 51–58. Beyond the two factors cited earlier, Arendt attributes the loss of the "public sphere" to the encroachment of "the social" on the community at large. Foucault strikingly agrees with this assessment: "In a society in which the principal elements are no longer the community and public life, but on the one hand, private individuals and, on the other, the state, relations can be regulated only in a form that is the exact reverse of the [ancient] spectacle" (Foucault, *Discipline and Punish*, p. 216).

85. Foucault, *Discipline and Punish*, p. 222. See also Foucault's statement that "the real, corporeal disciplines constituted the foundation of the formal, juridical liberties" (ibid.). See also p. 194: "The [modern] individual is no doubt the fictitious atom of an 'ideological' representation of society; but he is also a reality fabricated by this specific technology of power that I have called 'discipline.'"

86. Deleuze and Guattari, *Nomadology*, p. 54.

87. Ibid., p. 34.

88. "The place of all the land animals is the earth and the air, namely, this part of the earth and the air, and furthermore rather that immediately encompassing place which both Aristotle and Archytas have explained" (Iamblichus, as cited in Sambursky, *The Concept of Place*, p. 51).

89. On "topoanalysis," see Gaston Bachelard, *The Poetics of Space*, trans. Maria Jolas (Boston: Beacon Press, 1994), pp. xxxii, 8, 10, 226. Heidegger says: "Das denkende Dichten ist in der Wahrheit die Topologie des Seyns. Sie sagt diesem die Ortschaft seines Wesens" (*Aus der Erfahrung des Denkens* [Pfullingen: Neske, 1954], p. 23).

90. Aristotle, *Physics* 4.12.220a27. I here modify Hussey's translation: "The least number, without qualification, is the two."

Index

A Priori, 110, 185–186, 226, 239, 406–407n.1
Above/Below, dimensional features of body in place, 76–82
Abram, David, 432n.108
Acculturation: vs. enculturation, 434n.20
Ackerman, James, 129
Addison, Joseph, 163
Ahead and Behind, 82–88
Alberti, Leon Battista, 118, 158, 346n.43, 418n.47, 424n.112
Alienation (from Place), 307–10, 313, 363–65
Alongside and Around, as modes of dwelling, 125–30
Altizer, T. J. J., 444n.11
Amboyna People, 91
Anaximines, 220–21, 236
Animal life, vs. plant life, xii, 64
Antaeus, 212, 329
Anthropocentrism, Humanocentrism, 187
Anthropology, 319–20, 323–24, 332–33, 347
Apache, stories of, 277, 305, 449n.77
Aquinas, 358
Arc: of abundance, 208–209; architectural, 131–32, 147; articulatory, 94, 96, 99, 110, 185; of desolation, defined, 199; of desolation as area of vanishing in wild places, 207, 216–18, 236, 261–62, 265; of earth, 298; of embodiment, 110–11, 147; horizonal, 62, 68, 94–97, 185–87; of reachability, 60, 110, 185; tensional, 55, 185
Architecture. See Building, Built places
Archytas/Archytian Axiom, 14–15, 98, 313, 319, 338, 346–47, 354, 459n.22
Arendt, Hannah, 363–65, 464n.84
Aristotle, xi, 8, 10, 12, 13, 14, 19, 23, 45, 75, 76, 90, 104, 226, 299–300, 308, 311, 319, 329, 335, 349–50, 355, 361, 366, 400n.48, 402n.69, 450n.92, 453n.30, 458nn.3,4, 459nn.11,15, 464n.90
Arnheim, Rudolph, 124
Art. See Heidegger, Martin, work of art
Articulation, to world via right- and left-handedness, 92–97
Atmosphere, feature of wild places, 219–22, 236, 262

Augustine, Saint: on time, 12, 13, 14, 20, 302, 377n.79, 378n.81, 448n.71
Aura, 129, 410n.42

Bachelard, Gaston, x, xv, xxi, 123, 228, 311, 319, 341, 366, 411n.51, 423n.94, 433n.3, 450nn.91,93, 464n.89
Bakhtin, Mikhail, 277, 444n.9
Barrenness, feature of desolate landscape, 195
Bashō, Matsuo, 280–83, 284, 285, 286, 305, 306, 309, 310
Basis-Place, 213
Basso, Keith, 305, 325, 369n.5, 443n.8, 446n.42, 449n.77
Before and After: as placial, not temporal, 12
Being-in-Place, xv, 179, 280, 289, 314, 345
Bellah, Robert, 284, 445n.28
Benjamin, Walter, 442n.137
Bergson, Henri, 9, 11, 16, 361, 374n.24, 450n.93
Berkeley, George, 67, 68, 386n.12
Berry, Wendell, 225, 239, 253, 324n.2, 430n.74, 432n.113, 435n.34, 436n.39, 438n.93, 441n.125
Beverley, Robert, 189
Binarist dogma, 338–40, 346
Bioregions, xxix–xxx
Biosphere, and atmosphere, 221–22, 432n.107
Birkerts, Sven, 37, 307, 311
Blondel, Jean-François, 163
Bloomer, Kent, 408n.21, 413n.68
Bly, Robert, 246
Body, Embodiment: basis of architecture, 412n.52; and culture, 348; model for built places, 117–20; and dwelling, 116–20, 132, 140–41, 153, 181; dyadic structures of, 48–105, 152–53; as habitual, 51–52, 78–79, 293, 295–97; as locus of here, 52–53, 71–72; and journeying, 153; knowing, 336–38; lived, 346; and perception, 325–27; role in memory, 129; role in navigation, 26–29; as orienting, 26, 312, 313, 314, 324–26; sustained and supported by place, 355–56; feature of wild places, 205, 213, 217, 222–25, 259–60, 262
Border, xxvii, xxx, xxxvi
Boundary: as active power, 355; in architecture,

465

EDWARD S. CASEY is Distinguished Professor at State University of New York at Stony Brook. His previous books include *Imagining* (Indiana University Press, 2d ed., 2000); *Remembering* (Indiana University Press, 2d ed., 2000); *The Fate of Place; Representing Place: Landscape Paintings and Maps; Earth-Mapping: Artists Reshaping Landscape;* and *The World at a Glance* (Indiana University Press, 2007).